סדור
נתיבות אמונה
SIDDUR NETIVOT EMUNAH

PATHS of FAITH

THE NEW
JEWISH PRAYER BOOK
for SYNAGOGUE and HOME

FOR WEEKDAYS, SHABBAT,
FESTIVALS & OTHER OCCASIONS

Compiled and Translated by

CHAIM STERN

PATHS OF FAITH: _The New Jewish Prayer Book For Synagogue and Home_

For further information, contact:

S.P.I. Books
99 Spring Street
New York, NY 10012
Tel: (212) 431-5011
Fax: (212) 431-8646
Email: sales@spibooks.com

10 9 8 7 6 5 4 3 2 1
First Edition

Mi Shebeirach from _And You Shall Be a Blessing_, music by Debbie Friedman, lyrics by Debbie Friedman and Drorah Setel, © 1988 by Debbie Lynn Friedman (ASCAP) is used by permission of the publisher, Sounds Write Productions, Inc. (ASCAP).

An Ian Shapolsky book

Published by S.P.I. Books in cooperation with:
ROSSEL BOOKS
Rabbi Seymour Rossel, _Executive Editor_
Melvin Wolfson, _Copy Editor_
Dr. Edward Graham, _Editorial Advisor_

Library of Congress Cataloging-in-Publication Data available.

S.P.I. Books' World Wide Web address: _www.spibooks.com_

ISBN: 1-56171-933-1

Printed in Canada

Temple Israel of Greater Miami. He had just begun to serve his new congregation when cancer overtook him. He worked courageously for three months—through the Days of Awe—inspiring worshipers and colleagues alike with his indomitable spirit, his power, and his spirituality.

Rabbi Stern learned that *Paths of Faith* was going to be published on the night before he entered the hospital for the last time. He was thrilled by the news, calling friends throughout the country to express his happiness. He had poured much of himself, and of what he had learned from years of creating liturgy, into the making of this prayer book. He understood that it would become a monument to his lifetime occupation with prayer, even as he understood that it would inspire young and old alike for years to come.

"This prayer book sums up my devotion to creating a liturgy for our people," he told his wife, Lea Lane Stern, a few weeks before he died. "Its poetry and power will uplift the spirit in this time of uncertainty. It is my legacy." Rabbi Stern died on November 5, 2001.

American Reform community—including *Gates of Prayer,* *Gates of Repentance, Gates of Forgiveness,* and *Gates of Joy.*

His other works include *Gates of Freedom,* a magnificent Passover Haggadah; *Pirke Avot: Wisdom of the Jewish Sages,* an innovative translation and commentary; *Day by Day,* a classic collection of spiritual readings; and *On the Doorposts of Your House,* a home worship resource. For *The Haftarah Commentary,* he provided fresh and inspiring translations of all the prophetic selections read in the yearly cycle of synagogue worship. His last works were a translation and commentary of *Genesis* (with W. Gunther Plaut) and this final prayer book, *Netivot Emunah: Paths of Faith.*

Rabbi Stern was born August 8, 1930, in Brooklyn, New York, the last of nine children, the only son, and the only child born outside Jerusalem. He came from a line of rabbis and Bible scholars stretching back to the eleventh century. He studied in a *yeshiva* but, as the darkening clouds descended on European Jewry, he turned from Orthodoxy to political activism. He attended City College of New York, then entered Harvard Law School. Midway through his law studies, he felt impelled to return to the calling of his ancestors—but now in the Reform movement.

He was ordained at Hebrew Union College-Jewish Institute of Religion in 1958, earned a Master's degree in Hebrew Literature, and was later honored with a Doctor of Divinity degree. During one of his frequent visits to England, he served as a research fellow in Hebrew Studies at Oxford University.

Rabbi Stern served temples in New Jersey, Milwaukee, and London; and for thirty-three years he was the senior rabbi at Temple Beth El of Northern Westchester in Chappaqua, New York. Upon his retirement, he accepted a position at

CHAIM STERN: A TRIBUTE

Rabbi Chaim Stern, ז״ל, was a superb liturgist, translator, and poet. He was often called "the poet laureate of the Reform movement." He was also a *mensch*, a true Jewish gentleman, with a smile that would light a room, and a sly, dry sense of humor that never stopped, even during his final illness.

Rabbi Stern was one-of-a-kind: brilliant, perceptive, gentle, and truthful. He believed in excellence and discipline—he combined these with his other gifts to produce a body of work that changed the course of Reform Judaism from the mid-twentieth to the twenty-first century. Gender-sensitive language, Hebrew prayers accompanied by lyrical English translations, use of insightful selections from literature and philosophy outside Reform Judaism—these were only a few of his contributions.

Rabbi Stern's translations and original liturgy were frequently put to music and adapted into other art forms. They became the touchstone for synagogue leaders and worshipers throughout the English-speaking world. Words from his liturgy were even quoted by President William Jefferson Clinton, who turned to *Gates of Repentance* in his own time of trouble.

Above all, Rabbi Stern was the most prolific liturgist in the history of Judaism. Together with Rabbi John D. Rayner, he created the modern prayer books *Service of the Heart*, *Gate of Repentance*, and *Siddur Lev Chadash* for the British Liberal Movement. And, through the last thirty years, he conceived and created each of the "Gates" series of prayerbooks for the

Netivot Emunah provides a complete liturgy for (Festival) *Yom Tov*, with similar special readings. It too follows the same pattern of innovation and tradition.

Finally, there is a special *Tefilah* with inserts for *Shabbat Shuvah, Chol Ha-Moeid Yom Tov, Rosh Chodesh,* and *Chanukah.* Thus the *Tefilah* for "ordinary" Sabbaths is not interrupted.

No liturgy by itself can solve the problems of communal worship with which many of us wrestle daily, but this new liturgy for weekdays, Shabbat, and *Yom Tov* for congregations and individuals is offered with the prayer that it may bring us all a little closer to the realization of the presence of God within the worshiping community. The paths of faith are various; may *Netivot Emunah* help us on our journey toward the Holy.

—Chaim Stern
Chappaqua, New York
September, 2001

other passages in the prayer book, to enhance the worshiper's appreciation of the text, and to invite the worshiper to make discoveries about the text and its interconnection. Furthermore, each preliminary section also has a brief "reflection" to awaken thought and feeling in the worshiper.

The *Shema* now includes an optional passage culled from Deuteronomy that restores the flavor of the traditional text (hitherto omitted in Reform prayer books).

In the *Tefilah*, proclaiming God as the source of eternal life, the *Gevurot* restores *mechayei hameitim*, and adds a passage about the seasons that goes beyond *tal* and *geshem*, the traditional seasonal inserts.

The English is of course gender-neutral throughout.

Special prayers and prayer-sections that are liturgical innovations include: Prayers for Healing (section); Betrothal prayer; an extensive selection from *Pirke Avot*, accompanied by commentary mainly from traditional sources; a selection of readings for "Troubled Times"; extensive reflections on God and on the human condition; a special selection of newly translated Psalms not found elsewhere in the prayer book. The section entitled "Blessings" contains blessings and rituals for individuals and communities, at home and in the synagogue.

Weekdays: The morning service includes much material from the traditional *Birchot ha-Shachar*. In addition we make available Psalms for each day, using some Psalms that are traditional and others that are new in this context. Similarly, we make available a complete *Kabbalat Shabbat* for the evening service and a complete *Birchot ha-Shachar* and *Pesukei deZimra* for the morning, and in addition offer alternative opening sections for evening and morning.

INTRODUCTION

I present the new prayer book, *Netivot Emunah: Paths of Faith*, to our community in the belief that this siddur will meet the needs of many congregations and individuals, and I offer it as the summing-up of a lifetime devoted to creating a liturgy for our people.

This prayer book respects the traditions of the classical liturgy and of Liberal-Reform Judaism. It retains and restores much of tradition, yet contains many innovations. It is our hope that worshipers will find in its pages pathways to a deeper spiritual life in their Jewish journey.

The structure of the service is an innovation in the North American liturgy. For each Shabbat, Festival, and weekday there is a choice of introductory materials, both traditional and innovative. The core of the service is fixed from the *Bar'chu* to the end of the *Tefilah*. All passages are freshly reconsidered and newly retranslated, not paraphrased; and transliterations accompany passages likely to be sung by the congregation.

The services include many new features. Among these: each service begins with a *Kavannah* (here called "Prayer Before Prayer") in the margin; the contents of these *Kavvanot* are ethical, and are taken from traditional texts. Thus the worshiper is encouraged to link prayer and meditation with the ethical behavior that ought to flow from the act of worship.

Another feature: alongside each of the classical prayers is a brief statement about its content or significance, establishing for the worshiper its place in the general structure of our liturgy. In addition, there are thematic cross-references to

Contents

CONTENTS

ACKNOWLEDGMENTS

The untimely death of Rabbi Chaim Stern came before the completion of the introductory materials for *Netivot Emunah: Paths of Faith*. The publishers therefore wish to thank those whose work strengthened the author's hand and made the publication of this prayer book possible.

Dr. Edward Graham of Larchmont, New York, read the manuscript for style, making many suggestions incorporated by the author in the months preceding his death.

Melvin Wolfson of Chappaqua, New York, longtime friend of Rabbi Stern, served in this work, as he had in so many of Rabbi Stern's previous works, as copy editor, lavishing inordinate time and effort right up to the moment of publication.

Both Lea Lane Stern and Michael Stern provided technical assistance to make available the manuscript and design work so nearly completed by Rabbi Stern.

The final touches—editorial and design—were undertaken by co-publisher, Rabbi Seymour Rossel of Chappaqua, New York, who worked in partnership with Rabbi Stern on this project and many others, including *The Haftarah Commentary* and *Gates of Freedom: The Passover Haggadah*.

In any acknowledgments, Rabbi Stern would surely have thanked his beloved wife, Lea Lane Stern, and his three sons—David, Philip, and Michael—for their love and support. It is only fitting that the publishers should include this note on his behalf.

סדור

נתיבות אמונה

SIDDUR NETIVOT EMUNAH

PATHS OF FAITH

והגינות REFLECTIONS

BEFORE PRAYER CAN BEGIN

Reflections on a variety of other topics begin with Pirke Avot on page 322 and continue through page 378.

פַּעַם שָׁאַל אוֹתוֹ חָסִיד אֶחָד, בַּמֶּה הוּא עוֹסֵק לִפְנֵי הַתְּפִלָּה. הֵשִׁיב לוֹ רַבֵּנוּ: פָּארְן דַאוַוענען דַאווֶן אִיךְ.

‌❧ A Chasid asked the Tzanzer Rebbe, "What does the Rabbi do before praying?" "Before praying," replied our master, "I pray [that I may be able to pray]." (Chasidic, 19th century)

‌❧ Prayer takes place only when the mind understands. . . . Therefore it is better that those who cannot pray in Hebrew should pray in a language they understand. (Sefer Chasidim, 12th century)

PRAYER AND ITS VALUE

‌❧ I do not pretend to understand how the divine Creator influences the human child. I feel as if spiritual forces were pouring constantly from the infinite source which is never poorer for all it gives forth. . . . Yet these influences of spirit make their way in different degrees—or not at all—to different souls. The windows of some souls are perhaps nearly shut. The windows of others have only a few chinks and crevices open. At some seasons—the seasons of prayer—those chinks and crevices may open a little wider so that a little more of God's light may enter in.

‌❧ I have always found prayer difficult. So often it seems like a fruitless game of hide-and-seek where we seek and God hides. . . . Yet I cannot leave prayer alone for long. My need drives me to God. And I have a feeling . . . that finally all my seeking will prove infinitely worthwhile. And I am

3

not sure what I mean by "finding." Some days my very seeking seems a kind of "finding." And, of course, if "finding" means the end of "seeking," it were better to go on seeking.

𝕮   True prayer is the opening of our hearts Godward, and the answer is a flow of light and influence from God.

𝕮   If anyone comes to public worship and leaves with the feeling that he or she has got nothing out of it, let that person ask: "Did I bring anything to it?" . . . It is true of public worship in a high degree that only they receive who give. The influence of public worship, like that of electricity, is felt only where there is a capacity for receiving it. Stone and ice are spiritual nonconductors.

𝕮   A congregation at worship is a society declaring its devotion to God, a community forged by faith in the Divine. If in public worship I realize that my prayers are also the prayers of the one by my side, it will make us effectively aware of our common humanity and engender a spirit potent for social good. They who worship God together bring God into their mutual relations. If public worship does not produce this result, it is but private worship in a public place. If it does bring people close together under the influence of God, then it sanctifies human society.

𝕮   Prayer gives us the guidance we need. It opens the mind to the illumination of God. . . . Through prayer, we can receive the guidance of God to strengthen our hold on truth, goodness, righteousness, and purity; the laws emanating from the nature of God.

𝕮   One who is about to pray should learn from a common laborer, who sometimes takes a whole day to prepare for a job. A wood-cutter, who spends most of the day sharpening the saw and only the last hour cutting the wood, has earned a day's wage.

❦ Prayer is opening the heart to God. It is not all petition. It has its listening side. Prayer is more than speaking to God; it is giving God an opportunity to speak to us.

❦ All the gates of Heaven are closed except the Gates of Tears. These are always open. (Talmud Berachot 32a)

A Chasidic master said: Why are the Gates of Tears always open? Because tears are a sign of grief, and grief cannot open gates that are closed. The other gates, however, need not be kept open, for they can be opened by joyful prayer.

SPIRITUAL LIFE

℘   Spiritual life and secure life do not go together. To save oneself one must struggle and take risks.

℘   If you divide your life between God and the world, through giving the world "what is its" to save for God "what is God's," you are denying God the service the Holy One demands: to hallow the everyday in the world and the soul.

℘   This is the vision of a great and noble life: to endure ambiguity and to make light shine through it; to stand fast in uncertainty; to prove capable of unlimited love and hope.

℘   The genius of Judaism resides . . . in raising the secular to the sacred, the material to the spiritual. Just as Judaism raises the seventh day to the Sabbath, so it seeks to raise every weekday to the Sabbath.

℘

The road that stretches before our feet
is a challenge to the heart
long before it tests the strength of our legs.
Our destiny is to run to the edge of the world
and beyond, off into the darkness;
sure, for all our blindness;
secure, for all our helplessness;
strong, for all our weakness;
gaily in love, for all the pressure on our hearts.
In that darkness beyond the world,
we can begin to know the world and ourselves.
We begin to understand that we are not made
to pace out our lives behind prison walls,
but to walk into the arms of God.

LIFE IN THE WORLD

❧   The Jews have always been a minority. But a minority is compelled to think; that is the blessing of its fate. The conviction of the few is expressed through the energy of constant searching and finding.

❧   Our life is fulfilled by what we become, not by what we were at birth. Endowment and heritage mean much and then again nothing; the essential thing is what we make of them.

❧   *When you come into the land and plant. . . .* (Leviticus 19:23) Though you find the land full of goodness, don't think of sitting idle. Make sure to plant trees. As you found trees that others planted, so you must plant for your children. Never say "I am old. How many more years do I have? Why should I trouble myself for the sake of others?" You found trees, so you must plant more even when you are old.

❧   Do not imagine that all other beings exist merely for the sake of the existence of human beings. On the contrary, all other beings exist for their own sakes, and not for the sake of something else.

שירים SONGS

שבת המלכה THE SUN ON THE TREETOPS

הַחַמָּה מֵרֹאשׁ הָאִילָנוֹת נִסְתַּלְּקָה,
בֹּאוּ וְנֵצֵא לִקְרַאת שַׁבָּת הַמַּלְכָּה.
הִנֵּה הִיא יוֹרֶדֶת, הַקְּדוֹשָׁה
הַבְּרוּכָה, וְעִמָּה מַלְאָכִים, צְבָא
שָׁלוֹם וּמְנוּחָה. בֹּאִי בֹּאִי
הַמַּלְכָּה! בֹּאִי בֹּאִי הַכַּלָּה!
שָׁלוֹם עֲלֵיכֶם, מַלְאֲכֵי הַשָּׁלוֹם.

Ha-cha-mah mei-rosh ha-i-la-not
nis-tal-kah, bo-u v'nei-tzei lik-rat
Shabbat ha-mal-kah.

Hi-nei hi yo-reh-det, ha-k'do-shah
ha-b'ru-chah, v'i-mah mal-a-chim,
tz'va sha-lom u-m'nu-chah.

Bo-i bo-i ha-mal-kah! Bo-i bo-i
ha-ka-lah! Sha-lom a-lei-chem,
mal-a-chei ha-shalom.

Additional song-texts begin on page 406.

The sun on the treetops no longer is seen,
Come gather to welcome the Sabbath, our queen.
Behold her descending, the holy, the blessed,
And with her the angels of peace and of rest.
Draw near, draw near, and here abide,
Draw near, draw near, O Sabbath bride.
Peace also to you, you angels of peace.

ידיד נפש HEART'S DELIGHT

יְדִיד נֶפֶשׁ, אָב הָרַחֲמָן, מְשׁוֹךְ עַבְדְּךָ אֶל רְצוֹנֶךָ.
יָרוּץ עַבְדְּךָ כְּמוֹ אַיָּל, יִשְׁתַּחֲוֶה אֶל מוּל הֲדָרֶךָ.
יֶעֱרַב לוֹ יְדִידוֹתֶיךָ מִנֹּפֶת צוּף וְכָל־טָעַם.

Y'did neh-fesh, Av ha-ra-cha-man, m'shoch av-d'cha el r'tzo-neh-cha.
Ya-rutz av-d'cha k'mo a-yal, yish-ta-cha-veh el mul ha-da-reh-cha.
Yeh-eh-rav lo y'di-do-teh-cha mi-no-fet tzuf v'chol ta-am.

Heart's delight, source of mercy, draw Your servant into Your arms. I
run toward You like a gazelle to gaze in adoration at Your beauty. Your
friendship is sweeter to me than honeyed taste.

8

שלום עליכם   PEACE BE TO YOU

שָׁלוֹם עֲלֵיכֶם, מַלְאֲכֵי הַשָּׁרֵת, מַלְאֲכֵי עֶלְיוֹן,

מִמֶּלֶךְ מַלְכֵי הַמְּלָכִים, הַקָּדוֹשׁ בָּרוּךְ הוּא.

בּוֹאֲכֶם לְשָׁלוֹם, מַלְאֲכֵי הַשָּׁלוֹם, מַלְאֲכֵי עֶלְיוֹן,

מִמֶּלֶךְ מַלְכֵי הַמְּלָכִים, הַקָּדוֹשׁ בָּרוּךְ הוּא.

בָּרְכוּנִי לְשָׁלוֹם, מַלְאֲכֵי הַשָּׁלוֹם, מַלְאֲכֵי עֶלְיוֹן,

מִמֶּלֶךְ מַלְכֵי הַמְּלָכִים, הַקָּדוֹשׁ בָּרוּךְ הוּא.

צֵאתְכֶם לְשָׁלוֹם, מַלְאֲכֵי הַשָּׁלוֹם, מַלְאֲכֵי עֶלְיוֹן,

מִמֶּלֶךְ מַלְכֵי הַמְּלָכִים, הַקָּדוֹשׁ בָּרוּךְ הוּא.

Sha-lom a-lei-chem mal-a-chei ha-sha-reit, mal-a-chei el-yon,

Mi-meh-lech ma-l'chei ha-m'la-chim, ha-ka-dosh ba-ruch hu.

Bo-a-chem l'sha-lom, mal-a-chei ha-sha-lom, mal-a-chei el-yon,

Mi-meh-lech ma-l'chei ha-m'la-chim, ha-ka-dosh ba-ruch hu.

Ba-r'chu-ni l'sha-lom, mal-a-chei ha-sha-lom, mal-a-chei el-yon,

Mi-meh-lech ma-l'chei ha-m'la-chim, ha-ka-dosh ba-ruch hu.

Tzei-t'chem l'sha-lom, mal-a-chei ha-sha-lom, mal-a-chei el-yon,

Mi-meh-lech ma-l'chei ha-m'la-chim, ha-ka-dosh ba-ruch hu.

Peace be to you, ministering angels, messengers of the Most High, of the supreme sovereign, the Holy One, ever to be praised.

Enter in peace, O messengers of the Most High, of the supreme sovereign, the Holy One, ever to be praised.

Bless us with peace, O messengers of the Most High, of the supreme sovereign, the Holy One, ever to be praised.

Depart in peace, O messengers of the Most High, of the supreme sovereign, the Holy One, ever to be praised.

אשא עיני   I LIFT UP MY EYES

אֶשָּׂא עֵינַי אֶל־הֶהָרִים: מֵאַיִן יָבֹא עֶזְרִי?
עֶזְרִי מֵעִם יהוה, עֹשֵׂה שָׁמַיִם וָאָרֶץ.

Eh-sa ei-nai el heh-ha-rim: mei-a-yin ya-vo ez-ri?
Ez-ri mei-im Adonai, o-seh sha-ma-yim va-a-retz.

I lift up my eyes unto the mountains: where will I find my help? My help
comes from Adonai, maker of heaven and earth.

וטהר לבנו   PURIFY OUR HEARTS

וְטַהֵר לִבֵּנוּ לְעָבְדְּךָ בֶּאֱמֶת.

V'ta-heir li-bei-nu l'ov-d'cha beh-eh-met.

Purify our hearts to serve You in truth.

מי האיש   WHO AMONG US?

מִי־הָאִישׁ הֶחָפֵץ חַיִּים,   Mi ha-ish heh-cha-feitz cha-yim,
אֹהֵב יָמִים לִרְאוֹת טוֹב?   o-heiv ya-mim lir-ot tov?
נְצֹר לְשׁוֹנְךָ מֵרָע,   N'tzor l'sho-n'cha mei-ra,
וּשְׂפָתֶיךָ מִדַּבֵּר מִרְמָה.   u-s'fa-teh-cha mi-da-beir mir-mah.
סוּר מֵרָע וַעֲשֵׂה־טוֹב,   Sur mei-ra va-a-sei tov,
בַּקֵּשׁ שָׁלוֹם וְרָדְפֵהוּ.   ba-keish shalom v'rod'fei-hu.

Who among us craves life, and longs for time to see the good? Then let
us keep our tongue from evil, our lips from deceitful speech. Let us turn
aside from evil and do good; seek peace and pursue it.

הנה מה טוב   HOW GOOD IT IS

הִנֵּה מַה־טּוֹב וּמַה־נָּעִים שֶׁבֶת אַחִים גַּם־יָחַד.

Hi-nei mah-tov u-mah na-im sheh-vet a-chim gam ya-chad.

How good it is, and how pleasant, to dwell together in unity.

אנעים זמירות   SWEET HYMNS

אַנְעִים זְמִירוֹת וְשִׁירִים אֶאֱרֹג,

כִּי אֵלֶיךָ נַפְשִׁי תַעֲרֹג.

נַפְשִׁי חִמְּדָה בְּצֵל יָדֶךָ,

לָדַעַת כָּל־רָז סוֹדֶךָ.

מִדֵּי דַבְּרִי בִּכְבוֹדֶךָ,

הוֹמֶה לִבִּי אֶל־דּוֹדֶיךָ.

יֶעֱרַב־נָא שִׂיחִי עָלֶיךָ,

כִּי נַפְשִׁי תַעֲרֹג אֵלֶיךָ.

Sweet hymns and songs I weave

for You, my soul's delight.

My soul yearns for You,

Yearns to know Your mysteries.

And as I declare Your glory,

Your love is my heart's desire.

Pleasing be my praise to You,

the one for whom my spirit longs.

שחר אבקשך   AT THE DAWN I SEEK YOU

שַׁחַר אֲבַקֶּשְׁךָ, צוּרִי וּמִשְׂגַּבִּי,

אֶעֱרוֹךְ לְפָנֶיךָ שַׁחֲרִי וְגַם

עַרְבִּי.

לִפְנֵי גְדֻלָּתָךְ אֶעֱמֹד וְאֶבָּהֵל,

כִּי עֵינְךָ תִרְאֶה כָּל־מַחְשְׁבוֹת

לִבִּי.

מַה־זֶּה אֲשֶׁר יוּכַל הַלֵּב

וְהַלָּשׁוֹן לַעֲשׂוֹת, וּמַה כֹּחַ

רוּחִי בְּתוֹךְ קִרְבִּי?

הִנֵּה לְךָ תִיטַב זִמְרַת אֱנוֹשׁ,

עַל כֵּן אוֹדְךָ בְּעוֹד תִּהְיֶה

נִשְׁמַת אֱלוֹהַ בִּי.

At the dawn do I seek You,

my rock and refuge strong,

setting my morning prayer before You,

my evening prayer as well.

Before Your greatness

I stand in awe and fear;

the thoughts my heart has hidden

to Your seeing eye are clear.

What, however, is it, that

heart and tongue can do?

What is this my strength,

my spirit's strength within me?

Yet You find it pleasing

to hear our human praise-songs;

therefore I will thank You all my days,

while Your spirit dwells within me.

OPENING PRAYERS

1

PREPARING FOR WORSHIP AS A FAMILY OF FAMILIES: AM YISRAEL.

Surrounded by the members of the community in which we live, we come before You, eternal God. We share our happiness and it becomes greater. We share our troubles and they seem smaller. May we never be too selfish to give, nor too proud to receive, for in giving and receiving we discover You and the meaning of our life.

Let us not separate ourselves from the true strength of our community: the experience and wisdom of old people, the hopes of the young, and the examples of care and courage that sustain us. Open our hearts and minds to welcome those who need us, thus to receive a measure of Your presence in our daily life.

2

PREPARING FOR WORSHIP AS A FAMILY OF FAMILIES: AM YISRAEL.

We thank You, O God, for this time of prayer, when we become especially conscious of Your presence, and place before You our desires, our hopes, and our gratitude. This consciousness, this inner certainty of Your presence, is our greatest blessing.

Holy One, bless our worship this day. May the gleams of Your light and the visions of Your truth that bless us here abide with us when we go out into the world, keeping us steadfast in loyalty to You and Your Mitzvot. Amen.

ברוך יהוה יום יום

SERVICES FOR
WEEKDAYS

A PRAYER
BEFORE
PRAYER:
May my
worship today
encourage me
to fulfill this
Mitzvah:
"You shall not
keep the wages
belonging to a
worker beyond
the time when
it is due."
(Leviticus
19:13)

In the dark of night and in the light of day, praise the ever-lasting God.

Praised be the one whose glory fills heaven and earth.

Praise the one who made this green earth our dwelling-place.

Praised be the one who filled the ocean-depths with life.

From generation to generation we give thanks to Your name;

to the end of time we will sing Your praise.

ALL RISE

OR

הִנֵּה, בָּרְכוּ אֶת־יהוה, כָּל־עַבְדֵי יהוה,

הָעֹמְדִים בְּבֵית־יהוה בַּלֵּילוֹת.

שְׂאוּ־יְדֵכֶם קֹדֶשׁ, וּבָרְכוּ אֶת־יהוה.

יְבָרֶכְךָ יהוה מִצִּיּוֹן, עֹשֵׂה שָׁמַיִם וָאָרֶץ.

בָּרוּךְ יהוה בַּיּוֹם, בָּרוּךְ יהוה בַּלֵּילָה.

בָּרוּךְ יהוה בְּשָׁכְבֵנוּ, בָּרוּךְ יהוה בְּקוּמֵנוּ.

Come, praise Adonai, all God's servants, you who stand at night in the house of God.

Raise yourselves toward holiness, and praise Adonai.

May God, the maker of heaven and earth, bless you out of Zion.

Praised be God by day, praised be God by night.

Praised be God when we lie down, praised be God when we rise up.

ALL RISE

13

שמע וברכותיה   THE SHEMA AND ITS BLESSINGS

בָּרְכוּ אֶת־יי הַמְבֹרָךְ.

בָּרוּךְ יי הַמְבֹרָךְ לְעוֹלָם וָעֶד.

Praise Adonai, to whom our praise is due.

We praise Adonai,

to whom our praise is due forever and ever.

מעריב ערבים   CREATION

בָּרוּךְ אַתָּה יי, אֱלֹהֵינוּ מֶלֶךְ הָעוֹלָם,

אֲשֶׁר בִּדְבָרוֹ מַעֲרִיב עֲרָבִים,

All creation
has one origin;
we celebrate
its creator
and sustainer.

✣ See page 355
and Psalm 148
(page 374).

We praise You, Adonai our God, sovereign of the universe, whose word makes evening fall.

בְּחָכְמָה פּוֹתֵחַ שְׁעָרִים,

וּבִתְבוּנָה מְשַׁנֶּה עִתִּים,

וּמַחֲלִיף אֶת־הַזְּמַנִּים,

וּמְסַדֵּר אֶת־הַכּוֹכָבִים

בְּמִשְׁמְרוֹתֵיהֶם בָּרָקִיעַ

כִּרְצוֹנוֹ. בּוֹרֵא יוֹם וָלַיְלָה,

גּוֹלֵל אוֹר מִפְּנֵי חֹשֶׁךְ

וְחֹשֶׁךְ מִפְּנֵי אוֹר,

וּמַעֲבִיר יוֹם וּמֵבִיא לַיְלָה,

וּמַבְדִּיל בֵּין יוֹם וּבֵין

לַיְלָה: יי צְבָאוֹת שְׁמוֹ.

Your wisdom opens the gates of heaven, Your understanding makes times pass and seasons change, Your law orders the stars in their courses through the skies.

Creator of day and night, You roll away light as darkness falls, and darkness with the coming of the light. You make day pass and bring on the night, to separate day from night: You are the God of time and space.

בָּרוּךְ אַתָּה יי, הַמַּעֲרִיב עֲרָבִים.

We praise You, O God, whose word makes evening fall.

14

REVELATION אהבת עולם

God, origin of space/time, is also the foundation of the moral order.

❧ See Pirke Avot, page 322, and Psalm 51 (page 364).

אַהֲבַת עוֹלָם בֵּית יִשְׂרָאֵל עַמְּךָ אָהָבְתָּ.

Unending love have You shown the House of Israel, Your people:

תּוֹרָה וּמִצְוֹת, חֻקִּים
וּמִשְׁפָּטִים אוֹתָנוּ לִמַּדְתָּ.
עַל־כֵּן, יְיָ אֱלֹהֵינוּ,
בְּשָׁכְבֵּנוּ וּבְקוּמֵנוּ נָשִׂיחַ
בְּחֻקֶּיךָ, וְנִשְׂמַח בְּדִבְרֵי
תוֹרָתְךָ וּבְמִצְוֹתֶיךָ לְעוֹלָם
וָעֶד. כִּי הֵם חַיֵּינוּ וְאֹרֶךְ
יָמֵינוּ, וּבָהֶם נֶהְגֶּה יוֹמָם
וָלָיְלָה. וְאַהֲבָתְךָ אַל־תָּסוּר
מִמֶּנּוּ לְעוֹלָמִים.

Torah and Mitzvot, laws and precepts have You taught us. And so, when we lie down and when we rise up, we will meditate on the meanings of Your law, and rejoice forever in Your Torah and Mitzvot. Day and night we will reflect on them, for they are our life and the length of our days. O may Your love never depart from our hearts!

בָּרוּךְ אַתָּה יְיָ, אוֹהֵב עַמּוֹ יִשְׂרָאֵל.

We praise You, O God: You love Your people Israel.

שְׁמַע יִשְׂרָאֵל: יהוה אֱלֹהֵינוּ, יהוה אֶחָד.
בָּרוּךְ שֵׁם כְּבוֹד מַלְכוּתוֹ לְעוֹלָם וָעֶד.

Hear, O Israel: Adonai is our God, Adonai alone.
Praised be God's glorious majesty forever and ever.

ALL ARE SEATED

וְאָהַבְתָּ אֵת יְהֹוָה אֱלֹהֶיךָ
בְּכָל־לְבָבְךָ וּבְכָל־נַפְשְׁךָ וּבְכָל־מְאֹדֶךָ:
וְהָיוּ הַדְּבָרִים הָאֵלֶּה אֲשֶׁר אָנֹכִי מְצַוְּךָ הַיּוֹם

15

עַל־לְבָבֶךָ: וְשִׁנַּנְתָּם לְבָנֶיךָ וְדִבַּרְתָּ בָּם

בְּשִׁבְתְּךָ בְּבֵיתֶךָ וּבְלֶכְתְּךָ בַדֶּרֶךְ וּבְשָׁכְבְּךָ וּבְקוּמֶךָ:

וּקְשַׁרְתָּם לְאוֹת עַל־יָדֶךָ וְהָיוּ לְטֹטָפֹת בֵּין עֵינֶיךָ:

וּכְתַבְתָּם עַל־מְזֻזֹת בֵּיתֶךָ וּבִשְׁעָרֶיךָ:

לְמַעַן תִּזְכְּרוּ וַעֲשִׂיתֶם אֶת־כָּל־מִצְוֹתָי

וִהְיִיתֶם קְדֹשִׁים לֵאלֹהֵיכֶם:

אֲנִי יְהֹוָה אֱלֹהֵיכֶם אֲשֶׁר הוֹצֵאתִי אֶתְכֶם מֵאֶרֶץ מִצְרַיִם

לִהְיוֹת לָכֶם לֵאלֹהִים: אֲנִי יְהֹוָה אֱלֹהֵיכֶם:

*V'a-hav-ta et Adonai Eh-lo-heh-cha b'chol l'va-v'cha u-v'chol naf-sh'cha
u-v'chol m'o-deh-cha. V'ha-yu ha-d'va-rim ha-ei-leh a-sher a-no-chi
m'tza-v'cha ha-yom al l'va-veh-cha. V'shi-nan-tam l'va-neh-cha v'di-bar-ta
bam b'shiv-t'cha b'vei-teh-cha u-v'lech-t'cha va-deh-rech u-v'shoch-b'cha
u-v'ku-meh-cha. U-k'shar-tam l'ot al ya-deh-cha v'ha-yu l'to-ta-fot bein
ei-neh-cha; uch'tav-tam al m'zu-zot bei-teh-cha u-vi-sh'a-reh-cha. L'ma-an
tiz-k'ru va-a-si-tem et kol mitz-vo-tai, vi-h'yi-tem k'do-shim lei-lo-hei-chem.
A-ni Adonai Eh-lo-hei-chem a-sher ho-tzei-ti et-chem mei-eh-retz mitz-ra-yim
li-h'yot la-chem lei-lo-him. A-ni Adonai Eh-lo-hei-chem.*

*You shall love Adonai your God with all your mind, with all
your heart, with all your might. Let these words, which I
command you this day, be upon your heart. Teach them
constantly to your children, speaking of them in your home and
on your way, when you lie down and when you rise up. Bind
them as a sign upon your hand; let them be symbols before your
eyes; and inscribe them on the doorposts of your house, and on
your gates: that you may be mindful of all my Mitzvot, and do
them; then shall you be consecrated to your God. I, Adonai, am
your God who led you out of Egypt to be your God; I, Adonai, am
your God.*

At times
we think
of You as a
question,
when we need
to feel You as
the question.
May my
life be the
response I
make, when
You *are* the
question.

❖ See "Looking
for God,"
pages 352-357.

SOME MAY WISH TO INCLUDE THE FOLLOWING

וְהָיָה אִם־שָׁמֹעַ תִּשְׁמְעוּ אֶל־מִצְוֹתַי אֲשֶׁר אָנֹכִי מְצַוֶּה אֶתְכֶם הַיּוֹם
לְאַהֲבָה אֶת־יְהֹוָה אֱלֹהֵיכֶם וּלְעָבְדוֹ בְּכָל־לְבַבְכֶם וּבְכָל־נַפְשְׁכֶם:
יְצַו יְהֹוָה אִתְּךָ אֶת־הַבְּרָכָה בַּאֲסָמֶיךָ וּבְכֹל מִשְׁלַח יָדֶךָ וּבֵרַכְךָ
בָּאָרֶץ אֲשֶׁר־יְהֹוָה אֱלֹהֶיךָ נֹתֵן לָךְ: יְקִימְךָ יְהֹוָה לוֹ לְעַם קָדוֹשׁ
כַּאֲשֶׁר נִשְׁבַּע־לָךְ כִּי תִשְׁמֹר אֶת־מִצְוֹת יְהֹוָה אֱלֹהֶיךָ וְהָלַכְתָּ
בִּדְרָכָיו: כִּי הַמִּצְוָה הַזֹּאת אֲשֶׁר אָנֹכִי מְצַוְּךָ הַיּוֹם לֹא־נִפְלֵאת
הִוא מִמְּךָ וְלֹא רְחֹקָה הִוא: כִּי־קָרוֹב אֵלֶיךָ הַדָּבָר מְאֹד בְּפִיךָ
וּבִלְבָבְךָ לַעֲשֹׂתוֹ: הַעִידֹתִי בָכֶם הַיּוֹם אֶת־הַשָּׁמַיִם וְאֶת־הָאָרֶץ
הַחַיִּים וְהַמָּוֶת נָתַתִּי לְפָנֶיךָ הַבְּרָכָה וְהַקְּלָלָה וּבָחַרְתָּ בַּחַיִּים
לְמַעַן תִּחְיֶה אַתָּה וְזַרְעֶךָ:

If you truly hearken to the Mitzvot that I command you this day, to love and serve Adonai your God with all your heart and mind, then your God will ordain blessing upon your homes and all your undertakings, and upon the soil on which your God has placed you. Adonai will affirm you as a holy people, when you keep the Mitzvot and walk in the ways of your God.

For this Mitzvah that I command you this day is not too difficult for you; nor is it far away—no, this word is very near you, in your mouth and in your heart—and you can do it. I call heaven and earth to witness before you this day: life and death have I placed before you, blessing and curse. Choose life, then, that you and your children may live.

(Deuteronomy 11:13; 28:8-9; 30:11,14,19)

৵

גאולה REDEMPTION

אֱמֶת וֶאֱמוּנָה כָּל־זֹאת, וְקַיָּם
עָלֵינוּ, כִּי הוּא יי אֱלֹהֵינוּ,
וְאֵין זוּלָתוֹ, וַאֲנַחְנוּ יִשְׂרָאֵל
עַמּוֹ. הַפּוֹדֵנוּ מִיַּד מְלָכִים,
הַגּוֹאֲלֵנוּ מִכַּף כָּל־הֶעָרִיצִים,
וַיּוֹצֵא אֶת־עַמּוֹ יִשְׂרָאֵל
מִמִּצְרַיִם לְחֵרוּת עוֹלָם.
וְרָאוּ בָנָיו גְּבוּרָתוֹ, שִׁבְּחוּ
וְהוֹדוּ לִשְׁמוֹ, וּמַלְכוּתוֹ
בְּרָצוֹן קִבְּלוּ עֲלֵיהֶם.
מֹשֶׁה וּמִרְיָם וְכָל־יִשְׂרָאֵל
לְךָ עָנוּ שִׁירָה בְּשִׂמְחָה
רַבָּה, וְאָמְרוּ כֻלָּם:

All this we hold to be true and sure: You are Adonai our God, there is none else, and we are Israel Your people.

You deliver us from the hand of oppressors and save us from the grip of every tyrant, as when You led us out of Egypt, forever to be free to serve You.

When Your children witnessed Your might, they acclaimed You and gave thanks to Your name; gladly they enthroned You; then, full of joy, Moses, Miriam, and all Israel sang together:

We remember the bitter root of bondage, and we remember, also, the first redemption, the taste and smell of sweet freedom's bread, and the song of Miriam, Moses, and all Israel. From all this we learned to hope that others, too, might come to know the joy of freedom.

✣ See page 348, foot of page, and Psalm 3 (page 358).

מִי־כָמֹכָה בָּאֵלִם, יהוה?
מִי כָּמֹכָה, נֶאְדָּר בַּקֹּדֶשׁ,
נוֹרָא תְהִלֹּת, עֹשֵׂה פֶלֶא?
מַלְכוּתְךָ רָאוּ בָנֶיךָ,
בּוֹקֵעַ יָם לִפְנֵי מֹשֶׁה;
זֶה אֵלִי! עָנוּ וְאָמְרוּ:
יהוה יִמְלֹךְ לְעֹלָם וָעֶד!

Mi cha-mo-cha ba-ei-lim, Adonai?

Mi ka-mo-cha, neh-dar ba-ko-desh,

no-ra t'hi-lot, o-sei feh-leh?

Mal-chu-t'cha ra-u va-neh-cha,

bo-kei-a yam li-f'nei Mo-sheh;

zeh Ei-li! A-nu v'a-m'ru:

Adonai yim-loch l'o-lam va-ed.

וַנֶּאֱמַר: V'neh-eh-mar:

כִּי פָדָה יי אֶת־יַעֲקֹב, Ki fa-da Adonai et Ya-a-kov,

וּגְאָלוֹ מִיַּד חָזָק מִמֶּנּוּ. u-g'a-lo mi-yad cha-zak mi-meh-nu.

בָּרוּךְ אַתָּה יי, גָּאַל Ba-ruch a-ta Adonai, ga-al

יִשְׂרָאֵל. Yis-ra-eil.

Who is like You, Adonai, among all that is worshiped? Who is like You, glorious in holiness, awesome in splendor, doing wonders?

With the parting of the waters, Your children perceived Your sovereign might. "This is my God!" they cried. "Adonai shall reign forever and ever."

And it has been said: "Adonai has delivered Jacob, and redeemed us from the hand of one stronger than ourselves."

We praise You, O God, redeemer of Israel.

הַשְׁכִּיבֵנוּ   DIVINE PROVIDENCE

✽ See page 379, Psalm 4 (page 359), and Psalm 131 (page 370).

הַשְׁכִּיבֵנוּ, יי אֱלֹהֵינוּ, לְשָׁלוֹם, וְהַעֲמִידֵנוּ, מַלְכֵּנוּ, לְחַיִּים.

וּפְרוֹשׁ עָלֵינוּ סֻכַּת שְׁלוֹמֶךָ, וְתַקְּנֵנוּ בְּעֵצָה טוֹבָה מִלְּפָנֶיךָ,

וְהוֹשִׁיעֵנוּ לְמַעַן שְׁמֶךָ, וְהָגֵן בַּעֲדֵנוּ.

וְהָסֵר מֵעָלֵינוּ אוֹיֵב דֶּבֶר וְחֶרֶב וְרָעָב וְיָגוֹן;

וְהָסֵר שָׂטָן מִלְּפָנֵינוּ וּמֵאַחֲרֵינוּ.

וּבְצֵל כְּנָפֶיךָ תַּסְתִּירֵנוּ, כִּי אֵל שׁוֹמְרֵנוּ וּמַצִּילֵנוּ אָתָּה,

כִּי אֵל מֶלֶךְ חַנּוּן וְרַחוּם אָתָּה.

וּשְׁמוֹר צֵאתֵנוּ וּבוֹאֵנוּ לְחַיִּים וּלְשָׁלוֹם מֵעַתָּה וְעַד עוֹלָם.

Help us to lie down in peace, Adonai our God, and help us rise up to life renewed. Spread over us the shelter of Your peace; guide us with Your good counsel; and for Your name's sake, be our help.

19

Be a shield about us; save us from hatred and sickness, from war, famine, and anguish; and help us to turn aside from evil.

Shelter us in the shadow of Your wings, for You are our guardian and helper, a gracious and merciful God.

And guard our going out and our coming in, that we may have life and peace, now and always.

בָּרוּךְ אַתָּה יי, שׁוֹמֵר עַמּוֹ יִשְׂרָאֵל לָעַד.

We praise You, O God, forever the guardian of Your people Israel.

A REFLECTION

❧   *The Holy One makes good intentions bear fruit.* (Talmud Kiddushin 40a) If, despite all your labors, you have not accomplished all that you set out to do, do not throw up your hands in despair: God takes note of your labors, even those that do not succeed, and reckons you as having accomplished your task. (Machzor Vitry, 11-12th century)

৵

THE READER'S KADDISH IS ON PAGE 43

৵

WHEN PUTTING ON THE TALLIT

בָּרְכִי נַפְשִׁי אֶת־יהוה! יהוה אֱלֹהַי, גָּדַלְתָּ מְּאֹד!
הוֹד וְהָדָר לָבָשְׁתָּ, עֹטֶה־אוֹר כַּשַּׂלְמָה, נוֹטֶה שָׁמַיִם כַּיְרִיעָה.

Praise Adonai, O my soul! Adonai my God, how very great You
are! Arrayed in glory and spendor, You wrap Yourself in light as
with a garment; You stretch out the heavens like a curtain.

בָּרוּךְ אַתָּה יי, אֱלֹהֵינוּ מֶלֶךְ הָעוֹלָם,
אֲשֶׁר קִדְּשָׁנוּ בְּמִצְוֹתָיו וְצִוָּנוּ לְהִתְעַטֵּף בַּצִּיצִת.

We praise You, Adonai our God, sovereign of the universe: You
hallow us with the Mitzvah of Tzitzit ["fringes"].

WHEN PUTTING ON TEFILLIN

On the hand

בָּרוּךְ אַתָּה יי, אֱלֹהֵינוּ מֶלֶךְ הָעוֹלָם,
אֲשֶׁר קִדְּשָׁנוּ בְּמִצְוֹתָיו וְצִוָּנוּ לְהָנִיחַ תְּפִלִּין.

We praise You, Adonai our God, sovereign of the universe: You
hallow·us with the Mitzvah of wearing Tefillin.

On the head

בָּרוּךְ אַתָּה יי, אֱלֹהֵינוּ מֶלֶךְ הָעוֹלָם,
אֲשֶׁר קִדְּשָׁנוּ בְּמִצְוֹתָיו וְצִוָּנוּ עַל־מִצְוַת תְּפִלִּין.

We praise You, Adonai our God, sovereign of the universe: You
hallow us with the Mitzvah of Tefillin.

Upon
winding the
Retzuah on
the finger.

וְאֵרַשְׂתִּיךְ לִי לְעוֹלָם; וְאֵרַשְׂתִּיךְ לִי בְּצֶדֶק וּבְמִשְׁפָּט, וּבְחֶסֶד
וּבְרַחֲמִים. וְאֵרַשְׂתִּיךְ לִי בֶּאֱמוּנָה, וְיָדַעַתְּ אֶת־יהוה.

May I bring head, heart, and hand to the service of the Holy One,
and prove worthy of the divine promise to us: "I will betroth you
to me forever; I will betroth you to me in righteousness and
justice, in love and compassion; I will betroth you to me in
faithfulness, and you shall know your God."

21

מְקוֹר הַחַיִּים, Fountain of Life, at break of day we invite Your presence. We enter Your house to worship, and You say: "Be holy: serve one another in love."

אוֹר הַחַיִּים, Light of the Living, at break of day we invite Your presence. Give wings to our hopes and dreams, and bless us each day as we go forth to do our work in the world. Amen.

A REFLECTION

❧ The Baal Shem Tov used to teach: If you understand that each day the world is created anew, and that you yourself are born anew each morning, your faith will grow, and every day you will find yourself newly eager to serve God. (Chasidic)

You made me in Your image, a creature able to walk in Your footsteps; You made me a creator, a dreaming child in a universe filled with wonder. Let me look with grateful eyes upon the world. Help me to see Your creation with new eyes, to draw new pictures in the sand—visible dreams of an invisible love. O God, for the love You daily show us by creating the world anew, I give thanks.

❧

CONTINUE WITH ONE OR MORE OF THE FOLLOWING
BIRCHOT HA-SHACHAR

אשר יצר   FOR THE BODY

בָּרוּךְ אַתָּה יְיָ, אֱלֹהֵינוּ מֶלֶךְ הָעוֹלָם,
אֲשֶׁר יָצַר אֶת־הָאָדָם בְּחָכְמָה,
וּבָרָא בוֹ נְקָבִים נְקָבִים, חֲלוּלִים חֲלוּלִים.
גָּלוּי וְיָדוּעַ לִפְנֵי כִסֵּא כְבוֹדֶךָ,

A PRAYER BEFORE PRAYER: May my worship today encourage me to fulfill this precept: "Sow for yourselves righteousness; reap the fruit of steadfast love; break up your fallow ground: for it is time to seek the Eternal One." (Hosea 10:12)

22

❋ See page
351 and
"Prayers for
Healing,"
pages 376-378.

שֶׁאִם יִפָּתֵחַ אֶחָד מֵהֶם אוֹ יִסָּתֵם אֶחָד מֵהֶם,

אִי אֶפְשַׁר לְהִתְקַיֵּם וְלַעֲמוֹד לְפָנֶיךָ.

בָּרוּךְ אַתָּה יי, רוֹפֵא כָל־בָּשָׂר וּמַפְלִיא לַעֲשׂוֹת.

We praise the eternal God, sovereign of the universe, who
with wisdom has fashioned us, making our vital organs, our
veins and arteries, our nerves and sinews—balancing all the
forces within us. O God enthroned in glory, were even one
of these organs to fail, we could not stand before You.

*We praise You, Adonai, wondrous source of healing and well-
being.*

THE READER'S KADDISH IS ON PAGE 43

אלהי נשמה   FOR THE SOVL

אֱלֹהַי, נְשָׁמָה שֶׁנָּתַתָּ בִּי טְהוֹרָה הִיא!

The soul that You have given me, O God, is pure!

❋ See page
182 and
"Looking at
Ourselves,"
pages 347-351.

אַתָּה בְרָאתָהּ, אַתָּה יְצַרְתָּהּ, אַתָּה נְפַחְתָּהּ בִּי, וְאַתָּה מְשַׁמְּרָהּ
בְּקִרְבִּי. כָּל־זְמַן שֶׁהַנְּשָׁמָה בְקִרְבִּי, מוֹדֶה אֲנִי לְפָנֶיךָ, יי אֱלֹהַי
וֵאלֹהֵי אֲבוֹתַי וְאִמּוֹתַי, רִבּוֹן כָּל־הַמַּעֲשִׂים, אֲדוֹן כָּל־הַנְּשָׁמוֹת.

*You created and formed it, breathed it into me, and within me
You sustain it. So long as I have breath, therefore, I will give
thanks to You, my God, God of my fathers and mothers, source of
all being, loving guide of every human spirit.*

בָּרוּךְ אַתָּה יי, אֲשֶׁר בְּיָדוֹ נֶפֶשׁ כָּל־חָי וְרוּחַ כָּל־בְּשַׂר־אִישׁ.

*We praise You, O God: In Your hand are the souls of all the
living and the spirits of all flesh.*

THE READER'S KADDISH IS ON PAGE 43

לעסוק בדברי תורה FOR TORAH

בָּרוּךְ אַתָּה יי, אֱלֹהֵינוּ מֶלֶךְ הָעוֹלָם, אֲשֶׁר קִדְּשָׁנוּ
בְּמִצְוֹתָיו וְצִוָּנוּ לַעֲסוֹק בְּדִבְרֵי תוֹרָה.

✤ See Pirke Avot, pages 322-340.

We praise You, Adonai our God, sovereign of the universe:
You hallow us with Your Mitzvot and command us to
immerse ourselves in Torah.

וְהַעֲרֶב־נָא, יי אֱלֹהֵינוּ, אֶת־דִּבְרֵי תוֹרָתְךָ
בְּפִינוּ וּבְפִי עַמְּךָ בֵּית יִשְׂרָאֵל,
וְנִהְיֶה אֲנַחְנוּ וְצֶאֱצָאֵינוּ,
וְצֶאֱצָאֵי עַמְּךָ בֵּית יִשְׂרָאֵל,
כֻּלָּנוּ יוֹדְעֵי שְׁמֶךָ וְלוֹמְדֵי תוֹרָתֶךָ לִשְׁמָהּ.
בָּרוּךְ אַתָּה יי, הַמְלַמֵּד תּוֹרָה לְעַמּוֹ יִשְׂרָאֵל.

*Adonai our God, let the words of Your Torah be sweet in our
mouths, and in the mouths of Your people Israel, that we and our
children may all come to know You through our loving study of
Torah. We praise You, Adonai, teacher of Torah to Your people
Israel.*

אֵלּוּ דְבָרִים שֶׁאֵין לָהֶם שִׁעוּר:
כִּבּוּד אָב וָאֵם, וּגְמִילוּת חֲסָדִים, וְהַשְׁכָּמַת בֵּית הַמִּדְרָשׁ
שַׁחֲרִית וְעַרְבִית, וְהַכְנָסַת אוֹרְחִים, וּבִקּוּר חוֹלִים,
וְהַכְנָסַת כַּלָּה, וּלְוָיַת הַמֵּת, וְעִיּוּן תְּפִלָּה, וַהֲבָאַת שָׁלוֹם
בֵּין אָדָם לַחֲבֵרוֹ. וְתַלְמוּד תּוֹרָה כְּנֶגֶד כֻּלָּם.

These are duties whose worth cannot be measured:

honoring one's father and mother,
acts of lovingkindness,
diligent pursuit of knowledge and wisdom,

hospitality to wayfarers,
visiting the sick,
rejoicing with bride and groom,
consoling the bereaved,
praying with sincerity,
and making peace when people quarrel.
And the study of Torah leads to them all.

THE READER'S KADDISH IS ON PAGE 43

ברכות יום יום   OUR DAILY BLESSINGS

❧ See "For a World of Wonders," pages 392-393.

בָּרוּךְ אַתָּה יי, אֱלֹהֵינוּ מֶלֶךְ הָעוֹלָם,
אֲשֶׁר נָתַן לַשֶּׂכְוִי בִינָה לְהַבְחִין בֵּין יוֹם וּבֵין לָיְלָה.

Praised be Adonai our God, who has given instinctive knowledge to every creature.

בָּרוּךְ אַתָּה יי, אֱלֹהֵינוּ מֶלֶךְ הָעוֹלָם, פּוֹקֵחַ עִוְרִים.

Praised be Adonai our God, who enlightens the blind.

בָּרוּךְ אַתָּה יי, אֱלֹהֵינוּ מֶלֶךְ הָעוֹלָם, מַלְבִּישׁ עֲרֻמִּים.

Praised be Adonai our God, who clothes the naked.

בָּרוּךְ אַתָּה יי, אֱלֹהֵינוּ מֶלֶךְ הָעוֹלָם, מַתִּיר אֲסוּרִים.

Praised be Adonai our God, who releases the captive.

בָּרוּךְ אַתָּה יי, אֱלֹהֵינוּ מֶלֶךְ הָעוֹלָם, זוֹקֵף כְּפוּפִים.

Praised be Adonai our God, who lifts up the fallen.

בָּרוּךְ אַתָּה יי, אֱלֹהֵינוּ מֶלֶךְ הָעוֹלָם, הַנּוֹתֵן לַיָּעֵף כֹּחַ.

Praised be Adonai our God, who gives strength to the weary.

בָּרוּךְ אַתָּה יי, אֱלֹהֵינוּ מֶלֶךְ הָעוֹלָם, עוֹטֵר יִשְׂרָאֵל בְּתִפְאָרָה.

Praised be Adonai our God, who crowns Israel with glory.

בָּרוּךְ אַתָּה יי, אֱלֹהֵינוּ מֶלֶךְ הָעוֹלָם, הַמַּעֲבִיר שֵׁנָה
מֵעֵינַי וּתְנוּמָה מֵעַפְעַפָּי.

Praised be Adonai our God, who opens our eyes to greet the new day.

THE READER'S KADDISH IS ON PAGE 43

FROM PSALM 19

הַשָּׁמַיִם מְסַפְּרִים כְּבוֹד־אֵל, וּמַעֲשֵׂה יָדָיו מַגִּיד הָרָקִיעַ.

יוֹם לְיוֹם יַבִּיעַ אֹמֶר, וְלַיְלָה לְּלַיְלָה יְחַוֶּה־דָּעַת.

✳ See "For a World of Wonders," pages 392-393.

The heavens declare the glory of God,

the sky proclaims God's handiwork.

Day unto day utters speech,

night unto night sends forth knowledge.

אֵין־אֹמֶר וְאֵין דְּבָרִים, בְּלִי נִשְׁמָע קוֹלָם.

בְּכָל־הָאָרֶץ יָצָא קַוָּם, וּבִקְצֵה תֵבֵל מִלֵּיהֶם.

Yet there is no speech, there are no words;

not a sound of them is heard!

And still their call goes out to all the earth,

their message to the end of the world.

A REFLECTION

❦   When I heard the learn'd astronomer,
When the proofs, the figures, were ranged in columns before me,
How soon unaccountable I became tired and sick,
Till rising and gliding out I wander'd off by myself,
In the mystical moist night-air, and from time to time,
Look'd up in perfect silence at the stars. (Walt Whitman)

THE READER'S KADDISH IS ON PAGE 43

26

A DAILY PSALM

SUNDAY

FROM PSALM 24

✢ See
"Selected
Psalms,"
pages 358-375.

A PRAISE-SONG OF DAVID

לְדָוִד מִזְמוֹר

לַיהוה הָאָרֶץ וּמְלוֹאָהּ, תֵּבֵל וְיֹשְׁבֵי בָהּ.

כִּי־הוּא עַל־יַמִּים יְסָדָהּ, וְעַל־נְהָרוֹת יְכוֹנְנֶהָ.

מִי־יַעֲלֶה בְהַר־יהוה, וּמִי־יָקוּם בִּמְקוֹם קָדְשׁוֹ?

נְקִי כַפַּיִם וּבַר־לֵבָב, אֲשֶׁר לֹא־נָשָׂא לַשָּׁוְא נַפְשִׁי,

וְלֹא נִשְׁבַּע לְמִרְמָה.

יִשָּׂא בְרָכָה מֵאֵת יהוה, וּצְדָקָה מֵאֱלֹהֵי יִשְׁעוֹ.

זֶה דּוֹר דֹּרְשָׁיו, מְבַקְשֵׁי פָנֶיךָ, יַעֲקֹב, סֶלָה.

The earth is Yours, Adonai, and the fullness thereof; the world and all who dwell in it.

For You set its foundation upon the seas, and established it upon the currents.

Who may ascend the mountain of Adonai, who may stand in God's holy place?

They that have clean hands and pure hearts, whose thought is not false, and whose word is good.

They will receive blessing from Adonai, justice from the God of their salvation.

This is the destiny of those who seek You, who seek Your presence, O God of Jacob.

ALL RISE

BAR'CHU IS ON PAGE 34

27

MONDAY

PSALM 1

אַשְׁרֵי הָאִישׁ אֲשֶׁר לֹא הָלַךְ בַּעֲצַת רְשָׁעִים,

וּבְדֶרֶךְ חַטָּאִים לֹא עָמָד, וּבְמוֹשַׁב לֵצִים לֹא יָשָׁב.

כִּי אִם בְּתוֹרַת יהוה חֶפְצוֹ, וּבְתוֹרָתוֹ יֶהְגֶּה יוֹמָם וָלָיְלָה.

וְהָיָה כְּעֵץ שָׁתוּל עַל־פַּלְגֵי מָיִם, אֲשֶׁר פִּרְיוֹ יִתֵּן בְּעִתּוֹ,

וְעָלֵהוּ לֹא־יִבּוֹל, וְכֹל אֲשֶׁר־יַעֲשֶׂה יַצְלִיחַ.

לֹא־כֵן הָרְשָׁעִים—כִּי אִם־כַּמֹּץ אֲשֶׁר־תִּדְּפֶנּוּ רוּחַ.

עַל־כֵּן לֹא־יָקֻמוּ רְשָׁעִים בַּמִּשְׁפָּט, וְחַטָּאִים בַּעֲדַת צַדִּיקִים.

כִּי־יוֹדֵעַ יהוה דֶּרֶךְ צַדִּיקִים, וְדֶרֶךְ רְשָׁעִים תֹּאבֵד.

❖ See "Selected Psalms," pages 358-375.

Blessed are they who do not follow the counsel of the wicked, who do not take the path of sinners, who do not join the company of cynics, who delight instead in God's teaching, as they meditate on it day and night.

They are like trees planted by running streams, trees that yield their fruit in season, whose leaves do not wither—the fruit of their labor is always good.

Not so the wicked—rootless, they drift, driven by the wind. For they cannot withstand scrutiny, nor stand among the righteous. Adonai values the way of the righteous, and causes the wicked to lose their way.

ALL RISE

BAR'CHU IS ON PAGE 34

TUESDAY

FROM PSALM 5

אֲמָרַי הַאֲזִינָה, יהוה, בִּינָה הֲגִיגִי.

הַקְשִׁיבָה לְקוֹל שַׁוְעִי, מַלְכִּי וֵאלֹהָי, כִּי־אֵלֶיךָ אֶתְפַּלָּל.

❖ See "Selected Psalms," pages 358-375.

יהוה, בְּקֶר תִּשְׁמַע קוֹלִי; בְּקֶר אֶעֱרָח־לְךָ, וַאֲצַפֶּה.

כִּי לֹא אֵל־חָפֵץ רֶשַׁע אָתָּה; לֹא יְגֻרְךָ רָע.

לֹא־יִתְיַצְּבוּ הוֹלְלִים לְנֶגֶד עֵינֶיךָ. שָׂנֵאתָ כָּל־פֹּעֲלֵי אָוֶן;

תְּאַבֵּד דֹּבְרֵי כָזָב; אִישׁ־דָּמִים וּמִרְמָה יְתָעֵב יהוה.

Give ear, Adonai, to my words; hear the whisper of my soul.
Listen to my cry for help, my sovereign God; for to You
alone do I pray.

*Hear my voice at daybreak; at daybreak I plead with You, and
wait.*

You are not a God who welcomes wickedness; evil cannot be
Your guest. The arrogant cannot look You in the eye—You
despise all who do evil. You make an end to liars; murderers
and traitors are abhorrent to You.

וַאֲנִי, בְּרֹב חַסְדְּךָ אָבוֹא בֵיתֶךָ,

אֶשְׁתַּחֲוֶה אֶל־הֵיכַל־קָדְשְׁךָ בְּיִרְאָתֶךָ.

וְיִשְׂמְחוּ כָל־חוֹסֵי בָךְ; לְעוֹלָם יְרַנֵּנוּ.

וְתָסֵךְ עָלֵימוֹ; וְיַעְלְצוּ בְךָ אֹהֲבֵי שְׁמֶךָ.

כִּי־אַתָּה תְּבָרֵךְ צַדִּיק, יהוה, כַּצִּנָּה רָצוֹן תַּעְטְרֶנּוּ.

*Your great love, O God, inspires me to enter Your house; with
awe I worship in Your sanctuary.*

*All who trust in You rejoice; they sing Your praise forever. You
give them shelter; and all who love Your name exult in You.*
*For You give Your blessing to the just; You throw Your favor
about them like a shield.*

ALL RISE

BAR'CHU IS ON PAGE 34

WEDNESDAY

FROM PSALM 8

✣ See "Selected Psalms," pages 358-375.

יהוה, אֲדֹנֵינוּ, מָה־אַדִּיר שִׁמְךָ בְּכָל־הָאָרֶץ!

אֲשֶׁר תְּנָה הוֹדְךָ עַל־הַשָּׁמָיִם!

כִּי־אֶרְאֶה שָׁמֶיךָ, מַעֲשֵׂי אֶצְבְּעֹתֶיךָ,

יָרֵחַ וְכוֹכָבִים אֲשֶׁר כּוֹנָנְתָּה,

מָה־אֱנוֹשׁ, כִּי־תִזְכְּרֶנּוּ, וּבֶן־אָדָם, כִּי תִפְקְדֶנּוּ?

וַתְּחַסְּרֵהוּ מְּעַט מֵאֱלֹהִים, וְכָבוֹד וְהָדָר תְּעַטְּרֵהוּ!

תַּמְשִׁילֵהוּ בְּמַעֲשֵׂי יָדֶיךָ, כֹּל שַׁתָּה תַחַת־רַגְלָיו:

צֹנֶה וַאֲלָפִים, כֻּלָּם; וְגַם בַּהֲמוֹת שָׂדָי,

צִפּוֹר שָׁמַיִם וּדְגֵי הַיָּם, עֹבֵר אָרְחוֹת יַמִּים.

יהוה, אֲדֹנֵינוּ, מָה־אַדִּיר שִׁמְךָ בְּכָל־הָאָרֶץ!

Adonai our God, how majestic is Your name in all the earth! You have impressed Your glory upon the heavens!

When I look at the heavens, the work of Your fingers, the moon and the stars that You have established,

What are we, that You are mindful of us, we mortals, that You care for us? Yet You have made us little lower than the angels, and crowned us with glory and honor!

You have appointed us to look after all that You have made; You have placed all creation in our care: sheep and cattle, all of them; beasts and birds and fishes, and all who travel the ocean's paths.

Adonai our God, how majestic is Your name in all the earth!

ALL RISE

BAR'CHU IS ON PAGE 34

30

THURSDAY

FROM PSALM 104

✽ See
"Selected
Psalms,"
pages 358-375.

בָּרְכִי, נַפְשִׁי, אֶת־יהוה. יהוה אֱלֹהַי, גָּדַלְתָּ מְּאֹד.
הוֹד וְהָדָר לָבָשְׁתָּ, עֹטֶה־אוֹר כַּשַּׂלְמָה. נוֹטֶה שָׁמַיִם כַּיְרִיעָה.
הַשָּׂם־עָבִים רְכוּבוֹ, הַמְהַלֵּךְ עַל־כַּנְפֵי־רֽוּחַ.
עֹשֶׂה מַלְאָכָיו רוּחוֹת, מְשָׁרְתָיו אֵשׁ לֹהֵט.

Praise Adonai, O my soul! Adonai my God, how very great
You are! Arrayed in glory and splendor, You wrap Yourself
in light as with a garment.

> *You stretch out the heavens like a curtain. The clouds are Your
> chariot; You ride on the wings of the wind.*

You make the winds Your messengers,

> *and flames of fire Your ministers.*

הַמְשַׁלֵּחַ מַעְיָנִים בַּנְּחָלִים; בֵּין הָרִים יְהַלֵּכוּן,
יַשְׁקוּ כָּל־חַיְתוֹ שָׂדָי, יִשְׁבְּרוּ פְרָאִים צְמָאָם.
עֲלֵיהֶם עוֹף־הַשָּׁמַיִם יִשְׁכּוֹן, מִבֵּין עֳפָאיִם יִתְּנוּ־קוֹל.
מַצְמִיחַ חָצִיר לַבְּהֵמָה, וְעֵשֶׂב לַעֲבֹדַת הָאָדָם,
לְהוֹצִיא לֶחֶם מִן־הָאָרֶץ, וְיַיִן יְשַׂמַּח לְבַב־אֱנוֹשׁ.

You send streams to spring forth in the valleys; they run
between the mountains, giving drink to the beasts of the
field, quenching the thirst of the wild asses.

> *The birds of the air nest on their banks, and sing among the
> leaves.*

You make grass grow for the cattle, and plants for people to
cultivate

> *that bread may come forth from the earth, and the wine that
> gladdens our hearts.*

עָשָׂה יָרֵחַ לְמוֹעֲדִים; שֶׁמֶשׁ יָדַע מְבוֹאוֹ.

תָּשֶׁת־חֹשֶׁךְ וִיהִי לָיְלָה, בּוֹ־תִרְמֹשׂ כָּל־חַיְתוֹ־יָעַר.

הַכְּפִירִים שֹׁאֲגִים לַטָּרֶף, וּלְבַקֵּשׁ מֵאֵל אָכְלָם.

תִּזְרַח הַשֶּׁמֶשׁ יֵאָסֵפוּן, וְאֶל־מְעוֹנֹתָם יִרְבָּצוּן.

You made the moon to mark the seasons;

the sun knows its time of setting.

You make darkness, and it is night, when all the beasts go prowling. The young lions roar for prey, demanding their food from God.

When the sun rises, they slink away, and go to their lairs for rest.

יֵצֵא אָדָם לְפָעֳלוֹ, וְלַעֲבֹדָתוֹ עֲדֵי־עָרֶב.

מָה־רַבּוּ מַעֲשֶׂיךָ, יהוה! כֻּלָּם בְּחָכְמָה עָשִׂיתָ,

מָלְאָה הָאָרֶץ קִנְיָנֶךָ.

יְהִי כְבוֹד יהוה לְעוֹלָם, יִשְׂמַח יהוה בְּמַעֲשָׂיו.

אָשִׁירָה לַיהוה בְּחַיָּי, אֲזַמְּרָה לֵאלֹהַי בְּעוֹדִי.

Then men and women go to their work, to their toil until evening.

How manifold are Your works, Adonai! In wisdom You have made them all; the earth is full of Your creations.

I will sing to Adonai all my days; I will sing praises to my God so long as I live.

ALL RISE

BAR'CHU IS ON PAGE 34

FRIDAY

FROM PSALM 112

✼ See
"Selected
Psalms,"
pages 358-375.

אַשְׁרֵי־אִישׁ יָרֵא אֶת־יהוה, בְּמִצְוֹתָיו חָפֵץ מְאֹד!

גִּבּוֹר בָּאָרֶץ יִהְיֶה זַרְעוֹ; דּוֹר יְשָׁרִים יְבֹרָךְ.

הוֹן־וָעֹשֶׁר בְּבֵיתוֹ, וְצִדְקָתוֹ עֹמֶדֶת לָעַד.

זָרַח בַּחֹשֶׁךְ אוֹר לַיְשָׁרִים; חַנּוּן וְרַחוּם וְצַדִּיק.

Blessed are they who revere Adonai, who delight greatly in God's commandments.

Their descendants shall be honored in the land; the generation of the upright shall be blessed.

Their households shall prosper, and their righteousness shall be remembered forever.

Light shall dawn in the darkness for the upright; for all who are gracious, merciful, and just.

טוֹב־אִישׁ חוֹנֵן וּמַלְוֶה, כִּי־לְעוֹלָם לֹא־יִמּוֹט, לְזֵכֶר

עוֹלָם יִהְיֶה צַדִּיק. מִשְּׁמוּעָה רָעָה לֹא יִירָא, נָכוֹן

לִבּוֹ, בָּטֻחַ בַּיהוה.

סָמוּךְ לִבּוֹ; לֹא יִירָא. פִּזַּר נָתַן לָאֶבְיוֹנִים;

צִדְקָתוֹ עֹמֶדֶת לָעַד; קַרְנוֹ תָּרוּם בְּכָבוֹד.

How good it is for the generous: they shall not fail; they shall ever be remembered as righteous. They shall not fear malicious rumors, for their minds are steady; they are safe in God's care. Their hearts are brave, and they do not fear.

They have been generous, and given freely to the poor; their righteousness endures; their lives shall be exalted in honor.

ALL RISE

שמע וברכותיה THE SHEMA AND ITS BLESSINGS

בָּרְכוּ אֶת־יי הַמְבֹרָךְ.
בָּרוּךְ יי הַמְבֹרָךְ לְעוֹלָם וָעֶד.

Praise the one to whom our praise is due.
We praise the Eternal One
to whom our praise is due forever and ever.

יוצר CREATION

בָּרוּךְ אַתָּה יי, אֱלֹהֵינוּ מֶלֶךְ הָעוֹלָם,
יוֹצֵר אוֹר וּבוֹרֵא חֹשֶׁךְ, עֹשֶׂה שָׁלוֹם וּבוֹרֵא אֶת־הַכֹּל.

We praise You, Adonai our God, sovereign of the universe,
maker of light and creator of darkness, author of peace and
creator of all things.

The creator of the universe is also its sustainer: each morning we awaken to the miracle of a creation ancient beyond imagining, yet newborn as the first dawn to an infant's eyes.

✣ See page 355 and Psalm 148 (page 374).

הַמֵּאִיר לָאָרֶץ וְלַדָּרִים עָלֶיהָ
בְּרַחֲמִים, וּבְטוּבוֹ מְחַדֵּשׁ
בְּכָל־יוֹם תָּמִיד מַעֲשֵׂה
בְרֵאשִׁית. מָה רַבּוּ מַעֲשֶׂיךָ,
יי! כֻּלָּם בְּחָכְמָה עָשִׂיתָ,
מָלְאָה הָאָרֶץ קִנְיָנֶךָ. תִּתְבָּרַךְ,
יי אֱלֹהֵינוּ, עַל־שֶׁבַח מַעֲשֵׂה
יָדֶיךָ וְעַל־מְאוֹרֵי־אוֹר שֶׁעָשִׂיתָ:
יְפָאֲרוּךָ סֶלָה.

In mercy You give light to the earth and all who dwell on it, and in Your goodness You continually renew—day by day—the work of creation.

How manifold are Your works, O God! In wisdom You have made them all. The work of Your hands proclaims Your praise, and the radiant stars bear witness to Your glory.

בָּרוּךְ אַתָּה יי, יוֹצֵר הַמְּאוֹרוֹת.

We praise You, O God, creator of light.

34

אהבה רבה REVELATION

אַהֲבָה רַבָּה אֲהַבְתָּנוּ, יְיָ אֱלֹהֵינוּ.
חֶמְלָה גְדוֹלָה וִיתֵרָה חָמַלְתָּ עָלֵינוּ.

Great is Your love for us, O God, and overflowing Your compassion.

Torah—
the moral
order—is the
theme of the
second of the
blessings that
precede the
Shema. It is a
gift of love; it
gives light to
our eyes. And
it incurs
obligation:
to learn, to
understand,
and to fulfill
the divine
mandate.

✣ See Pirke
Avot, page
322, and
Psalm 51
(page 364).

אָבִינוּ מַלְכֵּנוּ, בַּעֲבוּר אֲבוֹתֵינוּ וְאִמּוֹתֵינוּ שֶׁבָּטְחוּ בְךָ וַתְּלַמְּדֵם
חֻקֵּי חַיִּים, כֵּן תְּחָנֵּנוּ וּתְלַמְּדֵנוּ. אָבִינוּ, הָאָב הָרַחֲמָן, הַמְרַחֵם,
רַחֵם עָלֵינוּ וְתֵן בְּלִבֵּנוּ לְהָבִין וּלְהַשְׂכִּיל, לִשְׁמֹעַ, לִלְמֹד
וּלְלַמֵּד, לִשְׁמֹר וְלַעֲשׂוֹת וּלְקַיֵּם אֶת־כָּל־דִּבְרֵי תַלְמוּד תּוֹרָתֶךָ
בְּאַהֲבָה. וְהָאֵר עֵינֵינוּ בְּתוֹרָתֶךָ, וְדַבֵּק לִבֵּנוּ בְּמִצְוֹתֶיךָ, וְיַחֵד
לְבָבֵנוּ לְאַהֲבָה וּלְיִרְאָה אֶת־שְׁמֶךָ. וְלֹא־נֵבוֹשׁ לְעוֹלָם וָעֶד, כִּי
בְשֵׁם קָדְשְׁךָ הַגָּדוֹל וְהַנּוֹרָא בָּטָחְנוּ. נָגִילָה וְנִשְׂמְחָה בִּישׁוּעָתֶךָ,
כִּי אֵל פּוֹעֵל יְשׁוּעוֹת אָתָּה, וּבָנוּ בָחַרְתָּ וְקֵרַבְתָּנוּ לְשִׁמְךָ הַגָּדוֹל
סֶלָה בֶּאֱמֶת, לְהוֹדוֹת לְךָ וּלְיַחֶדְךָ בְּאַהֲבָה.

Our ancestors put their trust in You, and You taught them a living law. Now be gracious to us, Compassionate One, and teach us: fill our hearts with wisdom and insight, that we may love, understand, and follow Your Teaching.

Enlighten our eyes with Your Torah, help us cling to Your commandments, and inspire us with a ready heart to love and revere Your name.

We rejoice in You and exult in Your saving power, O God who have ever been our help. You have called us to Your service and have drawn us near to You in faithfulness, with joy to offer You praise and proclaim Your unity.

בָּרוּךְ אַתָּה יְיָ, הַבּוֹחֵר בְּעַמּוֹ יִשְׂרָאֵל בְּאַהֲבָה.

We praise You, O God, who call us in love to Your service.

35

שְׁמַע יִשְׂרָאֵל: יְהֹוָה אֱלֹהֵינוּ, יְהֹוָה אֶחָד.
בָּרוּךְ שֵׁם כְּבוֹד מַלְכוּתוֹ לְעוֹלָם וָעֶד.

Hear, O Israel: Adonai is our God, Adonai alone.
Praised be God's glorious majesty forever and ever.

ALL ARE SEATED

וְאָהַבְתָּ אֵת יְהֹוָה אֱלֹהֶיךָ
בְּכָל־לְבָבְךָ וּבְכָל־נַפְשְׁךָ וּבְכָל־מְאֹדֶךָ:
וְהָיוּ הַדְּבָרִים הָאֵלֶּה אֲשֶׁר אָנֹכִי מְצַוְּךָ הַיּוֹם
עַל־לְבָבֶךָ: וְשִׁנַּנְתָּם לְבָנֶיךָ וְדִבַּרְתָּ בָּם
בְּשִׁבְתְּךָ בְּבֵיתֶךָ וּבְלֶכְתְּךָ בַדֶּרֶךְ וּבְשָׁכְבְּךָ וּבְקוּמֶךָ:
וּקְשַׁרְתָּם לְאוֹת עַל־יָדֶךָ וְהָיוּ לְטֹטָפֹת בֵּין עֵינֶיךָ:
וּכְתַבְתָּם עַל־מְזֻזוֹת בֵּיתֶךָ וּבִשְׁעָרֶיךָ:
לְמַעַן תִּזְכְּרוּ וַעֲשִׂיתֶם אֶת־כָּל־מִצְוֺתָי
וִהְיִיתֶם קְדֹשִׁים לֵאלֹהֵיכֶם:
אֲנִי יְהֹוָה אֱלֹהֵיכֶם אֲשֶׁר הוֹצֵאתִי אֶתְכֶם מֵאֶרֶץ מִצְרַיִם
לִהְיוֹת לָכֶם לֵאלֹהִים: אֲנִי יְהֹוָה אֱלֹהֵיכֶם:

At times we
think of You
as a question,
when we need
to feel You as
the question.
May my life be
the response
I make, when
You *are* the
question.

✣ See "Looking
for God,"
pages 352-357.

*V'a-hav-ta et Adonai Eh-lo-heh-cha b'chol l'va-v'cha u-v'chol naf-sh'cha
u-v'chol m'o-deh-cha. V'ha-yu ha-d'va-rim ha-ei-leh a-sher a-no-chi
m'tza-v'cha ha-yom al l'va-veh-cha. V'shi-nan-tam l'va-neh-cha v'di-bar-ta
bam b'shiv-t'cha b'vei-teh-cha u-v'lech-t'cha va-deh-rech u-v'shoch-b'cha
u-v'ku-meh-cha. U-k'shar-tam l'ot al ya-deh-cha v'ha-yu l'to-ta-fot bein
ei-neh-cha; u-ch'tav-tam al m'zu-zot bei-teh-cha u-vi-sh'a-reh-cha. L'ma-an
tiz-k'ru va-a-si-tem et kol mitz-vo-tai, vi-h'yi-tem k'do-shim lei-lo-hei-chem.
A-ni Adonai Eh-lo-hei-chem a-sher ho-tzei-ti et-chem mei-eh-retz mitz-ra-yim
li-h'yot la-chem lei-lo-him. A-ni Adonai Eh-lo-hei-chem.*

You shall love Adonai your God with all your mind, with all
your heart, with all your might. Let these words, which I
command you this day, be upon your heart. Teach them

constantly to your children, speaking of them in your home and on your way, when you lie down and when you rise up. Bind them as a sign upon your hand; let them be symbols before your eyes; and inscribe them on the doorposts of your house, and on your gates: that you may be mindful of all my Mitzvot, and do them; then shall you be consecrated to your God. I, Adonai, am your God who led you out of Egypt to be your God; I, Adonai, am your God.

SOME MAY WISH TO INCLUDE THE FOLLOWING

וְהָיָה אִם־שָׁמֹעַ תִּשְׁמְעוּ אֶל־מִצְוֺתַי אֲשֶׁר אָנֹכִי מְצַוֶּה אֶתְכֶם הַיּוֹם לְאַהֲבָה אֶת־יְהוָה אֱלֹהֵיכֶם וּלְעָבְדוֹ בְּכָל־לְבַבְכֶם וּבְכָל־נַפְשְׁכֶם: יְצַו יְהוָה אִתְּךָ אֶת־הַבְּרָכָה בַּאֲסָמֶיךָ וּבְכֹל מִשְׁלַח יָדֶךָ וּבֵרַכְךָ בָּאָרֶץ אֲשֶׁר־יְהוָה אֱלֹהֶיךָ נֹתֵן לָךְ: יְקִימְךָ יְהוָה לוֹ לְעַם קָדוֹשׁ כַּאֲשֶׁר נִשְׁבַּע־לָךְ כִּי תִשְׁמֹר אֶת־מִצְוֺת יְהוָה אֱלֹהֶיךָ וְהָלַכְתָּ בִּדְרָכָיו: כִּי הַמִּצְוָה הַזֹּאת אֲשֶׁר אָנֹכִי מְצַוְּךָ הַיּוֹם לֹא־נִפְלֵאת הִוא מִמְּךָ וְלֹא רְחֹקָה הִוא: כִּי־קָרוֹב אֵלֶיךָ הַדָּבָר מְאֹד בְּפִיךָ וּבִלְבָבְךָ לַעֲשֹׂתוֹ: הַעִידֹתִי בָכֶם הַיּוֹם אֶת־הַשָּׁמַיִם וְאֶת־הָאָרֶץ הַחַיִּים וְהַמָּוֶת נָתַתִּי לְפָנֶיךָ הַבְּרָכָה וְהַקְּלָלָה וּבָחַרְתָּ בַּחַיִּים לְמַעַן תִּחְיֶה אַתָּה וְזַרְעֶךָ:

If you truly hearken to the Mitzvot that I command you this day, to love and serve Adonai your God with all your heart and mind, then your God will ordain blessing upon your homes and all your undertakings, and upon the soil on which your God has placed you. Adonai will affirm you as a holy people, when you keep the Mitzvot and walk in the ways of your God.

For this Mitzvah that I command you this day is not too difficult for you; nor is it far away—no, this word is very

near you, in your mouth and in your heart—and you can do it. I call heaven and earth to witness before you this day: life and death have I placed before you, blessing and curse. Choose life, then, that you and your children may live.
(Deuteronomy 11:13; 28:8-9; 30:11,14,19)

גאולה   REDEMPTION

אֱמֶת וְיַצִּיב וְיָשָׁר וְקַיָּם וְטוֹב וְיָפֶה הַדָּבָר הַזֶּה
עָלֵינוּ לְעוֹלָם וָעֶד.

True, enduring, good, and beautiful are these words, now and forever.

אֱמֶת שָׁאַתָּה הוּא יי אֱלֹהֵינוּ וֵאלֹהֵי אֲבוֹתֵינוּ וְאִמּוֹתֵינוּ, מַלְכֵּנוּ
מֶלֶךְ אֲבוֹתֵינוּ וְאִמּוֹתֵינוּ, יוֹצְרֵנוּ צוּר יְשׁוּעָתֵנוּ, פּוֹדֵנוּ וּמַצִּילֵנוּ
מֵעוֹלָם הוּא שְׁמֶךָ, אֵין אֱלֹהִים זוּלָתֶךָ. אֱמֶת אַתָּה הוּא רִאשׁוֹן
וְאַתָּה הוּא אַחֲרוֹן, וּמִבַּלְעָדֶיךָ אֵין לָנוּ מוֹשִׁיעַ. מִמִּצְרַיִם
גְּאַלְתָּנוּ, יי אֱלֹהֵינוּ, וּמִבֵּית עֲבָדִים פְּדִיתָנוּ. מֹשֶׁה וּמִרְיָם וּבְנֵי
יִשְׂרָאֵל לְךָ עָנוּ שִׁירָה בְּשִׂמְחָה רַבָּה, וְאָמְרוּ כֻלָּם:

True it is that You are our sovereign God, as You were the God of our mothers and fathers. You are our maker, the rock of our salvation; from of old we have known You as our helper and savior: there is no God but You. Truly, You are the first and the last, and we have no redeemer but You.

Out of Egypt You delivered us; You freed us from the house of bondage. Then, with great joy, Moses, Miriam, and all Israel sang this song to You:

מִי־כָמֹכָה בָּאֵלִם, יהוה?   *Mi cha-mo-cha ba-ei-lim, Adonai?*

מִי כָמֹכָה, נֶאְדָּר בַּקֹּדֶשׁ,   *Mi ka-mo-cha, neh-dar ba-ko-desh,*

Looking back at our first redemption from bondage, our people concluded that they could hope for and expect a redemption that would last for all time. The hope remains—along with our task of bringing about the redemption for which we yearn.

❧ See page 348, foot of page, and Psalm 3 (page 358).

38

נוֹרָא תְהִלֹת, עֹשֵׂה פֶלֶא?   *no-ra t'hi-lot, o-sei feh-leh?*

שִׁירָה חֲדָשָׁה שִׁבְּחוּ   *Shi-ra cha-da-sha shi-b'chu*

גְאוּלִים לְשִׁמְךָ עַל־שְׂפַת   *g'u-lim l'shi-m'cha al s'fat*

הַיָּם; יַחַד כֻּלָם הוֹדוּ   *ha-yam; ya-chad ku-lam ho-du*

וְהִמְלִיכוּ וְאָמְרוּ:   *v'him-li-chu v'a-m'ru:*

יהוה יִמְלֹךְ לְעֹלָם וָעֶד!   *Adonai yim-loch l'o-lam va-ed!*

צוּר יִשְׂרָאֵל, קוּמָה   *Tzur Yis-ra-eil, ku-mah*

בְּעֶזְרַת יִשְׂרָאֵל, וּפְדֵה   *b'ez-rat Yis-ra-eil, u-f'dei*

כִנְאֻמֶךָ יְהוּדָה וְיִשְׂרָאֵל.   *ki-n'u-meh-cha Y'hu-da v'Yis-ra-eil.*

גְאָלֵנוּ, יי צְבָאוֹת שְׁמוֹ,   *Go-a-lei-nu, Adonai tz'va-ot sh'mo,*

קָדוֹשׁ יִשְׂרָאֵל. בָּרוּךְ   *k'dosh Yis-ra-eil. Ba-ruch*

אַתָּה יי, גָּאַל יִשְׂרָאֵל.   *a-ta Adonai, ga-al Yis-ra-eil.*

Who is like You, Adonai, among all that is worshiped? Who is like You, glorious in holiness, awesome in splendor, doing wonders?

A new song the redeemed sang to Your name at the shore of the sea. With one voice they gave thanks and proclaimed Your sovereign power: "Adonai will reign forever and ever."

O Rock of Israel, rise up and help us. Keep Your promise to redeem Your people Israel. Our redeemer is the God of all being, the Holy One of Israel. We praise You, O God, redeemer of Israel.

⚛

THE READER'S KADDISH IS ON PAGE 43

אַשְׁרֵי

PSALMS 84:5 AND 144:15

אַשְׁרֵי יוֹשְׁבֵי בֵיתֶךָ, עוֹד יְהַלְלוּךָ סֶּלָה.

אַשְׁרֵי הָעָם שֶׁכָּכָה לּוֹ; אַשְׁרֵי הָעָם שֶׁיהוה אֱלֹהָיו.

Happy are those who dwell in Your house,
who continually sing Your praises.

Happy the people who are so blessed;
happy the people whose God You are.

FROM PSALM 145

A PSALM OF DAVID   תְּהִלָּה לְדָוִד

אֲרוֹמִמְךָ, אֱלוֹהַי הַמֶּלֶךְ, וַאֲבָרְכָה שִׁמְךָ לְעוֹלָם וָעֶד.

בְּכָל־יוֹם אֲבָרְכֶךָּ, וַאֲהַלְלָה שִׁמְךָ לְעוֹלָם וָעֶד.

Always we exalt You, and praise Your name forever.

B*ecause You are our maker, we extol Your name forever.*

גָּדוֹל יהוה וּמְהֻלָּל מְאֹד, וְלִגְדֻלָּתוֹ אֵין חֵקֶר.

דּוֹר לְדוֹר יְשַׁבַּח מַעֲשֶׂיךָ, וּגְבוּרֹתֶיךָ יַגִּידוּ.

Calling us to greatness, Eternal One, You teach us.

D*eclaring Your works tremendous, we witness to Your power.*

הֲדַר כְּבוֹד הוֹדֶךָ, וְדִבְרֵי נִפְלְאֹתֶיךָ אָשִׂיחָה.

וֶעֱזוּז נוֹרְאֹתֶיךָ יֹאמֵרוּ, וּגְדֻלָּתְךָ אֲסַפְּרֶנָּה.

Ever to tell Your glory, the wonder of Your mercies.

F*or as we praise Your marvels, so we laud Your greatness.*

The English
text can be
chanted as the
Hebrew might
be.

A PRAYER
BEFORE
PRAYER:
May my
worship
encourage
me to fulfill
this Mitzvah:
"Never curse
those who
cannot hear or
place a
stumbling-
block before
those who
cannot see; be
in awe of your
God—I am
Adonai."
(Leviticus
19:14)

✢ See "A Daily
Psalm," pages
27-33, and
"Selected
Psalms," pages
358-375.

זֵכֶר רַב־טוּבְךָ יַבִּיעוּ, וְצִדְקָתְךָ יְרַנֵּנוּ.

חַנּוּן וְרַחוּם יהוה, אֶרֶךְ אַפַּיִם וּגְדָל־חָסֶד.

Great the good we honor, singing of Your justice.

Holding us in kindness, in love You are abounding.

טוֹב־יהוה לַכֹּל, וְרַחֲמָיו עַל־כָּל־מַעֲשָׂיו.

יוֹדוּךָ יהוה כָּל־מַעֲשֶׂיךָ, וַחֲסִידֶיךָ יְבָרְכוּךָ.

In Your never-ending goodness, You teach Your creatures mercy.

Joyful, we all thank You; Your faithful ones shall praise You.

כְּבוֹד מַלְכוּתְךָ יֹאמֵרוּ, וּגְבוּרָתְךָ יְדַבֵּרוּ,

לְהוֹדִיעַ לִבְנֵי הָאָדָם גְּבוּרֹתָיו, וּכְבוֹד הֲדַר מַלְכוּתוֹ.

Knowing that You are sovereign, we all proclaim Your splendor.

Let all perceive Your power, the triumph of Your wisdom.

מַלְכוּתְךָ מַלְכוּת כָּל־עֹלָמִים, וּמֶמְשַׁלְתְּךָ בְּכָל־דּוֹר וָדוֹר.

סוֹמֵךְ יהוה לְכָל־הַנֹּפְלִים, וְזוֹקֵף לְכָל־הַכְּפוּפִים.

Majestic, You rule in glory; Your reign endures forever.

O God, support the helpless, and raise up all the fallen.

עֵינֵי־כֹל אֵלֶיךָ יְשַׂבֵּרוּ, וְאַתָּה נוֹתֵן־לָהֶם אֶת־אָכְלָם בְּעִתּוֹ.

פּוֹתֵחַ אֶת־יָדֶךָ וּמַשְׂבִּיעַ לְכָל־חַי רָצוֹן.

Pleading, they implore You; in their need, pray feed them.

Quickly Your hand be open, to comfort every creature.

41

צַדִּיק יהוה בְּכָל־דְּרָכָיו, וְחָסִיד בְּכָל־מַעֲשָׂיו.

קָרוֹב יְהוָה לְכָל־קֹרְאָיו, לְכֹל אֲשֶׁר יִקְרָאֻהוּ בֶאֱמֶת.

Righteous are You always, loving in Your actions.

So near to all who call You, to all in truth who call You.

רְצוֹן־יְרֵאָיו יַעֲשֶׂה, וְאֶת־שַׁוְעָתָם יִשְׁמַע וְיוֹשִׁיעֵם.

תְּהִלַּת יהוה יְדַבֶּר־פִּי וִיבָרֵךְ כָּל־בָּשָׂר

שֵׁם קָדְשׁוֹ לְעוֹלָם וָעֶד.

Those who seek You, call You; You hear their cry and help
them.

Unceasing, our lips sing praise-songs; rejoicing in You forever.

PSALM 115:18

וַאֲנַחְנוּ נְבָרֵךְ יָהּ מֵעַתָּה וְעַד־עוֹלָם. הַלְלוּיָהּ!

Let us extol the eternal God from this time forth and forever.
Halleluyah!

❧

42

ALL RISE

חצי קדיש READER'S KADDISH

יִתְגַּדַּל וְיִתְקַדַּשׁ שְׁמֵהּ רַבָּא בְּעָלְמָא דִי־בְרָא כִרְעוּתֵהּ,

וְיַמְלִיךְ מַלְכוּתֵהּ בְּחַיֵּיכוֹן וּבְיוֹמֵיכוֹן וּבְחַיֵּי

דְכָל־בֵּית יִשְׂרָאֵל, בַּעֲגָלָא וּבִזְמַן קָרִיב, וְאִמְרוּ: אָמֵן.

יְהֵא שְׁמֵהּ רַבָּא מְבָרַךְ לְעָלַם וּלְעָלְמֵי עָלְמַיָּא.

יִתְבָּרַךְ וְיִשְׁתַּבַּח, וְיִתְפָּאַר וְיִתְרוֹמַם וְיִתְנַשֵּׂא,

וְיִתְהַדָּר וְיִתְעַלֶּה וְיִתְהַלָּל שְׁמֵהּ דְקוּדְשָׁא, בְּרִיךְ הוּא,

לְעֵלָּא מִן־כָּל־בִּרְכָתָא וְשִׁירָתָא, תֻּשְׁבְּחָתָא וְנֶחֱמָתָא

דַּאֲמִירָן בְּעָלְמָא, וְאִמְרוּ: אָמֵן.

Yit-ga-dal v'yit-ka-dash sh'mei ra-ba b'al-ma di-v'ra chi-r'u'tei,
v'yam-lich mal-chu-tei b'cha-yei-chon u-v'yo-mei-chon u-v'cha-yei
d'chol beit Yis-ra-eil, ba-a-ga-la u-vi-z'man ka-riv, v'i-m'ru: A-mein.
Y'hei sh'mei ra-ba m'va-rach l'a-lam u-l'al-mei al-ma-ya.
Yit-ba-rach v'yish-ta-bach v'yit-pa-ar, v'yit-ro-mam, v'yit-na-sei,
v'yit-ha-dar, v'yit-a-leh, v'yit-ha-lal sh'mei d'kud-sha, b'rich hu,
l'ei-la min kol bir-cha-ta v'shi-ra-ta, tush-b'cha-ta v'neh-cheh-ma-ta
da-a-mi-ran b'al-ma, v'i-m'ru: A-mein.

Hallowed be Your great name on earth, Your creation; establish Your dominion in our own day, in our own lives, and in the life of the whole House of Israel.

Blessed be Your great name forever and ever.

Blessed, praised, honored, and exalted be the name of the Holy One, ever to be praised, though You are beyond all the blessings and songs of praise that the world may offer.

&

תפלה TEFILAH

אבות ואמהות GOD OF ALL GENERATIONS

בָּרוּךְ אַתָּה יְיָ, אֱלֹהֵינוּ
וֵאלֹהֵי אֲבוֹתֵינוּ וְאִמּוֹתֵינוּ:
אֱלֹהֵי אַבְרָהָם, אֱלֹהֵי
יִצְחָק וֵאלֹהֵי יַעֲקֹב:
אֱלֹהֵי שָׂרָה, אֱלֹהֵי רִבְקָה,
אֱלֹהֵי לֵאָה וֵאלֹהֵי רָחֵל;
הָאֵל הַגָּדוֹל הַגִּבּוֹר וְהַנּוֹרָא,
אֵל עֶלְיוֹן. גּוֹמֵל חֲסָדִים
טוֹבִים וְקוֹנֵה הַכֹּל,
וְזוֹכֵר חַסְדֵי אָבוֹת וְאִמָּהוֹת,
וּמֵבִיא גְאֻלָּה לִבְנֵי בְנֵיהֶם,
לְמַעַן שְׁמוֹ בְּאַהֲבָה.

Ba-ruch a-ta Adonai, Eh-lo-hei-nu
vei-lo-hei a-vo-tei-nu v'i-mo-tei-nu:
Eh-lo-hei Av-ra-ham, eh-lo-hei
Yitz-chak, vei-lo-hei Ya-a-kov.
Eh-lo-hei Sa-rah, eh-lo-hei Riv-kah,
eh-lo-hei Lei-ah, vei-lo-hei Ra-cheil;
ha-eil ha-ga-dol ha-gi-bor v'ha-no-ra,
eil el-yon. Go-meil cha-sa-dim
to-vim, v'ko-nei ha-kol,
v'zo-cheir chas-dei a-vot v'i-ma-hot,
u-mei-vi g'u-la li-v'nei v'nei-hem,
l'ma-an sh'mo, b'a-ha-vah.

The Weekday
Tefilah has
nineteen
prayers.
In the first, we
recall with
reverence the
founders of
our people and
faith. We say:
Each
generation
finds its own
way, and yet—
their God is
ours.

✿ See "Looking
for God,"
pages 352-357.

We praise You, Adonai, our God and God of our ancestors: of Abraham,
Isaac, and Jacob; of Sarah, Rebekah, Leah, and Rachel; the great, mighty,
and awesome God, God Most High.

You deal kindly with us and embrace us all. You remember the faithfulness of our ancestors, and in love bring redemption to their children's
children for the sake of Your name.

DURING THE TEN DAYS OF REPENTANCE ADD

זָכְרֵנוּ לְחַיִּים, *Zoch-rei-nu l'cha-yim,*

מֶלֶךְ חָפֵץ בַּחַיִּים, *meh-lech cha-feitz ba-cha-yim,*

וְכָתְבֵנוּ בְּסֵפֶר הַחַיִּים, *v'chot-vei-nu b'sefer ha-cha-yim,*

לְמַעַנְךָ אֱלֹהִים חַיִּים. *l'ma-a-n'cha, Eh-lo-him cha-yim.*

Remember us for life, because You, O sovereign, delight in life; and inscribe us in the Book of Life, for Your sake, O God of life.

מֶלֶךְ עוֹזֵר וּמוֹשִׁיעַ *Meh-lech o-zeir u-mo-shi-a*

וּמָגֵן. בָּרוּךְ אַתָּה יי, *u-ma-gein. Ba-ruch a-ta Adonai,*

מָגֵן אַבְרָהָם וְעֶזְרַת שָׂרָה. *ma-gein Av-ra-ham v'ez-rat Sa-rah.*

You are our sovereign and helper, our redeemer and shield.
We praise You, O God, Shield of Abraham and Protector of Sarah.

גבורות GOD'S POWER

In this prayer, we affirm the power of God, whose reach extends to this world— the world we walk in—and to a world we cannot imagine.

❉ See Psalm 103 (page 366) and Psalm 146 (page 371).

אַתָּה גִּבּוֹר לְעוֹלָם, אֲדֹנָי, *A-ta gi-bor l'o-lam, Adonai,*

מְחַיֵּה מֵתִים אַתָּה, רַב *m'cha-yei mei-tim a-ta, rav*

לְהוֹשִׁיעַ. *l'ho-shi-a. Ma-shiv ha-ru-ach*

מַשִּׁיב הָרוּחַ וּמוֹרִיד הַגָּשֶׁם, *u-mo-rid ha-ga-shem; maz-ri-ach*

מַזְרִיחַ הַשֶּׁמֶשׁ וּמוֹרִיד הַטָּל. *ha-she-mesh u-mo-rid ha-tal.*

מְכַלְכֵּל חַיִּים בְּחֶסֶד, *M'chal-keil cha-yim b'cheh-sed,*

מְחַיֵּה מֵתִים בְּרַחֲמִים רַבִּים. *m'cha-yei mei-tim b'ra-cha-mim*

סוֹמֵךְ נוֹפְלִים, וְרוֹפֵא *ra-bim. So-meich no-f'lim, v'ro-fei*

חוֹלִים, וּמַתִּיר אֲסוּרִים, *cho-lim, u-ma-tir a-su-rim,*

וּמְקַיֵּם אֱמוּנָתוֹ לִישֵׁנֵי *u-m'ka-yeim eh-mu-na-to li-shei-nei*

עָפָר. *a-far.*

45

מִי כָמְוֹךָ, בַּעַל גְּבוּרוֹת,   *Mi cha-mo-cha ba-al g'vu-rot,*

וּמִי דְוֹמֶה לָךְ, מֶלֶךְ מֵמִית   *u-mi do-meh lach, meh-lech mei-mit*

וּמְחַיֶּה וּמַצְמִיחַ יְשׁוּעָה?   *u-m'cha-yeh u-matz-mi-ach y'shu-a?*

Unending is Your might, Eternal One; You are the source of eternal life;
great is Your power to save. You cause the wind to blow and the rain to
fall, the sun to shine and the dew to descend. In Your love You sustain
the living; in Your compassion You grant us eternal life. You support the
falling and heal the sick; You free the captive and keep faith with those
who sleep in the dust. Who is like You, source of all strength? Who is
Your equal, sovereign author of life and death, who causes deliverance
to flower in our world?

DURING THE TEN DAYS OF REPENTANCE ADD

מִי כָמְוֹךָ, אַב הָרַחֲמִים,   *Mi cha-mo-cha, av ha-ra-cha-mim,*

זוֹכֵר יְצוּרָיו לַחַיִּים   *zo-cheir y'tzu-rav la-cha-yim*

בְּרַחֲמִים?   *b'ra-cha-mim?*

Who is like You, God of mercy? In Your mercy You remember Your
creatures, and grant them life.

וְנֶאֱמָן אַתָּה לְהַחֲיוֹת   *V'neh-eh-man a-ta l'ha-cha-yot*

מֵתִים. בָּרוּךְ אַתָּה יי,   *mei-tim. Ba-ruch a-ta Adonai,*

מְחַיֶּה הַמֵּתִים.   *m'cha-yei ha-mei-tim.*

Trusting in You, we see life beyond death.
We praise You, O God, source of eternal life.

FOR AN EVENING SERVICE

קדושת השם   GOD'S HOLINESS

As we walk beneath the stars, we are walking among them, and the mystery of being calls to us—and thus the Holy calls to us from within the heights and the depths of our hearts.

✶ See Psalm 42/3 (page 363) and Psalm 63 (page 365).

אַתָּה קָדוֹשׁ וְשִׁמְךָ קָדוֹשׁ,

A-ta ka-dosh v'shi-m'cha

וּקְדוֹשִׁים בְּכָל־יוֹם

ka-dosh, u-k'do-shim b'chol

יְהַלְלוּךָ סֶּלָה.

yom y'ha-l'lu-cha seh-lah.

You are holy, Your name is holy, and every day all creation sings Your praise.

DURING THE TEN DAYS OF REPENTANCE CONCLUDE

בָּרוּךְ אַתָּה יי, הַמֶּלֶךְ הַקָּדוֹשׁ.

Ba-ruch a-ta Adonai, ha-meh-lech ha-ka-dosh.

We praise You, Adonai, the God who reigns in holiness.

ON ALL OTHER DAYS

בָּרוּךְ אַתָּה יי, הָאֵל הַקָּדוֹשׁ.

Ba-ruch a-ta Adonai, ha-eil ha-ka-dosh.

We praise You, Adonai, the holy God.

ALL ARE SEATED

FOR A MORNING SERVICE

נְקַדֵּשׁ אֶת־שִׁמְךָ בָּעוֹלָם, כְּשֵׁם שֶׁמַּקְדִּישִׁים אוֹתוֹ

בִּשְׁמֵי מָרוֹם, כַּכָּתוּב עַל־יַד נְבִיאֶךָ:

וְקָרָא זֶה אֶל־זֶה וְאָמַר:

We hallow Your name on earth, even as all creation to the highest heavens proclaims Your holiness, and in the words of the prophet we say:

קָדוֹשׁ, קָדוֹשׁ, קָדוֹשׁ יהוה צְבָאוֹת,
מְלֹא כָל־הָאָרֶץ כְּבוֹדוֹ.

Holy, holy, holy is the God of all being! The whole earth is filled with God's glory!

אַדִּיר אַדִּירֵנוּ, יהוה אֲדֹנֵינוּ, מָה־אַדִּיר שִׁמְךָ בְּכָל־הָאָרֶץ!

God our strength, God of mercy, how majestic is Your name in all the earth!

בָּרוּךְ כְּבוֹד־יהוה מִמְּקוֹמוֹ.

Praised be the glory of God in heaven and earth.

אֶחָד הוּא אֱלֹהֵינוּ, הוּא אָבִינוּ, הוּא מַלְכֵּנוּ, הוּא מוֹשִׁיעֵנוּ;
וְהוּא יַשְׁמִיעֵנוּ בְּרַחֲמָיו לְעֵינֵי כָּל־חָי:

You alone are our God and maker, our ruler and helper; and in Your mercy You reveal Yourself to us in the sight of all the living:

אֲנִי יהוה אֱלֹהֵיכֶם!

I AM ADONAI YOUR GOD!

יִמְלֹךְ יהוה לְעוֹלָם; אֱלֹהַיִךְ, צִיּוֹן, לְדֹר וָדֹר. הַלְלוּיָהּ!

Adonai shall reign forever; Your God, O Zion, from generation to generation. Halleluyah!

In this prayer, the Sanctification, we echo the awe and wonder expressed by our psalmists, mystics, and prophets as they experienced God's presence in their lives.

❖ See pages 352-353 and page 400.

לְדוֹר וָדוֹר נַגִּיד גָּדְלֶךָ, וּלְנֵצַח נְצָחִים קְדֻשָּׁתְךָ נַקְדִּישׁ.
וְשִׁבְחֲךָ, אֱלֹהֵינוּ, מִפִּינוּ לֹא יָמוּשׁ לְעוֹלָם וָעֶד.

From generation to generation we will make known Your greatness, and to all eternity proclaim Your holiness. Your praise, O God, shall never depart from our lips.

DURING THE TEN DAYS OF REPENTANCE CONCLUDE	ON ALL OTHER DAYS
בָּרוּךְ אַתָּה יי, הַמֶּלֶךְ הַקָּדוֹשׁ.	בָּרוּךְ אַתָּה יי, הָאֵל הַקָּדוֹשׁ.
Ba-ruch a-ta Adonai, *ha-meh-lech ha-ka-dosh.*	*Ba-ruch a-ta Adonai,* *ha-eil ha-ka-dosh.*
We praise You, Adonai, the God who reigns in holiness.	*We praise You, Adonai, the holy God.*

ALL ARE SEATED

WISDOM בינה

On weekdays we think of our needs. From our prayers themselves we learn what to ask for, and we ask for help as we work to realize our hopes and achieve our goals.

אַתָּה חוֹנֵן לְאָדָם דַּעַת וּמְלַמֵּד לֶאֱנוֹשׁ בִּינָה.
חָנֵּנוּ מֵאִתְּךָ דֵּעָה, בִּינָה וְהַשְׂכֵּל.

For Your gracious gift of reason that enables us to search after knowledge and insight, we give thanks. May You continue to bless us with knowledge, understanding, and insight.

בָּרוּךְ אַתָּה יי, חוֹנֵן הַדָּעַת.

We praise You, O God, gracious giver of knowledge.

תשובה REPENTANCE

הֲשִׁיבֵנוּ אָבִינוּ לְתוֹרָתֶךָ, וְקָרְבֵנוּ מַלְכֵּנוּ לַעֲבוֹדָתֶךָ,
וְהַחֲזִירֵנוּ בִּתְשׁוּבָה שְׁלֵמָה לְפָנֶיךָ.

Help us to turn back to Torah, O God, and help us return to
You with whole hearts, to devote ourselves to Your service.

בָּרוּךְ אַתָּה יי, הָרוֹצֶה בִּתְשׁוּבָה.

We praise You, O God: You delight in repentance.

סליחה FORGIVENESS

סְלַח־לָנוּ אָבִינוּ כִּי חָטָאנוּ, מְחַל־לָנוּ מַלְכֵּנוּ כִּי פָשָׁעְנוּ,
כִּי מוֹחֵל וְסוֹלֵחַ אָתָּה.

Grant us forgiveness when we need to be forgiven, pardon
us when we transgress, for You are the source of pardon and
forgiveness.

בָּרוּךְ אַתָּה יי, חַנּוּן הַמַּרְבֶּה לִסְלֹחַ.

We praise You, O God, gracious and generous in forgiveness.

גאולה REDEMPTION

רְאֵה בְעָנְיֵנוּ וְרִיבָה רִיבֵנוּ, וּגְאָלֵנוּ מְהֵרָה לְמַעַן שְׁמֶךָ,
כִּי גוֹאֵל חָזָק אָתָּה.

O God, our mighty redeemer, when we are beset by troubles
and in need of help, look upon us and be our saving power
as You have been with our people from the beginning.

בָּרוּךְ אַתָּה יי, גּוֹאֵל יִשְׂרָאֵל.

We praise You, O God, redeemer of Israel.

רפואה HEALTH

רְפָאֵנוּ יְיָ וְנֵרָפֵא, הוֹשִׁיעֵנוּ וְנִוָּשֵׁעָה, וְהַעֲלֵה רְפוּאָה
שְׁלֵמָה לְכָל־מַכּוֹתֵינוּ.

Heal us—and we are healed; help us—and we are helped! O
grant us healing for all our ills.

בָּרוּךְ אַתָּה יְיָ, רוֹפֵא הַחוֹלִים.

We praise You, O God, healer of the sick.

ברכת השנים ABUNDANCE

בָּרֵךְ עָלֵינוּ, יְיָ אֱלֹהֵינוּ, אֶת־הַשָּׁנָה הַזֹּאת וְאֶת־כָּל־מִינֵי תְבוּאָתָהּ
לְטוֹבָה. וְתֵן בְּרָכָה עַל־פְּנֵי הָאֲדָמָה, וְשַׂבְּעֵנוּ מִטּוּבֶךָ.

Bless us this year with a good and lovely world. We give
thanks for the earth, for its abundance and its beauty: teach
us to care for it, and to rejoice in its goodness.

בָּרוּךְ אַתָּה יְיָ, מְבָרֵךְ הַשָּׁנִים.

We praise You, O God: You bless the earth from year to year.

חרות FREEDOM

תְּקַע בְּשׁוֹפָר גָּדוֹל לְחֵרוּתֵנוּ, וְשָׂא נֵס לְפְדּוֹת עֲשׁוּקֵינוּ,
וְקוֹל דְּרוֹר יִשָּׁמַע בְּאַרְבַּע כַּנְפוֹת הָאָרֶץ.

Sound the shofar of liberty for all who are oppressed, and
inspire us to work for their liberation: let the song of
freedom be heard in the world's four corners.

בָּרוּךְ אַתָּה יְיָ, פּוֹדֶה עֲשׁוּקִים.

We praise You, O God, redeemer of the oppressed.

משפט JUSTICE

הוֹשִׁיבָה שׁוֹפְטֵי צֶדֶק בְּתוֹךְ בְּנֵי עַמֶּךְ, וְיוֹעֲצֵי חֶסֶד בְּכָל־תֵּבֵל אַרְצֶךָ, וְאָז תִּמְלוֹךְ עָלֵינוּ אַתָּה לְבַדֶּךָ, בְּחֶסֶד וּבְרַחֲמִים.

Give the leaders and officials of all nations wise and understanding hearts, that they may be honest and just, and ever seek the good of their people. Then will Your sovereign rule of kindness and compassion be established in our midst.

בָּרוּךְ אַתָּה יי, מֶלֶךְ אוֹהֵב צְדָקָה וּמִשְׁפָּט.

We praise You, sovereign God: You love righteousness and justice.

על הרשעה ON WICKEDNESS

וְלָרִשְׁעָה עַל־תְּהִי תִקְוָה, וְהַתּוֹעִים אֵלֶיךָ יָשׁוּבוּ, וּמַלְכוּת זָדוֹן מְהֵרָה תַּעֲבִיר.

Let there be an end to wickedness in the world, and cause all who go wrong in arrogance to turn back to Your word, O God.

בָּרוּךְ אַתָּה יי, הַמַּעֲבִיר רֶשַׁע מִן־הָאָרֶץ.

We praise You, O God, whose will it is that evil shall pass away from the earth.

על הצדיקים THE RIGHTEOUS

עַל־הַצַּדִּיקִים וְעַל־הַחֲסִידִים וְעַל־גֵּרֵי הַצֶּדֶק, וְעַל־כָּל־עוֹשֵׂי רְצוֹנֶךָ, יֶהֱמוּ רַחֲמֶיךָ, יי אֱלֹהֵינוּ, וְשִׂים חֶלְקֵנוּ עִמָּהֶם לְעוֹלָם.

Be with all good and honest men and women of every race and faith, O God, and grant that we may be numbered among them.

בָּרוּךְ אַתָּה יי, מִשְׁעָן וּמִבְטָח לַצַּדִּיקִים.

We praise You, O God, the staff and support of the righteous.

בונה ירושלים JERUSALEM

וּבִירוּשָׁלַיִם עִירְךָ בְּרַחֲמִים תִּשְׁכּוֹן, וִיהִי שָׁלוֹם בִּשְׁעָרֶיהָ,

וְשַׁלְוָה בְּלֵב יוֹשְׁבֶיהָ, וְתוֹרָתְךָ מִצִּיּוֹן תֵּצֵא, וּדְבָרְךָ מִירוּשָׁלָיִם.

Let Your compassionate presence be manifest in Jerusalem
Your city, and may all who live there know peace and
tranquility. Then will Torah once more go forth from Zion,
Your word from Jerusalem.

בָּרוּךְ אַתָּה יי, בּוֹנֵה יְרוּשָׁלָיִם.

We praise You, O God, builder of Jerusalem.

ישועה DELIVERANCE

אֶת־צֶמַח צְדָקָה מְהֵרָה תַצְמִיחַ, וְקֶרֶן יְשׁוּעָה תָּרוּם

כִּנְאֻמֶךָ, כִּי לִישׁוּעָתְךָ קִוִּינוּ כָּל־הַיּוֹם.

Plant righteousness among us, O God, and help us and all
people everywhere, to bring the world nearer to deliverance
from war, poverty, and injustice, and from all hatred and
fear.

בָּרוּךְ אַתָּה יי, מַצְמִיחַ קֶרֶן יְשׁוּעָה.

We praise You, O God, who will cause the day of redemption to
dawn in all the world.

שומע תפלה PRAYER

שְׁמַע קוֹלֵנוּ, יי אֱלֹהֵינוּ, חוּס וְרַחֵם עָלֵינוּ, וּתְקַבֵּל בְּרַחֲמִים

וּבְרָצוֹן אֶת־תְּפִלָּתֵנוּ, כִּי אַתָּה שׁוֹמֵעַ תְּפִלַּת כָּל־פֶּה.

Adonai our God, in compassion hear our words and hearken
to our prayer, for You hear the prayer of every living being.

בָּרוּךְ אַתָּה יי, שׁוֹמֵעַ תְּפִלָּה.

We praise You, the God who hearkens to prayer.

עבודה   WORSHIP

רְצֵה, יי אֱלֹהֵינוּ, בְּעַמְּךָ יִשְׂרָאֵל וּתְפִלָּתָם בְּאַהֲבָה תְקַבֵּל,

וּתְהִי לְרָצוֹן תָּמִיד עֲבוֹדַת יִשְׂרָאֵל עַמֶּךָ.

בָּרוּךְ אַתָּה יי, שֶׁאוֹתְךָ לְבַדְּךָ בְּיִרְאָה נַעֲבוֹד.

Look with favor, Adonai our God, upon Your people Israel, and with love accept our prayers. May our worship ever be worthy of Your favor. We praise You, Adonai: You alone are the One we worship in awe.

This is a prayer for prayer itself, that our prayers may be worthy, for do we not become what we pray for?

❖ See "Prayer and Its Value," pages 3-5.

ON ROSH CHODESH AND CHOL HA-MOEID ADD

אֱלֹהֵינוּ וֵאלֹהֵי אֲבוֹתֵינוּ וְאִמּוֹתֵינוּ, יַעֲלֶה וְיָבֹא וְיִזָּכֵר

זִכְרוֹנֵנוּ וְזִכְרוֹן כָּל־עַמְּךָ בֵּית יִשְׂרָאֵל לְפָנֶיךָ לְטוֹבָה

לְחֵן לְחֶסֶד וּלְרַחֲמִים, לְחַיִּים וּלְשָׁלוֹם בְּיוֹם

❖ רֹאשׁ הַחֹדֶשׁ הַזֶּה.

❖ חַג הַמַּצּוֹת הַזֶּה.

❖ חַג הַסֻּכּוֹת הַזֶּה.

זָכְרֵנוּ, יי אֱלֹהֵינוּ, בּוֹ לְטוֹבָה. אָמֵן.

וּפָקְדֵנוּ בוֹ לִבְרָכָה. אָמֵן.

וְהוֹשִׁיעֵנוּ בוֹ לְחַיִּים. אָמֵן.

Our God of our fathers and mothers, be mindful of Your people Israel on this

❖ first day of the new month,

❖ festival of Pesach,

❖ festival of Sukkot,

and renew in us love and compassion, goodness, life, and peace.

This day remember us for well-being. Amen.

Bless us with Your nearness. Amen.

Help us to renew our life. Amen.

הוֹדָאָה   THANKSGIVING

מוֹדִים אֲנַחְנוּ לָךְ שָׁאַתָּה הוּא יי אֱלֹהֵינוּ וֵאלֹהֵי אֲבוֹתֵינוּ
וְאִמּוֹתֵינוּ, אֱלֹהֵי כָל־בָּשָׂר, יוֹצְרֵנוּ, יוֹצֵר בְּרֵאשִׁית. בְּרָכוֹת
וְהוֹדָאוֹת לְשִׁמְךָ הַגָּדוֹל וְהַקָּדוֹשׁ עַל־שֶׁהֶחֱיִיתָנוּ וְקִיַּמְתָּנוּ.
כֵּן תְּחַיֵּנוּ וּתְקַיְּמֵנוּ, יי אֱלֹהֵינוּ, וְתֶאֱסֹף גָּלֻיּוֹתֵינוּ לְשָׁמֹר חֻקֶּיךָ,
לַעֲשׂוֹת רְצוֹנֶךָ, וּלְעָבְדְּךָ בְּלֵבָב שָׁלֵם.

We affirm with gratitude that You, Adonai, are our God, the
God of our fathers and mothers, the God of all flesh, our
creator, the source of all being. We bless and praise Your
great and holy name, for keeping us in life and sustaining
us. Continue us in life and sustain us, Adonai our God;
strengthen us to observe Your laws, to do Your will, and to
serve You with a whole heart.

Every breath is precious, every moment a gift; our tradition teaches us gratitude: to be thankful for the gift of our life and its joys. And even for our sorrows.

❊ See "Giving Thanks," page 395, and Psalm 147 (page 371).

DURING THE TEN DAYS OF REPENTANCE ADD

וּכְתוֹב לְחַיִּים טוֹבִים כָּל־בְּנֵי בְרִיתֶךָ.

May all those loyal to Your covenant be inscribed for a good life.

בָּרוּךְ אֵל הַהוֹדָאוֹת.

Praised be God, to whom our thanks are due.

ON CHANUKAH ADD

עַל הַנִּסִּים, וְעַל הַפֻּרְקָן, וְעַל הַגְּבוּרוֹת, וְעַל הַתְּשׁוּעוֹת, וְעַל
הַנֶּחָמוֹת שֶׁעָשִׂיתָ לַאֲבוֹתֵינוּ וּלְאִמּוֹתֵינוּ בַּיָּמִים הָהֵם וּבַזְּמַן הַזֶּה.
בִּימֵי מַתִּתְיָהוּ בֶּן־יוֹחָנָן כֹּהֵן גָּדוֹל, חַשְׁמוֹנַאי וּבָנָיו,
כְּשֶׁעָמְדָה מַלְכוּת יָוָן הָרְשָׁעָה עַל עַמְּךָ יִשְׂרָאֵל, לְהַשְׁכִּיחָם
תּוֹרָתֶךָ וּלְהַעֲבִירָם מֵחֻקֵּי רְצוֹנֶךָ. וְאַתָּה בְּרַחֲמֶיךָ הָרַבִּים

עָמַדְתָּ לָהֶם בְּעֵת צָרָתָם, רַבְתָּ אֶת־רִיבָם, דַּנְתָּ אֶת־דִּינָם,
מָסַרְתָּ גִבּוֹרִים בְּיַד חַלָּשִׁים, וְרַבִּים בְּיַד מְעַטִּים, וּטְמֵאִים
בְּיַד טְהוֹרִים, וּרְשָׁעִים בְּיַד צַדִּיקִים, וְזֵדִים בְּיַד עוֹסְקֵי
תוֹרָתֶךָ. וּלְךָ עָשִׂיתָ שֵׁם גָּדוֹל וְקָדוֹשׁ בְּעוֹלָמֶךָ, וּלְעַמְּךָ
יִשְׂרָאֵל עָשִׂיתָ תְּשׁוּעָה גְדוֹלָה וּפֻרְקָן כְּהַיּוֹם הַזֶּה, וְאַחַר כֵּן
בָּאוּ בָנֶיךָ לִדְבִיר בֵּיתֶךָ, וּפִנּוּ אֶת־הֵיכָלֶךָ, וְטִהֲרוּ אֶת־מִקְדָּשֶׁךָ,
וְהִדְלִיקוּ נֵרוֹת בְּחַצְרוֹת קָדְשֶׁךָ, וְקָבְעוּ שְׁמוֹנַת יְמֵי חֲנֻכָּה אֵלּוּ,
לְהוֹדוֹת וּלְהַלֵּל לְשִׁמְךָ הַגָּדוֹל.

In days of old, at this season, You saved our people by wonders and
mighty deeds. In the days of the High Priest, Mattathias the Hasmonean,
the tyrannic Syrian-Greeks sought to destroy our people Israel by forcing
them to forget their Torah, and thus to abandon Your teaching.

But in great compassion You stood by them, so that the weak defeated
the strong, the few prevailed over the many, and the righteous prevailed.
For this great deliverance Your name was exalted and sanctified in the
world: Your children returned to Your house to purify the sanctuary and
to kindle its lights. And they dedicated these eight days of Chanukah to
give thanks and praise to Your great name.

ON PURIM ADD

עַל הַנִּסִּים, וְעַל הַפֻּרְקָן, וְעַל הַגְּבוּרוֹת, וְעַל הַתְּשׁוּעוֹת, וְעַל
הַנִּחָמוֹת שֶׁעָשִׂיתָ לַאֲבוֹתֵינוּ וּלְאִמּוֹתֵינוּ בַּיָּמִים הָהֵם וּבַזְּמַן הַזֶּה.
בִּימֵי מָרְדְּכַי וְאֶסְתֵּר בְּשׁוּשַׁן הַבִּירָה, כְּשֶׁעָמַד עֲלֵיהֶם הָמָן
הָרָשָׁע, בִּקֵּשׁ לְהַשְׁמִיד לַהֲרוֹג וּלְאַבֵּד אֶת־כָּל־הַיְּהוּדִים, מִנַּעַר
וְעַד־זָקֵן, טַף וְנָשִׁים, בְּיוֹם אֶחָד, בִּשְׁלֹשָׁה עָשָׂר לְחֹדֶשׁ
שְׁנֵים־עָשָׂר, הוּא־חֹדֶשׁ אֲדָר, וּשְׁלָלָם לָבוֹז. וְאַתָּה בְּרַחֲמֶיךָ
הָרַבִּים הֵפַרְתָּ אֶת־עֲצָתוֹ וְקִלְקַלְתָּ אֶת־מַחֲשַׁבְתּוֹ.

In days of old, at this season, You saved our people by wonders and mighty deeds. In the time of Mordechai and Esther, the wicked Haman arose in Persia, plotting the destruction of all the Jews, young and old alike. He planned to destroy them in a single day, the thirteenth of Adar, and to plunder their possessions. But by Your great mercy his plan was thwarted, his scheme frustrated. We therefore thank and bless You, O great and gracious God!

AT AN AFTERNOON OR EVENING SERVICE

ברכת שלום   PEACE

Our final prayer of the Tefilah is for peace and well-being, for ourselves, our people, and all people.

✽ *See Pirke Avot, pages 324-325, and page 351.*

שָׁלוֹם רָב עַל־יִשְׂרָאֵל עַמְּךָ תָּשִׂים לְעוֹלָם,
כִּי אַתָּה הוּא מֶלֶךְ אָדוֹן לְכָל הַשָּׁלוֹם.
וְטוֹב בְּעֵינֶיךָ לְבָרֵךְ אֶת־עַמְּךָ יִשְׂרָאֵל
וְאֶת־כָּל־הָעַמִּים בְּכָל־עֵת וּבְכָל־שָׁעָה בִּשְׁלוֹמֶךָ.

Supreme source of peace, grant true and lasting peace to our people Israel, for it is good in Your sight that Your people Israel, and all peoples, may be blessed at all times with Your gift of peace.

DURING THE TEN DAYS OF REPENTANCE ADD

בְּסֵפֶר חַיִּים וּבְרָכָה
נִכָּתֵב לְחַיִּים
טוֹבִים וּלְשָׁלוֹם.

May we be inscribed in the Book of Life and Blessing for a life of goodness and peace.

בָּרוּךְ אַתָּה יי, עוֹשֵׂה הַשָּׁלוֹם.

We praise You, O God, the source of peace.

AT A MORNING SERVICE

PEACE ברכת שלום

שִׂים שָׁלוֹם, טוֹבָה וּבְרָכָה, חֵן וָחֶסֶד וְרַחֲמִים,
עָלֵינוּ וְעַל כָּל־יִשְׂרָאֵל עַמֶּךָ .
בָּרְכֵנוּ, אָבִינוּ, כֻּלָּנוּ כְּאֶחָד בְּאוֹר פָּנֶיךָ,
כִּי בְאוֹר פָּנֶיךָ נָתַתָּ לָּנוּ, יְיָ אֱלֹהֵינוּ,
תּוֹרַת חַיִּים, וְאַהֲבַת חֶסֶד,
וּצְדָקָה וּבְרָכָה וְרַחֲמִים וְחַיִּים וְשָׁלוֹם.
וְטוֹב בְּעֵינֶיךָ לְבָרֵךְ אֶת־עַמְּךָ יִשְׂרָאֵל
וְאֶת־כָּל־הָעַמִּים בְּכָל־עֵת וּבְכָל־שָׁעָה בִּשְׁלוֹמֶךָ .

Our final prayer of the Tefilah is for peace and well-being, for ourselves, our people, and all people.

✤ See Pirke Avot, pages 324-325 and page 351.

Grant peace, goodness and blessing, grace, love, and mercy to us and to all Your people Israel. As a loving parent, bless us with the light of Your presence; for by that light, eternal God, You have revealed to us a Torah to live by: the love of kindness, righteousness, blessing, and mercy, bringing life and peace. For it is good in Your sight that Your people Israel and all peoples be blessed at all times with Your gift of peace.

DURING THE TEN DAYS OF REPENTANCE ADD

בְּסֵפֶר חַיִּים וּבְרָכָה
נִכָּתֵב לְחַיִּים
טוֹבִים וּלְשָׁלוֹם.

May we be inscribed in the Book of Life and Blessing for a life of goodness and peace.

בָּרוּךְ אַתָּה יְיָ, עוֹשֵׂה הַשָּׁלוֹם.

We praise You, O God, the source of peace.

SILENT PRAYER

אֱלֹהַי, נְצֹר לְשׁוֹנִי מֵרָע, וּשְׂפָתַי מִדַּבֵּר מִרְמָה. וְלִמְקַלְלַי נַפְשִׁי תִדּוֹם וְנַפְשִׁי כֶּעָפָר לַכֹּל תִּהְיֶה. פְּתַח לִבִּי בְּתוֹרָתֶךָ, וּבְמִצְוֹתֶיךָ תִּרְדֹּף נַפְשִׁי. עֲשֵׂה לְמַעַן שְׁמֶךָ, עֲשֵׂה לְמַעַן יְמִינֶךָ, עֲשֵׂה לְמַעַן קְדֻשָּׁתֶךָ, עֲשֵׂה לְמַעַן תּוֹרָתֶךָ; לְמַעַן יֵחָלְצוּן יְדִידֶיךָ, הוֹשִׁיעָה יְמִינְךָ וַעֲנֵנִי.

My God, keep my tongue from evil, my lips from deceptive speech. In the face of malice give me a quiet spirit; let me be humble wherever I go. Open my heart to Your teaching; make me eager to fulfill Your Mitzvot. Then will Your name be exalted, Your might manifest, Your holiness visible, and Your Torah magnified. Inspire me to love You, and be the answer to my prayer.

REFLECTIONS

SUNDAY

❧   Give me a quiet heart, and help me to hear the still, small voice that speaks within me, calling me to come closer to You and to grow in Your likeness. That voice teaches me to do my work faithfully, even when no one's eye is upon me, so that I may come to the end of each day feeling that I have used its gifts wisely and faced its trials bravely. It enables me to judge others with kindness and to love them freely. And it persuades me to see the divinity in everyone I meet.

MONDAY

❧   In my great need for light I look to You, Holy One. Help me to sense Your presence and to find the courage to affirm You, even when shadows darken my days. When my own weakness and the storms of life hide You from my

59

sight, teach me that You are near to me at all times. In Your great goodness give me trust, peace, and light. May my heart find its rest in You.

TUESDAY

℘ Something precious is taken from us, and we think of it as something we have lost, instead of something we have had. We remember only how empty our lives are now; we forget how full and rich they were before. . . . Let us count the past, happy days not as loss, but as gain. We have had them; and, now that they are ended, let us turn the present loss to glorious gain—the gain that comes with new courage, with noble tasks, with a wide outlook on life and duty.

WEDNESDAY

℘ The Baal Shem Tov said: No two people have the same abilities. You, like all others, must work to serve God according to your own talents. If you try to imitate another, you merely lose your opportunity to do good through your own merit; you cannot accomplish anything by imitating another person's way of service.

THURSDAY

℘ Do not neglect your own task in order to take one up for which someone else is responsible, however great that other task may be. Discern your own task and attend to it.

FRIDAY

℘ Guard me from despising others for their weaknesses, and, whatever may be my own faults and weaknesses, let me not come to despise myself. Instead, encourage me to search diligently for the good in others, that I may come to see that there is strength and goodness in everyone— including me!

☙

יְהְיוּ לְרָצוֹן אִמְרֵי־פִי	Yi-h'yu l'ra-tzon i-m'rei fi
וְהֶגְיוֹן לִבִּי לְפָנֶיךָ,	v'heg-yon li-bi l'fa-neh-cha,
יְהֹוָה, צוּרִי וְגֹאֲלִי.	Adonai tzu-ri v'go-a-li.

May the words of my mouth and the meditations of my heart be acceptable to You, O God, my rock and my redeemer. Amen.

☙

עֹשֶׂה שָׁלוֹם בִּמְרוֹמָיו,	O-seh sha-lom bi-m'ro-mav,
הוּא יַעֲשֶׂה שָׁלוֹם עָלֵינוּ	hu ya-a-seh sha-lom a-lei-nu
וְעַל־כָּל־יִשְׂרָאֵל, וְאִמְרוּ׃	v'al kol Yis-ra-eil, v'i-m'ru:
אָמֵן.	A-mein.

May the source of peace on high send peace to us, to all Israel, and to all the world, and let us say: Amen.

☙

כל מקדשי שביעי

SHABBAT WORSHIP

ערבית לשבת   SHABBAT EVENING SERVICE

קבלת שבת   WELCOMING THE SABBATH

1

הדלקת הנרות   THE KINDLING OF LIGHTS

וְקָרֵאתָ לַשַּׁבָּת עֹֽנֶג.

"You shall call the Sabbath a delight." These lights we kindle are a symbol of joy. May their brightness lift our spirits, and fill our hearts with happiness and peace.

בָּרוּךְ אַתָּה יי, אֱלֹהֵֽינוּ מֶֽלֶךְ הָעוֹלָם, אֲשֶׁר קִדְּשָֽׁנוּ בְּמִצְוֹתָיו וְצִוָּֽנוּ לְהַדְלִיק נֵר שֶׁל שַׁבָּת.

Ba-ruch a-ta Adonai, Eh-lo-hei-nu meh-lech ha-o-lam, a-sher ki-d'sha-nu b'mitz-vo-tav v'tzi-va-nu l'had-lik ner shel Shabbat.

We praise You, Adonai our God, sovereign of the universe: You hallow us with Your Mitzvot, and command us to kindle the lights of Shabbat.

A PRAYER BEFORE PRAYER: May my worship on this Shabbat encourage me to fulfill this precept: "Do justly, love mercy, and walk humbly with your God." (Micah 6:8)

A REFLECTION

𝕮   Every ethical deed and every decision for good is a sanctification of God's name; such deeds and decisions are a realization of the Divine, and through them is established a sanctuary of the good upon earth. (Leo Baeck)

෴

SELECT [FROM AMONG] THE FOLLOWING KABBALAT SHABBAT PSALMS

FROM PSALM 95

❧ See
"Selected
Psalms,"
pages 358-375,
and "A Daily
Psalm," pages
27-33.

לְכוּ נְרַנְּנָה לַיהוה, נָרִיעָה לְצוּר יִשְׁעֵנוּ. נְקַדְּמָה פָנָיו בְּתוֹדָה,
בִּזְמִרוֹת נָרִיעַ לוֹ. אֲשֶׁר בְּיָדוֹ מֶחְקְרֵי־אָרֶץ, וְתוֹעֲפוֹת הָרִים
לוֹ. אֲשֶׁר־לוֹ הַיָּם, וְהוּא עָשָׂהוּ, וְיַבֶּשֶׁת יָדָיו יָצָרוּ. בְּאוּ
נִשְׁתַּחֲוֶה וְנִכְרָעָה, נִבְרְכָה לִפְנֵי־יהוה עֹשֵׂנוּ. כִּי הוּא אֱלֹהֵינוּ, וַאֲנַחְנוּ
עַם מַרְעִיתוֹ וְצֹאן יָדוֹ. הַיּוֹם—אִם־בְּקֹלוֹ תִשְׁמָעוּ.

Come let us sing praise to Adonai, let us shout with joy to
our sheltering rock. Let us draw near with thanksgiving,
shouting praise-songs to our God.

*In Your hands are the depths of the earth; the mountain-peaks,
also, are Yours. Yours is the sea—You made it—and the dry land
was formed by Your hand.*

Come, let us bow the head and bend the knee before Adonai
our maker, our God whose flock we are: This day we could
be redeemed—if only we would hearken to God's voice!

PSALM 92 IS ON PAGE 68; L'CHA DODI IS ON PAGE 70

FROM PSALM 96

❧ See
"Selected
Psalms,"
pages 358-375,
and "A Daily
Psalm," pages
27-33.

שִׁירוּ לַיהוה שִׁיר חָדָשׁ; שִׁירוּ לַיהוה כָּל־הָאָרֶץ!
שִׁירוּ לַיהוה, בָּרְכוּ שְׁמוֹ; בַּשְּׂרוּ מִיּוֹם־לְיוֹם יְשׁוּעָתוֹ.
סַפְּרוּ בַגּוֹיִם כְּבוֹדוֹ, בְּכָל־הָעַמִּים נִפְלְאוֹתָיו.
כִּי גָדוֹל יהוה, וּמְהֻלָּל מְאֹד, נוֹרָא הוּא עַל־כָּל־אֱלֹהִים.

Sing to Adonai a new song; sing to Adonai, all the earth!

*We shall sing to You, Adonai, praising Your name; we shall tell
of Your deliverance from day to day.*

We shall proclaim Your splendor among the nations, Your wondrous deeds among the peoples.

For great are You, beyond all praise, inspiring awe in all the mighty: in Your presence are brightness and glory, in Your holy place, beauty and brilliance.

הוֹד־וְהָדָר לְפָנָיו, עֹז וְתִפְאֶרֶת בְּמִקְדָּשׁוֹ.

הָבוּ לַיהוה, מִשְׁפְּחוֹת עַמִּים, הָבוּ לַיהוה כָּבוֹד וָעֹז.

הָבוּ לַיהוה כְּבוֹד שְׁמוֹ; הִשְׁתַּחֲווּ לַיהוה בְּהַדְרַת־קֹדֶשׁ.

חִילוּ מִפָּנָיו כָּל־הָאָרֶץ. אִמְרוּ בַגּוֹיִם: יהוה מָלָךְ;

אַף־תִּכּוֹן תֵּבֵל, בַּל־תִּמּוֹט: יָדִין עַמִּים בְּמֵישָׁרִים.

Pay homage to God, O families of nations, pay homage to God's glory and might.

Pay homage to the glory of God's name; worship Adonai in the beauty of holiness.

Let all the earth tremble before You, as we proclaim among the nations: "Adonai reigns!" Yes, the world is established; it cannot be moved, for You rule the peoples in righteousness.

יִשְׂמְחוּ הַשָּׁמַיִם וְתָגֵל הָאָרֶץ; יִרְעַם הַיָּם וּמְלֹאוֹ. יַעֲלֹז שָׂדַי

וְכָל־אֲשֶׁר־בּוֹ; אָז יְרַנְּנוּ כָּל־עֲצֵי־יָעַר לִפְנֵי יהוה. כִּי בָא,

כִּי בָא לִשְׁפֹּט הָאָרֶץ: יִשְׁפֹּט־תֵּבֵל בְּצֶדֶק, וְעַמִּים בֶּאֱמוּנָתוֹ.

Be glad, O heavens; rejoice, O earth; let the sea and its fullness roar. Let the field exult, and all that is in it: then all the trees of the forest shall sing for joy before Adonai, who comes, who comes to judge the earth:

To judge the world with justice, and the peoples with faithfulness.

PSALM 92 IS ON PAGE 68; L'CHA DODI IS ON PAGE 70

FROM PSALM 97

❊ See
"Selected
Psalms,"
pages 358-375,
and "A Daily
Psalm," pages
27-33.

יהוה מָלָךְ: תָּגֵל הָאָרֶץ, יִשְׂמְחוּ אִיִּים רַבִּים. עָנָן
וַעֲרָפֶל סְבִיבָיו; צֶדֶק וּמִשְׁפָּט מְכוֹן כִּסְאוֹ. הִגִּידוּ
הַשָּׁמַיִם צִדְקוֹ, וְרָאוּ כָל־הָעַמִּים כְּבוֹדוֹ. שָׁמְעָה
וַתִּשְׂמַח צִיּוֹן; וַתָּגֵלְנָה בְּנוֹת יְהוּדָה, לְמַעַן מִשְׁפָּטֶיךָ,
יהוה. כִּי־אַתָּה, יהוה, עֶלְיוֹן עַל־כָּל־הָאָרֶץ:
מְאֹד נַעֲלֵיתָ עַל־כָּל־אֱלֹהִים.
אוֹר זָרֻעַ לַצַּדִּיק, וּלְיִשְׁרֵי־לֵב שִׂמְחָה.
שִׂמְחוּ צַדִּיקִים בַּיהוה, וְהוֹדוּ לְזֵכֶר קָדְשׁוֹ.

Adonai reigns: let the earth rejoice, let the many isles be glad.

Cloud and mist surround You; righteousness and justice are the foundation of Your throne.

The heavens proclaim Your righteousness, and all the peoples behold Your glory.

Zion hears and is glad; the cities of Judah rejoice because of Your judgments, O God.

For You, Adonai, are high above all the earth, far beyond all other gods.

Light is sown for the righteous, and gladness for the upright in heart.

Let the righteous rejoice in Adonai, and give thanks to God's holy name.

PSALM 92 IS ON PAGE 68; L'CHA DODI IS ON PAGE 70

FROM PSALM 98

מִזְמוֹר. שִׁירוּ לַיהוה שִׁיר חָדָשׁ, כִּי־נִפְלָאוֹת עָשָׂה.
הוֹדִיעַ יהוה יְשׁוּעָתוֹ; לְעֵינֵי הַגּוֹיִם גִּלָּה צִדְקָתוֹ.
זָכַר חַסְדּוֹ וֶאֱמוּנָתוֹ לְבֵית יִשְׂרָאֵל.
רָאוּ כָל־אַפְסֵי־אָרֶץ אֵת יְשׁוּעַת אֱלֹהֵינוּ.
הָרִיעוּ לַיהוה כָּל־הָאָרֶץ; פִּצְחוּ וְרַנְּנוּ וְזַמֵּרוּ!
בַּחֲצֹצְרוֹת וְקוֹל שׁוֹפָר הָרִיעוּ לִפְנֵי הַמֶּלֶךְ יהוה.

❖ See "Selected Psalms," pages 358-375, and "A Daily Psalm," pages 27-33.

Sing a new song to Adonai, who has done wonders.

You have made known Your saving power; You have revealed Your righteousness in the sight of the nations.

You fulfill Your promise of faithful love to the House of Israel.

All the ends of the earth have seen the saving power of our God.

Shout praise to Adonai all the earth; break out in songs of praise. With trumpets and shofar-blasts shout praise to the sovereign God.

יִרְעַם הַיָּם וּמְלֹאוֹ; תֵּבֵל וְיֹשְׁבֵי בָהּ.
נְהָרוֹת יִמְחֲאוּ־כָף! יַחַד הָרִים יְרַנֵּנוּ
לִפְנֵי־יהוה, כִּי בָא לִשְׁפֹּט הָאָרֶץ:
יִשְׁפֹּט־תֵּבֵל בְּצֶדֶק, וְעַמִּים בְּמֵישָׁרִים.

Let the sea roar, and its fullness; the world, and all who dwell in it. Let rivers clap hands! Together let mountains sing praise before Adonai, who comes to judge the earth:

To judge the world with justice, and the peoples with righteousness.

PSALM 92 IS ON PAGE 68; L'CHA DODI IS ON PAGE 70

PSALM 29

❈ See "Selected
Psalms," pages
358-375, and
"A Daily
Psalm," pages
27-33.

A PRAISE-SONG OF DAVID

מִזְמוֹר לְדָוִד

הָבוּ לַיהוה, בְּנֵי אֵלִים, הָבוּ לַיהוה כָּבוֹד וָעֹז!

הָבוּ לַיהוה כְּבוֹד שְׁמוֹ, הִשְׁתַּחֲווּ לַיהוה בְּהַדְרַת־קֹדֶשׁ.

קוֹל יהוה עַל־הַמָּיִם! אֵל־הַכָּבוֹד הִרְעִים! יהוה עַל־מַיִם רַבִּים!

קוֹל־יהוה בַּכֹּחַ, קוֹל יהוה בֶּהָדָר, קוֹל יהוה שֹׁבֵר אֲרָזִים,

וַיְשַׁבֵּר יהוה אֶת־אַרְזֵי הַלְּבָנוֹן.

וַיַּרְקִידֵם כְּמוֹ־עֵגֶל לְבָנוֹן וְשִׂרְיֹן כְּמוֹ בֶן־רְאֵמִים.

קוֹל־יהוה חֹצֵב לַהֲבוֹת אֵשׁ!

קוֹל יהוה יָחִיל מִדְבָּר! יָחִיל יהוה מִדְבַּר קָדֵשׁ;

קוֹל יהוה יְחוֹלֵל אַיָּלוֹת, וַיֶּחֱשֹׂף יְעָרוֹת,

וּבְהֵיכָלוֹ כֻּלּוֹ אֹמֵר: כָּבוֹד!

יהוה לַמַּבּוּל יָשָׁב, וַיֵּשֶׁב יהוה מֶלֶךְ לְעוֹלָם.

יהוה עֹז לְעַמּוֹ יִתֵּן, יהוה יְבָרֵךְ אֶת־עַמּוֹ בַשָּׁלוֹם.

Pay homage to God, you mighty ones, pay homage to God's glory and might.
Pay homage to the glory of God's name; worship Adonai in the beauty of holiness.
Adonai's voice above the waters! Thunder of the glorious God!
Adonai over the raging waters!
God's voice in power, God's voice in splendor,
The voice of Adonai breaks cedars,
Adonai shatters the cedars of Lebanon,
making them skip like a calf, Lebanon and Sirion, like young rams.
Adonai's voice sparks fiery flames!
Adonai's voice shakes the desert! Adonai shakes the Kadesh desert!
Adonai's voice uproots oaks, and strips the forests, as in God's temple all cry: "Glory!"
God sits enthroned over the torrents; God is sovereign forever.
Adonai: You give strength to Your people. Adonai: You bless Your people with peace.

FROM PSALM 92

A PRAISE-SONG TO THE SABBATH DAY

מִזְמוֹר שִׁיר לְיוֹם הַשַּׁבָּת

✥ See "Selected Psalms," pages 358-375, and "A Daily Psalm," pages 27-33.

טוֹב לְהֹדוֹת לַיהוה, וּלְזַמֵּר לְשִׁמְךָ עֶלְיוֹן,

לְהַגִּיד בַּבֹּקֶר חַסְדֶּךָ, וֶאֱמוּנָתְךָ בַּלֵּילוֹת,

עֲלֵי־עָשׂוֹר וַעֲלֵי־נָבֶל, עֲלֵי הִגָּיוֹן בְּכִנּוֹר.

כִּי שִׂמַּחְתַּנִי, יהוה, בְּפָעֳלֶךָ, בְּמַעֲשֵׂי יָדֶיךָ אֲרַנֵּן.

מַה־גָּדְלוּ מַעֲשֶׂיךָ, יהוה! מְאֹד עָמְקוּ מַחְשְׁבֹתֶיךָ.

It is good to give thanks to Adonai,
to sing praises to Your name, O Most High,

to tell of Your love in the morning,
Your faithfulness in the night,

to the sound of harp and lute,
the sweet viol's song.

Oh, how You gladden me with Your deeds, Adonai;
so I sing for joy over the works of Your hands.

צַדִּיק כַּתָּמָר יִפְרָח, כְּאֶרֶז בַּלְּבָנוֹן יִשְׂגֶּה.

שְׁתוּלִים בְּבֵית יהוה, בְּחַצְרוֹת אֱלֹהֵינוּ יַפְרִיחוּ.

עוֹד יְנוּבוּן בְּשֵׂיבָה, דְּשֵׁנִים וְרַעֲנַנִּים יִהְיוּ,

לְהַגִּיד כִּי־יָשָׁר יהוה, צוּרִי, וְלֹא־עַוְלָתָה בּוֹ.

The righteous shall flourish like palms,
reach high like a cedar in Lebanon.

Rooted in Your house, Adonai,
they shall flourish in the courts of our God.
Fresh and green shall they be
still vigorous in old age.
Proclaiming that Adonai is just,
my God, my flawless rock.

PSALM 93

❊ See "Selected
Psalms," pages
358-375, and
"A Daily
Psalm," pages
27-33.

יְהוָה מָלָךְ, גֵּאוּת לָבֵשׁ;

לָבֵשׁ יְהוָה, עֹז הִתְאַזָּר;

אַף־תִּכּוֹן תֵּבֵל, בַּל־תִּמּוֹט.

נָכוֹן כִּסְאֲךָ מֵאָז, מֵעוֹלָם אָתָּה.

נָשְׂאוּ נְהָרוֹת, יְהוָה,

נָשְׂאוּ נְהָרוֹת קוֹלָם,

יִשְׂאוּ נְהָרוֹת דָּכְיָם;

מִקֹּלוֹת מַיִם רַבִּים, אַדִּירִים

מִשְׁבְּרֵי־יָם, אַדִּיר בַּמָּרוֹם

יְהוָה.

עֵדֹתֶיךָ נֶאֶמְנוּ מְאֹד;

לְבֵיתְךָ נַאֲוָה־קֹדֶשׁ, יְהוָה,

לְאֹרֶךְ יָמִים.

Adonai reigns, robed in majesty,

Adonai is robed, girded with might.

The world is established, not to be moved.

Your throne is established from of old;

You are from everlasting.

The torrents lift up, Adonai,

the torrents lift up their voice,

the torrents howl their rage;

yet above the raging waters,

the mighty breakers of the sea,

is the majesty of God on high.

The truth of Your words is constant;

Adonai, holiness befits Your house for all time.

❧

L'CHA DODI   לכה דודי

לְכָה דוֹדִי לִקְרַאת כַּלָּה, פְּנֵי שַׁבָּת נְקַבְּלָה.
לְכָה דוֹדִי לִקְרַאת כַּלָּה, פְּנֵי שַׁבָּת נְקַבְּלָה.

L'cha do-di lik-rat ka-la, p'nei Shabbat n'ka-b'la.
L'cha do-di lik-rat ka-la, p'nei Shabbat n'ka-b'la.

> As we welcome Shabbat with L'cha Dodi, we turn to welcome each other, and extend the hand of friendship.

שָׁמוֹר וְזָכוֹר, בְּדִבּוּר אֶחָד, הִשְׁמִיעָנוּ אֵל הַמְיֻחָד.
יְיָ אֶחָד וּשְׁמוֹ אֶחָד, לְשֵׁם וּלְתִפְאֶרֶת וְלִתְהִלָּה. לכה ...

Sha-mor v'za-chor, b'di-bur eh-chad, hish-mi-a-nu Eil ha-m'yu-chad;
Adonai Eh-chad u-sh'mo Eh-chad, l'sheim u-l'tif-eh-ret v'li-t'hi-la.
L'cha do-di . . .

לִקְרַאת שַׁבָּת לְכוּ וְנֵלְכָה, כִּי הִיא מְקוֹר הַבְּרָכָה.
מֵרֹאשׁ מִקֶּדֶם נְסוּכָה, סוֹף מַעֲשֶׂה בְּמַחֲשָׁבָה תְּחִלָּה.
לכה ...

Lik-rat Shabbat l'chu v'nei-l'cha, ki hi m'kor ha-b'ra-cha.
Mei-rosh mi-keh-dem n'su-cha, sof ma-a-seh b'ma-cha-sha-va t'chi-la.
L'cha do-di . . .

הִתְעוֹרְרִי, הִתְעוֹרְרִי, כִּי בָא אוֹרֵךְ! קוּמִי, אוֹרִי,
עוּרִי עוּרִי, שִׁיר דַּבֵּרִי; כְּבוֹד יְיָ עָלַיִךְ נִגְלָה. לכה ...

Hit-o-r'ri, hit-o-r'ri, ki va o-reich! Ku-mi, o-ri,
u-ri u-ri, shir da-bei-ri; k'vod Adonai a-la-yich nig-la.
L'cha do-di . . .

בּוֹאִי בְשָׁלוֹם עֲטֶרֶת בַּעְלָהּ, גַּם בְּשִׂמְחָה וּבְצָהֳלָה,
תּוֹךְ אֱמוּנֵי עַם סְגֻלָּה, בּוֹאִי כַלָּה! בּוֹאִי כַלָּה! לכה ...

Bo-i v'sha-lom, a-teh-ret ba-a-lah, gam b'sim-chah u-v'tso-ho-la,
Toch eh-mu-nei am s'gu-la, bo-i cha-la! Bo-i cha-la!
L'cha do-di . . .

BELOVED

Beloved, come to meet the bride; beloved, come to greet Shabbat.

"Keep" and "Remember": a single command, the only God caused us to hear; the Eternal is one, God's name is one, for honor and glory and praise.

Beloved, come to meet the bride; beloved, come to greet Shabbat.

Come with me to meet Shabbat, forever a fountain of blessing. Still it flows, as from the start: the last of days, for which the first was made.

Beloved, come to meet the bride; beloved, come to greet Shabbat.

Awake, awake, your light has come! Arise, shine, awake and sing; the Eternal's glory dawns upon you.

Beloved, come to meet the bride; beloved, come to greet Shabbat.

Enter in peace, O crown of your husband; enter in gladness, enter in joy. Come to the people that keeps its faith. Enter, O bride! Enter, O bride!

Beloved, come to meet the bride; beloved, come to greet Shabbat.

"Keep" and "Remember"— The Torah's two versions of the fifth (Shabbat) commandment differ in their first word. The Rabbis thought that both words were uttered simultaneously.

As we welcome Shabbat with L'cha Dodi, we turn to welcome each other, and extend the hand of friendship.

THE READER'S KADDISH IS ON PAGE 90

71

2

הדלקת הנרות THE KINDLING OF LIGHTS

וְקָרֵאתָ לַשַּׁבָּת עֹנֶג.

In the spirit of our ancient tradition, which unites and sanctifies the House of Israel in all lands and ages, we welcome Shabbat by kindling these lights.

בָּרוּךְ אַתָּה יי, אֱלֹהֵינוּ מֶלֶךְ הָעוֹלָם, אֲשֶׁר קִדְּשָׁנוּ בְּמִצְוֹתָיו וְצִוָּנוּ לְהַדְלִיק נֵר שֶׁל שַׁבָּת.

Ba-ruch a-ta Adonai, Eh-lo-hei-nu meh-lech ha-o-lam, a-sher ki-d'sha-nu b'mitz-vo-tav v'tzi-va-nu l'had-lik ner shel Shabbat.

We praise You, Adonai our God, sovereign of the universe: You hallow us with Your Mitzvot, and command us to kindle the lights of Shabbat.

❧

Holy One, Your glory fills the universe. We are never beyond the reach of Your hand, yet we are especially grateful for sacred times and places, for they help us to reach out to You. Let us sense Your nearness at this hour, let us hear Your voice speaking in our hearts in the stillness of Sabbath peace, as we turn to You.

❧

A PRAYER BEFORE PRAYER: May my worship on this Shabbat encourage me to fulfill this Mitzvah: "Love your neighbor as yourself." (Leviticus 19:18)

72

כִּי אֶשְׁמְרָה שַׁבָּת, אֵל יִשְׁמְרֵנִי.
אוֹת הִיא לְעוֹלְמֵי עַד, בֵּינוֹ וּבֵינִי.

Ki esh-m'ra Shabbat, Eil yish-m'rei-ni.
Ot hi l'o-l'mei ad, bei-no u-vei-ni.

When we keep Shabbat, God keeps us;
It it a sign between God and Israel forever . . .

FROM PSALM 92

✽ See
"Selected
Psalms,"
pages 358-375,
and "A Daily
Psalm," pages
27-33.

A PRAISE-SONG TO THE SABBATH DAY

מִזְמוֹר שִׁיר לְיוֹם הַשַּׁבָּת
טוֹב לְהֹדוֹת לַיהוה, וּלְזַמֵּר לְשִׁמְךָ עֶלְיוֹן,
לְהַגִּיד בַּבֹּקֶר חַסְדֶּךָ, וֶאֱמוּנָתְךָ בַּלֵּילוֹת,
עֲלֵי־עָשׂוֹר וַעֲלֵי־נָבֶל, עֲלֵי הִגָּיוֹן בְּכִנּוֹר.
כִּי שִׂמַּחְתַּנִי, יהוה, בְּפָעֳלֶךָ, בְּמַעֲשֵׂי יָדֶיךָ אֲרַנֵּן.
מַה־גָּדְלוּ מַעֲשֶׂיךָ, יהוה! מְאֹד עָמְקוּ מַחְשְׁבֹתֶיךָ.

It is good to give thanks to Adonai,
to sing praises to Your name, O Most High,

> to tell of Your love in the morning,
> Your faithfulness in the night,

to the sound of harp and lute,
the sweet viol's song.

> Oh, how You gladden me with Your deeds, Adonai;
> so I sing for joy over the works of Your hands.

צַדִּיק כַּתָּמָר יִפְרָח, כְּאֶרֶז בַּלְּבָנוֹן יִשְׂגֶּה.
שְׁתוּלִים בְּבֵית יהוה, בְּחַצְרוֹת אֱלֹהֵינוּ יַפְרִיחוּ.
עוֹד יְנוּבוּן בְּשֵׂיבָה, דְּשֵׁנִים וְרַעֲנַנִּים יִהְיוּ,
לְהַגִּיד כִּי־יָשָׁר יהוה, צוּרִי, וְלֹא־עַוְלָתָה בּוֹ.

The righteous shall flourish like palms,
reach high like a cedar in Lebanon.

Rooted in Your house, Adonai,
they shall flourish in the courts of our God.
Fresh and green shall they be, still vigorous in old age.
Proclaiming that Adonai is just, my God, my flawless rock.

A REFLECTION

⁶   If you wish to fulfill the commandment to judge your
neighbor with justice, judge every human being for the best.

❦

לכה דודי   L'CHA DODI

As we welcome Shabbat with L'cha Dodi, we turn to welcome each other, and extend the hand of friendship.

לְכָה דוֹדִי לִקְרַאת כַּלָּה, פְּנֵי שַׁבָּת נְקַבְּלָה.

לְכָה דוֹדִי לִקְרַאת כַּלָּה, פְּנֵי שַׁבָּת נְקַבְּלָה.

L'cha do-di lik-rat ka-la, p'nei Shabbat n'ka-b'la.

L'cha do-di lik-rat ka-la, p'nei Shabbat n'ka-b'la.

שָׁמוֹר וְזָכוֹר, בְּדִבּוּר אֶחָד, הִשְׁמִיעָנוּ אֵל הַמְיֻחָד.

יי אֶחָד וּשְׁמוֹ אֶחָד, לְשֵׁם וּלְתִפְאֶרֶת וְלִתְהִלָּה. לכה ...

Sha-mor v'za-chor, b'di-bur eh-chad, hish-mi-a-nu Eil ha-m'yu-chad;

Adonai Eh-chad u-sh'mo Eh-chad, l'sheim u-l'tif-eh-ret v'li-t'hi-la.

L'cha do-di . . .

לִקְרַאת שַׁבָּת לְכוּ וְנֵלְכָה, כִּי הִיא מְקוֹר הַבְּרָכָה.

מֵרֹאשׁ מִקֶּדֶם נְסוּכָה, סוֹף מַעֲשֶׂה בְּמַחֲשָׁבָה תְּחִלָּה.
לכה ...

Lik-rat Shabbat l'chu v'nei-l'cha, ki hi m'kor ha-b'ra-cha.

Mei-rosh mi-keh-dem n'su-cha, sof ma-a-seh b'ma-cha-sha-va t'chi-la.

L'cha do-di . . .

הִתְעוֹרְרִי, הִתְעוֹרְרִי, כִּי בָא אוֹרֵךְ! קוּמִי, אוֹרִי,

עוּרִי עוּרִי, שִׁיר דַּבֵּרִי; כְּבוֹד יי עָלַיִךְ נִגְלָה. לכה ...

Hit-o-r'ri, hit-o-r'ri, ki va o-reich! Ku-mi, o-ri,

u-ri u-ri, shir da-bei-ri; k'vod Adonai a-la-yich nig-la.

L'cha do-di . . .

בּוֹאִי בְשָׁלוֹם עֲטֶרֶת בַּעְלָהּ, גַּם בְּשִׂמְחָה וּבְצָהֳלָה,

תּוֹךְ אֱמוּנֵי עַם סְגֻלָּה, בּוֹאִי כַלָּה! בּוֹאִי כַלָּה! לכה ...

Bo-i v'sha-lom, a-teh-ret ba-a-lah, gam b'sim-chah u-v'tso-ho-la,

Toch eh-mu-nei am s'gu-la, bo-i cha-la! Bo-i cha-la!

L'cha do-di . . .

BELOVED

Beloved, come to meet the bride; beloved, let us greet Shabbat.

"Keep" and "Remember": a single command, the only God caused us to hear; the Eternal is one, God's name is one, for honor and glory and praise.

Beloved, come to meet the bride; beloved, come to greet Shabbat.

Come with me to meet Shabbat, forever a fountain of blessing. Still it flows, as from the start: the last of days, for which the first was made.

Beloved, come to meet the bride; beloved, come to greet Shabbat.

Awake, awake, your light has come! Arise, shine, awake and sing; the Eternal's glory dawns upon you.

Beloved, come to meet the bride; beloved, come to greet Shabbat.

Enter in peace, O crown of your husband; enter in gladness, enter in joy. Come to the people that keeps its faith. Enter, O bride! Enter, O bride!

Beloved, come to meet the bride; beloved, come to greet Shabbat.

"Keep" and "Remember"— The Torah's two versions of the fifth (Shabbat) commandment differ in their first word. The Rabbis thought that both words were uttered simultaneously.

As we welcome Shabbat with L'cha Dodi, we turn to welcome each other, and extend the hand of friendship.

THE READER'S KADDISH IS ON PAGE 88

3

הדלקת הנרות   THE KINDLING OF LIGHTS

הָעָם הַהֹלְכִים בַּחֹשֶׁךְ רָאוּ אוֹר גָּדוֹל.

A PRAYER
BEFORE
PRAYER:
May my
worship on
this Shabbat
encourage me
to fulfill this
Mitzvah:
"If your kin
become poor
and cannot
sustain
themselves,
you must
assist them."
(Leviticus
25:35)

"The people who walked in darkness have seen a great light." But in the past week some have known sorrow or disappointment; some have endured hours and days of pain. Let this Shabbat be an oasis, a time of of healing: To the lonely may it bring companionship; to the sorrowing, comfort; to the dispirited, courage; to all of us, peaceful minds and hope for the future.

בָּרוּךְ אַתָּה יי, אֱלֹהֵינוּ מֶלֶךְ הָעוֹלָם, אֲשֶׁר קִדְּשָׁנוּ
בְּמִצְוֹתָיו וְצִוָּנוּ לְהַדְלִיק נֵר שֶׁל שַׁבָּת.

Ba-ruch a-ta Adonai, Eh-lo-hei-nu meh-lech ha-o-lam, a-sher ki-d'sha-nu
b'mitz-vo-tav v'tzi-va-nu l'had-lik ner shel Shabbat.

We praise You, Adonai our God, sovereign of the universe: You hallow us with Your Mitzvot, and command us to kindle the lights of Shabbat.

🙠

Happy is the people by whom the Sabbath is sanctified; happy are they who rejoice in its blessing. For as one who brings good tidings and promises peace, Shabbat brings its message of healing and love.

שלום עליכם SHALOM ALEICHEM

שָׁלוֹם עֲלֵיכֶם, מַלְאֲכֵי הַשָּׁרֵת, מַלְאֲכֵי עֶלְיוֹן,
מִמֶּלֶךְ מַלְכֵי הַמְּלָכִים, הַקָּדוֹשׁ בָּרוּךְ הוּא.

בּוֹאֲכֶם לְשָׁלוֹם, מַלְאֲכֵי הַשָּׁלוֹם, מַלְאֲכֵי עֶלְיוֹן,
מִמֶּלֶךְ מַלְכֵי הַמְּלָכִים, הַקָּדוֹשׁ בָּרוּךְ הוּא.

בָּרְכוּנִי לְשָׁלוֹם, מַלְאֲכֵי הַשָּׁלוֹם, מַלְאֲכֵי עֶלְיוֹן,
מִמֶּלֶךְ מַלְכֵי הַמְּלָכִים, הַקָּדוֹשׁ בָּרוּךְ הוּא.

צֵאתְכֶם לְשָׁלוֹם, מַלְאֲכֵי הַשָּׁלוֹם, מַלְאֲכֵי עֶלְיוֹן,
מִמֶּלֶךְ מַלְכֵי הַמְּלָכִים, הַקָּדוֹשׁ בָּרוּךְ הוּא.

Sha-lom a-lei-chem mal-a-chei ha-sha-reit, mal-a-chei el-yon,
Mi-meh-lech ma-l'chei ha-m'la-chim, ha-ka-dosh ba-ruch hu.

Bo-a-chem l'sha-lom, mal-a-chei ha-sha-lom, mal-a-chei el-yon,
Mi-meh-lech ma-l'chei ha-m'la-chim, ha-ka-dosh ba-ruch hu.

Ba-r'chu-ni l'sha-lom, mal-a-chei ha-sha-lom, mal-a-chei el-yon,
Mi-meh-lech ma-l'chei ha-m'la-chim, ha-ka-dosh ba-ruch hu.

Tzei-t'chem l'sha-lom, mal-a-chei ha-sha-lom, mal-a-chei el-yon,
Mi-meh-lech ma-l'chei ha-m'la-chim, ha-ka-dosh ba-ruch hu.

Peace be to you, ministering angels, messengers of the Most High, of the supreme sovereign, the Holy One, ever to be praised.

Enter in peace, O messengers of the Most High, of the supreme sovereign, the Holy One, ever to be praised.

Bless us with peace, O messengers of the Most High, of the supreme sovereign, the Holy One, ever to be praised.

Depart in peace, O messengers of the Most High, of the supreme sovereign, the Holy One, ever to be praised.

A HYMN OF LONGING AND PRAISE

❋ See
"Selected
Psalms,"
pages 358-375,
and "A Daily
Psalm," pages
27-33.

מַה־יְּדִידוֹת מִשְׁכְּנוֹתֶיךָ, יהוה צְבָאוֹת!

נִכְסְפָה וְגַם־כָּלְתָה נַפְשִׁי לְחַצְרוֹת יהוה;

לִבִּי וּבְשָׂרִי יְרַנְּנוּ אֶל אֵל־חָי.

How lovely are Your dwelling-places, God of all being!

My soul longs and yearns for the courts of my God; my heart and flesh sing for joy to the living God.

גַּם־צִפּוֹר מָצְאָה בַיִת, וּדְרוֹר קֵן לָהּ,

אֲשֶׁר־שָׁתָה אֶפְרֹחֶיהָ אֶת־מִזְבְּחוֹתֶיךָ,

יהוה צְבָאוֹת, מַלְכִּי וֵאלֹהָי.

As the sparrow finds a home, and the swallow has a nest where she rears her young,

so do I seek out Your altars, God of all being, my sovereign God.

אַשְׁרֵי יוֹשְׁבֵי בֵיתֶךָ, עוֹד יְהַלְלוּךָ סֶּלָה ...

אַשְׁרֵי אָדָם עוֹז־לוֹ בָךְ; מְסִלּוֹת בִּלְבָבָם.

Blessed are they that dwell in Your house, who never cease to praise You.

Blessed are they that find their strength in You; their hearts are highways to Your presence.

A REFLECTION

❧ Help me, Holy One, to strengthen the goodness within me. Help me to see clearly what is worthwhile, and to keep to it faithfully. Then when this day and this week have passed, they will mark another step on my way through life, a step taken in the awareness that You go with me.

79

FROM PSALM 98

✣ See "Selected Psalms," pages 358-375, and "A Daily Psalm," pages 27-33.

מִזְמוֹר . שִׁירוּ לַיהוה שִׁיר חָדָשׁ, כִּי־נִפְלָאוֹת עָשָׂה.

הוֹדִיעַ יהוה יְשׁוּעָתוֹ; לְעֵינֵי הַגּוֹיִם גִּלָּה צִדְקָתוֹ.

זָכַר חַסְדּוֹ וֶאֱמוּנָתוֹ לְבֵית יִשְׂרָאֵל.

רָאוּ כָל־אַפְסֵי־אָרֶץ אֵת יְשׁוּעַת אֱלֹהֵינוּ.

הָרִיעוּ לַיהוה כָּל־הָאָרֶץ; פִּצְחוּ וְרַנְּנוּ וְזַמֵּרוּ!

בַּחֲצֹצְרוֹת וְקוֹל שׁוֹפָר הָרִיעוּ לִפְנֵי הַמֶּלֶךְ יהוה.

Sing a new song to Adonai, who has done wonders.

You have made known Your saving power; You have revealed Your righteousness in the sight of the nations.

You fulfill Your promise of faithful love to the House of Israel.

All the ends of the earth have seen the saving power of our God.

Shout praise to Adonai all the earth; break out in songs of praise. With trumpets and shofar-blasts shout praise to the sovereign God.

יִרְעַם הַיָּם וּמְלֹאוֹ; תֵּבֵל וְיֹשְׁבֵי בָהּ.

נְהָרוֹת יִמְחֲאוּ־כָף! יַחַד הָרִים יְרַנֵּנוּ

לִפְנֵי־יהוה, כִּי בָא לִשְׁפֹּט הָאָרֶץ:

יִשְׁפֹּט־תֵּבֵל בְּצֶדֶק, וְעַמִּים בְּמֵישָׁרִים.

Let the sea roar, and its fullness; the world, and all who dwell in it. Let rivers clap hands! Together let mountains sing praise before Adonai, who comes to judge the earth:

To judge the world with justice, and the peoples with righteousness.

L'CHA DODI   לכה דודי

As we
welcome
Shabbat
with
L'cha Dodi,
we turn to
welcome
each other,
and extend
the hand of
friendship.

לְכָה דוֹדִי לִקְרַאת כַּלָּה, פְּנֵי שַׁבָּת נְקַבְּלָה.
לְכָה דוֹדִי לִקְרַאת כַּלָּה, פְּנֵי שַׁבָּת נְקַבְּלָה.

L'cha do-di lik-rat ka-la, p'nei Shabbat n'ka-b'la.
L'cha do-di lik-rat ka-la, p'nei Shabbat n'ka-b'la.

שָׁמוֹר וְזָכוֹר, בְּדִבּוּר אֶחָד, הִשְׁמִיעָנוּ אֵל הַמְיֻחָד.
יְיָ אֶחָד וּשְׁמוֹ אֶחָד, לְשֵׁם וּלְתִפְאֶרֶת וְלִתְהִלָּה. לכה ...

Sha-mor v'za-chor, b'di-bur eh-chad, hish-mi-a-nu Eil ha-m'yu-chad;
Adonai Eh-chad u-sh'mo Eh-chad, l'sheim u-l'tif-eh-ret v'li-t'hi-la.
L'cha do-di . . .

לִקְרַאת שַׁבָּת לְכוּ וְנֵלְכָה, כִּי הִיא מְקוֹר הַבְּרָכָה.
מֵרֹאשׁ מִקֶּדֶם נְסוּכָה, סוֹף מַעֲשֶׂה בְּמַחֲשָׁבָה תְּחִלָּה. לכה ...

Lik-rat Shabbat l'chu v'nei-l'cha, ki hi m'kor ha-b'ra-cha.
Mei-rosh mi-keh-dem n'su-cha, sof ma-a-seh b'ma-cha-sha-va t'chi-la.
L'cha do-di . . .

הִתְעוֹרְרִי, הִתְעוֹרְרִי, כִּי בָא אוֹרֵךְ! קוּמִי, אוֹרִי,
עוּרִי עוּרִי, שִׁיר דַּבֵּרִי; כְּבוֹד יְיָ עָלַיִךְ נִגְלָה. לכה ...

Hit-o-r'ri, hit-o-r'ri, ki va o-reich! Ku-mi, o-ri,
u-ri u-ri, shir da-bei-ri; k'vod Adonai a-la-yich nig-la.
L'cha do-di . . .

בּוֹאִי בְשָׁלוֹם עֲטֶרֶת בַּעֲלָהּ, גַּם בְּשִׂמְחָה וּבְצָהֳלָה,
תּוֹךְ אֱמוּנֵי עַם סְגֻלָּה, בּוֹאִי כַלָּה! בּוֹאִי כַלָּה! לכה ...

Bo-i v'sha-lom, a-teh-ret ba-a-lah, gam b'sim-chah u-v'tso-ho-la,
Toch eh-mu-nei am s'gu-la, bo-i cha-la! Bo-i cha-la!
L'cha do-di . . .

BELOVED

Beloved, come to meet the bride; beloved, let us greet Shabbat.

"Keep" and "Remember": a single decree, the only God caused us to hear; Adonai is one, God's name is one, to be honored, exalted, and praised.

Beloved, come to meet the bride; beloved, let us greet Shabbat.

Come let us greet Shabbat, for she is the fountain of blessing. Still it flows, as from the start: the last of days, for which the first was made.

Beloved, come to meet the bride; beloved, let us greet Shabbat.

Awake, awake, your light has come! Arise, shine, awake and sing; Awake, awake, your light has come! An eternal glory dawns upon you.

Beloved, come to meet the bride; beloved, let us greet Shabbat.

Enter in peace, O crown of your husband; enter in gladness, enter in joy. Come to the faithful, to Israel's folk. Enter, O bride! Enter, O bride!

Beloved, come to meet the bride; beloved, let us greet Shabbat.

"Keep" and "Remember"— The Torah's two versions of the fifth (Shabbat) commandment differ in their first word. The Rabbis thought that both words were uttered simultaneously.

As we welcome Shabbat with L'cha Dodi, we turn to welcome each other, and extend the hand of friendship.

THE READER'S KADDISH IS ON PAGE 88

ערבית לשבת   SHABBAT EVENING SERVICE

קבלת שבת   WELCOMING THE SABBATH

4

הדלקת הנרות   THE KINDLING OF LIGHTS

A PRAYER
BEFORE
PRAYER:
May my
worship on
this Shabbat
encourage me
to fulfill this
precept: "Do
not judge
your friend
until you are
in his or her
place." (Pirke
Avot 2:4)

Draw near, O Holy One, from our working days to the joys of Shabbat. You have been with us all the week, yet at times we have forgotten You. Kindling these lights, we say Your name, remembering the love You have shown us. We turn to You in gratitude, to nourish our needy souls with Your tenderness.

בָּרוּךְ אַתָּה יי, אֱלֹהֵינוּ מֶלֶךְ הָעוֹלָם, אֲשֶׁר קִדְּשָׁנוּ בְּמִצְוֹתָיו וְצִוָּנוּ לְהַדְלִיק נֵר שֶׁל שַׁבָּת.

Ba-ruch a-ta Adonai, Eh-lo-hei-nu meh-lech ha-o-lam, a-sher ki-d'sha-nu b'mitz-vo-tav v'tzi-va-nu l'had-lik ner shel Shabbat.

We praise You, Adonai our God, sovereign of the universe: You hallow us with Your Mitzvot, and command us to kindle the lights of Shabbat.

⇛

Shabbat has descended, with its promise of rest, its precious gift of time: time to embrace family and friends, to reflect more deeply on the meaning and purpose of our lives, and to worship in the beauty of holiness, bringing contentment to our hearts. May every Shabbat be a sanctuary of love and devotion: thus shall we find happiness in our homes, and blessing for us all.

⇛

FROM PSALM 95

❖ See "Selected Psalms," pages 358-375, and "A Daily Psalm," pages 27-33.

לְכוּ נְרַנְּנָה לַיהוה, נָרִיעָה לְצוּר יִשְׁעֵנוּ.

נְקַדְּמָה פָנָיו בְּתוֹדָה, בִּזְמִרוֹת נָרִיעַ לוֹ.

אֲשֶׁר בְּיָדוֹ מֶחְקְרֵי־אָרֶץ, וְתוֹעֲפוֹת הָרִים לוֹ.

אֲשֶׁר־לוֹ הַיָּם, וְהוּא עָשָׂהוּ, וְיַבֶּשֶׁת יָדָיו יָצָרוּ.

בֹּאוּ נִשְׁתַּחֲוֶה וְנִכְרָעָה, נִבְרְכָה לִפְנֵי־יהוה עֹשֵׂנוּ.

כִּי הוּא אֱלֹהֵינוּ, וַאֲנַחְנוּ עַם מַרְעִיתוֹ וְצֹאן יָדוֹ

הַיּוֹם—אִם־בְּקֹלוֹ תִשְׁמָעוּ.

Come let us sing praise to Adonai, let us shout with joy to our sheltering rock. Let us draw near with thanksgiving, shouting praise-songs to our God.

In Your hands are the depths of the earth; the mountain-peaks, also, are Yours. Yours is the sea—You made it—and the dry land was formed by Your hand.

Come, let us bow the head and bend the knee before Adonai our maker, our God whose flock we are: This day we could be redeemed—if only we would hearken to God's voice!

⊷

מַה־יָּפֶה הַיּוֹם: שַׁבָּת שָׁלוֹם.

Mah ya-feh ha-yom: Shabbat Shalom.

How beautiful is this day: Shabbat Shalom.

⊷

A REFLECTION

   Rav Beroka of Bei Chozai often came to the market of Bei Lapat. There, from time to time, he would encounter Elijah the Prophet.

At one of their meetings, he said to Elijah: "Is there anyone in this market who has earned Paradise?"

Elijah's answer was: "No."

For a time, there was a silence between them. Then two men came along.

When he saw them, Elijah said: "These two will enter Paradise."

Rav Beroka went to them and said: "Who are you and what are your deeds?"

They answered: "We are jesters."

"And your deeds: what are they?"

"When people are dejected we make them laugh. When people quarrel we find a way to help them make peace."
(Talmud Ta'anit 22a)

Ω

הִנֵּה מַה־טּוֹב וּמַה־נָּעִים שֶׁבֶת אַחִים גַּם־יָחַד.

Hi-nei mah-tov u-mah na-im sheh-vet a-chim gam ya-chad.

How good it is, and how pleasant, when we dwell together in unity.

Ω

L'CHA DODI   לכה דודי

לְכָה דוֹדִי לִקְרַאת כַּלָּה, פְּנֵי שַׁבָּת נְקַבְּלָה.
לְכָה דוֹדִי לִקְרַאת כַּלָּה, פְּנֵי שַׁבָּת נְקַבְּלָה.

L'cha do-di lik-rat ka-la, p'nei Shabbat n'ka-b'la.
L'cha do-di lik-rat ka-la, p'nei Shabbat n'ka-b'la.

As we welcome Shabbat with L'cha Dodi, we turn to welcome each other, and extend the hand of friendship.

שָׁמוֹר וְזָכוֹר, בְּדִבּוּר אֶחָד, הִשְׁמִיעָנוּ אֵל הַמְיֻחָד.
יְיָ אֶחָד וּשְׁמוֹ אֶחָד, לְשֵׁם וּלְתִפְאֶרֶת וְלִתְהִלָּה. לכה ...

Sha-mor v'za-chor, b'di-bur eh-chad, hish-mi-a-nu Eil ha-m'yu-chad.
Adonai Eh-chad u-sh'mo Eh-chad, l'sheim u-l'tif-eh-ret v'li-t'hi-la.
L'cha do-di . . .

לִקְרַאת שַׁבָּת לְכוּ וְנֵלְכָה, כִּי הִיא מְקוֹר הַבְּרָכָה.
מֵרֹאשׁ מִקֶּדֶם נְסוּכָה, סוֹף מַעֲשֶׂה בְּמַחֲשָׁבָה תְּחִלָּה. לכה ...

Lik-rat Shabbat l'chu v'nei-l'cha, ki hi m'kor ha-b'ra-cha.
Mei-rosh mi-keh-dem n'su-cha, sof ma-a-seh b'ma-cha-sha-va t'chi-la.
L'cha do-di . . .

הִתְעוֹרְרִי, הִתְעוֹרְרִי, כִּי בָא אוֹרֵךְ! קוּמִי, אוֹרִי,
עוּרִי עוּרִי, שִׁיר דַּבֵּרִי; כְּבוֹד יְיָ עָלַיִךְ נִגְלָה. לכה ...

Hit-o-r'ri, hit-o-r'ri, ki va o-reich! Ku-mi, o-ri,
u-ri u-ri, shir da-bei-ri; k'vod Adonai a-la-yich nig-la.
L'cha do-di . . .

בּוֹאִי בְשָׁלוֹם עֲטֶרֶת בַּעְלָהּ, גַּם בְּשִׂמְחָה וּבְצָהֳלָה,
תּוֹךְ אֱמוּנֵי עַם סְגֻלָּה, בּוֹאִי כַלָּה! בּוֹאִי כַלָּה! לכה ...

Bo-i v'sha-lom, a-teh-ret ba-a-lah, gam b'sim-chah u-v'tso-ho-la,
Toch eh-mu-nei am s'gu-la, bo-i cha-la! Bo-i cha-la!
L'cha do-di . . .

BELOVED

"Keep" and "Remember"—
The two versions of the fifth (Shabbat) commandment differ in their first word. The Rabbis thought that both words were uttered simultaneously.

Beloved, come to meet the bride; beloved, come to greet Shabbat.

"Keep" and "Remember": a single decree, the only God caused us to hear; the Eternal is one, God's name is one, for honor and glory and praise.

Beloved, come to meet the bride; beloved, come to greet Shabbat.

Come with me to meet Shabbat, forever a fountain of blessing. Still it flows, as from the start: the last of days, for which the first was made.

Beloved, come to meet the bride; beloved, come to greet Shabbat.

As we welcome Shabbat with L'cha Dodi, we turn to welcome each other, to extend the hand of friendship.

Awake, awake, your light has come! Arise, shine, awake and sing; the Eternal's glory dawns upon you.

Beloved, come to meet the bride; beloved, come to greet Shabbat.

Enter in peace, O crown of your husband; enter in gladness, enter in joy. Come to the people that keeps its faith. Enter, O bride! Enter, O bride!

Beloved, come to meet the bride; beloved, come to greet Shabbat.

ALL RISE

חֲצִי קַדִּישׁ READER'S KADDISH

יִתְגַּדַּל וְיִתְקַדַּשׁ שְׁמֵהּ רַבָּא בְּעָלְמָא דִי־בְרָא כִרְעוּתֵהּ,
וְיַמְלִיךְ מַלְכוּתֵהּ בְּחַיֵּיכוֹן וּבְיוֹמֵיכוֹן וּבְחַיֵּי דְכָל־בֵּית
יִשְׂרָאֵל, בַּעֲגָלָא וּבִזְמַן קָרִיב, וְאִמְרוּ: אָמֵן.
יְהֵא שְׁמֵהּ רַבָּא מְבָרַךְ לְעָלַם וּלְעָלְמֵי עָלְמַיָּא.
יִתְבָּרַךְ וְיִשְׁתַּבַּח, וְיִתְפָּאַר וְיִתְרוֹמַם וְיִתְנַשֵּׂא, וְיִתְהַדָּר
וְיִתְעַלֶּה וְיִתְהַלָּל שְׁמֵהּ דְּקוּדְשָׁא, בְּרִיךְ הוּא,
לְעֵלָּא מִן־כָּל־בִּרְכָתָא וְשִׁירָתָא, תֻּשְׁבְּחָתָא וְנֶחֱמָתָא
דַּאֲמִירָן בְּעָלְמָא, וְאִמְרוּ: אָמֵן.

Yit-ga-dal v'yit-ka-dash sh'mei ra-ba b'al-ma di-v'ra chi-r'u'tei,
v'yam-lich mal-chu-tei b'cha-yei-chon u-v'yo-mei-chon u-v'cha-yei d'chol beit
Yis-ra-eil, ba-a-ga-la u-vi-z'man ka-riv, v'i-m'ru: A-mein.

Y'hei sh'mei ra-ba m'va-rach l'a-lam u-l'al-mei al-ma-ya.

Yit-ba-rach v'yish-ta-bach, v'yit-pa-ar v'yit-ro-mam v'yit-na-sei, v'yit-ha-dar
v'yit-a-leh v'yit-ha-lal sh'mei d'kud-sha, b'rich hu,

l'ei-la min kol bir-cha-ta v'shi-ra-ta, tush-b'cha-ta v'neh-cheh-ma-ta
da-a-mi-ran b'al-ma, v'i-m'ru: A-mein.

Hallowed be Your great name on earth, Your creation; establish Your dominion in our own day, in our own lives, and in the life of the whole House of Israel.

Blessed be Your great name forever and ever.

Blessed, praised, honored, and exalted be the name of the Holy One, ever to be praised, though You are beyond all the blessings and songs of praise that the world may offer.

❧

בָּרְכוּ אֶת־יְיָ הַמְבֹרָךְ.

בָּרוּךְ יְיָ הַמְבֹרָךְ לְעוֹלָם וָעֶד.

Praise Adonai, to whom our praise is due.

We praise Adonai

to whom our praise is due forever and ever.

מעריב ערבים   CREATION

בָּרוּךְ אַתָּה יְיָ, אֱלֹהֵינוּ מֶלֶךְ הָעוֹלָם,

אֲשֶׁר בִּדְבָרוֹ מַעֲרִיב עֲרָבִים,

We praise You, Adonai our God, sovereign of the universe, whose word makes evening fall.

All creation
has one
origin; we
celebrate its
creator and
sustainer.

❁ See page
355 and Psalm
148 (page
374).

בְּחׇכְמָה פּוֹתֵחַ שְׁעָרִים,

וּבִתְבוּנָה מְשַׁנֶּה עִתִּים,

וּמַחֲלִיף אֶת־הַזְּמַנִּים,

וּמְסַדֵּר אֶת־הַכּוֹכָבִים

בְּמִשְׁמְרוֹתֵיהֶם בָּרָקִיעַ

כִּרְצוֹנוֹ. בּוֹרֵא יוֹם וָלַיְלָה,

גּוֹלֵל אוֹר מִפְּנֵי חֹשֶׁךְ

וְחֹשֶׁךְ מִפְּנֵי אוֹר,

וּמַעֲבִיר יוֹם וּמֵבִיא לָיְלָה,

וּמַבְדִּיל בֵּין יוֹם וּבֵין

לָיְלָה: יְיָ צְבָאוֹת שְׁמוֹ.

Your wisdom opens the gates of heaven, Your understanding makes times pass and seasons change, Your law orders the stars in their courses through the skies.

Creator of day and night, You roll away light as darkness falls, and darkness with the coming of the light. You make day pass and bring on the night, to separate day from night: You are the God of time and space.

בָּרוּךְ אַתָּה יְיָ, הַמַּעֲרִיב עֲרָבִים.

We praise You, O God: Your word makes evening fall.

אהבת עולם   REVELATION

אַהֲבַת עוֹלָם בֵּית יִשְׂרָאֵל עַמְּךָ אָהָבְתָּ.

Unending love have You shown the House of Israel, Your people:

God, origin of space/time, is also the foundation of the moral order.

✤ See Pirke Avot, pages 322 and 340.

תּוֹרָה וּמִצְוֹת, חֻקִּים
וּמִשְׁפָּטִים אוֹתָנוּ לִמַּדְתָּ.
עַל־כֵּן, יְיָ אֱלֹהֵינוּ,
בְּשָׁכְבֵּנוּ וּבְקוּמֵנוּ נָשִׂיחַ
בְּחֻקֶּיךָ, וְנִשְׂמַח בְּדִבְרֵי
תוֹרָתְךָ וּבְמִצְוֹתֶיךָ לְעוֹלָם
וָעֶד. כִּי הֵם חַיֵּינוּ וְאֹרֶךְ
יָמֵינוּ, וּבָהֶם נֶהְגֶּה יוֹמָם
וָלָיְלָה. וְאַהֲבָתְךָ אַל־תָּסוּר
מִמֶּנּוּ לְעוֹלָמִים.

Torah and Mitzvot, laws and precepts have You taught us. And so, when we lie down and when we rise up, we will meditate on the meanings of Your law, and rejoice forever in Your Torah and Mitzvot. Day and night we will reflect on them, for they are our life and the length of our days. O may Your love never depart from our hearts!

בָּרוּךְ אַתָּה יְיָ, אוֹהֵב עַמּוֹ יִשְׂרָאֵל.

We praise You, O God: You love Your people Israel.

שְׁמַע יִשְׂרָאֵל: יהוה אֱלֹהֵינוּ, יהוה אֶחָד.
בָּרוּךְ שֵׁם כְּבוֹד מַלְכוּתוֹ לְעוֹלָם וָעֶד.

Hear, O Israel: Adonai is our God, Adonai alone.

Praised be God's glorious majesty forever and ever.

ALL ARE SEATED

וְאָהַבְתָּ אֵת יְהֹוָה אֱלֹהֶיךָ
בְּכָל־לְבָבְךָ וּבְכָל־נַפְשְׁךָ וּבְכָל־מְאֹדֶךָ:
וְהָיוּ הַדְּבָרִים הָאֵלֶּה אֲשֶׁר אָנֹכִי מְצַוְּךָ הַיּוֹם
עַל־לְבָבֶךָ: וְשִׁנַּנְתָּם לְבָנֶיךָ וְדִבַּרְתָּ בָּם בְּשִׁבְתְּךָ
בְּבֵיתֶךָ וּבְלֶכְתְּךָ בַדֶּרֶךְ וּבְשָׁכְבְּךָ וּבְקוּמֶךָ:
וּקְשַׁרְתָּם לְאוֹת עַל־יָדֶךָ וְהָיוּ לְטֹטָפֹת בֵּין עֵינֶיךָ:
וּכְתַבְתָּם עַל־מְזוּזֹת בֵּיתֶךָ וּבִשְׁעָרֶיךָ:
לְמַעַן תִּזְכְּרוּ וַעֲשִׂיתֶם אֶת־כָּל־מִצְוֹתָי
וִהְיִיתֶם קְדֹשִׁים לֵאלֹהֵיכֶם:
אֲנִי יְהֹוָה אֱלֹהֵיכֶם אֲשֶׁר הוֹצֵאתִי אֶתְכֶם מֵאֶרֶץ
מִצְרַיִם לִהְיוֹת לָכֶם לֵאלֹהִים: אֲנִי יְהֹוָה אֱלֹהֵיכֶם:

At times we
think of You
as a question,
when we
need to feel
You as *the*
question.
May my
life be the
response I
make, when
You *are* the
question.

❋ See
"Looking for
God," pages
352-357.

*V'a-hav-ta et Adonai Eh-lo-heh-cha b'chol l'va-v'cha u-v'chol naf-sh'cha
u-v'chol m'o-deh-cha. V'ha-yu ha-d'va-rim ha-ei-leh a-sher a-no-chi
m'tza-v'cha ha-yom al l'va-veh-cha. V'shi-nan-tam l'va-neh-cha v'di-bar-ta
bam b'shiv-t'cha b'vei-teh-cha u-v'lech-t'cha va-deh-rech u-v'shoch-b'cha
u-v'ku-meh-cha. U-k'shar-tam l'ot al ya-deh-cha v'ha-yu l'to-ta-fot bein
ei-neh-cha; u-ch'tav-tam al m'zu-zot bei-teh-cha u-vi-sh'a-reh-cha. L'ma-an
tiz-k'ru va-a-si-tem et kol mitz-vo-tai, vi-h'yi-tem k'do-shim lei-lo-hei-chem.
A-ni Adonai Eh-lo-hei-chem a-sher ho-tzei-ti et-chem mei-eh-retz
mitz-ra-yim li-h'yot la-chem lei-lo-him. A-ni Adonai Eh-lo-hei-chem.*

*You shall love Adonai your God with all your mind, with all
your heart, with all your might. Let these words, which I command you this day, be upon your heart. Teach them constantly to
your children, speaking of them in your home and on your way,
when you lie down and when you rise up. Bind them as a sign
upon your hand; let them be symbols before your eyes; and
inscribe them on the doorposts of your house, and on your gates:
that you may be mindful of all my Mitzvot, and do them; then
shall you be consecrated to your God. I, Adonai, am your God*

who led you out of Egypt to be your God; I, Adonai, am your God.

SOME MAY WISH TO INCLUDE THE FOLLOWING

וְהָיָ֗ה אִם־שָׁמֹ֤עַ תִּשְׁמְעוּ֙ אֶל־מִצְוֺתַ֔י אֲשֶׁ֧ר אָנֹכִ֛י מְצַוֶּ֥ה אֶתְכֶ֖ם הַיּ֑וֹם
לְאַהֲבָ֞ה אֶת־יְהֹוָ֤ה אֱלֹֽהֵיכֶם֙ וּלְעׇבְד֔וֹ בְּכׇל־לְבַבְכֶ֖ם וּבְכׇל־נַפְשְׁכֶֽם׃
יְצַ֨ו יְהֹוָ֤ה אִתְּךָ֙ אֶת־הַבְּרָכָ֔ה בַּאֲסָמֶ֕יךָ וּבְכֹ֖ל מִשְׁלַ֣ח יָדֶ֑ךָ וּבֵרַכְךָ֗
בָּאָ֕רֶץ אֲשֶׁר־יְהֹוָ֥ה אֱלֹהֶ֖יךָ נֹתֵ֥ן לָֽךְ׃ יְקִֽימְךָ֨ יְהֹוָ֥ה לוֹ֙ לְעַ֣ם קָד֔וֹשׁ
כַּאֲשֶׁ֖ר נִֽשְׁבַּֽע־לָ֑ךְ כִּ֣י תִשְׁמֹ֗ר אֶת־מִצְוֺת֙ יְהֹוָ֣ה אֱלֹהֶ֔יךָ וְהָלַכְתָּ֖
בִּדְרָכָֽיו׃ כִּ֚י הַמִּצְוָ֣ה הַזֹּ֔את אֲשֶׁ֧ר אָנֹכִ֛י מְצַוְּךָ֖ הַיּ֑וֹם לֹֽא־נִפְלֵ֥את
הִוא֙ מִמְּךָ֔ וְלֹ֥א רְחֹקָ֖ה הִֽוא׃ כִּֽי־קָר֥וֹב אֵלֶ֛יךָ הַדָּבָ֖ר מְאֹ֑ד בְּפִ֥יךָ
וּבִֽלְבָבְךָ֖ לַעֲשֹׂתֽוֹ׃ הַעִדֹ֨תִי בָכֶ֜ם הַיּ֗וֹם אֶת־הַשָּׁמַ֙יִם֙ וְאֶת־הָאָ֔רֶץ
הַֽחַיִּ֤ים וְהַמָּ֙וֶת֙ נָתַ֣תִּי לְפָנֶ֔יךָ הַבְּרָכָ֖ה וְהַקְּלָלָ֑ה וּבָֽחַרְתָּ֙ בַּֽחַיִּ֔ים
לְמַ֥עַן תִּחְיֶ֖ה אַתָּ֥ה וְזַרְעֶֽךָ׃

If you truly hearken to the Mitzvot that I command you this day, to love and serve Adonai your God with all your heart and mind, then your God will ordain blessing upon your homes and all your undertakings, and upon the soil on which your God has placed you. Adonai will affirm you as a holy people, when you keep the Mitzvot and walk in the ways of your God.

For this Mitzvah that I command you this day is not too difficult for you; nor is it far away—no, this word is very near you, in your mouth and in your heart—and you can do it. I call heaven and earth to witness before you this day: life and death have I placed before you, blessing and curse. Choose life, then, that you and your children may live. (Deuteronomy 11:13; 28:8-9; 30:11,14,19)

גאולה REDEMPTION

Looking back at our first redemption from bondage, our people concluded that they could hope for and expect a redemption that would last for all time. The hope remains— along with our task of bringing about the redemption for which we yearn.

אֱמֶת וֶאֱמוּנָה כָּל־זֹאת,
וְקַיָּם עָלֵינוּ, כִּי הוּא
יי אֱלֹהֵינוּ, וְאֵין זוּלָתוֹ,
וַאֲנַחְנוּ יִשְׂרָאֵל עַמּוֹ.

All this we hold to be true and sure: You are Adonai our God, there is none else, and we are Israel Your people.

הַפּוֹדֵנוּ מִיַּד מְלָכִים,
הַגּוֹאֲלֵנוּ מִכַּף כָּל־הֶעָרִיצִים,
וַיּוֹצֵא אֶת־עַמּוֹ יִשְׂרָאֵל
מִמִּצְרַיִם לְחֵרוּת עוֹלָם.

You deliver us from the hand of oppressors, and save us from the fist of every tyrant, as when You led us out of Egypt, forever to be free to serve You.

וְרָאוּ בָנָיו גְּבוּרָתוֹ, שִׁבְּחוּ
וְהוֹדוּ לִשְׁמוֹ, וּמַלְכוּתוֹ
בְּרָצוֹן קִבְּלוּ עֲלֵיהֶם.
מֹשֶׁה וּמִרְיָם וְכָל־יִשְׂרָאֵל
לְךָ עָנוּ שִׁירָה בְּשִׂמְחָה
רַבָּה, וְאָמְרוּ כֻלָּם:

When Your children witnessed Your might, they acclaimed You and gave thanks to Your name; gladly they enthroned You; then, full of joy, Moses, Miriam, and all Israel sang together:

מִי־כָמֹכָה בָּאֵלִם, יהוה?

Mi cha-mo-cha ba-ei-lim, Adonai?

מִי כָּמֹכָה, נֶאְדָּר בַּקֹּדֶשׁ,

Mi ka-mo-cha, neh-dar ba-ko-desh,

נוֹרָא תְהִלֹּת, עֹשֵׂה פֶלֶא?

no-ra t'hi-lot, o-sei feh-leh?

מַלְכוּתְךָ רָאוּ בָנֶיךָ,

Mal-chu-t'cha ra-u va-neh-cha,

בּוֹקֵעַ יָם לִפְנֵי מֹשֶׁה;

bo-kei-a yam li-f'nei Mo-sheh;

זֶה אֵלִי! עָנוּ וְאָמְרוּ:

zeh Ei-li! A-nu v'a-m'ru:

יהוה יִמְלֹךְ לְעֹלָם וָעֶד!

Adonai yim-loch l'o-lam va-ed!

וְנֶאֱמַר: V'neh-eh-mar:

כִּי פָדָה יי אֶת־יַעֲקֹב,   Ki fa-da Adonai et Ya-a-kov,

וּגְאָלוֹ מִיַּד חָזָק מִמֶּנּוּ.   u-g'a-lo mi-yad cha-zak mi-meh-nu.

בָּרוּךְ אַתָּה יי, גָּאַל יִשְׂרָאֵל.   Ba-ruch a-ta Adonai, ga-al Yis-ra-eil.

Who is like You, Adonai, among all that is worshiped? Who is like You, glorious in holiness, awesome in splendor, doing wonders?

With the parting of the waters, Your children perceived Your sovereign might. "This is my God!" they cried. "Adonai shall reign forever and ever."

And it has been said: "Adonai has delivered Jacob, and redeemed us from the hand of one stronger than ourselves."

We praise You, O God, redeemer of Israel.

A REFLECTION

   It is one thing to be redeemed from Egypt; it is another to know what to do next. It is hard to gain freedom, and harder still to remain free. And what are we now to do with the "freedom" we speak of? One reason to be here in this place is to ask this question.

השכיבנו   DIVINE PROVIDENCE

הַשְׁכִּיבֵנוּ, יי אֱלֹהֵינוּ, לְשָׁלוֹם, וְהַעֲמִידֵנוּ, מַלְכֵּנוּ, לְחַיִּים.

וּפְרוֹשׂ עָלֵינוּ סֻכַּת שְׁלוֹמֶךָ, וְתַקְּנֵנוּ בְּעֵצָה טוֹבָה

מִלְּפָנֶיךָ, וְהוֹשִׁיעֵנוּ לְמַעַן שְׁמֶךָ, וְהָגֵן בַּעֲדֵנוּ.

וְהָסֵר מֵעָלֵינוּ אוֹיֵב דֶּבֶר וְחֶרֶב וְרָעָב וְיָגוֹן;

וְהָסֵר שָׂטָן מִלְּפָנֵינוּ וּמֵאַחֲרֵינוּ.

וּבְצֵל כְּנָפֶיךָ תַּסְתִּירֵנוּ, כִּי אֵל שׁוֹמְרֵנוּ וּמַצִּילֵנוּ אָתָּה,

כִּי אֵל מֶלֶךְ חַנּוּן וְרַחוּם אָתָּה.

וּשְׁמוֹר צֵאתֵנוּ וּבוֹאֵנוּ לְחַיִּים וּלְשָׁלוֹם מֵעַתָּה וְעַד עוֹלָם.

❊ See page 379, Psalm 4 (page 359), and Psalm 131 (page 370).

Help us to lie down in peace, Adonai our God, and help us rise up to life renewed. Spread over us the shelter of Your peace; guide us with Your good counsel; and for Your name's sake, be our help.

Be a shield about us; save us from hatred and sickness, from war, famine, and anguish; and help us to turn aside from evil.

Shelter us in the shadow of Your wings, for You are our guardian and helper, a gracious and merciful God.

And guard our going out and our coming in, that we may have life and peace, now and always.

בָּרוּךְ אַתָּה יי, הַפּוֹרֵשׂ סֻכַּת שָׁלוֹם עָלֵינוּ וְעַל־כָּל־עַמּוֹ
יִשְׂרָאֵל וְעַל־יְרוּשָׁלָיִם.

We praise You, O God: may Your sheltering peace descend on us, all Israel, and all who dwell on earth.

וּשְׁמְרוּ   THE COVENANT OF SHABBAT

וְשָׁמְרוּ בְנֵי־יִשְׂרָאֵל אֶת־הַשַּׁבָּת, לַעֲשׂוֹת אֶת־הַשַּׁבָּת
לְדֹרֹתָם בְּרִית עוֹלָם. בֵּינִי וּבֵין בְּנֵי יִשְׂרָאֵל
אוֹת הִיא לְעֹלָם. כִּי־שֵׁשֶׁת יָמִים עָשָׂה יהוה אֶת־הַשָּׁמַיִם
וְאֶת־הָאָרֶץ, וּבַיּוֹם הַשְּׁבִיעִי שָׁבַת וַיִּנָּפַשׁ.

V'sha-m'ru v'nei Yis-ra-eil et ha-Shabbat, la-a-sot et ha-Shabbat
l'do-ro-tam, b'rit o-lam. Bei-ni u-vein b'nei Yis-ra-eil
ot hi l'o-lam. Ki shei-shet ya-mim a-sa Adonai et ha-sha-ma-yim
v'et ha-a-retz, u-va-yom ha-sh'vi-i sha-vat va-yi-na-fash.

The people of Israel shall keep the Sabbath, observing the Sabbath in every generation as a covenant forever. It is a sign between me and the people of Israel forever. For in six days Adonai made heaven and earth, but on the seventh day God rested and was refreshed.

&

REFLECTIONS

𝕮   O God, I give thanks for the days to come and for the strength You have given me that will bring me through its difficulties and dangers. I thank You for the joys that will lighten my days. If in the swift-passing days I fail to hear Your voice, and if in their blinding glare I do not recognize Your presence, open my ears and my eyes to You.

Help me, then; strengthen the goodness within me. Help me to see what is worthwhile, and to keep to it faithfully. Then when this day and this week have passed, they will mark another step on my way through life, a step taken in the awareness that You are with me.

⪙

𝕮   When I discarded
all the baggage I had prepared
for the journey,
there remained
the journey itself.

⪙

ALL RISE

תפלה TEFILAH

The Tefilah for
Shabbat
Shuvah, Chol
Ha-Moeid,
Chanukah, and
Rosh Chodesh
is on page 270.

אֲדֹנָי שְׂפָתַי תִּפְתָּח, וּפִי יַגִּיד תְּהִלָּתֶךָ.

Eternal God, open my lips, and my mouth will declare Your praise.

אבות ואמהות GOD OF ALL GENERATIONS

The Shabbat
Tefilah has
seven prayers.
In the first, we
recall with
reverence the
founders of
our people and
faith. We say:
Each
generation
finds its own
way, and yet—
their God is
ours.

✢ See "Looking
for God,"
pages 352-357.

בָּרוּךְ אַתָּה יי, אֱלֹהֵינוּ
 Ba-ruch a-ta Adonai, Eh-lo-hei-nu

וֵאלֹהֵי אֲבוֹתֵינוּ וְאִמּוֹתֵינוּ:
 vei-lo-hei a-vo-tei-nu v'i-mo-tei-nu:

אֱלֹהֵי אַבְרָהָם, אֱלֹהֵי
 Eh-lo-hei Av-ra-ham, eh-lo-hei

יִצְחָק וֵאלֹהֵי יַעֲקֹב:
 Yitz-chak, vei-lo-hei Ya-a-kov.

אֱלֹהֵי שָׂרָה, אֱלֹהֵי רִבְקָה,
 Eh-lo-hei Sa-rah, eh-lo-hei Riv-kah,

אֱלֹהֵי לֵאָה וֵאלֹהֵי רָחֵל;
 eh-lo-hei Lei-ah, vei-lo-hei Ra-cheil.

הָאֵל הַגָּדוֹל הַגִּבּוֹר
 Ha-eil ha-ga-dol ha-gi-bor

וְהַנּוֹרָא, אֵל עֶלְיוֹן. גּוֹמֵל
 v'ha-no-ra, eil el-yon. Go-meil

חֲסָדִים טוֹבִים וְקוֹנֵה הַכֹּל,
 cha-sa-dim to-vim, v'ko-nei ha-kol,

וְזוֹכֵר חַסְדֵי אָבוֹת וְאִמָּהוֹת,
 v'zo-cheir chas-dei a-vot v'i-ma-hot,

וּמֵבִיא גְאֻלָּה לִבְנֵי בְנֵיהֶם,
 u-mei-vi g'u-la li-v'nei v'nei-hem,

לְמַעַן שְׁמוֹ בְּאַהֲבָה. מֶלֶךְ
 l'ma-an sh'mo, b'a-ha-vah. Meh-lech

עוֹזֵר וּמוֹשִׁיעַ וּמָגֵן.
 o-zeir u-mo-shi-a u-ma-gein.

בָּרוּךְ אַתָּה יי, מָגֵן
 Ba-ruch a-ta Adonai, ma-gein

אַבְרָהָם וְעֶזְרַת שָׂרָה.
 Av-ra-ham v'ez-rat Sa-rah.

We praise You, Adonai our God and God of our ancestors: of Abraham, Isaac, and Jacob; of Sarah, Rebekah, Leah, and Rachel; the great, mighty, and awesome God, God Most High. You deal kindly with us and embrace us all. You remember the faithfulness of our ancestors, and in love bring redemption to their children's children for the sake of Your name. You are our sovereign and helper, our redeemer and shield. We praise You, Adonai, Shield of Abraham and Protector of Sarah.

גבורות   GOD'S POWER

אַתָּה גִבּוֹר לְעוֹלָם, אֲדֹנָי,
מְחַיֵּה מֵתִים אַתָּה, רַב
לְהוֹשִׁיעַ.
מַשִּׁיב הָרוּחַ וּמוֹרִיד הַגֶּשֶׁם,
מַזְרִיחַ הַשֶּׁמֶשׁ וּמוֹרִיד הַטָּל.
מְכַלְכֵּל חַיִּים בְּחֶסֶד,
מְחַיֵּה מֵתִים בְּרַחֲמִים רַבִּים.
סוֹמֵךְ נוֹפְלִים, וְרוֹפֵא
חוֹלִים, וּמַתִּיר אֲסוּרִים,
וּמְקַיֵּם אֱמוּנָתוֹ לִישֵׁנֵי עָפָר.
מִי כָמוֹךָ, בַּעַל גְּבוּרוֹת, וּמִי
דוֹמֶה לָךְ, מֶלֶךְ מֵמִית וּמְחַיֶּה
וּמַצְמִיחַ יְשׁוּעָה? וְנֶאֱמָן
אַתָּה לְהַחֲיוֹת מֵתִים.
בָּרוּךְ אַתָּה יי, מְחַיֵּה
הַמֵּתִים.

A-ta gi-bor l'o-lam, Adonai,
m'cha-yei mei-tim a-ta, rav
l'ho-shi-a. Ma-shiv ha-ru-ach
u-mo-rid ha-ga-shem; maz-ri-ach
ha-she-mesh u-mo-rid ha-tal.
M'chal-keil cha-yim b'cheh-sed,
m'cha-yei mei-tim b'ra-cha-mim
ra-bim. So-meich no-f'lim, v'ro-fei
cho-lim, u-ma-tir a-su-rim,
u-m'ka-yeim eh-mu-na-to li-shei-nei
a-far. Mi cha-mo-cha ba-al g'vu-rot,
u-mi do-meh lach, meh-lech mei-mit
u-m'cha-yeh u-matz-mi-ach y'shu-a?
V'neh-eh-man a-ta l'ha-cha-yot
mei-tim. Ba-ruch a-ta Adonai,
m'cha-yei ha-mei-tim.

In this prayer, we affirm the power of God, whose reach extends to this world—the world we walk in—and to a world we cannot imagine.

✣ See Psalm 103 (page 366) and Psalm 146 (page 371).

Unending is Your might, Eternal One; You are the source of eternal life; great is Your power to save. You cause the wind to blow and the rain to fall, the sun to shine and the dew to descend.

In Your love You sustain the living; in Your compassion You grant us eternal life. You support the falling and heal the sick; You free the captive and keep faith with those who sleep in the dust. Who is like You, source of all strength? Who is Your equal, sovereign author of life and death, who causes deliverance to flower in our world?

Trusting in You, we see life beyond death.

We praise You, O God, source of eternal life.

קְדוּשַׁת הַשֵּׁם   THE HOLINESS OF GOD

As we walk beneath the stars, we are walking among them, and the mystery of being calls to us—and thus the Holy calls to us from within the heights and the depths of our hearts.

✣ See Psalm 42/3 (page 363) and Psalm 63 (page 365).

אַתָּה קָדוֹשׁ וְשִׁמְךָ קָדוֹשׁ,   *A-ta ka-dosh v'shi-m'cha ka-dosh,*

וּקְדוֹשִׁים בְּכָל־יוֹם   *u-k'do-shim b'chol yom*

יְהַלְלוּךָ סֶּלָה.   *y'ha-l'lu-cha seh-lah.*

בָּרוּךְ אַתָּה יי,   *Ba-ruch a-ta Adonai,*

הָאֵל הַקָּדוֹשׁ.   *ha-eil ha-ka-dosh.*

You are holy, Your name is holy, and day by day all creation sings Your praise.

We praise You, Adonai, the holy God.

ALL ARE SEATED

קְדוּשַׁת הַיּוֹם   THE HOLINESS OF SHABBAT

EITHER

יִשְׂמְחוּ   MOST PRECIOUS OF DAYS

יִשְׂמְחוּ בְמַלְכוּתְךָ שׁוֹמְרֵי שַׁבָּת וְקוֹרְאֵי עֹנֶג.

עַם מְקַדְּשֵׁי שְׁבִיעִי כֻּלָּם יִשְׂבְּעוּ וְיִתְעַנְּגוּ מִטּוּבֶךָ.

וְהַשְּׁבִיעִי רָצִיתָ בּוֹ וְקִדַּשְׁתּוֹ.

חֶמְדַּת יָמִים אוֹתוֹ קָרָאתָ, זֵכֶר לְמַעֲשֵׂה בְרֵאשִׁית.

Yis-m'chu v'ma-l'chu-t'cha sho-m'rei Shabbat v'ko-r'ei o-neg.
Am m'ka-d'shei sh'vi-i ku-lam yis-b'u v'yit-a-n'gu mi-tu-veh-cha.
V'ha-sh'vi-i ra-tzi-ta bo v'ki-dash-to.
Chem-dat ya-mim o-to ka-ra-ta, zei-cher l'ma-a-sei v'rei-sheet.

Those who keep the Sabbath and call it a delight shall rejoice in Your sovereign presence. All who hallow the seventh day shall taste the joy of Your bounty. This is the day You delight in and sanctify. "Loveliest of days," You called it, "a reminder of the work of creation."

☙

OR

וַיְכֻלּוּ הַשָּׁמַיִם וְהָאָרֶץ וְכָל־
צְבָאָם: וַיְכַל אֱלֹהִים בַּיּוֹם
הַשְּׁבִיעִי מְלַאכְתּוֹ אֲשֶׁר עָשָׂה:
וַיִּשְׁבֹּת בַּיּוֹם הַשְּׁבִיעִי מִכָּל־
מְלַאכְתּוֹ אֲשֶׁר עָשָׂה: וַיְבָרֶךְ
אֱלֹהִים אֶת־יוֹם הַשְּׁבִיעִי
וַיְקַדֵּשׁ אֹתוֹ כִּי בוֹ שָׁבַת מִכָּל־
מְלַאכְתּוֹ אֲשֶׁר־בָּרָא אֱלֹהִים
לַעֲשׂוֹת:

*Va-y'chu-lu ha-sha-ma-yim
v'ha-a-retz v'chol tz'va-am. Va-y'chal
Eh-lo-him ba-yom ha-sh'vi-i m'lach-to
a-sher a-sah, va-yish-bot ba-yom
ha-sh'vi-i mi-kol m'lach-to a-sher
a-sah. Va-y'va-rech Eh-lo-him et-yom
ha-sh'vi-i va-y'ka-deish o-to, ki vo
sha-vat mi-kol m'lach-to a-sher ba-ra
Eh-lo-him la-a-sot.*

For a day we can drop our weekday ambitions, and aim for other things. In the middle blessing of the Seven, we celebrate Shabbat, the seventh day of creation.

Completed now were heaven and earth and all their host. On the seventh day God had completed the work that had been done, ceasing then on the seventh day from all the work that [God] had done. Then God blessed the seventh day and made it holy, and ceased from all the creative work that God [had chosen] to do.

&

אֱלֹהֵינוּ וֵאלֹהֵי אֲבוֹתֵינוּ וְאִמּוֹתֵינוּ, רְצֵה בִמְנוּחָתֵנוּ.

Our God, God of our fathers and mothers, may our Sabbath rest be pleasing in Your sight.

קַדְּשֵׁנוּ בְּמִצְוֹתֶיךָ וְתֵן חֶלְקֵנוּ בְּתוֹרָתֶךָ. שַׂבְּעֵנוּ מִטּוּבֶךָ, וְשַׂמְּחֵנוּ
בִּישׁוּעָתֶךָ, וְטַהֵר לִבֵּנוּ לְעָבְדְּךָ בֶּאֱמֶת. וְהַנְחִילֵנוּ, יְיָ אֱלֹהֵינוּ,
בְּאַהֲבָה וּבְרָצוֹן שַׁבַּת קָדְשֶׁךָ, וְיָנוּחוּ בָהּ יִשְׂרָאֵל מְקַדְּשֵׁי שְׁמֶךָ.

*Eh-lo-hei-nu vei-lo-hei a-vo-tei-nu v'i-mo-tei-nu, r'tzei vi-m'nu-cha-tei-nu.
Ka-d'shei-nu b'mitz-vo-teh-cha v-tein chel-kei-nu b'toh-ra-teh-cha. Sab-ei-nu
mi-tu-veh-cha, v'sam-chei-nu bi-shu-a-teh-cha, v'ta-heir li-bei-nu l-ov-d'cha*

beh-eh-met. V'han-chi-lei-nu, Adonai Eh-lo-hei-nu, b'a-ha-va u-v'ra-tzon
Shabbat kod-sheh-cha, v'ya-nu-chu va Yis-ra-eil m'ka-d'shei sh'meh-cha.

Sanctify us with Your Mitzvot, and make Your Torah our life's portion. Satisfy us with Your goodness, gladden us with Your salvation, and purify our hearts to serve You in truth. In Your gracious love, Adonai our God, let the holiness of Shabbat enter our hearts, that all Israel, hallowing Your name, may find rest and peace.

בָּרוּךְ אַתָּה יי, מְקַדֵּשׁ הַשַּׁבָּת.

Ba-ruch a-ta Adonai, m'ka-deish ha-Shabbat.

We praise You, the God who hallows Shabbat.

עבודה WORSHIP

רְצֵה, יי אֱלֹהֵינוּ, בְּעַמְּךָ יִשְׂרָאֵל
וּתְפִלָּתָם בְּאַהֲבָה תְקַבֵּל,
וּתְהִי לְרָצוֹן תָּמִיד עֲבוֹדַת יִשְׂרָאֵל עַמֶּךָ.
בָּרוּךְ אַתָּה יי, שֶׁאוֹתְךָ לְבַדְּךָ בְּיִרְאָה נַעֲבוֹד.

This is a prayer for prayer itself—that our prayers may be worthy, for do we not become what we pray for?

❊ See "Prayer and Its Value," pages 3-5.

Look with favor, Adonai our God, upon Your people Israel, and with love accept our prayers. May our worship ever be worthy of Your favor. We praise You, Adonai: You alone are the One we worship in awe.

הודאה   THANKSGIVING

מוֹדִים אֲנַחְנוּ לָךְ שָׁאַתָּה הוּא יי אֱלֹהֵינוּ וֵאלֹהֵי אֲבוֹתֵינוּ
וְאִמּוֹתֵינוּ, אֱלֹהֵי כָל־בָּשָׂר, יוֹצְרֵנוּ יוֹצֵר בְּרֵאשִׁית.
בְּרָכוֹת וְהוֹדָאוֹת לְשִׁמְךָ הַגָּדוֹל וְהַקָּדוֹשׁ עַל־שֶׁהֶחֱיִיתָנוּ
וְקִיַּמְתָּנוּ. כֵּן תְּחַיֵּנוּ וּתְקַיְּמֵנוּ, יי אֱלֹהֵינוּ, וּתְאַמְּצֵנוּ
לִשְׁמֹר חֻקֶּיךָ, לַעֲשׂוֹת רְצוֹנֶךָ, וּלְעָבְדְּךָ בְּלֵבָב שָׁלֵם.
בָּרוּךְ אֵל הַהוֹדָאוֹת.

We affirm with gratitude that You, Adonai, are our God, the
God of our fathers and mothers, the God of all flesh, our
creator, the source of all being. We bless and praise Your
great and holy name, for keeping us in life and sustaining
us.

Continue us in life and sustain us, Adonai our God; strengthen
us to observe Your laws, to do Your will, and to serve You with a
whole heart.

In this prayer we express our gratitude for worldly life, and for the life of the spirit that existence makes possible.

❖ *See "Giving Thanks," page 398, and Psalm 147 (page 372).*

ברכת שלום   PEACE

שָׁלוֹם רָב עַל־יִשְׂרָאֵל עַמְּךָ תָּשִׂים לְעוֹלָם, כִּי אַתָּה הוּא מֶלֶךְ
אָדוֹן לְכָל־הַשָּׁלוֹם. וְטוֹב בְּעֵינֶיךָ לְבָרֵךְ אֶת־עַמְּךָ יִשְׂרָאֵל
וְאֶת־כָּל־הָעַמִּים בְּכָל־עֵת וּבְכָל־שָׁעָה בִּשְׁלוֹמֶךָ.

Supreme source of peace, grant true and lasting peace to our
people Israel, for it is good in Your sight that Your people
Israel, and all peoples, may be blessed at all times with Your
gift of peace.

The Amidah concludes with a prayer for peace, serenity, well-being, for ourselves and our people, and for all people.

❖ *See Pirke Avot, pages 324-325, and page 351.*

בָּרוּךְ אַתָּה יי, הַמְבָרֵךְ אֶת־עַמּוֹ יִשְׂרָאֵל בַּשָּׁלוֹם.

We praise You, O God, for the blessing of peace that You have
willed for Your people Israel and for all peoples.

SILENT PRAYER

אֱלֹהַי, נְצֹר לְשׁוֹנִי מֵרָע, וּשְׂפָתַי מִדַּבֵּר מִרְמָה. וְלִמְקַלְלַי נַפְשִׁי
תִדּוֹם וְנַפְשִׁי כֶּעָפָר לַכֹּל תִּהְיֶה. פְּתַח לִבִּי בְּתוֹרָתֶךָ, וּבְמִצְוֹתֶיךָ
תִּרְדּוֹף נַפְשִׁי. עֲשֵׂה לְמַעַן שְׁמֶךָ, עֲשֵׂה לְמַעַן יְמִינֶךָ, עֲשֵׂה
לְמַעַן קְדֻשָּׁתֶךָ, עֲשֵׂה לְמַעַן תּוֹרָתֶךָ; לְמַעַן יֵחָלְצוּן יְדִידֶיךָ,
הוֹשִׁיעָה יְמִינְךָ וַעֲנֵנִי.

My God, keep my tongue from evil, my lips from deceptive speech. In the face of malice give me a quiet spirit; let me be humble wherever I go. Open my heart to Your teaching, make me eager to fulfill Your Mitzvot. Thus will Your name be exalted, Your might manifest, Your holiness visible, and Your Torah magnified. Inspire me to love You, and be the answer to my prayer.

REFLECTIONS

1

⚭   There are objects in life higher than success. The Sabbath, with its exhortation to the worship of God and the doing of kindly deeds, reminds us week by week of these higher objects. It prevents us reducing our life to the level of a machine. The Sabbath is one of the glories of our humanity. For if to labor is noble, of our own free will to pause in that labor may be nobler still. (Claude Montefiore)

2

⚭   Today my work is to rest from work, and to turn my mind to eternal things. This day can then become a gift for body and soul, helping me realize that it is not by bread alone that I live—bread for the body—but by something eternal in my spirit. Even the bread I eat today will be more than bread, as I eat it bathed in the light of the Eternal. For, having been created in Your image, I bear the impress of Your eternity. On Shabbat, especially, I can experience some sense of that eternity.

3

ও Fill me with Your spirit. Let me so open my heart to You that I become aware of Your indwelling presence. I ask this gift in humility, trusting to Your lovingkindness that my eager heart seeking You may find You. Holy One, give me tranquility of spirit, and with it, the will to work for righteousness with all my might. So will Your love and power lead me to blessing.

יִהְיוּ לְרָצוֹן אִמְרֵי־פִי וְהֶגְיוֹן לִבִּי לְפָנֶיךָ,
יהוה, צוּרִי וְגֹאֲלִי.

Yi-h'yu l'ra-tzon i-m'rei fi v'heg-yon li-bi l'fa-neh-cha,

Adonai tzu-ri v'go-a-li.

May the words of my mouth and the meditations of my heart be acceptable to You, O God, my rock and my redeemer. Amen.

עֹשֶׂה שָׁלוֹם בִּמְרוֹמָיו, *O-seh sha-lom bi-m'ro-mav,*

הוּא יַעֲשֶׂה שָׁלוֹם עָלֵינוּ *hu ya-a-seh sha-lom a-lei-nu*

וְעַל־כָּל־יִשְׂרָאֵל, וְאִמְרוּ: *v'al kol Yis-ra-eil, v'i-m'ru:*

אָמֵן. *A-mein.*

May the source of peace on high send peace to us, to all Israel, and to all the world, and let us say: Amen.

שחרית לשבת   SHABBAT MORNING SERVICE

THE TALLIT RITUAL IS ON PAGE 21

ברכות השחר   MORNING BLESSINGS

מה טבו   THE BLESSING OF WORSHIP

A PRAYER
BEFORE
PRAYER:
May my
worship on
this Shabbat
encourage me
to fulfill this
Mitzvah:
"Justice,
justice shall
you pursue."
(Deuteron-
omy 16:20)

מַה־טֹּבוּ אֹהָלֶיךָ, יַעֲקֹב,
Mah to-vu o-ha-leh-cha, Ya-a-kov,

מִשְׁכְּנֹתֶיךָ, יִשְׂרָאֵל! וַאֲנִי,
mish-k'no-teh-cha, Yis-ra-eil! Va-a-ni,

בְּרֹב חַסְדְּךָ אָבוֹא בֵיתֶךָ,
b'rov chas-d'cha a-vo vei-teh-cha,

אֶשְׁתַּחֲוֶה אֶל־הֵיכַל־
esh-ta-cha-veh el hei-chal

קָדְשְׁךָ בְּיִרְאָתֶךָ.
kod-sh'cha b'yir-a-teh-cha.

יהוה, אָהַבְתִּי מְעוֹן בֵּיתֶךָ,
Adonai, a-hav-ti m'on bei-teh-cha

וּמְקוֹם מִשְׁכַּן כְּבוֹדֶךָ.
u-m'kom mish-kan k'vo-deh-cha.

וַאֲנִי אֶשְׁתַּחֲוֶה וְאֶכְרָעָה,
Va-a-ni esh-ta-cha-veh v'ech-ra-ah,

אֶבְרְכָה לִפְנֵי־יהוה עֹשִׂי.
ev-r'cha li-f'nei Adonai o-si.

וַאֲנִי תְפִלָּתִי־לְךָ, יהוה,
Va-a-ni t'fi-la-ti l'cha, Adonai,

עֵת רָצוֹן.
eit ra-tzon.

אֱלֹהִים, בְּרָב־חַסְדֶּךָ,
Eh-lo-him b'rov chas-deh-cha

עֲנֵנִי בֶּאֱמֶת יִשְׁעֶךָ.
a-nei-ni beh-eh-met yish-eh-cha.

How lovely are your tents, O Jacob, your dwelling-places, O Israel! Your great love, O God, inspires me to enter Your house; with awe I worship in Your sanctuary.

Adonai, I love the house where Your glory dwells; humbly I worship before my God and maker.

May my prayer be acceptable to You, Adonai. In Your great kindness, answer me with Your saving truth.

CHOOSE ONE OR MORE OF THE FOLLOWING BIRCHOT HA-SHACHAR;
PESUKEI DEZIMRA BEGINS ON PAGE 111;
OTHER "MORNING BLESSINGS" BEGIN ON PAGE 125.

1

אשר יצר FOR THE BODY

בָּרוּךְ אַתָּה יי, אֱלֹהֵינוּ מֶלֶךְ הָעוֹלָם, אֲשֶׁר יָצַר אֶת־הָאָדָם
בְּחָכְמָה, וּבָרָא בוֹ נְקָבִים נְקָבִים, חֲלוּלִים חֲלוּלִים.
גָּלוּי וְיָדוּעַ לִפְנֵי כִסֵּא כְבוֹדֶךָ, שֶׁאִם יִפָּתֵחַ אֶחָד מֵהֶם
אוֹ יִסָּתֵם אֶחָד מֵהֶם, אִי אֶפְשָׁר לְהִתְקַיֵּם וְלַעֲמוֹד לְפָנֶיךָ.
בָּרוּךְ אַתָּה יי, רוֹפֵא כָל־בָּשָׂר וּמַפְלִיא לַעֲשׂוֹת.

❖ See "Prayers
for Healing,"
pages 376-378,
and page 351.

We praise the eternal God, sovereign of the universe, who
with wisdom has fashioned us, making our vital organs, our
veins and arteries, our nerves and sinews—balancing all the
forces within us. O God enthroned in glory, were even one
of these organs to fail, we could not stand alive before You.

*We praise You, Adonai, wondrous source of healing and well-
being.*

PESUKEI
DEZIMRA
BEGINS ON
PAGE III.

אלהי נשמה FOR THE SOUL

אֱלֹהַי, נְשָׁמָה שֶׁנָּתַתָּ בִּי טְהוֹרָה הִיא!

❖ See page 182
and "Looking
at Ourselves,
pages 347-351.

The soul that You have given me, O God, is pure!

אַתָּה בְרָאתָהּ, אַתָּה יְצַרְתָּהּ, אַתָּה נְפַחְתָּהּ בִּי, וְאַתָּה מְשַׁמְּרָהּ
בְּקִרְבִּי. כָּל־זְמַן שֶׁהַנְּשָׁמָה בְּקִרְבִּי, מוֹדֶה אֲנִי לְפָנֶיךָ, יי אֱלֹהַי
וֵאלֹהֵי אֲבוֹתַי וְאִמּוֹתַי, רִבּוֹן כָּל־הַמַּעֲשִׂים, אֲדוֹן כָּל־הַנְּשָׁמוֹת.

*You created and formed it, breathed it into me, and within me
You sustain it. So long as I have breath, therefore, I will give
thanks to You, my God, God of all ages, source of all being,
loving guide of every human spirit.*

בָּרוּךְ אַתָּה יי, אֲשֶׁר בְּיָדוֹ נֶפֶשׁ כָּל־חָי וְרוּחַ כָּל־בְּשַׂר־אִישׁ.

*We praise You, O God: In Your hand are the souls of all the
living and the spirits of all flesh.*

PESUKEI
DEZIMRA
BEGINS ON
PAGE III.

FOR TORAH לעסוק בדברי תורה

❁ See Pirke
Avot, pages
322-340.

בָּרוּךְ אַתָּה יי, אֱלֹהֵינוּ
מֶלֶךְ הָעוֹלָם, אֲשֶׁר קִדְּשָׁנוּ
בְּמִצְוֹתָיו וְצִוָּנוּ לַעֲסוֹק
בְּדִבְרֵי תוֹרָה.

We praise You, Adonai our God, sovereign of the universe: You hallow us with Your Mitzvot and command us to immerse ourselves in Torah.

וְהַעֲרֶב־נָא, יי אֱלֹהֵינוּ, אֶת־דִּבְרֵי תוֹרָתְךָ בְּפִינוּ וּבְפִי עַמְּךָ
בֵּית יִשְׂרָאֵל, וְנִהְיֶה אֲנַחְנוּ וְצֶאֱצָאֵינוּ, וְצֶאֱצָאֵי עַמְּךָ בֵּית
יִשְׂרָאֵל, כֻּלָּנוּ יוֹדְעֵי שְׁמֶךָ וְלוֹמְדֵי תוֹרָתֶךָ לִשְׁמָהּ.
בָּרוּךְ אַתָּה יי, הַמְלַמֵּד תּוֹרָה לְעַמּוֹ יִשְׂרָאֵל.

Adonai our God, let the words of Your Torah be sweet in our mouths, and in the mouths of Your people Israel, that we and our children may all come to know You through our loving study of Torah. We praise You, Adonai, teacher of Torah to Your people Israel.

אֵלּוּ דְבָרִים שֶׁאֵין לָהֶם שִׁעוּר:
כִּבּוּד אָב וָאֵם, וּגְמִילוּת חֲסָדִים, וְהַשְׁכָּמַת בֵּית הַמִּדְרָשׁ
שַׁחֲרִית וְעַרְבִית, וְהַכְנָסַת אוֹרְחִים, וּבִקּוּר חוֹלִים,
וְהַכְנָסַת כַּלָּה, וּלְוָיַת הַמֵּת, וְעִיּוּן תְּפִלָּה, וַהֲבָאַת שָׁלוֹם
בֵּין אָדָם לַחֲבֵרוֹ. וְתַלְמוּד תּוֹרָה כְּנֶגֶד כֻּלָּם.

These are duties whose worth cannot be measured:

*honoring one's father and mother,
acts of love and kindness,
diligent pursuit of knowledge and wisdom,
hospitality to wayfarers,
visiting the sick,
rejoicing with bride and groom,*

consoling the bereaved,
praying with sincerity,
and making peace when people quarrel.
And the study of Torah leads to them all.

PESUKEI
DEZIMRA
BEGINS ON
PAGE III.

ברכות יום יום   OUR DAILY BLESSINGS

בָּרוּךְ אַתָּה יי, אֱלֹהֵינוּ מֶלֶךְ הָעוֹלָם,
אֲשֶׁר נָתַן לַשֶּׂכְוִי בִינָה לְהַבְחִין בֵּין יוֹם וּבֵין לָיְלָה.

Praised be Adonai our God, who has given instinctive knowledge to every creature.

❖ See "For a
World of
Wonders,"
pages 398-399.

בָּרוּךְ אַתָּה יי, אֱלֹהֵינוּ מֶלֶךְ הָעוֹלָם, פּוֹקֵחַ עִוְרִים.

Praised be Adonai our God, who enlightens the blind.

בָּרוּךְ אַתָּה יי, אֱלֹהֵינוּ מֶלֶךְ הָעוֹלָם, מַלְבִּישׁ עֲרֻמִּים.

Praised be Adonai our God, who clothes the naked.

בָּרוּךְ אַתָּה יי, אֱלֹהֵינוּ מֶלֶךְ הָעוֹלָם, מַתִּיר אֲסוּרִים.

Praised be Adonai our God, who releases the captive.

בָּרוּךְ אַתָּה יי, אֱלֹהֵינוּ מֶלֶךְ הָעוֹלָם, זוֹקֵף כְּפוּפִים.

Praised be Adonai our God, who lifts up the fallen.

בָּרוּךְ אַתָּה יי, אֱלֹהֵינוּ מֶלֶךְ הָעוֹלָם, הַנּוֹתֵן לַיָּעֵף כֹּחַ.

Praised be Adonai our God, who gives strength to the weary.

בָּרוּךְ אַתָּה יי, אֱלֹהֵינוּ מֶלֶךְ הָעוֹלָם, הַמַּעֲבִיר שֵׁנָה
מֵעֵינָי וּתְנוּמָה מֵעַפְעַפָּי.

Praised be Adonai our God, who opens our eyes to greet the new day.

PESUKEI
DEZIMRA
BEGINS ON
PAGE III.

יְהִי רָצוֹן מִלְּפָנֶיךָ, יְיָ אֱלֹהֵינוּ וֵאלֹהֵי אֲבוֹתֵינוּ וְאִמּוֹתֵינוּ,
שֶׁתַּרְגִּילֵנוּ בְּתוֹרָתֶךָ, וְדַבְּקֵנוּ בְּמִצְוֹתֶיךָ. וְאַל
תְּבִיאֵנוּ לֹא לִידֵי חֵטְא, וְלֹא לִידֵי עֲבֵרָה וְעָוֹן,
וְלֹא לִידֵי נִסָּיוֹן, וְלֹא לִידֵי בִזָּיוֹן, וְאַל תַּשְׁלֶט־בָּנוּ
יֵצֶר הָרָע, וְהַרְחִיקֵנוּ מֵאָדָם רָע וּמֵחָבֵר רָע, וְדַבְּקֵנוּ
בְּיֵצֶר הַטּוֹב וּבְמַעֲשִׂים טוֹבִים, וְכֹף אֶת־יִצְרֵנוּ
לְהִשְׁתַּעְבֶּד־לָךְ, וּתְנֵנוּ הַיּוֹם וּבְכָל־יוֹם לְחֵן וּלְחֶסֶד
וּלְרַחֲמִים בְּעֵינֶיךָ וּבְעֵינֵי כָל־רוֹאֵינוּ, וְתִגְמְלֵנוּ חֲסָדִים
טוֹבִים. בָּרוּךְ אַתָּה יְיָ, גּוֹמֵל חֲסָדִים טוֹבִים.

❖ See
"Looking at
Ourselves,"
pages 347-351.

Our God and God of our mothers and fathers, guide us with
Your teaching, and help us embrace Your commandments.
Keep us from succumbing to temptation, and shield us from
evil, and from all that brings shame upon us. Strengthen our
every inclination toward goodness, so that all our powers
lead us to to serve You with good deeds and noble actions.
Today and every day may we merit kindness and compassion in Your sight, and in the sight of all who behold us;
let us ever be worthy of Your love.

PESUKEI
DEZIMRA
BEGINS ON
PAGE III.

We praise You, O God, for the love You show us every day.

&

לְעוֹלָם יְהֵא אָדָם יְרֵא שָׁמַיִם בַּסֵּתֶר וּבַגָּלוּי,
וּמוֹדֶה עַל הָאֱמֶת, וְדוֹבֵר אֱמֶת בִּלְבָבוֹ.

Aways revere God in what you do, privately as well as publicly; acknowledge the truth, and speak it in your heart.

* See "Looking at Ourselves," pages 347-351.

רִבּוֹן כָּל־הָעוֹלָמִים, לֹא עַל־צִדְקוֹתֵינוּ אֲנַחְנוּ מַפִּילִים תַּחֲנוּנֵינוּ
לְפָנֶיךָ, כִּי עַל רַחֲמֶיךָ הָרַבִּים. מָה אֲנַחְנוּ, מֶה חַיֵּינוּ, מֶה
חַסְדֵּנוּ, מַה־יְשׁוּעָתֵנוּ, מַה־צִּדְקֵנוּ, מַה־כֹּחֵנוּ, מַה־גְּבוּרָתֵנוּ?
מַה־נֹּאמַר לְפָנֶיךָ, יְיָ אֱלֹהֵינוּ וֵאלֹהֵי אֲבוֹתֵינוּ וְאִמּוֹתֵינוּ?
הֲלֹא כָּל־הַגִּבּוֹרִים כְּאַיִן לְפָנֶיךָ, וְאַנְשֵׁי הַשֵּׁם כְּלֹא הָיוּ,
וַחֲכָמִים כִּבְלִי מַדָּע, וּנְבוֹנִים כִּבְלִי הַשְׂכֵּל?
כִּי רֹב מַעֲשֵׂיהֶם תֹּהוּ, וִימֵי חַיֵּיהֶם הֶבֶל לְפָנֶיךָ;

Sovereign of all worlds, we pour out our hearts to You, relying not on our virtues but on Your compassion. For what are we? What is our life, and what our purity? What is our goodness, and what our strength? What can we say in Your presence, Adonai our God, God of our mothers and fathers? Are not the mighty as nothing before You, the illustrious as though they had never lived, the learned as if they had no knowledge, the wise as if without understanding? Most of our deeds are vain, and in Your sight our life passes away like the wind.

אֲבָל אֲנַחְנוּ עַמְּךָ בְּנֵי בְרִיתֶךָ, וְאוֹתָנוּ קָרֵאתָ לַעֲבוֹדָתֶךָ. לְפִיכָךְ
אֲנַחְנוּ חַיָּבִים לְהוֹדוֹת לְךָ וּלְשַׁבֵּחֲךָ, וּלְבָרֵךְ וּלְקַדֵּשׁ אֶת־שְׁמֶךָ.

Yet we are Your people, bound to Your covenant, and called to Your service. We must therefore thank and praise You, and pro-claim the holiness of Your name.

אַשְׁרֵינוּ!	How blessed we are!
מַה־טּוֹב חֶלְקֵנוּ!	How good is our portion!
וּמַה־נָּעִים גּוֹרָלֵנוּ!	How pleasant our lot!
וּמַה־יָּפָה יְרֻשָּׁתֵנוּ!	How beautiful our heritage!

פסוקי דזמרא   SONGS OF PRAISE

✣ See Psalm
108 (page 367)
and Psalm 148
(page 374).

בָּרוּךְ שֶׁאָמַר וְהָיָה הָעוֹלָם, בָּרוּךְ הוּא.

בָּרוּךְ עוֹשֶׂה בְרֵאשִׁית, בָּרוּךְ אוֹמֵר וְעוֹשֶׂה.

בָּרוּךְ מְרַחֵם עַל הָאָרֶץ, בָּרוּךְ מְרַחֵם עַל הַבְּרִיּוֹת.

בָּרוּךְ אַתָּה יי, אֱלֹהֵינוּ מֶלֶךְ הָעוֹלָם, הַמְהֻלָּל בְּפִי עַמּוֹ,

מְשֻׁבָּח וּמְפֹאָר בִּלְשׁוֹן חֲסִידָיו וַעֲבָדָיו. בִּשְׁבָחוֹת וּבִזְמִירוֹת

נְגַדֶּלְךָ וּנְמַלִּיכְךָ, מַלְכֵּנוּ, יָחִיד, חֵי הָעוֹלָמִים.

בָּרוּךְ אַתָּה יי, מֶלֶךְ מְהֻלָּל בַּתִּשְׁבָּחוֹת.

Praised be the one who commanded the world to be.

Praised be the creator of the cosmos; praised be the one whose word is deed.

Praised be the one whose compassion extends to the earth and its creatures.

We praise You, Adonai our God, sovereign of the universe: Your people acclaim You, and those who love and serve You declare Your glory. With songs of praise we extol You, and proclaim Your sovereignty, the Only One, life of all worlds.

We praise You, sovereign God, to whom our praise is due.

THE READER'S KADDISH IS ON PAGE 132

FROM PSALM 19

✣ See "For a
World of
Wonders,"
pages 398-399,
and Psalm 8
(page 30).

הַשָּׁמַיִם מְסַפְּרִים כְּבוֹד־אֵל, וּמַעֲשֵׂה יָדָיו מַגִּיד הָרָקִיעַ.

יוֹם לְיוֹם יַבִּיעַ אֹמֶר, וְלַיְלָה לְּלַיְלָה יְחַוֶּה־דָּעַת.

The heavens declare the glory of God,

the skies proclaim God's handiwork.

111

Day unto day utters speech,

night unto night sends forth knowledge.

אֵין־אֹמֶר וְאֵין דְּבָרִים, בְּלִי נִשְׁמָע קוֹלָם.

בְּכָל־הָאָרֶץ יָצָא קַוָּם, וּבִקְצֵה תֵבֵל מִלֵּיהֶם.

There is no speech, there are no words;

not a sound of them is heard!

Yet still their call goes out to all the earth,

their message to the end of the world.

תּוֹרַת יהוה תְּמִימָה, מְשִׁיבַת נָפֶשׁ.

עֵדוּת יהוה נֶאֱמָנָה, מַחְכִּימַת פֶּתִי.

פִּקּוּדֵי יהוה יְשָׁרִים, מְשַׂמְּחֵי־לֵב.

מִצְוַת יהוה בָּרָה, מְאִירַת עֵינָיִם.

יִרְאַת יהוה טְהוֹרָה, עוֹמֶדֶת לָעַד.

מִשְׁפְּטֵי־יהוה אֱמֶת, צָדְקוּ יַחְדָּו.

הַנֶּחֱמָדִים מִזָּהָב וּמִפַּז רָב,

וּמְתוּקִים מִדְּבַשׁ וְנֹפֶת צוּפִים.

God's teaching is perfect, reviving the soul.

God's word is unfailing, making wise the simple.

God's precepts are right, delighting the mind.

God's commandment is clear, enlightening the eyes.

God's doctrine is pure, enduring forever.

God's ordinances are true, and altogether just.

They are more to be desired than gold,
than any amount of fine gold;

sweeter than honey from the honeycomb.

When I heard
the learn'd
astronomer,/
When the
proofs, the
figures, were
ranged in
columns before
me,/
How soon
unaccountable
I became tired
and sick,/
Till rising and
gliding out I
wander'd off
by myself,/
In the mystical
moist night-air,
and from time
to time,/
Look'd up in
perfect silence
at the stars.
(Walt Whitman)

112

גַּם־עַבְדְּךָ נִזְהָר בָּהֶם, בְּשָׁמְרָם עֵקֶב רָב.

שְׁגִיאוֹת מִי־יָבִין? מִנִּסְתָּרוֹת נַקֵּנִי.

גַּם מִזֵּדִים חֲשֹׂךְ עַבְדֶּךָ, אַל־יִמְשְׁלוּ־בִי.

אָז אֵיתָם, וְנִקֵּיתִי מִפֶּשַׁע רָב.

Your servant does well to heed them,

for great is the reward of keeping them.

Who can recognize all one's errors?

Cleanse me, therefore, of unconscious sins.

From willful sins, too, keep Your servant safe,

let them not hold me in thrall;

then I shall be blameless,

and innocent of grave transgressions.

יִהְיוּ לְרָצוֹן אִמְרֵי־פִי, May the words of my mouth, and the meditations of my heart, be
וְהֶגְיוֹן לִבִּי לְפָנֶיךָ, יְהֹוָה, acceptable to You, O God, my rock
צוּרִי וְגֹאֲלִי. and my redeemer.

THE READER'S KADDISH IS ON PAGE 132

FROM PSALM 34

❋ See Psalm 104 (page 31) and Psalm 147 (page 372).

אֲבָרְכָה אֶת־יהוה בְּכָל־עֵת; תָּמִיד תְּהִלָּתוֹ בְּפִי.

בַּיהוה תִּתְהַלֵּל נַפְשִׁי; יִשְׁמְעוּ עֲנָוִים וְיִשְׂמָחוּ.

גַּדְּלוּ לַיהוה אִתִּי, וּנְרוֹמְמָה שְׁמוֹ יַחְדָּו.

דָּרַשְׁתִּי אֶת־יהוה וְעָנָנִי, וּמִכָּל־מְגוּרוֹתַי הִצִּילָנִי.

I will honor Adonai at all times; God's praise shall continually be in my mouth.

My soul shall delight in Adonai; let the humble see this and be glad.

113

O magnify the Eternal One with me, and together let us exalt God's name.

I sought Adonai, who answered me, saving me from many woes.

זֶה עָנִי קָרָא וַיהוה שָׁמֵעַ, וּמִכָּל־צָרוֹתָיו הוֹשִׁיעוֹ.

טַעֲמוּ וּרְאוּ כִּי־טוֹב יהוה; אַשְׁרֵי הַגֶּבֶר יֶחֱסֶה־בּוֹ.

This poor soul cried out; Adonai heard, and redeemed me from my many troubles.

Taste and see that Adonai is good; blessed is the one who takes refuge in God.

כְּפִירִים רָשׁוּ וְרָעֵבוּ, וְדֹרְשֵׁי יהוה לֹא־יַחְסְרוּ כָל־טוֹב.

לְכוּ־בָנִים, שִׁמְעוּ־לִי: יִרְאַת יהוה אֲלַמֶּדְכֶם.

מִי־הָאִישׁ הֶחָפֵץ חַיִּים, אֹהֵב יָמִים לִרְאוֹת טוֹב.

נְצֹר לְשׁוֹנְךָ מֵרָע, וּשְׂפָתֶיךָ מִדַּבֵּר מִרְמָה.

סוּר מֵרָע וַעֲשֵׂה־טוֹב; בַּקֵּשׁ שָׁלוֹם וְרָדְפֵהוּ.

Lions may roar and rave and go hungry,

but those who turn to Adonai never lack for good.

Come, people, and listen to me: I will teach You the meaning of faith. Who among you craves life, and longs for time to see the good?

Then keep your tongue from evil, your lips from deceitful speech. Turn aside from evil and do good; seek peace and pursue it.

קָרוֹב יהוה לְנִשְׁבְּרֵי־לֵב, וְאֶת־דַּכְּאֵי־רוּחַ יוֹשִׁיעַ.

רַבּוֹת רָעוֹת צַדִּיק; וּמִכֻּלָּם יַצִּילֶנּוּ יהוה.

פּוֹדֶה יהוה נֶפֶשׁ עֲבָדָיו; וְלֹא יֶאְשְׁמוּ כָּל־הַחֹסִים בּוֹ.

114

Adonai is near to the brokenhearted, and comes to help the despairing. Many are the pains of the righteous; and they find deliverance from all of them in Adonai.

Adonai: You redeem the lives of those who serve You; all who trust in You are not forsaken.

THE READER'S KADDISH IS ON PAGE 132

FROM PSALM 33

❋ See "Selected Psalms," pages 358-375, and "A Daily Psalm," pages 27-33.

רַנְּנוּ צַדִּיקִים בַּיהוה, לַיְשָׁרִים נָאוָה תְהִלָּה.
הוֹדוּ לַיהוה בְּכִנּוֹר, בְּנֵבֶל עָשׂוֹר זַמְּרוּ־לוֹ.
שִׁירוּ־לוֹ שִׁיר חָדָשׁ, הֵיטִיבוּ נַגֵּן בִּתְרוּעָה.

Sing for joy to Adonai, you righteous,
  for the upright do well to give praise.

Give thanks to Adonai with a lyre,
  make music to God with a ten-stringed harp.

Sing to God a new song,
  play well, with shouts of joy.

כִּי־יָשָׁר דְּבַר־יהוה, וְכָל־מַעֲשֵׂהוּ בֶּאֱמוּנָה.
אֹהֵב צְדָקָה וּמִשְׁפָּט; חֶסֶד יהוה מָלְאָה הָאָרֶץ.
בִּדְבַר יהוה שָׁמַיִם נַעֲשׂוּ, וּבְרוּחַ פִּיו כָּל־צְבָאָם.
כֹּנֵס כַּנֵּד מֵי הַיָּם, נֹתֵן בְּאוֹצָרוֹת תְּהוֹמוֹת.
יִירְאוּ מֵיהוה כָּל־הָאָרֶץ, מִמֶּנּוּ יָגוּרוּ כָּל־יֹשְׁבֵי תֵבֵל.
כִּי הוּא אָמַר וַיֶּהִי; הוּא־צִוָּה וַיַּעֲמֹד.

For God's word holds good;
  And God's deeds are faithfully done.

Adonai loves righteousness and justice;
God's kindness fills the earth.

By the word of Adonai the heavens were made,
and all their host by the breath of God's mouth.

At the divine command the ocean waves rise,
or gather instead in the vaults of the deep.

Let all the earth revere Adonai,
let all who dwell there stand in awe of God,

Who spoke, and it came to be,
who commanded, and it stood firm.

THE READER'S KADDISH IS ON PAGE 132

FROM PSALM 92

A PRAISE-SONG TO THE SABBATH DAY

מִזְמוֹר שִׁיר לְיוֹם הַשַּׁבָּת

טוֹב לְהֹדוֹת לַיהוה, וּלְזַמֵּר לְשִׁמְךָ עֶלְיוֹן,
לְהַגִּיד בַּבֹּקֶר חַסְדֶּךָ, וֶאֱמוּנָתְךָ בַּלֵּילוֹת,
עֲלֵי־עָשׂוֹר וַעֲלֵי־נָבֶל, עֲלֵי הִגָּיוֹן בְּכִנּוֹר.

✢ See "Selected Psalms," pages 358-375, and "A Daily Psalm," pages 27-33.

It is good to give thanks to Adonai,
to sing praises to Your name, O Most High,

To tell of Your love in the morning,
Your faithfulness in the night,
to the sound of harp and lute,
the sweet viol's song.

כִּי שִׂמַּחְתַּנִי, יהוה, בְּפָעֳלֶךָ, בְּמַעֲשֵׂי יָדֶיךָ אֲרַנֵּן.
מַה־גָּדְלוּ מַעֲשֶׂיךָ, יהוה! מְאֹד עָמְקוּ מַחְשְׁבֹתֶיךָ.
צַדִּיק כַּתָּמָר יִפְרָח, כְּאֶרֶז בַּלְּבָנוֹן יִשְׂגֶּה.

116

שְׁתוּלִים בְּבֵית יהוה, בְּחַצְרוֹת אֱלֹהֵינוּ יַפְרִיחוּ.

עוֹד יְנוּבוּן בְּשֵׂיבָה, דְּשֵׁנִים וְרַעֲנַנִּים יִהְיוּ,

לְהַגִּיד כִּי־יָשָׁר יהוה, צוּרִי, וְלֹא־עַוְלָתָה בּוֹ.

Oh, how You gladden me with Your deeds, Adonai;
so I sing for joy over the work of Your hands.

> *How great are Your works, Adonai!*
> *How very deep Your design!*

The righteous shall flourish like palms,
reach high like the Lebanon in cedar.

> *Rooted in Your house, Adonai, they shall flourish in the courts of*
> *our God. Fresh and green shall they be, still vigorous in old age.*
> *Proclaiming that Adonai is just, my God, my flawless rock.*

THE READER'S KADDISH IS ON PAGE 132

PSALM 93

❈ See
"Selected
Psalms,"
pages 358-375,
and "A Daily
Psalm," pages
27-33.

יהוה מָלָךְ, גֵּאוּת לָבֵשׁ; לָבֵשׁ יהוה, עֹז הִתְאַזָּר;

אַף־תִּכּוֹן תֵּבֵל, בַּל־תִּמּוֹט.

נָכוֹן כִּסְאֲךָ מֵאָז, מֵעוֹלָם אָתָּה.

נָשְׂאוּ נְהָרוֹת, יהוה, נָשְׂאוּ נְהָרוֹת קוֹלָם,

יִשְׂאוּ נְהָרוֹת דָּכְיָם;

מִקֹּלוֹת מַיִם רַבִּים, אַדִּירִים מִשְׁבְּרֵי־יָם,

אַדִּיר בַּמָּרוֹם יהוה. עֵדֹתֶיךָ נֶאֶמְנוּ מְאֹד;

לְבֵיתְךָ נַאֲוָה־קֹּדֶשׁ, יהוה, לְאֹרֶךְ יָמִים.

Adonai reigns, robed in majesty,
Adonai is robed, girded with might.
The world is established,
not to be moved.
Your throne is established from of old;

You are from everlasting.
The torrents lift up, Adonai,
the torrents lift up their voice,
the torrents howl their rage;
yet above the raging waters,
the mighty breakers of the sea,
is the majesty of God on high.
The truth of Your words is constant;
Adonai, holiness befits Your house for all time.

THE READER'S KADDISH IS ON PAGE 132

אַשְׁרֵי

PSALMS 84:5 AND 144:15

אַשְׁרֵי יוֹשְׁבֵי בֵיתֶךָ, עוֹד יְהַלְלוּךָ סֶּלָה.

אַשְׁרֵי הָעָם שֶׁכָּכָה לּוֹ; אַשְׁרֵי הָעָם שֶׁיהוה אֱלֹהָיו.

The English text can be chanted as the Hebrew might be.

Happy are those who dwell in Your house,
who continually sing Your praises.

Happy the people who are so blessed;
happy the people whose God You are.

FROM PSALM 145

A PSALM OF DAVID   תְּהִלָּה לְדָוִד

❀ See "Selected Psalms," pages 358-375, and "A Daily Psalm," pages 27-33.

אֲרוֹמִמְךָ, אֱלוֹהַי הַמֶּלֶךְ, וַאֲבָרְכָה שִׁמְךָ לְעוֹלָם וָעֶד.

בְּכָל־יוֹם אֲבָרְכֶךָ, וַאֲהַלְלָה שִׁמְךָ לְעוֹלָם וָעֶד.

Always we exalt You, and praise Your name forever.

Because You are our maker, we extol Your name forever.

גָּדוֹל יהוה וּמְהֻלָּל מְאֹד, וְלִגְדֻלָּתוֹ אֵין חֵקֶר.

דּוֹר לְדוֹר יְשַׁבַּח מַעֲשֶׂיךָ, וּגְבוּרֹתֶיךָ יַגִּידוּ.

Calling us to greatness, Eternal One, You teach us.

Declaring Your works tremendous, we witness to Your power.

הֲדַר כְּבוֹד הוֹדֶךָ, וְדִבְרֵי נִפְלְאֹתֶיךָ אָשִׂיחָה.

וֶעֱזוּז נוֹרְאֹתֶיךָ יֹאמֵרוּ, וּגְדֻלָּתְךָ אֲסַפְּרֶנָּה.

Ever we tell Your glory, the wonder of Your mercies.

For as we praise Your marvels, so we laud Your greatness.

זֵכֶר רַב־טוּבְךָ יַבִּיעוּ, וְצִדְקָתְךָ יְרַנֵּנוּ.

חַנּוּן וְרַחוּם יהוה, אֶרֶךְ אַפַּיִם וּגְדָל־חָסֶד.

Great the good we honor, singing of Your justice.

Holding us in kindness, in love You are abounding.

טוֹב־יהוה לַכֹּל, וְרַחֲמָיו עַל־כָּל־מַעֲשָׂיו.

יוֹדוּךָ יהוה כָּל־מַעֲשֶׂיךָ, וַחֲסִידֶיךָ יְבָרְכוּךָ.

In Your boundless goodness, You teach Your creatures mercy.

Joyful, we all thank You; Your faithful ones shall praise You.

כְּבוֹד מַלְכוּתְךָ יֹאמֵרוּ, וּגְבוּרָתְךָ יְדַבֵּרוּ,

לְהוֹדִיעַ לִבְנֵי הָאָדָם גְּבוּרֹתָיו, וּכְבוֹד הֲדַר מַלְכוּתוֹ.

Knowing that You are sovereign, we all proclaim Your splendor.

Let all perceive Your power, the triumph of Your wisdom.

מַלְכוּתְךָ מַלְכוּת כָּל־עֹלָמִים, וּמֶמְשַׁלְתְּךָ בְּכָל־דּוֹר וָדוֹר.

סוֹמֵךְ יהוה לְכָל־הַנֹּפְלִים, וְזוֹקֵף לְכָל־הַכְּפוּפִים.

Majestic, You rule in glory; Your reign endures forever.

O God, support the helpless, and raise up all the fallen.

עֵינֵי־כֹל אֵלֶיךָ יְשַׂבֵּרוּ, וְאַתָּה נוֹתֵן־לָהֶם אֶת־אָכְלָם בְּעִתּוֹ.

פּוֹתֵחַ אֶת־יָדֶךָ וּמַשְׂבִּיעַ לְכָל־חַי רָצוֹן.

Pleading, they implore You; in their need, pray feed them.

Quickly Your hand be open, to comfort every creature.

צַדִּיק יהוה בְּכָל־דְּרָכָיו, וְחָסִיד בְּכָל־מַעֲשָׂיו.

קָרוֹב יְהֹוָה לְכָל־קֹרְאָיו, לְכֹל אֲשֶׁר יִקְרָאֻהוּ בֶאֱמֶת.

Righteous are You always, loving in Your actions.

So near to all who call You, to all who call upon You.

רְצוֹן־יְרֵאָיו יַעֲשֶׂה, וְאֶת־שַׁוְעָתָם יִשְׁמַע וְיוֹשִׁיעֵם.

תְּהִלַּת יהוה יְדַבֶּר־פִּי וִיבָרֵךְ כָּל־בָּשָׂר

שֵׁם קָדְשׁוֹ לְעוֹלָם וָעֶד.

Those who seek You, call You; You hear their cry and help them.

Unceasing, our lips sing praise-songs; rejoicing in You forever.

PSALM 115:18

וַאֲנַחְנוּ נְבָרֵךְ יָהּ מֵעַתָּה וְעַד־עוֹלָם. הַלְלוּיָהּ!

And now let us extol the eternal God from this time and forever. Halleluyah!

THE READER'S KADDISH IS ON PAGE 132

PSALM 150

✽ See
"Selected
Psalms,"
pages 358-375,
and "A Daily
Psalm," pages
27-33.

הַלְלוּיָהּ! Halleluyah!

הַלְלוּ־אֵל בְּקָדְשׁוֹ, Praise God in the sanctuary,

הַלְלוּהוּ בִּרְקִיעַ עֻזּוֹ. Praise God whose power the heavens proclaim.

הַלְלוּהוּ בִגְבוּרֹתָיו, Praise God's mighty deeds,

הַלְלוּהוּ כְּרֹב גֻּדְלוֹ. Praise God's abundant greatness.

הַלְלוּהוּ בְּתֵקַע שׁוֹפָר, Praise with shofar-blast,
Praise with lyre and harp.

הַלְלוּהוּ בְּנֵבֶל וְכִנּוֹר. Praise with timbrel and dance,

הַלְלוּהוּ בְתֹף וּמָחוֹל, Praise with lute and pipe.

הַלְלוּהוּ בְּמִנִּים וְעֻגָב. Praise with cymbals sounding,

הַלְלוּהוּ בְצִלְצְלֵי־שָׁמַע, Praise with cymbals resounding.

הַלְלוּהוּ בְּצִלְצְלֵי תְרוּעָה.

כֹּל הַנְּשָׁמָה תְּהַלֵּל יָהּ. Let every soul praise the Eternal One.

הַלְלוּיָהּ! Halleluyah!

THE READER'S KADDISH IS ON PAGE 132

נִשְׁמַת כָּל־חַי תְּבָרֵךְ אֶת־שִׁמְךָ, יְיָ אֱלֹהֵינוּ, וְרוּחַ כָּל־בָּשָׂר
תְּפָאֵר וּתְרוֹמֵם זִכְרְךָ, מַלְכֵּנוּ, תָּמִיד. מִן הָעוֹלָם וְעַד־הָעוֹלָם
אַתָּה אֵל. אֱלֹהֵי הָרִאשׁוֹנִים וְהָאַחֲרוֹנִים, אֱלוֹהַּ כָּל־בְּרִיּוֹת,
אֲדוֹן כָּל־תּוֹלָדוֹת, הַמְהֻלָּל בְּרֹב הַתִּשְׁבָּחוֹת, הַמְנַהֵג עוֹלָמוֹ
בְּחֶסֶד וּבְרִיּוֹתָיו בְּרַחֲמִים. לְךָ לְבַדְּךָ אֲנַחְנוּ מוֹדִים.

The souls of all the living shall praise Your name, Adonai our God; the spirits of all flesh shall ever proclaim Your majesty. From eternity to eternity You are God.

God of the first and the last, creator of all living creatures, hope of all generations, beyond all praise, You guide Your world with love and its creatures with compassion. To You alone we give thanks.

אִלּוּ פִֽינוּ מָלֵא שִׁירָה כַּיָּם, וּלְשׁוֹנֵֽנוּ כַּהֲמוֹן גַּלָּיו,

וְשִׂפְתוֹתֵֽינוּ שֶֽׁבַח כְּמֶרְחֲבֵי רָקִֽיעַ, וְעֵינֵֽינוּ מְאִירוֹת כַּשֶּֽׁמֶשׁ

וְכַיָּרֵֽחַ, וְיָדֵֽינוּ פְרוּשׂוֹת כְּנִשְׁרֵי שָׁמָֽיִם, וְרַגְלֵֽינוּ קַלּוֹת

כָּאַיָּלוֹת—אֵין אֲנַֽחְנוּ מַסְפִּיקִים לְהוֹדוֹת לָךְ, וּלְבָרֵךְ אֶת־שְׁמֶֽךָ,

עַל־אַחַת מֵאֶֽלֶף אֶֽלֶף אַלְפֵי אֲלָפִים וְרֹבֵּי רְבָבוֹת

פְּעָמִים הַטּוֹבוֹת שֶׁעָשִֽׂיתָ עִם־אֲבוֹתֵֽינוּ וְאִמּוֹתֵֽינוּ וְעִמָּֽנוּ.

Yet were our mouths full of song as the sea, our tongues eloquent as its waves, our lips praiseful as the heavens' expanse; were our eyes bright as the sun and the moon, our arms spread out like an eagle's wings, and our feet quick as a deer's—we could not begin to thank You or praise Your name enough for even one of the countless blessings You have bestowed upon our mothers and fathers, and upon us.

עַל כֵּן אֵבָרִים שֶׁפִּלַּֽגְתָּ בָּֽנוּ, וְרֽוּחַ וּנְשָׁמָה שֶׁנָּפַֽחְתָּ בְּאַפֵּֽינוּ,

וְלָשׁוֹן אֲשֶׁר שַֽׂמְתָּ בְּפִֽינוּ, הֵן הֵם יוֹדוּ וִיבָרְכוּ וִישַׁבְּחוּ

וִיפָאֲרוּ אֶת־שְׁמֶֽךָ, מַלְכֵּֽנוּ.

כִּי כָל־פֶּה לְךָ יוֹדֶה, וְכָל־בֶּֽרֶךְ לְךָ תִכְרַע,

וְכָל־קוֹמָה לְפָנֶֽיךָ תִשְׁתַּחֲוֶה, וְכָל־לְבָבוֹת יִירָאֽוּךָ,

וְכָל־קֶֽרֶב וּכְלָיוֹת יְזַמְּרוּ לִשְׁמֶֽךָ.

Therefore the limbs that You formed in us, the ethereal spirit that You have breathed into us, the tongue that

You have put in our mouths—how they will dance and sing in praise of Your majestic name! Every mouth will thank You, every tongue will swear allegiance, every knee will bend, and every head bow down before You.

The hearts of all shall be in awe of You, and our innermost being shall sing praise to Your name.

כַּדָּבָר שֶׁכָּתוּב: כָּל־עַצְמוֹתַי

As it is written: "All my bones shall say: Adonai, who is like You?" O how we praise You, extol You, and honor Your holy name, as it is said:

תֹאמַרְנָה: יְיָ, מִי כָמְוֹךָ?

נְהַלֶּלְךָ וּנְשַׁבֵּחֲךָ וּנְפָאֶרְךָ

וּנְבָרֵךְ אֶת־שֵׁם קָדְשֶׁךָ,

כָּאָמוּר: בָּרְכִי, נַפְשִׁי, אֶת־יְיָ,

"Give praise to Adonai, O my soul, and let all that is in me honor God's holy name!"

וְכָל־קְרָבַי אֶת־שֵׁם קָדְשׁוֹ!

הָאֵל בְּתַעֲצֻמוֹת עֻזֶּךָ, הַגָּדוֹל בִּכְבוֹד שְׁמֶךָ, הַגִּבּוֹר לָנֶצַח

וְהַנּוֹרָא בְּנוֹרְאוֹתֶיךָ. הַמֶּלֶךְ הַיּוֹשֵׁב עַל כִּסֵּא רָם וְנִשָּׂא.

שׁוֹכֵן עַד, מָרוֹם וְקָדוֹשׁ שְׁמוֹ. וְכָתוּב: רַנְּנוּ צַדִּיקִים בַּיְיָ,

לַיְשָׁרִים נָאוָה תְהִלָּה. בְּפִי יְשָׁרִים תִּתְהַלָּל; וּבְדִבְרֵי צַדִּיקִים

תִּתְבָּרַךְ; וּבִלְשׁוֹן חֲסִידִים תִּתְרוֹמָם; וּבְקֶרֶב קְדוֹשִׁים תִּתְקַדָּשׁ.

Tremendous in power, great in the glory of Your being, mighty forever and awesome in Your works, supreme and exalted, You sit enthroned in majesty.

You abide forever, the high and holy God. As it is written: "Sing for joy to Adonai, you righteous, for the upright do well to give praise."

The songs of the righteous extol You; the words of the upright give You praise; the speech of the faithful exalts You; and among the holy You are hallowed.

וּבְמַקְהֲלוֹת רִבְבוֹת עַמְּךָ בֵּית יִשְׂרָאֵל בְּרִנָּה יִתְפָּאֵר
שִׁמְךָ, מַלְכֵּנוּ, בְּכָל־דּוֹר וָדוֹר.

And in joyful assembly Your people, the House of Israel, in every generation glorify Your name in song.

৯৫

יִשְׁתַּבַּח שִׁמְךָ לָעַד, מַלְכֵּנוּ,
הָאֵל הַמֶּלֶךְ הַגָּדוֹל וְהַקָּדוֹשׁ
בַּשָּׁמַיִם וּבָאָרֶץ. כִּי לְךָ נָאֶה,
יי אֱלֹהֵינוּ וֵאלֹהֵי אֲבוֹתֵינוּ
וְאִמּוֹתֵינוּ, שִׁיר וּשְׁבָחָה, הַלֵּל
וְזִמְרָה, בְּרָכוֹת וְהוֹדָאוֹת,
מֵעַתָּה וְעַד עוֹלָם. בָּרוּךְ אַתָּה
יי, הַבּוֹחֵר בְּשִׁירֵי זִמְרָה.

Praised be Your name, sovereign God, in heaven and on earth. To You, our God and God of our ancestors, let hymns and psalms be sung; to You all praise and thanks are due now and forever.

We praise You, O God: may You accept our songs of praise.

৯৫

THE READER'S KADDISH IS ON PAGE 132

124

SHABBAT MORNING SERVICE שחרית לשבת

OPENING PRAYERS

2

MA TOVU IS ON PAGE 105

MA TOVU IS ON PAGE 105

הִנֵּה מַה־טוֹב וּמַה־נָּעִים שֶׁבֶת אַחִים גַּם־יָֽחַד.

Hi-nei ma-tov u-ma na-im sheh-vet a-chim gam ya-chad.

How good it is, and how pleasant,
to dwell together in unity.

&

אלהי נשמה FOR THE SOUL

אֱלֹהַי, נְשָׁמָה שֶׁנָּתַֽתָּ בִּי טְהוֹרָה הִיא!

The soul that You have given me, O God, is pure!

אַתָּה בְרָאתָהּ, אַתָּה יְצַרְתָּהּ, אַתָּה נְפַחְתָּהּ בִּי, וְאַתָּה מְשַׁמְּרָהּ
בְּקִרְבִּי. כָּל־זְמַן שֶׁהַנְּשָׁמָה בְקִרְבִּי, מוֹדֶה אֲנִי לְפָנֶֽיךָ, יי אֱלֹהַי
וֵאלֹהֵי אֲבוֹתַי וְאִמּוֹתַי, רִבּוֹן כָּל־הַמַּעֲשִׂים, אֲדוֹן כָּל־הַנְּשָׁמוֹת.

*You created and formed it, breathed it into me, and within me
You sustain it. So long as I have breath, therefore, I will give
thanks to You, my God, God of all ages, source of all being,
loving guide of every human spirit.*

בָּרוּךְ אַתָּה יי, אֲשֶׁר בְּיָדוֹ נֶֽפֶשׁ כָּל־חָי וְרֽוּחַ כָּל־בְּשַׂר־אִישׁ.

*We praise You, O God, in whose embrace are all the living—body
and soul.*

&

A PRAYER
BEFORE
PRAYER:
May my
worship on
this Shabbat
encourage me
to fulfill this
precept: "The
righteous
shall live by
their faith."
(Habakkuk
2:4)

❀ See page
182 and
"Looking at
Ourselves,"
pages 347-351.

יְהִי רָצוֹן מִלְּפָנֶיךָ, יי אֱלֹהֵינוּ,

שֶׁתַּשְׁכֵּן בְּפוּרֵינוּ אַהֲבָה וְאַחֲוָה

וְשָׁלוֹם וְרֵעוּת, וְתַצְלִיחַ סוֹפֵנוּ

אַחֲרִית וְתִקְוָה, וְתַקְּנֵנוּ בְּחָבֵר

טוֹב וְיֵצֶר טוֹב בְּעוֹלָמֶךָ,

וְנַשְׁכִּים וְנִמְצָא יְחוּל לְבָבֵנוּ

לְיִרְאָה אֶת־שְׁמֶךָ, וְתָבוֹא

לְפָנֶיךָ קוֹרַת נַפְשֵׁנוּ לְטוֹבָה.

Adonai our God, let love and harmony, peace and friendship dwell among us, and fill our new day with the courage of hope.

Guide us in Your world with good companions and good intentions. May we rise up in the morning to find our hearts ready to do Your will, and may our deepest longings be fulfilled for good.

※ See page 182 and "Looking at Ourselves," pages 347-351.

&

THE READER'S KADDISH IS ON PAGE 132

3

MA TOVU IS ON PAGE 105

כִּי אֶשְׁמְרָה שַׁבָּת, אֵל יִשְׁמְרֵנִי.

אוֹת הִיא לְעוֹלְמֵי עַד, בֵּינוֹ וּבֵינִי.

Ki esh-m'ra Shabbat, Eil yish-m'rei-ni.

Ot hi l'o-l'mei ad, bei-no u-vei-ni.

When we keep Shabbat, God keeps us;
It it a sign between God and Israel forever.

A PRAYER BEFORE PRAYER: May my worship on this Shabbat encourage me to fulfill this precept: "Serve Adonai with awe, and rejoice with trembling." (Psalm 2:11)

❊ See Psalm
139 (page
356), and
Psalm 148
(page 374).

כָּל־כּוֹכְבֵי בֹקֶר לְךָ יָשִׁירוּ,

כִּי זָהֳרֵיהֶם מִמְּךָ יַזְהִירוּ.

וּבְנֵי אֱלֹהִים עוֹמְדִים עַל

מִשְׁמְרוֹת לַיְל וָיוֹם,

שֵׁם נֶאְדָּר יַאְדִּירוּ,

וּקְהַל קְדֹשִׁים קִבְּלוּ מֵהֶם

וְכָל־שַׁחַר לְשַׁחַר בֵּיתְךָ

יָעִירוּ.

To You the stars of morning sing,
from You their radiance bright must spring.
And steadfast in their vigils, day and night,
Your angels, flooded with fervor, ring
Your praise; they teach the holy ones to bring
into Your house the breath of early light.

We thank You, O God, for this time of prayer, when as one we strive to become aware of Your presence and place before You our desires, our hopes, and our gratitude.

Eternal God, bless our worship this day. May the gleams of Your light and the visions of Your truth that bless us here, remain with us when we go out into the world, keeping us steadfast in loyalty to You and to Your commandments. Amen.

☙

מְקוֹר הַחַיִּים, Fountain of Life, at break of day we invite Your presence. We enter Your house to worship, and You say: "Be holy: serve one another in love."

אוֹר הַחַיִּים, Light of the Living, at break of day we invite Your presence. Give wings to our hopes and dreams; bless the work of our hands, and make us Your partners in the building of a world where the prophetic vision will be fulfilled, and all will dwell in harmony and peace. Amen.

THE READER'S KADDISH IS ON PAGE 132

4

MA TOVU IS ON PAGE 105

עַל שְׁלֹשָׁה דְבָרִים הָעוֹלָם עוֹמֵד:
עַל הַתּוֹרָה, וְעַל הָעֲבוֹדָה, וְעַל גְּמִילוּת חֲסָדִים.

Al sh'lo-sha d'va-rim ha-o-lam o-meid:
Al ha-Torah, v'al ha-a-vo-da, v'al g'mi-lut cha-sa-dim.

The world rests on three things:
On Torah, worship, and loving deeds.

FOR TORAH לעסוק בדברי תורה

בָּרוּךְ אַתָּה יי, אֱלֹהֵינוּ מֶלֶךְ הָעוֹלָם, אֲשֶׁר קִדְּשָׁנוּ בְּמִצְוֹתָיו וְצִוָּנוּ לַעֲסוֹק בְּדִבְרֵי תוֹרָה.

We praise You, Adonai our God, sovereign of the universe: You hallow us with Your Mitzvot and command us to immerse ourselves in Torah.

A PRAYER BEFORE PRAYER: May my worship on this Shabbat encourage me to fulfill this Mitzvah: "Let these words, which I command you this day, be upon your heart. Teach them constantly to your children . . . ." (Deuteronomy 6:6-7a)

וְהַעֲרֶב־נָא, יי אֱלֹהֵינוּ, אֶת־דִּבְרֵי תוֹרָתְךָ בְּפִינוּ וּבְפִי עַמְּךָ בֵּית יִשְׂרָאֵל, וְנִהְיֶה אֲנַחְנוּ וְצֶאֱצָאֵינוּ, וְצֶאֱצָאֵי עַמְּךָ בֵּית יִשְׂרָאֵל, כֻּלָּנוּ יוֹדְעֵי שְׁמֶךָ וְלוֹמְדֵי תוֹרָתֶךָ לִשְׁמָהּ. בָּרוּךְ אַתָּה יי, הַמְלַמֵּד תּוֹרָה לְעַמּוֹ יִשְׂרָאֵל.

Adonai our God, let the words of Your Torah be sweet in our mouths, and in the mouths of Your people Israel, that we and our children may all come to know You through our loving study of Torah. We praise You, Adonai, teacher of Torah to Your people Israel.

✤ See Pirke Avot, pages 322-340.

אֵלּוּ דְבָרִים שֶׁאֵין לָהֶם שִׁעוּר:
כִּבּוּד אָב וָאֵם, וּגְמִילוּת חֲסָדִים,
וְהַשְׁכָּמַת בֵּית הַמִּדְרָשׁ שַׁחֲרִית וְעַרְבִית,

וְהַכְנָסַת אוֹרְחִים, וּבִקּוּר חוֹלִים,

וְהַכְנָסַת כַּלָּה, וּלְוָיַת הַמֵּת, וְעִיּוּן תְּפִלָּה,

וַהֲבָאַת שָׁלוֹם בֵּין אָדָם לַחֲבֵרוֹ.

וְתַלְמוּד תּוֹרָה כְּנֶגֶד כֻּלָּם.

These are duties whose worth cannot be measured:

honoring one's father and mother,
acts of love and kindness,
diligent pursuit of knowledge and wisdom,
hospitality to wayfarers,
visiting the sick,
rejoicing with bride and groom,
consoling the bereaved,
praying with sincerity,
and making peace when people quarrel.
And the study of Torah leads to them all.

THE READER'S KADDISH IS ON PAGE 132

5

MA TOVU IS ON PAGE 105

מַה־יָּפֶה הַיּוֹם: שַׁבָּת שָׁלוֹם.

Mah ya-feh ha-yom: Shabbat Shalom

How beautiful is this day: Shabbat Shalom.

A PRAYER BEFORE PRAYER: May my worship on this Shabbat encourage me to fulfill this precept: "Turn away from wrong-doing, and do good; seek peace and pursue it." (Psalm 34:15)

We thank You, O God, for this Sabbath day, which draws us nearer to You and to one another. Though You are truly the breath of our life, we feel Your presence most powerfully when we turn to You in worship and meditation. May this service renew in our hearts the sense of Your presence, and bring us peace.

A REFLECTION

℘   May my life be a link in the chain of goodness. As I say the prayers of my fathers and mothers, help me to hear in every word their devotion and faithfulness, their joy and suffering. Holiness is my heritage; may I be worthy of it.

I pray that this tradition will live in me and pass from me to generations I shall never know, enriched by the truth I have found and such good deeds as I have done. So may I fulfill my task on earth and be blessed.

And when this service ends and the prayers have ceased, help me to bring their spirit back to the world in which I live. May I love God and my neighbor as myself, and be a living witness to the vision of a better world that has come to me from generations past.

FROM MICAH 6

בַּמָּה אֲקַדֵּם יהוה? אִכַּף לֵאלֹהֵי מָרוֹם?

הַאֲקַדְּמֶנּוּ בְעוֹלוֹת? בַּעֲגָלִים בְּנֵי שָׁנָה?

הֲיִרְצֶה יהוה בְּאַלְפֵי אֵילִים, בְּרִבְבוֹת נַחֲלֵי־שָׁמֶן?

הִגִּיד לְךָ אָדָם מַה־טּוֹב; וּמָה־יהוה דּוֹרֵשׁ מִמְּךָ?

כִּי אִם־עֲשׂוֹת מִשְׁפָּט, וְאַהֲבַת חֶסֶד,

וְהַצְנֵעַ לֶכֶת עִם־אֱלֹהֶיךָ.

✻ See Psalm 51 (page 364).

With what shall I approach Adonai?
How shall I worship the God of heaven?

Shall I come before God with burnt-offerings,
or with yearling calves?

Will God be pleased with thousands of rams,

or with ten thousand rivers of oil?

130

People tell You what is good; but what does the eternal God require of You?

Only to do justly, and love mercy, and walk humbly with Your God.

❧

Revere God in all that you do, privately as well as publicly, acknowledge the truth, and speak it in your heart.

Our God and God of our ancestors, teach us to see each new day as a token of Your love. Open our eyes to Your presence in our daily life. Strengthen in us the voice of conscience, prompt us to deeds of goodness, and, when we are tempted to take advantage of the weaknesses of others, help us instead to show generosity and kindness. Amen.

❧

ALL RISE

חֲצִי קַדִּישׁ　READER'S KADDISH

יִתְגַּדַּל וְיִתְקַדַּשׁ שְׁמֵהּ רַבָּא בְּעָלְמָא דִי־בְרָא כִרְעוּתֵהּ,

וְיַמְלִיךְ מַלְכוּתֵהּ בְּחַיֵּיכוֹן וּבְיוֹמֵיכוֹן וּבְחַיֵּי

דְכָל־בֵּית יִשְׂרָאֵל, בַּעֲגָלָא וּבִזְמַן קָרִיב, וְאִמְרוּ: אָמֵן.

יְהֵא שְׁמֵהּ רַבָּא מְבָרַךְ לְעָלַם וּלְעָלְמֵי עָלְמַיָּא.

יִתְבָּרַךְ וְיִשְׁתַּבַּח, וְיִתְפָּאַר, וְיִתְרוֹמַם וְיִתְנַשֵּׂא,

וְיִתְהַדָּר וְיִתְעַלֶּה וְיִתְהַלָּל שְׁמֵהּ דְּקוּדְשָׁא, בְּרִיךְ הוּא,

לְעֵלָּא מִן־כָּל־בִּרְכָתָא וְשִׁירָתָא, תֻּשְׁבְּחָתָא וְנֶחֱמָתָא

דַּאֲמִירָן בְּעָלְמָא, וְאִמְרוּ: אָמֵן.

Yit-ga-dal v'yit-ka-dash sh'mei ra-ba b'al-ma di-v'ra chi-r'u'tei,
v'yam-lich mal-chu-tei b'cha-yei-chon u-v'yo-mei-chon u-v'cha-yei
d'chol beit Yis-ra-eil, ba-a-ga-la u-vi-z'man ka-riv, v'i-m'ru: A-mein.

Y'hei sh'mei ra-ba m'va-rach l'a-lam u-l'al-mei al-ma-ya.

Yit-ba-rach v'yish-ta-bach v'yit-pa-ar, v'yit-ro-mam, v'yit-na-sei,
v'yit-ha-dar, v'yit-a-leh, v'yit-ha-lal sh'mei d'kud-sha, b'rich hu,
l'ei-la min kol bir-cha-ta v'shi-ra-ta, tush-b'cha-ta v'neh-cheh-ma-ta
da-a-mi-ran b'al-ma, v'i-m'ru: A-mein.

Hallowed be Your great name on earth, Your creation; establish Your dominion in our own day, in our own lives, and in the life of the whole House of Israel.

Blessed be Your great name forever and ever.

Blessed, praised, honored, and exalted be the name of the Holy One, ever to be praised, though You are beyond all the blessings and songs of praise that the world may offer.

בָּרְכוּ אֶת־יי הַמְבֹרָךְ.
בָּרוּךְ יי הַמְבֹרָךְ לְעוֹלָם וָעֶד.

Praise Adonai, to whom our praise is due.

We praise Adonai,
to whom our praise is due forever and ever.

יוצר CREATION

בָּרוּךְ אַתָּה יי, אֱלֹהֵינוּ מֶלֶךְ הָעוֹלָם,
יוֹצֵר אוֹר וּבוֹרֵא חֹשֶׁךְ, עֹשֶׂה שָׁלוֹם וּבוֹרֵא אֶת־הַכֹּל.

We praise You, Adonai our God, sovereign of the universe, maker of light and creator of darkness, author of peace and creator of all things.

הַמֵּאִיר לָאָרֶץ וְלַדָּרִים עָלֶיהָ
בְּרַחֲמִים, וּבְטוּבוֹ מְחַדֵּשׁ
בְּכָל־יוֹם תָּמִיד מַעֲשֵׂה
בְרֵאשִׁית. מָה רַבּוּ מַעֲשֶׂיךָ,
יי! כֻּלָּם בְּחָכְמָה עָשִׂיתָ,
מָלְאָה הָאָרֶץ קִנְיָנֶךָ. תִּתְבָּרַךְ,
יי אֱלֹהֵינוּ, עַל־שֶׁבַח מַעֲשֵׂה
יָדֶיךָ וְעַל־מְאוֹרֵי־אוֹר שֶׁעָשִׂיתָ:
יְפָאֲרוּךָ סֶּלָה.

In mercy You give light to the earth and all who dwell on it, and in Your goodness You continually renew—day by day—the work of creation.

How manifold are Your works, O God! With wisdom You have made them all. The work of Your hands declares Your praise, and the radiant stars bear witness to Your glory.

The creator of the universe is also its sustainer: Each morning we awaken to the miracle of a creation ancient beyond imagining, yet new as the first dawn to an infant's eyes.

✽ See page 355 and Psalm 148 (page 374).

בָּרוּךְ אַתָּה יי, יוֹצֵר הַמְּאוֹרוֹת.

We praise You, O God, creator of light.

REVELATION אהבה רבה

אַהֲבָה רַבָּה אֲהַבְתָּנוּ, יְיָ אֱלֹהֵינוּ.
חֶמְלָה גְדוֹלָה וִיתֵרָה חָמַלְתָּ עָלֵינוּ.

Great is Your love for us, O God, and overflowing Your compassion.

אָבִינוּ מַלְכֵּנוּ, בַּעֲבוּר אֲבוֹתֵינוּ וְאִמּוֹתֵינוּ שֶׁבָּטְחוּ בְךָ וַתְּלַמְּדֵם
חֻקֵּי חַיִּים, כֵּן תְּחָנֵּנוּ וּתְלַמְּדֵנוּ. אָבִינוּ, הָאָב הָרַחֲמָן, הַמְרַחֵם,
רַחֵם עָלֵינוּ וְתֵן בְּלִבֵּנוּ לְהָבִין וּלְהַשְׂכִּיל, לִשְׁמֹעַ, לִלְמֹד
וּלְלַמֵּד, לִשְׁמֹר וְלַעֲשׂוֹת וּלְקַיֵּם אֶת־כָּל־דִּבְרֵי תַלְמוּד תּוֹרָתֶךָ
בְּאַהֲבָה. וְהָאֵר עֵינֵינוּ בְּתוֹרָתֶךָ, וְדַבֵּק לִבֵּנוּ בְּמִצְוֹתֶיךָ, וְיַחֵד
לְבָבֵנוּ לְאַהֲבָה וּלְיִרְאָה אֶת־שְׁמֶךָ. וְלֹא־נֵבוֹשׁ לְעוֹלָם וָעֶד, כִּי
בְשֵׁם קָדְשְׁךָ הַגָּדוֹל וְהַנּוֹרָא בָּטָחְנוּ. נָגִילָה וְנִשְׂמְחָה בִּישׁוּעָתֶךָ,
כִּי אֵל פּוֹעֵל יְשׁוּעוֹת אָתָּה, וּבָנוּ בָחַרְתָּ וְקֵרַבְתָּנוּ לְשִׁמְךָ הַגָּדוֹל
סֶלָה בֶּאֱמֶת, לְהוֹדוֹת לְךָ וּלְיַחֶדְךָ בְּאַהֲבָה.

Our ancestors put their trust in You, and You taught them a living law. Now be gracious to us, Compassionate One, and teach us: fill our hearts with wisdom and insight, that we may love, understand, and follow Your Teaching.

Enlighten our eyes with Your Torah, help us cling to Your commandments, and inspire us to love and revere Your name with a ready heart.

We rejoice in You and exult in Your saving power, for You have ever been our help. You have called us to serve You and have drawn us near to You in faithfulness, with joy to offer You praise and proclaim Your unity.

בָּרוּךְ אַתָּה יְיָ, הַבּוֹחֵר בְּעַמּוֹ יִשְׂרָאֵל בְּאַהֲבָה.

We praise You, O God, for You call us in love to Your service.

Torah is the theme of the second of the blessings that precede the Shema. It is a gift of love, it gives light to our eyes. And it imposes obligation: to learn, to understand, and to fulfill the divine mandate.

✣ See Pirke Avot, page 322, and Psalm 51 (page 364).

134

שְׁמַע יִשְׂרָאֵל: יהוה אֱלֹהֵינוּ, יהוה אֶחָד.

בָּרוּךְ שֵׁם כְּבוֹד מַלְכוּתוֹ לְעוֹלָם וָעֶד.

Hear, O Israel: Adonai is our God, Adonai alone.
Praised be God's glorious majesty forever and ever.

ALL ARE SEATED

At times we
think of You
as a question,
when we
need to feel
You as *the*
question.
May my life
be the
response I
make, when
You *are* the
question.

✳ See
"Looking for
God," pages
352-357.

וְאָהַבְתָּ אֵת יְהֹוָה אֱלֹהֶיךָ

בְּכָל־לְבָבְךָ וּבְכָל־נַפְשְׁךָ וּבְכָל־מְאֹדֶךָ:

וְהָיוּ הַדְּבָרִים הָאֵלֶּה אֲשֶׁר אָנֹכִי מְצַוְּךָ הַיּוֹם

עַל־לְבָבֶךָ: וְשִׁנַּנְתָּם לְבָנֶיךָ וְדִבַּרְתָּ בָּם

בְּשִׁבְתְּךָ בְּבֵיתֶךָ וּבְלֶכְתְּךָ בַדֶּרֶךְ וּבְשָׁכְבְּךָ וּבְקוּמֶךָ:

וּקְשַׁרְתָּם לְאוֹת עַל־יָדֶךָ וְהָיוּ לְטֹטָפֹת בֵּין עֵינֶיךָ:

וּכְתַבְתָּם עַל־מְזוּזֹת בֵּיתֶךָ וּבִשְׁעָרֶיךָ:

לְמַעַן תִּזְכְּרוּ וַעֲשִׂיתֶם אֶת־כָּל־מִצְוֹתָי

וִהְיִיתֶם קְדֹשִׁים לֵאלֹהֵיכֶם:

אֲנִי יְהֹוָה אֱלֹהֵיכֶם אֲשֶׁר הוֹצֵאתִי אֶתְכֶם מֵאֶרֶץ

מִצְרַיִם לִהְיוֹת לָכֶם לֵאלֹהִים: אֲנִי יְהֹוָה אֱלֹהֵיכֶם:

V'a-hav-ta et Adonai Eh-lo-heh-cha b'chol l'va-v'cha u-v'chol naf-sh'cha
u-v'chol m'o-deh-cha. V'ha-yu ha-d'va-rim ha-ei-leh a-sher a-no-chi
m'tza-v'cha ha-yom al l'va-veh-cha. V'shi-nan-tam l'va-neh-cha v'di-bar-ta
bam b'shiv-t'cha b'vei-teh-cha u-v'lech-t'cha va-deh-rech u-v'shoch-b'cha
u-v'ku-meh-cha. U-k'shar-tam l'ot al ya-deh-cha v'ha-yu l'to-ta-fot bein
ei-neh-cha; u-ch'tav-tam al m'zu-zot bei-teh-cha u-vi-sh'a-reh-cha. L'ma-an
tiz-k'ru va-a-si-tem et kol mitz-vo-tai, vi-h'yi-tem k'do-shim lei-lo-hei-chem.
A-ni Adonai Eh-lo-hei-chem a-sher ho-tzei-ti et-chem mei-eh-retz
mitz-ra-yim li-h'yot la-chem lei-lo-him. A-ni Adonai Eh-lo-hei-chem.

You shall love Adonai your God with all your heart, with all your soul, with all your might. Let these words, which I command you this day, be upon your heart. Teach them constantly to your children, and speak of them in your home and on your way, when you lie down and when you rise up. Bind them as a sign upon your hand and let them be symbols before your eyes; inscribe them on the doorposts of your house, and on your gates: that you may be mindful of all my Mitzvot, and do them; then shall you be consecrated to your God. I, Adonai, am your God who led you out of Egypt to be your God; I, Adonai, am your God.

SOME MAY WISH TO INCLUDE THE FOLLOWING

וְהָיָה אִם־שָׁמֹעַ תִּשְׁמְעוּ אֶל־מִצְוֹתַי אֲשֶׁר אָנֹכִי מְצַוֶּה אֶתְכֶם הַיּוֹם
לְאַהֲבָה אֶת־יְהֹוָה אֱלֹהֵיכֶם וּלְעָבְדוֹ בְּכָל־לְבַבְכֶם וּבְכָל־נַפְשְׁכֶם:
יְצַו יְהֹוָה אִתְּךָ אֶת־הַבְּרָכָה בַּאֲסָמֶיךָ וּבְכָל מִשְׁלַח יָדֶךָ וּבֵרַכְךָ
בָּאָרֶץ אֲשֶׁר־יְהֹוָה אֱלֹהֶיךָ נֹתֵן לָךְ: יְקִימְךָ יְהֹוָה לוֹ לְעַם קָדוֹשׁ
כַּאֲשֶׁר נִשְׁבַּע־לָךְ כִּי תִשְׁמֹר אֶת־מִצְוֹת יְהֹוָה אֱלֹהֶיךָ וְהָלַכְתָּ
בִּדְרָכָיו: כִּי הַמִּצְוָה הַזֹּאת אֲשֶׁר אָנֹכִי מְצַוְּךָ הַיּוֹם לֹא־נִפְלֵאת
הִוא מִמְּךָ וְלֹא רְחֹקָה הִוא: כִּי־קָרוֹב אֵלֶיךָ הַדָּבָר מְאֹד בְּפִיךָ
וּבִלְבָבְךָ לַעֲשֹׂתוֹ: הַעִידֹתִי בָכֶם הַיּוֹם אֶת־הַשָּׁמַיִם וְאֶת־הָאָרֶץ
הַחַיִּים וְהַמָּוֶת נָתַתִּי לְפָנֶיךָ הַבְּרָכָה וְהַקְּלָלָה וּבָחַרְתָּ בַּחַיִּים
לְמַעַן תִּחְיֶה אַתָּה וְזַרְעֶךָ:

If you truly hearken to the Mitzvot that I command you this day, to love and serve Adonai your God with all your heart and mind, then your God will ordain blessing upon your homes and all your undertakings, and upon the soil on which your God has placed you. Adonai will affirm you as a holy people, when you keep the Mitzvot and walk in the ways of your God.

For this Mitzvah that I command you this day is not too difficult for you; nor is it far away—no, this word is very near you, in your mouth and in your heart—and you can do it. I call heaven and earth to witness before you this day: life and death have I placed before you, blessing and curse. Choose life, then, that you and your children may live.
(Deuteronomy 11:13; 28:8-9; 30:11,14,19)

גְּאוּלָה REDEMPTION

אֱמֶת וְיַצִּיב וְיָשָׁר וְקַיָּם וְטוֹב וְיָפֶה הַדָּבָר הַזֶּה
עָלֵינוּ לְעוֹלָם וָעֶד.

True, enduring, good, and beautiful are these words, now and forever.

אֱמֶת שָׁאַתָּה הוּא יי אֱלֹהֵינוּ וֵאלֹהֵי אֲבוֹתֵינוּ וְאִמּוֹתֵינוּ, מַלְכֵּנוּ
מֶלֶךְ אֲבוֹתֵינוּ וְאִמּוֹתֵינוּ, יוֹצְרֵנוּ צוּר יְשׁוּעָתֵנוּ, פּוֹדֵנוּ וּמַצִּילֵנוּ
מֵעוֹלָם הוּא שְׁמֶךָ, אֵין אֱלֹהִים זוּלָתֶךָ. אֱמֶת אַתָּה הוּא רִאשׁוֹן
וְאַתָּה הוּא אַחֲרוֹן, וּמִבַּלְעָדֶיךָ אֵין לָנוּ מוֹשִׁיעַ. מִמִּצְרַיִם
גְּאַלְתָּנוּ, יי אֱלֹהֵינוּ, וּמִבֵּית עֲבָדִים פְּדִיתָנוּ. מֹשֶׁה וּמִרְיָם וּבְנֵי
יִשְׂרָאֵל לְךָ עָנוּ שִׁירָה בְּשִׂמְחָה רַבָּה, וְאָמְרוּ כֻלָּם:

True it is that You are our sovereign God, as You were the God of our ancestors; You are our maker, the rock of our salvation. We have known You always as our helper and savior; there is no God but You. Truly You are the first and the last, and we have no redeemer but You.

Out of Egypt You delivered us; You freed us from the house of bondage. Then, with great joy, Moses, Miriam, and all Israel sang this song to You:

Looking back at our first redemption from bondage, our people concluded that they could hope and expect a redemption that would last for all time. The hope remains—along with the task of doing our share of the work of redemption.

❧ See page 348, foot of page, and Psalm 3 (page 358).

137

מִי־כָמֹֽכָה בָּאֵלִם, יהוה?   *Mi cha-mo-cha ba-ei-lim, Adonai?*

מִי כָּמֹֽכָה, נֶאְדָּר בַּקֹּֽדֶשׁ,   *Mi ka-mo-cha, neh-dar ba-ko-desh,*

נוֹרָא תְהִלֹּת, עֹשֵׂה פֶֽלֶא?   *no-ra t'hi-lot, o-sei feh-leh?*

שִׁירָה חֲדָשָׁה שִׁבְּחוּ   *Shi-ra cha-da-sha shi-b'chu*

גְאוּלִים לְשִׁמְךָ עַל־שְׂפַת   *g'u-lim l'shi-m'cha al s'fat*

הַיָּם; יַֽחַד כֻּלָּם הוֹדוּ   *ha-yam; ya-chad ku-lam ho-du*

וְהִמְלִֽיכוּ וְאָמְרוּ:   *v'him-li-chu v'a-m'ru:*

יהוה יִמְלֹךְ לְעֹלָם וָעֶד!   *Adonai yim-loch l'o-lam va-ed!*

צוּר יִשְׂרָאֵל, קוּמָה   *Tzur Yis-ra-eil, ku-mah*

בְּעֶזְרַת יִשְׂרָאֵל, וּפְדֵה   *b'ez-rat Yis-ra-eil, u-f'dei*

כִנְאֻמֶֽךָ יְהוּדָה וְיִשְׂרָאֵל.   *chi-n'u-meh-cha Y'hu-da v'Yis-ra-eil.*

גֹּאֲלֵֽנוּ, יי צְבָאוֹת שְׁמוֹ,   *Go-a-lei-nu, Adonai Tz'va-ot sh'mo,*

קְדוֹשׁ יִשְׂרָאֵל. בָּרוּךְ   *k'dosh Yis-ra-eil. Ba-ruch*

אַתָּה יי, גָּאַל יִשְׂרָאֵל.   *a-ta Adonai, ga-al Yis-ra-eil.*

Who is like You, Adonai, among all that is worshiped? Who is like You, glorious in holiness, awesome in splendor, doing wonders?

A new song the redeemed sang to Your name at the shore of the sea. With one voice they gave thanks and proclaimed Your sovereign power: "Adonai shall reign forever and ever."

O Rock of Israel, rise up and help us. Keep Your promise to redeem Your people Israel. Our redeemer is the God of all being, the Holy One of Israel. We praise You, O God, redeemer of Israel.

A REFLECTION

&

הַשְׁמִיעֵנִי בַבֹּקֶר חַסְדֶּךָ, כִּי־בְךָ
בָטָחְתִּי. הוֹדִיעֵנִי דֶּרֶךְ־זוּ אֵלֵךְ;
הַדְרִיכֵנִי בַאֲמִתֶּךָ וְלַמְּדֵנִי,
כִּי־אַתָּה אֱלֹהֵי יִשְׁעִי, אוֹתְךָ
קִוִּיתִי כָּל־הַיּוֹם. שְׁלַח־אוֹרְךָ
וַאֲמִתְּךָ: הֵמָּה יַנְחוּנִי; יְבִיאוּנִי
אֶל־הַר־קָדְשְׁךָ וְאֶל־מִשְׁכְּנוֹתֶיךָ.
לֵב טָהוֹר בְּרָא־לִי, אֱלֹהִים,
וְרוּחַ נָכוֹן חַדֵּשׁ בְּקִרְבִּי.

Reveal Your lovingkindness in the morning, O God in whom my trust abides. Let me know the way I should go; guide me in Your truth and teach me, God of my salvation, my constant hope. Send forth Your light and Your truth: they will lead me; they will bring me to Your holy mountain, to Your dwelling-place. Create in me a clean heart, O God, and renew a willing spirit within me.

&

ALL RISE

תפלה TEFILAH

אֲדֹנָי שְׂפָתַי תִּפְתָּח, וּפִי יַגִּיד תְּהִלָּתֶךָ.

Eternal God, open my lips, and my mouth will declare Your praise.

אבות ואמהות GOD OF ALL GENERATIONS

The Tefilah for
Shabbat
Shuvah, Chol
Ha-Moeid,
Chanukah, and
Rosh Chodesh
is on page 270.

בָּרוּךְ אַתָּה יי, אֱלֹהֵינוּ
Ba-ruch a-ta Adonai, Eh-lo-hei-nu

וֵאלֹהֵי אֲבוֹתֵינוּ וְאִמּוֹתֵינוּ:
vei-lo-hei a-vo-tei-nu v'i-mo-tei-nu:

אֱלֹהֵי אַבְרָהָם, אֱלֹהֵי
Eh-lo-hei Av-ra-ham, eh-lo-hei

יִצְחָק וֵאלֹהֵי יַעֲקֹב:
Yitz-chak, vei-lo-hei Ya-a-kov.

אֱלֹהֵי שָׂרָה, אֱלֹהֵי רִבְקָה,
Eh-lo-hei Sa-rah, eh-lo-hei Riv-kah,

אֱלֹהֵי לֵאָה וֵאלֹהֵי רָחֵל;
eh-lo-hei Lei-ah, vei-lo-hei Ra-cheil.

הָאֵל הַגָּדוֹל הַגִּבּוֹר
Ha-eil ha-ga-dol ha-gi-bor

וְהַנּוֹרָא, אֵל עֶלְיוֹן. גּוֹמֵל
v'ha-no-ra, eil el-yon. Go-meil

חֲסָדִים טוֹבִים, וְקוֹנֵה הַכֹּל,
cha-sa-dim to-vim, v'ko-nei ha-kol,

וְזוֹכֵר חַסְדֵי אָבוֹת וְאִמָּהוֹת,
v'zo-cheir chas-dei a-vot v'i-ma-hot,

וּמֵבִיא גְאֻלָּה לִבְנֵי בְנֵיהֶם,
u-mei-vi g'u-la li-v'nei v'nei-hem,

לְמַעַן שְׁמוֹ בְּאַהֲבָה. מֶלֶךְ
l'ma-an sh'mo, b'a-ha-vah. Meh-lech

עוֹזֵר וּמוֹשִׁיעַ וּמָגֵן.
o-zeir u-mo-shi-a u-ma-gein.

בָּרוּךְ אַתָּה יי,
Ba-ruch a-ta Adonai,

מָגֵן אַבְרָהָם וְעֶזְרַת שָׂרָה.
ma-gein Av-ra-ham v'ez-rat Sa-rah.

The Shabbat
Tefilah has
seven prayers.
In the first, we
recall with
reverence the
founders of
our people and
faith. We say:
Each
generation
finds its own
way, and
yet—their God
is ours.

✤ See "Looking
for God,"
pages 352-357.

We praise You, Adonai our God and God of our ancestors: of Abraham, Isaac, and Jacob; of Sarah, Rebekah, Leah, and Rachel; the great, mighty, and awesome God, God Most High. You deal kindly with us and embrace us all. You remember the faithfulness of our ancestors, and in love bring redemption to their children's children for the sake of Your name. You are our sovereign and helper, our redeemer and shield. We praise You, Adonai, Shield of Abraham and Protector of Sarah.

גבורות   GOD'S POWER

In this prayer,
we affirm the
power of God,
whose reach
extends to this
world—the
world we walk
in—and to a
world we
cannot
imagine.

❧ See Psalm
103 (page 366)
and Psalm 146
(page 371).

אַתָּה גִבּוֹר לְעוֹלָם, אֲדֹנָי,

A-ta gi-bor l'o-lam, Adonai,

מְחַיֵּה מֵתִים אַתָּה, רַב

m'cha-yei mei-tim a-ta, rav

לְהוֹשִׁיעַ.

l'ho-shi-a. Ma-shiv ha-ru-ach

מַשִּׁיב הָרוּחַ וּמוֹרִיד הַגֶּשֶׁם,

u-mo-rid ha-ga-shem; maz-ri-ach

מַזְרִיחַ הַשֶּׁמֶשׁ וּמוֹרִיד הַטָּל.

ha-she-mesh u-mo-rid ha-tal.

מְכַלְכֵּל חַיִּים בְּחֶסֶד,

M'chal-keil cha-yim b'cheh-sed,

מְחַיֵּה מֵתִים בְּרַחֲמִים רַבִּים.

m'cha-yei mei-tim b'ra-cha-mim

סוֹמֵךְ נוֹפְלִים, וְרוֹפֵא

ra-bim. So-meich no-f'lim, v'ro-fei

חוֹלִים, וּמַתִּיר אֲסוּרִים,

cho-lim, u-ma-tir a-su-rim,

וּמְקַיֵּם אֱמוּנָתוֹ לִישֵׁנֵי עָפָר.

u-m'ka-yeim eh-mu-na-to li-shei-nei

מִי כָמְוֹךָ, בַּעַל גְּבוּרוֹת, וּמִי

a-far. Mi cha-mo-cha ba-al g'vu-rot,

דְוֹמֶה לָךְ, מֶלֶךְ מֵמִית וּמְחַיֶּה

u-mi do-meh lach, meh-lech mei-mit

וּמַצְמִיחַ יְשׁוּעָה? וְנֶאֱמָן

u-m'cha-yeh u-matz-mi-ach y'shu-a?

אַתָּה לְהַחֲיוֹת מֵתִים.

V'neh-eh-man a-ta l'ha-cha-yot

בָּרוּךְ אַתָּה יי, מְחַיֵּה

mei-tim. Ba-ruch a-ta Adonai,

הַמֵּתִים.

m'cha-yei ha-mei-tim.

Unending is Your might, Eternal One; You are the source of eternal life;
great is Your power to save. You cause the wind to blow and the rain to
fall, the sun to shine and the dew to descend.

In Your love You sustain the living; in Your compassion You grant us
eternal life. You support the falling and heal the sick; You free the
captive and keep faith with those who sleep in the dust.

Who is like You, source of all strength? Who is Your equal, sovereign
author of life and death, who causes deliverance to flower in our world?

Trusting in You, we see life beyond death.

We praise You, O God, source of eternal life.

קְדוּשָׁה SANCTIFICATION

נְקַדֵּשׁ אֶת־שִׁמְךָ בָּעוֹלָם, כְּשֵׁם שֶׁמַּקְדִּישִׁים אוֹתוֹ
בִּשְׁמֵי מָרוֹם, כַּכָּתוּב עַל־יַד נְבִיאֶךָ:
וְקָרָא זֶה אֶל־זֶה וְאָמַר:

We hallow Your name on earth, even as all creation, to the
highest heavens, proclaims Your holiness, and in the words
of the prophet we say:

קָדוֹשׁ, קָדוֹשׁ, קָדוֹשׁ יהוה צְבָאוֹת,
מְלֹא כָל־הָאָרֶץ כְּבוֹדוֹ.

Holy, holy, holy is the God of all being! The whole earth is filled
with Your glory!

אַדִּיר אַדִּירֵנוּ, יהוה אֲדֹנֵינוּ, מָה־אַדִּיר שִׁמְךָ בְּכָל־הָאָרֶץ!

God our strength, God of mercy, how majestic is Your name
in all the earth!

בָּרוּךְ כְּבוֹד־יהוה מִמְּקוֹמוֹ.

Praised be the glory of God in heaven and earth.

אֶחָד הוּא אֱלֹהֵינוּ, הוּא אָבִינוּ, הוּא מַלְכֵּנוּ, הוּא מוֹשִׁיעֵנוּ;
וְהוּא יַשְׁמִיעֵנוּ בְּרַחֲמָיו לְעֵינֵי כָּל־חָי:

You alone are our God and maker, our ruler and helper; and
in Your mercy You reveal Yourself to us in the sight of all
the living:

אֲנִי יהוה אֱלֹהֵיכֶם!

I AM ADONAI YOUR GOD!

In the
Sanctification,
we echo the awe
and wonder
expressed by
our psalmists,
mystics, and
prophets as they
experienced
God's presence
in their lives.

❊ See pages 352-353 and page 397.

יִמְלֹךְ יהוה לְעוֹלָם, אֱלֹהַיִךְ צִיּוֹן, לְדֹר וָדֹר. הַלְלוּיָהּ!

Adonai shall reign forever; your God, O Zion, from generation to generation. Halleluyah!

לְדוֹר וָדוֹר נַגִּיד גָּדְלֶךָ, וּלְנֵצַח נְצָחִים קְדֻשָּׁתְךָ נַקְדִּישׁ. וְשִׁבְחֲךָ, אֱלֹהֵינוּ, מִפִּינוּ לֹא יָמוּשׁ לְעוֹלָם וָעֶד.

From generation to generation we will make known Your greatness, and to all eternity proclaim Your holiness. Your praise, O God, shall never depart from our lips.

בָּרוּךְ אַתָּה יי, הָאֵל הַקָּדוֹשׁ.

We praise You, Adonai, the holy God.

ALL ARE SEATED

קְדוּשַׁת הַיּוֹם **THE HOLINESS OF SHABBAT**

EITHER

וְשָׁמְרוּ **THE COVENANT OF SHABBAT**

וְשָׁמְרוּ בְנֵי־יִשְׂרָאֵל אֶת־הַשַּׁבָּת, לַעֲשׂוֹת אֶת־הַשַּׁבָּת לְדֹרֹתָם בְּרִית עוֹלָם. בֵּינִי וּבֵין בְּנֵי יִשְׂרָאֵל אוֹת הִיא לְעֹלָם. כִּי־שֵׁשֶׁת יָמִים עָשָׂה יהוה אֶת־הַשָּׁמַיִם וְאֶת־הָאָרֶץ, וּבַיּוֹם הַשְּׁבִיעִי שָׁבַת וַיִּנָּפַשׁ.

We do not
ask for
material
blessings
on the day
devoted to
God.
The gifts
we seek on
Shabbat
are spiritual.

V'sha-m'ru v'nei Yis-ra-eil et ha-Shabbat, la-a-sot et ha-Shabbat l'do-ro-tam, b'rit o-lam. Bei-ni u-vein b'nei Yis-ra-eil ot hi l'o-lam. Ki shei-shet ya-mim a-sa Adonai et ha-sha-ma-yim v'et ha-a-retz, u-va-yom ha-sh'vi-i sha-vat va-yi-na-fash.

The people of Israel shall keep the Sabbath, observing the Sabbath in every generation as a covenant forever. It is a sign between me and the people of Israel forever. For in six days Adonai made heaven and earth, but on the seventh day God rested and was refreshed.

OR

ישמחו MOST PRECIOUS OF DAYS

יִשְׂמְחוּ בְמַלְכוּתְךָ שׁוֹמְרֵי שַׁבָּת וְקוֹרְאֵי עֹנֶג.
עַם מְקַדְּשֵׁי שְׁבִיעִי כֻּלָם יִשְׂבְּעוּ וְיִתְעַנְּגוּ מִטּוּבֶךָ.
וְהַשְּׁבִיעִי רָצִיתָ בּוֹ וְקִדַּשְׁתּוֹ. חֶמְדַּת יָמִים אוֹתוֹ קָרָאתָ,
זֵכֶר לְמַעֲשֵׂה בְרֵאשִׁית.

Yis-m'chu v'ma-l'chu-t'cha sho-m'rei Shabbat v'ko-r'ei o-neg.
Am m'ka-d'shei sh'vi-i ku-lam yis-b'u v'yit-a-n'gu mi-tu-veh-cha.
V'ha-sh'vi-i ra-tzi-ta bo v'ki-dash-to. Chem-dat ya-mim o-to ka-ra-ta,
zei-cher l'ma-a-sei v'rei-sheet.

Those who keep the Sabbath and call it a delight shall rejoice in Your
sovereign presence. All who hallow the seventh day shall taste the joy of
Your bounty. This is the day You delight in and sanctify. "Loveliest of
days," You have called it, "a reminder of the work of creation."

אֱלֹהֵינוּ וֵאלֹהֵי אֲבוֹתֵינוּ וְאִמּוֹתֵינוּ, רְצֵה בִמְנוּחָתֵנוּ.

Our God, God of our fathers and mothers, may our Sabbath
rest be pleasing in Your sight.

קַדְּשֵׁנוּ בְּמִצְוֹתֶיךָ וְתֵן חֶלְקֵנוּ בְּתוֹרָתֶךָ.
שַׂבְּעֵנוּ מִטּוּבֶךָ, וְשַׂמְּחֵנוּ בִּישׁוּעָתֶךָ,
וְטַהֵר לִבֵּנוּ לְעָבְדְּךָ בֶּאֱמֶת.
וְהַנְחִילֵנוּ, יְיָ אֱלֹהֵינוּ, בְּאַהֲבָה וּבְרָצוֹן
שַׁבַּת קָדְשֶׁךָ, וְיָנוּחוּ בָהּ יִשְׂרָאֵל מְקַדְּשֵׁי שְׁמֶךָ.

Ka-d'shei-nu b'mitz-vo-teh-cha v-tein chel-kei-nu b'toh-ra-teh-cha.
Sab-ei-nu mi-tu-veh-cha, v'sam-chei-nu bi-shu-a-teh-cha,
v'ta-heir li-bei-nu l-ov-d'cha beh-eh-met.
V'han-chi-lei-nu, Adonai Eh-lo-hei-nu, b'a-ha-va u-v'ra-tzon
Shabbat kod-sheh-cha, v'ya-nu-chu va Yis-ra-eil m'ka-d'shei sh'meh-cha.

Sanctify us with Your Mitzvot, and make Your Torah our life's portion. Satisfy us with Your goodness, gladden us with Your salvation, and purify our hearts to serve You in truth. In Your gracious love, Adonai our God, let the holiness of Shabbat enter our hearts, that all Israel, hallowing Your name, may find rest and peace.

בָּרוּךְ אַתָּה יי, מְקַדֵּשׁ הַשַׁבָּת.

We praise You, the God who hallows Shabbat.

עבודה WORSHIP

We pray now that our prayer be acceptable! And at all times, we pray for the insight that God is with us, now and always—for that truly is the answer to our prayers.

❀ See "Prayer and Its Value," pages 3-5.

רְצֵה, יי אֱלֹהֵינוּ, בְּעַמְּךָ יִשְׂרָאֵל, וּתְפִלָּתָם בְּאַהֲבָה תְקַבֵּל, וּתְהִי לְרָצוֹן תָּמִיד עֲבוֹדַת יִשְׂרָאֵל עַמֶּךָ.

Look with favor, Adonai our God, upon Your people Israel, and with love accept our prayers. May our worship ever be worthy of Your favor.

אֵל קָרוֹב לְכָל־קֹרְאָיו,
פְּנֵה אֶל עֲבָדֶיךָ וְחָנֵנוּ; שְׁפוֹךְ רוּחֲךָ עָלֵינוּ,
וְתֶחֱזֶינָה עֵינֵינוּ בְּשׁוּבְךָ לְצִיּוֹן בְּרַחֲמִים.

O God near to every seeker,
turn to Your servants and show us grace.
Shower Your spirit upon us,
and let Zion and all Israel behold
Your compassionate presence.

בָּרוּךְ אַתָּה יי, הַמַּחֲזִיר שְׁכִינָתוֹ לְצִיּוֹן.

We praise You, Adonai, whose presence restores Zion and all Israel.

145

הודאה   THANKSGIVING

A PERSONAL PRAYER OF THANKSGIVING

מוֹדִים אֲנַחְנוּ לָךְ שָׁאַתָּה הוּא יי אֱלֹהֵינוּ וֵאלֹהֵי אֲבוֹתֵינוּ

וְאִמּוֹתֵינוּ, אֱלֹהֵי כָל־בָּשָׂר, יוֹצְרֵנוּ יוֹצֵר בְּרֵאשִׁית. בְּרָכוֹת

וְהוֹדָאוֹת לְשִׁמְךָ הַגָּדוֹל וְהַקָּדוֹשׁ עַל־שֶׁהֶחֱיִיתָנוּ וְקִיַּמְתָּנוּ.

כֵּן תְּחַיֵּנוּ וּתְקַיְּמֵנוּ, יי אֱלֹהֵינוּ, וְתֶאֶסֹף גָּלֻיוֹתֵינוּ לְשָׁמְרֵ חֻקֶּיךָ,

לַעֲשׂוֹת רְצוֹנֶךָ, וּלְעָבְדְּךָ בְּלֵבָב שָׁלֵם. בָּרוּךְ אֵל הַהוֹדָאוֹת.

We affirm with gratitude that You, Adonai, are our God, the God of our fathers and mothers, the God of all flesh, our creator, the source of all being. We bless and praise Your great and holy name, for keeping us in life and sustaining us. Continue us in life and sustain us, Adonai our God; strengthen us to observe Your laws, to do Your will, and to serve You with a whole heart.

THE PUBLIC PRAYER OF THANKSGIVING

מוֹדִים אֲנַחְנוּ לָךְ, שָׁאַתָּה הוּא יי אֱלֹהֵינוּ

וֵאלֹהֵי אֲבוֹתֵינוּ וְאִמּוֹתֵינוּ לְעוֹלָם וָעֶד.

צוּר חַיֵּינוּ, מָגֵן יִשְׁעֵנוּ, אַתָּה הוּא לְדוֹר וָדוֹר.

Gratefully we acknowledge that You, Adonai, are our God, the God of our fathers and our mothers, our God forever. In every age You are the rock of our life, our protecting shield.

Every breath is precious and every moment a gift. Our tradition teaches us gratitude: to be thankful for the gift of our life, its joys— and even for our sorrows.

❖ See "Giving Thanks," page 398, and Psalm 147 (page 372).

נוֹדֶה לְךָ וּנְסַפֵּר תְּהִלָּתֶךָ, עַל־חַיֵּינוּ הַמְּסוּרִים בְּיָדֶךָ,

וְעַל־נִשְׁמוֹתֵינוּ הַפְּקוּדוֹת לָךְ, וְעַל־נִסֶּיךָ שֶׁבְּכָל־יוֹם עִמָּנוּ,

וְעַל־נִפְלְאוֹתֶיךָ וְטוֹבוֹתֶיךָ שֶׁבְּכָל־עֵת, עֶרֶב וָבֹקֶר וְצָהֳרָיִם.

הַטּוֹב: כִּי לֹא־כָלוּ רַחֲמֶיךָ, וְהַמְרַחֵם: כִּי־לֹא תַמּוּ חֲסָדֶיךָ,

מֵעוֹלָם קִוִּינוּ לָךְ.

וְעַל כֻּלָּם יִתְבָּרַךְ וְיִתְרוֹמַם שִׁמְךָ, מַלְכֵּנוּ, תָּמִיד לְעוֹלָם וָעֶד.

וְכֹל הַחַיִּים יוֹדוּךָ סֶּלָה, וִיהַלְלוּ אֶת־שִׁמְךָ בֶּאֱמֶת,

הָאֵל יְשׁוּעָתֵנוּ וְעֶזְרָתֵנוּ סֶלָה.

We thank You and sing Your praises: for our lives, which are in Your hand; for our souls, which are in Your keeping; for the signs of Your presence we encounter every day; and for Your wondrous gifts at all times, morning, noon, and night.

Source of goodness, Your mercies do not end; Compassionate One, Your kindness does not fail. From of old You have been our hope.

For all these gifts, let Your name ever be exalted in praise.

Let all the living affirm You and in faithfulness give thanks to Your name, O God our deliverer and help!

בָּרוּךְ אַתָּה יְיָ, הַטּוֹב שִׁמְךָ וּלְךָ נָאֶה לְהוֹדוֹת.

We praise You Adonai, source of good, to whom our thanks are due.

PEACE ברכת שלום

שִׂים שָׁלוֹם, טוֹבָה וּבְרָכָה, חֵן וָחֶסֶד וְרַחֲמִים,
עָלֵינוּ וְעַל כָּל־יִשְׂרָאֵל עַמֶּךָ.
בָּרְכֵנוּ, אָבִינוּ, כֻּלָּנוּ כְּאֶחָד בְּאוֹר פָּנֶיךָ,
כִּי בְאוֹר פָּנֶיךָ נָתַתָּ לָּנוּ, יְיָ אֱלֹהֵינוּ,
תּוֹרַת חַיִּים, וְאַהֲבַת חֶסֶד,
וּצְדָקָה וּבְרָכָה וְרַחֲמִים וְחַיִּים וְשָׁלוֹם.
וְטוֹב בְּעֵינֶיךָ לְבָרֵךְ אֶת־עַמְּךָ יִשְׂרָאֵל
וְאֶת־כָּל־הָעַמִּים בְּכָל־עֵת וּבְכָל־שָׁעָה בִּשְׁלוֹמֶךָ.

In our prayer for peace we pray for our people and for all the peoples of the world. Only when all are at peace can we truly say that we are at peace.

❧ See Pirke Avot, pages 324-325, and page 351.

Grant peace, goodness and blessing, grace, love and mercy to us and to all Your people Israel. As a loving parent, bless us with the light of Your presence; for by that light, eternal God, You have revealed to us a Torah to live by: the love of kindness, righteousness, blessing, and mercy, bringing life and peace. For it is good in Your sight that Your people Israel and all peoples be blessed at all times with Your gift of peace.

בָּרוּךְ אַתָּה יְיָ, הַמְּבָרֵךְ אֶת־עַמּוֹ יִשְׂרָאֵל בַּשָּׁלוֹם.

We praise You, O God: You bless Your people Israel with peace.

SILENT PRAYER

אֱלֹהַי, נְצֹר לְשׁוֹנִי מֵרָע, וּשְׂפָתַי מִדַּבֵּר מִרְמָה. וְלִמְקַלְלַי נַפְשִׁי
תִדּוֹם וְנַפְשִׁי כֶּעָפָר לַכֹּל תִּהְיֶה. פְּתַח לִבִּי בְּתוֹרָתֶךָ, וּבְמִצְוֹתֶיךָ
תִּרְדּוֹף נַפְשִׁי. עֲשֵׂה לְמַעַן שְׁמֶךָ, עֲשֵׂה לְמַעַן יְמִינֶךָ, עֲשֵׂה
לְמַעַן קְדֻשָּׁתֶךָ, עֲשֵׂה לְמַעַן תּוֹרָתֶךָ; לְמַעַן יֵחָלְצוּן יְדִידֶיךָ,
הוֹשִׁיעָה יְמִינְךָ וַעֲנֵנִי.

My God, keep my tongue from evil, my lips from deceptive speech. In the face of malice give me a quiet spirit; let me be humble wherever I go. Open my heart to Your teaching, make me eager to fulfill Your Mitzvot. Then will Your name be exalted, Your might manifest, Your holiness visible, Your Torah magnified. Inspire me to love You, and be the answer to my prayer.

REFLECTIONS

1

☾ You have called me into life, setting me in the midst of purposes I cannot measure or fully understand. Yet I thank You for the good I know, for the life I have, and for the gifts that—in sickness and in health—have been my daily portion: the beauty of earth and sky, the visions that have stirred me from my ease to quicken my endeavors, the demands of truth and justice that move me to acts of goodness, and the contemplation of Your eternal presence, which fill me with hope that what is good and lovely cannot perish. For all these gifts, I give thanks.

2

☾ Your word comes in stillness, and as I hear it, it comes to me alone. I cannot pretend that I need not respond with all my heart and soul because the commandment is meant for my neighbor: I am my neighbor, my nearest neighbor!

3

☾ There is the laughter that is born out of the pure joy of living, the spontaneous expression of health and energy—the sweet laughter of the child. This is a gift of God. There is the warm laughter of the kindly soul that heartens the discouraged, gives health to the sick and comfort to the dying. . . . There is, above all, the laughter that comes from the eternal joy of creation, the joy of making the world new, the joy of expressing the inner riches of the soul—laughter that triumphs over pain and hardship in the passion for an enduring ideal, the joy of bringing the light of happiness, of truth and beauty into a dark world. This is divine laughter par excellence.

4

❦   On Shabbat I can relax. For a time I can stop running, because I've arrived in time's favored resting-place. Give me this day of rest to realize that much of my restlessness doesn't have to be; and help me to bring some Shabbat rest into the week.

&

יִהְיוּ לְרָצוֹן אִמְרֵי־פִי   *Yi-h'yu l'ra-tzon i-m'rei fi*

וְהֶגְיוֹן לִבִּי לְפָנֶיךָ,   *v'heg-yon li-bi l'fa-neh-cha,*

יהוה, צוּרִי וְגֹאֲלִי.   *Adonai tzu-ri v'go-a-li.*

May the words of my mouth and the meditations of my heart be acceptable to You, O God, my rock and my redeemer. Amen.

&

עֹשֶׂה שָׁלוֹם בִּמְרוֹמָיו,   *O-seh sha-lom bi-m'ro-mav,*

הוּא יַעֲשֶׂה שָׁלוֹם עָלֵינוּ   *hu ya-a-seh sha-lom a-lei-nu*

וְעַל־כָּל־יִשְׂרָאֵל, וְאִמְרוּ:   *v'al kol Yis-ra-eil, v'i-m'ru:*

אָמֵן.   *A-mein.*

May the source of peace on high send peace to us, to all Israel, and to all the world, and let us say: Amen.

THE LITURGY FOR THE READING OF TORAH
BEGINS ON PAGE 168 OR PAGE 169

AFTERNOON SERVICE FOR SHABBAT AND YOM TOV

אַשְׁרֵי

PSALMS 84:5 AND 14:15

אַשְׁרֵי יוֹשְׁבֵי בֵיתֶךָ, עוֹד יְהַלְלוּךָ סֶּלָה.

אַשְׁרֵי הָעָם שֶׁכָּכָה לּוֹ; אַשְׁרֵי הָעָם שֶׁיהוה אֱלֹהָיו.

Happy are those who dwell in Your house,
who continually sing Your praises.

Happy the people who are so blessed;
happy the people whose God You are.

FROM PSALM 145

A PSALM OF DAVID   תְּהִלָּה לְדָוִד

אֲרוֹמִמְךָ, אֱלוֹהַי הַמֶּלֶךְ, וַאֲבָרְכָה שִׁמְךָ לְעוֹלָם וָעֶד.

בְּכָל־יוֹם אֲבָרְכֶךָּ, וַאֲהַלְלָה שִׁמְךָ לְעוֹלָם וָעֶד.

Always we exalt You, and praise Your name forever.

Because *You are our maker, we extol Your name forever.*

גָּדוֹל יהוה וּמְהֻלָּל מְאֹד, וְלִגְדֻלָּתוֹ אֵין חֵקֶר.

דּוֹר לְדוֹר יְשַׁבַּח מַעֲשֶׂיךָ, וּגְבוּרֹתֶיךָ יַגִּידוּ.

Calling us to greatness, Eternal One, You teach us.

Declaring *Your works tremendous, we witness to Your power.*

The English text can be chanted as the Hebrew might be.

A PRAYER BEFORE PRAYER: May my worship on this Shabbat encourage me to fulfill this precept: "Guard your tongue from evil, and your lips from deceitful speech. Seek peace and pursue it." (Psalm 34:14)

✽ See "A Daily Psalm," pages 27-33, and "Selected Psalms," pages 358-375.

151

הֲדַר כְּבוֹד הוֹדֶךָ, וְדִבְרֵי נִפְלְאוֹתֶיךָ אָשִׂיחָה.

וֶעֱזוּז נוֹרְאוֹתֶיךָ יֹאמֵרוּ, וּגְדֻלָּתְךָ אֲסַפְּרֶנָּה.

Ever we tell Your glory, the wonder of Your mercies.

For as we praise Your marvels, so we laud Your greatness.

זֵכֶר רַב־טוּבְךָ יַבִּיעוּ, וְצִדְקָתְךָ יְרַנֵּנוּ.

חַנּוּן וְרַחוּם יהוה, אֶרֶךְ אַפַּיִם וּגְדָל־חָסֶד.

Great the good we honor, singing of Your justice.

Holding us in kindness, in love You are abounding.

טוֹב־יהוה לַכֹּל, וְרַחֲמָיו עַל־כָּל־מַעֲשָׂיו.

יוֹדוּךָ יהוה כָּל־מַעֲשֶׂיךָ, וַחֲסִידֶיךָ יְבָרְכוּכָה.

In Your boundless goodness, You teach Your creatures mercy.

Joyful, we all thank You; Your faithful ones shall praise You.

כְּבוֹד מַלְכוּתְךָ יֹאמֵרוּ, וּגְבוּרָתְךָ יְדַבֵּרוּ,

לְהוֹדִיעַ לִבְנֵי הָאָדָם גְּבוּרֹתָיו, וּכְבוֹד הֲדַר מַלְכוּתוֹ.

Knowing that You are sovereign, we all proclaim Your splendor.

Let all perceive Your power, the triumph of Your wisdom.

מַלְכוּתְךָ מַלְכוּת כָּל־עֹלָמִים, וּמֶמְשַׁלְתְּךָ בְּכָל־דּוֹר וָדוֹר.

סוֹמֵךְ יהוה לְכָל־הַנֹּפְלִים, וְזוֹקֵף לְכָל־הַכְּפוּפִים.

Majestic, You rule in glory; Your reign endures forever.

O God, support the helpless, and raise up all the fallen.

152

עֵינֵי־כֹל אֵלֶיךָ יְשַׂבֵּרוּ, וְאַתָּה נוֹתֵן־לָהֶם אֶת־אָכְלָם בְּעִתּוֹ.
פּוֹתֵחַ אֶת־יָדֶךָ וּמַשְׂבִּיעַ לְכָל־חַי רָצוֹן.

Pleading, they implore You; in their need, pray feed them.
  Q*uick Your hand be open, to comfort every creature.*

צַדִּיק יהוה בְּכָל־דְּרָכָיו, וְחָסִיד בְּכָל־מַעֲשָׂיו.
קָרוֹב יְהֹוָה לְכָל־קֹרְאָיו, לְכֹל אֲשֶׁר יִקְרָאֻהוּ בֶאֱמֶת.

Righteous are You always, loving in Your actions.
  S*o near to all who call You, to all who call upon You.*

רְצוֹן־יְרֵאָיו יַעֲשֶׂה, וְאֶת־שַׁוְעָתָם יִשְׁמַע וְיוֹשִׁיעֵם.
תְּהִלַּת יהוה יְדַבֶּר־פִּי וִיבָרֵךְ כָּל־בָּשָׂר
שֵׁם קָדְשׁוֹ לְעוֹלָם וָעֶד.

Those who seek You, call You; You hear their cry and help
them.
  U*nceasing, our lips sing praise-songs; rejoicing in You forever.*

PSALM 115:18

וַאֲנַחְנוּ נְבָרֵךְ יָהּ מֵעַתָּה וְעַד־עוֹלָם. הַלְלוּיָהּ!

And now let us extol the eternal God from this time and
forever. Halleluyah!

❧

בָּרוּךְ יְיָ, יוֹם יוֹם יַעֲמָס
לָנוּ; הָאֵל יְשׁוּעָתֵנוּ, סֶלָה.

We give You thanks, O God our helper: day by day You uphold us.

יְהִי רָצוֹן מִלְּפָנֶיךָ, יְיָ אֱלֹהֵינוּ
וֵאלֹהֵי אֲבוֹתֵינוּ וְאִמּוֹתֵינוּ,
שֶׁנִּשְׁמוֹר חֻקֶּיךָ בָּעוֹלָם הַזֶּה,
וְנִזְכֶּה וְנִחְיֶה וְנִרְאֶה, וְנִירַשׁ
טוֹבָה וּבְרָכָה, לִשְׁנֵי יְמוֹת
הַגְּאוּלָה, וּלְחַיֵּי הָעוֹלָם הַבָּא.

Adonai our God and God of our ancestors, may we abide by Your precepts in our daily lives, and prove worthy of a life filled with goodness; bless us with the will to redeem the world from its many ills, and may our vision of the world to come bring us joy.

כֹּה־אָמַר יְהוָה גֹּאֲלֵךְ, קְדוֹשׁ
יִשְׂרָאֵל: וַאֲנִי זֹאת בְּרִיתִי
אוֹתָם, אָמַר יְהוָה: רוּחִי אֲשֶׁר
עָלֶיךָ, וּדְבָרַי אֲשֶׁר־שַׂמְתִּי
בְּפִיךָ, לֹא־יָמוּשׁוּ מִפִּיךָ, וּמִפִּי
זַרְעֲךָ, וּמִפִּי זֶרַע זַרְעֲךָ, אָמַר
יְהוָה, מֵעַתָּה וְעַד־עוֹלָם.

Thus says Adonai your redeemer, the Holy One of Israel: This is my covenant with them: my spirit that is within you, and the words that I have put in your mouth, shall not depart from your lips, or from those of your children or children's children, from now until the end of time.

בָּרוּךְ אֱלֹהֵינוּ שֶׁבְּרָאָנוּ לִכְבוֹדוֹ, וּקְרָאָנוּ לַעֲבוֹדָתוֹ, וְנָתַן לָנוּ
תּוֹרַת אֱמֶת, וְחַיֵּי עוֹלָם נָטַע בְּתוֹכֵנוּ. הוּא יִפְתַּח לִבֵּנוּ בְּתוֹרָתוֹ,
וְיָשֵׂם בְּלִבֵּנוּ אַהֲבָתוֹ וְיִרְאָתוֹ, וְלַעֲשׂוֹת רְצוֹנוֹ בְּלֵבָב שָׁלֵם.

We praise You, our God: You have created us for Your glory, called us to Your service, given us true teachings, and implanted within us eternal life. May our minds be open to Your teaching, filling us with love and reverence, that we may ever do Your will with a whole heart.

ALL RISE

חצי קדיש   READER'S KADDISH

יִתְגַּדַּל וְיִתְקַדַּשׁ שְׁמֵהּ רַבָּא בְּעָלְמָא דִי־בְרָא כִרְעוּתֵהּ,
וְיַמְלִיךְ מַלְכוּתֵהּ בְּחַיֵּיכוֹן וּבְיוֹמֵיכוֹן וּבְחַיֵּי דְכָל־בֵּית
יִשְׂרָאֵל, בַּעֲגָלָא וּבִזְמַן קָרִיב, וְאִמְרוּ: אָמֵן.

יְהֵא שְׁמֵהּ רַבָּא מְבָרַךְ לְעָלַם וּלְעָלְמֵי עָלְמַיָּא.

יִתְבָּרַךְ וְיִשְׁתַּבַּח, וְיִתְפָּאַר וְיִתְרוֹמַם וְיִתְנַשֵּׂא, וְיִתְהַדַּר
וְיִתְעַלֶּה וְיִתְהַלָּל שְׁמֵהּ דְּקוּדְשָׁא, בְּרִיךְ הוּא,
לְעֵלָּא מִן־כָּל־בִּרְכָתָא וְשִׁירָתָא, תֻּשְׁבְּחָתָא וְנֶחֱמָתָא
דַּאֲמִירָן בְּעָלְמָא, וְאִמְרוּ: אָמֵן.

Yit-ga-dal v'yit-ka-dash sh'mei ra-ba b'al-ma di-v'ra chi-r'u'tei,
v'yam-lich mal-chu-tei b'cha-yei-chon u-v'yo-mei-chon u-v'cha-yei d'chol beit
Yis-ra-eil, ba-a-ga-la u-vi-z'man ka-riv, v'i-m'ru: A-mein.

Y'hei sh'mei ra-ba m'va-rach l'a-lam u-l'al-mei al-ma-ya.

Yit-ba-rach v'yish-ta-bach, v'yit-pa-ar v'yit-ro-mam v'yit-na-sei, v'yit-ha-dar
v'yit-a-leh v'yit-ha-lal sh'mei d'kud-sha, b'rich hu,
l'ei-la min kol bir-cha-ta v'shi-ra-ta, tush-b'cha-ta v'neh-cheh-ma-ta
da-a-mi-ran b'al-ma, v'i-m'ru: A-mein.

Hallowed be Your great name on earth, Your creation; establish Your dominion in our own day, in our own lives, and in the life of the whole House of Israel. Blessed be Your great name forever and ever. Blessed, praised, honored, and exalted be the name of the Holy One, ever to be praised, though You are beyond all the blessings and songs of praise that the world may offer.

תפלה TEFILAH

אֲדֹנָי שְׂפָתַי תִּפְתָּח, וּפִי יַגִּיד תְּהִלָּתֶךָ.

Eternal God, open my lips, that my mouth may declare Your praise.

אבות ואמהות GOD OF ALL GENERATIONS

<table>
<tr><td>בָּרוּךְ אַתָּה יְיָ, אֱלֹהֵינוּ</td><td>Ba-ruch a-ta Adonai, Eh-lo-hei-nu</td></tr>
<tr><td>וֵאלֹהֵי אֲבוֹתֵינוּ וְאִמּוֹתֵינוּ:</td><td>vei-lo-hei a-vo-tei-nu v'i-mo-tei-nu:</td></tr>
<tr><td>אֱלֹהֵי אַבְרָהָם, אֱלֹהֵי</td><td>Eh-lo-hei Av-ra-ham, eh-lo-hei</td></tr>
<tr><td>יִצְחָק וֵאלֹהֵי יַעֲקֹב:</td><td>Yitz-chak, vei-lo-hei Ya-a-kov.</td></tr>
<tr><td>אֱלֹהֵי שָׂרָה, אֱלֹהֵי רִבְקָה,</td><td>Eh-lo-hei Sa-rah, eh-lo-hei Riv-kah,</td></tr>
<tr><td>אֱלֹהֵי לֵאָה וֵאלֹהֵי רָחֵל;</td><td>eh-lo-hei Lei-ah, vei-lo-hei Ra-cheil.</td></tr>
<tr><td>הָאֵל הַגָּדוֹל הַגִּבּוֹר</td><td>Ha-eil ha-ga-dol ha-gi-bor</td></tr>
<tr><td>וְהַנּוֹרָא, אֵל עֶלְיוֹן. גּוֹמֵל</td><td>v'ha-no-ra, eil el-yon. Go-meil</td></tr>
<tr><td>חֲסָדִים טוֹבִים וְקוֹנֵה הַכֹּל,</td><td>cha-sa-dim to-vim, v'ko-nei ha-kol,</td></tr>
<tr><td>וְזוֹכֵר חַסְדֵי אָבוֹת וְאִמָּהוֹת,</td><td>v'zo-cheir chas-dei a-vot v'i-ma-hot,</td></tr>
<tr><td>וּמֵבִיא גְאֻלָּה לִבְנֵי בְנֵיהֶם,</td><td>u-mei-vi g'u-la li-v'nei v'nei-hem,</td></tr>
<tr><td>לְמַעַן שְׁמוֹ בְּאַהֲבָה. מֶלֶךְ</td><td>l'ma-an sh'mo, b'a-ha-vah. Meh-lech</td></tr>
<tr><td>עוֹזֵר וּמוֹשִׁיעַ וּמָגֵן.</td><td>o-zeir u-mo-shi-a u-ma-gein.</td></tr>
<tr><td>בָּרוּךְ אַתָּה יְיָ,</td><td>Ba-ruch a-ta Adonai,</td></tr>
<tr><td>מָגֵן אַבְרָהָם וְעֶזְרַת שָׂרָה.</td><td>ma-gein Av-ra-ham v'ez-rat Sa-rah.</td></tr>
</table>

We praise You, Adonai our God and God of our ancestors: of Abraham, Isaac, and Jacob; of Sarah, Rebekah, Leah, and Rachel; the great, mighty, and awesome God, God Most High. You deal kindly with us and embrace us all. You remember the faithfulness of our ancestors, and in love bring redemption to their children's children for the sake of Your name. You are our sovereign and helper, our redeemer and shield. We praise You, Adonai, Shield of Abraham and Protector of Sarah.

The Tefilah for Shabbat Shuvah, Chol Ha-Moeid, Chanukah, and Rosh Chodesh is on page 270.

The Shabbat and Yom Tov Tefilah has seven prayers. In the first, we recall with reverence the founders of our people and faith. We say: Each generation finds its own way, and yet—their God is ours.

❋ See "Looking for God," pages 352-357.

156

גבורות   GOD'S POWER

In this prayer, we affirm the power of God, whose reach extends to all worlds, from the world we walk in, to worlds we cannot imagine.

✿ See Psalm 103 (page 366) and Psalm 146 (page 371).

אַתָּה גִבּוֹר לְעוֹלָם, אֲדֹנָי,
A-ta gi-bor l'o-lam, Adonai,

מְחַיֵּה מֵתִים אַתָּה, רַב
m'cha-yei mei-tim a-ta, rav

לְהוֹשִׁיעַ.
l'ho-shi-a. Ma-shiv ha-ru-ach

מַשִּׁיב הָרוּחַ וּמוֹרִיד הַגֶּשֶׁם,
u-mo-rid ha-ga-shem; maz-ri-ach

מַזְרִיחַ הַשֶּׁמֶשׁ וּמוֹרִיד הַטָּל.
ha-she-mesh u-mo-rid ha-tal.

מְכַלְכֵּל חַיִּים בְּחֶסֶד,
M'chal-keil cha-yim b'cheh-sed,

מְחַיֵּה מֵתִים בְּרַחֲמִים רַבִּים.
m'cha-yei mei-tim b'ra-cha-mim

סוֹמֵךְ נוֹפְלִים, וְרוֹפֵא
ra-bim. So-meich no-f'lim, v'ro-fei

חוֹלִים, וּמַתִּיר אֲסוּרִים,
cho-lim, u-ma-tir a-su-rim,

וּמְקַיֵּם אֱמוּנָתוֹ לִישֵׁנֵי עָפָר.
u-m'ka-yeim eh-mu-na-to li-shei-nei

מִי כָמוֹךָ, בַּעַל גְּבוּרוֹת, וּמִי
a-far. Mi cha-mo-cha ba-al g'vu-rot,

דּוֹמֶה לָּךְ, מֶלֶךְ מֵמִית וּמְחַיֵּה
u-mi do-meh lach, meh-lech mei-mit

וּמַצְמִיחַ יְשׁוּעָה? וְנֶאֱמָן
u-m'cha-yeh u-matz-mi-ach y'shu-a?

אַתָּה לְהַחֲיוֹת מֵתִים.
V'neh-eh-man a-ta l'ha-cha-yot

בָּרוּךְ אַתָּה יי, מְחַיֵּה
mei-tim. Ba-ruch a-ta Adonai,

הַמֵּתִים.
m'cha-yei ha-mei-tim.

Unending is Your might, Eternal One; You are the source of eternal life; great is Your power to save. You cause the wind to blow and the rain to fall, the sun to shine and the dew to descend.

In Your love You sustain the living; in Your compassion You grant us eternal life. You support the falling and heal the sick; You free the captive and keep faith with those who sleep in the dust. Who is like You, source of all strength? Who is Your equal, sovereign author of life and death, who causes deliverance to flower in our world?

Trusting in You, we see life beyond death.

We praise You, O God, source of eternal life.

קְדוּשָׁה SANCTIFICATION

נְקַדֵּשׁ אֶת־שִׁמְךָ בָּעוֹלָם, כְּשֵׁם שֶׁמַּקְדִּישִׁים אוֹתוֹ
בִּשְׁמֵי מָרוֹם, כַּכָּתוּב עַל־יַד נְבִיאֶךָ:
וְקָרָא זֶה אֶל־זֶה וְאָמַר:

Wherever we walk, the ground on which we stand is holy.

❖ See Psalm 42/3 (page 363) and Psalm 63 (page 365).

We hallow Your name on earth, even as all creation, to the highest heavens, proclaims Your holiness, and in the words of the prophet we say:

קָדוֹשׁ, קָדוֹשׁ, קָדוֹשׁ יהוה צְבָאוֹת,
מְלֹא כָל־הָאָרֶץ כְּבוֹדוֹ.

Holy, holy, holy is the God of all being! The whole earth is filled with Your glory!

אַדִּיר אַדִּירֵנוּ, יהוה אֲדֹנֵינוּ, מָה־אַדִּיר שִׁמְךָ בְּכָל־הָאָרֶץ!

God our strength, God of mercy, how majestic is Your name in all the earth!

בָּרוּךְ כְּבוֹד־יהוה מִמְּקוֹמוֹ.

Praised be the glory of God in heaven and earth.

אֶחָד הוּא אֱלֹהֵינוּ, הוּא אָבִינוּ, הוּא מַלְכֵּנוּ, הוּא מוֹשִׁיעֵנוּ;
וְהוּא יַשְׁמִיעֵנוּ בְּרַחֲמָיו לְעֵינֵי כָּל־חָי:

You alone are our God and maker, our ruler and helper; and in Your mercy You reveal Yourself to us in the sight of all the living:

אֲנִי יהוה אֱלֹהֵיכֶם!

I AM ADONAI YOUR GOD!

יִמְלֹךְ יהוה לְעוֹלָם, אֱלֹהַיִךְ צִיּוֹן, לְדֹר וָדֹר. הַלְלוּיָהּ!

Adonai shall reign forever; Your God, O Zion, from generation to generation. Halleluyah!

לְדוֹר וָדוֹר נַגִּיד גָּדְלֶךָ, וּלְנֵצַח נְצָחִים קְדֻשָּׁתְךָ נַקְדִּישׁ. וְשִׁבְחֲךָ, אֱלֹהֵינוּ, מִפִּינוּ לֹא יָמוּשׁ לְעוֹלָם וָעֶד.

From generation to generation we will make known Your greatness, and to all eternity proclaim Your holiness. Your praise, O God, shall never depart from our lips.

בָּרוּךְ אַתָּה יְיָ, הָאֵל הַקָּדוֹשׁ.

We praise You, Adonai, the holy God.

ALL ARE SEATED

A REFLECTION

   Three things conspire together in my eyes
to bring the remembrance of You ever before me:
the starry heavens,
the broad green earth,
the depths of my heart. (Solomon ibn Gabirol)

ON YOM TOV, CONTINUE WITH ATA V'CHARTANU ON PAGE 162

קדושת היום   THE HOLINESS OF SHABBAT

אתה אחד   YOU ARE ONE

אַתָּה אֶחָד וְשִׁמְךָ אֶחָד, וּמִי
כְּעַמְּךָ יִשְׂרָאֵל, גּוֹי אֶחָד
בָּאָרֶץ? תִּפְאֶרֶת גְּדֻלָּה
וַעֲטֶרֶת יְשׁוּעָה, יוֹם מְנוּחָה
וּקְדֻשָּׁה לְעַמְּךָ נָתָתָּ. מְנוּחַת
אַהֲבָה וּנְדָבָה, מְנוּחַת אֱמֶת
וֶאֱמוּנָה, מְנוּחַת שָׁלוֹם וְשַׁלְוָה
וְהַשְׁקֵט וָבֶטַח, מְנוּחָה שְׁלֵמָה
שָׁאַתָּה רוֹצֶה בָּהּ. יַכִּירוּ בָנֶיךָ
וְיֵדְעוּ כִּי מֵאִתְּךָ הִיא מְנוּחָתָם,
וְעַל־מְנוּחָתָם יַקְדִּישׁוּ
אֶת־שְׁמֶךָ.

You are one, Your name is one.
Who is like Your people Israel,
a people unique on the earth? A
garland of glory have You
given us, a crown of salvation:
a day of rest and holiness. May
our rest on this day be one of
love and devotion, sincerity
and faithfulness, peace and
tranquility, quietness and confi-
dence: the perfect rest that You
desire. Cause Your children to
know and understand that their
rest comes from You, and that
by it they hallow Your name.

Shabbat—
the word
means
"stopping."
Stopping to
rest: rest for
the body,
rest for the
spirit, rest for
the world we
live in.

OR

ישמחו   MOST PRECIOUS OF DAYS

יִשְׂמְחוּ בְמַלְכוּתְךָ שׁוֹמְרֵי שַׁבָּת וְקוֹרְאֵי עֹנֶג. עַם מְקַדְּשֵׁי
שְׁבִיעִי כֻּלָּם יִשְׂבְּעוּ וְיִתְעַנְּגוּ מִטּוּבֶךָ. וְהַשְּׁבִיעִי רָצִיתָ בּוֹ
וְקִדַּשְׁתּוֹ. חֶמְדַּת יָמִים אוֹתוֹ קָרָאתָ, זֵכֶר לְמַעֲשֵׂה בְרֵאשִׁית.

*Yis-m'chu v'ma-l'chu-t'cha sho-m'rei Shabbat v'ko-r'ei o-neg. Am m'ka-d'shei
sh'vi-i ku-lam yis-b'u v'yit-a-n'gu mi-tu-veh-cha. V'ha-sh'vi-i ra-tzi-ta bo
v'ki-dash-to. Chem-dat ya-mim o-to ka-ra-ta, zei-cher l'ma-a-sei v'rei-sheet.*

160

Those who keep the Sabbath and call it a delight shall rejoice in Your sovereign presence. All who hallow the seventh day shall taste the joy of Your bounty. This is the day You delight in and sanctify. "Loveliest of days," You have called it, "a reminder of the work of creation."

אֱלֹהֵינוּ וֵאלֹהֵי אֲבוֹתֵינוּ וְאִמּוֹתֵינוּ, רְצֵה בִמְנוּחָתֵנוּ.

Our God, God of our fathers and mothers, may our Sabbath rest be pleasing in Your sight.

קַדְּשֵׁנוּ בְּמִצְוֹתֶיךָ וְתֵן חֶלְקֵנוּ בְּתוֹרָתֶךָ.
שַׂבְּעֵנוּ מִטּוּבֶךָ, וְשַׂמְּחֵנוּ בִּישׁוּעָתֶךָ,
וְטַהֵר לִבֵּנוּ לְעָבְדְּךָ בֶּאֱמֶת.
וְהַנְחִילֵנוּ, יְיָ אֱלֹהֵינוּ, בְּאַהֲבָה וּבְרָצוֹן
שַׁבַּת קָדְשֶׁךָ, וְיָנְוּחוּ בָה יִשְׂרָאֵל מְקַדְּשֵׁי שְׁמֶךָ.

Ka-d'shei-nu b'mitz-vo-teh-cha v-tein chel-kei-nu b'toh-ra-teh-cha.
Sab-ei-nu mi-tu-veh-cha, v'sam-chei-nu bi-shu-a-teh-cha,
v'ta-heir li-bei-nu l-ov-d'cha beh-eh-met.
V'han-chi-lei-nu, Adonai Eh-lo-hei-nu, b'a-ha-va u-v'ra-tzon
Shabbat kod-sheh-cha, v'ya-nu-chu va Yis-ra-eil m'ka-d'shei sh'meh-cha.

Sanctify us with Your Mitzvot, and make Your Torah our life's portion. Satisfy us with Your goodness, gladden us with Your salvation, and purify our hearts to serve You in truth. In Your gracious love, Adonai our God, let the holiness of Shabbat enter our hearts, that all Israel, hallowing Your name, may find rest and peace.

בָּרוּךְ אַתָּה יְיָ, מְקַדֵּשׁ הַשַּׁבָּת.

We praise You, the God who hallows Shabbat.

ON SHABBAT, CONTINUE WITH R'TZEI ON PAGE 164

קְדֻשַּׁת הַיּוֹם THE HOLINESS OF YOM TOV

אַתָּה בְחַרְתָּנוּ מִכָּל־הָעַמִּים,
אָהַבְתָּ אוֹתָנוּ וְרָצִיתָ בָּנוּ,
וְקִדַּשְׁתָּנוּ בְּמִצְוֹתֶיךָ, וְקֵרַבְתָּנוּ,
מַלְכֵּנוּ, לַעֲבוֹדָתֶךָ, וְשִׁמְךָ
הַגָּדוֹל וְהַקָּדוֹשׁ עָלֵינוּ קָרָאתָ.
וַתִּתֶּן לָנוּ, יְיָ אֱלֹהֵינוּ, בְּאַהֲבָה
(שַׁבָּתוֹת לִמְנוּחָה וּ) מוֹעֲדִים
לְשִׂמְחָה, חַגִּים וּזְמַנִּים לְשָׂשׂוֹן,
אֶת־יוֹם (הַשַּׁבָּת הַזֶּה וְאֶת־יוֹם)

You have called us to a sacred task among the peoples. In Your love and favor You have hallowed us by Your Mitzvot, drawn us near to Your service, and charged us to make known Your great and holy name. And in Your love, Adonai our God, You have given us (Sabbaths of rest,) feasts of joy and seasons of gladness, among them this (Sabbath day and this)

❖ חַג הַמַּצּוֹת הַזֶּה, זְמַן חֵרוּתֵנוּ,

❖ חַג הַשָּׁבוּעוֹת הַזֶּה, זְמַן מַתַּן תּוֹרָתֵנוּ,

❖ חַג הַסֻּכּוֹת הַזֶּה, זְמַן שִׂמְחָתֵנוּ,

❖ הַשְּׁמִינִי חַג הָעֲצֶרֶת הַזֶּה, זְמַן שִׂמְחָתֵנוּ,

❖ Festival of Pesach, season of our freedom,

❖ Festival of Shavuot, season of revelation,

❖ Festival of Sukkot, season of our gladness,

❖ Festival of Sh'mini Atzeret (Simchat Torah), season of our gladness,

(בְּאַהֲבָה) מִקְרָא קֹדֶשׁ, זֵכֶר
לִיצִיאַת מִצְרָיִם.

to unite us in worship, and in remembrance of the Exodus from Egypt.

אֱלֹהֵינוּ וֵאלֹהֵי אֲבוֹתֵינוּ וְאִמּוֹתֵינוּ, יַעֲלֶה וְיָבֹא וְיִזָּכֵר
זִכְרוֹנֵנוּ וְזִכְרוֹן כָּל־עַמְּךָ בֵּית יִשְׂרָאֵל לְפָנֶיךָ לְטוֹבָה
לְחֵן לְחֶסֶד וּלְרַחֲמִים, לְחַיִּים וּלְשָׁלוֹם בְּיוֹם

162

❖ חַג הַמַּצּוֹת הַזֶּה.

❖ חַג הַשָּׁבוּעוֹת הַזֶּה.

❖ חַג הַסֻּכּוֹת הַזֶּה.

❖ הַשְּׁמִינִי חַג הָעֲצֶרֶת הַזֶּה.

זָכְרֵנוּ, יְיָ אֱלֹהֵינוּ, בּוֹ לְטוֹבָה. אָמֵן.

וּפָקְדֵנוּ בוֹ לִבְרָכָה. אָמֵן.

וְהוֹשִׁיעֵנוּ בוֹ לְחַיִּים. אָמֵן.

Our God of our fathers and mothers, be mindful of Your people Israel on this

❖ Festival of Pesach,
❖ Festival of Shavuot,
❖ Festival of Sukkot,
❖ Festival of Sh'mini Atzeret (Simchat Torah),

and renew in us love and compassion, goodness, life, and peace.

This day remember us for well-being. Amen.

Bless us with Your nearness. Amen.

Help us to renew our life. Amen.

וְהַשִּׂיאֵנוּ, יְיָ אֱלֹהֵינוּ, אֶת־בִּרְכַּת מוֹעֲדֶיךָ לְשִׂמְחָה וּלְשָׂשׂוֹן,

כַּאֲשֶׁר רָצִיתָ וְאָמַרְתָּ לְבָרְכֵנוּ. קַדְּשֵׁנוּ בְּמִצְוֹתֶיךָ וְתֵן חֶלְקֵנוּ

בְּתוֹרָתֶךָ. שַׂבְּעֵנוּ מִטּוּבֶךָ, וְשַׂמְּחֵנוּ בִּישׁוּעָתֶךָ, וְטַהֵר לִבֵּנוּ

לְעָבְדְּךָ בֶּאֱמֶת. וְהַנְחִילֵנוּ, יְיָ אֱלֹהֵינוּ, בְּשִׂמְחָה וּבְשָׂשׂוֹן

(שַׁבָּת וּ) מוֹעֲדֵי קָדְשֶׁךָ.

בָּרוּךְ אַתָּה יְיָ, מְקַדֵּשׁ (הַשַּׁבָּת וְ) יִשְׂרָאֵל וְהַזְּמַנִּים.

Eternal God, may our observance of the festivals bring us blessing, happiness, and joy. Sanctify us with Your Mitzvot, and let Your Torah be our life's portion. Satisfy us with Your

goodness, gladden us with Your salvation, and purify our hearts to serve You in truth.

And grant, eternal God, that the joy of (Shabbat and) *Yom Tov may be with us always.*

We praise You, O God, for the holiness of (Shabbat,) *Israel and the Festivals.*

עבודה   WORSHIP

רְצֵה, יְיָ אֱלֹהֵינוּ, בְּעַמְּךָ יִשְׂרָאֵל, וּתְפִלָּתָם בְּאַהֲבָה תְקַבֵּל,
וּתְהִי לְרָצוֹן תָּמִיד עֲבוֹדַת יִשְׂרָאֵל עַמֶּךָ.

אֵל קָרוֹב לְכָל־קֹרְאָיו, פְּנֵה אֶל עֲבָדֶיךָ וְחָנֵּנוּ; שְׁפוֹךְ רוּחֲךָ
עָלֵינוּ, וְתֶחֱזֶינָה עֵינֵינוּ בְּשׁוּבְךָ לְצִיּוֹן בְּרַחֲמִים.

Look with favor, Adonai our God, upon Your people Israel, and with love accept our prayers. May our worship ever be worthy of Your favor.

O God near to every seeker,

turn to Your servants and show us grace.

Shower Your spirit upon us, and let Zion and all Israel behold Your compassionate presence.

בָּרוּךְ אַתָּה יְיָ, הַמַּחֲזִיר שְׁכִינָתוֹ לְצִיּוֹן.

We praise You, Adonai, whose presence restores Zion and all Israel.

Are there other creatures able to worship? Perhaps their very being is a hymn of praise to their creator.

❧ See "Prayer and Its Value," pages 3-5.

הודאה   THANKSGIVING

מוֹדִים אֲנַחְנוּ לָךְ שָׁאַתָּה הוּא יְיָ אֱלֹהֵינוּ וֵאלֹהֵי אֲבוֹתֵינוּ
וְאִמּוֹתֵינוּ, אֱלֹהֵי כָל־בָּשָׂר, יוֹצְרֵנוּ יוֹצֵר בְּרֵאשִׁית.
בְּרָכוֹת וְהוֹדָאוֹת לְשִׁמְךָ הַגָּדוֹל וְהַקָּדוֹשׁ עַל־שֶׁהֶחֱיִיתָנוּ
וְקִיַּמְתָּנוּ. כֵּן תְּחַיֵּנוּ וּתְקַיְּמֵנוּ, יְיָ אֱלֹהֵינוּ, וְתֶאֱסֹף גָּלֻיּוֹתֵינוּ לְשָׁמֵר חֻקֶּיךָ,
לַעֲשׂוֹת רְצוֹנֶךָ, וּלְעָבְדְּךָ בְּלֵבָב שָׁלֵם. בָּרוּךְ אֵל הַהוֹדָאוֹת.

Let us be grateful that our tradition has taught us how to give thanks.

❧ See "Giving Thanks," page 395, and Psalm 147 (page 372).

We affirm with gratitude that You, Adonai, are our God, the God of our fathers and mothers, the God of all flesh, our creator, the source of all being. We bless and praise Your great and holy name, for keeping us in life and sustaining us.

Continue us in life and sustain us, Adonai our God; strengthen us to observe Your laws, to do Your will, and to serve You with a whole heart. Praised be God, to whom our thanks are due.

ברכת שלום   PEACE

שָׁלוֹם רָב עַל־יִשְׂרָאֵל עַמְּךָ תָּשִׂים לְעוֹלָם,
כִּי אַתָּה הוּא מֶלֶךְ אָדוֹן לְכָל־הַשָּׁלוֹם.
וְטוֹב בְּעֵינֶיךָ לְבָרֵךְ אֶת־עַמְּךָ יִשְׂרָאֵל
וְאֶת־כָּל־הָעַמִּים בְּכָל־עֵת וּבְכָל־שָׁעָה בִּשְׁלוֹמֶךָ.

Supreme source of peace, grant true and lasting peace to our people Israel, for it is good in Your sight that Your people Israel, and all peoples, may be blessed at all times with Your gift of peace.

בָּרוּךְ אַתָּה יי, עוֹשֵׂה הַשָּׁלוֹם.

We praise You, O God, the source of peace.

SILENT PRAYER

אֱלֹהַי, נְצֹר לְשׁוֹנִי מֵרָע, וּשְׂפָתַי מִדַּבֵּר מִרְמָה. וְלִמְקַלְלַי נַפְשִׁי תִדּוֹם וְנַפְשִׁי כֶּעָפָר לַכֹּל תִּהְיֶה. פְּתַח לִבִּי בְּתוֹרָתֶךָ, וּבְמִצְוֹתֶיךָ תִּרְדּוֹף נַפְשִׁי. עֲשֵׂה לְמַעַן שְׁמֶךָ, עֲשֵׂה לְמַעַן יְמִינֶךָ, עֲשֵׂה לְמַעַן קְדֻשָׁתֶךָ, עֲשֵׂה לְמַעַן תּוֹרָתֶךָ; לְמַעַן יֵחָלְצוּן יְדִידֶיךָ, הוֹשִׁיעָה יְמִינְךָ וַעֲנֵנִי.

My God, keep my tongue from evil, my lips from deceptive speech. In the face of malice give me a quiet spirit; let me be

We are called to add some Shalom to God's creation. Small as each contribution may be, our collective additions can change the world.

✽ See Pirke Avot, pages 324-325, and page 351.

165

humble wherever I go. Open my heart to Your teaching, make me eager to fulfill Your Mitzvot. Then will Your name be exalted, Your might manifest, Your holiness visible, Your Torah magnified. Inspire me to love You, and be the answer to my prayer.

REFLECTIONS

1

ℂ   Even when a virtue has become second nature, do not be overconfident and say, "It can never leave me." There is always the possibility that it will. Therefore, never neglect an opportunity to do good, thus to strengthen yourself in that habit. (Maimonides)

2

ℂ   Holy One, give me a quiet heart, and help me to hear the still, small voice that speaks within me. It calls me to come close to you and to grow in your likeness. It teaches me to do my work faithfully, even when no one's eye is upon me. It counsels me to judge others kindly and to love them freely, for it persuades me to see the divinity in everyone I meet. Help me, O God, to come to the end of each day feeling that I used its gifts wisely and faced its trials bravely.

3

ℂ   What a blessing it is to work, and then to rest. Especially today I feel rich in blessing—the blessing of Your spirit that pervades all things living and inanimate, the joy of family love, and the gift of friendship. Give me always a heart grateful as in my sunniest days, a soul thankful as in the hour of my highest joy.

4

℆   As I reflect upon the blessings I daily receive, I think above all that I am called to *be* a blessing. More than getting, let me give, give with a full heart and an open spirit.

5

℆   The Holy One said to Israel: What do I seek of you? All I ask is that you love one another, and honor one another, and respect one another, and that there be found in you neither transgression nor theft nor anything ugly, so that you do not become tainted. As it is said: *...walk humbly with your God.* (Micah 6:8) Read it this way: *Walk humbly, and your God will be with you.* (Midrash)

יִהְיוּ לְרָצוֹן אִמְרֵי־פִי וְהֶגְיוֹן לִבִּי לְפָנֶיךָ, יהוה, צוּרִי וְגֹאֲלִי.

Yi-h'yu l'ra-tzon i-m'rei fi v'heg-yon li-bi l'fa-neh-cha, Adonai tzu-ri v'go-a-li.

May the words of my mouth and the meditations of my heart be acceptable to You, O God, my rock and my redeemer. Amen.

&

עֹשֶׂה שָׁלוֹם בִּמְרוֹמָיו,	*O-seh sha-lom bi-m'ro-mav,*
הוּא יַעֲשֶׂה שָׁלוֹם עָלֵינוּ	*hu ya-a-seh sha-lom a-lei-nu*
וְעַל־כָּל־יִשְׂרָאֵל, וְאִמְרוּ:	*v'al kol Yis-ra-eil, v'i-m'ru:*
אָמֵן.	*A-mein.*

May the source of peace on high let peace descend on us, on all Israel, and all the world, and let us say: Amen.

THE LITURGY FOR THE READING OF TORAH ON SHABBAT
BEGINS ON THE NEXT PAGE

THE LITURGY FOR THE READING OF TORAH ON YOM TOV
BEGINS ON PAGE 250

ALEINU BEGINS ON PAGE 284 OR PAGE 286.

THE READING OF TORAH   קריאת התורה

FOR SHABBAT

אֵין־כָּמְוֹךָ בָאֱלֹהִים, אֲדֹנָי,
וְאֵין כְּמַעֲשֶׂיךָ. מַלְכוּתְךָ
מַלְכוּת כָּל־עוֹלָמִים,
וּמֶמְשַׁלְתְּךָ בְּכָל־דּוֹר וָדֹר.

יְהֹוָה מֶלֶךְ, יְהֹוָה מָלָךְ,
יְהֹוָה יִמְלֹךְ לְעוֹלָם וָעֶד.

יְהֹוָה עֹז לְעַמּוֹ יִתֵּן,

יְהֹוָה יְבָרֵךְ אֶת־עַמּוֹ בַשָּׁלוֹם.

None are like You, Adonai, among the gods, and there are no deeds like Yours. Your sovereignty is everlasting; Your dominion endures through all generations.

Adonai reigns; Adonai will reign forever and ever. Eternal God, You give strength to Your people; eternal God, You bless Your people with peace.

Standing before the Ark, we can imagine ourselves at Sinai; and we can reaffirm our covenant with the Eternal, whose word goes forth continually to each generation and every individual. We pray to know before whom we stand.

ALL RISE

אֵל הָרַחֲמִים, הֵיטִיבָה
בִרְצוֹנְךָ אֶת־צִיּוֹן;
תִּבְנֶה חוֹמוֹת יְרוּשָׁלָיִם.
כִּי בְךָ לְבַד בָּטָחְנוּ,
מֶלֶךְ אֵל רָם וְנִשָּׂא,
אֲדוֹן עוֹלָמִים.

Av ha-ra-cha-mim, hei-ti-vah

vir'tzo-n'cha et tzi-on;

tiv-neh cho-mot Y'ru-sha-la-yim.

Ki v'cha l'vad ba-tach-nu,

meh-lech eil ram v'ni-sa,

a-don o-la-mim.

Source of mercy, favor Zion with goodness: build up Jerusalem's walls.
In You alone we trust, O sovereign and supreme, high and exalted God.

CONTINUE WITH THE OPENING OF THE ARK ON PAGE 170

168

קְרִיאַת הַתּוֹרָה THE READING OF TORAH

FOR SHABBAT OR WEEKDAYS

Standing
before the
Ark, we can
imagine
ourselves at
Sinai; and we
can reaffirm
our covenant
with the
Eternal,
whose word
goes forth
continually to
each
generation
and every
individual.
We pray to
know before
whom we
stand.

הַקְהֵל אֶת־הָעָם, הָאֲנָשִׁים
וְהַנָּשִׁים וְהַטַּף וְגֵרְךָ אֲשֶׁר
בִּשְׁעָרֶיךָ, לְמַעַן יִשְׁמְעוּ
וּלְמַעַן יִלְמְדוּ וְיָרְאוּ אֶת־
יהוה אֱלֹהֵיכֶם, וְשָׁמְרוּ
לַעֲשׂוֹת אֶת־כָּל־דִּבְרֵי
הַתּוֹרָה הַזֹּאת.
וּבְנֵיהֶם אֲשֶׁר לֹא־יָדְעוּ
יִשְׁמְעוּ וְלָמְדוּ לְיִרְאָה
אֶת־יהוה אֱלֹהֵיכֶם.

Assemble the people—men, women, and children, and the strangers in your towns—to hear, and learn to revere Adonai your God, and faithfully to observe all the precepts of the Torah. And let their children who do not yet know it hear, that they too may learn to revere Adonai your God.

ALL RISE

וְהָאֵר עֵינֵינוּ בְּתוֹרָתֶךָ, וְדַבֵּק לִבֵּנוּ בְּמִצְוֹתֶיךָ,
וְיַחֵד לְבָבֵנוּ לְאַהֲבָה וּלְיִרְאָה אֶת־שְׁמֶךָ.

V'ha-eir ei-nei-nu b'to-ra-teh-cha, v'da-beik li-bei-nu b'mitz-vo-teh-cha,
v'ya-cheid l'va-vei-nu l'a-ha-va u-l'yir-ah et sh'meh-cha.

Enlighten our eyes with Your Torah, help us cling to Your commandments, and inspire us to love and revere Your name with a ready heart.

THE ARK IS OPENED

הָבוּ גֹדֶל לֵאלֹהֵינוּ, וּתְנוּ כָבוֹד לַתּוֹרָה.

Let us declare the greatness of our God,
and give honor to the Torah.

כִּי מִצִּיּוֹן תֵּצֵא תוֹרָה, וּדְבַר־יהוה מִירוּשָׁלֶָיִם.
בָּרוּךְ שֶׁנָּתַן תּוֹרָה לְעַמּוֹ יִשְׂרָאֵל בִּקְדֻשָּׁתוֹ.

Ki mi-tzi-yon tei-tzei Torah, u-d'var Adonai mi-y'ru-sha-la-yim.
Ba-ruch sheh-na-tan Torah l'a-mo Yisrael bi-k'du-sha-to.

For Torah shall go forth from Zion, and the word of God from Jerusalem.
Praised be the one who in holiness has given Torah to our people Israel.

გა

גַּדְּלוּ לַיהוה אִתִּי, וּנְרוֹמְמָה שְׁמוֹ יַחְדָּו.

O magnify the Eternal One with me,
and together let us exalt God's name.

שְׁמַע יִשְׂרָאֵל: יהוה אֱלֹהֵינוּ, יהוה אֶחָד!

Shema Yisrael, Adonai Eh-lo-hei-nu, Adonai Eh-chad!

אֶחָד אֱלֹהֵינוּ, גָּדוֹל אֲדֹנֵינוּ, קָדוֹשׁ שְׁמוֹ!

Eh-chad Eh-lo-hei-nu, ga-dol A-do-nei-nu, ka-dosh sh'mo.

Hear, O Israel: Adonai is our God, Adonai alone!
Our God is one; great and holy is Adonai.

გა

בֵּית יַעֲקֹב, לְכוּ וְנֵלְכָה בְּאוֹר יהוה.

O House of Jacob, come, let us walk
in the light of the Eternal.

SOME CONGREGATIONS CONTINUE WITH A PROCESSION (HAKAFAH)

לְךָ, יהוה, הַגְּדֻלָּה וְהַגְּבוּרָה וְהַתִּפְאֶרֶת

וְהַנֵּצַח וְהַהוֹד, כִּי כֹל בַּשָּׁמַיִם וּבָאָרֶץ.

לְךָ, יהוה, הַמַּמְלָכָה וְהַמִּתְנַשֵּׂא לְכֹל לְרֹאשׁ.

L'cha, Adonai, ha-g'du-lah v'ha-g'vu-rah v'ha-tif-eh-ret

v'ha-nei-tzach v'ha-hod, ki chol ba-sha-ma-yim u-va-a-retz.

L'cha, Adonai, ha-ma-m'la-chah v'ha-mit-na-sei l'chol l'rosh.

Yours, Adonai, is the greatness, the power, the glory, the victory, and the majesty; for all that is in heaven and earth is Yours. You, Adonai, are sovereign; You are supreme over all.

ALL ARE SEATED

THE TORAH IS READ

BEFORE AN ALIYAH

בָּרְכוּ אֶת־יי הַמְבֹרָךְ!

בָּרוּךְ יי הַמְבֹרָךְ לְעוֹלָם וָעֶד!

בָּרוּךְ יי הַמְבֹרָךְ לְעוֹלָם וָעֶד!

בָּרוּךְ אַתָּה יי, אֱלֹהֵינוּ מֶלֶךְ הָעוֹלָם,

אֲשֶׁר בָּחַר־בָּנוּ מִכָּל־הָעַמִּים, וְנָתַן־לָנוּ אֶת־תּוֹרָתוֹ.

בָּרוּךְ אַתָּה יי, נוֹתֵן הַתּוֹרָה.

READER: Ba-r'chu et Adonai ha-m'vo-rach!

CONGREGATION: Ba-ruch Adonai ha-m'vo-rach l'o-lam va-ed!

READER: Ba-ruch Adonai ha-m'vo-rach l'o-lam va-ed!

Ba-ruch a-ta Adonai, Eh-lo-hei-nu meh-lech ha-o-lam,

a-sher ba-char ba-nu mi-kol ha-a-mim, v'na-tan la-nu et Torah-to.

Ba-ruch a-ta Adonai, no-tein ha-Torah.

Praise the one to whom our praise is due!

Praised be the one to whom our praise is due, now and forever!

We praise You, Adonai our God, sovereign of the universe: You have called us to Your service by giving us the Torah. We praise You, O God, giver of the Torah.

AFTER AN ALIYAH

בָּרוּךְ אַתָּה יי, אֱלֹהֵינוּ מֶלֶךְ הָעוֹלָם,

אֲשֶׁר נָתַן־לָנוּ תּוֹרַת אֱמֶת, וְחַיֵּי עוֹלָם נָטַע בְּתוֹכֵנוּ.

בָּרוּךְ אַתָּה יי, נוֹתֵן הַתּוֹרָה.

READER: *Ba-ruch a-ta Adonai, Eh-lo-hei-nu meh-lech ha-o-lam,*
a-sher na-tan la-nu To-rat eh-met, v'cha-yei o-lam na-ta b'to-chei-nu.
Ba-ruch a-ta Adonai, no-tein ha-Torah.

We praise You, Adonai our God, sovereign of the universe: You have given us a Torah of truth, implanting within us eternal life. We praise You, O God, giver of the Torah.

SPECIAL PRAYERS THAT MIGHT BE INCLUDED BEFORE THE HAFTARAH
OR BEFORE THE TORAH IS RETURNED TO THE ARK ARE ON PAGES 175-181

&

WHEN THE READING OF TORAH HAS BEEN COMPLETED

הגבהה—HAGBAHA—LIFTING THE TORAH

וְזֹאת הַתּוֹרָה אֲשֶׁר־שָׂם מֹשֶׁה לִפְנֵי בְּנֵי יִשְׂרָאֵל,

עַל־פִּי יי בְּיַד־מֹשֶׁה.

V'zot ha-Torah a-sher sam Mo-sheh li-f'nei b'nei Yisrael,
al pi Adonai b'yad Mo-sheh.

This is the Torah that Moses placed before the people of Israel.

&

THE HAFTARAH IS READ

BEFORE THE READING

בָּרוּךְ אַתָּה יְיָ, אֱלֹהֵינוּ מֶלֶךְ הָעוֹלָם, אֲשֶׁר בָּחַר
בִּנְבִיאִים טוֹבִים, וְרָצָה בְדִבְרֵיהֶם הַנֶּאֱמָרִים בֶּאֱמֶת.
בָּרוּךְ אַתָּה יְיָ, הַבּוֹחֵר בַּתּוֹרָה, וּבְמֹשֶׁה עַבְדּוֹ,
וּבְיִשְׂרָאֵל עַמּוֹ, וּבִנְבִיאֵי הָאֱמֶת וָצֶדֶק.

We praise You, Adonai our God, sovereign of the universe: You have called faithful prophets to speak words of truth. We praise You, O God, for the revelation of Torah, for Moses Your servant and Israel Your people, and for the prophets of truth and righteousness.

AFTER THE READING

בָּרוּךְ אַתָּה יְיָ, אֱלֹהֵינוּ מֶלֶךְ הָעוֹלָם, צוּר כָּל־הָעוֹלָמִים,
צַדִּיק בְּכָל־הַדּוֹרוֹת, הָאֵל הַנֶּאֱמָן, הָאוֹמֵר וְעוֹשֶׂה, הַמְדַבֵּר
וּמְקַיֵּם, שֶׁכָּל־דְּבָרָיו אֱמֶת וָצֶדֶק.

We praise You, Adonai our God, sovereign of the universe, rock of all worlds, righteous in every generations, the faithful God whose word is deed, whose every teaching is justice and truth.

❧

Some will wish to include this and the following blessing.

נֶאֱמָן אַתָּה הוּא, יְיָ אֱלֹהֵינוּ, וְנֶאֱמָנִים דְּבָרֶיךָ, וְדָבָר אֶחָד
מִדְּבָרֶיךָ אָחוֹר לֹא יָשׁוּב רֵיקָם, כִּי אֵל מֶלֶךְ נֶאֱמָן
וְרַחֲמָן אָתָּה. בָּרוּךְ אַתָּה יְיָ, הָאֵל הַנֶּאֱמָן בְּכָל־דְּבָרָיו.

True are You, Adonai our God, and true are Your words: not one word of Yours goes unfulfilled, for You are the sovereign God, true and compassionate. We praise You, Adonai, the God whose words are true.

רַחֵם עַל צִיּוֹן, כִּי הִיא בֵּית חַיֵּינוּ. וְלַעֲלוּבַת נֶפֶשׁ תּוֹשִׁיעַ
בִּמְהֵרָה בְיָמֵינוּ. בָּרוּךְ אַתָּה יי, מְשַׂמֵּחַ צִיּוֹן בְּבָנֶיהָ.

Some will wish to include this and the previous blessing.

Have compassion upon Zion, for it is the house of our life. Long were we bowed down: Now, in our own days, help us to find deliverance. We praise You, O God: You bring joy to Zion's children.

⊰⊱

עַל־הַתּוֹרָה, וְעַל־הָעֲבוֹדָה, וְעַל־הַנְּבִיאִים,
וְעַל־יוֹם הַשַּׁבָּת הַזֶּה, שֶׁנָּתַתָּ־לָּנוּ, יי אֱלֹהֵינוּ,
לִקְדֻשָּׁה וְלִמְנוּחָה, לְכָבוֹד וּלְתִפְאָרֶת, עַל־הַכֹּל,
יי אֱלֹהֵינוּ, אֲנַחְנוּ מוֹדִים לָךְ וּמְבָרְכִים אוֹתָךְ.
יִתְבָּרַךְ שִׁמְךָ בְּפִי כָּל־חַי תָּמִיד לְעוֹלָם וָעֶד.
בָּרוּךְ אַתָּה יי, מְקַדֵּשׁ הַשַּׁבָּת.

For the Torah, for this, our time of worship, for the prophets, and for this Shabbat that You, Adonai our God, have given us for holiness and rest, for honor and glory, for all of these we thank and praise You. May Your name continually be praised by every living being. We praise You, the God who hallows Shabbat.

THE LITURGY FOR RETURNING
THE TORAH TO THE ARK IS ON PAGE 182.

174

MI SHEBEIRACH   מי שברך

FOR A BAR OR BAT MITZVAH OR OTHER SPECIAL OCCASION

מִי שֶׁבֵּרַךְ אֲבוֹתֵינוּ אַבְרָהָם, יִצְחָק וְיַעֲקֹב,

וְאִמּוֹתֵינוּ שָׂרָה, רִבְקָה, לֵאָה וְרָחֵל, הוּא יְבָרֵךְ

EITHER אֶת־ _____ בֶּן _____ שֶׁעָלָה לַתּוֹרָה

OR אֶת־ _____ בַּת _____ שֶׁעָלְתָה לַתּוֹרָה

לִכְבוֹד הַמָּקוֹם, וְלִכְבוֹד הַשַּׁבָּת (וְלִכְבוֹד הָרֶגֶל).

EITHER הַקָּדוֹשׁ בָּרוּךְ הוּא יְבָרֵךְ אוֹתוֹ וְאֶת־כָּל־מִשְׁפַּחְתּוֹ,

OR הַקָּדוֹשׁ בָּרוּךְ הוּא יְבָרֵךְ אוֹתָהּ וְאֶת־כָּל־מִשְׁפַּחְתָּהּ

וְיִשְׁלַח בְּרָכָה וְהַצְלָחָה בְּכָל־מַעֲשֵׂה

EITHER יָדָיו, עִם כָּל־יִשְׂרָאֵל אֶחָיו וְאַחְיוֹתָיו, וְנֹאמַר: אָמֵן.

OR יָדֶיהָ, עִם כָּל־יִשְׂרָאֵל אַחֶיהָ וְאַחְיוֹתֶיהָ, וְנֹאמַר: אָמֵן.

May the one who blessed our ancestors Abraham, Isaac, and
Jacob, Sarah, Rebekah, Leah, and Rachel bless _____ who has
come up to the Torah in honor of God and of Shabbat [Yom
Tov]. May the Holy One bless him and his family/ her and
her family/, and prosper him/her in all that he/she
undertakes, together with all the House of Israel, and let us
say: *Amen.*

ON BEHALF OF A BAR OR BAT MITZVAH

May the one who blessed our ancestors Abraham, Isaac, and
Jacob, Sarah, Rebekah, Leah, and Rachel bless _____ who,
having reached the age of Bar/Bat Mitzvah, has been called
to the Torah. May he/she ever be eager to perform Mitzvot,
be a source of pride to his/her family and friends as a
worthy member of our community, and become a blessing to
future generations. And let us say: *Amen.*

175

מִי שֶׁבֵּרַךְ   MI SHEBEIRACH

A PRAYER FOR HEALING

A musical version of Mi Shebeirach and other prayers for healing begin on page 376.

We pray now for all who are afflicted: Let the healing powers that God has implanted within them, and the love of family and friends, sustain them in their time of need.

Be with all Your children, O God: be with us all.

בָּרוּךְ אַתָּה יי, רוֹפֵא הַחוֹלִים.

Ba-ruch a-ta Adonai, ro-fei ha-cho-lim.

Praised be the God who gives us the power to heal.

מִי שֶׁבֵּרַךְ אֲבוֹתֵינוּ אַבְרָהָם, יִצְחָק, וְיַעֲקֹב,

וְאִמּוֹתֵינוּ שָׂרָה, רִבְקָה, לֵאָה, וְרָחֵל, הוּא יְבָרֵךְ אוֹתָנוּ.

הַקָּדוֹשׁ בָּרוּךְ הוּא יִמָּלֵא רַחֲמִים עַל־ _____

וְעַל־כָּל הַחוֹלִים, וְיִשְׁלַח לָנוּ בִמְהֵרָה רְפוּאַת הַנֶּפֶשׁ

וּרְפוּאַת הַגּוּף. וְנֹאמַר: אָמֵן.

May the one who blessed our ancestors Abraham, Isaac, and Jacob, Sarah, Rebekah, Leah, and Rachel bless [_____ and] all who are in need of healing. Holy One, in the fullness of Your compassion bestow upon them renewed health and strength. Guide their healers, O God, and give them skill and compassion, and the joy that comes from selfless service. And let us say: *Amen.*

ברכת החדש   FOR THE NEW MONTH

יְהִי רָצוֹן מִלְּפָנֶיךָ, יי אֱלֹהֵינוּ וֵאלֹהֵי אֲבוֹתֵינוּ וְאִמּוֹתֵינוּ, שֶׁתְּחַדֵּשׁ
עָלֵינוּ אֶת־הַחְדֶשׁ הַזֶּה, (הַבָּא,) לְטוֹבָה וְלִבְרָכָה. וְתִתֶּן־לָנוּ חַיִּים
אֲרֻכִּים, חַיִּים שֶׁל־שָׁלוֹם, חַיִּים שֶׁל־טוֹבָה, חַיִּים שֶׁל־בְּרָכָה,
חַיִּים שֶׁל־פַּרְנָסָה, חַיִּים שֶׁל־חִלּוּץ עֲצָמוֹת, חַיִּים שֶׁיֵּשׁ בָּהֶם
יִרְאַת חֵטְא, חַיִּים שֶׁתְּהֵא בָנוּ אַהֲבַת תּוֹרָה וְיִרְאַת שָׁמַיִם,
חַיִּים שֶׁיִּמָּלְאוּ מִשְׁאֲלוֹת לִבֵּנוּ לְטוֹבָה. אָמֵן.

Our God and God of our ancestors, may the month to come
bring us renewed good and blessing, with long life, peace,
prosperity, and health, a life full of blessing, one exalted by
love of Torah and reverence for the Divine, a life in which
the longings of our hearts are fulfilled for good. Amen.

מִי שֶׁעָשָׂה נִסִּים לַאֲבוֹתֵינוּ וּלְאִמּוֹתֵינוּ וְגָאַל אוֹתָם מֵעַבְדוּת לְחֵרוּת,
הוּא יִגְאַל אוֹתָנוּ בְּקָרוֹב, חֲבֵרִים כָּל־יִשְׂרָאֵל, וְנֹאמַר: אָמֵן.

Wondrous God, in ancient days You led our mothers and
fathers from bondage to freedom; redeem us yet again,
making all Israel one united people.

EITHER רֹאשׁ חֹדֶשׁ . . . יִהְיֶה בְּיוֹם . . .

The new month of _____ will begin on _____

OR רֹאשׁ חֹדֶשׁ . . . הוּא הַיּוֹם.

The new month of _____ begins today.

יְחַדְּשֵׁהוּ הַקָּדוֹשׁ בָּרוּךְ הוּא עָלֵינוּ וְעַל־כָּל־עַמּוֹ בֵּית יִשְׂרָאֵל
לְחַיִּים וּלְשָׁלוֹם, לְשָׂשׂוֹן וּלְשִׂמְחָה, לִישׁוּעָה וּלְנֶחָמָה, וְנֹאמַר: אָמֵן.

Holy One, let the new month bring for us, and for the whole
House of Israel, life and peace, happiness and joy, deliverance and comfort; and let us say: *Amen.*

FOR OUR CONGREGATION

Eternal God, we pray for the whole House of Israel, united by a common heritage of faith and hope.

Bless this holy congregation and all who serve it, together with all other holy congregations in lands near and far. Uphold us, shield us, and bestow upon us abundant life and health and peace.

O God, send healing to the sick, comfort to all who are suffering in body or spirit, and Your tender love to the sorrowing hearts among us. Be a refuge through their time of trial, and help them rise from weakness to strength, from suffering to consolation, from lonely fear to the courage of faith. *Amen.*

FOR OUR NATION

We pray for our country and for all who hold positions of leadership and responsibility in our national life. Let Your blessing rest upon them, and make them responsive to Your will, so that our nation may be an example of justice and compassion to all the world.

Deepen our desire to serve our nation, and teach us to uphold its good name by our own right-conduct. Imbue us with zeal for the cause of liberty in our own land and in all lands; and may our homes be safe from affliction, strife, and war. *Amen.*

FOR THE STATE OF ISRAEL

We pray for the Land of Israel and its people. May its borders know peace, its inhabitants tranquility. And may the bonds of faith and fate that unite Jews everywhere be a source of strength to Israel and to us all. God of all lands and ages, answer our constant prayer with a Zion once more aglow with light for us and for all the world, and let us say: *Amen.*

ספירת העמר   COUNTING OF THE OMER

וּסְפַרְתֶּם לָכֶם מִמָּחֳרַת הַשַּׁבָּת, "Count seven weeks from the
day after the sabbath, when a
מִיּוֹם הֲבִיאֲכֶם אֶת־עֹמֶר sheaf (omer) of grain is to be
הַתְּנוּפָה שֶׁבַע שַׁבָּתוֹת תְּמִימֹת brought as an offering, so
that the day after the seventh
תִּהְיֶינָה. עַד מִמָּחֳרַת הַשַּׁבָּת week will make it fifty days."
הַשְּׁבִיעִת תִּסְפְּרוּ חֲמִשִּׁים יוֹם. (Leviticus 23:15-16)

We count the days of the early harvest season of ancient
Israel, from Pesach to Shavuot, and so we walk once more
the road from Egypt to Mount Sinai, from liberty to law,
from freedom to responsibility.

בָּרוּךְ אַתָּה יי, *Ba-ruch a-ta Adonai,*

אֱלֹהֵינוּ מֶלֶךְ הָעוֹלָם, *Eh-lo-hei-nu meh-lech ha-o-lam,*

אֲשֶׁר קִדְּשָׁנוּ בְּמִצְוֹתָיו *a-sher ki-d'sha-nu b'mitz-vo-tav*

וְצִוָּנוּ עַל סְפִירַת הָעֹמֶר. *v'tzi-va-nu al s'fi-rat ha-omer.*

*We praise You, Adonai our God, sovereign of the universe: You
hallow us with Your Mitzvot, and invite us to count the days of
the Omer.*

EXAMPLES

הַיּוֹם יוֹם אֶחָד לָעֹמֶר...

הַיּוֹם שְׁנֵי יָמִים לָעֹמֶר...

הַיּוֹם שִׁבְעָה יָמִים שֶׁהֵם שָׁבוּעַ אֶחָד לָעֹמֶר...

הַיּוֹם חֲמִשָּׁה עָשָׂר יוֹם שֶׁהֵם שְׁנֵי שָׁבוּעוֹת וְיוֹם אֶחָד לָעֹמֶר...

Today is the first day of the Omer. . . .

Today is the second day of the Omer. . . .

Today is the seventh day, making one week, of the Omer. . . .

Today is the fifteenth day, making two weeks and one day, of the Omer. . . .

UPON RECOVERY FROM SERIOUS ILLNESS
OR UPON ESCAPE FROM DANGER

לְךָ־אֶזְבַּח זֶבַח תּוֹדָה וּבְשֵׁם יהוה אֶקְרָא.

L'cha ez-bach zeh-vach to-dah, u-v'sheim Adonai ek-ra.

To You, O God, I offer my thanksgiving, and glorify Your name.

בָּרוּךְ אַתָּה יי, אֱלֹהֵינוּ מֶלֶךְ הָעוֹלָם, שֶׁגְּמָלַנִי כָּל־טוֹב.

Ba-ruch a-ta Adonai, Eh-lo-hei-nu meh-lech ha-o-lam, sheh-g'ma'la'ni kol-tov.

We praise You, Adonai our God, sovereign of the universe, for the great goodness You have bestowed upon me.

THE CONGREGATION RESPONDS

מִי שֶׁגְּמָלְנוּ כָּל־טוֹב, הוּא יִגְמְלֵנוּ כָּל־טוֹב סֶלָה.

Mi sheh-g'ma'la'nu kol-tov, hu yig-m'lei-nu kol-tov seh-lah.

May the one who has been gracious to us continue to favor us with all that is good.

THE CONGREGATION CONTINUES

בָּרוּךְ אַתָּה יי, אֱלֹהֵינוּ מֶלֶךְ הָעוֹלָם, שֶׁהֶחֱיָנוּ
וְקִיְּמָנוּ וְהִגִּיעָנוּ לַזְּמַן הַזֶּה.

Ba-ruch a-ta Adonai, Eh-lo-hei-nu meh-lech ha-o-lam, sheh-heh-cheh-ya-nu,
v'ki-y'ma-nu, v'hi-gi-a-nu la-z'man ha-zeh.

We praise You, Adonai our God, sovereign of the universe, for keeping us in life, for sustaining us, and for enabling us to reach this season.

৯৪

BETROTHAL PRAYER

מִי שֶׁבֵּרַךְ אֲבוֹתֵינוּ אַבְרָהָם, יִצְחָק, וְיַעֲקֹב,
וְאִמּוֹתֵינוּ שָׂרָה, רִבְקָה, לֵאָה, וְרָחֵל, הוּא יְבָרֵךְ אֶת־
הֶחָתָן וְאֶת־הַכַּלָּה _____, וְיַצְלִיחַ דַּרְכָּם, וְיִזְכּוּ לִבְנוֹת
בַּיִת בְּיִשְׂרָאֵל לְשֵׁם וְלִתְהִלָּה. הַקָּדוֹשׁ בָּרוּךְ הוּא יְבָרֵךְ
אוֹתָם וְיִשְׁלַח בְּרָכָה וְהַצְלָחָה בְּכָל־מַעֲשֵׂה יְדֵיהֶם
עִם כָּל־יִשְׂרָאֵל אֲחֵיהֶם וְאַחְיוֹתֵיהֶם, וְנֹאמַר: אָמֵן.

Source of all life, God who blessed our ancestors Abraham, Isaac, and Jacob, Sarah, Rebekah, Leah, and Rachel bless _____ and _____, that the sacred commitments of their wedding day may sustain them all the days of their lives.

May the love that binds them be strong and lasting, and let their hearts be filled with patience, forbearance, and understanding.

Bless them with health, courage, and good fortune; grant that their love and friendship deepen through the years, so that they always find joy together.

_____ and _____: *May the Holy One make smooth your life's path as you create a home worthy of praise, a secure dwelling-place. May God prosper all that you undertake, together with all your brothers and sisters of the House of Israel: Amen.*

The Reading of Torah

RETURNING THE TORAH TO THE ARK

ALL RISE

יְהַלְלוּ אֶת־שֵׁם יהוה, כִּי־נִשְׂגָּב שְׁמוֹ לְבַדּוֹ.

Let us praise the eternal God,
whose name alone is exalted.

הוֹדוֹ עַל־אֶרֶץ וְשָׁמָיִם, וַיָּרֶם קֶרֶן לְעַמּוֹ, תְּהִלָּה
לְכָל־חֲסִידָיו, לִבְנֵי יִשְׂרָאֵל, עַם־קְרֹבוֹ, הַלְלוּיָהּ!

Ho-do al eh-retz v'sha-ma-yim, va-ya-rem ke-ren l'a-mo, t'hi-lah
l'chol cha-si-dav, li-v'nei Yisrael am k'ro-vo, halleluyah!

Your splendor covers heaven and earth; You are the strength of Your
people, a glory to Your faithful ones, to Israel, a people close to You.
Halleluyah!

כִּי זֹאת הַבְּרִית אֲשֶׁר אֶכְרֹת אֶת־בֵּית יִשְׂרָאֵל
אַחֲרֵי הַיָּמִים הָהֵם, נְאֻם־יהוה: נָתַתִּי אֶת־תּוֹרָתִי
בְּקִרְבָּם, וְעַל־לִבָּם אֶכְתֲּבֶנָּה, וְהָיִיתִי לָהֶם לֵאלֹהִים,
וְהֵמָּה יִהְיוּ־לִי לְעָם. וְלֹא יְלַמְּדוּ עוֹד אִישׁ אֶת־רֵעֵהוּ
וְאִישׁ אֶת־אָחִיו לֵאמֹר, דְּעוּ אֶת־יהוה, כִּי־כֻלָּם יֵדְעוּ
אוֹתִי, לְמִקְטַנָּם וְעַד־גְּדוֹלָם, נְאֻם־יהוה.

This is the covenant I will make with the House of Israel in
time to come, says Adonai: I will put my teaching within
them, and inscribe it on their hearts; I will be their God, and
they shall be my people. No longer shall anyone teach a
friend or a neighbor to know me, for they all shall know me,
young and old alike!

Behold, I have given you a good doctrine; do not forsake it. It is a
tree of life to those who hold it fast, and all who cling to it find
blessing. Its ways are ways of pleasantness, and all its paths are
peace.

182

כִּי לֶקַח טוֹב נָתַתִּי לָכֶם, תּוֹרָתִי אַל־תַּעֲזֹבוּ.

Ki leh-kach tov na-ta-ti la-chem, to-ra-ti al ta-a-zo-vu.

עֵץ־חַיִּים הִיא לַמַּחֲזִיקִים בָּהּ, וְתֹמְכֶיהָ מְאֻשָּׁר.
דְּרָכֶיהָ דַרְכֵי־נֹעַם, וְכָל־נְתִיבוֹתֶיהָ שָׁלוֹם.
הֲשִׁיבֵנוּ יהוה אֵלֶיךָ, וְנָשׁוּבָה.
חַדֵּשׁ יָמֵינוּ כְּקֶדֶם.

Eitz cha-yim hi la-ma-cha-zi-kim ba, v'to-m'cheh-ha m'u-shar.
D'ra-cheh-ha dar'chei no-am, v'chol n'ti-vo-teh-ha sha-lom.
Ha-shi-vei-nu Adonai ei-leh-cha, v'na-shu-vah.
Cha-deish ya-mei-nu k'keh-dem.

Help us to return to You, O God; then truly shall we return. Renew our days as of old.

THE ARK IS CLOSED

ALL ARE SEATED

❧

183

חגים וזמנים לששון

FESTIVAL WORSHIP

ערבית ליום טוב   YOM TOV EVENING SERVICE

וְשָׂמַחְתָּ בְּחַגֶּךָ.

"You shall rejoice in your festival."

With gratitude and joy we welcome (Shabbat and) the Festival of: ❖ Pesach ❖ Shavuot ❖ Sukkot ❖ Atzeret-Simchat Torah ❖ by kindling these lights.

בָּרוּךְ אַתָּה יי, אֱלֹהֵינוּ	Ba-ruch a-ta Adonai, Eh-lo-hei-nu
מֶלֶךְ הָעוֹלָם, אֲשֶׁר	meh-lech ha-o-lam, a-sher
קִדְּשָׁנוּ בְּמִצְוֹתָיו וְצִוָּנוּ	ki-d'sha-nu b'mitz-vo-tav v'tzi-va-nu
לְהַדְלִיק נֵר שֶׁל	l'had-lik ner shel
(שַׁבָּת וְשֶׁל) יוֹם טוֹב.	(Shabbat v'shel) Yom Tov.
בָּרוּךְ אַתָּה יי,	Ba-ruch a-ta Adonai,
אֱלֹהֵינוּ מֶלֶךְ הָעוֹלָם,	Eh-lo-hei-nu meh-lech ha-o-lam,
שֶׁהֶחֱיָנוּ וְקִיְּמָנוּ	sheh-heh-cha-ya-nu v'ki-y'ma-nu
וְהִגִּיעָנוּ לַזְּמַן הַזֶּה.	v'hi-gi-a-nu la-z'man ha-zeh.

We praise You, Adonai our God, sovereign of the universe: You hallow us with Your Mitzvot, and command us to kindle the lights of (Shabbat and) Yom Tov.

We praise You, Adonai our God, sovereign of the universe, for keeping us in life, for sustaining us, and for enabling us to reach this season.

❀

A PRAYER BEFORE PRAYER: May my worship on this Yom Tov encourage me to fulfill this Mitzvah: "Love the stranger, therefore, for you were strangers in the land of Egypt." And it is written: "Adonai your God … seeks justice for the orphan and widow, and loves and provides for the stranger." (Deuteronomy 19:18-19)

WELCOMING YOM TOV   קבלת יום טוב

FOR PESACH

זָכוֹר אֶת־הַיּוֹם הַזֶּה, אֲשֶׁר יְצָאתֶם מִמִּצְרַיִם, מִבֵּית עֲבָדִים,
כִּי בְּחֹזֶק יָד הוֹצִיא יהוה אֶתְכֶם מִזֶּה.

Remember this day, the day you went forth from Egypt,
from the house of bondage, for with a mighty hand Adonai
led you out of there.

וְזָכַרְתָּ כִּי־עֶבֶד הָיִיתָ בְּמִצְרָיִם.

Remember that you were a slave in the land of Egypt.

וְשָׂמַחְתָּ לִפְנֵי יהוה אֱלֹהֶיךָ—אַתָּה, וּבִנְךָ וּבִתֶּךָ, וְהַגֵּר,
וְהַיָּתוֹם, וְהָאַלְמָנָה אֲשֶׁר בְּקִרְבֶּךָ—

As you rejoice before Adonai your God—you, your son and
daughter, the stranger, the orphan, and the widow in your
midst—

וְזָכַרְתָּ כִּי־עֶבֶד הָיִיתָ בְּמִצְרָיִם.

Remember that you were a slave in the land of Egypt.

כְּאֶזְרָח מִכֶּם יִהְיֶה לָכֶם הַגֵּר הַגָּר אִתְּכֶם,
וְאָהַבְתָּ לוֹ כָּמוֹךָ, כִּי־גֵרִים הֱיִיתֶם בְּאֶרֶץ מִצְרָיִם.

The strangers in your midst shall be to you as the native-
born, and you shall love them as yourselves, for you were
strangers in the land of Egypt.

וְזָכַרְתָּ כִּי־עֶבֶד הָיִיתָ בְּמִצְרָיִם.

Remember that you were a slave in the land of Egypt.

כִּי־לִי בְנֵי־יִשְׂרָאֵל עֲבָדִים: עֲבָדַי הֵם, אֲשֶׁר־הוֹצֵאתִי אוֹתָם
מֵאֶרֶץ מִצְרָיִם. אֲנִי יהוה אֱלֹהֵיכֶם.

The people of Israel shall serve only me; they are my servants whom I brought out of the land of Egypt; I, Adonai,
am your God.

וַיְדַבֵּר מֹשֶׁה אֶת־מֹעֲדֵי יהוה אֶל־בְּנֵי יִשְׂרָאֵל.

And Moses proclaimed God's festivals to the people of Israel.

❧

ON WEEKDAYS, CONTINUE ON PAGE 190

ON SHABBAT, CONTINUE ON PAGE 191

❧

FOR SHAVUOT

Shavuot is the season of Revelation; on Pesach we went forth
to freedom; now, in the gift of Torah, we celebrate the
freedom of spirit that Torah brings to those who hold it dear.

FROM EXODUS 19

כֹּה תֹאמַר לְבֵית יַעֲקֹב וְתַגֵּיד לִבְנֵי יִשְׂרָאֵל:
אַתֶּם רְאִיתֶם אֲשֶׁר עָשִׂיתִי לְמִצְרָיִם, וָאֶשָּׂא אֶתְכֶם
עַל־כַּנְפֵי נְשָׁרִים וָאָבִא אֶתְכֶם אֵלָי.
וְעַתָּה אִם־שָׁמוֹעַ תִּשְׁמְעוּ בְּקֹלִי וּשְׁמַרְתֶּם אֶת־בְּרִיתִי,
וִהְיִיתֶם לִי סְגֻלָּה מִכָּל־הָעַמִּים. כִּי־לִי כָּל־הָאָרֶץ,
וְאַתֶּם תִּהְיוּ־לִי מַמְלֶכֶת כֹּהֲנִים וְגוֹי קָדוֹשׁ.

Say this to the House of Jacob; tell this to the people of Israel:
You have seen what I did to the Egyptians, how I carried
you on the wings of eagles, and brought you here to me.

186

Now, if you really listen to me and keep my covenant, you shall be my own treasured people. For all the world is mine, and you shall be to me a community of priests, a holy nation.

וַיָּבֹא מֹשֶׁה וַיִּקְרָא לְזִקְנֵי הָעָם, וַיָּשֶׂם לִפְנֵיהֶם אֵת כָּל־הַדְּבָרִים הָאֵלֶּה אֲשֶׁר צִוָּהוּ יהוה.

וַיַּעֲנוּ כָל־הָעָם יַחְדָּו וַיֹּאמְרוּ: כֹּל אֲשֶׁר־דִּבֶּר יהוה נַעֲשֶׂה!

So Moses went down and called the elders of the people together, and put before them all that God had commanded him.

Then all the people answered as one, saying: All that God has spoken we will do!

וַיְדַבֵּר מֹשֶׁה אֶת־מֹעֲדֵי יהוה אֶל־בְּנֵי יִשְׂרָאֵל.

And Moses proclaimed God's festivals to the people of Israel.

৶

ON WEEKDAYS, CONTINUE ON PAGE 190

ON SHABBAT, CONTINUE ON PAGE 191

৶

FOR SUKKOT

FROM DEUTERONOMY 24

כִּי תִקְצֹר קְצִירְךָ בְשָׂדֶךָ וְשָׁכַחְתָּ עֹמֶר בַּשָּׂדֶה, לֹא תָשׁוּב
לְקַחְתּוֹ; לַגֵּר לַיָּתוֹם וְלָאַלְמָנָה יִהְיֶה: לְמַעַן יְבָרֶכְךָ יְהֹוָה
אֱלֹהֶיךָ בְּכֹל מַעֲשֵׂה יָדֶיךָ.

כִּי תַחְבֹּט זֵיתְךָ, לֹא תְפָאֵר אַחֲרֶיךָ, לַגֵּר לַיָּתוֹם וְלָאַלְמָנָה
יִהְיֶה. כִּי תִבְצֹר כַּרְמְךָ, לֹא תְעוֹלֵל אַחֲרֶיךָ, לַגֵּר לַיָּתוֹם
וְלָאַלְמָנָה יִהְיֶה. וְזָכַרְתָּ כִּי־עֶבֶד הָיִיתָ בְּאֶרֶץ מִצְרָיִם:
עַל־כֵּן אָנֹכִי מְצַוְּךָ לַעֲשׂוֹת אֶת־הַדָּבָר הַזֶּה.

When you reap your harvest in your field and forget a sheaf there, do not go back to get it:

Let it be for the stranger, the orphan, and the widow: then Adonai your God will bless all your undertakings.

When you beat your olive trees, do not strip the branches bare:

Let it be for the stranger, the orphan, and the widow.

When you gather the grapes of your vineyard, do not glean what remains:

Let it be for the stranger, the orphan, and the widow.

Remember that you were a slave in the land of Egypt; therefore I command you to do this.

וַיְדַבֵּר מֹשֶׁה אֶת־מֹעֲדֵי יְהֹוָה אֶל־בְּנֵי יִשְׂרָאֵל.

And Moses proclaimed God's festivals to the people of Israel.

&

ON WEEKDAYS, CONTINUE ON PAGE 190

ON SHABBAT, CONTINUE ON PAGE 191

&

FOR SIMCHAT TORAH

FROM PSALM 119

❀ See
"Selected
Psalms,"
pages 358-375,
and "A Daily
Psalm," pages
27-33.

אַשְׁרֵי תְמִימֵי־דָרֶךְ, הַהֹלְכִים בְּתוֹרַת יהוה.

אוֹדְךָ בְּיֹשֶׁר לֵבָב, בְּלָמְדִי מִשְׁפְּטֵי צִדְקֶךָ.

Blessed are they whose way is upright,
who follow the path of God's teaching.

As we learn Your laws of justice,
we thank You with a whole heart.

זֹאת נֶחָמָתִי בְעָנְיִי, כִּי אִמְרָתְךָ חִיָּתְנִי.

יְבֹאוּנִי רַחֲמֶיךָ וְאֶחְיֶה, כִּי־תוֹרָתְךָ שַׁעֲשֻׁעָי.

This comforts us when we are brought low:
Your teaching gives us new life.

In Your compassion You give me life,
for Your Torah is my delight.

לוּלֵי תוֹרָתְךָ שַׁעֲשֻׁעָי, אָז אָבַדְתִּי בְעָנְיִי.

נֵר־לְרַגְלִי דְבָרֶךָ, וְאוֹר לִנְתִיבָתִי.

Were not Your Torah my delight,
I would perish in my affliction

Your words are a lamp for our feet,
a light for our path.

נָחַלְתִּי עֵדְוֹתֶיךָ לְעוֹלָם, כִּי־שְׂשׂוֹן לִבִּי הֵמָּה.

עַל־כֵּן אָהַבְתִּי מִצְוֹתֶיךָ מִזָּהָב וּמִפָּז.

We will cherish Your testimonies always,
for they are the joy of our hearts.

Therefore we prize Your commandments more than gold,
than refined gold.

צִדְקָתְךָ צֶדֶק לְעוֹלָם; וְתוֹרָתְךָ אֱמֶת.

שָׂשׂ אָנֹכִי עַל־אִמְרָתֶךָ, כְּמוֹצֵא שָׁלָל רָב.

Your righteousness is everlasting; Your Torah is truth.

So we rejoice in Your teaching,
as one who finds great treasure.

וַיְדַבֵּר מֹשֶׁה אֶת־מֹעֲדֵי יהוה אֶל־בְּנֵי יִשְׂרָאֵל.

And Moses proclaimed God's festivals to the people of Israel.

&

ON WEEKDAYS

FROM PSALM 67

אֱלֹהִים יְחָנֵּנוּ וִיבָרְכֵנוּ, יָאֵר פָּנָיו אִתָּנוּ סֶלָה,

לָדַעַת בָּאָרֶץ דַּרְכֶּךָ, בְּכָל־גּוֹיִם יְשׁוּעָתֶךָ.

God, be gracious to us and bless us,
and let Your face shine upon us,

that Your way may be known upon earth,
Your deliverance among all nations.

❋ See "Selected Psalms," pages 358-375, and "A Daily Psalm," pages 27-33.

יוֹדוּךָ עַמִּים אֱלֹהִים, יוֹדוּךָ עַמִּים כֻּלָּם.

יִשְׂמְחוּ וִירַנְּנוּ לְאֻמִּים, כִּי־תִשְׁפֹּט עַמִּים מִישׁוֹר,

וּלְאֻמִּים בָּאָרֶץ תַּנְחֵם סֶלָה.

יוֹדוּךָ עַמִּים אֱלֹהִים, יוֹדוּךָ עַמִּים כֻּלָּם.

אֶרֶץ נָתְנָה יְבוּלָהּ; יְבָרְכֵנוּ אֱלֹהִים אֱלֹהֵינוּ.

יְבָרְכֵנוּ אֱלֹהִים, וְיִירְאוּ אֹתוֹ כָּל־אַפְסֵי־אָרֶץ.

Let the peoples praise You, O God;
let all the peoples praise You!

Let the nations shout for joy,
for You rule the world with justice,
and guide the nations of the earth.

Let the peoples praise You, O God;
let all the peoples praise You!

The earth has brought forth its harvest;
God, our God, has blessed us.

God has blessed us;
let all the earth give praise.

&

ON SHABBAT
FROM PSALM 92

❊ See "Selected
Psalms," pages
358-375, and
"A Daily
Psalm," pages
27-33.

A PRAISE-SONG TO THE SABBATH DAY

מִזְמוֹר שִׁיר לְיוֹם הַשַּׁבָּת

טוֹב לְהֹדוֹת לַיהוה, וּלְזַמֵּר לְשִׁמְךָ עֶלְיוֹן,

לְהַגִּיד בַּבֹּקֶר חַסְדֶּךָ, וֶאֱמוּנָתְךָ בַּלֵּילוֹת,

עֲלֵי־עָשׂוֹר וַעֲלֵי־נָבֶל, עֲלֵי הִגָּיוֹן בְּכִנּוֹר.

כִּי שִׂמַּחְתַּנִי, יהוה, בְּפָעֳלֶךָ, בְּמַעֲשֵׂי יָדֶיךָ אֲרַנֵּן.

מַה־גָּדְלוּ מַעֲשֶׂיךָ, יהוה! מְאֹד עָמְקוּ מַחְשְׁבֹתֶיךָ.

It is good to give thanks to Adonai,
to sing praises to Your name, O Most High,

to tell of Your love in the morning,
Your faithfulness in the night,

to the sound of harp and lute,
the sweet viol's song.

Oh, how You gladden me with Your deeds, Adonai;
so I sing for joy over the works of Your hands.

צַדִּיק כַּתָּמָר יִפְרָח, כְּאֶרֶז בַּלְּבָנוֹן יִשְׂגֶּה.
שְׁתוּלִים בְּבֵית יהוה, בְּחַצְרוֹת אֱלֹהֵינוּ יַפְרִיחוּ.
עוֹד יְנוּבוּן בְּשֵׂיבָה, דְּשֵׁנִים וְרַעֲנַנִּים יִהְיוּ,
לְהַגִּיד כִּי־יָשָׁר יהוה, צוּרִי, וְלֹא־עַוְלָתָה בּוֹ.

The righteous shall flourish like palms,
reach high like a cedar in Lebanon.

Rooted in Your house, Adonai,
they shall flourish in the courts of our God.
Fresh and green shall they be,
vigorous still in old age.
Proclaiming that Adonai is just,
my God, my flawless rock.

ALL RISE

חצי קדיש READER'S KADDISH

יִתְגַּדַּל וְיִתְקַדַּשׁ שְׁמֵהּ רַבָּא בְּעָלְמָא דִי־בְרָא כִרְעוּתֵהּ,
וְיַמְלִיךְ מַלְכוּתֵהּ בְּחַיֵּיכוֹן וּבְיוֹמֵיכוֹן וּבְחַיֵּי דְכָל־בֵּית
יִשְׂרָאֵל, בַּעֲגָלָא וּבִזְמַן קָרִיב, וְאִמְרוּ: אָמֵן.
יְהֵא שְׁמֵהּ רַבָּא מְבָרַךְ לְעָלַם וּלְעָלְמֵי עָלְמַיָּא.
יִתְבָּרַךְ וְיִשְׁתַּבַּח, וְיִתְפָּאַר וְיִתְרוֹמַם וְיִתְנַשֵּׂא, וְיִתְהַדָּר
וְיִתְעַלֶּה וְיִתְהַלָּל שְׁמֵהּ דְּקוּדְשָׁא, בְּרִיךְ הוּא,
לְעֵלָּא מִן־כָּל־בִּרְכָתָא וְשִׁירָתָא, תֻּשְׁבְּחָתָא וְנֶחֱמָתָא
דַּאֲמִירָן בְּעָלְמָא, וְאִמְרוּ: אָמֵן.

Yit-ga-dal v'yit-ka-dash sh'mei ra-ba b'al-ma di-v'ra chi-r'u'tei,
v'yam-lich mal-chu-tei b'cha-yei-chon u-v'yo-mei-chon u-v'cha-yei d'chol beit
Yis-ra-eil, ba-a-ga-la u-vi-z'man ka-riv, v'i-m'ru: A-mein.
Y'hei sh'mei ra-ba m'va-rach l'a-lam u-l'al-mei al-ma-ya.
Yit-ba-rach v'yish-ta-bach, v'yit-pa-ar v'yit-ro-mam v'yit-na-sei, v'yit-ha-dar
v'yit-a-leh v'yit-ha-lal sh'mei d'kud-sha, b'rich hu,
l'ei-la min kol bir-cha-ta v'shi-ra-ta, tush-b'cha-ta v'neh-cheh-ma-ta
da-a-mi-ran b'al-ma, v'i-m'ru: A-mein.

Hallowed be Your great name on earth, Your creation; establish Your dominion in our own day, in our own lives, and in the life of the whole House of Israel.

Blessed be Your great name forever and ever.

Blessed, praised, honored, and exalted be the name of the Holy One, ever to be praised, though You are beyond all the blessings and songs of praise that the world may offer.

בָּרְכוּ אֶת־יִי הַמְבֹרָךְ.

בָּרוּךְ יִי הַמְבֹרָךְ לְעוֹלָם וָעֶד.

Praise Adonai, to whom our praise is due.
We praise Adonai,
to whom our praise is due forever and ever.

מעריב ערבים   CREATION

בָּרוּךְ אַתָּה יִי, אֱלֹהֵינוּ מֶלֶךְ הָעוֹלָם,

אֲשֶׁר בִּדְבָרוֹ מַעֲרִיב עֲרָבִים,

We praise You, Adonai our God, sovereign of the universe, whose word makes evening fall.

All creation has one origin; we celebrate its creator and sustainer.

בְּחָכְמָה פּוֹתֵחַ שְׁעָרִים,

וּבִתְבוּנָה מְשַׁנֶּה עִתִּים,

וּמַחֲלִיף אֶת־הַזְּמַנִּים,

וּמְסַדֵּר אֶת־הַכּוֹכָבִים

בְּמִשְׁמְרוֹתֵיהֶם בָּרָקִיעַ

כִּרְצוֹנוֹ. בּוֹרֵא יוֹם וָלַיְלָה,

גּוֹלֵל אוֹר מִפְּנֵי חֹשֶׁךְ

וְחֹשֶׁךְ מִפְּנֵי אוֹר,

וּמַעֲבִיר יוֹם וּמֵבִיא לַיְלָה,

וּמַבְדִּיל בֵּין יוֹם וּבֵין

לָיְלָה: יִי צְבָאוֹת שְׁמוֹ.

Your wisdom opens the gates of heaven, Your understanding makes times pass and seasons change, Your law orders the stars in their courses through the skies.

Creator of day and night, You roll light away as darkness falls, and darkness with the coming of the light, making day pass and bringing on the night, to separate day from night: You are the God of time and space.

❖ See page 355 and Psalm 148 (page 374).

בָּרוּךְ אַתָּה יִי, הַמַּעֲרִיב עֲרָבִים.

We praise You, O God: Your word makes evening fall.

אהבת עולם REVELATION

אַהֲבַת עוֹלָם בֵּית יִשְׂרָאֵל עַמְּךָ אָהַבְתָּ.

Unending love have You shown the House of Israel, Your people:

God, origin of space/time, is also the foundation of the moral order.

❊ See Pirke Avot, pages 322 and 340.

תּוֹרָה וּמִצְוֹת, חֻקִּים
וּמִשְׁפָּטִים אוֹתָנוּ לִמַּדְתָּ.
עַל־כֵּן, יְיָ אֱלֹהֵינוּ,
בְּשָׁכְבֵּנוּ וּבְקוּמֵנוּ נָשִׂיחַ
בְּחֻקֶּיךָ, וְנִשְׂמַח בְּדִבְרֵי
תוֹרָתֶךָ וּבְמִצְוֹתֶיךָ לְעוֹלָם
וָעֶד. כִּי הֵם חַיֵּינוּ וְאֹרֶךְ
יָמֵינוּ, וּבָהֶם נֶהְגֶּה יוֹמָם
וָלַיְלָה. וְאַהֲבָתְךָ אַל־תָּסוּר
מִמֶּנּוּ לְעוֹלָמִים.

Torah and Mitzvot, laws and precepts have You taught us. And so, when we lie down and when we rise up, we will meditate on the meanings of Your law, and rejoice forever in Your Torah and Mitzvot. Day and night we will reflect on them, for they are our life and the length of our days. O may Your love never depart from our hearts!

בָּרוּךְ אַתָּה יְיָ, אוֹהֵב עַמּוֹ יִשְׂרָאֵל.

We praise You, O God: You love Your people Israel.

שְׁמַע יִשְׂרָאֵל: יהוה אֱלֹהֵינוּ, יהוה אֶחָד.
בָּרוּךְ שֵׁם כְּבוֹד מַלְכוּתוֹ לְעוֹלָם וָעֶד.

Hear, O Israel: Adonai is our God, Adonai alone.
Praised be God's glorious majesty forever and ever.

ALL ARE SEATED

וְאָהַבְתָּ אֵת יְהֹוָה אֱלֹהֶיךָ
בְּכָל־לְבָבְךָ וּבְכָל־נַפְשְׁךָ וּבְכָל־מְאֹדֶךָ:
וְהָיוּ הַדְּבָרִים הָאֵלֶּה אֲשֶׁר אָנֹכִי מְצַוְּךָ הַיּוֹם

195

עַל־לְבָבֶךָ: וְשִׁנַּנְתָּם לְבָנֶיךָ וְדִבַּרְתָּ בָּם
בְּשִׁבְתְּךָ בְּבֵיתֶךָ וּבְלֶכְתְּךָ בַדֶּרֶךְ וּבְשָׁכְבְּךָ וּבְקוּמֶךָ:
וּקְשַׁרְתָּם לְאוֹת עַל־יָדֶךָ וְהָיוּ לְטֹטָפֹת בֵּין עֵינֶיךָ:
וּכְתַבְתָּם עַל־מְזוּזֹת בֵּיתֶךָ וּבִשְׁעָרֶיךָ:
לְמַעַן תִּזְכְּרוּ וַעֲשִׂיתֶם אֶת־כָּל־מִצְוֹתָי
וִהְיִיתֶם קְדֹשִׁים לֵאלֹהֵיכֶם:
אֲנִי יְהֹוָה אֱלֹהֵיכֶם אֲשֶׁר הוֹצֵאתִי אֶתְכֶם מֵאֶרֶץ מִצְרַיִם
לִהְיוֹת לָכֶם לֵאלֹהִים: אֲנִי יְהֹוָה אֱלֹהֵיכֶם:

*V'a-hav-ta et Adonai Eh-lo-heh-cha b'chol l'va-v'cha u-v'chol naf-sh'cha
u-v'chol m'o-deh-cha. V'ha-yu ha-d'va-rim ha-ei-leh a-sher a-no-chi
m'tza-v'cha ha-yom al l'va-veh-cha. V'shi-nan-tam l'va-neh-cha v'di-bar-ta
bam b'shiv-t'cha b'vei-teh-cha u-v'lech-t'cha va-deh-rech u-v'shoch-b'cha
u-v'ku-meh-cha. U-k'shar-tam l'ot al ya-deh-cha v'ha-yu l'to-ta-fot bein
ei-neh-cha; u-ch'tav-tam al m'zu-zot bei-teh-cha u-vi-sh'a-reh-cha. L'ma-an
tiz-k'ru va-a-si-tem et kol mitz-vo-tai, vi-h'yi-tem k'do-shim lei-lo-hei-chem.
A-ni Adonai Eh-lo-hei-chem a-sher ho-tzei-ti et-chem mei-eh-retz mitz-ra-yim
li-h'yot la-chem lei-lo-him. A-ni Adonai Eh-lo-hei-chem.*

*You shall love Adonai your God with all your heart, with all
your soul, with all your might. Let these words, which I
command you this day, be upon your heart. Teach them
constantly to your children, speaking of them in your home and
on your way, when you lie down and when you rise up. Bind
them as a sign upon your hand and let them be symbols before
your eyes; inscribe them on the doorposts of your house, and on
your gates: that you may be mindful of all my Mitzvot, and do
them; then shall you be consecrated to your God. I, Adonai, am
your God who led you out of Egypt to be your God; I, Adonai, am
your God.*

At times we
think of You
as a question,
when we
need to feel
You as *the*
question.
May my
life be the
response I
make, when
You *are* the
question.

❀ See
"Looking for
God," pages
352-357.

196

SOME MAY WISH TO INCLUDE THE FOLLOWING

וְהָיָה אִם־שָׁמֹעַ תִּשְׁמְעוּ אֶל־מִצְוֹתַי אֲשֶׁר אָנֹכִי מְצַוֶּה אֶתְכֶם הַיּוֹם
לְאַהֲבָה אֶת־יְהֹוָה אֱלֹהֵיכֶם וּלְעָבְדוֹ בְּכָל־לְבַבְכֶם וּבְכָל־נַפְשְׁכֶם:
יְצַו יְהֹוָה אִתְּךָ אֶת־הַבְּרָכָה בַּאֲסָמֶיךָ וּבְכֹל מִשְׁלַח יָדֶךָ וּבֵרַכְךָ
בָּאָרֶץ אֲשֶׁר־יְהֹוָה אֱלֹהֶיךָ נֹתֵן לָךְ: יְקִימְךָ יְהֹוָה לוֹ לְעַם קָדוֹשׁ
כַּאֲשֶׁר נִשְׁבַּע־לָךְ כִּי תִשְׁמֹר אֶת־מִצְוֹת יְהֹוָה אֱלֹהֶיךָ וְהָלַכְתָּ
בִּדְרָכָיו: כִּי הַמִּצְוָה הַזֹּאת אֲשֶׁר אָנֹכִי מְצַוְּךָ הַיּוֹם לֹא־נִפְלֵאת
הִוא מִמְּךָ וְלֹא רְחֹקָה הִוא: כִּי־קָרוֹב אֵלֶיךָ הַדָּבָר מְאֹד בְּפִיךָ
וּבִלְבָבְךָ לַעֲשֹׂתוֹ: הַעִידֹתִי בָכֶם הַיּוֹם אֶת־הַשָּׁמַיִם וְאֶת־הָאָרֶץ
הַחַיִּים וְהַמָּוֶת נָתַתִּי לְפָנֶיךָ הַבְּרָכָה וְהַקְּלָלָה וּבָחַרְתָּ בַּחַיִּים
לְמַעַן תִּחְיֶה אַתָּה וְזַרְעֶךָ:

If you truly hearken to the Mitzvot that I command you this day, to love and serve Adonai your God with all your heart and mind, then your God will ordain blessing upon your homes and all your undertakings, and upon the soil on which your God has placed you. Adonai will affirm you as a holy people, when you keep the Mitzvot and walk in the ways of your God.

For this Mitzvah that I command you this day is not too difficult for you; nor is it far away—no, this word is very near you, in your mouth and in your heart—and you can do it. I call heaven and earth to witness before you this day: life and death have I placed before you, blessing and curse. Choose life, then, that you and your children may live.
(Deuteronomy 11:13; 28:8-9; 30:11,14,19)

જી

גאולה   REDEMPTION

אֱמֶת וֶאֱמוּנָה כָּל־זֹאת,
וְקַיָּם עָלֵינוּ, כִּי הוּא
יי אֱלֹהֵינוּ, וְאֵין זוּלָתוֹ,
וַאֲנַחְנוּ יִשְׂרָאֵל עַמּוֹ.
הַפּוֹדֵנוּ מִיַּד מְלָכִים,
הַגּוֹאֲלֵנוּ מִכַּף כָּל־הֶעָרִיצִים,
וַיּוֹצֵא אֶת־עַמּוֹ יִשְׂרָאֵל
מִמִּצְרַיִם לְחֵרוּת עוֹלָם.
וְרָאוּ בָנָיו גְּבוּרָתוֹ, שִׁבְּחוּ
וְהוֹדוּ לִשְׁמוֹ, וּמַלְכוּתוֹ
בְּרָצוֹן קִבְּלוּ עֲלֵיהֶם.
מֹשֶׁה וּמִרְיָם וְכָל־יִשְׂרָאֵל
לְךָ עָנוּ שִׁירָה בְּשִׂמְחָה
רַבָּה, וְאָמְרוּ כֻלָּם:

All this we hold to be true and sure: You are Adonai our God, there is none else, and we are Israel Your people.

You deliver us from the hand of oppressors, and save us from the fist of every tyrant, as when You led us out of Egypt, forever to be free to serve You.

When Your children witnessed Your might, they acclaimed You and gave thanks to Your name; gladly they enthroned You; then, full of joy, Moses, Miriam, and all Israel sang together:

Looking back at our first redemption from bondage, our people concluded that they could hope and expect a redemption that would last for all time. The hope remains—along with our task of briging about the redemption for which we yearn.

✣ See page 348, foot of page, and Psalm 3 (page 358).

מִי־כָמֹכָה בָּאֵלִם, יהוה?
מִי כָּמֹכָה, נֶאְדָּר בַּקֹּדֶשׁ,
נוֹרָא תְהִלֹּת, עֹשֵׂה פֶלֶא?
מַלְכוּתְךָ רָאוּ בָנֶיךָ,
בּוֹקֵעַ יָם לִפְנֵי מֹשֶׁה;
זֶה אֵלִי! עָנוּ וְאָמְרוּ:
יהוה יִמְלֹךְ לְעֹלָם וָעֶד!

Mi cha-mo-cha ba-ei-lim, Adonai?

Mi ka-mo-cha, neh-dar ba-ko-desh,

no-ra t'hi-lot, o-sei feh-leh?

Mal-chu-t'cha ra-u va-neh-cha,

bo-kei-a yam li-f'nei Mo-sheh;

zeh Ei-li! A-nu v'a-m'ru:

Adonai yim-loch l'o-lam va-ed.

וְנֶאֱמַר: *V'neh-eh-mar:*

כִּי פָדָה יי אֶת־יַעֲקֹב,   *Ki fa-da Adonai et Ya-a-kov,*

וּגְאָלוֹ מִיַּד חָזָק מִמֶּנּוּ.   *u-g'a-lo mi-yad cha-zak mi-meh-nu.*

בָּרוּךְ אַתָּה יי, גָּאַל   *Ba-ruch a-ta Adonai, ga-al*

יִשְׂרָאֵל.   *Yis-ra-eil.*

Who is like You, Adonai, all that is worshiped? Who is like You, glorious in holiness, awesome in splendor, doing wonders?

In the parting of the waters, Your children perceived Your sovereign might. "This is my God!" they cried. "Adonai shall reign forever and ever." And it has been said: "Adonai has delivered Jacob, and redeemed us from the hand of one stronger than ourselves."

We praise You, O God, redeemer of Israel.

הַשְׁכִּיבֵנוּ   DIVINE PROVIDENCE

✢ See page 379, Psalm 4 (page 359), and Psalm 131 (page 370).

הַשְׁכִּיבֵנוּ, יי אֱלֹהֵינוּ, לְשָׁלוֹם, וְהַעֲמִידֵנוּ, מַלְכֵּנוּ, לְחַיִּים.

וּפְרוֹשׂ עָלֵינוּ סֻכַּת שְׁלוֹמֶךָ, וְתַקְּנֵנוּ בְּעֵצָה טוֹבָה מִלְּפָנֶיךָ,

וְהוֹשִׁיעֵנוּ לְמַעַן שְׁמֶךָ, וְהָגֵן בַּעֲדֵנוּ.

Help us to lie down in peace, Adonai our God, and help us rise up to life renewed. Spread over us the shelter of Your peace; guide us with Your good counsel; and for Your name's sake, be our help.

וְהָסֵר מֵעָלֵינוּ אוֹיֵב דֶּבֶר וְחֶרֶב וְרָעָב וְיָגוֹן; וְהָסֵר שָׂטָן

מִלְּפָנֵינוּ וּמֵאַחֲרֵינוּ. וּבְצֵל כְּנָפֶיךָ תַּסְתִּירֵנוּ, כִּי אֵל שׁוֹמְרֵנוּ

וּמַצִּילֵנוּ אָתָּה, כִּי אֵל מֶלֶךְ חַנּוּן וְרַחוּם אָתָּה.

וּשְׁמוֹר צֵאתֵנוּ וּבוֹאֵנוּ לְחַיִּים וּלְשָׁלוֹם מֵעַתָּה וְעַד עוֹלָם.

Be a shield about us; save us from hatred and sickness, from war, famine, and anguish; and help us to turn aside from evil. Shelter us in the shadow of Your wings, for You are our guardian and

helper, a gracious and merciful God. And guard our going out and our coming in, that we may have life and peace, now and always.

בָּרוּךְ אַתָּה יי, הַפּוֹרֵשׂ סֻכַּת שָׁלוֹם עָלֵינוּ וְעַל־כָּל־עַמּוֹ יִשְׂרָאֵל וְעַל־יְרוּשָׁלָיִם.

We praise You, O God: may Your sheltering peace descend on us, all Israel, and all who dwell on earth.

ON SHABBAT

ושמרו   THE COVENANT OF SHABBAT

וְשָׁמְרוּ בְנֵי־יִשְׂרָאֵל אֶת־הַשַּׁבָּת, לַעֲשׂוֹת אֶת־הַשַּׁבָּת לְדֹרֹתָם בְּרִית עוֹלָם. בֵּינִי וּבֵין בְּנֵי יִשְׂרָאֵל אוֹת הִיא לְעֹלָם. כִּי־שֵׁשֶׁת יָמִים עָשָׂה יהוה אֶת־הַשָּׁמַיִם וְאֶת־הָאָרֶץ, וּבַיּוֹם הַשְּׁבִיעִי שָׁבַת וַיִּנָּפַשׁ.

V'sha-m'ru v'nei Yis-ra-eil et ha-Shabbat, la-a-sot et ha-Shabbat l'do-ro-tam,
b'rit o-lam. Bei-ni u-vein b'nei Yis-ra-eil ot hi l'o-lam.
Ki shei-shet ya-mim a-sa Adonai et ha-sha-ma-yim v'et ha-a-retz,
u-va-yom ha-sh'vi-i sha-vat va-yi-na-fash.

The people of Israel shall keep the Sabbath, observing the Sabbath in every generation as a covenant forever. It is a sign between me and the people of Israel forever. For in six days Adonai made heaven and earth, but on the seventh day God rested and was refreshed.

A REFLECTION

❧   *It is good to sing to our God.* (Psalm 147:1) It is good if you can have God sing within you. (Chasidic)

Thou hast given so much to me
Give me one thing more—a grateful heart.

ALL RISE

תפלה TEFILAH

אֲדֹנָי שְׂפָתַי תִּפְתָּח, וּפִי יַגִּיד תְּהִלָּתֶךָ.

Eternal God, open my lips, and my mouth will declare Your praise.

אבות ואמהות GOD OF ALL GENERATIONS

The Yom Tov Tefilah has seven prayers. In the first, we recall with reverence the founders of our people and faith. We say: Each generation finds its own way, and yet— their God is ours.

✻ See "Looking for God," pages 352-357.

בָּרוּךְ אַתָּה יי, אֱלֹהֵינוּ
   Ba-ruch a-ta Adonai, Eh-lo-hei-nu

וֵאלֹהֵי אֲבוֹתֵינוּ וְאִמּוֹתֵינוּ:
   vei-lo-hei a-vo-tei-nu v'i-mo-tei-nu:

אֱלֹהֵי אַבְרָהָם, אֱלֹהֵי
   Eh-lo-hei Av-ra-ham, eh-lo-hei

יִצְחָק וֵאלֹהֵי יַעֲקֹב:
   Yitz-chak, vei-lo-hei Ya-a-kov.

אֱלֹהֵי שָׂרָה, אֱלֹהֵי רִבְקָה,
   Eh-lo-hei Sa-rah, eh-lo-hei Riv-kah,

אֱלֹהֵי לֵאָה וֵאלֹהֵי רָחֵל;
   eh-lo-hei Lei-ah, vei-lo-hei Ra-cheil;

הָאֵל הַגָּדוֹל הַגִּבּוֹר וְהַנּוֹרָא,
   Ha-eil ha-ga-dol ha-gi-bor v'ha-no-ra,

אֵל עֶלְיוֹן. גוֹמֵל חֲסָדִים
   eil el-yon. Go-meil cha-sa-dim

טוֹבִים וְקוֹנֵה הַכֹּל,
   to-vim, v'ko-nei ha-kol,

וְזוֹכֵר חַסְדֵי אָבוֹת וְאִמָּהוֹת,
   v'zo-cheir chas-dei a-vot v'i-ma-hot,

וּמֵבִיא גְאֻלָּה לִבְנֵי בְנֵיהֶם,
   u-mei-vi g'u-la li-v'nei v'nei-hem,

לְמַעַן שְׁמוֹ בְּאַהֲבָה. מֶלֶךְ
   l'ma-an sh'mo, b'a-ha-vah. Meh-lech

עוֹזֵר וּמוֹשִׁיעַ וּמָגֵן.
   o-zeir u-mo-shi-a u-ma-gein.

בָּרוּךְ אַתָּה יי,
   Ba-ruch a-ta Adonai,

מָגֵן אַבְרָהָם וְעֶזְרַת שָׂרָה.
   ma-gein Av-ra-ham v'ez-rat Sa-rah.

We praise You, Adonai our God and God of our ancestors: of Abraham, Isaac, and Jacob; of Sarah, Rebekah, Leah, and Rachel; the great, mighty, and awesome God, God Most High. You deal kindly with us and embrace us all. You remember the faithfulness of our ancestors, and in love bring redemption to their children's children for the sake of Your name. You are our sovereign and helper, our redeemer and shield. We praise You, Adonai, Shield of Abraham and Protector of Sarah.

גבורות GOD'S POWER

אַתָּה גִבּוֹר לְעוֹלָם, אֲדֹנָי,

מְחַיֵּה מֵתִים אַתָּה, רַב

לְהוֹשִׁיעַ.

מַשִּׁיב הָרוּחַ וּמוֹרִיד הַגֶּשֶׁם,

מַזְרִיחַ הַשֶּׁמֶשׁ וּמוֹרִיד הַטָּל.

מְכַלְכֵּל חַיִּים בְּחֶסֶד,

מְחַיֵּה מֵתִים בְּרַחֲמִים רַבִּים.

סוֹמֵךְ נוֹפְלִים, וְרוֹפֵא

חוֹלִים, וּמַתִּיר אֲסוּרִים,

וּמְקַיֵּם אֱמוּנָתוֹ לִישֵׁנֵי עָפָר.

מִי כָמְוֹךָ, בַּעַל גְּבוּרוֹת,

וּמִי דְּוֹמֶה לָּךְ,

מֶלֶךְ מֵמִית וּמְחַיֶּה

וּמַצְמִיחַ יְשׁוּעָה? וְנֶאֱמָן

אַתָּה לְהַחֲיוֹת מֵתִים.

בָּרוּךְ אַתָּה יי, מְחַיֵּה הַמֵּתִים.

A-ta gi-bor l'o-lam, Adonai,
m'cha-yei mei-tim a-ta, rav
l'ho-shi-a. Ma-shiv ha-ru-ach
u-mo-rid ha-ga-shem; maz-ri-ach
ha-she-mesh u-mo-rid ha-tal.
M'chal-keil cha-yim b'cheh-sed,
m'cha-yei mei-tim b'ra-cha-mim
ra-bim. So-meich no-f'lim, v'ro-fei
cho-lim, u-ma-tir a-su-rim,
u-m'ka-yeim eh-mu-na-to li-shei-nei
a-far. Mi cha-mo-cha ba-al g'vu-rot,
u-mi do-meh lach, meh-lech mei-mit
u-m'cha-yeh u-matz-mi-ach y'shu-a?
V'neh-eh-man a-ta l'ha-cha-yot
mei-tim. Ba-ruch a-ta Adonai,
m'cha-yei ha-mei-tim.

In this prayer we affirm the power of God, whose reach extends to all worlds—from the world we walk in, to worlds we cannot imagine.

✢ See Psalm 103 (page 366) and Psalm 146 (page 371).

Unending is Your might, Eternal One; You are the source of eternal life; great is Your power to save. You cause the wind to blow and the rain to fall, the sun to shine and the dew to descend.

In Your love You sustain the living; in Your compassion You grant us eternal life. You support the falling and heal the sick; You free the captive and keep faith with those who sleep in the dust. Who is like You, source of all strength? Who is Your equal, sovereign author of life and death, who causes deliverance to flower in our world?

Trusting in You, we see life beyond death.

We praise You, O God, source of eternal life.

קדושת השם   THE HOLINESS OF GOD

As we walk beneath the stars, we walk among them, and the mystery of being calls to us— this prayer proclaims the holiness of God.

אַתָּה קָדוֹשׁ וְשִׁמְךָ קָדוֹשׁ,   A-ta ka-dosh v'shi-m'cha ka-dosh,

וּקְדוֹשִׁים בְּכָל־יוֹם   u-k'do-shim b'chol yom

יְהַלְלוּךָ סֶּלָה. בָּרוּךְ   y'ha-l'lu-cha seh-lah. Ba-ruch

אַתָּה יְיָ, הָאֵל הַקָּדוֹשׁ.   a-ta Adonai, ha-eil ha-ka-dosh.

You are holy, Your name is holy, and every day all creation sings Your praise. We praise You, Adonai, the holy God.

ALL ARE SEATED

✳ See Psalm 42/3 (page 363) and Psalm 63 (page 365).

קדושת היום   THE HOLINESS OF YOM TOV

Our Tefilah's middle blessing celebrates the holiness of the day. Yom Tov is an in-vitation to live a life filled with joyful celebration.

אַתָּה בְחַרְתָּנוּ מִכָּל־הָעַמִּים, אָהַבְתָּ אוֹתָנוּ וְרָצִיתָ בָּנוּ,

וְקִדַּשְׁתָּנוּ בְּמִצְוֹתֶיךָ, וְקֵרַבְתָּנוּ, מַלְכֵּנוּ, לַעֲבוֹדָתֶךָ, וְשִׁמְךָ

הַגָּדוֹל וְהַקָּדוֹשׁ עָלֵינוּ קָרָאתָ.

וַתִּתֶּן לָנוּ, יְיָ אֱלֹהֵינוּ, בְּאַהֲבָה (שַׁבָּתוֹת לִמְנוּחָה וּ) מוֹעֲדִים

לְשִׂמְחָה, חַגִּים וּזְמַנִּים לְשָׂשׂוֹן, אֶת־יוֹם (הַשַּׁבָּת הַזֶּה וְאֶת־יוֹם)

❖ חַג הַמַּצּוֹת הַזֶּה, זְמַן חֵרוּתֵנוּ,

❖ חַג הַשָּׁבוּעוֹת הַזֶּה, זְמַן מַתַּן תּוֹרָתֵנוּ,

❖ חַג הַסֻּכּוֹת הַזֶּה, זְמַן שִׂמְחָתֵנוּ,

❖ הַשְּׁמִינִי חַג הָעֲצֶרֶת הַזֶּה, זְמַן שִׂמְחָתֵנוּ,

(בְּאַהֲבָה) מִקְרָא קֹדֶשׁ, זֵכֶר לִיצִיאַת מִצְרָיִם.

You have called us to a sacred task among the peoples. In Your love and favor You have hallowed us by Your Mitzvot, drawn us near to Your service, and charged us to make known Your great and holy name. And in Your love, Adonai our God, You have given us (Sabbaths of rest,) feasts of joy and seasons of gladness, among them this (Sabbath day and this)

❖ Festival of Pesach, season of our freedom,

❖ Festival of Shavuot, season of revelation,

❖ Festival of Sukkot, season of our gladness,

❖ Festival of Sh'mini Atzeret (Simchat Torah), season of our gladness,

to unite us in worship, and in remembrance of the Exodus from Egypt.

אֱלֹהֵינוּ וֵאלֹהֵי אֲבוֹתֵינוּ וְאִמּוֹתֵינוּ, יַעֲלֶה וְיָבֹא וְיִזָּכֵר

זִכְרוֹנֵנוּ וְזִכְרוֹן כָּל־עַמְּךָ בֵּית יִשְׂרָאֵל לְפָנֶיךָ לְטוֹבָה

לְחֵן לְחֶסֶד וּלְרַחֲמִים, לְחַיִּים וּלְשָׁלוֹם בְּיוֹם

❖ חַג הַמַּצּוֹת הַזֶּה.

❖ חַג הַשָּׁבוּעוֹת הַזֶּה.

❖ חַג הַסֻּכּוֹת הַזֶּה.

❖ הַשְּׁמִינִי חַג הָעֲצֶרֶת הַזֶּה.

זָכְרֵנוּ, יְיָ אֱלֹהֵינוּ, בּוֹ לְטוֹבָה. אָמֵן.

וּפָקְדֵנוּ בוֹ לִבְרָכָה. אָמֵן.

וְהוֹשִׁיעֵנוּ בוֹ לְחַיִּים. אָמֵן.

Our God of our fathers and mothers, be mindful of Your people Israel on this

❖ Festival of Pesach,

❖ Festival of Shavuot,

❖ Festival of Sukkot,

❖ Festival of Sh'mini Atzeret (Simchat Torah),

and renew in us love and compassion, goodness, life, and peace.

This day remember us for well-being. Amen.
Bless us with Your nearness. Amen.
Help us to renew our life. Amen.

וְהַשִּׂיאֵנוּ, יְיָ אֱלֹהֵינוּ, אֶת־בִּרְכַּת מוֹעֲדֶיךָ לְשִׂמְחָה וּלְשָׂשׂוֹן,
כַּאֲשֶׁר רָצִיתָ וְאָמַרְתָּ לְבָרְכֵנוּ. קַדְּשֵׁנוּ בְּמִצְוֹתֶיךָ וְתֵן חֶלְקֵנוּ
בְּתוֹרָתֶךָ. שַׂבְּעֵנוּ מִטּוּבֶךָ, וְשַׂמְּחֵנוּ בִּישׁוּעָתֶךָ, וְטַהֵר לִבֵּנוּ
לְעָבְדְּךָ בֶּאֱמֶת. וְהַנְחִילֵנוּ, יְיָ אֱלֹהֵינוּ, בְּשִׂמְחָה וּבְשָׂשׂוֹן
(שַׁבָּת וּ) מוֹעֲדֵי קָדְשֶׁךָ.

בָּרוּךְ אַתָּה יְיָ, מְקַדֵּשׁ (הַשַּׁבָּת וְ) יִשְׂרָאֵל וְהַזְּמַנִּים.

*Eternal God, may our observance of the festivals bring us
blessing, happiness, and joy. Sanctify us with Your Mitzvot, and
let Your Torah be our life's portion. Satisfy us with Your
goodness, gladden us with Your salvation, and purify our hearts
to serve You in truth*

Grant also, eternal God, that the joy of (Shabbat and) *Yom Tov
may be with us always.*

We praise You, O God, for the holiness of (Shabbat,) *Israel and the
Festivals.*

עבודה WORSHIP

רְצֵה, יְיָ אֱלֹהֵינוּ, בְּעַמְּךָ יִשְׂרָאֵל
וּתְפִלָּתָם בְּאַהֲבָה תְקַבֵּל,
וּתְהִי לְרָצוֹן תָּמִיד עֲבוֹדַת יִשְׂרָאֵל עַמֶּךָ.
בָּרוּךְ אַתָּה יְיָ, שֶׁאוֹתְךָ לְבַדְּךָ בְּיִרְאָה נַעֲבוֹד.

Look with favor, Adonai our God, upon Your people Israel,
and with love accept our prayers. May our worship ever be
worthy of Your favor. We praise You, Adonai: You alone are
the One we worship in awe.

This is a
prayer for
prayer itself,
that our
prayers may
be worthy, for
do we not
become what
we pray for?

❖ See "Prayer
and Its
Value," pages
3-5.

הודאה   THANKSGIVING

מוֹדִים אֲנַחְנוּ לָךְ שָׁאַתָּה הוּא יי אֱלֹהֵינוּ וֵאלֹהֵי אֲבוֹתֵינוּ
וְאִמּוֹתֵינוּ, אֱלֹהֵי כָל־בָּשָׂר, יוֹצְרֵנוּ יוֹצֵר בְּרֵאשִׁית.
בְּרָכוֹת וְהוֹדָאוֹת לְשִׁמְךָ הַגָּדוֹל וְהַקָּדוֹשׁ עַל־שֶׁהֶחֱיִיתָנוּ
וְקִיַּמְתָּנוּ. כֵּן תְּחַיֵּנוּ וּתְקַיְּמֵנוּ, יי אֱלֹהֵינוּ, וְתֶאֱסוֹף גָּלֻיּוֹתֵינוּ
לְשָׁמֹר חֻקֶּיךָ, לַעֲשׂוֹת רְצוֹנֶךָ, וּלְעָבְדְּךָ בְּלֵבָב שָׁלֵם.
בָּרוּךְ אֵל הַהוֹדָאוֹת.

We affirm with gratitude that You, Adonai, are our God, the
God of our fathers and mothers, the God of all flesh, our
creator, the source of all being. We bless and praise Your
great and holy name, for keeping us in life and sustaining
us.

*Continue us in life and sustain us, Adonai our God; strengthen
us to observe Your laws, to do Your will, and to serve You with a
whole heart. Praised be God, to whom our thanks are due.*

We are taught
to be grateful
for life and for
all that life
makes
possible.

❖ See "Giving
Thanks," page
399, and Psalm
147 (page 372).

ברכת שלום   PEACE

שָׁלוֹם רָב עַל־יִשְׂרָאֵל עַמְּךָ תָּשִׂים לְעוֹלָם,
כִּי אַתָּה הוּא מֶלֶךְ אָדוֹן לְכָל־הַשָּׁלוֹם.
וְטוֹב בְּעֵינֶיךָ לְבָרֵךְ אֶת־עַמְּךָ יִשְׂרָאֵל
וְאֶת־כָּל־הָעַמִּים בְּכָל־עֵת וּבְכָל־שָׁעָה בִּשְׁלוֹמֶךָ.

Supreme source of peace, grant true and lasting peace to our
people Israel, for it is good in Your sight that Your people
Israel, and all peoples, may be blessed at all times with Your
gift of peace.

Our final
prayer is for
peace, serenity,
well-being,
for ourselves
and our
people, and
for all people.

❖ See Pirke
Avot, pages
324–325, and
page 351.

בָּרוּךְ אַתָּה יי, הַמְבָרֵךְ אֶת־עַמּוֹ יִשְׂרָאֵל בַּשָּׁלוֹם.
We praise You, O God: You bless Your people Israel with peace.

SILENT PRAYER

אֱלֹהַי, נְצֹר לְשׁוֹנִי מֵרָע, וּשְׂפָתַי מִדַּבֵּר מִרְמָה. וְלִמְקַלְלַי נַפְשִׁי
תִדּוֹם וְנַפְשִׁי כֶּעָפָר לַכֹּל תִּהְיֶה. פְּתַח לִבִּי בְּתוֹרָתֶךָ, וּבְמִצְוֹתֶיךָ
תִּרְדֹּף נַפְשִׁי. עֲשֵׂה לְמַעַן שְׁמֶךָ, עֲשֵׂה לְמַעַן יְמִינֶךָ, עֲשֵׂה
לְמַעַן קְדֻשָּׁתֶךָ, עֲשֵׂה לְמַעַן תּוֹרָתֶךָ; לְמַעַן יֵחָלְצוּן יְדִידֶיךָ,
הוֹשִׁיעָה יְמִינְךָ וַעֲנֵנִי.

My God, keep my tongue from evil, my lips from deceptive speech. In the face of malice give me a quiet spirit; let me be humble wherever I go. Open my heart to Your teaching, make me eager to fulfill Your Mitzvot. Then will Your name be exalted, Your might manifest, Your holiness visible, Your Torah magnified. Inspire me to love You, and be the answer to my prayer.

PESACH

  ❧   "Why?" is of all questions the deepest, the most profound. And so the right to ask is the primary means to the liberation of mind and soul. The ability to question is a precious gift that parents must nurture within their children.

SHAVUOT

  ❧   The Koretzer Rebbe said: Within us are all the worlds, and we can therefore be in contact with them all. Within us are all the qualities, good and evil, but they are unborn, and we have the power to beget them. We can transform evil qualities into good, and good into evil. By studying Torah and performing Mitzvot we give birth to the angelic within us. (Chasidic)

SUKKOT AND SH'MINI ATZERET (SIMCHAT TORAH)

☾ Thank You, O God, for all the changing seasons—all that is sweet in my life, on days that swiftly pass—all that I have learned in bitter hours and days, even when they seem reluctant to end: all the changeful moments of being are a gift, the gift of life.

I saw how rows of white raindrops
From bare boughs shone,
And how the storm had stript leaves,
Forgetting none
Save one left high on a top twig
Swinging alone;
Then that too bursting into song
Fled and was gone. (Andrew Young)

&

יִהְיוּ לְרָצוֹן אִמְרֵי־פִי   *Yi-h'yu l'ra-tzon i-m'rei fi*

וְהֶגְיוֹן לִבִּי לְפָנֶיךָ,   *v'heg-yon li-bi l'fa-neh-cha,*

יהוה, צוּרִי וְגֹאֲלִי.   *Adonai tzu-ri v'go-a-li.*

May the words of my mouth and the meditations of my heart be acceptable to You, O God, my rock and my redeemer. Amen.

&

עֹשֶׂה שָׁלוֹם בִּמְרוֹמָיו,   *O-seh sha-lom bi-m'ro-mav,*

הוּא יַעֲשֶׂה שָׁלוֹם עָלֵינוּ   *hu ya-a-seh sha-lom a-lei-nu*

וְעַל־כָּל־יִשְׂרָאֵל, וְאִמְרוּ:   *v'al kol Yis-ra-eil, v'i-m'ru:*

אָמֵן.   *A-mein.*

May the source of peace on high send peace to us, to all Israel, and to all the world, and let us say: Amen.

הלל קטן   SHORT FORM OF HALLEL

PSALM 117

❧ See
"Selected
Psalms,"
pages 358-375,
and "A Daily
Psalm," pages
27-33.

הַלְלוּ אֶת־יהוה כָּל־גּוֹיִם;
שַׁבְּחוּהוּ כָּל־הָאֻמִּים,
כִּי גָבַר עָלֵינוּ חַסְדּוֹ,
וֶאֱמֶת־יהוה לְעוֹלָם,
הַלְלוּיָהּ!

Praise Adonai, all you nations; extol the Eternal One, all you peoples, for God's love for us is tremendous, and God's faithfulness is everlasting. Halleluyah!

FROM PSALM 118

הוֹדוּ לַיהוה כִּי־טוֹב, כִּי לְעוֹלָם חַסְדּוֹ.

יֹאמַר־נָא יִשְׂרָאֵל: כִּי לְעוֹלָם חַסְדּוֹ.

יֹאמְרוּ־נָא בֵית־אַהֲרֹן: כִּי לְעוֹלָם חַסְדּוֹ.

יֹאמְרוּ־נָא יִרְאֵי יהוה: כִּי לְעוֹלָם חַסְדּוֹ.

בָּרוּךְ הַבָּא בְּשֵׁם יהוה; בֵּרַכְנוּכֶם מִבֵּית יהוה.

אֵלִי אַתָּה, וְאוֹדֶךָּ; אֱלֹהַי, אֲרוֹמְמֶךָּ.

הוֹדוּ לַיהוה כִּי־טוֹב, כִּי לְעוֹלָם חַסְדּוֹ.

Give thanks to Adonai, who is good,

whose love endures forever.

Let Israel declare:

God's love endures forever.

Let the House of Aaron declare:

God's love endures forever.

Let all who fear God declare:

God's love endures forever.

Blessed are you who come in God's name;
here, in God's house, may you be blessed.

You are my God, and I thank You;
You are my God, I exalt You.

Give thanks to Adonai, who is good,

whose love endures forever.

৯৯

שחרית ליום טוב   YOM TOV MORNING SERVICE

THE RITUAL FOR PUTTING ON THE TALLIT IS ON PAGE 21

❧

ברכות השחר   MORNING BLESSINGS

מה טבו   THE BLESSING OF WORSHIP

A PRAYER
BEFORE
PRAYER:
May my
worship on
this Yom Tov
encourage me
to fulfill this
precept: "You
shall rejoice
before Adonai
your God."

מַה־טֹּבוּ אֹהָלֶיךָ, יַעֲקֹב,

מִשְׁכְּנֹתֶיךָ, יִשְׂרָאֵל! וַאֲנִי,

בְּרֹב חַסְדְּךָ אָבוֹא בֵיתֶךָ,

אֶשְׁתַּחֲוֶה אֶל־הֵיכַל־

קָדְשְׁךָ בְּיִרְאָתֶךָ.

יהוה, אָהַבְתִּי מְעוֹן בֵּיתֶךָ,

וּמְקוֹם מִשְׁכַּן כְּבוֹדֶךָ.

וַאֲנִי אֶשְׁתַּחֲוֶה וְאֶכְרָעָה,

אֶבְרְכָה לִפְנֵי־יהוה עֹשִׂי.

וַאֲנִי תְפִלָּתִי־לְךָ, יהוה, עֵת

רָצוֹן. אֱלֹהִים, בְּרָב־חַסְדֶּךָ,

עֲנֵנִי בֶּאֱמֶת יִשְׁעֶךָ.

Mah to-vu o-ha-leh-cha, Ya-a-kov,

mish-k'no-teh-cha, Yis-ra-eil! Va-a-ni,

b'rov chas-d'cha a-vo vei-teh-cha,

esh-ta-cha-veh el hei-chal

kod-sh'cha b'yir-a-teh-cha.

Adonai, a-hav-ti m'on bei-teh-cha

u-m'kom mish-kan k'vo-deh-cha.

Va-a-ni esh-ta-cha-veh v'ech-ra-ah,

ev-r'cha li-f'nei Adonai o-si.

Va-a-ni t'fi-la-ti l'cha, Adonai, eit

ra-tzon. Eh-lo-him b'rov chas-deh-cha

a-nei-ni beh-eh-met yish-eh-cha.

How lovely are your tents, O Jacob, your dwelling-places, O Israel! Your great love, O God, inspires me to enter Your house; with awe I worship in Your sanctuary.

Adonai, I love the house where Your glory dwells; humbly I worship before my God and maker.

May my prayer be acceptable to You, Adonai. In Your great kindness, answer me with Your saving truth.

211

FOR ALL FESTIVALS

FROM PSALM 57

נָכוֹן לִבִּי, אֱלֹהִים,

נָכוֹן לִבִּי!

אָשִׁירָה וַאֲזַמֵּרָה!

עוּרָה כְבוֹדִי!

עוּרָה הַנֵּבֶל וְכִנּוֹר!

אָעִירָה שָּׁחַר!

אוֹדְךָ בָעַמִּים, אֲדֹנָי,

אֲזַמֶּרְךָ בַּלְאֻמִּים.

כִּי גָדֹל עַד־שָׁמַיִם חַסְדֶּךָ,

וְעַד־שְׁחָקִים אֲמִתֶּךָ.

My heart is ready, O God, my heart is ready!
I will sing, I will sing praises!
Awake, O my soul!
Awake, O harp and lyre!
I will arouse the dawn!
I will give thanks to You, Adonai,
among the peoples,
and sing Your praises among the nations.
For Your love
is high as the heavens, and Your faithfulness
reaches to the clouds.

✣ See Psalm 108 (page 367).

FOR PESACH

You led forth Your people with joy, Your loved ones with singing. Your way, O God, is holiness; what god is so great as God?

You do wonders, O God. You have shown the nations Your power.

With strength You redeemed Your people, the children of Jacob and Joseph.

Your path was through the sea, Your way through raging waters.

Though mortal eyes could not see, You led Your people like a flock.

During this festival we celebrate the birth of our people: our going forth from the house of bondage; and life's annual rebirth, the earth's renewal, the God who embraces us

קוּמִי לָךְ, רַעְיָתִי, יָפָתִי,	*Rise up, my love,*
וּלְכִי־לָךְ.	*my fair one, come away!*
כִּי־הִנֵּה הַסְּתָיו עָבָר,	*For now the winter is past,*
הַגֶּשֶׁם חָלַף הָלַךְ לוֹ.	*the rains are over and gone.*
הַנִּצָּנִים נִרְאוּ בָאָרֶץ,	*The flowers appear on the earth,*
עֵת הַזָּמִיר הִגִּיעַ.	*the time of singing has come.*
וְקוֹל הַתּוֹר	*The voice of the turtledove*
נִשְׁמַע בְּאַרְצֵנוּ.	*is heard in our land.*

❧

ON WEEKDAYS, CONTINUE ON PAGE 217

ON SHABBAT, CONTINUE ON PAGE 218

❧

Shavuot is the season of revelation; on Pesach we went forth to freedom; now, in the gift of Torah, we celebrate the freedom of spirit that Torah brings to those who hold it dear.

FOR SHAVUOT

FROM HOSEA 2

לָכֵן הִנֵּה אָנֹכִי מְפַתֶּיהָ, וְהֹלַכְתִּיהָ הַמִּדְבָּר, וְדִבַּרְתִּי עַל־לִבָּהּ.
וְכָרַתִּי לָהֶם בְּרִית בַּיּוֹם הַהוּא עִם־חַיַּת הַשָּׂדֶה, וְעִם־עוֹף
הַשָּׁמַיִם וְרֶמֶשׂ הָאֲדָמָה: וְקֶשֶׁת וְחֶרֶב וּמִלְחָמָה אֶשְׁבּוֹר
מִן־הָאָרֶץ, וְהִשְׁכַּבְתִּים לָבֶטַח.

213

Now I will draw you to me, lead you through the wasted land, and speak to your heart. I will make a covenant for you, that day, with animals, birds, and every creature: I will break the tools of war—the bow, the sword—and remove them from the world, so that you shall dwell in safety, for I am the God who embraces you:

וְאֵרַשְׂתִּיךְ לִי לְעוֹלָם, וְאֵרַשְׂתִּיךְ לִי בְּצֶדֶק וּבְמִשְׁפָּט,

וּבְחֶסֶד וּבְרַחֲמִים, וְאֵרַשְׂתִּיךְ לִי בֶּאֱמוּנָה, וְיָדַעַתְּ אֶת־יהוה.

I will betroth you to me forever; I will betroth you to me in righteousness and justice, in kindness and in love. I will betroth you to me in faithfulness, and you shall know the Eternal One.

&

ON WEEKDAYS, CONTINUE ON PAGE 217

ON SHABBAT, CONTINUE ON PAGE 218

&

FOR SUKKOT

FROM ECCLESIASTES 3 AND 12

לַכֹּל זְמָן, וְעֵת לְכָל־חֵפֶץ תַּחַת הַשָּׁמָיִם:

עֵת לָלֶדֶת וְעֵת לָמוּת;

עֵת לָטַעַת וְעֵת לַעֲקוֹר נָטוּעַ;

עֵת לִפְרוֹץ וְעֵת לִבְנוֹת;

עֵת לִבְכּוֹת וְעֵת לִשְׂחוֹק;

עֵת סְפוֹד וְעֵת רְקוֹד;

עֵת לְהַשְׁלִיךְ אֲבָנִים וְעֵת כְּנוֹס אֲבָנִים;

עֵת לַחֲבוֹק וְעֵת לִרְחֹק מֵחַבֵּק;

The cycle of the festivals moves on, and in the fall we begin to look toward winter, and consider our changing lives.

214

For everything there is a season,
and a time for every desire under heaven:

A time to be born and a time to die;

A time to plant and a time to uproot;

A time to tear down and a time to build up;

A time to weep and a time to laugh;

A time to grieve and a time to dance;

A time to cast away stones,

and a time to gather stones;

A time to embrace,

and a time to refrain from embracing;

עֵת לְבַקֵּשׁ וְעֵת לְאַבֵּד; עֵת לִשְׁמוֹר וְעֵת לְהַשְׁלִיךְ;
עֵת לִקְרוֹעַ וְעֵת לִתְפּוֹר; עֵת לַחֲשׁוֹת וְעֵת לְדַבֵּר.
סוֹף דָּבָר, הַכֹּל נִשְׁמָע: אֶת־הָאֱלֹהִים יְרָא
וְאֶת־מִצְוֺתָיו שְׁמוֹר, כִּי־זֶה כָּל־הָאָדָם.

A time to seek and a time to lose;

A time to keep and a time to give away;

A time to rend and a time to mend;

A time to keep silence and a time to speak.

The end of the matter, all having been heard:

Revere God and keep God's commandments,
for that gives life its meaning

⚬

ON WEEKDAYS, CONTINUE ON PAGE 217

ON SHABBAT, CONTINUE ON PAGE 218

⚬

215

FOR ATZERET–SIMCHAT TORAH

FROM PSALM 119

בְּחֻקֹּתֶיךָ אֶשְׁתַּעֲשָׁע; לֹא אֶשְׁכַּח דְּבָרֶךָ.

גַּל־עֵינַי, וְאַבִּיטָה נִפְלָאוֹת מִתּוֹרָתֶךָ.

דֶּרֶךְ־פִּקּוּדֶיךָ הֲבִינֵנִי, וְאָשִׂיחָה בְּנִפְלְאוֹתֶיךָ.

הֲבִינֵנִי וְאֶצְּרָה תוֹרָתֶךָ, וְאֶשְׁמְרֶנָּה בְכָל־לֵב.

✤ See "Selected Psalms," pages 358-375, and "A Daily Psalm," pages 27-33.

I delight in Your statutes; I will not forget Your word.

Open my eyes, that Your Torah may show me wonders.

Make me understand the way of Your precepts, and I will reflect on Your wondrous works.

Give me understanding, that I may keep Your law, and observe it with a whole heart.

וְאֶשְׁתַּעֲשַׁע בְּמִצְוֹתֶיךָ אֲשֶׁר אָהָבְתִּי.

טוֹב־לִי תוֹרַת־פִּיךָ מֵאַלְפֵי זָהָב וָכָסֶף.

יְבֹאֻנִי רַחֲמֶיךָ וְאֶחְיֶה, כִּי־תוֹרָתְךָ שַׁעֲשֻׁעָי.

מַה־נִּמְלְצוּ לְחִכִּי אִמְרָתֶךָ, מִדְּבַשׁ לְפִי.

I delight in Your commandments, because I love them.

The instruction of Your mouth is better to me than thousands of gold and silver pieces.

Let Your mercy come to me and give me life; for Your law is my delight.

How sweet are Your words to my taste, sweeter than honey to my mouth!

פָּנֶיךָ הָאֵר בְּעַבְדֶּךָ, וְלַמְּדֵנִי אֶת־חֻקֶּיךָ.

תַּעַן לְשׁוֹנִי אִמְרָתֶךָ, כִּי כָל־מִצְוֹתֶיךָ צֶּדֶק.

216

Smile upon Your servant, and teach me Your statutes.

My tongue will sing of Your word, for all Your commandments are just.

ON SHABBAT, CONTINUE ON PAGE 218

ON WEEKDAYS

PSALM 100

מִזְמוֹר לְתוֹדָה A PSALM OF THANKSGIVING

✻ See "Selected Psalms," pages 358-375, and "A Daily Psalm," pages 27-33.

הָרִיעוּ לַיהוָה, כָּל־הָאָרֶץ;	Shout for joy to Adonai, all the earth,
עִבְדוּ אֶת־יהוה בְּשִׂמְחָה;	serve Adonai with gladness,
בֹּאוּ לְפָנָיו בִּרְנָנָה.	come before God with praiseful song.
דְּעוּ כִּי־יהוה הוּא אֱלֹהִים.	Know that Adonai, the one who made us, is God.
הוּא־עָשָׂנוּ וְלוֹ אֲנַחְנוּ;	*We are Your people; You are our maker;*
עַמּוֹ וְצֹאן מַרְעִיתוֹ.	*we are Your flock; You are our shepherd.*
בֹּאוּ שְׁעָרָיו בְּתוֹדָה,	*With thanksgiving we enter Your gates,*
חֲצֵרֹתָיו בִּתְהִלָּה.	*Your courts with acclaim.*
הוֹדוּ־לוֹ, בָּרְכוּ שְׁמוֹ.	*We give You thanks; we praise Your name.*
כִּי־טוֹב יהוה, לְעוֹלָם חַסְדּוֹ,	*For You are good, Adonai; Your love is everlasting,*
וְעַד־דֹּר וָדֹר אֱמוּנָתוֹ.	*and Your faithfulness to all generations.*

ON SHABBAT

FROM PSALM 92

A PRAISE-SONG TO THE SABBATH DAY

מִזְמוֹר שִׁיר לְיוֹם הַשַּׁבָּת

טוֹב לְהֹדוֹת לַיהוה, וּלְזַמֵּר לְשִׁמְךָ עֶלְיוֹן,

לְהַגִּיד בַּבֹּקֶר חַסְדֶּךָ, וֶאֱמוּנָתְךָ בַּלֵּילוֹת,

עֲלֵי־עָשׂוֹר וַעֲלֵי־נָבֶל, עֲלֵי הִגָּיוֹן בְּכִנּוֹר.

כִּי שִׂמַּחְתַּנִי, יהוה, בְּפָעֳלֶךָ, בְּמַעֲשֵׂי יָדֶיךָ אֲרַנֵּן.

מַה־גָּדְלוּ מַעֲשֶׂיךָ, יהוה! מְאֹד עָמְקוּ מַחְשְׁבֹתֶיךָ.

✣ See "Selected Psalms," pages 358-375, and "A Daily Psalm," pages 27-33.

It is good to give thanks to Adonai,
to sing praises to Your name, O Most High,

*To tell of Your love in the morning, Your faithfulness in the
night, to the sound of harp and lute, the sweet viol's song.*

Oh, how You gladden me with Your deeds, Adonai;
so I sing for joy over the work of Your hands.

How great are Your works, Adonai!
How very deep Your design!

צַדִּיק כַּתָּמָר יִפְרָח, כְּאֶרֶז בַּלְּבָנוֹן יִשְׂגֶּה.

שְׁתוּלִים בְּבֵית יהוה, בְּחַצְרוֹת אֱלֹהֵינוּ יַפְרִיחוּ.

עוֹד יְנוּבוּן בְּשֵׂיבָה, דְּשֵׁנִים וְרַעֲנַנִּים יִהְיוּ,

לְהַגִּיד כִּי־יָשָׁר יהוה, צוּרִי, וְלֹא־עַוְלָתָה בּוֹ.

The righteous shall flourish like palms,
reach high like a cedar in Lebanon.

Rooted in Your house, Adonai,
they shall flourish in the courts of our God.
Fresh and green shall they be, still vigorous in old age.
Proclaiming that Adonai is just, my God, my flawless rock.

ALL RISE

יצי קדיש READER'S KADDISH

יִתְגַּדַּל וְיִתְקַדַּשׁ שְׁמֵהּ רַבָּא בְּעָלְמָא דִי־בְרָא כִרְעוּתֵהּ,
וְיַמְלִיךְ מַלְכוּתֵהּ בְּחַיֵּיכוֹן וּבְיוֹמֵיכוֹן וּבְחַיֵּי דְכָל־בֵּית
יִשְׂרָאֵל, בַּעֲגָלָא וּבִזְמַן קָרִיב, וְאִמְרוּ: אָמֵן.
יְהֵא שְׁמֵהּ רַבָּא מְבָרַךְ לְעָלַם וּלְעָלְמֵי עָלְמַיָּא.
יִתְבָּרַךְ וְיִשְׁתַּבַּח, וְיִתְפָּאַר וְיִתְרוֹמַם וְיִתְנַשֵּׂא, וְיִתְהַדָּר
וְיִתְעַלֶּה וְיִתְהַלָּל שְׁמֵהּ דְּקוּדְשָׁא, בְּרִיךְ הוּא,
לְעֵלָּא מִן־כָּל־בִּרְכָתָא וְשִׁירָתָא, תֻּשְׁבְּחָתָא וְנֶחֱמָתָא
דַּאֲמִירָן בְּעָלְמָא, וְאִמְרוּ: אָמֵן.

Yit-ga-dal v'yit-ka-dash sh'mei ra-ba b'al-ma di-v'ra chi-r'u'tei,
v'yam-lich mal-chu-tei b'cha-yei-chon u-v'yo-mei-chon u-v'cha-yei d'chol beit
Yis-ra-eil, ba-a-ga-la u-vi-z'man ka-riv, v'i-m'ru: A-mein.

Y'hei sh'mei ra-ba m'va-rach l'a-lam u-l'al-mei al-ma-ya.

Yit-ba-rach v'yish-ta-bach, v'yit-pa-ar v'yit-ro-mam v'yit-na-sei, v'yit-ha-dar
v'yit-a-leh v'yit-ha-lal sh'mei d'kud-sha, b'rich hu,

l'ei-la min kol bir-cha-ta v'shi-ra-ta, tush-b'cha-ta v'neh-cheh-ma-ta
da-a-mi-ran b'al-ma, v'i-m'ru: A-mein.

Hallowed be Your great name on earth, Your creation; establish Your
dominion in our own day, in our own lives, and in the life of the whole
House of Israel.

Blessed be Your great name forever and ever.

Blessed, praised, honored, and exalted be the name of the Holy One, ever
to be praised, though You are beyond all the blessings and songs of
praise that the world may offer.

שמע וברכותיה THE SHEMA AND ITS BLESSINGS

בָּרְכוּ אֶת־יְיָ הַמְבֹרָךְ.

בָּרוּךְ יְיָ הַמְבֹרָךְ לְעוֹלָם וָעֶד.

Praise Adonai, to whom our praise is due.
We praise Adonai,
to whom our praise is due forever and ever.

יוצר CREATION

בָּרוּךְ אַתָּה יְיָ, אֱלֹהֵינוּ מֶלֶךְ הָעוֹלָם,

יוֹצֵר אוֹר וּבוֹרֵא חֹשֶׁךְ, עֹשֶׂה שָׁלוֹם וּבוֹרֵא אֶת־הַכֹּל.

We praise You, Adonai our God, sovereign of the universe,
maker of light and creator of darkness, author of peace and
creator of all things.

The creator of the universe is also its sustainer: Each morning we awaken to the miracle of a creation ancient beyond imagining, yet new as the first dawn to an infant's eyes.

✻ See page 355 and Psalm 148 (page 374).

הַמֵּאִיר לָאָרֶץ וְלַדָּרִים
עָלֶיהָ בְּרַחֲמִים, וּבְטוּבוֹ
מְחַדֵּשׁ בְּכָל־יוֹם תָּמִיד
מַעֲשֵׂה בְרֵאשִׁית. מָה
רַבּוּ מַעֲשֶׂיךָ, יְיָ! כֻּלָּם
בְּחָכְמָה עָשִׂיתָ, מָלְאָה
הָאָרֶץ קִנְיָנֶךָ. תִּתְבָּרַךְ,
יְיָ אֱלֹהֵינוּ, עַל־שֶׁבַח
מַעֲשֵׂה יָדֶיךָ וְעַל־מְאוֹרֵי־
אוֹר שֶׁעָשִׂיתָ: יְפָאֲרוּךָ סֶלָה.

In mercy You give light to
the earth and all who dwell
on it, and in Your goodness
You continually renew—day
by day—the work of
creation.

*How manifold are Your works,
O God! With wisdom You
have made them all. The work
of Your hands declares Your
praise, and the radiant stars
bear witness to Your glory.*

בָּרוּךְ אַתָּה יְיָ, יוֹצֵר הַמְּאוֹרוֹת.

We praise You, O God, creator of light.

220

REVELATION אהבה רבה

אַהֲבָה רַבָּה אֲהַבְתָּנוּ, יי אֱלֹהֵינוּ.
חֶמְלָה גְדוֹלָה וִיתֵרָה חָמַלְתָּ עָלֵינוּ.

Torah—
the moral
order—is the
theme of the
second of the
blessings that
precede the
Shema. It is a
gift of love. It
gives light to
our eyes. And
it incurs
obligation:
to learn, to
understand,
and to fulfill
the divine
mandate.

❉ See Pirke
Avot, page
322, and
Psalm 51
(page 364).

Great is Your love for us, O God, and overflowing Your
compassion.

אָבִינוּ מַלְכֵּנוּ, בַּעֲבוּר אֲבוֹתֵינוּ וְאִמּוֹתֵינוּ שֶׁבָּטְחוּ בְךָ וַתְּלַמְּדֵם
חֻקֵּי חַיִּים, כֵּן תְּחָנֵּנוּ וּתְלַמְּדֵנוּ. אָבִינוּ, הָאָב הָרַחֲמָן, הַמְרַחֵם,
רַחֵם עָלֵינוּ וְתֵן בְּלִבֵּנוּ לְהָבִין וּלְהַשְׂכִּיל, לִשְׁמֹעַ, לִלְמֹד,
וּלְלַמֵּד, לִשְׁמֹר וְלַעֲשׂוֹת וּלְקַיֵּם אֶת־כָּל־דִּבְרֵי תַלְמוּד תּוֹרָתֶךָ
בְּאַהֲבָה. וְהָאֵר עֵינֵינוּ בְּתוֹרָתֶךָ, וְדַבֵּק לִבֵּנוּ בְּמִצְוֹתֶיךָ, וְיַחֵד
לְבָבֵנוּ לְאַהֲבָה וּלְיִרְאָה אֶת־שְׁמֶךָ. וְלֹא־נֵבוֹשׁ לְעוֹלָם וָעֶד, כִּי
בְשֵׁם קָדְשְׁךָ הַגָּדוֹל וְהַנּוֹרָא בָּטָחְנוּ. נָגִילָה וְנִשְׂמְחָה בִּישׁוּעָתֶךָ,
כִּי אֵל פּוֹעֵל יְשׁוּעוֹת אָתָּה, וּבָנוּ בָחַרְתָּ וְקֵרַבְתָּנוּ לְשִׁמְךָ הַגָּדוֹל
סֶלָה בֶּאֱמֶת, לְהוֹדוֹת לְךָ וּלְיַחֶדְךָ בְּאַהֲבָה.

Our ancestors put their trust in You, and You taught them a
living law. Now be gracious to us, Compassionate One, and
teach us: fill our hearts with wisdom and insight, that we
may love, understand, and follow Your Teaching.

*Enlighten our eyes with Your Torah, help us cling to Your
commandments, and inspire us to love and revere Your name
with a ready heart.*

We rejoice in You and exult in Your saving power, for You
have ever been our help. You have called us to serve You
and have drawn us near to You in faithfulness, with joy to
offer You praise and proclaim Your unity.

בָּרוּךְ אַתָּה יי, הַבּוֹחֵר בְּעַמּוֹ יִשְׂרָאֵל בְּאַהֲבָה.

We praise You, O God, for You call us in love to Your service.

221

שְׁמַ֫ע יִשְׂרָאֵל: יהוה אֱלֹהֵ֫ינוּ, יהוה אֶחָֽד.
בָּרוּךְ שֵׁם כְּבוֹד מַלְכוּתוֹ לְעוֹלָם וָעֶד.

Hear, O Israel: Adonai is our God, Adonai alone.
Praised be God's glorious majesty forever and ever.

ALL ARE SEATED

וְאָהַבְתָּ֗ אֵ֚ת יְהֹוָ֣ה אֱלֹהֶ֔יךָ בְּכָל־לְבָבְךָ֥ וּבְכָל־נַפְשְׁךָ֖
וּבְכָל־מְאֹדֶֽךָ: וְהָי֞וּ הַדְּבָרִ֣ים הָאֵ֗לֶּה אֲשֶׁ֨ר אָנֹכִ֧י מְצַוְּךָ֛
הַיּ֖וֹם עַל־לְבָבֶֽךָ: וְשִׁנַּנְתָּ֣ם לְבָנֶ֔יךָ וְדִבַּרְתָּ֖ בָּ֑ם
בְּשִׁבְתְּךָ֤ בְּבֵיתֶ֨ךָ֙ וּבְלֶכְתְּךָ֣ בַדֶּ֔רֶךְ וּֽבְשָׁכְבְּךָ֖ וּבְקוּמֶֽךָ:
וּקְשַׁרְתָּ֥ם לְא֖וֹת עַל־יָדֶ֑ךָ וְהָי֥וּ לְטֹטָפֹ֖ת בֵּ֥ין עֵינֶֽיךָ:
וּכְתַבְתָּ֛ם עַל־מְזוּז֥וֹת בֵּיתֶ֖ךָ וּבִשְׁעָרֶֽיךָ: לְמַ֣עַן תִּזְכְּר֗וּ
וַעֲשִׂיתֶ֖ם אֶת־כָּל־מִצְוֺתָ֑י וִהְיִיתֶ֥ם קְדֹשִׁ֖ים לֵֽאלֹהֵיכֶֽם:
אֲנִ֞י יְהֹוָ֣ה אֱלֹֽהֵיכֶ֗ם אֲשֶׁ֨ר הוֹצֵ֤אתִי אֶתְכֶם֙ מֵאֶ֣רֶץ מִצְרַ֔יִם
לִהְי֥וֹת לָכֶ֖ם לֵֽאלֹהִ֑ים אֲנִ֖י יְהֹוָ֥ה אֱלֹהֵיכֶֽם:

*V'a-hav-ta et Adonai Eh-lo-heh-cha b'chol l'va-v'cha u-v'chol naf-sh'cha
u-v'chol m'o-deh-cha. V'ha-yu ha-d'va-rim ha-ei-leh a-sher a-no-chi
m'tza-v'cha ha-yom al l'va-veh-cha. V'shi-nan-tam l'va-neh-cha v'di-bar-ta
bam b'shiv-t'cha b'vei-teh-cha u-v'lech-t'cha va-deh-rech u-v'shoch-b'cha
u-v'ku-meh-cha. U-k'shar-tam l'ot al ya-deh-cha v'ha-yu l'to-ta-fot bein
ei-neh-cha; u-ch'tav-tam al m'zu-zot bei-teh-cha u-vi-sh'a-reh-cha. L'ma-an
tiz-k'ru va-a-si-tem et kol mitz-vo-tai, vi-h'yi-tem k'do-shim lei-lo-hei-chem.
A-ni Adonai Eh-lo-hei-chem a-sher ho-tzei-ti et-chem mei-eh-retz mitz-ra-yim
li-h'yot la-chem lei-lo-him. A-ni Adonai Eh-lo-hei-chem.*

*You shall love Adonai your God with all your heart, with all
your soul, with all your might. Let these words, which I
command you this day, be upon your heart. Teach them
constantly to your children, speaking of them in your home and
on your way, when you lie down and when you rise up. Bind*

At times we
think of You
as a question,
when we
need to feel
You as *the*
question.
May my life
be the
response I
make, when
You *are* the
question.

❖ See
"Looking for
God," pages
352-357).

222

them as a sign upon your hand and let them be symbols before your eyes; inscribe them on the doorposts of your house, and on your gates: that you may be mindful of all my Mitzvot, and do them; then shall you be consecrated to your God. I, Adonai, am your God who led you out of Egypt to be your God; I, Adonai, am your God.

SOME MAY WISH TO INCLUDE THE FOLLOWING

וְהָיָה אִם־שָׁמֹעַ תִּשְׁמְעוּ אֶל־מִצְוֹתַי אֲשֶׁר אָנֹכִי מְצַוֶּה אֶתְכֶם הַיּוֹם לְאַהֲבָה אֶת־יְהוָה אֱלֹהֵיכֶם וּלְעָבְדוֹ בְּכָל־לְבַבְכֶם וּבְכָל־נַפְשְׁכֶם: יְצַו יְהוָה אִתְּךָ אֶת־הַבְּרָכָה בַּאֲסָמֶיךָ וּבְכֹל מִשְׁלַח יָדֶךָ וּבֵרַכְךָ בָּאָרֶץ אֲשֶׁר־יְהוָה אֱלֹהֶיךָ נֹתֵן לָךְ: יְקִימְךָ יְהוָה לוֹ לְעַם קָדוֹשׁ כַּאֲשֶׁר נִשְׁבַּע־לָךְ כִּי תִשְׁמֹר אֶת־מִצְוֹת יְהוָה אֱלֹהֶיךָ וְהָלַכְתָּ בִּדְרָכָיו: כִּי הַמִּצְוָה הַזֹּאת אֲשֶׁר אָנֹכִי מְצַוְּךָ הַיּוֹם לֹא־נִפְלֵאת הִוא מִמְּךָ וְלֹא רְחֹקָה הִוא: כִּי־קָרוֹב אֵלֶיךָ הַדָּבָר מְאֹד בְּפִיךָ וּבִלְבָבְךָ לַעֲשֹׂתוֹ: הַעִידֹתִי בָכֶם הַיּוֹם אֶת־הַשָּׁמַיִם וְאֶת־הָאָרֶץ הַחַיִּים וְהַמָּוֶת נָתַתִּי לְפָנֶיךָ הַבְּרָכָה וְהַקְּלָלָה וּבָחַרְתָּ בַּחַיִּים לְמַעַן תִּחְיֶה אַתָּה וְזַרְעֶךָ:

If you truly hearken to the Mitzvot that I command you this day, to love and serve Adonai your God with all your heart and mind, then your God will ordain blessing upon your homes and all your undertakings, and upon the soil on which your God has placed you. Adonai will affirm you as a holy people, when you keep the Mitzvot and walk in the ways of your God.

For this Mitzvah that I command you this day is not too difficult for you; nor is it far away—no, this word is very near you, in your mouth and in your heart—and you can do it. I call heaven and earth to witness before you this day: life and death have I placed before you, blessing and curse. Choose life, then, that you and your children may live. (Deuteronomy 11:13; 28:8-9; 30:11,14,19)

גְּאוּלָה   REDEMPTION

אֱמֶת וְיַצִּיב וְיָשָׁר וְקַיָּם וְטוֹב וְיָפֶה הַדָּבָר הַזֶּה עָלֵינוּ לְעוֹלָם וָעֶד.

True, enduring, good, and beautiful are these words, now and forever.

Looking back at our first redemption from bondage, our people concluded that they could hope for and expect a redemption that would last for all time. The hope remains—along with our task of bringing about the redemption for which we yearn.

אֱמֶת שָׁאַתָּה הוּא יי אֱלֹהֵינוּ וֵאלֹהֵי אֲבוֹתֵינוּ וְאִמּוֹתֵינוּ, מַלְכֵּנוּ מֶלֶךְ אֲבוֹתֵינוּ וְאִמּוֹתֵינוּ, יוֹצְרֵנוּ צוּר יְשׁוּעָתֵנוּ, פּוֹדֵנוּ וּמַצִּילֵנוּ מֵעוֹלָם הוּא שְׁמֶךָ, אֵין אֱלֹהִים זוּלָתֶךָ. אֱמֶת אַתָּה הוּא רִאשׁוֹן וְאַתָּה הוּא אַחֲרוֹן, וּמִבַּלְעָדֶיךָ אֵין לָנוּ מוֹשִׁיעַ. מִמִּצְרַיִם גְּאַלְתָּנוּ, יי אֱלֹהֵינוּ, וּמִבֵּית עֲבָדִים פְּדִיתָנוּ. מֹשֶׁה וּמִרְיָם וּבְנֵי יִשְׂרָאֵל לְךָ עָנוּ שִׁירָה בְּשִׂמְחָה רַבָּה, וְאָמְרוּ כֻלָּם:

True it is that You are our sovereign God, as You were the God of our ancestors; You are our maker, the rock of our salvation. We have known You always as our helper and savior; there is no God but You. Truly You are the first and the last, and we have no redeemer but You.

✣ See page 348, foot of page, and Psalm 3 (page 358).

Out of Egypt You delivered us; You freed us from the house of bondage. Then, with great joy, Moses, Miriam, and all Israel sang this song to You:

מִי־כָמֹכָה בָּאֵלִם, יהוה?   *Mi cha-mo-cha ba-ei-lim, Adonai?*

מִי כָּמֹכָה, נֶאְדָּר בַּקֹּדֶשׁ,   *Mi ka-mo-cha, neh-dar ba-ko-desh,*

נוֹרָא תְהִלֹּת, עֹשֵׂה פֶלֶא?   *no-ra t'hi-lot, o-sei feh-leh?*

שִׁירָה חֲדָשָׁה שִׁבְּחוּ   *Shi-ra cha-da-sha shi-b'chu*

גְּאוּלִים לְשִׁמְךָ עַל־שְׂפַת   *g'u-lim l'shi-m'cha al s'fat*

הַיָּם; יַחַד כֻּלָּם הוֹדוּ   *ha-yam; ya-chad ku-lam ho-du*

וְהִמְלִיכוּ וְאָמְרוּ:   *v'him-li-chu v'a-m'ru:*

יהוה יִמְלֹךְ לְעֹלָם וָעֶד!   *Adonai yim-loch l'o-lam va-ed!*

צוּר יִשְׂרָאֵל, קוּמָה   *Tzur Yis-ra-eil, ku-mah*

בְּעֶזְרַת יִשְׂרָאֵל, וּפְדֵה   *b'ez-rat Yis-ra-eil, u-f'dei*

כִנְאֻמֶךָ יְהוּדָה וְיִשְׂרָאֵל.   *chi-n'u-meh-cha Y'hu-da v'Yis-ra-eil.*

גֹּאֲלֵנוּ, יי צְבָאוֹת שְׁמוֹ,   *Go-a-lei-nu, Adonai tz'va-ot sh'mo,*

קְדוֹשׁ יִשְׂרָאֵל. בָּרוּךְ   *k'dosh Yis-ra-eil. Ba-ruch*

אַתָּה יי, גָּאַל יִשְׂרָאֵל.   *a-ta Adonai, ga-al Yis-ra-eil.*

Who is like You, Adonai, among all that is worshiped? Who is like You, glorious in holiness, awesome in splendor, doing wonders?

A new song the redeemed sang to Your name at the shore of the sea. With one voice they all gave thanks and proclaimed Your sovereign power: "Adonai shall reign forever and ever."

O rock of Israel, come to Israel's help. Our redeemer is the God of all being, the Holy One of Israel. We praise You, O God, redeemer of Israel.

A REFLECTION

I have done all that You have commanded me (Deuteronomy 26:14). That means: I have rejoiced, and caused others to rejoice. (Midrash) On Yom Tov we rejoice—and help each other to rejoice—in the ever-renewed cycle of the seasons, in the undying memory of our people's liberation from bondage, and in our continual discovery of Torah.

ALL RISE

תפלה TEFILAH

אֲדֹנָי שְׂפָתַי תִּפְתָּח, וּפִי יַגִּיד תְּהִלָּתֶךָ.

Eternal God, open my lips, and my mouth will declare Your praise.

אבות ואמהות GOD OF ALL GENERATIONS

בָּרוּךְ אַתָּה יי, אֱלֹהֵינוּ
Ba-ruch a-ta Adonai, Eh-lo-hei-nu

וֵאלֹהֵי אֲבוֹתֵינוּ וְאִמּוֹתֵינוּ:
vei-lo-hei a-vo-tei-nu v'i-mo-tei-nu:

אֱלֹהֵי אַבְרָהָם, אֱלֹהֵי
Eh-lo-hei Av-ra-ham, eh-lo-hei

יִצְחָק וֵאלֹהֵי יַעֲקֹב:
Yitz-chak, vei-lo-hei Ya-a-kov.

אֱלֹהֵי שָׂרָה, אֱלֹהֵי רִבְקָה,
Eh-lo-hei Sa-rah, eh-lo-hei Riv-kah,

אֱלֹהֵי לֵאָה וֵאלֹהֵי רָחֵל;
eh-lo-hei Lei-ah, vei-lo-hei Ra-cheil.

הָאֵל הַגָּדוֹל הַגִּבּוֹר
Ha-eil ha-ga-dol ha-gi-bor

וְהַנּוֹרָא, אֵל עֶלְיוֹן. גּוֹמֵל
v'ha-no-ra, eil el-yon. Go-meil

חֲסָדִים טוֹבִים וְקוֹנֵה הַכֹּל,
cha-sa-dim to-vim, v'ko-nei ha-kol,

וְזוֹכֵר חַסְדֵי אָבוֹת וְאִמָּהוֹת,
v'zo-cheir chas-dei a-vot v'i-ma-hot,

וּמֵבִיא גְאֻלָּה לִבְנֵי בְנֵיהֶם,
u-mei-vi g'u-la li-v'nei v'nei-hem,

לְמַעַן שְׁמוֹ בְּאַהֲבָה. מֶלֶךְ
l'ma-an sh'mo, b'a-ha-vah. Meh-lech

עוֹזֵר וּמוֹשִׁיעַ וּמָגֵן.
o-zeir u-mo-shi-a u-ma-gein.

בָּרוּךְ אַתָּה יי,
Ba-ruch a-ta Adonai,

מָגֵן אַבְרָהָם וְעֶזְרַת שָׂרָה.
ma-gein Av-ra-ham v'ez-rat Sa-rah.

The Yom Tov Tefilah has seven prayers. In the first, we recall with reverence the founders of our people and faith. We say: Each generation finds its own way, and yet—their God is ours.

❖ See "Looking for God," pages 352-357.

We praise You, Adonai our God and God of our ancestors: of Abraham, Isaac, and Jacob; of Sarah, Rebekah, Leah, and Rachel; the great, mighty, and awesome God, God Most High. You deal kindly with us and embrace us all. You remember the faithfulness of our ancestors, and in love bring redemption to their children's children for the sake of Your name. You are our sovereign and helper, our redeemer and shield.
We praise You, Adonai, Shield of Abraham and Protector of Sarah.

גבורות GOD'S POWER

In this prayer, we affirm the power of God, whose reach extends to this world—the world we walk in—and to a world we cannot imagine.

✣ See Psalm 103 (page 366) and Psalm 146 (page 371).

אַתָּה גִּבּוֹר לְעוֹלָם, אֲדֹנָי,
מְחַיֵּה מֵתִים אַתָּה, רַב
לְהוֹשִׁיעַ.
מַשִּׁיב הָרוּחַ וּמוֹרִיד הַגֶּשֶׁם,
מַזְרִיחַ הַשֶּׁמֶשׁ וּמוֹרִיד הַטָּל.
מְכַלְכֵּל חַיִּים בְּחֶסֶד,
מְחַיֵּה מֵתִים בְּרַחֲמִים רַבִּים.
סוֹמֵךְ נוֹפְלִים, וְרוֹפֵא
חוֹלִים, וּמַתִּיר אֲסוּרִים,
וּמְקַיֵּם אֱמוּנָתוֹ לִישֵׁנֵי עָפָר.
מִי כָמוֹךָ, בַּעַל גְּבוּרוֹת, וּמִי
דוֹמֶה לָךְ, מֶלֶךְ מֵמִית וּמְחַיֶּה
וּמַצְמִיחַ יְשׁוּעָה? וְנֶאֱמָן
אַתָּה לְהַחֲיוֹת מֵתִים.
בָּרוּךְ אַתָּה יי, מְחַיֵּה
הַמֵּתִים.

A-ta gi-bor l'o-lam, Adonai,
m'cha-yei mei-tim a-ta, rav
l'ho-shi-a. Ma-shiv ha-ru-ach u-mo-
rid ha-ga-shem; maz-ri-ach
ha-she-mesh u-mo-rid ha-tal.
M'chal-keil cha-yim b'cheh-sed,
m'cha-yei mei-tim b'ra-cha-mim
ra-bim. So-meich no-f'lim, v'ro-fei
cho-lim, u-ma-tir a-su-rim,
u-m'ka-yeim eh-mu-na-to li-shei-nei
a-far. Mi cha-mo-cha ba-al g'vu-rot,
u-mi do-meh lach, meh-lech mei-mit
u-m'cha-yeh u-matz-mi-ach y'shu-a?
V'neh-eh-man a-ta l'ha-cha-yot
mei-tim. Ba-ruch a-ta Adonai, m'cha-
yei ha-mei-tim.

Unending is Your might, Eternal One; You are the source of eternal life; great is Your power to save. You cause the wind to blow and the rain to fall, the sun to shine and the dew to descend.

In Your love You sustain the living; in Your compassion You grant us eternal life. You support the falling and heal the sick; You free the captive and keep faith with those who sleep in the dust. Who is like You, source of all strength? Who is Your equal, sovereign author of life and death, who causes deliverance to flower in our world?

Trusting in You, we see life beyond death.

We praise You, O God, source of eternal life.

227

קְדוּשָׁה   SANCTIFICATION

נְקַדֵּשׁ אֶת־שִׁמְךָ בָּעוֹלָם, כְּשֵׁם שֶׁמַּקְדִּישִׁים אוֹתוֹ

בִּשְׁמֵי מָרוֹם, כַּכָּתוּב עַל־יַד נְבִיאֶךָ:

וְקָרָא זֶה אֶל־זֶה וְאָמַר:

We hallow Your name on earth, even as all creation, to the highest heavens, proclaims Your holiness, and in the words of the prophet we say:

קָדוֹשׁ, קָדוֹשׁ, קָדוֹשׁ יהוה צְבָאוֹת,

מְלֹא כָל־הָאָרֶץ כְּבוֹדוֹ.

Holy, holy, holy is the God of all being! The whole earth is filled with Your glory!

אַדִּיר אַדִּירֵנוּ, יהוה אֲדֹנֵינוּ, מָה־אַדִּיר שִׁמְךָ בְּכָל־הָאָרֶץ!

God our strength, God of mercy, how majestic is Your name in all the earth!

בָּרוּךְ כְּבוֹד־יהוה מִמְּקוֹמוֹ.

Praised be the glory of God in heaven and earth.

אֶחָד הוּא אֱלֹהֵינוּ, הוּא אָבִינוּ, הוּא מַלְכֵּנוּ, הוּא מוֹשִׁיעֵנוּ;

וְהוּא יַשְׁמִיעֵנוּ בְּרַחֲמָיו לְעֵינֵי כָּל־חָי:

You alone are our God and maker, our ruler and helper; and in Your mercy You reveal Yourself to us in the sight of all the living:

אֲנִי יהוה אֱלֹהֵיכֶם!

I AM ADONAI YOUR GOD!

In the Sanctification we echo the awe and wonder expressed by our psalmists, mystics, and prophets as they experienced God's presence in their lives.

✥ See pages 352-353 and page 400.

228

יִמְלֹךְ יהוה לְעוֹלָם, אֱלֹהַיִךְ צִיּוֹן, לְדֹר וָדֹר. הַלְלוּיָהּ!

Adonai shall reign forever; Your God, O Zion, from generation to generation. Halleluyah!

לְדוֹר וָדוֹר נַגִּיד גָּדְלֶךָ, וּלְנֵצַח נְצָחִים קְדֻשָּׁתְךָ נַקְדִּישׁ. וְשִׁבְחֲךָ, אֱלֹהֵינוּ, מִפִּינוּ לֹא יָמוּשׁ לְעוֹלָם וָעֶד.

From generation to generation we will make known Your greatness, and to all eternity proclaim Your holiness. Your praise, O God, shall never depart from our lips.

בָּרוּךְ אַתָּה יי, הָאֵל הַקָּדוֹשׁ.

We praise You, Adonai, the holy God.

ALL ARE SEATED

קְדוּשַׁת הַיּוֹם   THE HOLINESS OF YOM TOV

אַתָּה בְחַרְתָּנוּ מִכָּל־הָעַמִּים, אָהַבְתָּ אוֹתָנוּ וְרָצִיתָ בָּנוּ, וְקִדַּשְׁתָּנוּ בְּמִצְוֹתֶיךָ, וְקֵרַבְתָּנוּ, מַלְכֵּנוּ, לַעֲבוֹדָתֶךָ, וְשִׁמְךָ הַגָּדוֹל וְהַקָּדוֹשׁ עָלֵינוּ קָרָאתָ.
וַתִּתֶּן לָנוּ, יי אֱלֹהֵינוּ, בְּאַהֲבָה (שַׁבָּתוֹת לִמְנוּחָה וּ) מוֹעֲדִים לְשִׂמְחָה, חַגִּים וּזְמַנִּים לְשָׂשׂוֹן, אֶת־יוֹם (הַשַּׁבָּת הַזֶּה וְאֶת־יוֹם)

❖ חַג הַמַּצּוֹת הַזֶּה, זְמַן חֵרוּתֵנוּ,

❖ חַג הַשָּׁבוּעוֹת הַזֶּה, זְמַן מַתַּן תּוֹרָתֵנוּ,

❖ חַג הַסֻּכּוֹת הַזֶּה, זְמַן שִׂמְחָתֵנוּ,

❖ הַשְּׁמִינִי חַג הָעֲצֶרֶת הַזֶּה, זְמַן שִׂמְחָתֵנוּ,

(בְּאַהֲבָה) מִקְרָא קֹדֶשׁ, זֵכֶר לִיצִיאַת מִצְרָיִם.

You have called us to a sacred task among the peoples. In Your love and favor You have hallowed us by Your Mitzvot,

Our Yom Tov Tefilah's middle blessing celebrates the Holiness of the Day. Yom Tov is a time of celebration and joy.

229

drawn us near to Your service, and charged us to make known Your great and holy name. And in Your love, Adonai our God, You have given us (Sabbaths of rest,) feasts of joy and seasons of gladness, among them this (Sabbath day and this)

❖ Festival of Pesach, season of our freedom,
❖ Festival of Shavuot, season of revelation,
❖ Festival of Sukkot, season of our gladness,
❖ Festival of Sh'mini Atzeret (Simchat Torah), season of our gladness,

to unite us in worship, and in remembrance of the Exodus from Egypt.

אֱלֹהֵינוּ וֵאלֹהֵי אֲבוֹתֵינוּ וְאִמּוֹתֵינוּ, יַעֲלֶה וְיָבֹא וְיִזָּכֵר
זִכְרוֹנֵנוּ וְזִכְרוֹן כָּל־עַמְּךָ בֵּית יִשְׂרָאֵל לְפָנֶיךָ לְטוֹבָה
לְחֵן לְחֶסֶד וּלְרַחֲמִים, לְחַיִּים וּלְשָׁלוֹם בְּיוֹם

❖ חַג הַמַּצּוֹת הַזֶּה.

❖ חַג הַשָּׁבוּעוֹת הַזֶּה.

❖ חַג הַסֻּכּוֹת הַזֶּה.

❖ הַשְּׁמִינִי חַג הָעֲצֶרֶת הַזֶּה.

זָכְרֵנוּ, יְיָ אֱלֹהֵינוּ, בּוֹ לְטוֹבָה. אָמֵן.

וּפָקְדֵנוּ בוֹ לִבְרָכָה. אָמֵן.

וְהוֹשִׁיעֵנוּ בוֹ לְחַיִּים. אָמֵן.

Our God , God of our fathers and our mothers, be mindful of Your people Israel on this

❖ Festival of Pesach,
❖ Festival of Shavuot,
❖ Festival of Sukkot,
❖ Festival of Sh'mini Atzeret (Simchat Torah),

and renew in us love and compassion, goodness, life, and peace.

This day remember us for well-being. Amen.
Bless us with Your nearness. Amen.
Help us to renew our life. Amen.

וְהַשִּׂיאֵנוּ, יְיָ אֱלֹהֵינוּ, אֶת־בִּרְכַּת מוֹעֲדֶיךָ לְשִׂמְחָה וּלְשָׂשׂוֹן,
כַּאֲשֶׁר רָצִיתָ וְאָמַרְתָּ לְבָרְכֵנוּ. קַדְּשֵׁנוּ בְּמִצְוֹתֶיךָ וְתֵן חֶלְקֵנוּ
בְּתוֹרָתֶךָ. שַׂבְּעֵנוּ מִטּוּבֶךָ, וְשַׂמְּחֵנוּ בִּישׁוּעָתֶךָ, וְטַהֵר לִבֵּנוּ
לְעָבְדְּךָ בֶּאֱמֶת. וְהַנְחִילֵנוּ, יְיָ אֱלֹהֵינוּ, בְּשִׂמְחָה וּבְשָׂשׂוֹן (שַׁבָּת וּ)
מוֹעֲדֵי קָדְשֶׁךָ. בָּרוּךְ אַתָּה יְיָ, מְקַדֵּשׁ (הַשַּׁבָּת וְ) יִשְׂרָאֵל וְהַזְּמַנִּים.

Eternal God, may our observance of the festivals bring us bless-
ing, happiness, and joy. Sanctify us with Your Mitzvot, and let
Your Torah be our life's portion. Satisfy us with Your goodness,
gladden us with Your salvation, and purify our hearts to serve
You in truth
Grant also, Eternal God, that the joy of (Shabbat and) Yom Tov
may be with us always. We praise You, O God, for the holiness of
(Shabbat,) Israel and the Festivals.

We pray now
that our
prayer be
acceptable.
One such
prayer:
"May we pray
for the under-
standing that
God is with
us wherever
we go."

❁ See "Prayer
and Its
Value," pages
3-5.

עבודה   **WORSHIP**

רְצֵה, יְיָ אֱלֹהֵינוּ, בְּעַמְּךָ יִשְׂרָאֵל,
וּתְפִלָּתָם בְּאַהֲבָה תְקַבֵּל,
וּתְהִי לְרָצוֹן תָּמִיד עֲבוֹדַת יִשְׂרָאֵל עַמֶּךָ.
אֵל קָרוֹב לְכָל־קֹרְאָיו,
פְּנֵה אֶל עֲבָדֶיךָ וְחָנֵּנוּ; שְׁפוֹךְ רוּחֲךָ עָלֵינוּ,
וְתֶחֱזֶינָה עֵינֵינוּ בְּשׁוּבְךָ לְצִיּוֹן בְּרַחֲמִים.

Look with favor, Adonai our God, upon Your people Israel,
and with love accept our prayers. May our worship ever be
worthy of Your favor.

O God near to every seeker,
turn to Your servants and show us grace.
Shower Your spirit upon us, and let Zion and all Israel
behold Your compassionate presence.

בָּרוּךְ אַתָּה יי, הַמַּחֲזִיר שְׁכִינָתוֹ לְצִיּוֹן.

We praise You, Adonai, whose presence restores Zion and all Israel.

הודאה   THANKSGIVING

PERSONAL PRAYER

מוֹדִים אֲנַחְנוּ לָךְ שָׁאַתָּה הוּא יי אֱלֹהֵינוּ וֵאלֹהֵי אֲבוֹתֵינוּ
וְאִמּוֹתֵינוּ, אֱלֹהֵי כָל־בָּשָׂר, יוֹצְרֵנוּ יוֹצֵר בְּרֵאשִׁית. בְּרָכוֹת
וְהוֹדָאוֹת לְשִׁמְךָ הַגָּדוֹל וְהַקָּדוֹשׁ עַל־שֶׁהֶחֱיִיתָנוּ וְקִיַּמְתָּנוּ.
כֵּן תְּחַיֵּנוּ וּתְקַיְּמֵנוּ, יי אֱלֹהֵינוּ, וְתֶאֶמְצֵנוּ לִשְׁמֹר חֻקֶּיךָ,
לַעֲשׂוֹת רְצוֹנֶךָ, וּלְעָבְדְּךָ בְּלֵבָב שָׁלֵם. בָּרוּךְ אֵל הַהוֹדָאוֹת.

We affirm with gratitude that You, Adonai, are our God, the
God of our fathers and mothers, the God of all flesh, our
creator, the source of all being. We bless and praise Your
great and holy name, for keeping us in life and sustaining
us. Continue and sustain us in life, Adonai our God;
strengthen us to observe Your laws, to do Your will, and to
serve You with a whole heart. Praised be God, to whom our
thanks are due.

Every breath is precious and every moment a gift. Our tradition teaches us gratitude: to be thankful for the gift of our life, its joys— and even for our sorrows.

✢ See "Giving Thanks," page 398, and Psalm 147 (page 372).

PUBLIC PRAYER

מוֹדִים אֲנַחְנוּ לָךְ, שָׁאַתָּה הוּא יי אֱלֹהֵינוּ וֵאלֹהֵי אֲבוֹתֵינוּ
וְאִמּוֹתֵינוּ לְעוֹלָם וָעֶד. צוּר חַיֵּינוּ, מָגֵן יִשְׁעֵנוּ, אַתָּה הוּא
לְדוֹר וָדוֹר.

Gratefully we acknowledge that You, Adonai, are our God, the God of our fathers and our mothers, our God forever. In every age You are the rock of our life, our protecting shield.

נוֹדֶה לְךָ וּנְסַפֵּר תְּהִלָּתֶךָ, עַל־חַיֵּינוּ הַמְּסוּרִים בְּיָדֶךָ,

וְעַל־נִשְׁמוֹתֵינוּ הַפְּקוּדוֹת לָךְ, וְעַל־נִסֶּיךָ שֶׁבְּכָל־יוֹם עִמָּנוּ,

וְעַל־נִפְלְאוֹתֶיךָ וְטוֹבוֹתֶיךָ שֶׁבְּכָל־עֵת, עֶרֶב וָבֹקֶר וְצָהֳרָיִם.

הַטּוֹב: כִּי לֹא־כָלוּ רַחֲמֶיךָ, וְהַמְרַחֵם: כִּי־לֹא תַמּוּ חֲסָדֶיךָ,

מֵעוֹלָם קִוִּינוּ לָךְ.

וְעַל כֻּלָּם יִתְבָּרַךְ וְיִתְרוֹמַם שִׁמְךָ, מַלְכֵּנוּ, תָּמִיד לְעוֹלָם וָעֶד.

וְכֹל הַחַיִּים יוֹדוּךָ סֶּלָה, וִיהַלְלוּ אֶת־שִׁמְךָ בֶּאֱמֶת, הָאֵל

יְשׁוּעָתֵנוּ וְעֶזְרָתֵנוּ סֶלָה.

We thank You and sing Your praises: for our lives, which are in Your hand; for our souls, which are in Your keeping; for the signs of Your presence we encounter every day; and for Your wondrous gifts at all times, morning, noon, and night.

Source of goodness, Your mercies do not end; Compassionate One, Your kindness does not fail. From of old You have been our hope.

For all these gifts, let Your name ever be exalted in praise.
Let all the living affirm You and in faithfulness give thanks to Your name, O God our deliverer and help!

בָּרוּךְ אַתָּה יְיָ, הַטּוֹב שִׁמְךָ וּלְךָ נָאֶה לְהוֹדוֹת.

We praise You, Adonai, source of good, to whom our thanks are due.

233

ברכת שלום   PEACE

אֱלֹהֵינוּ וֵאלֹהֵי אֲבוֹתֵינוּ וְאִמּוֹתֵינוּ: בָּרְכֵנוּ בַּבְּרָכָה
הַמְשֻׁלֶּשֶׁת הַכְּתוּבָה בַּתּוֹרָה:

יְבָרֶכְךָ יהוה וְיִשְׁמְרֶךָ. כֵּן יְהִי רָצוֹן.

יָאֵר יהוה פָּנָיו אֵלֶיךָ וִיחֻנֶּךָּ. כֵּן יְהִי רָצוֹן.

יִשָּׂא יהוה פָּנָיו אֵלֶיךָ וְיָשֵׂם לְךָ שָׁלוֹם. כֵּן יְהִי רָצוֹן.

Our God and God of our ancestors, bless us with the three-
fold benediction of the Torah:

May God bless you and keep you. *Let this be God's will.*

May God smile upon you, and be gracious to you. *Let this be
God's will.*

May God reach out to you in tenderness, and give you
peace. *Amen. Let this be God's will.*

In our prayer
for peace we
pray for our
people and
for all
the world's
peoples.
Only when
all are at
peace can we
truly say: "We
are at peace."

✤ See Pirke
Avot, pages
324-325, and
page 351.

שִׂים שָׁלוֹם, טוֹבָה וּבְרָכָה, חֵן וָחֶסֶד וְרַחֲמִים, עָלֵינוּ וְעַל כָּל־
יִשְׂרָאֵל עַמֶּךָ. בָּרְכֵנוּ, אָבִינוּ, כֻּלָּנוּ כְּאֶחָד בְּאוֹר פָּנֶיךָ, כִּי בְאוֹר
פָּנֶיךָ נָתַתָּ לָּנוּ, יי אֱלֹהֵינוּ, תּוֹרַת חַיִּים, וְאַהֲבַת חֶסֶד, וּצְדָקָה
וּבְרָכָה וְרַחֲמִים וְחַיִּים וְשָׁלוֹם. וְטוֹב בְּעֵינֶיךָ לְבָרֵךְ אֶת־עַמְּךָ
יִשְׂרָאֵל וְאֶת־כָּל־הָעַמִּים בְּכָל־עֵת וּבְכָל־שָׁעָה בִּשְׁלוֹמֶךָ.

Grant peace, goodness and blessing, grace, love and mercy
to us and to all Your people Israel. As a loving parent, bless
us with the light of Your presence; for by that light, eternal
God, You have revealed to us a Torah to live by: the love of
kindness, righteousness, blessing, and mercy, bringing life
and peace. For it is good in Your sight that Your people
Israel and all peoples be blessed at all times with Your gift of
peace.

בָּרוּךְ אַתָּה יי, הַמְבָרֵךְ אֶת־עַמּוֹ יִשְׂרָאֵל בַּשָּׁלוֹם.

We praise You, O God: You bless Your people Israel with peace.

SILENT PRAYER

אֱלֹהַי, נְצֹר לְשׁוֹנִי מֵרָע, וּשְׂפָתַי מִדַּבֵּר מִרְמָה. וְלִמְקַלְלַי נַפְשִׁי
תִדּוֹם וְנַפְשִׁי כֶּעָפָר לַכֹּל תִּהְיֶה. פְּתַח לִבִּי בְּתוֹרָתֶךָ, וּבְמִצְוֹתֶיךָ
תִּרְדֹּף נַפְשִׁי. עֲשֵׂה לְמַעַן שְׁמֶךָ, עֲשֵׂה לְמַעַן יְמִינֶךָ, עֲשֵׂה
לְמַעַן קְדֻשָּׁתֶךָ, עֲשֵׂה לְמַעַן תּוֹרָתֶךָ; לְמַעַן יֵחָלְצוּן יְדִידֶיךָ,
הוֹשִׁיעָה יְמִינְךָ וַעֲנֵנִי.

My God, keep my tongue from evil, my lips from deceptive speech. In the face of malice give me a quiet spirit; let me be humble wherever I go. Open my heart to Your teaching, make me eager to fulfill Your Mitzvot. Thus will Your name be exalted, Your might manifest, Your holiness visible, Your Torah magnified. Inspire me to love You, and be the answer to my prayer.

PESACH

𝄞 There are times when I feel like a boy. As long as you are able to admire and to love, you are young. And there is so much to admire and to love. . . . Look at the sea, the sky, trees, flowers! A single tree—what a miracle it is! What a fantastic, wonderful creation this world is, with such diversity.

SHAVUOT

𝄞 "Teach me the whole Torah," someone said, "while I stand on one foot." Shammai cursed and drove him away. He went to Hillel, who said: "What is hateful to you, do not do to anyone else: that is the whole Torah. The rest will follow—go now and learn it." (Talmud)

SUKKOT AND SH'MINI ATZERET (SIMCHAT TORAH)

ℭ   Help me to understand the meaning of the word "enough." Some things I surely have enough of, enough to be grateful for. Other things I don't have. Some I may in time acquire, others not. Do not let me enmesh myself in the web of endless desires. Let today be enough for today: tomorrow hasn't come, and never will come—until tomorrow.

&

יִהְיוּ לְרָצוֹן אִמְרֵי־פִי וְהֶגְיוֹן לִבִּי לְפָנֶיךָ, יהוה, צוּרִי וְגֹאֲלִי.

Yi-h'yu l'ra-tzon i-m'rei fi v'heg-yon li-bi l'fa-neh-cha, Adonai tzu-ri v'go-a-li.

May the words of my mouth and the meditations of my heart be acceptable to You, O God, my rock and my redeemer. Amen.

&

עֹשֶׂה שָׁלוֹם בִּמְרוֹמָיו,   *O-seh sha-lom bi-m'ro-mav,*

הוּא יַעֲשֶׂה שָׁלוֹם עָלֵינוּ   *hu ya-a-seh sha-lom a-lei-nu*

וְעַל־כָּל־יִשְׂרָאֵל, וְאִמְרוּ:   *v'al kol Yis-ra-eil, v'i-m'ru:*

אָמֵן.   *A-mein.*

May the source of peace on high send peace to us, to all Israel, and to all the world, and let us say: Amen.

&

HOLDING THE LULAV AND ETROG ON SUKKOT

בָּרוּךְ אַתָּה יי, אֱלֹהֵינוּ מֶלֶךְ הָעוֹלָם, אֲשֶׁר קִדְּשָׁנוּ בְּמִצְוֹתָיו וְצִוָּנוּ עַל־נְטִילַת לוּלָב.

Ba-ruch a-ta Adonai, Eh-lo-hei-nu meh-lech ha-o-lam, a-sher ki-d'sha-nu b'mitz-vo-tav v'tzi-va-nu al n'ti-lat lu-lav.

We praise You, Adonai our God, sovereign of the universe: You hallow us with Your Mitzvot and command us to raise high the Lulav.

הלל HALLEL

❊ See "Selected Psalms," pages 358-375, and "A Daily Psalm," pages 27-33.

בָּרוּךְ אַתָּה יְיָ,

Ba-ruch a-ta Adonai,

אֱלֹהֵינוּ מֶלֶךְ הָעוֹלָם,

Eh-lo-hei-nu meh-lech ha-o-lam,

אֲשֶׁר קִדְּשָׁנוּ בְּמִצְוֹתָיו

a-sher ki-d'sha-nu b'mitz-vo-tav

וְצִוָּנוּ לִקְרֹא אֶת־הַהַלֵּל.

v'tzi-va-nu lik-ro et-ha-Hallel.

We praise You, Adonai our God, sovereign of the universe: You hallow us with Your Mitzvot and inspire us to recite the Psalms of Praise.

FROM PSALM 113

הַלְלוּיָהּ! הַלְלוּ עַבְדֵי יהוה, הַלְלוּ אֶת־שֵׁם יהוה.

יְהִי שֵׁם יהוה מְבֹרָךְ מֵעַתָּה וְעַד־עוֹלָם.

מִמִּזְרַח־שֶׁמֶשׁ עַד־מְבוֹאוֹ מְהֻלָּל שֵׁם יהוה.

Halleluyah! Sing praises, you servants of Adonai, praise the name of God. Let God's name be praised, now and forever.

From the rising of the sun to its setting, God's name is praised.

רָם עַל־כָּל־גּוֹיִם יהוה, עַל הַשָּׁמַיִם כְּבוֹדוֹ.

מִי כַּיהוה אֱלֹהֵינוּ, הַמַּגְבִּיהִי לָשָׁבֶת, הַמַּשְׁפִּילִי לִרְאוֹת

בַּשָּׁמַיִם וּבָאָרֶץ? מְקִימִי מֵעָפָר דָּל, מֵאַשְׁפֹּת יָרִים אֶבְיוֹן.

לְהוֹשִׁיבִי עִם־נְדִיבִים, עִם נְדִיבֵי עַמּוֹ. הַלְלוּיָהּ!

Far above the nations is Adonai,

whose glory is higher than the heavens.

Who is like Adonai our God, enthroned on high,
and yet looks down upon heaven and earth?

Who raises the poor from the dust, who lifts the wretched from the dirt, to give them a place among the great, among the great ones of the people. Halleluyah!

PSALM 114

בְּצֵאת יִשְׂרָאֵל מִמִּצְרָיִם, בֵּית יַעֲקֹב מֵעַם לֹעֵז,

הָיְתָה יְהוּדָה לְקָדְשׁוֹ, יִשְׂרָאֵל מַמְשְׁלוֹתָיו.

הַיָּם רָאָה וַיָּנֹס, הַיַּרְדֵּן יִסֹּב לְאָחוֹר.

הֶהָרִים רָקְדוּ כְאֵילִים, גְּבָעוֹת כִּבְנֵי־צֹאן.

When Israel went forth from Egypt, the House of Jacob from
a people foreign to them, Judah became God's sanctuary;
Israel, God's dominion.

*The sea saw it and fled, the Jordan turned back. The mountains
skipped like rams, the hills like young lambs.*

מַה־לְּךָ הַיָּם כִּי תָנוּס, הַיַּרְדֵּן תִּסֹּב לְאָחוֹר?

הֶהָרִים תִּרְקְדוּ כְאֵילִים, גְּבָעוֹת כִּבְנֵי־צֹאן?

O sea, what made you run away? O Jordan, why did you
turn back?

*O mountains, why did you skip like rams? O hills, like young
lambs?*

מִלִּפְנֵי אָדוֹן חוּלִי אָרֶץ, מִלִּפְנֵי אֱלוֹהַּ יַעֲקֹב,

הַהֹפְכִי הַצּוּר אֲגַם־מָיִם, חַלָּמִישׁ לְמַעְיְנוֹ־מָיִם.

Tremble, O earth, before the Eternal One, before the God of
Jacob, who turns rocks into pools of water, stony ground
into flowing springs.

238

PSALM 115

לֹא לָנוּ, יהוה, לֹא לָנוּ, כִּי־לְשִׁמְךָ תֵּן כָּבוֹד
עַל־חַסְדְּךָ עַל־אֲמִתֶּךָ.
לָמָּה יֹאמְרוּ הַגּוֹיִם, אַיֵּה־נָא אֱלֹהֵיהֶם,
וֵאלֹהֵינוּ בַשָּׁמָיִם, כֹּל אֲשֶׁר־חָפֵץ עָשָׂה?

Not to us, Adonai, not to us, but to Your name
let honor be given for Your love and faithfulness.

Why should the nations say, "Where is their God?"
when our God is on high, and God's will prevails?

עֲצַבֵּיהֶם כֶּסֶף וְזָהָב, מַעֲשֵׂה יְדֵי אָדָם.
פֶּה־לָהֶם, וְלֹא יְדַבֵּרוּ; עֵינַיִם לָהֶם, וְלֹא יִרְאוּ.
אָזְנַיִם לָהֶם, וְלֹא יִשְׁמָעוּ; אַף לָהֶם, וְלֹא יְרִיחוּן.
יְדֵיהֶם, וְלֹא יְמִישׁוּן, רַגְלֵיהֶם, וְלֹא יְהַלֵּכוּ;
לֹא־יֶהְגּוּ בִּגְרוֹנָם.
כְּמוֹהֶם יִהְיוּ עֹשֵׂיהֶם, כֹּל אֲשֶׁר־בֹּטֵחַ בָּהֶם.

Their idols are silver and gold, the work of human hands.

They have mouths, yet they cannot speak;
eyes, yet they cannot see.
They have ears, yet they cannot hear;
noses, yet they cannot smell.
They have hands, yet they cannot touch;
feet, yet they cannot walk;
from their throats no sound is heard.
Those who make them,
all who trust in them, become like them!

יִשְׂרָאֵל, בְּטַח בַּיהוה; עֶזְרָם וּמָגִנָּם הוּא.
בֵּית אַהֲרֹן, בִּטְחוּ בַיהוה, עֶזְרָם וּמָגִנָּם הוּא.

יִרְאֵי יהוה, בִּטְחוּ בַיהוה, עֶזְרָם וּמָגִנָּם הוּא.

יהוה זְכָרָנוּ, יְבָרֵךְ, יְבָרֵךְ אֶת־בֵּית יִשְׂרָאֵל, יְבָרֵךְ
אֶת־בֵּית אַהֲרֹן. יְבָרֵךְ יִרְאֵי יהוה, הַקְּטַנִּים עִם־הַגְּדֹלִים.

O Israel, trust in Adonai, your help and your shield.

O House of Aaron, trust in Adonai, your help and your shield.

All God-fearing people, trust in Adonai, your help and your
shield.

*God is mindful of us and will bless us, will bless the House of
Israel, will bless the House of Aaron, will bless all God-fearing
people, young and old alike.*

יֹסֵף יהוה עֲלֵיכֶם, עֲלֵיכֶם וְעַל־בְּנֵיכֶם.

בְּרוּכִים אַתֶּם לַיהוה, עֹשֵׂה שָׁמַיִם וָאָרֶץ.

הַשָּׁמַיִם שָׁמַיִם לַיהוה, וְהָאָרֶץ נָתַן לִבְנֵי־אָדָם.

לֹא הַמֵּתִים יְהַלְלוּ־יָהּ, וְלֹא כָּל־יֹרְדֵי דוּמָה.

וַאֲנַחְנוּ נְבָרֵךְ יָהּ מֵעַתָּה וְעַד־עוֹלָם. הַלְלוּיָהּ!

May God increase your blessings, yours and your children's.

May you be blessed by Adonai, maker of heaven and earth.
The heavens belong to God, who has given the earth to
human beings.

For the dead do not praise God, nor do those who go down
to silence.

But we will praise God now and forever. Halleluyah!

FROM PSALM 116

אָהַבְתִּי כִּי־יִשְׁמַע יהוה אֶת־קוֹלִי תַּחֲנוּנָי,

כִּי־הִטָּה אָזְנוֹ לִי וּבְיָמַי אֶקְרָא.

אֲפָפוּנִי חֶבְלֵי־מָוֶת; וּמְצָרֵי שְׁאוֹל מְצָאוּנִי;

צָרָה וְיָגוֹן אֶמְצָא, וּבְשֵׁם־יהוה אֶקְרָא:

אָנָּה, יהוה, מַלְּטָה נַפְשִׁי!

חַנּוּן יהוה וְצַדִּיק, וֵאלֹהֵינוּ מְרַחֵם.

שֹׁמֵר פְּתָאִים יהוה; דַּלּוֹתִי וְלִי יְהוֹשִׁיעַ.

שׁוּבִי, נַפְשִׁי, לִמְנוּחָיְכִי, כִּי־יהוה גָּמַל עָלָיְכִי.

כִּי חִלַּצְתָּ נַפְשִׁי מִמָּוֶת, אֶת־עֵינִי מִן־דִּמְעָה, אֶת־רַגְלִי מִדֶּחִי.

אֶתְהַלֵּךְ לִפְנֵי יהוה בְּאַרְצוֹת הַחַיִּים.

הֶאֱמַנְתִּי, כִּי אֲדַבֵּר אֲנִי עָנִיתִי מְאֹד.

אֲנִי אָמַרְתִּי בְחָפְזִי, כָּל־הָאָדָם כֹּזֵב.

I love Adonai, who hears my entreaties,
whose ear is turned to me whenever I call.
Death's snare was round about me;
the torments of Sheol found me out;
I met trouble and sorrow, and cried out to Adonai:
"Save me, O God, save me!"
God is gracious and just; our God is compassionate.
Adonai protects the simple;
I was brought low and God saved me.
Be at ease again, my soul, for God has been good to you.
O God, You have spared my soul from death, my eyes from
tears, my feet from stumbling.
I shall walk before You, Adonai, in the land of the living.
I remain faithful even when I cry out:
"How great is my affliction!"
And when in my folly I say: "All people are frauds."

מָה־אָשִׁיב לַיהוה כָּל־תַּגְמוּלְוֹהִי עָלָי?

כּוֹס־יְשׁוּעוֹת אֶשָּׂא, וּבְשֵׁם יהוה אֶקְרָא.

לְךָ־אֶזְבַּח זֶבַח תּוֹדָה, וּבְשֵׁם יהוה אֶקְרָא.

How can I repay You, O God, for all that You have given me?

I shall lift up the cup of salvation, and invoke Your name in praise.

I shall bring You my offering of thanks, and invoke Your name in praise.

PSALM 117

הַלְלוּ אֶת־יהוה, Praise Adonai, all you na-
כָּל־גּוֹיִם; tions; extol the Eternal One,
שַׁבְּחוּהוּ, כָּל־הָאֻמִּים, all you peoples, for God's
כִּי גָבַר עָלֵינוּ חַסְדּוֹ; love for us is tremendous,
וֶאֱמֶת־יהוה לְעוֹלָם, and God's faithfulness is
הַלְלוּיָהּ! everlasting. Halleluyah!

FROM PSALM 118

הוֹדוּ לַיהוה כִּי־טוֹב, כִּי לְעוֹלָם חַסְדּוֹ.

יֹאמַר־נָא יִשְׂרָאֵל: כִּי לְעוֹלָם חַסְדּוֹ.

יֹאמְרוּ־נָא בֵית־אַהֲרֹן: כִּי לְעוֹלָם חַסְדּוֹ.

יֹאמְרוּ־נָא יִרְאֵי יהוה: כִּי לְעוֹלָם חַסְדּוֹ.

Give thanks to Adonai, who is good,

whose love is everlasting.

Let Israel declare:

God's love is everlasting.

Let the House of Aaron declare:

God's love is everlasting.

Let God-fearing people declare:

God's love is everlasting.

מִן־הַמֵּצַר קָרָאתִי יָּה, עָנָנִי בַמֶּרְחָב יָה.

יהוה לִי, לֹא אִירָא; מַה־יַּעֲשֶׂה לִי אָדָם?

טוֹב לַחֲסוֹת בַּיהוה מִבְּטֹחַ בָּאָדָם.

טוֹב לַחֲסוֹת בַּיהוה מִבְּטֹחַ בִּנְדִיבִים.

עָזִּי וְזִמְרָת יָה, וַיְהִי־לִי לִישׁוּעָה.

קוֹל רִנָּה וִישׁוּעָה בְּאָהֳלֵי צַדִּיקִים. יְמִין יהוה עֹשָׂה חָיִל.

יְמִין יהוה רוֹמֵמָה; יְמִין יהוה עֹשָׂה חָיִל.

לֹא אָמוּת, כִּי־אֶחְיֶה וַאֲסַפֵּר מַעֲשֵׂי יָה.

פִּתְחוּ־לִי שַׁעֲרֵי־צֶדֶק; אָבֹא־בָם אוֹדֶה יָה.

In dire straits I cried out to God,
who answered me and set me free.

God is with me, I am not afraid; what can others do to me?

It is better to take refuge in God
than to rely on human beings.

It is better to take refuge in God than to rely on princes.

God is my strength and my shield,

and has become my salvation.

Hear! Glad songs of triumph in the tents of the righteous!

Adonai does mighty deeds.

God's power is supreme;

Adonai does mighty deeds.

243

I shall not die, but live to tell of God's deeds.

Open for me the gates of righteousness;
let me enter them and give thanks to God.

זֶה־הַשַּׁעַר לַיהוה; צַדִּיקִים יָבֹאוּ בוֹ.

אוֹדְךָ, כִּי עֲנִיתָנִי, וַתְּהִי־לִי לִישׁוּעָה.

אֶבֶן מָאֲסוּ הַבּוֹנִים הָיְתָה לְרֹאשׁ פִּנָּה.

מֵאֵת יהוה הָיְתָה זֹּאת; הִיא נִפְלָאת בְּעֵינֵינוּ.

זֶה־הַיּוֹם עָשָׂה יהוה, נָגִילָה וְנִשְׂמְחָה בוֹ.

This is the gate of Adonai;
the righteous shall enter it.

I thank You, for You have answered me,
and have become my salvation.

The stone that the builders rejected
has become the chief cornerstone.

This has come from God; it is marvelous in our sight.

This is the day Adonai has made—

let us rejoice and be glad in it.

אָנָּא יהוה, הוֹשִׁיעָה נָּא!   *Eternal God, deliver us!*

אָנָּא יהוה, הוֹשִׁיעָה נָּא!   *Eternal God, deliver us!*

אָנָּא יהוה, הַצְלִיחָה נָא!   *Eternal God, prosper us!*

אָנָּא יהוה, הַצְלִיחָה נָא!   *Eternal God, prosper us!*

בָּרוּךְ הַבָּא בְּשֵׁם יהוה; בֵּרַכְנוּכֶם מִבֵּית יהוה.

אֵלִי אַתָּה, וְאוֹדֶךָּ; אֱלֹהַי, אֲרוֹמְמֶךָּ.

הוֹדוּ לַיהוה כִּי־טוֹב, כִּי לְעוֹלָם חַסְדּוֹ.

Blessed are you who come in God's name;
here, in God's house, may you be blessed.

You are my God, and I thank You;
You are my God, I exalt You.

Give thanks to Adonai, who is good,

whose love is everlasting.

ॐ

קריאת התורה THE READING OF TORAH

FOR YOM TOV

וְהָיָה בְּאַחֲרִית הַיָּמִים נָכוֹן
יִהְיֶה הַר בֵּית־יהוה בְּרֹאשׁ
הֶהָרִים, וְנִשָּׂא מִגְּבָעוֹת וְנָהֲרוּ
אֵלָיו כָּל־הַגּוֹיִם. וְהָלְכוּ עַמִּים
רַבִּים וְאָמְרוּ: לְכוּ וְנַעֲלֶה
אֶל־הַר־יהוה, אֶל־בֵּית אֱלֹהֵי
יַעֲקֹב, וְיֹרֵנוּ מִדְּרָכָיו, וְנֵלְכָה
בְּאֹרְחֹתָיו.

And it shall come to pass in days to come, that the mountain of God's house shall be established as the highest of mountains, towering above the hills, and all the nations shall stream to it. Then the peoples shall say: "Come, let us go up to the mountain of Adonai, to the house of the God of Jacob, so that we may learn God's ways, and walk in God's paths."

Standing before the Ark, we can imagine ourselves at Sinai; and we can reaffirm our covenant with the Eternal, whose word goes forth continually to each generation and every individual. We pray to know before whom we stand.

ALL RISE

וְהָאֵר עֵינֵינוּ בְּתוֹרָתֶךָ, וְדַבֵּק לִבֵּנוּ בְּמִצְוֹתֶיךָ,
וְיַחֵד לְבָבֵנוּ לְאַהֲבָה וּלְיִרְאָה אֶת־שְׁמֶךָ.

V'ha-eir ei-nei-nu b'to-ra-teh-cha, v'da-beik li-bei-nu b'mitz-vo-teh-cha,
v'ya-cheid l'va-vei-nu l'a-ha-va u-l'yir-ah et sh'meh-cha.

Enlighten our eyes with Your Torah, help us cling to Your commandments, and inspire us to love and revere Your name with a ready heart.

THE ARK IS OPENED

יהוה, יהוה אֵל רַחוּם וְחַנּוּן, אֶרֶךְ אַפַּיִם וְרַב־חֶסֶד וֶאֱמֶת,
נֹצֵר חֶסֶד לָאֲלָפִים, נֹשֵׂא עָוֹן וָפֶשַׁע וְחַטָּאָה וְנַקֵּה.

Adonai, Adonai is a merciful and gracious God, endlessly patient, kind and faithful, showing mercy to thousands, forgiving sin and transgression, and granting pardon.

246

הָבוּ גֹדֶל לֵאלֹהֵינוּ, וּתְנוּ כָבוֹד לַתּוֹרָה.

Let us declare the greatness of our God,
and give honor to the Torah.

כִּי מִצִּיּוֹן תֵּצֵא תוֹרָה, וּדְבַר־יהוה מִירוּשָׁלָיִם.
בָּרוּךְ שֶׁנָּתַן תּוֹרָה לְעַמּוֹ יִשְׂרָאֵל בִּקְדֻשָּׁתוֹ.

Ki mi-tzion tei-tzei Torah, u-d'var Adonai mi-y'ru-sha-la-yim.
Ba-ruch sheh-na-tan Torah l'a-mo Yisrael bi-k'du-sha-to.

For Torah shall go forth from Zion, and the word of God from Jerusalem.
Praised be the one who in holiness has given Torah to our people Israel.

גַּדְּלוּ לַיהוה אִתִּי, וּנְרוֹמְמָה שְׁמוֹ יַחְדָּו.

O magnify the Eternal One with me,
and together let us exalt God's name.

שְׁמַע יִשְׂרָאֵל: יהוה אֱלֹהֵינוּ, יהוה אֶחָד!

Shema Yisrael, Adonai Eh-lo-hei-nu, Adonai Eh-chad!

אֶחָד אֱלֹהֵינוּ, גָּדוֹל אֲדֹנֵינוּ, קָדוֹשׁ שְׁמוֹ!

Eh-chad Eh-lo-hei-nu, ga-dol A-do-nei-nu, ka-dosh sh'mo!

Hear, O Israel: Adonai is our God, Adonai alone!
Our God is one; great and holy is the Eternal One.

בֵּית יַעֲקֹב, לְכוּ וְנֵלְכָה בְּאוֹר יהוה.

O House of Jacob, come, let us walk
by the light of our God.

SOME CONGREGATIONS CONTINUE WITH A PROCESSION (HAKAFAH)

THE BLESSINGS FOR THE READING OF TORAH ARE ON PAGE 257

קריאת התורה THE READING OF TORAH

FOR SIMCHAT TORAH

אַשְׁרֵי תְמִימֵי־דָרֶךְ,
הַהֹלְכִים בְּתוֹרַת יהוה.

Blessed are those whose way is sure, who walk in the Torah's path.

אַשְׁרֵי נֹצְרֵי עֵדֹתָיו,
בְּכָל־לֵב יִדְרְשׁוּהוּ.

Blessed are those who follow Your teachings, O God, who seek You with a whole heart.

נֵר־לְרַגְלִי דְבָרֶךָ,
וְאוֹר לִנְתִיבָתִי;
וְתוֹרָתְךָ שַׁעֲשֻׁעָי.

Your word is a lamp for our feet and a light for our path; Your Torah is our joy.

אַשְׁרֵי הָעָם שֶׁכָּכָה לּוֹ;
אַשְׁרֵי הָעָם שֶׁיהוה אֱלֹהָיו.

Happy the people who are so blessed; happy the people whose God You are.

Standing before the Ark, we can imagine ourselves at Sinai; and we can reaffirm our covenant with the Eternal, whose word goes forth continually to each generation and every individual. We pray to know before whom we stand.

ALL RISE

אַתָּה הָרְאֵתָ לָדַעַת, כִּי יהוה
הוּא הָאֱלֹהִים; אֵין עוֹד מִלְבַדּוֹ.

You have been shown, that you may know that Adonai is God; there is none else.

לְעֹשֵׂה נִפְלָאוֹת גְּדֹלוֹת
לְבַדּוֹ, כִּי לְעוֹלָם חַסְדּוֹ.

We praise the one who does great wonders, whose love endures forever.

אֵין־כָּמוֹךָ בָאֱלֹהִים, אֲדֹנָי,
וְאֵין כְּמַעֲשֶׂיךָ.

No one is like You, Adonai, among all that is worshiped, and there are no deeds like Yours.

Some may wish to choose from among the following verses.

יְהִי כְבוֹד יהוה לְעוֹלָם, יִשְׂמַח יהוה בְּמַעֲשָׂיו.

Let Your glory endure forever, Adonai; may You rejoice in Your works.

יְהִי שֵׁם יהוה מְבֹרָךְ מֵעַתָּה וְעַד־עוֹלָם.

Let Your name be praised now and forever.

יְהִי יהוה אֱלֹהֵינוּ עִמָּנוּ, כַּאֲשֶׁר הָיָה עִם־אֲבֹתֵינוּ וְאִמּוֹתֵינוּ; אַל־יַעַזְבֵנוּ וְאַל־יִטְּשֵׁנוּ.

Be with us, O God, as You were with our ancestors; do not forsake us.

וְאִמְרוּ: הוֹשִׁיעֵנוּ, אֱלֹהֵי יִשְׁעֵנוּ, לְהֹדוֹת לְשֵׁם קָדְשֶׁךָ, לְהִשְׁתַּבֵּחַ בִּתְהִלָּתֶךָ.

And let us say: Deliver us, O God of our salvation, that we may acclaim Your holy name and glory in Your praise.

יי מֶלֶךְ, יי מָלָךְ, יי יִמְלֹךְ לְעוֹלָם וָעֶד. יהוה עֹז לְעַמּוֹ יִתֵּן, יהוה יְבָרֵךְ אֶת־עַמּוֹ בַשָּׁלוֹם.

Adonai reigns; Adonai will reign forever and ever. Eternal God, You give strength to Your people; Eternal God, You bless Your people with peace.

THE ARK IS OPENED

שְׁמַע יִשְׂרָאֵל: יהוה אֱלֹהֵינוּ, יהוה אֶחָד!

Shema Yisrael, Adonai Eh-lo-hei-nu, Adonai Eh-chad!

אֶחָד אֱלֹהֵינוּ, גָּדוֹל אֲדֹנֵינוּ, קָדוֹשׁ וְנוֹרָא שְׁמוֹ!

Eh-chad Eh-lo-hei-nu, ga-dol A-do-nei-nu, ka-dosh v'no-ra sh'mo!

Hear, O Israel: Adonai is our God, Adonai alone!
Our God is one; great and holy and awesome
is Adonai.

בֵּית יַעֲקֹב, לְכוּ וְנֵלְכָה בְּאוֹר יהוה.

O House of Jacob, come, let us walk
by the light of our God.

אַשְׁרֵיכֶם יִשְׂרָאֵל, אַשְׁרֵיכֶם יִשְׂרָאֵל, אַשְׁרֵיכֶם יִשְׂרָאֵל,
אֲשֶׁר בָּחַר בָּכֶם אֵל, וְהִנְחִילְכֶם הַתּוֹרָה.

How blessed, how fortunate, how privileged you are, O
Israel, called to serve God, inheritors of the Torah!

CONSECRATION OF CHILDREN

CHILDREN RECITE THE SHEMA

READER

Eternal God, bless these children who stand here today: our
hope for the future. May the words of Torah always be
sweet to them, bringing light to their eyes and joy to their
hearts. This day we consecrate them to the study of Your
word. As they grow in learning, may they grow in wisdom,
bringing honor to themselves, their families, this congregation, and the whole House of Israel. Amen.

PARENTS

*We give thanks for our children, a precious gift entrusted to us, a
sacred responsibility. May we find the wisdom to raise them in
the tradition of our people: the tradition of Torah and Mitzvot, of
love and good deeds.*

*Here and now we consecrate our children and ourselves to learn
Torah and to live it. Let such joy as we feel now always be with
us, as together with our children we walk the paths of life.*

THE CHILDREN ARE BLESSED AND RETURN TO THEIR PARENTS

הוֹדוּ לַיהוה כִּי־טוֹב, כִּי לְעוֹלָם חַסְדּוֹ.

Ho-du l'Adonai ki tov, ki l'o-lam chas-do.

Give thanks to Adonai, who is good, whose love is everlasting.

HAKAFOT (PROCESSIONS)

Some may wish to choose from among the following verses. In some congregations it is the practice instead to sing a series of songs that are known and can be sung by all who are present.

אָנָּא יי, הוֹשִׁיעָה נָא.
Eternal God, be our help.

אָנָּא יי, הַצְלִיחָה נָא.
Eternal God, prosper us.

אָנָּא יי, עֲנֵנוּ בְיוֹם קָרְאֵנוּ.
Eternal God, be our answer when we call upon You.

אֱלֹהֵי הָרוּחוֹת, הוֹשִׁיעָה נָא.
God of all beings, be our help.

בּוֹחֵן לְבָבוֹת, הַצְלִיחָה נָא.
Searcher of hearts, prosper us.

גּוֹאֵל חָזָק, עֲנֵנוּ בְיוֹם קָרְאֵנוּ.
Mighty redeemer, be our answer when we call upon You.

דּוֹבֵר צְדָקוֹת, הוֹשִׁיעָה נָא.
Teacher of justice, be our help.

הָדוּר בִּלְבוּשׁוֹת, הַצְלִיחָה נָא.
God robed in glory, prosper us.

וָתִיק וְחָסִיד, עֲנֵנוּ בְיוֹם קָרְאֵנוּ.
Eternally gracious one, be our answer when we call upon You.

זַךְ וְיָשָׁר, הוֹשִׁיעָה נָא.
God pure and upright, be our help.

חוֹמֵל דַּלִּים, הַצְלִיחָה נָא.
Champion of the poor, prosper us.

טוֹב וּמֵטִיב, עֲנֵנוּ בְיוֹם קָרְאֵנוּ.
Good and beneficent, be our answer when we call upon You.

יוֹדֵעַ מַחֲשָׁבוֹת, הוֹשִׁיעָה נָא.
Searcher of minds, be our help.

כַּבִּיר וְנָאוֹר, הַצְלִיחָה נָא.
Mighty and radiant, prosper us.

לוֹבֵשׁ צְדָקוֹת, עֲנֵנוּ בְיוֹם קָרְאֵנוּ.
Robed in righteousness, be our answer when we call upon You.

מֶֽלֶךְ עוֹלָמִים, הוֹשִֽׁיעָה נָא. Eternal sovereign, be our help.

נָאוֹר וְאַדִּיר, הַצְלִיחָה נָא. God radiant and glorious, prosper us.

סוֹמֵךְ נוֹפְלִים, עֲנֵֽנוּ בְּיוֹם קָרְאֵֽנוּ. Upholder of the falling, be our answer when we call upon You.

עוֹזֵר דַּלִּים, הוֹשִֽׁיעָה נָא. Helper of the weak, be our help.

פּוֹדֶה וּמַצִּיל, הַצְלִיחָה נָא. Redeemer and deliverer, prosper us.

צוּר עוֹלָמִים, עֲנֵֽנוּ בְּיוֹם קָרְאֵֽנוּ. Eternal Rock, be our answer when we call upon You.

קָדוֹשׁ וְנוֹרָא, הוֹשִֽׁיעָה נָא. Holy and awesome, be our help.

רַחוּם וְחַנּוּן, הַצְלִיחָה נָא. Merciful and gracious, prosper us.

שׁוֹמֵר הַבְּרִית, עֲנֵֽנוּ בְּיוֹם קָרְאֵֽנוּ. Keeper of the covenant, be our answer when we call upon You.

תּוֹמֵךְ תְּמִימִים, הוֹשִֽׁיעָה נָא. Supporter of the upright, be our help.

תַּקִּיף לָעַד, הַצְלִיחָה נָא. God whose power is everlasting, prosper us.

תָּמִים בְּמַעֲשָׂיו, עֲנֵֽנוּ בְּיוֹם קָרְאֵֽנוּ. God whose ways are pure, be our answer when we call upon You.

TWO SCROLLS ARE PREPARED FOR READING

252

שִׂישׂוּ וְשִׂמְחוּ בְּשִׂמְחַת תּוֹרָה,
וּתְנוּ כָבוֹד לַתּוֹרָה.

Rejoice and be glad on Simchat Torah, and give honor to the Torah.

כִּי טוֹב סַחֲרָה מִכָּל־סְחוֹרָה,
מִפָּז וּמִפְּנִינִים יְקָרָה.

For it is better than all other goods, more precious than gold and diamonds.

נָגִיל וְנָשִׂישׂ בְּזֹאת הַתּוֹרָה,
כִּי הִיא לָנוּ עֹז וְאוֹרָה.

Let us rejoice in this Torah of ours, for it gives us strength and light.

תּוֹרָה הִיא עֵץ חַיִּים, לְכֻלָּם
חַיִּים, כִּי עִמְּךָ מְקוֹר חַיִּים.

It is a tree of life, of life for all; for You, O God, are our fountain of life.

ALL ARE SEATED

THE TORAH IS READ

BEFORE AN ALIYAH

בָּרְכוּ אֶת־יְיָ הַמְבֹרָךְ!
בָּרוּךְ יְיָ הַמְבֹרָךְ לְעוֹלָם וָעֶד!
בָּרוּךְ יְיָ הַמְבֹרָךְ לְעוֹלָם וָעֶד!
בָּרוּךְ אַתָּה יְיָ, אֱלֹהֵינוּ מֶלֶךְ הָעוֹלָם,
אֲשֶׁר בָּחַר־בָּנוּ מִכָּל־הָעַמִּים, וְנָתַן־לָנוּ אֶת־תּוֹרָתוֹ.
בָּרוּךְ אַתָּה יְיָ, נוֹתֵן הַתּוֹרָה.

READER: *Ba-r'chu et Adonai ha-m'vo-rach!*

CONGREGATION: *Ba-ruch Adonai ha-m'vo-rach l'o-lam va-ed!*

READER: *Ba-ruch Adonai ha-m'vo-rach l'o-lam va-ed!*

Ba-ruch a-ta Adonai, Eh-lo-hei-nu meh-lech ha-o-lam,
a-sher ba-char ba-nu mi-kol ha-a-mim, v'na-tan la-nu et Torah-to.
Ba-ruch a-ta Adonai, no-tein ha-Torah.

Praise the one to whom our praise is due!

Praised be the one to whom our praise is due, now and forever!

We praise You, Adonai our God, sovereign of the universe: You have called us to Your service by giving us the Torah. We praise You, O God, giver of the Torah.

AFTER AN ALIYAH

בָּרוּךְ אַתָּה יי, אֱלֹהֵינוּ מֶלֶךְ הָעוֹלָם,

אֲשֶׁר נָתַן־לָנוּ תּוֹרַת אֱמֶת, וְחַיֵּי עוֹלָם נָטַע בְּתוֹכֵנוּ.

בָּרוּךְ אַתָּה יי, נוֹתֵן הַתּוֹרָה.

READER: *Ba-ruch a-ta Adonai, Eh-lo-hei-nu meh-lech ha-o-lam,*
a-sher na-tan la-nu To-rat eh-met, v'cha-yei o-lam na-ta b'to-chei-nu.
Ba-ruch a-ta Adonai, no-tein ha-Torah.

We praise You, Adonai our God, sovereign of the universe: You have given us a Torah of truth, implanting within us eternal life. We praise You, O God, giver of the Torah.

SPECIAL PRAYERS THAT MIGHT BE INCLUDED BEFORE THE HAFTARAH OR BEFORE THE TORAH IS RETURNED TO THE ARK ARE ON PAGES 175-181

WHEN THE READING OF TORAH HAS BEEN COMPLETED

הגבהה—HAGBAHA—THE TORAH IS LIFTED AND WE SAY

וְזֹאת הַתּוֹרָה אֲשֶׁר־שָׂם מֹשֶׁה לִפְנֵי בְּנֵי יִשְׂרָאֵל,

עַל־פִּי יי בְּיַד־מֹשֶׁה.

V'zot ha-Torah a-sher sam Mo-sheh li-f'nei b'nei Yisrael,
al pi Adonai b'yad Mo-sheh.

This is the Torah that Moses placed before the people of Israel.

❦

THE HAFTARAH IS READ

BEFORE THE READING

בָּרוּךְ אַתָּה יי, אֱלֹהֵינוּ מֶלֶךְ הָעוֹלָם, אֲשֶׁר בָּחַר
בִּנְבִיאִים טוֹבִים, וְרָצָה בְדִבְרֵיהֶם הַנֶּאֱמָרִים בֶּאֱמֶת.
בָּרוּךְ אַתָּה יי, הַבּוֹחֵר בַּתּוֹרָה, וּבְמֹשֶׁה עַבְדּוֹ,
וּבְיִשְׂרָאֵל עַמּוֹ, וּבִנְבִיאֵי הָאֱמֶת וָצֶדֶק.

We praise You, Adonai our God, sovereign of the universe: You have
called faithful prophets to speak words of truth. We praise You, O God,
for the revelation of Torah, for Moses Your servant and Israel Your
people, and for the prophets of truth and righteousness.

AFTER THE READING

בָּרוּךְ אַתָּה יי, אֱלֹהֵינוּ מֶלֶךְ הָעוֹלָם, צוּר כָּל־הָעוֹלָמִים,
צַדִּיק בְּכָל־הַדּוֹרוֹת, הָאֵל הַנֶּאֱמָן, הָאוֹמֵר וְעוֹשֶׂה,
הַמְדַבֵּר וּמְקַיֵּם, שֶׁכָּל־דְּבָרָיו אֱמֶת וָצֶדֶק.

We praise You, Adonai our God, sovereign of the universe, rock of all
worlds, righteous in every generations, the faithful God whose word is
deed, whose every teaching is justice and truth.

※

נֶאֱמָן אַתָּה הוּא, יי אֱלֹהֵינוּ, וְנֶאֱמָנִים דְּבָרֶיךָ, וְדָבָר
אֶחָד מִדְּבָרֶיךָ אָחוֹר לֹא יָשׁוּב רֵיקָם, כִּי אֵל מֶלֶךְ נֶאֱמָן
וְרַחֲמָן אָתָּה. בָּרוּךְ אַתָּה יי, הָאֵל הַנֶּאֱמָן בְּכָל־דְּבָרָיו.

Some will wish
to include this
and the
following
blessing.

True are You, Adonai our God, and true are Your words: not one
word of Yours goes unfulfilled, for You are the sovereign God,
true and compassionate. We praise You, Adonai, the God whose
words are true.

רַחֵם עַל צִיּוֹן כִּי הִיא בֵּית חַיֵּינוּ. וְלַעֲלוּבַת נֶפֶשׁ תּוֹשִׁיעַ
בִּמְהֵרָה בְיָמֵינוּ. בָּרוּךְ אַתָּה יי, מְשַׂמֵּחַ צִיּוֹן בְּבָנֶיהָ.

Some may wish
to include this
blessing.

Have compassion upon Zion, for it is the house of our life, and
let every humbled spirit find deliverance. We praise You, O God:
You give joy to Zion's children.

&

עַל־הַתּוֹרָה וְעַל־הָעֲבוֹדָה וְעַל־הַנְּבִיאִים וְעַל־הַיּוֹם (הַשַּׁבָּת הַזֶּה,
וְעַל־יוֹם)

❖ חַג הַמַּצּוֹת הַזֶּה,

❖ חַג הַשָּׁבֻעוֹת הַזֶּה,

❖ חַג הַסֻּכּוֹת הַזֶּה,

❖ הַשְּׁמִינִי חַג הָעֲצֶרֶת הַזֶּה,

שֶׁנָּתַתָּ־לָּנוּ, יי אֱלֹהֵינוּ, (לִקְדֻשָּׁה וְלִמְנוּחָה,) לְשָׂשׂוֹן וּלְשִׂמְחָה,
לְכָבוֹד וּלְתִפְאָרֶת, עַל־הַכֹּל, יי אֱלֹהֵינוּ, אֲנַחְנוּ מוֹדִים לָךְ
וּמְבָרְכִים אוֹתָךְ. יִתְבָּרַךְ שִׁמְךָ בְּפִי כָּל־חַי תָּמִיד לְעוֹלָם
וָעֶד. בָּרוּךְ אַתָּה יי, מְקַדֵּשׁ (הַשַּׁבָּת וְ) יִשְׂרָאֵל וְהַזְּמַנִּים.

For the Torah, for worship, for the prophets, and for this (Shabbat and this)

❖ Festival of Matzot,
❖ Festival of Shavuot,
❖ Festival of Sukkot,
❖ Festival of Sh'mini Atzeret (Simchat Torah)

that You, Adonai our God, have given us for (holiness and rest,) for joy and
gladness, for honor and glory: we thank and praise You. May Your name
ever be praised by every living being. We praise You, O God: You
hallow (Shabbat,) Israel and Yom Tov.

THE LITURGY FOR RETURNING THE TORAH TO THE ARK IS ON PAGE 257.

RETURNING THE TORAH TO THE ARK

ALL RISE

יְהַלְלוּ אֶת־שֵׁם יהוה, כִּי־נִשְׂגָּב שְׁמוֹ לְבַדּוֹ.

Let us praise the eternal God,
whose name alone is exalted.

הוֹדוֹ עַל־אֶרֶץ וְשָׁמָיִם, וַיָּרֶם קֶרֶן לְעַמּוֹ, תְּהִלָּה
לְכָל־חֲסִידָיו, לִבְנֵי יִשְׂרָאֵל, עַם־קְרֹבוֹ, הַלְלוּיָהּ!

Ho-do al eh-retz v'sha-ma-yim, va-ya-rem keh-ren l'a-mo, t'hi-lah
l'chol cha-si-dav, li-v'nei Yisrael am k'ro-vo, halleluyah!

Your splendor covers heaven and earth; You are the strength of Your
people, making glorious Your faithful ones, Israel, a people close to You.
Halleluyah!

כִּי זֹאת הַבְּרִית אֲשֶׁר אֶכְרֹת אֶת־בֵּית יִשְׂרָאֵל
אַחֲרֵי הַיָּמִים הָהֵם, נְאֻם־יהוה: נָתַתִּי אֶת־תּוֹרָתִי
בְּקִרְבָּם, וְעַל־לִבָּם אֶכְתֲּבֶנָּה, וְהָיִיתִי לָהֶם לֵאלֹהִים,
וְהֵמָּה יִהְיוּ־לִי לְעָם. וְלֹא יְלַמְּדוּ עוֹד אִישׁ אֶת־רֵעֵהוּ
וְאִישׁ אֶת־אָחִיו לֵאמֹר, דְּעוּ אֶת־יהוה, כִּי־כֻלָּם יֵדְעוּ
אוֹתִי, לְמִקְטַנָּם וְעַד־גְּדוֹלָם, נְאֻם־יהוה.

This is the covenant I will make with the House of Israel in
time to come, says Adonai: I will put my teaching within
them, and inscribe it on their hearts; I will be their God, and
they shall be my people. No longer shall anyone need to
teach a friend or a neighbor to know me, for they all shall
know me, young and old alike!

Behold, I have given you a good doctrine; do not forsake it. It is a
tree of life to those who hold it fast, and all who cling to it find
blessing. Its ways are ways of pleasantness, and all its paths are
peace.

כִּי לֶקַח טוֹב נָתַתִּי לָכֶם, תּוֹרָתִי אַל־תַּעֲזֹבוּ.

Ki leh-kach tov na-ta-ti la-chem, to-ra-ti al ta-a-zo-vu.

עֵץ־חַיִּים הִיא לַמַּחֲזִיקִים בָּהּ, וְתֹמְכֶיהָ מְאֻשָּׁר.
דְּרָכֶיהָ דַרְכֵי־נֹעַם, וְכָל־נְתִיבוֹתֶיהָ שָׁלוֹם.
הֲשִׁיבֵנוּ יהוה אֵלֶיךָ, וְנָשׁוּבָה. חַדֵּשׁ יָמֵינוּ כְּקֶדֶם.

Eitz cha-yim hi la-ma-cha-zi-kim ba, v'to-m'cheh-ha m'u-shar.

D'ra-cheh-ha dar'chei no-am, v'chol n'ti-vo-teh-ha sha-lom.

Ha-shi-vei-nu Adonai ei-leh-cha, v'na-shu-vah. Cha-deish ya-mei-nu k'keh-dem.

Help us to return to You, O God; then truly shall we return. Renew our days as of old.

THE ARK IS CLOSED

ALL ARE SEATED

☙

YIZKOR   יזכור

MEMORIAL SERVICE   הזכרת נשמות

✻ See
"Reflections
for Troubled
Hours," pages
341-346.

יהוה, מָה־אָדָם וַתֵּדָעֵהוּ;
בֶּן־אֱנוֹשׁ וַתְּחַשְּׁבֵהוּ?
אָדָם לַהֶבֶל דָּמָה;
יָמָיו כְּצֵל עוֹבֵר.
בַּבְּקֶר כְּחָצִיר יַחֲלֹף.
בַּבְּקֶר יָצִיץ וְחָלָף;
לָעֶרֶב יְמוֹלֵל וְיָבֵשׁ.
תָּשֵׁב אֱנוֹשׁ עַד־דַּכָּא,
וַתְּאמֶר: שׁוּבוּ בְנֵי־אָדָם.

Adonai, what are we, that You take note of us; what are we, that You take account of us?

We are like air; our days are like a shadow passing, like grass that springs up in the morning: in the morning it flourishes and is renewed; in the evening it fades and withers.

You cause us to return to dust, saying: Return, O mortal creatures!

FROM ECCLESIASTES 3

לַכֹּל זְמָן, וְעֵת לְכָל־חֵפֶץ תַּחַת הַשָּׁמָיִם:
עֵת לָלֶדֶת וְעֵת לָמוּת; עֵת לִבְכּוֹת וְעֵת לִשְׂחוֹק.

For everything there is a season, and a time for every desire under heaven:

A time to be born and a time to die;

A time to weep and a time to laugh.

עֵת סְפוֹד וְעֵת רְקוֹד; עֵת לַחֲבוֹק וְעֵת לִרְחֹק מֵחַבֵּק.

A time to grieve and a time to dance;

A time to embrace and a time to refrain from embracing.

עֵת לְבַקֵּשׁ וְעֵת לְאַבֵּד; עֵת לִשְׁמוֹר וְעֵת לְהַשְׁלִיךְ.

A time to seek and a time to lose;

A time to keep and a time to give away.

Yizkor

FROM PSALM 36

מַה־יָּקָר חַסְדְּךָ, אֱלֹהִים; How precious is Your
lovingkindness, O God, and
וּבְנֵי אָדָם בְּצֵל כְּנָפֶיךָ we all take refuge in the
יֶחֱסָיוּן. shadow of Your wings.

יִרְוְיֻן מִדֶּשֶׁן בֵּיתֶךָ, We feast on the abundance
of Your house, and You
וְנַחַל עֲדָנֶיךָ תַשְׁקֵם. give us drink from the river
of Your delights.

כִּי־עִמְּךָ מְקוֹר חַיִּים; For with You is the fountain
of life; in Your light we see
בְּאוֹרְךָ נִרְאֶה־אוֹר. light.

A REFLECTION

❧ When we are dead, and people weep and grieve for
us, let it be because we touched their lives with beauty and
simplicity. Let it not be said that life was good to us, but,
rather, that we were good to life. (Rabbi Jacob Philip Rudin)

FROM PSALM 90

אֲדֹנָי, מָעוֹן אַתָּה הָיִיתָ לָּנוּ בְּדֹר וָדֹר.
בְּטֶרֶם הָרִים יֻלָּדוּ, וַתְּחוֹלֵל אֶרֶץ וְתֵבֵל,
וּמֵעוֹלָם עַד־עוֹלָם אַתָּה אֵל.

Adonai, You have been our refuge in all generations.

Before the mountains were born, or earth and universe brought
forth, from eternity to eternity You are God.

כִּי אֶלֶף שָׁנִים בְּעֵינֶיךָ כְּיוֹם אֶתְמוֹל כִּי יַעֲבֹר,
וְאַשְׁמוּרָה בַלָּיְלָה.

כְּלִינוּ שָׁנֵינוּ כְמוֹ־הֶגֶה. כִּי־גָז חִישׁ וַנָּעֻפָה.

לִמְנוֹת יָמֵינוּ כֵּן הוֹדַע, וְנָבִא לְלֵבַב חָכְמָה.

A thousand years in Your sight are but as yesterday when it
is past, or as a watch in the night.

*Our years come to an end like a sigh, for they are soon gone, and
we fly away. So teach us to number our days, that we may grow
wise in heart.*

שַׂבְּעֵנוּ בַבֹּקֶר חַסְדֶּךָ, וּנְרַנְּנָה וְנִשְׂמְחָה בְּכָל־יָמֵינוּ.

יֵרָאֶה אֶל־עֲבָדֶיךָ פָּעֳלֶךָ, וַהֲדָרְךָ עַל־בְּנֵיהֶם.

וִיהִי נֹעַם אֲדֹנָי אֱלֹהֵינוּ עָלֵינוּ, וּמַעֲשֵׂה יָדֵינוּ כּוֹנְנָה עָלֵינוּ,

וּמַעֲשֵׂה יָדֵינוּ כּוֹנְנֵהוּ.

Satisfy us in the morning with Your lovingkindness, that we
may rejoice and be glad all our days.

*Let Your servants understand Your ways, and their children see
Your glory.*

Let Your favor, Adonai our God, be with us, and may our
work have lasting meaning.

Let the work of our hands endure!

A REFLECTION

❧   The path of the righteous is like a shining light, ever
more bright until the day is full. (Proverbs)

FROM PSALM 16

שָׁמְרֵנִי אֵל, כִּי־חָסִיתִי בָךְ.

אָמַרְתִּי לַיהוה: אֲדֹנָי אָתָּה, טוֹבָתִי בַּל־עָלֶיךָ.

יהוה מְנָת־חֶלְקִי וְכוֹסִי, אַתָּה תּוֹמִיךְ גּוֹרָלִי.

חֲבָלִים נָפְלוּ־לִי בַּנְּעִמִים, אַף־נַחֲלָת שָׁפְרָה עָלָי.

אֲבָרֵךְ אֶת־יהוה אֲשֶׁר יְעָצָנִי, אַף־לֵילוֹת יִסְּרוּנִי כִלְיוֹתָי.

Hold me, O God, for in You I find refuge,
and in You, Adonai, my happiness lies.

Guardian of all my days,
You are the cup from which I drink,
You are my life's portion.

The days of my life have fallen in pleasant places;
a goodly heritage has been my lot.

I thank You for guiding me,
for the inner voice that instructs me.

שִׁוִּיתִי יהוה לְנֶגְדִּי תָמִיד, כִּי מִימִינִי בַּל־אֶמּוֹט.

לָכֵן שָׂמַח לִבִּי וַיָּגֶל כְּבוֹדִי, אַף־בְּשָׂרִי יִשְׁכֹּן לָבֶטַח.

This passage might be read or sung.

I have set You before me always;
with You beside me I cannot fail.
And so my heart is glad,
my soul rejoices, and I can rest secure:

כִּי לֹא־תַעֲזֹב נַפְשִׁי לִשְׁאוֹל, לֹא־תִתֵּן חֲסִידְךָ לִרְאוֹת שָׁחַת.

תּוֹדִיעֵנִי אֹרַח חַיִּים; שְׂבַע שְׂמָחוֹת אֶת־פָּנֶיךָ; נְעִמוֹת בִּימִינְךָ נֶצַח.

for You will not abandon me in death.
You show me the path of life,
and Your presence is fullness of joy.

WE REMEMBER

We remember our loved ones. In the rising of the sun and in its going down, we remember them.

In the blowing of the wind and in the chill of winter, we remember them.

In the opening buds and in the rebirth of spring, we remember them.

In the blueness of the sky and in the warmth of summer, we remember them.

In the rustling of leaves and in the beauty of autumn, we remember them.

In the beginning of the year and when it ends, we remember them.

When we are weary and in need of strength, we remember them.

When we are lost and sick at heart, we remember them.

When we have joys we yearn to share, we remember them.

So long as we live, they too shall live, for they are now a part of us, as we remember them.

We give thanks: remembering is a gift. We give thanks: their lives are a blessing.

We give thanks for what we had. We give thanks for what we have.

Remembering is a gift, a gift of love passing back and forth among yesterdays, among those that were and those that are, those we walk with now, and yesterday's companions for whose journeys we are glad.

We give thanks for what we had. We give thanks for what we have.

SILENT PRAYER

יִזְכֹּר אֱלֹהִים נִשְׁמוֹת יַקִּירַי _____ שֶׁהָלְכוּ לְעוֹלָמָם. אָנָּא
תִּהְיֶינָה נַפְשׁוֹתֵיהֶם צְרוּרוֹת בִּצְרוֹר הַחַיִּים וּתְהִי מְנוּחָתָם
כָּבוֹד. שֹׂבַע שְׂמָחוֹת אֶת־פָּנֶיךָ, נְעִימוֹת בִּימִינְךָ נֶצַח. אָמֵן.

May God forever remember my dear ones _____ who have
gone to their eternal rest. They are at one with the one who
is life eternal. May the beauty of their lives shine evermore,
and inspire me always to bring honor to their memory.

יִזְכֹּר אֱלֹהִים נִשְׁמוֹת כָּל־אַחֵינוּ בְּנֵי יִשְׂרָאֵל שֶׁמָּסְרוּ
אֶת־נַפְשׁוֹתֵיהֶם עַל קִדּוּשׁ הַשֵּׁם. אָנָּא תִּהְיֶינָה נַפְשׁוֹתֵיהֶם
צְרוּרוֹת בִּצְרוֹר הַחַיִּים וּתְהִי מְנוּחָתָם כָּבוֹד. שֹׂבַע שְׂמָחוֹת
אֶת־פָּנֶיךָ, נְעִימוֹת בִּימִינְךָ נֶצַח. אָמֵן.

May God forever remember our brothers and sisters of the
House of Israel who gave their lives for the sanctification of
the Divine Name. They are at one with the one who is life
eternal. May the beauty of their lives shine evermore, and
may my life always bring honor to their memory.

PSALM 23

A SONG OF DAVID   מִזְמוֹר לְדָוִד

יְהוָה רֹעִי, לֹא אֶחְסָר. בִּנְאוֹת דֶּשֶׁא יַרְבִּיצֵנִי, עַל־מֵי מְנֻחוֹת
יְנַהֲלֵנִי. נַפְשִׁי יְשׁוֹבֵב; יַנְחֵנִי בְמַעְגְּלֵי־צֶדֶק לְמַעַן שְׁמוֹ.
גַּם כִּי־אֵלֵךְ בְּגֵיא צַלְמָוֶת לֹא־אִירָא רָע, כִּי־אַתָּה עִמָּדִי;
שִׁבְטְךָ וּמִשְׁעַנְתֶּךָ, הֵמָּה יְנַחֲמֻנִי. תַּעֲרֹךְ לְפָנַי שֻׁלְחָן נֶגֶד צֹרְרָי,
דִּשַּׁנְתָּ בַשֶּׁמֶן רֹאשִׁי, כּוֹסִי רְוָיָה. אַךְ טוֹב וָחֶסֶד יִרְדְּפוּנִי
כָּל־יְמֵי חַיָּי, וְשַׁבְתִּי בְּבֵית־יְהוָה לְאֹרֶךְ יָמִים.

*Adonai, You are my shepherd, I shall not want. You make me lie
down in green pastures, You lead me beside still waters. You*

restore my soul; You guide me in paths of righteousness for the sake of Your name. Yes, even when I walk through the valley of the shadow of death, I shall fear no evil, for You are with me; with rod and staff You comfort me. You prepare a table before me in the presence of my enemies; You have anointed my head with oil; my cup overflows. Surely, goodness and mercy shall follow me all the days of my life, and I shall dwell in the house of my God forever.

ALL RISE

אֵל מָלֵא רַחֲמִים, שׁוֹכֵן בַּמְּרוֹמִים, הַמְצֵא מְנוּחָה נְכוֹנָה תַּחַת
כַּנְפֵי הַשְּׁכִינָה עִם קְדוֹשִׁים וּטְהוֹרִים כְּזֹהַר הָרָקִיעַ מַזְהִירִים
לְנִשְׁמוֹת יַקִּירֵינוּ שֶׁהָלְכוּ לְעוֹלָמָם. בַּעַל הָרַחֲמִים יַסְתִּירֵם
בְּסֵתֶר כְּנָפָיו לְעוֹלָמִים. וְיִצְרוֹר בִּצְרוֹר הַחַיִּים אֶת־נִשְׁמָתָם.
יְיָ הוּא נַחֲלָתָם. וְיָנוּחוּ בְשָׁלוֹם עַל מִשְׁכָּבָם, וְנֹאמַר: אָמֵן.

God full of compassion, You who dwell on high, grant perfect rest under the wings of Your presence together with the holy and pure whose radiance illuminates the world, to our loved ones who have entered eternity. God, abounding in mercies, let them find refuge forever in the shadow of Your wings, and let their souls be bound up in the bond of eternal life. Adonai, You are their inheritance; may they rest in peace, and let us say: *Amen.*

TEFILAH FOR SPECIAL SABBATHS

ALL RISE

אֲדֹנָי שְׂפָתַי תִּפְתָּח, וּפִי יַגִּיד תְּהִלָּתֶךָ.

Adonai, open my lips, and my mouth will declare Your praise.

אבות ואמהות   GOD OF ALL GENERATIONS

בָּרוּךְ אַתָּה יי, אֱלֹהֵינוּ
Ba-ruch a-ta Adonai, Eh-lo-hei-nu

וֵאלֹהֵי אֲבוֹתֵינוּ וְאִמּוֹתֵינוּ:
vei-lo-hei a-vo-tei-nu v'i-mo-tei-nu:

אֱלֹהֵי אַבְרָהָם, אֱלֹהֵי
Eh-lo-hei Av-ra-ham, eh-lo-hei

יִצְחָק וֵאלֹהֵי יַעֲקֹב:
Yitz-chak, vei-lo-hei Ya-a-kov:

אֱלֹהֵי שָׂרָה, אֱלֹהֵי רִבְקָה,
Eh-lo-hei Sa-rah, eh-lo-hei Riv-kah,

אֱלֹהֵי לֵאָה וֵאלֹהֵי רָחֵל;
eh-lo-hei Lei-ah, vei-lo-hei Ra-cheil;

הָאֵל הַגָּדוֹל הַגִּבּוֹר
Ha-eil ha-ga-dol ha-gi-bor

וְהַנּוֹרָא, אֵל עֶלְיוֹן. גּוֹמֵל
v'ha-no-ra, eil el-yon. Go-meil

חֲסָדִים טוֹבִים וְקוֹנֵה הַכֹּל,
cha-sa-dim to-vim, v'ko-nei ha-kol,

וְזוֹכֵר חַסְדֵי אָבוֹת וְאִמָּהוֹת,
v'zo-cheir chas-dei a-vot v'i-ma-hot,

וּמֵבִיא גְּאֻלָּה לִבְנֵי בְנֵיהֶם,
u-mei-vi g'u-la li-v'nei v'nei-hem,

לְמַעַן שְׁמוֹ בְּאַהֲבָה.
l'ma-an sh'mo, b'a-ha-vah.

The Shabbat Tefilah has seven prayers. In the first, we recall with reverence the founders of our people and faith. We say: Each generation finds its own way, and yet—their God is ours.

❋ See "Looking for God," pages 352-357.

We praise You, Adonai our God and God of our ancestors: of Abraham, Isaac, and Jacob; of Sarah, Rebekah, Leah, and Rachel; the great, mighty, and awesome God, God Most High.

You deal kindly with us and embrace us all. You remember the faith-fulness of our ancestors, and in love bring redemption to their children's children for the sake of Your name.

ON SHABBAT SHUVAH ADD

זָכְרֵנוּ לְחַיִּים,   Zoch-rei-nu l'cha-yim,

מֶלֶךְ חָפֵץ בַּחַיִּים,   meh-lech cha-feitz ba-cha-yim,

וְכָתְבֵנוּ בְּסֵפֶר הַחַיִּים,   v'chot-vei-nu b'sefer ha-cha-yim,

לְמַעַנְךָ אֱלֹהִים חַיִּים.   l'ma-a-n'cha, Eh-lo-him cha-yim.

Remember us for life, for You, O sovereign, delight in life; and inscribe us in the Book of Life, for Your sake, O God of life.

מֶלֶךְ עוֹזֵר וּמוֹשִׁיעַ   Meh-lech o-zeir u-mo-shi-a

וּמָגֵן. בָּרוּךְ אַתָּה יי,   u-ma-gein. Ba-ruch a-ta Adonai,

מָגֵן אַבְרָהָם וְעֶזְרַת שָׂרָה.   ma-gein Av-ra-ham v'ez-rat Sa-rah.

You are our sovereign and helper, our redeemer and shield.
We praise You, O God, Shield of Abraham and Protector of Sarah.

גבורות   GOD'S POWER

In this prayer, we affirm the power of God, whose reach extends to this world—the world we walk in—and to a world we cannot imagine.

✣ See Psalm 103 (page 366) and Psalm 146 (page 371).

אַתָּה גִבּוֹר לְעוֹלָם, אֲדֹנָי,   A-ta gi-bor l'o-lam, Adonai,

מְחַיֵּה מֵתִים אַתָּה, רַב   m'cha-yei mei-tim a-ta, rav

לְהוֹשִׁיעַ.   l'ho-shi-a. Ma-shiv ha-ru-ach

מַשִּׁיב הָרוּחַ וּמוֹרִיד הַגֶּשֶׁם,   u-mo-rid ha-ga-shem; maz-ri-ach

מַזְרִיחַ הַשֶּׁמֶשׁ וּמוֹרִיד הַטָּל.   ha-she-mesh u-mo-rid ha-tal.

מְכַלְכֵּל חַיִּים בְּחֶסֶד,   M'chal-keil cha-yim b'cheh-sed,

מְחַיֵּה מֵתִים בְּרַחֲמִים רַבִּים.   m'cha-yei mei-tim b'ra-cha-mim

סוֹמֵךְ נוֹפְלִים, וְרוֹפֵא   ra-bim. So-meich no-f'lim, v'ro-fei

חוֹלִים, וּמַתִּיר אֲסוּרִים,   cho-lim, u-ma-tir a-su-rim,

וּמְקַיֵּם אֱמוּנָתוֹ לִישֵׁנֵי   u-m'ka-yeim eh-mu-na-to li-shei-nei

עָפָר.   a-far.

מִי כָמֽוֹךָ, בַּעַל גְּבוּרוֹת, וּמִי   *Mi cha-mo-cha ba-al g'vu-rot, u-mi*

דֽוֹמֶה לָּךְ, מֶֽלֶךְ מֵמִית וּמְחַיֶּה   *do-meh lach, meh-lech mei-mit*

וּמַצְמִֽיחַ יְשׁוּעָה?   *u-m'cha-yeh u-matz-mi-ach y'shu-a?*

Unending is Your might, Eternal One; You are the source of eternal life; great is Your power to save.

You cause the wind to blow and the rain to fall, the sun to shine and the dew to descend. In Your love You sustain the living; in Your compassion You grant us eternal life. You support the falling and heal the sick; You free the captive and keep faith with those who sleep in the dust. Who is like You, source of all strength? Who is Your equal, sovereign author of life and death, who causes deliverance to flower in our world?

ON SHABBAT SHUVAH ADD

מִי כָמֽוֹךָ, אַב הָרַחֲמִים,   *Mi cha-mo-cha, av ha-ra-cha-mim,*

זוֹכֵר יְצוּרָיו לַחַיִּים   *zo-cheir y'tzu-rav la-cha-yim*

בְּרַחֲמִים?   *b'ra-cha-mim?*

Who is like You, God of mercy? In Your mercy You remember Your creatures, and grant them life.

וְנֶאֱמָן אַתָּה לְהַחֲיוֹת   *V'neh-eh-man a-ta l'ha-cha-yot*

מֵתִים. בָּרוּךְ אַתָּה יְיָ,   *mei-tim. Ba-ruch a-ta Adonai,*

מְחַיֵּה הַמֵּתִים.   *m'cha-yei ha-mei-tim.*

Trusting in You, we see life beyond death.

We praise You, O God, source of eternal life.

FOR AN EVENING SERVICE

קדושת השם GOD'S HOLINESS

As we walk beneath the stars, we walk among them, and the mystery of being calls to us—our third prayer proclaims the holiness of God.

❁ See Psalm 42/3 (page 363) and Psalm 63 (page 365).

אַתָּה קָדוֹשׁ וְשִׁמְךָ קָדוֹשׁ,

וּקְדוֹשִׁים בְּכָל־יוֹם

יְהַלְלוּךָ סֶּלָה.

Ata ka-dosh v'shi-m'cha ka-dosh,

u-k'do-shim b'chol yom

y'ha-l'lu-cha seh-lah.

You are holy, Your name is holy, and every day all creation sings Your praise.

ON SHABBAT SHUVAH CONCLUDE	ON ALL OTHER DAYS CONCLUDE
בָּרוּךְ אַתָּה יי, הַמֶּלֶךְ הַקָּדוֹשׁ.	בָּרוּךְ אַתָּה יי, הָאֵל הַקָּדוֹשׁ.
Ba-ruch a-ta Adonai, ha-meh-lech ha-ka-dosh.	*Ba-ruch a-ta Adonai, ha-eil ha-ka-dosh.*
We praise You, Adonai, the God who reigns in holiness.	*We praise You, Adonai, the holy God.*

ALL ARE SEATED

FOR A MORNING SERVICE

נְקַדֵּשׁ אֶת־שִׁמְךָ בָּעוֹלָם, כְּשֵׁם שֶׁמַּקְדִּישִׁים אוֹתוֹ

בִּשְׁמֵי מָרוֹם, כַּכָּתוּב עַל־יַד נְבִיאֶךָ:

וְקָרָא זֶה אֶל־זֶה וְאָמַר:

We hallow Your name on earth, even as all creation, to the highest heavens, proclaims Your holiness, and in the words of the prophet we say:

קָדוֹשׁ, קָדוֹשׁ, קָדוֹשׁ יהוה צְבָאוֹת,

מְלֹא כָל־הָאָרֶץ כְּבוֹדוֹ.

Holy, holy, holy is the God of all being! The whole earth is filled with Your glory!

אַדִּיר אַדִּירֵנוּ, יהוה אֲדֹנֵינוּ, מָה־אַדִּיר שִׁמְךָ בְּכָל־הָאָרֶץ!

God our strength, God of mercy, how majestic is Your name in all the earth!

בָּרוּךְ כְּבוֹד־יהוה מִמְּקוֹמוֹ.

Praised be the glory of God in heaven and earth.

אֶחָד הוּא אֱלֹהֵינוּ, הוּא אָבִינוּ, הוּא מַלְכֵּנוּ, הוּא מוֹשִׁיעֵנוּ;

וְהוּא יַשְׁמִיעֵנוּ בְּרַחֲמָיו לְעֵינֵי כָּל־חָי:

You alone are our God and maker, our ruler and helper; and in Your mercy You reveal Yourself to us in the sight of all the living:

אֲנִי יהוה אֱלֹהֵיכֶם!

I AM ADONAI YOUR GOD!

יִמְלֹךְ יהוה לְעוֹלָם, אֱלֹהַיִךְ צִיּוֹן, לְדֹר וָדֹר. הַלְלוּיָהּ!

Adonai shall reign forever, Your God, O Zion, from generation to generation. Halleluyah!

In the Sanctification we echo the awe and wonder expressed by our psalmists, mystics, and prophets as they experienced God's presence in their lives.

❧ See pages 352-353 and page 397.

לְדוֹר וָדוֹר נַגִּיד גָּדְלֶךָ, וּלְנֵצַח נְצָחִים קְדֻשָּׁתְךָ נַקְדִּישׁ.
וְשִׁבְחֲךָ, אֱלֹהֵינוּ, מִפִּינוּ לֹא יָמוּשׁ לְעוֹלָם וָעֶד.

From generation to generation we will make known Your
greatness, and to all eternity proclaim Your holiness. Your
praise, O God, shall never depart from our lips.

ON SHABBAT SHUVAH CONCLUDE	ON ALL OTHER DAYS CONCLUDE
בָּרוּךְ אַתָּה יי, הַמֶּלֶךְ הַקָּדוֹשׁ.	בָּרוּךְ אַתָּה יי, הָאֵל הַקָּדוֹשׁ.
Ba-ruch a-ta Adonai,	*Ba-ruch a-ta Adonai,*
ha-meh-lech ha-ka-dosh.	*ha-eil ha-ka-dosh.*
We praise You, Adonai, the	*We praise You, Adonai,*
God who reigns in holiness.	*the holy God.*

ALL ARE SEATED

קְדוּשַׁת הַיּוֹם   **THE HOLINESS OF SHABBAT**

EITHER

וְשָׁמְרוּ   **THE COVENANT OF SHABBAT**

We do not
ask for
material
blessings
on the day
devoted to
God.
The gifts we
seek on
Shabbat
are spiritual.

וְשָׁמְרוּ בְנֵי־יִשְׂרָאֵל אֶת־הַשַּׁבָּת, לַעֲשׂוֹת אֶת־הַשַּׁבָּת לְדֹרֹתָם,
בְּרִית עוֹלָם. בֵּינִי וּבֵין בְּנֵי יִשְׂרָאֵל אוֹת הִיא לְעֹלָם.
כִּי־שֵׁשֶׁת יָמִים עָשָׂה יהוה אֶת־הַשָּׁמַיִם וְאֶת־הָאָרֶץ,
וּבַיּוֹם הַשְּׁבִיעִי שָׁבַת וַיִּנָּפַשׁ.

V'sha-m'ru v'nei Yis-ra-eil et ha-Shabbat, la-a-sot et ha-Shabbat l'do-ro-tam,
b'rit o-lam. Bei-ni u-vein b'nei Yis-ra-eil ot hi l'o-lam.
Ki shei-shet ya-mim a-sa Adonai et ha-sha-ma-yim v'et ha-a-retz,
u-va-yom ha-sh'vi-i sha-vat va-yi-na-fash.

The people of Israel shall keep the Sabbath, observing the Sabbath in every generation as a covenant forever. It is a sign between me and the people of Israel forever. For in six days Adonai made heaven and earth, but on the seventh day God rested and was refreshed.

OR

ישמחו MOST PRECIOUS OF DAYS

יִשְׂמְחוּ בְמַלְכוּתְךָ שׁוֹמְרֵי שַׁבָּת וְקוֹרְאֵי עְׂנֶג.

עַם מְקַדְּשֵׁי שְׁבִיעִי כֻּלָּם יִשְׂבְּעוּ וְיִתְעַנְּגוּ מִטּוּבֶךָ.

וְהַשְּׁבִיעִי רָצִיתָ בּוֹ וְקִדַּשְׁתּוֹ. חֶמְדַּת יָמִים אוֹתוֹ קָרָאתָ,

זֵכֶר לְמַעֲשֵׂה בְרֵאשִׁית.

Yis-m'chu v'ma-l'chu-t'cha sho-m'rei Shabbat v'ko-r'ei o-neg.
Am m'ka-d'shei sh'vi-i ku-lam yis-b'u v'yit-a-n'gu mi-tu-veh-cha.
V'ha-sh'vi-i ra-tzi-ta bo v'ki-dash-to. Chem-dat ya-mim o-to ka-ra-ta,
zei-cher l'ma-a-sei v'rei-sheet.

Those who keep the Sabbath and call it a delight shall rejoice in Your sovereign presence. All who hallow the seventh day shall taste the joy of Your bounty. This is the day You delight in and sanctify. "Loveliest of days," You have called it, "a reminder of the work of creation."

אֱלֹהֵינוּ וֵאלֹהֵי אֲבוֹתֵינוּ וְאִמּוֹתֵינוּ, רְצֵה בִמְנוּחָתֵנוּ.

Our God, God of our fathers and mothers, may our Sabbath rest
be pleasing in Your sight.

קַדְּשֵׁנוּ בְּמִצְוֹתֶיךָ וְתֵן חֶלְקֵנוּ בְּתוֹרָתֶךָ.

שַׂבְּעֵנוּ מִטּוּבֶךָ, וְשַׂמְּחֵנוּ בִּישׁוּעָתֶךָ,

וְטַהֵר לִבֵּנוּ לְעָבְדְּךָ בֶּאֱמֶת.

וְהַנְחִילֵנוּ, יי אֱלֹהֵינוּ, בְּאַהֲבָה וּבְרָצוֹן

שַׁבַּת קָדְשֶׁךָ, וְיָנוּחוּ בָהּ יִשְׂרָאֵל מְקַדְּשֵׁי שְׁמֶךָ.

Ka-d'shei-nu b'mitz-vo-teh-cha v'tein chel-kei-nu b'toh-ra-teh-cha.
Sab-ei-nu mi-tu-veh-cha, v'sam-chei-nu bi-shu-a-teh-cha,

v'ta-heir li-bei-nu l-ov-d'cha beh-eh-met.

V'han-chi-lei-nu, Adonai Eh-lo-hei-nu, b'a-ha-va u-v'ra-tzon

Shabbat kod-sheh-cha, v'ya-nu-chu va Yis-ra-eil m'ka-d'shei sh'meh-cha.

Sanctify us with Your Mitzvot, and make Your Torah our life's portion. Satisfy us with Your goodness, gladden us with Your salvation, and purify our hearts to serve You in truth. In Your gracious love, Adonai our God, let the holiness of Shabbat enter our hearts, that all Israel, hallowing Your name, may find rest and peace.

בָּרוּךְ אַתָּה יי, מְקַדֵּשׁ הַשַּׁבָּת.

Ba-ruch a-ta Adonai, m'ka-deish ha-Shabbat.

We praise You, the God who hallows Shabbat.

WORSHIP עבודה

רְצֵה, יי אֱלֹהֵינוּ, בְּעַמְּךָ יִשְׂרָאֵל,

וּתְפִלָּתָם בְּאַהֲבָה תְקַבֵּל,

וּתְהִי לְרָצוֹן תָּמִיד עֲבוֹדַת יִשְׂרָאֵל עַמֶּךָ.

We pray now that our prayer be acceptable! And at all times, we pray for the insight that God is with us, now and always— for that truly is the answer to our prayers.

❃ See "Prayer and Its Value," pages 3-5.

Look with favor, Adonai our God, upon Your people Israel, and with love accept our prayers. May our worship ever be worthy of Your favor.

273

ON ROSH CHODESH AND CHOL HA-MOEID ADD

אֱלֹהֵינוּ וֵאלֹהֵי אֲבוֹתֵינוּ
וְאִמּוֹתֵינוּ, יַעֲלֶה וְיָבֹא וְיִזָּכֵר
זִכְרוֹנֵנוּ וְזִכְרוֹן כָּל־עַמְּךָ
בֵּית יִשְׂרָאֵל לְפָנֶיךָ לְטוֹבָה
לְחֵן לְחֶסֶד וּלְרַחֲמִים,
לְחַיִּים וּלְשָׁלוֹם בְּיוֹם

Our God of our fathers and mothers, be mindful of Your people Israel on this

❖ day of Rosh Chodesh,
❖ day of Pesach,
❖ day of Sukkot,

❖ רֹאשׁ הַחֹדֶשׁ הַזֶּה.

❖ חַג הַמַּצּוֹת הַזֶּה.

❖ חַג הַסֻּכּוֹת הַזֶּה.

and renew in us love and compassion, goodness, life, and peace.

זָכְרֵנוּ, יי אֱלֹהֵינוּ, בּוֹ
לְטוֹבָה. אָמֵן.

This day remember us for well-being. Amen.
Bless us with Your nearness. Amen.
Help us to renew our life. Amen.

וּפָקְדֵנוּ בוֹ לִבְרָכָה. אָמֵן.

וְהוֹשִׁיעֵנוּ בוֹ לְחַיִּים. אָמֵן.

בָּרוּךְ אַתָּה יי, שֶׁאוֹתְךָ לְבַדְּךָ בְּיִרְאָה נַעֲבוֹד.

We praise You, Adonai: You alone are the One we worship with awe.

הודאה   THANKSGIVING

מוֹדִים אֲנַחְנוּ לָךְ שָׁאַתָּה הוּא יי אֱלֹהֵינוּ וֵאלֹהֵי אֲבוֹתֵינוּ
וְאִמּוֹתֵינוּ, אֱלֹהֵי כָל־בָּשָׂר, יוֹצְרֵנוּ יוֹצֵר בְּרֵאשִׁית. בְּרְכוֹת
וְהוֹדָאוֹת לְשִׁמְךָ הַגָּדוֹל וְהַקָּדוֹשׁ עַל־שֶׁהֶחֱיִיתָנוּ וְקִיַּמְתָּנוּ.
כֵּן תְּחַיֵּנוּ וּתְקַיְּמֵנוּ, יי אֱלֹהֵינוּ, וְתֶאֱמְצֵנוּ לִשְׁמֹר חֻקֶּיךָ,
לַעֲשׂוֹת רְצוֹנֶךָ, וּלְעָבְדְּךָ בְּלֵבָב שָׁלֵם.

Every breath is precious, every moment a gift; our tradition teaches us gratitude: to be thankful for the gift of our life and its joys. And even for our sorrows.

✥ See "Giving Thanks," page 395, and Psalm 147 (page 372).

We now affirm that You, Adonai, are our God, the God of our fathers and mothers, the God of all flesh, our creator, source of all being. For keeping us in life and sustaining us, we bless and praise Your great and holy name.

Continue us in life and sustain us, Adonai our God; strengthen us to observe Your laws, to do Your will, and to serve You with a whole heart.

ON SHABBAT SHUVAH ADD

וּכְתוֹב לְחַיִּים טוֹבִים כָּל־בְּנֵי בְרִיתֶךָ.

May all who are loyal to Your covenant be inscribed for a good life.

בָּרוּךְ אֵל הַהוֹדָאוֹת.

Praised be God, to whom our thanks are due.

ON CHANUKAH ADD

עַל הַנִּסִּים, וְעַל הַפֻּרְקָן, וְעַל הַגְּבוּרוֹת, וְעַל הַתְּשׁוּעוֹת, וְעַל
הַנִּחָמוֹת שֶׁעָשִׂיתָ לַאֲבוֹתֵינוּ וּלְאִמּוֹתֵינוּ בַּיָּמִים הָהֵם וּבַזְּמַן הַזֶּה.
בִּימֵי מַתִּתְיָהוּ בֶּן־יוֹחָנָן כֹּהֵן גָּדוֹל, חַשְׁמוֹנַאי וּבָנָיו,
כְּשֶׁעָמְדָה מַלְכוּת יָוָן הָרְשָׁעָה עַל עַמְּךָ יִשְׂרָאֵל, לְהַשְׁכִּיחָם
תּוֹרָתֶךָ וּלְהַעֲבִירָם מֵחֻקֵּי רְצוֹנֶךָ. וְאַתָּה בְּרַחֲמֶיךָ הָרַבִּים
עָמַדְתָּ לָהֶם בְּעֵת צָרָתָם, רַבְתָּ אֶת־רִיבָם, דַּנְתָּ אֶת־דִּינָם,
מָסַרְתָּ גִבּוֹרִים בְּיַד חַלָּשִׁים, וְרַבִּים בְּיַד מְעַטִּים, וּטְמֵאִים
בְּיַד טְהוֹרִים, וּרְשָׁעִים בְּיַד צַדִּיקִים, וְזֵדִים בְּיַד עוֹסְקֵי
תוֹרָתֶךָ. וּלְךָ עָשִׂיתָ שֵׁם גָּדוֹל וְקָדוֹשׁ בְּעוֹלָמֶךָ, וּלְעַמְּךָ
יִשְׂרָאֵל עָשִׂיתָ יְשׁוּעָה גְדוֹלָה וּפֻרְקָן כְּהַיּוֹם הַזֶּה, וְאַחַר כֵּן
בָּאוּ בָנֶיךָ לִדְבִיר בֵּיתֶךָ, וּפִנּוּ אֶת־הֵיכָלֶךָ, וְטִהֲרוּ אֶת־מִקְדָּשֶׁךָ,

וְהִדְלִיקוּ נֵרוֹת בְּחַצְרוֹת קָדְשֶׁךָ, וְקָבְעוּ שְׁמוֹנַת יְמֵי חֲנֻכָּה אֵלּוּ,
לְהוֹדוֹת וּלְהַלֵּל לְשִׁמְךָ הַגָּדוֹל.

In days of old, at this season, You saved our people by wonders and mighty deeds. In the days of the High Priest, Mattathias the Hasmonean, the tyrannic Syrian-Greeks sought to destroy our people Israel by forcing them to forget their Torah, and thus to abandon Your teaching.

But in great compassion You stood by them, so that the weak defeated the strong, the few prevailed over the many, and the righteous prevailed. By this great deliverance Your name was exalted and sanctified in the world: Your children returned to Your house to purify the sanctuary and to kindle its lights. And they dedicated these eight days of Chanukah to give thanks and praise to Your great name.

ON SHABBAT EVENING AND SHABBAT AFTERNOON

PEACE ברכת שלום

שָׁלוֹם רָב עַל־יִשְׂרָאֵל עַמְּךָ תָּשִׂים לְעוֹלָם,
כִּי אַתָּה הוּא מֶלֶךְ אָדוֹן לְכָל־הַשָּׁלוֹם.
וְטוֹב בְּעֵינֶיךָ לְבָרֵךְ אֶת־עַמְּךָ יִשְׂרָאֵל
וְאֶת־כָּל־הָעַמִּים בְּכָל־עֵת וּבְכָל־שָׁעָה בִּשְׁלוֹמֶךָ.

Supreme source of peace, grant true and lasting peace to Your people Israel, for it is good in Your sight that Your people Israel, and all peoples, may be blessed at all times with Your gift of peace.

In our prayer for peace we pray for our people and for all the peoples of the world. Only when all are at peace can we truly say that we are at peace.

ON SHABBAT SHUVAH ADD

בְּסֵפֶר חַיִּים וּבְרָכָה נִכָּתֵב
לְחַיִּים טוֹבִים וּלְשָׁלוֹם.

May we be inscribed in the Book of Life and Blessing for a life of goodness and peace.

✻ *See Pirke Avot, pages 324-325, and page 351.*

בָּרוּךְ אַתָּה יי, עוֹשֵׂה הַשָּׁלוֹם.

We praise You, O God, the source of peace.

ON SHABBAT MORNING

PEACE   ברכת שלום

Our prayer is
for peace,
serenity, and
well-being,
for ourselves
and our
people, and
for all people.

✤ See Pirke
Avot, pages
324-325, and
page 351.

שִׂים שָׁלוֹם, טוֹבָה וּבְרָכָה, חֵן וָחֶסֶד וְרַחֲמִים,
עָלֵינוּ וְעַל כָּל־יִשְׂרָאֵל עַמֶּךָ.
בָּרְכֵנוּ, אָבִינוּ, כֻּלָּנוּ כְּאֶחָד בְּאוֹר פָּנֶיךָ,
כִּי בְאוֹר פָּנֶיךָ נָתַתָּ לָּנוּ, יי אֱלֹהֵינוּ,
תּוֹרַת חַיִּים, וְאַהֲבַת חֶסֶד,
וּצְדָקָה וּבְרָכָה וְרַחֲמִים וְחַיִּים וְשָׁלוֹם.
וְטוֹב בְּעֵינֶיךָ לְבָרֵךְ אֶת־עַמְּךָ יִשְׂרָאֵל
וְאֶת־כָּל־הָעַמִּים בְּכָל־עֵת וּבְכָל־שָׁעָה בִּשְׁלוֹמֶךָ.

Grant peace, goodness and blessing, grace, love and mercy
to us and to all Israel, Your people. As a loving parent, bless
us, one and all, with the light of Your presence; for by that
light, eternal God, You have revealed to us a living law: the
love of kindness, righteousness, blessing, and mercy,
bringing life and peace. For it is good in Your sight that Your
people Israel and all peoples be blessed at all times with
Your gift of peace.

ON SHABBAT SHUVAH ADD

בְּסֵפֶר חַיִּים וּבְרָכָה נִכָּתֵב
לְחַיִּים טוֹבִים וּלְשָׁלוֹם.

*May we be inscribed in the
Book of Life and Blessing for a
life of goodness and peace.*

בָּרוּךְ אַתָּה יי, עוֹשֵׂה הַשָּׁלוֹם.

We praise You, O God, the source of peace.

SILENT PRAYER

אֱלֹהַי, נְצֹר לְשׁוֹנִי מֵרָע, וּשְׂפָתַי מִדַּבֵּר מִרְמָה. וְלִמְקַלְלַי נַפְשִׁי
תִדֹּם וְנַפְשִׁי כֶּעָפָר לַכֹּל תִּהְיֶה. פְּתַח לִבִּי בְּתוֹרָתֶךָ, וּבְמִצְוֹתֶיךָ
תִּרְדֹּף נַפְשִׁי. עֲשֵׂה לְמַעַן שְׁמֶךָ, עֲשֵׂה לְמַעַן יְמִינֶךָ, עֲשֵׂה
לְמַעַן קְדֻשָּׁתֶךָ, עֲשֵׂה לְמַעַן תּוֹרָתֶךָ; לְמַעַן יֵחָלְצוּן יְדִידֶיךָ,
הוֹשִׁיעָה יְמִינְךָ וַעֲנֵנִי.

My God, keep my tongue from evil, my lips from deceptive
speech. In the face of malice, give me a quiet spirit; let me be
humble wherever I go. Open my heart to Your teaching,
make me eager to fulfill Your Mitzvot. Then will Your name
be exalted, Your might manifest, Your holiness visible, Your
Torah magnified. Inspire me to love You, and be the answer
to my prayer.

☾ FROM PSALM 15

יְהוָה, מִי־יָגוּר בְּאָהֳלֶךָ?   Adonai, who may abide in
מִי־יִשְׁכֹּן בְּהַר קָדְשֶׁךָ?   Your house? Who may dwell in
Your holy mountain?

הוֹלֵךְ תָּמִים, וּפֹעֵל צֶדֶק,   Those who walk with integrity,
וְדֹבֵר אֱמֶת בִּלְבָבוֹ.   and do justly, and speak truth
from the heart.

לֹא־רָגַל עַל־לְשֹׁנוֹ,   Who have no malice on their
לֹא־עָשָׂה לְרֵעֵהוּ רָעָה,   tongues, who do no evil to
others, who never bring shame
וְחֶרְפָּה לֹא־נָשָׂא עַל־קְרֹבוֹ.   upon their kin.

נִשְׁבַּע לְהָרַע וְלֹא יָמִר,   Who do not go back on their
word, even to their loss, who
כַּסְפּוֹ לֹא־נָתַן בְּנֶשֶׁךְ,   do not take advantage of
וְשֹׁחַד עַל־נָקִי לֹא לָקָח.   others, who never take bribes.

עֹשֵׂה־אֵלֶּה לֹא יִמּוֹט לְעוֹלָם.   They that live in this way shall
never fail.

❧ See
"Selected
Psalms,"
pages 358-375,
and "A Daily
Psalm," pages
27-33.

❧

יִהְיוּ לְרָצוֹן אִמְרֵי־פִי   *Yi-h'yu l'ra-tzon i-m'rei fi*

וְהֶגְיוֹן לִבִּי לְפָנֶיךָ,   *v'heg-yon li-bi l'fa-neh-cha,*

יהוה, צוּרִי וְגֹאֲלִי.   *Adonai tzu-ri v'go-a-li.*

May the words of my mouth and the meditations of my heart be acceptable to You, O God, my rock and my redeemer. Amen.

❧

עֹשֶׂה שָׁלוֹם בִּמְרוֹמָיו,   *O-seh sha-lom bi-m'ro-mav,*

הוּא יַעֲשֶׂה שָׁלוֹם עָלֵינוּ   *hu ya-a-seh sha-lom a-lei-nu*

וְעַל־כָּל־יִשְׂרָאֵל, וְאִמְרוּ:   *v'al kol Yis-ra-eil, v'i-m'ru:*

אָמֵן.   *A-mein.*

May the source of peace on high send peace to us, to all Israel, and to all the world, and let us say: Amen.

❧

עלינו ALEINU

BEGIN HERE OR ON PAGE 282

ALL RISE

עָלֵינוּ לְשַׁבֵּחַ לַאֲדוֹן הַכֹּל, לָתֵת גְּדֻלָּה לְיוֹצֵר
בְּרֵאשִׁית, שֶׁלֹּא עָשָׂנוּ כְּגוֹיֵי הָאֲרָצוֹת, וְלֹא שָׂמָנוּ
כְּמִשְׁפְּחוֹת הָאֲדָמָה; שֶׁלֹּא שָׂם חֶלְקֵנוּ כָּהֶם, וְגוֹרָלֵנוּ
כְּכָל־הֲמוֹנָם. וַאֲנַחְנוּ כּוֹרְעִים וּמִשְׁתַּחֲוִים וּמוֹדִים
לִפְנֵי מֶלֶךְ מַלְכֵי הַמְּלָכִים, הַקָּדוֹשׁ בָּרוּךְ הוּא.

A-lei-nu l'sha-bei-ach la-a-don ha-kol, la-teit g'du-la l'yo-tzeir
b'rei-sheet, sheh-lo a-sa-nu k'go-yei ha-a-ra-tzot, v'lo sa-ma-nu
k'mish-p'chot ha-a-da-ma; sheh-lo sam chel-kei-nu ka-hem, v'go-ra-lei-nu
k'chol ha-mo-nam. Va-a-nach-nu ko-r'im u-mish-ta-cha-vim u-mo-dim
li-f'nei meh-lech ma-l'chei ha-m'la-chim, ha-ka-dosh ba-ruch hu.

We are called to praise the God of all, to proclaim the greatness of the world's creator, who summoned us to be a singular people, with a destiny of our own among the nations.

We therefore bow in awe and thanksgiving before the one who is sovereign over all, the Holy One, ever to be praised.

Aleinu is one of the great prayers of humanity. It begins by affirming the uniqueness of our people Israel; it concludes by affirming the essential unity of humankind and our hope that all peoples may come to recognize our common humanity as the children of the one creator, God.

&

שֶׁהוּא נוֹטֶה שָׁמַיִם וְיוֹסֵד אָרֶץ, וּמוֹשַׁב יְקָרוֹ בַּשָּׁמַיִם
מִמַּעַל, וּשְׁכִינַת עֻזּוֹ בְּגָבְהֵי מְרוֹמִים. הוּא אֱלֹהֵינוּ,
אֵין עוֹד. אֱמֶת מַלְכֵּנוּ, אֶפֶס זוּלָתוֹ, כַּכָּתוּב בְּתוֹרָתוֹ:
וְיָדַעְתָּ הַיּוֹם וַהֲשֵׁבֹתָ אֶל־לְבָבֶךָ, כִּי יהוה הוּא
הָאֱלֹהִים בַּשָּׁמַיִם מִמַּעַל וְעַל הָאָרֶץ מִתָּחַת, אֵין עוֹד.
עַל־כֵּן נְקַוֶּה לְּךָ, יי אֱלֹהֵינוּ, לִרְאוֹת מְהֵרָה בְּתִפְאֶרֶת
עֻזֶּךָ, לְהַעֲבִיר גִּלּוּלִים מִן הָאָרֶץ, וְהָאֱלִילִים כָּרוֹת

יְכָרֵתוּן. לְתַקֵּן עוֹלָם בְּמַלְכוּת שַׁדַּי, וְכָל־בְּנֵי בָשָׂר
יִקְרְאוּ בִשְׁמֶךָ, לְהַפְנוֹת אֵלֶיךָ כָּל־רִשְׁעֵי אָרֶץ.

You spread out the heavens and established the earth; Your splendor fills the highest heavens, Your might extends throughout all space. In truth You alone are our sovereign God, as it is written: "Know then this day and take it to heart: Adonai is God in the heavens above and on the earth below; there is none else."

Trusting in You, Adonai our God, we hope soon to behold the glory of Your might, when false gods shall vanish from our hearts. Help us to perfect the world under Your unchallenged rule, when all men and women shall invoke Your name, abandon evil, and turn to You alone.

יַכִּירוּ וְיֵדְעוּ כָּל־יוֹשְׁבֵי תֵבֵל כִּי לְךָ תִּכְרַע כָּל־בֶּרֶךְ,
תִּשָּׁבַע כָּל־לָשׁוֹן. לְפָנֶיךָ, יי אֱלֹהֵינוּ, יִכְרְעוּ וְיִפְּלוּ,
וְלִכְבוֹד שִׁמְךָ יְקָר יִתֵּנוּ, וִיקַבְּלוּ כֻלָּם אֶת־עֹל מַלְכוּתֶךָ,
וְתִמְלֹךְ עֲלֵיהֶם מְהֵרָה לְעוֹלָם וָעֶד. כִּי הַמַּלְכוּת שֶׁלְּךָ
הִיא, וּלְעוֹלְמֵי עַד תִּמְלוֹךְ בְּכָבוֹד. כַּכָּתוּב בְּתוֹרָתֶךָ:
יהוה יִמְלֹךְ לְעֹלָם וָעֶד.

May all who dwell on earth come to know that every knee must bend, and every tongue swear loyalty to You alone. Before You, Adonai our God, let them humble themselves, and to Your glorious name let them give honor. Let all accept Your sovereign rule; may that time come soon, and last forever.

For dominion is Yours, and to all eternity You will reign in glory, as it is written: Adonai shall reign forever and ever. And it is said: Adonai shall reign over all the earth; on that day, O God, You shall be one and Your name shall be one.

וְנֶאֱמַר: וְהָיָה יהוה לְמֶלֶךְ עַל־כָּל־הָאָרֶץ;

בַּיּוֹם הַהוּא יִהְיֶה יהוה אֶחָד וּשְׁמוֹ אֶחָד.

V'neh-eh-mar: V'ha-yah Adonai l'meh-lech al kol ha-a-retz;
ba-yom ha-hu yi-h'yeh Adonai eh-chad, u-sh'mo eh-chad.

&

עלינו ALEINU

ALL RISE

עָלֵינוּ לְשַׁבֵּחַ לַאֲדוֹן הַכֹּל, לָתֵת גְּדֻלָּה לְיוֹצֵר

בְּרֵאשִׁית, שֶׁלֹּא עָשָׂנוּ כְּגוֹיֵי הָאֲרָצוֹת, וְלֹא שָׂמָנוּ

כְּמִשְׁפְּחוֹת הָאֲדָמָה; שֶׁלֹּא שָׂם חֶלְקֵנוּ כָּהֶם, וְגוֹרָלֵנוּ

כְּכָל־הֲמוֹנָם. וַאֲנַחְנוּ כּוֹרְעִים וּמִשְׁתַּחֲוִים וּמוֹדִים

לִפְנֵי מֶלֶךְ מַלְכֵי הַמְּלָכִים, הַקָּדוֹשׁ בָּרוּךְ הוּא.

A-lei-nu l'sha-bei-ach la-a-don ha-kol, la-teit g'du-la l'yo-tzeir
b'rei-sheet, sheh-lo a-sa-nu k'go-yei ha-a-ra-tzot, v'lo sa-ma-nu
k'mish-p'chot ha-a-da-ma; sheh-lo sam chel-kei-nu ka-hem, v'go-ra-lei-nu
k'chol ha-mo-nam. Va-a-nach-nu ko-r'im u-mish-ta-cha-vim u-mo-dim
li-f'nei meh-lech ma-l'chei ha-m'la-chim, ha-ka-dosh ba-ruch hu.

Aleinu is one of the great prayers of humanity. It begins by affirming the uniqueness of our people Israel; it concludes by affirming the essential unity of humankind and our hope that all peoples may come to recognize our common humanity as the children of the one creator, God.

We are called to praise You, the God who gave birth to creation; we rejoice to be one family among the families of the earth, each unique in history, destined to walk on different paths toward the arms of God. So do we affirm and thank You, Holy One, source of our being.

Creator of skies, maker of worlds: Your glory is stamped on the heavens above; Your love is revealed in our days as they pass. You are our God; there is none else.

As You endow our fleeting days
with abiding worth,

so do we affirm and thank You,
  Holy One, source of our being.

May the time not be distant, O God,
when all shall turn to You in love,
and all our gifts shall be devoted to Your service.
We turn to You in hope, O God.
We yearn to see the promised day,
of justice, freedom, and peace,
the day when all shall sit
under their vines and fig-trees,
and none shall make them afraid.

  Then the prophet's word shall be fulfilled. On that day, O God,
  You shall be one and Your name shall be one.

וְנֶאֱמַר: וְהָיָה יהוה לְמֶֽלֶךְ עַל־כָּל־הָאָֽרֶץ;
בַּיּוֹם הַהוּא יִהְיֶה יהוה אֶחָד וּשְׁמוֹ אֶחָד.

V'neh-eh-mar: V'ha-yah Adonai l'meh-lech al kol ha-a-retz;
ba-yom ha-hu yi-h'yeh Adonai eh-chad, u-sh'mo eh-chad.

෨

BEFORE THE KADDISH

We think now of those who stand here with us no more: family, friends, neighbors, the great and good of every race and nation—all who have been a blessing to us and to all humanity.

זִכְרוֹנָם לִבְרָכָה—Their memory blesses us now and always; their life lives within us still.

REFLECTIONS

1.   FACING DEATH

As we pray before You, O God, we think of those who once shared with us the joys and burdens of life, and who are no longer in our midst. The sorrow of bereavement is softened by the bond of love that continues to unite us with our dear ones, and by the memories that we will always carry in our hearts. May all that was fine and beautiful in their lives remain with us as an influence for good. O God, grant consolation to those in sorrow, and light to those in darkness. Teach us at all times to put our trust in You, the source and sustainer of our life.

2.   A FAITHFUL LIFE

The growing good of the world is partly dependent on unhistoric acts; and that things are not so ill with you and me as they might have been, is half owing to the number who lived faithfully a hidden life, and rest in unvisited tombs. (George Eliot)

3.   THE MYSTERY AND ITS ANSWER

God, a mystery surrounds my life. What comes before it and what lies after it are hidden from me. My life is short, and Your universe is vast. But in the darkness is Your presence, and in the mystery, Your love. I put my trust in You, as did those who came before me. We praise You, eternal God: You see what is hidden from our sight.

4.   THE BLESSING OF MEMORY

Our beloved are with us through the blessing of memory and the power of their example. They help us to live as they themselves sought to live. We think of them now; they live in our hearts; they are a continual blessing.

5.   TO FEEL YOUR PRESENCE

In our great need for light we look to You. Holy One, help us to feel Your presence and to find the courage to affirm You, even when the shadows fall upon us. When our own weakness and the storms of life hide You from our sight, teach us that You are always near. Give us trust, give us peace, and give us light. May our hearts find their comfort and rest in You.

ॐ

Our time on earth may be brief, O God, yet You endow our fleeting days with abiding worth. We now recall the loved ones whom death has recently taken from us _____. We think, too, of those who died at this season in years past _____. As one family, united in sympathy, we all rise to say the sacred words that link us to one another, and to all past generations:

MOURNER'S KADDISH   קדיש יתום

יִתְגַּדַּל וְיִתְקַדַּשׁ שְׁמֵהּ רַבָּא בְּעָלְמָא דִּי־בְרָא כִרְעוּתֵהּ,
וְיַמְלִיךְ מַלְכוּתֵהּ בְּחַיֵּיכוֹן וּבְיוֹמֵיכוֹן וּבְחַיֵּי
דְּכָל־בֵּית יִשְׂרָאֵל, בַּעֲגָלָא וּבִזְמַן קָרִיב, וְאִמְרוּ: אָמֵן.

Yit-ga-dal v'yit-ka-dash sh'mei ra-ba b'al-ma di-v'ra chi-r'u'tei,
v'yam-lich mal-chu-tei b'cha-yei-chon u-v'yo-mei-chon u-v'cha-yei
d'chol beit Yis-ra-eil, ba-a-ga-la u-vi-z'man ka-riv, v'im'ru: A-mein.

יְהֵא שְׁמֵהּ רַבָּא מְבָרַךְ לְעָלַם וּלְעָלְמֵי עָלְמַיָּא.

Y'hei sh'mei ra-ba m'va-rach l'a-lam u-l'al-mei al-ma-ya.

יִתְבָּרַךְ וְיִשְׁתַּבַּח, וְיִתְפָּאַר וְיִתְרוֹמַם וְיִתְנַשֵּׂא,
וְיִתְהַדָּר וְיִתְעַלֶּה וְיִתְהַלָּל שְׁמֵהּ דְּקוּדְשָׁא, בְּרִיךְ הוּא,

Yit-ba-rach v'yish-ta-bach v'yit-pa-ar, v'yit-ro-mam, v'yit-na-sei,
v'yit-ha-dar, v'yit-a-leh, v'yit-ha-lal sh'mei d'ku-d'sha, b'rich hu,

לְעֵלָּא מִן־כָּל־בִּרְכָתָא וְשִׁירָתָא, תֻּשְׁבְּחָתָא וְנֶחֱמָתָא
דַּאֲמִירָן בְּעָלְמָא, וְאִמְרוּ: אָמֵן.

l'ei-la min kol bir-cha-ta v'shi-ra-ta, tush-b'cha-ta v'neh-cheh-ma-ta
da-a-mi-ran b'al-ma, v'im'ru: A-mein.

יְהֵא שְׁלָמָא רַבָּא מִן־שְׁמַיָּא וְחַיִּים עָלֵינוּ
וְעַל־כָּל־יִשְׂרָאֵל, וְאִמְרוּ: אָמֵן.

Y'hei sh'la-ma ra-ba min sh'ma-ya v'cha-yim, a-lei-nu
v'al kol Yis-ra-el, v'im'ru: A-mein.

עֹשֶׂה שָׁלוֹם בִּמְרוֹמָיו, הוּא יַעֲשֶׂה שָׁלוֹם עָלֵינוּ וְעַל
כָּל־יִשְׂרָאֵל, וְאִמְרוּ: אָמֵן.

O-seh sha-lom bi-m'ro-mav, hu ya-a-seh sha-lom a-lei-nu v'al
kol Yis-ra-eil, v'i-m'ru: A-mein.

☙

Hallowed be Your great name on earth, Your creation; establish Your dominion in our own day, in our own lives, and in the life of the whole House of Israel.

Blessed be Your great name forever and ever.

Blessed, praised, honored, and exalted be the name of the Holy One, ever to be praised, though You are beyond all the blessings and songs of praise that all the world may offer. Amen.

May true peace descend upon us from on high and bring new life to us and all Israel, and let us say: Amen.

May the source of peace on high send peace to us, to all Israel, and to all the world, and let us say: Amen.

❧

Holy One, in Your love and compassion comfort all who mourn, and give strength to all who are bereaved. Amen.

❧

ואני תפלתי לך

תפלות וקריאות שונות

PRAYERS AND READINGS FOR VARIOUS OCCASIONS

FOR VARIOUS OCCASIONS

קדוש לליל שבת KIDDUSH FOR THE EVE OF SHABBAT

בָּרוּךְ אַתָּה יי, אֱלֹהֵינוּ מֶלֶךְ הָעוֹלָם, בּוֹרֵא פְּרִי הַגָּפֶן.
בָּרוּךְ אַתָּה יי, אֱלֹהֵינוּ מֶלֶךְ הָעוֹלָם, אֲשֶׁר קִדְּשָׁנוּ
בְּמִצְוֹתָיו וְרָצָה בָנוּ, וְשַׁבַּת קָדְשׁוֹ בְּאַהֲבָה וּבְרָצוֹן
הִנְחִילָנוּ, זִכָּרוֹן לְמַעֲשֵׂה בְרֵאשִׁית. כִּי הוּא יוֹם תְּחִלָּה
לְמִקְרָאֵי קֹדֶשׁ, זֵכֶר לִיצִיאַת מִצְרָיִם. כִּי־בָנוּ בָחַרְתָּ
וְאוֹתָנוּ קִדַּשְׁתָּ מִכָּל־הָעַמִּים, וְשַׁבַּת קָדְשְׁךָ בְּאַהֲבָה
וּבְרָצוֹן הִנְחַלְתָּנוּ. בָּרוּךְ אַתָּה יי, מְקַדֵּשׁ הַשַׁבָּת.

Ba-ruch a-ta Adonai, Eh-lo-hei-nu meh-lech ha-o-lam, bo-rei p'ri ha-ga-fen.
Ba-ruch a-ta Adonai, Eh-lo-hei-nu meh-lech ha-o-lam, a-sher ki-d'sha-nu
b'mitz-vo-tav v'ra-tza va-nu, v'Shabbat kod-sho b'a-ha-va u-v'ra-tzon
hin-chi-la-nu, zi-ka-ron l'ma-a-sei v'rei-sheet. Ki hu yom t'chi-la
l'mik-ra-ei ko-desh, zei-cher li-tzi-at Mitz-ra-yim. Ki va-nu va-char-ta
v'o-ta-nu ki-dash-ta mi-kol ha-a-mim, v'Shabbat kod-sh'cha b'a-ha-va
u-v'ra-tzon hin-chal-ta-nu. Ba-ruch a-ta Adonai, m'ka-deish ha-Shabbat.

We praise You, Adonai our God, sovereign of the universe, creator of the fruit of the vine.

We praise You, Adonai our God, sovereign of the universe: You call us to holiness with the Mitzvah of Shabbat—a sign of Your love, a reminder of Your creative work, and of our liberation from Egyptian bondage—our day of days. On Shabbat especially, we hearken to Your call to serve You as a holy people.

We praise You, O God, for the holiness of Shabbat.

קדוש לשבת בבקר KIDDUSH FOR SHABBAT MORNING

וְשָׁמְרוּ בְנֵי־יִשְׂרָאֵל אֶת־הַשַּׁבָּת,

לַעֲשׂוֹת אֶת־הַשַּׁבָּת לְדֹרֹתָם בְּרִית עוֹלָם.

בֵּינִי וּבֵין בְּנֵי יִשְׂרָאֵל אוֹת הִיא לְעֹלָם.

כִּי־שֵׁשֶׁת יָמִים עָשָׂה יהוה אֶת־הַשָּׁמַיִם וְאֶת־הָאָרֶץ,

וּבַיּוֹם הַשְּׁבִיעִי שָׁבַת וַיִּנָּפַשׁ.

V'sha-m'ru v'nei Yis-ra-eil et ha-Shabbat,

la-a-sot et ha-Shabbat l'do-ro-tam, b'rit o-lam.

Bei-ni u-vein b'nei Yis-ra-eil ot hi l'o-lam.

Ki shei-shet ya-mim a-sa Adonai et ha-sha-ma-yim v'et ha-a-retz,

u-va-yom ha-sh'vi-i sha-vat va-yi-na-fash.

The people of Israel shall keep the Sabbath, observing the Sabbath in every generation as a covenant forever. It is a sign between me and the people of Israel forever. For in six days Adonai made heaven and earth, but on the seventh day God rested and was refreshed.

עַל־כֵּן בֵּרַךְ יהוה אֶת־יוֹם הַשַּׁבָּת וַיְקַדְּשֵׁהוּ.

Al kein bei-rach Adonai et yom ha-Shabbat va-y'ka-d'shei-hu.

Adonai therefore blessed the Sabbath day and called it holy.

בָּרוּךְ אַתָּה יי, אֱלֹהֵינוּ מֶלֶךְ הָעוֹלָם, בּוֹרֵא פְּרִי הַגָּפֶן.

Ba-ruch a-ta Adonai, Eh-lo-hei-nu meh-lech ha-o-lam, bo-rei p'ri ha-ga-fen.

We praise You, Adonai our God, sovereign of the universe, creator of the fruit of the vine.

קדוש לליל יום טוב KIDDVSH FOR THE EVE OF YOM TOV

בָּרוּךְ אַתָּה יְיָ, אֱלֹהֵינוּ מֶלֶךְ הָעוֹלָם, בּוֹרֵא פְּרִי הַגָּפֶן.

בָּרוּךְ אַתָּה יְיָ, אֱלֹהֵינוּ מֶלֶךְ הָעוֹלָם, אֲשֶׁר בָּחַר בָּנוּ

מִכָּל־עָם, וְרוֹמְמָנוּ מִכָּל־לָשׁוֹן, וְקִדְּשָׁנוּ בְּמִצְוֹתָיו.

וַתִּתֶּן לָנוּ, יְיָ אֱלֹהֵינוּ, בְּאַהֲבָה (שַׁבָּתוֹת לִמְנוּחָה וּ)

מוֹעֲדִים לְשִׂמְחָה, חַגִּים וּזְמַנִּים לְשָׂשׂוֹן

אֶת־יוֹם (הַשַּׁבָּת הַזֶּה וְאֶת־יוֹם)

❖ חַג הַמַּצּוֹת הַזֶּה, זְמַן חֵרוּתֵנוּ,

❖ חַג הַשָּׁבוּעוֹת הַזֶּה, זְמַן מַתַּן תּוֹרָתֵנוּ,

❖ חַג הַסֻּכּוֹת הַזֶּה, זְמַן שִׂמְחָתֵנוּ,

❖ הַשְּׁמִינִי חַג הָעֲצֶרֶת הַזֶּה, זְמַן שִׂמְחָתֵנוּ,

מִקְרָא קֹדֶשׁ, זֵכֶר לִיצִיאַת מִצְרָיִם.

כִּי־בָנוּ בָחַרְתָּ וְאוֹתָנוּ קִדַּשְׁתָּ מִכָּל־הָעַמִּים, (וְשַׁבָּת)

וּמוֹעֲדֵי קָדְשֶׁךָ (בְּאַהֲבָה וּבְרָצוֹן), בְּשִׂמְחָה וּבְשָׂשׂוֹן הִנְחַלְתָּנוּ.

בָּרוּךְ אַתָּה יְיָ, מְקַדֵּשׁ (הַשַּׁבָּת וְ) יִשְׂרָאֵל וְהַזְּמַנִּים.

Ba-ruch a-ta Adonai, Eh-lo-hei-nu meh-lech ha-o-lam, bo-rei p'ri ha-ga-fen.

Ba-ruch a-ta Adonai, Eh-lo-hei-nu meh-lech ha-o-lam, a-sher ba-char ba-nu

mi-kol am, v'ro-m'ma-nu mi-kol la-shon, v'kid'sha-nu b'mitz-vo-tav.

Va-ti-ten la-nu, Adonai Eh-lohei-nu, b'a-ha-va (sha-ba-tot li-m'nu-cha u-)

mo-a-dim l'sim-cha, cha-gim u-z'ma-nim l'sa-son,

et yom (ha-Shabbat ha-zeh v'et yom)

❖ *chag ha-matzot ha-zeh, z'man chei-ru-tei-nu,*

❖ *chag ha-shavuot ha-zeh, z'man ma-tan to-ra-tei-nu,*

❖ *chag ha-sukkot ha-zeh, z'man sim-cha-tei-nu,*

❖ *ha-sh'mini chag ha-atzeret ha-zeh, z'man sim-cha-tei-nu,*

mik-ra ko-desh, zei-cher li-tzi-at mitz-ra-yim.

Ki va-nu va-char-ta v'o-ta-nu ki-dash-ta mi-kol ha-a-mim, (v'sha-bat)
u-mo-a-dei kod-sh'cha (b'a-ha-va u-v'ra-tzon,) b'sim-cha u-v'sa-son hin-chal-ta-nu.
Ba-ruch a-ta Adonai, m'ka-deish (ha-Shabbat v') Yis-ra-eil v'ha-z'ma-nim.

We praise You, Adonai our God, sovereign of the universe, creator of the fruit of the vine.

Eternal God, You call us to Your service and hallow us with Mitzvot. In Your love You have given us (Shabbat and its rest,) festive times and seasons, and their joys. They are sacred meeting-days, reminders of our liberation from Egyptian bondage.

We praise You, O God, for these days sacred to Israel.

OMIT ON THE LAST DAY OF PESACH

בָּרוּךְ אַתָּה יי, אֱלֹהֵינוּ מֶלֶךְ הָעוֹלָם, שֶׁהֶחֱיָנוּ
וְקִיְּמָנוּ וְהִגִּיעָנוּ לַזְּמַן הַזֶּה.

Ba-ruch a-ta Adonai, Eh-lo-hei-nu meh-lech ha-o-lam, sheh-heh-cha-ya-nu
v'ki-y'ma-nu v'hi-gi-a-nu la-z'man ha-zeh.

We praise You, Adonai our God, sovereign of the universe, for keeping us alive, for sustaining us, and for enabling us to reach this season.

IN THE SUKKAH

בָּרוּךְ אַתָּה יי, אֱלֹהֵינוּ מֶלֶךְ הָעוֹלָם, אֲשֶׁר קִדְּשָׁנוּ
בְּמִצְוֹתָיו וְצִוָּנוּ לֵשֵׁב בַּסֻּכָּה.

Ba-ruch a-ta Adonai, Eh-lo-hei-nu meh-lech ha-o-lam, a-sher ki-d'sha-nu
b'mitz-vo-tav v'tzi-va-nu lei-sheiv ba-su-kah.

We praise You, Adonai our God: You hallow us with Your Mitzvot and call us to celebrate in the Sukkah.

FOR FOOD

בָּרוּךְ אַתָּה יי, אֱלֹהֵינוּ מֶלֶךְ הָעוֹלָם,
הַמּוֹצִיא לֶחֶם מִן הָאָרֶץ.

Ba-ruch a-ta Adonai, Eh-lo-hei-nu meh-lech ha-o-lam,
ha-mo-tzi leh-chem min ha-a-retz.

We praise You, Adonai our God, for the bread You bring forth from the earth.

ליום טוב בבקר   FOR THE MORNING OF YOM TOV

ON WEEKDAYS, BEGIN ON THE NEXT PAGE

ON SHABBAT

וְשָׁמְרוּ בְנֵי־יִשְׂרָאֵל אֶת־הַשַּׁבָּת, לַעֲשׂוֹת אֶת־הַשַּׁבָּת
לְדֹרֹתָם בְּרִית עוֹלָם. בֵּינִי וּבֵין בְּנֵי יִשְׂרָאֵל אוֹת
הִיא לְעֹלָם. כִּי־שֵׁשֶׁת יָמִים עָשָׂה יהוה אֶת־הַשָּׁמַיִם
וְאֶת־הָאָרֶץ, וּבַיּוֹם הַשְּׁבִיעִי שָׁבַת וַיִּנָּפַשׁ.

V'sha-m'ru v'nei Yis-ra-eil et ha-Shabbat, la-a-sot et ha-Shabbat
l'do-ro-tam, b'rit o-lam. Bei-ni u-vein b'nei Yis-ra-eil ot
hi l'o-lam. Ki shei-shet ya-mim a-sa Adonai et ha-sha-ma-yim
v'et ha-a-retz, u-va-yom ha-sh'vi-i sha-vat va-yi-na-fash.

The people of Israel shall keep the Sabbath, observing the Sabbath in every generation as a covenant forever. It is a sign between me and the people of Israel forever. For in six days Adonai made heaven and earth, but on the seventh day God rested and was refreshed.

עַל־כֵּן בֵּרַךְ יהוה אֶת־יוֹם הַשַּׁבָּת וַיְקַדְּשֵׁהוּ.

Al kein bei-rach Adonai et yom ha-Shabbat va-y'ka-d'shei-hu.

Adonai therefore blessed the Sabbath day and called it holy.

ON WEEKDAYS

אֵלֶּה מוֹעֲדֵי יהוה, מִקְרָאֵי קֹדֶשׁ, אֲשֶׁר תִּקְרְאוּ אֹתָם בְּמוֹעֲדָם.
וַיְדַבֵּר מֹשֶׁה אֶת־מֹעֲדֵי יהוה אֶל־בְּנֵי יִשְׂרָאֵל.

Ei-leh mo-a-dei Adonai, mik-ra-ei ko-desh, a-sher tik-r'u o-tam b'mo-a-dam.
Va-y'da-beir Mo-sheh et mo-a-dei Adonai el b'nei Yis-ra-eil.

These are the festivals appointed by God, the sacred meeting-times, that you shall proclaim at their appointed times. And Moses proclaimed God's festivals to the people of Israel.

בָּרוּךְ אַתָּה יי, אֱלֹהֵינוּ מֶלֶךְ הָעוֹלָם, בּוֹרֵא פְּרִי הַגָּפֶן.

Ba-ruch a-ta Adonai, Eh-lo-hei-nu meh-lech ha-o-lam, bo-rei p'ri ha-ga-fen.

We praise You, Adonai our God, sovereign of the universe, creator of the fruit of the vine.

IN THE SUKKAH

בָּרוּךְ אַתָּה יי, אֱלֹהֵינוּ מֶלֶךְ הָעוֹלָם, אֲשֶׁר קִדְּשָׁנוּ
בְּמִצְוֹתָיו וְצִוָּנוּ לֵשֵׁב בַּסֻּכָּה.

Ba-ruch a-ta Adonai, Eh-lo-hei-nu meh-lech ha-o-lam, a-sher ki-d'sha-nu
b'mitz-vo-tav v'tzi-va-nu lei-sheiv ba-su-kah.

We praise You, Adonai our God: You hallow us with Your Mitzvot and call us to celebrate in the Sukkah.

FOR FOOD

בָּרוּךְ אַתָּה יי, אֱלֹהֵינוּ מֶלֶךְ הָעוֹלָם,
הַמּוֹצִיא לֶחֶם מִן הָאָרֶץ.

Ba-ruch a-ta Adonai, Eh-lo-hei-nu meh-lech ha-o-lam,
ha-mo-tzi leh-chem min ha-a-retz.

We praise You, Adonai our God, who brings forth bread from the earth.

הבדלה HAVDALAH

AT THE CONCLUSION OF SHABBAT

THE LEADER LIGHTS THE HAVDALAH CANDLE;
THE YOUNGEST PERSON PRESENT MAY HOLD IT.

הִנֵּה אֵל יְשׁוּעָתִי, אֶבְטַח וְלֹא אֶפְחָד.

כִּי־עָזִּי וְזִמְרָת יָהּ יהוה, וַיְהִי־לִי לִישׁוּעָה.

וּשְׁאַבְתֶּם־מַֽיִם בְּשָׂשׂוֹן מִמַּעַיְנֵי הַיְשׁוּעָה.

לַיהוה הַיְשׁוּעָה, עַל־עַמְּךָ בִרְכָתֶךָ, סֶּלָה.

יהוה צְבָאוֹת עִמָּֽנוּ, מִשְׂגָּב־לָֽנוּ אֱלֹהֵי יַעֲקֹב, סֶּלָה.

יהוה צְבָאוֹת, אַשְׁרֵי אָדָם בֹּטֵחַ בָּךְ!

יהוה הוֹשִׁיעָה; הַמֶּֽלֶךְ יַעֲנֵֽנוּ בְיוֹם־קָרְאֵֽנוּ.

לַיְּהוּדִים הָיְתָה אוֹרָה וְשִׂמְחָה וְשָׂשׂוֹן וִיקָר, כֵּן תִּהְיֶה לָּֽנוּ.

כּוֹס־יְשׁוּעוֹת אֶשָּׂא, וּבְשֵׁם יהוה אֶקְרָא.

Hi-nei eil y'shu-a-ti, ev-tach v'lo ef-chad.

Ki o-zi v'zim-rat ya Adonai, va-y'hi li li-shu-a.

U-sh'av-tem ma-yim b'sa-son mi-ma-a-y'nei ha-y'shu-a.

La-Adonai ha-y'shu-ah, al a-m'cha bir-cha-teh-cha, seh-la.

Adonai tz'va-ot i-ma-nu, mis-gav la-nu Eh-lo-hei Ya-a-kov, seh-la.

Adonai tz'va-ot, ash-rei a-dam bo-tei-ach bach!

Adonai ho-shi-a; ha-meh-lech ya-a-nei-nu v'yom kor-ei-nu.

La-y'hu-dim ha-y'ta o-ra v'sim-cha v'sa-son vi-kar; kein ti-h'yeh la-nu.

Kos y'shu-ot eh-sa, u-v'sheim Adonai ek-ra.

Behold, God is my help; trusting in the Eternal One, I am not afraid. For Adonai is my strength and my song, and has become my salvation. With joy we draw water from the wells of salvation. Adonai brings deliverance, and blessing to the people. The God of all being is with us; the God of Jacob is our stronghold. God of all being, blessed is the one who trusts in You! God our help: answer us when we call upon You. As we have had light and joy, gladness and honor in ages past, so may it be for us today. And so we lift up the cup to rejoice in Your saving power, and invoke Your name with praise.

THE WINE OR GRAPE JUICE

בָּרוּךְ אַתָּה יי, אֱלֹהֵינוּ מֶלֶךְ הָעוֹלָם, בּוֹרֵא פְּרִי הַגָּפֶן.

Ba-ruch a-ta Adonai, Eh-lo-hei-nu meh-lech ha-o-lam, bo-rei p'ri ha-ga-fen.

We praise You, Adonai our God, sovereign of the universe, creator of the fruit of the vine.

THE LEADER DOES NOT DRINK THE WINE OR GRAPE JUICE UNTIL AFTER THE FINAL BLESSING, WHEN HAVDALAH HAS BEEN COMPLETED.

THE SPICES

בָּרוּךְ אַתָּה יי, אֱלֹהֵינוּ מֶלֶךְ הָעוֹלָם, בּוֹרֵא מִינֵי בְשָׂמִים.

Ba-ruch a-ta Adonai, Eh-lo-hei-nu meh-lech ha-o-lam, bo-rei mi-nei v'sa-mim.

We praise You, Adonai our God, sovereign of the universe, creator of all the spices.

THE SPICE-BOX, SYMBOL OF THE "ADDITIONAL SOUL" THAT MAKES SHABBAT SWEETER THAN THE WEEKDAYS, IS NOW CIRCULATED, THAT WE MAY INHALE SOME OF THAT SWEETNESS.

THE LIGHT
RAISE THE HAVDALAH CANDLE

בָּרוּךְ אַתָּה יי, אֱלֹהֵינוּ מֶלֶךְ הָעוֹלָם, בּוֹרֵא מְאוֹרֵי הָאֵשׁ.

Ba-ruch a-ta Adonai, Eh-lo-hei-nu meh-lech ha-o-lam, bo-rei m'o-rei ha-eish.

We praise You, Adonai our God, sovereign of the universe, creator of radiant fire.

THE CANDLE IS HELD HIGH AS THE LEADER SAYS:

בָּרוּךְ אַתָּה יי, אֱלֹהֵינוּ מֶלֶךְ הָעוֹלָם, הַמַּבְדִּיל
בֵּין קֹדֶשׁ לְחוֹל, בֵּין אוֹר לְחֹשֶׁךְ, בֵּין יִשְׂרָאֵל לָעַמִּים,
בֵּין יוֹם הַשְּׁבִיעִי לְשֵׁשֶׁת יְמֵי הַמַּעֲשֶׂה.
בָּרוּךְ אַתָּה יי, הַמַּבְדִּיל בֵּין קֹדֶשׁ לְחוֹל.

Ba-ruch a-ta Adonai, Eh-lo-hei-nu meh-lech ha-o-lam, ha-mav-dil
bein ko-desh l'chol, bein or l'cho-shech, bein Yis-ra-eil la-a-mim,
bein yom ha-sh'vi-i l'shei-shet y'mei ha-ma-a-seh.
Ba-ruch a-ta Adonai, ha-mav-dil bein ko-desh l'chol.

We praise You, Adonai our God, sovereign of the universe. You separate the holy from the commonplace, light from darkness, Israel from the nations, the seventh day of rest from the six days of labor.

We praise You, O God: You separate the holy from the commonplace.

SIP THE WINE OR GRAPE JUICE, THEN EXTINGUISH THE HAVDALAH
CANDLE IN THE REMAINING WINE OR GRAPE JUICE.

הַמַּבְדִּיל בֵּין קֹדֶשׁ לְחוֹל, חַטֹּאתֵינוּ הוּא יִמְחֹל,
זַרְעֵנוּ וְכַסְפֵּנוּ יַרְבֶּה כַחוֹל, וְכַכּוֹכָבִים בַּלָּיְלָה.

Ha-mav-dil bein ko-desh l'chol, cha-to-tei-nu hu yim-chol,
zar-ei-nu v'chas-pei-nu yar-beh ka-chol, v'cha-ko-cha-vim ba-lai-la.

שָׁבוּעַ טוֹב ...   *Sha-vu-a tov . . .*

A good week, a week of peace.
May gladness reign and joy increase.

אליהו הנביא   EILIYAHU HANAVI

אֵלִיָּהוּ הַנָּבִיא, אֵלִיָּהוּ הַתִּשְׁבִּי, אֵלִיָּהוּ, אֵלִיָּהוּ, אֵלִיָּהוּ
הַגִּלְעָדִי. בִּמְהֵרָה בְיָמֵינוּ, יָבֹא אֵלֵינוּ, עִם מָשִׁיחַ בֶּן דָּוִד.
עִם מָשִׁיחַ בֶּן דָּוִד. אֵלִיָּהוּ ...

Ei-li-ya-hu ha-na-vi, Ei-li-ya-hu ha-tish-bi, Ei-li-ya-hu, Ei-li-ya-hu, Ei-li-ya-hu
ha-gil-a-di. Bi-m'hei-ra v'ya-mei-nu, ya-vo ei-lei-nu, im Ma-shi-ach ben Da-vid.
Im Ma-shi-ach ben Da-vid. Ei-li-ya-hu . . .

Elijah the prophet, Elijah the Tishbite, Elijah the Gileadite: come to us soon, to herald our redemption. . . .

הבדלה HAVDALAH

We give thanks for the joy we have experienced during our celebration of Yom Tov. May we be blessed in time to come, and observe Yom Tov together again and again.

בָּרוּךְ אַתָּה יי, אֱלֹהֵינוּ מֶלֶךְ הָעוֹלָם, בּוֹרֵא פְּרִי הַגָּפֶן.

Ba-ruch a-ta Adonai, Eh-lo-hei-nu meh-lech ha-o-lam, bo-rei p'ri ha-ga-fen.

We praise You, Adonai our God, sovereign of the universe, creator of the fruit of the vine.

בָּרוּךְ אַתָּה יי, אֱלֹהֵינוּ מֶלֶךְ הָעוֹלָם, הַמַּבְדִיל
בֵּין קֹדֶשׁ לְחוֹל, בֵּין אוֹר לְחְשֶׁךְ, בֵּין יִשְׂרָאֵל לָעַמִּים,
בֵּין יוֹם הַשְּׁבִיעִי לְשֵׁשֶׁת יְמֵי הַמַּעֲשֶׂה.
בָּרוּךְ אַתָּה יי, הַמַּבְדִיל בֵּין קֹדֶשׁ לְחוֹל.

Ba-ruch a-ta Adonai, Eh-lo-hei-nu meh-lech ha-o-lam, ha-mav-dil
bein ko-desh l'chol, bein or l'cho-shech, bein Yis-ra-eil la-a-mim,
bein yom ha-sh'vi-i l'shei-shet y'mei ha-ma-a-seh.
Ba-ruch a-ta Adonai, ha-mav-dil bein ko-desh l'chol.

We praise You, Adonai our God, sovereign of the universe. You separate the holy from the commonplace, light from darkness, Israel from the nations, the seventh day of rest from the six days of labor.

We praise You, O God: You separate the holy from the commonplace.

BAR MITZVAH OR BAT MITZVAH

"And great shall be the peace of your children."
With joy we stand here with our child, whom we have
nurtured and cherished since birth.

_____, as you have grown in body and mind since
first we beheld you, years ago, so may you continue to grow.
Be strong in body, firm in mind, and faithful in heart, today
and every day of your life.

May this day, so joyous for you, your family, and your
friends, inspire you ever to go on learning, seeking, and
doing. Let your membership in the House of Israel bring you
contentment and challenge you to works of justice and love.
Then your life as a Jew will be a blesssing to you and to us
all. God grant us the strength to walk with you as you
continue your life's journey. Amen.

AND/OR

May God bless and keep you. May God always be in your
heart and inspire you to bring honor to our family and to the
House of Israel. May you grow in the love of Torah, develop
in body and mind, and fulfill your life with Mitzvot and
good deeds. Amen.

בָּרוּךְ אַתָּה יי, אֱלֹהֵינוּ מֶלֶךְ הָעוֹלָם, שֶׁהֶחֱיָנוּ
וְקִיְּמָנוּ וְהִגִּיעָנוּ לַזְּמַן הַזֶּה.

Ba-ruch a-ta Adonai, Eh-lo-hei-nu meh-lech ha-o-lam, sheh-heh-cheh-ya-nu,
v'ki-y'ma-nu, v'hi-gi-a-nu la-z'man ha-zeh.

We praise You, Adonai our God, sovereign of the universe, for keeping
us alive, for sustaining us, and for enabling us to reach this season.

שבת זכור   THE SHABBAT BEFORE PURIM

We come before You, O God, to give thanks for all our deliverances and blessings. On this Shabbat we remember how the Hamans of the world have sought our downfall over the ages, and give thanks that we have outlived them all.

FROM PSALM 124

❊ See "Selected Psalms," pages 358-375, and "A Daily Psalm," pages 27-33.

לוּלֵי יהוה שֶׁהָיָה לָנוּ (יֹאמַר־נָא יִשְׂרָאֵל)

לוּלֵי יהוה שֶׁהָיָה לָנוּ, בְּקוּם עָלֵינוּ אָדָם,

אֲזַי חַיִּים בְּלָעוּנוּ בַּחֲרוֹת אַפָּם בָּנוּ.

בָּרוּךְ יהוה, שֶׁלֹּא נְתָנָנוּ טֶרֶף לְשִׁנֵּיהֶם.

Had Adonai not been with us,

Had Adonai not been with us, when people rose up against us, they would have swallowed us up alive in their fury. Praised be Adonai, who did not give us up to be prey in their jaws.

נַפְשֵׁנוּ כְּצִפּוֹר נִמְלְטָה מִפַּח יוֹקְשִׁים;

הַפַּח נִשְׁבָּר, וַאֲנַחְנוּ נִמְלָטְנוּ.

עֶזְרֵנוּ בְּשֵׁם יהוה, עֹשֵׂה שָׁמַיִם וָאָרֶץ.

We are like a bird escaped from the fowler's trap; the trap broke, and we escaped.

Our help comes from Adonai, maker of heaven and earth.

299

THE SHABBAT BEFORE YOM HA-SHOAH

FROM PSALM 30

אֵלֶיךָ, יהוה, אֶקְרָא; וְאֶל־אֲדֹנָי אֶתְחַנָּן. מַה־בֶּצַע בְּדָמִי בְּרִדְתִּי
אֶל־שָׁחַת? הֲיוֹדְךָ עָפָר? הֲיַגִּיד אֲמִתֶּךָ? שְׁמַע־יהוה וְחָנֵּנִי; יהוה,
הֱיֵה־עֹזֵר לִי.

To You I cry out, O God; my plea ascends to You. What
good will be served if I go down silently to destruction? Will
the dust praise You? Will it declare Your faithfulness?

Hear, Adonai, and be gracious; be a help to me, O God!

ALL RISE

We remember a time when evil darkened the earth, and a
third of our people perished. We remember those of whom
we know, and those whose very names are lost.

*We honor the memory of those who died as martyrs, those who
died resisting, and those who died in terror.*

We weep for all that died with them: their goodness, their
wisdom, their richness of spirit. We lament the loss of wit
and learning; we mourn the death of laughter.

*Let us not forget the suffering of our people. Let their memory
strengthen us to struggle against cruelty and injustice, tyranny
and persecution.*

We salute those men and women who had the courage to
stand against the mob: to save us, and to suffer with us.
They, too, are witnesses to God's presence even in a world
that had lost hope.

*They are candles that shine from the darkness of those years, and
in their light we see what goodness is.*

In anguished silence we now remember those who were
called to sanctify God's name.

ALL ARE SEATED

300

THE SHABBAT BEFORE YOM HA-ATZMAUT

Eternal God, we give thanks that we have seen the miracle of Israel's rebirth. The vision of its pioneers, the devotion of its builders, and the courage of its defenders have yielded good fruit. The land, desolate for generations, is restored, and many have traveled from distant shores, there to begin new lives. For all this, O God, we thank You and praise Your holy name, as we echo the psalmist's words:

אִם־אֶשְׁכָּחֵךְ, יְרוּשָׁלָיִם, תִּשְׁכַּח יְמִינִי.

תִּדְבַּק־לְשׁוֹנִי לְחִכִּי אִם־לֹא אֶזְכְּרֵכִי,

אִם־לֹא אַעֲלֶה אֶת־יְרוּשָׁלַיִם עַל רֹאשׁ שִׂמְחָתִי.

If I forget you, O Jerusalem, let my right hand wither. Let my tongue cleave to the roof of my mouth if I do not remember you, if I do not set Jerusalem above my highest joy.

FROM PSALM 122

❈ See "Selected Psalms," pages 358-375, and "A Daily Psalm," pages 27-33.

שָׂמַחְתִּי בְּאֹמְרִים לִי: בֵּית יהוה נֵלֵךְ!

עֹמְדוֹת הָיוּ רַגְלֵינוּ בִּשְׁעָרַיִךְ יְרוּשָׁלָיִם!

יְרוּשָׁלַיִם הַבְּנוּיָה כְּעִיר שֶׁחֻבְּרָה־לָּהּ יַחְדָּו.

I rejoiced when they said to me: "Let us go to the house of Adonai!" Our feet have stood within your gates, O Jerusalem!

Jerusalem rebuilt, a city tied together and whole.

שַׁאֲלוּ שְׁלוֹם יְרוּשָׁלָיִם: יִשְׁלָיוּ אֹהֲבָיִךְ.

יְהִי־שָׁלוֹם בְּחֵילֵךְ, שַׁלְוָה בְּאַרְמְנוֹתָיִךְ.

לְמַעַן אַחַי וְרֵעָי אֲדַבְּרָה־נָּא שָׁלוֹם בָּךְ.

לְמַעַן בֵּית־יהוה אֱלֹהֵינוּ אֲבַקְשָׁה טוֹב לָךְ.

Pray for the peace of Jerusalem: may those who love you prosper.

Let there be peace within your walls, prosperity in your homes.

For the sake of my kin, my friends, I pray you find peace.

For the sake of the house of Adonai our God, I will seek your good.

৵

יום השואה YOM HA-SHOAH

On this day we remember the Shoah. From year to year it recedes further into the past, but its horrors remain beyond comprehension, and the losses it inflicted upon our people are beyond the powers of consolation. But we know for certain that we have a duty to remember: for the sake of those who perished; for the sake of those who survived; for our own sakes; and for the sake of future generations, so that they may commit themselves to preventing such a *shoah* from happening again, to our people or to any people.

We pledge ourselves to remember.

And should a wonder happen and I live on
To see the world illumined with new light,
The light of justice, love, and peace,
I shall praise that generation
From the depth of my sorrow, from the deepest abyss
Of my shattered soul.
But my wound will not be healed.
Its blood will flow as long as my heart beats,
As the blood of my brothers flowed, till their hearts froze. . . .
And even should You, God, in all Your mercy
Offer me the cup of forgetfulness—
I will not touch it! I shall say: Forgive me, God!
But if I taste the cup of forgetfulness,
I will no longer be I! . . .
And so, as long as my heart beats, . . .
I am unable to forget, and unwilling to forget! . . .

We pledge ourselves not to forget.

נָדַרְתִּי הַנֶּדֶר: לִזְכֹּר אֶת־הַכֹּל,
לִזְכֹּר—וְדָבָר לֹא לִשְׁכֹּחַ.
דָּבָר לֹא לִשְׁכֹּחַ—עַד דּוֹר עֲשִׂירִי,
עַד שֹׁךְ עֶלְבּוֹנִי, עַד כֻּלָּם,
עַד כֻּלָּהֶם,
עֲדֵי יִכְלוּ כָּל־שִׁבְטֵי מוּסָרִי.
קוֹנָם אִם לָרִיק יַעֲבֹר לֵיל הַזַּעַם,
קוֹנָם אִם לַבֹּקֶר אֶחֱזֹר לְסוּרִי
וּמְאוּם לֹא אֶלְמַד גַּם הַפַּעַם.

I have taken this oath: —
to remember it all.
To remember, and never to
forget.

Forgetting nothing of this,
till ten generations pass,
and the grief disappears,
and all the pain,
and the punishing blows are
ended for good.

I swear this night of terror
shall not have passed in vain;
I swear this morning I'll not
live unchanged,
As if I were no wiser even
now, even now.

One evening, when we were already resting on the floor of
our hut, dead tired, soup bowls in hand, a fellow prisoner
rushed in and asked us to run out to the assembly grounds
and see the wonderful sunset. Standing outside, we saw
sinister clouds glowing in the west and the whole sky alive
with clouds of ever-changing shapes and colors, from steel-
blue to blood-red. The desolate gray mud huts provided a
sharp contrast, while the puddles on the muddy ground
reflected the glowing sky. Then, after minutes of moving
silence, one prisoner said to another: "How beautiful the
world could be!"

ALL RISE

We remember a time when evil darkened the earth, and a third of our people perished. We remember those of whom we know, and those whose very names are lost.

We honor the memory of those who died as martyrs, those who died resisting, and those who died in terror.

We weep for all that died with them: their goodness, their wisdom, their richness of spirit. We lament the loss of wit and learning; we mourn the death of laughter.

Let us not forget the suffering of our people. Let their memory strengthen us to struggle against cruelty and injustice, tyranny and persecution.

We salute those men and women who had the courage to stand against the mob: to save us, and to suffer with us. They, too, are witnesses to God's presence in a world that had lost hope.

They are candles that shine from the darkness of those years, and in their light we see what goodness is.

We stand in gratitude for the lives of those who were the Congregation of Israel. Their spiritual resistance remains as an enduring testimony to a community where light persisted in darkness. We remember them all in love and compassion. We remember those who sanctified God's name.

אֵל מָלֵא רַחֲמִים, שׁוֹכֵן בַּמְּרוֹמִים, הַמְצֵא מְנוּחָה נְכוֹנָה תַּחַת
כַּנְפֵי הַשְּׁכִינָה עִם קְדוֹשִׁים וּטְהוֹרִים כְּזֹהַר הָרָקִיעַ מַזְהִירִים
לְנִשְׁמוֹת רִבְבוֹת אַלְפֵי יִשְׂרָאֵל שֶׁמְּתוּ עַל קִדּוּשׁ הַשֵּׁם. בְּעַל
הָרַחֲמִים יַסְתִּירֵם בְּסֵתֶר כְּנָפָיו לְעוֹלָמִים. וְיִצְרוֹר בִּצְרוֹר
הַחַיִּים אֶת־נִשְׁמָתָם. יי הוּא נַחֲלָתָם. וְיָנוּחוּ בְּשָׁלוֹם עַל
מִשְׁכָּבָם, וְנֹאמַר: אָמֵן.

God full of compassion, transcendent presence, grant perfect rest under the wings of Your presence along with the holy and pure whose radiance illumines the world, to the souls of the millions of our people who died for the sanctification of Your name. God abounding in mercies, let them find refuge forever in the shadow of Your wings, and let their souls be bound up in the bond of eternal life. As You, Adonai, are their inheritance, may they rest in peace, and let us say: Amen.

ALL ARE SEATED

But there is hope. There is hope because even in times of deepest darkness, there was courage, compassion and decency; the human spirit was not entirely defeated, and a remnant of our people survived.

There are stars whose light reaches the earth only after they themselves have disintegrated and are no more.
And there are men and women whose shining memory lights the world after they have passed from it.
These lights that shine in the darkest night are the ones that illumine the path for us.

There is hope because goodness is a mighty force.
From prophets, teachers, workers in every age, we have learned to hope, never to despair: the time will come, and we can help it come, when men and women and children will live in peace, and none shall make them afraid.

כֹּה אָמַר יהוה: מִנְעִי קוֹלֵךְ מִבֶּכִי, וְעֵינַיִךְ מִדִּמְעָה, כִּי יֵשׁ
שָׂכָר לִפְעֻלָּתֵךְ. וְיֵשׁ־תִּקְוָה לְאַחֲרִיתֵךְ, נְאֻם־יהוה. כִּי אָנֹכִי
יָדַעְתִּי אֶת־הַמַּחֲשָׁבֹת אֲשֶׁר אָנֹכִי חֹשֵׁב עֲלֵיכֶם, נְאֻם־יהוה,
מַחְשְׁבוֹת שָׁלוֹם, וְלֹא לְרָעָה, לָתֵת לָכֶם אַחֲרִית וְתִקְוָה.
וּקְרָאתֶם אֹתִי, וַהֲלַכְתֶּם וְהִתְפַּלַּלְתֶּם אֵלַי, וְשָׁמַעְתִּי אֲלֵיכֶם.
וּבִקַּשְׁתֶּם אֹתִי וּמְצָאתֶם, כִּי תִדְרְשֻׁנִי בְּכָל־לְבַבְכֶם.

Thus says Adonai: Keep your voice from weeping, and your eyes from tears, for there is a reward for your labors.

And there is hope for your future, says your God.

For I know the thoughts I have for you, says Adonai, thoughts of peace, and not of evil, to give you a future and a hope. You will call on me, you will come and pray to me, and I will hear you.

You will seek me and find me, when you search for me with all your heart.

For thus says the eternal God:
I will make a covenant with you,
a covenant that will endure forever;
for as the new heavens and the new earth
that I am making shall endure,
so shall your descendants endure,
so shall your name endure.
and from new moon to new moon,
and from Sabbath to Sabbath,
all flesh shall come to worship me.
And you shall have peace.

A MOMENT OF SILENCE

THE MOURNER'S KADDISH IS ON PAGE 286

יום העצמאות ISRAEL INDEPENDENCE DAY

FROM EZEKIEL 37

לָכֵן הִנָּבֵא וְאָמַרְתָּ אֲלֵיהֶם כֹּה־אָמַר אֲדֹנָי יְהוִה הִנֵּה אֲנִי פֹתֵחַ
אֶת־קִבְרוֹתֵיכֶם אֶתְכֶם מִקִּבְרוֹתֵיכֶם וְהַעֲלֵיתִי עַמִּי וְהֵבֵאתִי
אֶתְכֶם אֶל־אַדְמַת יִשְׂרָאֵל: וִידַעְתֶּם כִּי־אֲנִי יְהוָה בְּפִתְחִי
אֶת־קִבְרוֹתֵיכֶם וּבְהַעֲלוֹתִי אֶתְכֶם עַמִּי: וְנָתַתִּי רוּחִי בָכֶם
וִחְיִיתֶם וְהִנַּחְתִּי אֶתְכֶם מִקִּבְרוֹתֵיכֶם עַל־אַדְמַתְכֶם וִידַעְתֶּם
כִּי־אֲנִי יְהוָה דִּבַּרְתִּי וְעָשִׂיתִי נְאֻם־יְהוָה:

The hand of Adonai was upon me, leading me out by God's spirit and setting me down in the middle of a valley. It was full of bones. There were a great many of them spread on the surface of the valley, and they were very dry. God said to me: Mortal, can these bones live? I answered: O God Eternal, You [alone] know. Then God said to me: Prophesy to these bones, and say to them: You dry bones, hear the word of Adonai.

Behold, I will cause breath to enter you, and you shall live. I will put sinews on you, and cover you with flesh, and spread skin over you. I will put breath into you, and you shall live.

Then God said to me: Thus says God Eternal: Come, breath, from the four quarters of the earth, and breathe into these slain bodies, that they may live again. . . . and the breath came into them, and they came to life. They stood on their feet, an exceedingly great army. Then God said to me: Mortal, these bones are the whole House of Israel. They say: *Our bones are dried up, our hope is lost; we are cut off [from life]!* Therefore prophesy to them and say: Thus says God Eternal:

I am going to open your graves, my people; I will lift you out of your graves and bring you home to the Land of Israel. And when I have opened your graves and lifted you out of them, my people, you shall know that I am Adonai. I will put my breath into you and you shall live again, and I will place you in your own land. Then, says Adonai, you shall know that I, Adonai, have spoken and acted.

♣

Today we turn our thoughts to the Land of Israel, cradle of our faith, a land hallowed by memories of prophets and poets, mystics and sages. In all the ages of our history, and in all the places of our wanderings, we have remembered it with love and longing, saying with the Psalmist:

אִם־אֶשְׁכָּחֵךְ יְרוּשָׁלָ͏ִם, תִּשְׁכַּח יְמִינִי;

תִּדְבַּק־לְשׁוֹנִי לְחִכִּי אִם־לֹא אֶזְכְּרֵכִי,

אִם־לֹא אַעֲלֶה אֶת־יְרוּשָׁלַ͏ִם עַל רֹאשׁ שִׂמְחָתִי.

If I forget you, O Jerusalem, let my right hand wither; let my tongue cleave to the roof of my mouth if I do not remember you, if I do not set Jerusalem above my highest joy!

Eternal God, we give thanks for having lived to see the miracle of Israel's rebirth. The vision of its pioneers, the devotion of its builders, and the courage of its defenders have yielded good fruit. The land, desolate for generations, is restored, and many have traveled from distant shores, there to begin new lives. For all this, O God, we thank You and praise Your holy name.

שִׁירוּ לַיהוה שִׁיר חָדָשׁ, כִּי־נִפְלָאוֹת עָשָׂה.
זָכַר חַסְדּוֹ וֶאֱמוּנָתוֹ לְבֵית יִשְׂרָאֵל.

Sing a new song to Adonai, who has done wonderful things.

You have remembered Your love and faithfulness to the House of Israel.

כִּי־נִחַם יהוה עַמּוֹ וַעֲנִיָּו יְרַחֵם.
כִּי־נִחַם יהוה צִיּוֹן, נִחַם כָּל־חָרְבֹתֶיהָ.

You have comforted Your people, and shown compassion for the afflicted.

You have comforted Zion, brought comfort to her ruins.

וַיָּשֶׂם מִדְבָּרָהּ כְּעֵדֶן, וְעַרְבָתָהּ כְּגַן־יהוה.
שָׂשׂוֹן וְשִׂמְחָה יִמָּצֵא בָהּ; תּוֹדָה וְקוֹל זִמְרָה.

You have made her wilderness like Eden, her desert like a divine garden.

Joy and gladness shall be found there; thanksgiving and jubilant song.

יְשֻׂשׂוּם מִדְבָּר וְצִיָּה; וְתָגֵל עֲרָבָה, וְתִפְרַח כַּחֲבַצָּלֶת.
וּפְדוּיֵי יהוה יְשֻׁבוּן, וּבָאוּ צִיּוֹן בְּרִנָּה, וְשִׂמְחַת עוֹלָם עַל־רֹאשָׁם;
שָׂשׂוֹן וְשִׂמְחָה יַשִּׂיגוּ; וְנָסוּ יָגוֹן וַאֲנָחָה.

The wilderness and the dry land shall be glad;

The desert shall rejoice, and blossom as the rose.

Those whom God has ransomed shall return, and come to Zion with singing, with everlasting joy upon their heads;

They shall obtain joy and gladness; sorrow and sighing shall flee away.

בָּרוּךְ אַתָּה יי, אֱלֹהֵינוּ מֶלֶךְ הָעוֹלָם, שֶׁהֶחֱיָנוּ
וְקִיְּמָנוּ וְהִגִּיעָנוּ לַזְּמַן הַזֶּה.

*Ba-ruch a-ta Adonai, Eh-lo-hei-nu meh-lech ha-o-lam, sheh-heh-cha-ya-nu
v'ki-y'ma-nu v'hi-gi-a-nu la-z'man ha-zeh.*

We praise You, Adonai our God, sovereign of the universe, for keeping
us alive, for sustaining us, and for enabling us to reach this season.

FROM ISRAEL'S DECLARATION OF INDEPENDENCE

מְדִינַת יִשְׂרָאֵל תְּהֵא פְּתוּחָה לַעֲלִיָּה יְהוּדִית וּלְקִבּוּץ
גָּלֻיּוֹת, תִּשְׁקֹד עַל פִּתּוּחַ הָאָרֶץ לְטוֹבַת כָּל־תּוֹשְׁבֶיהָ,
תְּהֵא מֻשְׁתֶּתֶת עַל יְסוֹדוֹת הַחֵרוּת, הַצֶּדֶק וְהַשָּׁלוֹם לְאוֹר
חֲזוֹנָם שֶׁל נְבִיאֵי יִשְׂרָאֵל; תְּקַיֵּם שִׁוְיוֹן זְכֻיּוֹת חֶבְרָתִי
וּמְדִינִי גָּמוּר לְכָל־אֶזְרָחֶיהָ בְּלִי הֶבְדֵּל דָּת, גֶּזַע וּמִין;
תַּבְטִיחַ חֹפֶשׁ דָּת, מַצְפּוּן, לָשׁוֹן, חִנּוּךְ וְתַרְבּוּת; תִּשְׁמֹר
עַל הַמְּקוֹמוֹת הַקְּדוֹשִׁים שֶׁל כָּל־הַדָּתוֹת; וְתִהְיֶה נֶאֱמָנָה
לְעֶקְרוֹנוֹתֶיהָ שֶׁל מְגִלַּת אֻמּוֹת הַמְּאֻחָדוֹת.

The State of Israel will be open to the immigration of Jews
from all countries of their dispersion; will promote the
development of the country for the benefit of all its
inhabitants; will be based on the principles of liberty, justice,
and peace as conceived by the Prophets of Israel; will
uphold the full social and political equality of all its citizens,
without distinction of religion, race, or gender; will
guarantee freedom of religion, conscience, education, and
culture; will safeguard the holy places of all religions; and
will loyally uphold the principles of the United Nations
Charter.

ALL RISE

הַתִּקְוָה   THE HOPE

כָּל־עוֹד בַּלֵּבָב פְּנִימָה, נֶפֶשׁ יְהוּדִי הוֹמִיָּה;

וּלְפַאֲתֵי מִזְרָח קָדִימָה, עַיִן לְצִיּוֹן צוֹפִיָּה.

עוֹד לֹא אָבְדָה תִקְוָתֵנוּ, הַתִּקְוָה שְׁנוֹת אַלְפַּיִם,

לִהְיוֹת עַם חָפְשִׁי בְּאַרְצֵנוּ, בְּאֶרֶץ צִיּוֹן וִירוּשָׁלָיִם.

Kol od ba-lei-vav p'ni-mah, neh-fesh y'hudi ho-mi-yah;
u-l'fa-a-tei miz-rach ka-di-mah, a-yin l'tzi-yon tzo-fi-yah.
Od lo ov-dah tik-va-tei-nu, ha-tik-vah sh'not al-pa-yim,
li-h'yot am chof-shi b'ar-tzei-nu, b'eh-retz tzi-yon vi-y'ru-sha-la-yim.

As long as the Jewish heart still yearns, and looks east to Zion, so long our hope has not yet perished, the hope of two millennia, to be a free people in our land, the land of Zion and Jerusalem.

ALL ARE SEATED

Eternal God, guardian of Israel and redeemer of humanity, grant that Zion may be a safe shelter for its children, and a light to the nations. Give its people strength to build a land of justice and mercy for the good of all its inhabitants. Then shall the brightness of truth, compasssion, and peace shine forth from Zion, as it is written:

כִּי מִצִּיּוֹן תֵּצֵא תוֹרָה, וּדְבַר־יהוה מִירוּשָׁלָיִם.

Ki mi-tzi-yon tei-tzei Torah u-d'var Adonai mi-y'ru-sha-la-yim.

For out of Zion shall go forth Torah, and the word of God from Jerusalem.

✿

312

On this ancient day of mourning, we think of all God's children, in every corner of the earth, whose homes and houses of worship have been turned to rubble, who have been slain, enslaved, and brutalized. We think of them all. And especially today we remember the agonies inflicted on our own people, the House of Israel, ever and again, from earliest times.

FROM THE BOOK OF LAMENTATIONS

אֵיכָה יָשְׁבָה בָדָד הָעִיר רַבָּתִי עָם הָיְתָה כְּאַלְמָנָה
רַבָּתִי בַגּוֹיִם שָׂרָתִי בַּמְּדִינוֹת הָיְתָה לָמַס:
בָּכוֹ תִבְכֶּה בַּלַּיְלָה וְדִמְעָתָהּ עַל לֶחֱיָהּ אֵין־לָהּ מְנַחֵם
מִכָּל־אֹהֲבֶיהָ כָּל־רֵעֶיהָ בָּגְדוּ בָהּ הָיוּ לָהּ לְאֹיְבִים:

How lonely sits the city, once so full of people; once great among the nations, now a widow; a princess among states, become a vassal!

She weeps in the night, and tears run down her cheeks. There is none to comfort her among all her friends. All her allies have betrayed her, and have become her foes.

גָּלְתָה יְהוּדָה מֵעֹנִי וּמֵרֹב עֲבֹדָה הִיא יָשְׁבָה בַגּוֹיִם
לֹא מָצְאָה מָנוֹחַ כָּל־רֹדְפֶיהָ הִשִּׂיגוּהָ בֵּין הַמְּצָרִים:
לוֹא אֲלֵיכֶם כָּל־עֹבְרֵי דֶרֶךְ הַבִּיטוּ וּרְאוּ אִם־יֵשׁ
מַכְאוֹב כְּמַכְאֹבִי אֲשֶׁר עוֹלַל לִי:

Oppressed, enslaved, Judah has gone into exile. Living among the nations, she finds no resting place; her pursuers overtake her in the narrow passes.

Is it nothing to you, all you passersby? Look and see: is there any pain like the pain that has been inflicted on me?

313

מָה־אֲעִידֵךְ מָה אֲדַמֶּה־לָּךְ הַבַּת יְרוּשָׁלַם
מָה אַשְׁוֶה־לָּךְ וַאֲנַחֲמֵךְ בְּתוּלַת בַּת־צִיּוֹן
כִּי־גָדוֹל כַּיָּם שִׁבְרֵךְ מִי יִרְפָּא־לָךְ:
זְכֹר יְהֹוָה מֶה־הָיָה לָנוּ הַבִּיטָה וּרְאֵה אֶת־חֶרְפָּתֵנוּ:
נַחֲלָתֵנוּ נֶהֶפְכָה לְזָרִים בָּתֵּינוּ לְנָכְרִים:
יְתוֹמִים הָיִינוּ אֵין [וְאֵין] אָב אִמֹּתֵינוּ כְּאַלְמָנוֹת:
שָׁבַת מְשׂוֹשׂ לִבֵּנוּ נֶהְפַּךְ לְאֵבֶל מְחֹלֵנוּ:

What can I testify for you, with what compare you, O daughter of Jerusalem? To what can I liken you, that I may comfort you, O innocent daughter of Zion?

For your ruin is vast as the sea; who can heal you?

Remember, O God, what has befallen us; look, and see our degradation!

Our heritage has been turned over to strangers, our homes to aliens.

We have become orphans, fatherless; our mothers are like widows.

Gone is the joy of our hearts; our dancing is turned into mourning.

So it was for us at this season in the days of Babylon, and so it was again in the days of Rome.

A REFLECTION

𝕮   On the 9th of Av, the Judeans made another desperate sally, but were driven back by an overpowering force of the besiegers. The besieged attempted one more furious onslaught upon their enemies. They were again defeated, and again driven back to their sheltering walls. But this time they were closely followed by the Romans, one of whom, seizing a burning firebrand, mounted upon a comrade's shoulder, and flung his terrible missile through the so-called golden window of the Temple. The fire blazed up; it caught the wooden beams of the sanctuary, and rose in flames heavenward.

&

אֱלִי צִיּוֹן וְעָרֶיהָ כְּמוֹ אִשָּׁה בְּצִירֶיהָ,
וְכִבְתוּלָה חֲגוּרַת שַׂק עַל בַּעַל נְעוּרֶיהָ.

I mourn for Zion and her cities like a mother in her anguish, like a young woman in mourning for the husband of her youth.

How often has our pain seemed beyond bearing, as it was beyond comprehension! We saw that our tormentors would not rest until we were no more, until this was a world without Jews!

קוֹל בְּרָמָה נִשְׁמָע, נְהִי בְּכִי תַמְרוּרִים! רָחֵל מְבַכָּה עַל־בָּנֶיהָ,
מֵאֲנָה לְהִנָּחֵם עַל־בָּנֶיהָ, כִּי אֵינֶנּוּ.

A voice is heard in Ramah, lamentation and bitter weeping! Rachel is weeping for her children, refusing to be comforted for her children, for they are no more.

כָּל־זֹאת בָּאַתְנוּ וְלֹא שְׁכַחֲנוּךָ, וְלֹא־שִׁקַּרְנוּ בִּבְרִיתֶךָ.
כִּי־עָלֶיךָ הֹרַגְנוּ כָל־הַיּוֹם, נֶחְשַׁבְנוּ כְּצֹאן טִבְחָה.
אֱלֹהִים, אַל־דֳּמִי־לָךְ; אַל־תֶּחֱרַשׁ וְאַל־תִּשְׁקֹט אֵל.
כִּי־הִנֵּה אוֹיְבֶיךָ יֶהֱמָיוּן, וּמְשַׂנְאֶיךָ נָשְׂאוּ רֹאשׁ.
עַל־עַמְּךָ יַעֲרִימוּ סוֹד, וְיִתְיָעֲצוּ עַל־צְפוּנֶיךָ.
אָמְרוּ, לְכוּ וְנַכְחִידֵם מִגּוֹי; וְלֹא־יִזָּכֵר שֵׁם־יִשְׂרָאֵל עוֹד.

All this has come upon us, yet we have not forgotten You, or been false to Your covenant.

For Your sake we have been slain continually, and accounted as sheep for the slaughter.

O God, do not be silent; do not hold Your peace nor be still.

For Your enemies rage, and those who hate You hold their heads high.

They plot against Your people, and conspire against those who seek Your shelter.

They say, "Come, let us wipe them out as a nation; let the name of Israel be remembered no more."

But there is hope. There is hope because even in times of deepest darkness, there was courage, compassion, and decency; the human spirit was not entirely defeated, and a remnant of our people survived.

כֹּה אָמַר יהוה: מִנְעִי קוֹלֵךְ מִבֶּכִי, וְעֵינַיִךְ מִדִּמְעָה, כִּי
יֵשׁ שָׂכָר לִפְעֻלָּתֵךְ. וְיֵשׁ־תִּקְוָה לְאַחֲרִיתֵךְ, נְאֻם־יהוה.
כִּי אָנֹכִי יָדַעְתִּי אֶת־הַמַּחֲשָׁבֹת אֲשֶׁר אָנֹכִי חֹשֵׁב עֲלֵיכֶם,
נְאֻם־יהוה, מַחְשְׁבוֹת שָׁלוֹם, וְלֹא לְרָעָה, לָתֵת לָכֶם אַחֲרִית
וְתִקְוָה. וּקְרָאתֶם אֹתִי, וַהֲלַכְתֶּם וְהִתְפַּלַּלְתֶּם אֵלַי, וְשָׁמַעְתִּי
אֲלֵיכֶם. וּבִקַּשְׁתֶּם אֹתִי וּמְצָאתֶם, כִּי תִדְרְשֻׁנִי בְּכָל־לְבַבְכֶם.

Thus says Adonai: "Restrain your voice from weeping, and your eyes from tears, for your work shall be rewarded."

"And there is hope for your future," says Adonai.

"For I know the plans I have for you," says Adonai, "thoughts of peace, and not of evil, to give you a future and a hope. You will call on me, you will come and pray to me, and I will hear you."

"You will seek me and find me, when you search for me with all your heart."

FROM THE BOOK OF LAMENTATIONS

זֹאת אָשִׁיב אֶל־לִבִּי עַל־כֵּן אוֹחִיל:

חַסְדֵי יְהֹוָה כִּי לֹא־תָֽמְנוּ כִּי לֹא־כָלוּ רַחֲמָיו:

חֲדָשִׁים לַבְּקָרִים רַבָּה אֱמוּנָתֶֽךָ:

חֶלְקִי יְהֹוָה אָמְרָה נַפְשִׁי עַל־כֵּן אוֹחִיל לוֹ:

This I call to mind, therefore I have hope.

Surely Your love, O God, never ceases; surely Your mercies are unending.

They are new every morning; great is Your faithfulness.

"You, Adonai, are my portion," says my soul; "therefore I will hope in You."

נַחְפְּשָׂה דְרָכֵֽינוּ וְנַחְקֹֽרָה, וְנָשֽׁוּבָה עַד־יְהֹוָה.

Let us search and examine our ways, and return to God.

הֲשִׁיבֵֽנוּ יהוה אֵלֶֽיךָ, וְנָשֽׁוּבָה. חַדֵּשׁ יָמֵֽינוּ כְּקֶֽדֶם.

Help us to return to You, O God; then we shall return.
Renew our days as of old.

❧

317

THE SHABBAT BEFORE CHANUKAH

On the Festival of Light, another candle glows alongside the lights we kindle—the candle of hope. We call to mind the prophet's word summoning us to be God's servants, a light to the nations. First that light must glow within us. Let it grow as do the lights of Chanukah when, from night to night, the candles increase, and with them, the light that fills our rooms. And our eyes. That growing light is the miracle we celebrate year after year.

We have struggled to keep the flame burning. In 1944 the young poet Hannah Senesh with other young heroes went into Nazi-occupied Europe in an effort to save Jewish lives. She gave her life to keep alight the flame of life. Before her death she wrote:

אַשְׁרֵי הַגַּפְרוּר שֶׁנִּשְׂרַף וְהִצִּית לְהָבוֹת.

אַשְׁרֵי הַלֶּהָבָה שֶׁבָּעֲרָה בְּסִתְרֵי לְבָבוֹת.

אַשְׁרֵי הַלְּבָבוֹת שֶׁיָּדְעוּ לַחֲדוֹל בְּכָבוֹד.

אַשְׁרֵי הַגַּפְרוּר שֶׁנִּשְׂרַף וְהִצִּית לְהָבוֹת.

Blessed is the match that is consumed in kindling flame.
Blessed is the flame that burns in the heart's secret places.
Blessed is the heart that knows when to stop its beating with honor.
Blessed is the match that is consumed in kindling flame.

We pray now for all whose lives are made dark by oppressors: let light shine upon them. We pray for the hungry, the poor, the weak: let the sun of a better day rise upon them. May we be among those who kindle such light.

❧

חנוכה CHANUKAH

בָּרוּךְ אַתָּה יי, אֱלֹהֵינוּ
מֶלֶךְ הָעוֹלָם, אֲשֶׁר קִדְּשָׁנוּ
בְּמִצְוֹתָיו וְצִוָּנוּ לְהַדְלִיק
נֵר שֶׁל חֲנֻכָּה.

Ba-ruch a-ta Adonai, Eh-lo-hei-nu
meh-lech ha-o-lam, a-sher ki-d'sha-nu
b'mitz-vo-tav v'tzi-va-nu l'had-lik
ner shel Chanukah.

We praise You, Eternal One, Sovereign God of the universe: You call us to holiness, and enjoin us to kindle the Chanukah lights.

בָּרוּךְ אַתָּה יי, אֱלֹהֵינוּ
מֶלֶךְ הָעוֹלָם, שֶׁעָשָׂה נִסִּים
לַאֲבוֹתֵינוּ וּלְאִמּוֹתֵינוּ
בַּיָּמִים הָהֵם, בַּזְּמַן הַזֶּה.

Ba-ruch a-ta Adonai, Eh-lo-hei-nu
meh-lech ha-o-lam, sheh-a-sah ni-sim
la-a-vo-tei-nu u-l'i-mo-tei-nu
ba-ya-mim ha-heim, ba-z'man ha-zeh.

We praise You, Eternal One, Sovereign God of the universe: You did wonders for our fathers and our mothers in days of old, at this season.

ON THE FIRST NIGHT ONLY

בָּרוּךְ אַתָּה יי, אֱלֹהֵינוּ
מֶלֶךְ הָעוֹלָם, שֶׁהֶחֱיָנוּ
וְקִיְּמָנוּ וְהִגִּיעָנוּ
לַזְּמַן הַזֶּה.

Ba-ruch a-ta Adonai, Eh-lo-hei-nu
meh-lech ha-o-lam, sheh-heh-cha-ya-nu
v'ki-y'ma-nu v'hi-gi-a-nu
la-z'man ha-zeh.

We praise You, Eternal One, Sovereign God of the universe, for keeping us alive, for sustaining us, and for enabling us to reach this season.

THE FOLLOWING VERSES MAY BE RECITED AS THE LIGHTS ARE KINDLED.

1. הָעָם הַהֹלְכִים בַּחֹשֶׁךְ רָאוּ אוֹר גָּדוֹל.

The people who walked in darkness have seen a great light.

2. כִּי נָפַלְתִּי קָמְתִּי; כִּי־אֵשֵׁב בַּחֹשֶׁךְ יהוה אוֹר לִי.

Though I fall, I shall rise; though I sit in darkness, God shall be a light to me.

319

3. כִּי־אַתָּה תָּאִיר נֵרִי; יהוה אֱלֹהַי יַגִּיהַּ חָשְׁכִּי.

For You light my lamp; the everlasting God makes bright my darkness.

4. זָרַח בַּחֹשֶׁךְ אוֹר לַיְשָׁרִים; חַנּוּן וְרַחוּם וְצַדִּיק.

Light dawns in the darkness for the upright; for the one who is gracious, compassionate, and just.

5. יהוה אוֹרִי וְיִשְׁעִי; מִמִּי אִירָא?

God is my light and my help; whom shall I fear?

6. כִּי נֵר מִצְוָה, וְתוֹרָה אוֹר.

For the Mitzvah is a lamp, and Torah is light.

7. קוּמִי, אוֹרִי, כִּי בָא אוֹרֵךְ, וּכְבוֹד יהוה עָלַיִךְ זָרָח.

Arise, shine, for your light has come, and God's splendor shall dawn upon you.

8. בֵּית יַעֲקֹב, לְכוּ וְנֵלְכָה בְּאוֹר יהוה.

O House of Jacob, come, let us walk by the light of our God.

הַנֵּרוֹת הַלָּלוּ אֲנַחְנוּ מַדְלִיקִין עַל הַנִּסִּים, וְעַל הַתְּשׁוּעוֹת, וְעַל הַנִּפְלָאוֹת שֶׁעָשִׂיתָ לַאֲבוֹתֵינוּ וּלְאִמּוֹתֵינוּ. וְכָל־שְׁמוֹנַת יְמֵי חֲנֻכָּה הַנֵּרוֹת הַלָּלוּ קֹדֶשׁ; וְאֵין לָנוּ רְשׁוּת לְהִשְׁתַּמֵּשׁ בָּהֶם, אֶלָּא לִרְאוֹתָם בִּלְבָד, כְּדֵי לְהוֹדוֹת לְשִׁמְךָ עַל נִסֶּיךָ וְעַל נִפְלְאוֹתֶיךָ וְעַל יְשׁוּעָתֶךָ.

We kindle these lights in remembrance of the wonderful deliverance You performed for our ancestors. During all the eight days of Chanukah these lights are sacred; we are not to use them but only to gaze upon them, so that their glow may move us to give thanks for Your wonderful acts of deliverance.

FOR CHANUKAH SONGS, SEE PAGES 423-424

THE SHABBAT BEFORE TV BI-SH'VAT

Today we look forward to רֹאשׁ הַשָּׁנָה לָאִילָנוֹת, the New Year of the Trees. In the Land of Israel, especially, our people have expressed their love of trees and of all growing things on the fifteenth day of the month of Sh'vat. It is written:

One who goes out in springtime and sees trees sprouting should say:

בָּרוּךְ שֶׁלֹּא חִסֵּר בְּעוֹלָמוֹ כְּלוּם וּבָרָא בּוֹ בְּרִיּוֹת טוֹבוֹת
וְאִילָנוֹת טוֹבוֹת לְהִתְנָאוֹת בָּהֶן בְּנֵי אָדָם.

Ba-ruch sheh-lo chi-seir b'o-la-mo k'lum u-va-ra bo b'ri-yot to-vot
v'i-la-not to-vot l'hit-na-ot ba-hen b'nei a-dam.

Praised be the One whose world lacks nothing, who has created in it goodly creatures and goodly trees for us to enjoy.

From the very beginning of Creation, God's first concern was with planting, for that is what Scripture implies when it says, "God Eternal planted a garden in Eden." Therefore you, too, when you enter the land, should concern your-selves first of all with planting, for that is what Scripture teaches when it says, "When you come into the land, you shall plant trees that bear fruit." And it is written:

If you hold a sapling ready for planting in your hand, and they tell you, "The Messiah has come!", go ahead and plant your sapling, and then go to greet the Messiah.

Adonai our God, You have given us trees and plants and flowers: They provide food for the body and bring joy to the eye. Each year You make the world green again. It springs up afresh after the sleep of winter. Revive our spirits now, and fill us with love for You and the blossoming world You give us this and every year. And let us say: *Amen.*

נר־לרגלי דברך

תוספת

ADDITIONAL
READINGS

FOR REFLECTION AND STUDY

AND COMMENTARIES

FROM CHAPTER I

מֹשֶׁה קִבֵּל תּוֹרָה מִסִּינַי וּמְסָרָהּ לִיהוֹשֻׁעַ, וִיהוֹשֻׁעַ לִזְקֵנִים,
וּזְקֵנִים לִנְבִיאִים, וּנְבִיאִים מְסָרוּהָ לְאַנְשֵׁי כְנֶסֶת הַגְּדוֹלָה.
הֵם אָמְרוּ שְׁלֹשָׁה דְבָרִים: הֱווּ מְתוּנִים בַּדִּין, וְהַעֲמִידוּ
תַלְמִידִים הַרְבֵּה, וַעֲשׂוּ סְיָג לַתּוֹרָה.

Moses received Torah from Sinai and handed it on to Joshua, and Joshua [handed it on] to the elders, and the elders to the prophets. And the prophets handed it on to the members of the Great Assembly, who said three things: Be deliberate in judgment. Raise up many disciples. Make a fence for the Torah.

ℒ We are judged by our own standard of judgment. (Talmud Sotah 5b)
ℒ *a fence*—It is better to have a vineyard surrounded by a fence. Do not, however, make the fence more important than what it surrounds: should the fence fall in, all would then be lost. (Avot d'Rabbi Natan)

The symbol "ℒ" indicates a comment on the preceding text.

שִׁמְעוֹן הַצַּדִּיק הָיָה מִשְּׁיָרֵי כְנֶסֶת הַגְּדוֹלָה. הוּא הָיָה אוֹמֵר:
עַל שְׁלֹשָׁה דְבָרִים הָעוֹלָם עוֹמֵד: עַל הַתּוֹרָה, וְעַל הָעֲבוֹדָה,
וְעַל גְּמִילוּת חֲסָדִים.

Simeon the Rightous was one of the [last] members of the Great Assembly. He used to say: The world is based on three things: on the Torah, on worship, on deeds of lovingkindness.

ℒ Once when Rabbi Tarfon, Rabbi Yose the Galilean, and Rabbi Akiba were together in Lydda, the question arose: Which is more important, study or practice? Tarfon argued, "practice." Akiba argued, "study." They concluded: "Study is more important, for it leads to practice." (Midrash Sifrei to Deuteronomy 41) [Rabbi Yose's view is not stated.]

322

אַנְטִיגְנוֹס אִישׁ סוֹכוֹ קִבֵּל מִשִּׁמְעוֹן הַצַּדִּיק. הוּא הָיָה אוֹמֵר:
אַל תִּהְיוּ כַעֲבָדִים הַמְשַׁמְּשִׁין אֶת־הָרַב עַל מְנָת לְקַבֵּל פְּרָס,
אֶלָּא הֱווּ כַעֲבָדִים הַמְשַׁמְּשִׁין אֶת־הָרַב שֶׁלֹּא עַל מְנָת לְקַבֵּל
פְּרָס. וִיהִי מוֹרָא שָׁמַיִם עֲלֵיכֶם.

Antigonus of Socho received [Torah] from Simeon the Righteous.
He [Antigonus] would say: Do not be like servants who serve
their master in the hope of reward—be rather like servants who
serve their master without thought of reward. And let the fear of
Heaven be upon you.

꙳ The Hebrew word נוֹרָא has many meanings, but we should not con-
fuse "fear of Heaven" with being afraid. The "God-fearing" person is one
who lives reverently and acts ethically. (Rabbi Chaim Stern)

יוֹסֵי בֶּן יוֹעֶזֶר, אִישׁ צְרֵדָה, וְיוֹסֵי בֶּן יוֹחָנָן, אִישׁ יְרוּשָׁלַיִם,
קִבְּלוּ מִמֶּנּוּ. יוֹסֵי בֶּן יוֹעֶזֶר אוֹמֵר: יְהִי בֵיתְךָ בֵּית וַעַד
לַחֲכָמִים, וֶהֱוֵי מִתְאַבֵּק בַּעֲפַר רַגְלֵיהֶם, וֶהֱוֵי שׁוֹתֶה בְצָמָא
אֶת־דִּבְרֵיהֶם.

Yose ben Yo'ezer of Zareida and Yose ben Yochanan of Jerusalem
were next to receive [Torah]. Yose ben Yo'ezer said: Let your
home be a meeting-place for the wise, sit in the dust of their feet,
and thirstily drink in their words.

יוֹסֵי בֶּן יוֹחָנָן, אִישׁ יְרוּשָׁלַיִם, אוֹמֵר: יְהִי בֵיתְךָ פָּתוּחַ לִרְוָחָה,
וְיִהְיוּ עֲנִיִּים בְּנֵי בֵיתֶךָ.

Yose ben Yochanan of Jerusalem said: Let your house be opened
wide, and let the poor be members of your household.

꙳ Our sages taught: The non-Jewish poor are to be sustained along with
the Jewish poor, the non-Jewish sick are to be visited along with the
Jewish sick, and the non-Jewish dead are to be buried along with the
Jewish dead, for the sake of [the ways of] peace. (Talmud Gittin 61a)

יְהוֹשֻׁעַ בֶּן פְּרַחְיָה אוֹמֵר: עֲשֵׂה לְךָ רַב, וּקְנֵה לְךָ חָבֵר,
וֶהֱוֵי דָן אֶת־כָּל־הָאָדָם לְכַף זְכוּת.

Joshua ben Perachiah said: Find yourself a teacher, get yourself a
friend, and give everyone the benefit of the doubt.

✷ A friend is acquired only with the greatest of effort. (Sifre, Vayeilech)

✷ Three things ingratiate us to others: an open hand, a prepared table, a
light heart. (Avot d'Rabbi Natan B 31, S. Buber, ed.)

הִלֵּל אוֹמֵר: הֱוֵי מִתַּלְמִידָיו שֶׁל אַהֲרֹן, אוֹהֵב שָׁלוֹם וְרוֹדֵף
שָׁלוֹם, אוֹהֵב אֶת־הַבְּרִיּוֹת וּמְקָרְבָן לַתּוֹרָה.

Hillel said: Be a disciple of Aaron, loving peace and pursuing
peace, loving people and drawing them near to the Torah.

הוּא הָיָה אוֹמֵר: נְגַד שְׁמָא, אֲבַד שְׁמֵהּ. וּדְלָא מוֹסִיף יָסוּף.
וּדְלָא יָלֵף קְטָלָא חַיָּב. וּדְאִשְׁתַּמַּשׁ בְּתָגָא חֲלָף.

He [Hillel] would say: A name puffed up is a name lost. Who does
not add, subtracts. Who does not learn is as good as dead. Who
uses the crown [of Torah] for gain passes away.

✷ Honor flees the one who pursues it, and pursues the one who flees it.
(Talmud Eruvin 13b)

הוּא הָיָה אוֹמֵר: אִם אֵין אֲנִי לִי, מִי לִי? וּכְשֶׁאֲנִי לְעַצְמִי
מָה אֲנִי? וְאִם לֹא עַכְשָׁיו אֵימָתַי?

He [Hillel] would say: If I am not for myself, who will be for me?
And if I am [only] for myself, what am I? And if not now, when?

✷ If I do not work at perfecting myself today, I may not get the chance
tomorrow. But even if I do, today's chance to serve God has been lost,
never to return. (Rabbi Jonah ben Abraham, Spain, 13th century)

שַׁמַּאי אוֹמֵר: עֲשֵׂה תוֹרָתְךָ קֶבַע. אָמֹר מְעַט וַעֲשֵׂה הַרְבֵּה.
וֶהֱוִי מְקַבֵּל אֶת־כָּל־הָאָדָם בְּסֵבֶר פָּנִים יָפוֹת.

Shammai says: Make your Torah [learning] a fixed routine. Say little, do much. And greet everyone with a cheerful countenance.

✣ "Say little, do much." This teaches that the righteous promise little but do much; the wicked promise much but do not do even little. (Avot d'Rabbi Natan)

✣ "Greet everyone with a cheerful countenance." This teaches that you can shower someone with gifts, but if you do it with a downcast face, you have given nothing; if you greet someone with nothing more than a cheerful countenance, however, you have given the most precious of all gifts. (Avot d'Rabbi Natan)

רַבָּן שִׁמְעוֹן בֶּן גַּמְלִיאֵל אוֹמֵר: עַל שְׁלֹשָׁה דְבָרִים הָעוֹלָם
קַיָּם: עַל הַדִּין, וְעַל הָאֱמֶת, וְעַל הַשָּׁלוֹם.

Rabban Simeon ben Gamaliel says: The world is sustained by three things: by justice, by truth, and by peace.

✣ Rabbi Chanina said: The seal of the Holy One is truth. (Talmud Shabbat 55a)

FROM CHAPTER II

רַבִּי אוֹמֵר: אֵיזוֹ הִיא דֶרֶךְ יְשָׁרָה שֶׁיָּבוֹר לוֹ הָאָדָם?
כָּל־שֶׁהִיא תִפְאֶרֶת לְעֹשֶׂיהָ וְתִפְאֶרֶת לוֹ מִן הָאָדָם.

Rabbi [Judah ha-Nasi] says: What is a right path to choose? Whatever honors the one who follows it, and thus is beautiful in the eyes of others.

✣ As it is in many other cultures, the image of a path or way is frequently encountered in Jewish thought. The entire system of law is called הלכה, *Halachah*, from the root הלך, *halach*, to walk or go; the life of the spirit is pictured as a journey: "Walk before me with integrity," says God to Abraham and all his descendants; no single path can be right for all, even if they have a common destination. (Rabbi Chaim Stern)

הִלֵּל אוֹמֵר: אַל תִּפְרשׁ מִן הַצִּבּוּר. וְאַל תַּאֲמֵן בְּעַצְמְךָ
עַד יוֹם מוֹתָךְ. וְאַל תָּדִין אֶת־חֲבֵרְךָ עַד שֶׁתַּגִּיעַ לִמְקוֹמוֹ.
וְאַל תֹּאמַר דָּבָר שֶׁאִי אֶפְשָׁר לִשְׁמֹעַ, שֶׁסּוֹפוֹ לְהִשָּׁמֵעַ.
וְאַל תֹּאמַר: לִכְשֶׁאֶפָּנֶה אֶשְׁנֶה, שֶׁמָּא לֹא תִפָּנֶה.

Hillel says: Do not separate yourself from the community. Do not be too sure of yourself until the day you die. Do not judge your friends until you are in their place. Say nothing that cannot be understood [at once], hoping that in the end it will be understood. And do not say, "When I have time I will study"—you may never have the time.

℘ *Do not judge.* This goes along with the injunction not to be too sure of yourself. When people behave unjustly, it is easy to say, "Had I been in their position I would not have done that." You might have done just as badly, had you been in their position. (Rabbi Jonah ben Abraham)

הוּא הָיָה אוֹמֵר: אֵין בּוּר יְרֵא חֵטְא, וְלֹא עַם הָאָרֶץ חָסִיד,
וְלֹא הַבַּיְשָׁן לָמֵד, וְלֹא הַקַּפְּדָן מְלַמֵּד, וּבְמָקוֹם שֶׁאֵין אֲנָשִׁים,
הִשְׁתַּדֵּל לִהְיוֹת אִישׁ.

He [Hillel] would say: A boor does not fear sin; the ignorant are not pious; the bashful do not learn; the hot-tempered do not teach; and where none has integrity, you must strive for integrity.

℘ No one who wants to learn should say, "How can a fool like me ask questions of a brilliant sage? I neither know nor understand enough to ask." Feeling like this, how will you ever acquire wisdom? (Rabbi Jonah ben Abraham)

אָמַר לָהֶם: צְאוּ וּרְאוּ אֵיזוֹהִי דֶרֶךְ יְשָׁרָה שֶׁיִּדְבַּק בָּהּ הָאָדָם.
רַבִּי אֱלִיעֶזֶר אוֹמֵר: עַיִן טוֹבָה. רַבִּי יְהוֹשֻׁעַ אוֹמֵר: חָבֵר טוֹב.

רַבִּי יוֹסֵי אוֹמֵר: שָׁכֵן טוֹב. רַבִּי שִׁמְעוֹן אוֹמֵר: הָרוֹאֶה
אֶת־הַנּוֹלָד. רַבִּי אֶלְעָזָר אוֹמֵר: לֵב טוֹב. אָמַר לָהֶם: רוֹאֶה
אֲנִי אֶת־דִּבְרֵי אֶלְעָזָר בֶּן עֲרָךְ, שֶׁבִּכְלָל דְּבָרָיו דִּבְרֵיכֶם.

He [Yochanan ben Zakkai] said to them: What is a right path for one to take? Rabbi Eliezer says: A kindly eye. Rabbi Joshua says: A good friend. Rabbi Yose says: A good neighbor. Rabbi Simeon says: Foresight. Rabbi Elazar says: A good heart. He said to them: I prefer the words of Elazar ben Arach, for his words include all of yours.

A good heart. Such a person is generous, cultivates good companions (and is one), makes sure to seek out and dwell near good neighbors (and is one), and practices foresight, lest an impulsive act be the cause of harm. Such a person is at peace with God and with others. (Duran, Spain-North Africa, 14th-15th century)

רַבִּי אֱלִיעֶזֶר אוֹמֵר: יְהִי כְבוֹד חֲבֵרְךָ חָבִיב עָלֶיךָ כְּשֶׁלָּךְ;
וְאַל תְּהִי נוֹחַ לִכְעוֹס; וְשׁוּב יוֹם אֶחָד לִפְנֵי מִיתָתְךָ.

Rabbi Eliezer says: Let your friend's honor be as dear to you as your own. Do not be easily angered. Return [to God] one day before you die.

Resh Lakish said: If you raise your hand against another you are called wicked even if you don't strike a blow. (Talmud Sanhedrin 58b)

"Return [to God] one day before you die." His disciples asked Rabbi Eliezer: How can we know the day of our death? He answered: Let us then repent every day. (Abridged from Avot d'Rabbi Natan)

רַבִּי יְהוֹשֻׁעַ אוֹמֵר: עַיִן הָרַע, וְיֵצֶר הָרַע, וְשִׂנְאַת הַבְּרִיּוֹת
מוֹצִיאִין אֶת־הָאָדָם מִן הָעוֹלָם.

Rabbi Joshua says: Ill will, the evil impulse, and hatred of others destroy the world's social order.

✑ At first the evil impulse is like the thread of a spider's web; in the end it is as thick as wagon-rope. (Talmud Sukkah 52a)

רַבִּי יוֹסֵי אוֹמֵר: יְהִי מָמוֹן חֲבֵרְךָ חָבִיב עָלֶיךָ כְּשֶׁלָּךְ.
וְהַתְקֵן עַצְמְךָ לִלְמוֹד תּוֹרָה, שֶׁאֵינָה יְרֻשָּׁה לָךְ; וְכָל־מַעֲשֶׂיךָ
יִהְיוּ לְשֵׁם שָׁמָיִם.

Rabbi Yose said: Let your friend's property be as dear to you as your own. Discipline yourself to learn Torah, for it is not something you inherit. And let your every deed be for the sake of Heaven.

רַבִּי שִׁמְעוֹן אוֹמֵר: וּכְשֶׁאַתָּה מִתְפַּלֵּל, אַל תַּעַשׂ תְּפִלָּתְךָ קֶבַע,
אֶלָּא רַחֲמִים וְתַחֲנוּנִים לִפְנֵי הַמָּקוֹם בָּרוּךְ הוּא. וְאַל תְּהִי רָשָׁע
בִּפְנֵי עַצְמְךָ.

Rabbi Simeon said: When you pray, never let your prayer be routine, but [let it be] a plea for compassion and grace from the Blessed Presence. And do not regard yourself as wicked.

✑ "And do not regard yourself as wicked." Do not do something today for which you won't be able to face yourself tomorrow. (Rashi)

רַבִּי טַרְפוֹן אוֹמֵר: הַיּוֹם קָצָר, וְהַמְּלָאכָה מְרֻבָּה, וְהַפּוֹעֲלִים
עֲצֵלִים, וְהַשָּׂכָר הַרְבֵּה, וּבַעַל הַבַּיִת דּוֹחֵק.

Rabbi Tarfon said: The day is short, the work incessant, the workers lazy, the wages high, the employer pressing.

הוּא הָיָה אוֹמֵר: לֹא עָלֶיךָ הַמְּלָאכָה לִגְמוֹר, וְלֹא אַתָּה
בֶן־חוֹרִין לִבָּטֵל מִמֶּנָּה.

He would say: You are not required to complete the work—but neither are you free to abandon it.

FROM CHAPTER III

רַבִּי חֲנַנְיָה בֶּן תְּרַדְיוֹן אוֹמֵר: שְׁנַיִם שֶׁיוֹשְׁבִין וְיֵשׁ בֵּינֵיהֶן
דִּבְרֵי תוֹרָה, שְׁכִינָה שְׁרוּיָה בֵּינֵיהֶם.

Rabbi Chananiah ben Teradion says: When two are sitting and words of Torah pass between them, the Divine Presence hovers between them.

רַבִּי חֲנִינָא בֶּן דּוֹסָא אוֹמֵר: כָּל־שֶׁיִּרְאַת חֶטְאוֹ קוֹדֶמֶת לְחָכְמָתוֹ,
חָכְמָתוֹ מִתְקַיֶּמֶת. וְכָל־שֶׁחָכְמָתוֹ קוֹדֶמֶת לְיִרְאַת חֶטְאוֹ, אֵין
חָכְמָתוֹ מִתְקַיֶּמֶת. הוּא הָיָה אוֹמֵר: כָּל־שֶׁמַּעֲשָׂיו מְרֻבִּין מֵחָכְמָתוֹ,
חָכְמָתוֹ מִתְקַיֶּמֶת. וְכָל־שֶׁחָכְמָתוֹ מְרֻבִּין מִמַּעֲשָׂיו, אֵין חָכְמָתוֹ
מִתְקַיֶּמֶת.

Rabbi Chanina ben Dosa says: If you fear sin more than you covet wisdom, you will acquire enduring wisdom. But if you covet wisdom more than you fear sin, you will not acquire enduring wisdom. He would say: If your actions are louder than your words, you will acquire enduring wisdom. But if your words are louder than your actions, you will not acquire enduring wisdom.

✒ Wisdom may be understood as "skill," "mastery of technique," "science." The passage, thus construed, teaches that morality should inform skill, a warning against the use of "wisdom" for destructive purposes, and praise for its constructive use. (Rabbi Chaim Stern)

הוּא הָיָה אוֹמֵר: כָּל־שֶׁרוּחַ הַבְּרִיּוֹת נוֹחָה הֵימֶנּוּ, רוּחַ הַמָּקוֹם
נוֹחָה הֵימֶנּוּ. וְכָל־שֶׁאֵין רוּחַ הַבְּרִיּוֹת נוֹחָה הֵימֶנּוּ, אֵין רוּחַ
הַמָּקוֹם נוֹחָה הֵימֶנּוּ.

He would say: If others receive joy from you, God too receives joy from you. But if others receive no joy from you, God too receives no joy from you.

𝒵 This does not say all "others," for it is impossible to please everyone; no one is acceptable to all others [nor need one be]. So Esther 10:3 says of Mordechai, esteemed by most of his brethren—not by all. (Nachmias, Spain, 14th century)

הוּא הָיָה אוֹמֵר: חָבִיב אָדָם, שֶׁנִּבְרָא בְּצֶלֶם.

[Rabbi Akiva] would say: Beloved is humankind, for we are created in the divine image.

𝒵 "Image" cannot mean physical likeness; it refers to intelligence and understanding. (Nachmias)

הַכֹּל צָפוּי, וְהָרְשׁוּת נְתוּנָה. וּבְטוֹב הָעוֹלָם נִדּוֹן, וְהַכֹּל לְפִי רֹב הַמַּעֲשֶׂה.

All is foreseen, yet free choice is given. The world is judged as good, but all depends on the balance of our deeds.

𝒵 Three things are under our control: mouth, hands, and feet. Three things are not under our control: eyes, ears, and nose. (Midrash Tanchuma, Tol'dot)
𝒵 If you didn't do it, you didn't do it; but if you did do it, you should have done it right. (Talmud Yoma 77a)
𝒵 Some people choose the vinegar and leave the wine to others. (Talmud Bava Batra 84b)

רַבִּי אֶלְעָזָר בֶּן עֲזַרְיָה אוֹמֵר: אִם אֵין תּוֹרָה, אֵין דֶּרֶךְ אֶרֶץ;
אִם אֵין דֶּרֶךְ אֶרֶץ, אֵין תּוֹרָה. אִם אֵין חָכְמָה, אֵין יִרְאָה;
אִם אֵין יִרְאָה, אֵין חָכְמָה. אִם אֵין בִּינָה, אֵין דַּעַת;
אִם אֵין דַּעַת, אֵין בִּינָה. אִם אֵין קֶמַח, אֵין תּוֹרָה;
אִם אֵין תּוֹרָה, אֵין קֶמַח.

Rabbi Elazar ben Azariah says: Where there is no Torah, there is no civility; where there is no civility, there is no Torah. Where there is no wisdom, there is no reverence; where there is no reverence, there is no wisdom. Where there is no understanding, there is no knowledge; where there is no knowledge, there is no understanding. Where there is no bread, there is no Torah; where there is no Torah, there is no bread.

℘ This series of oppositions leads us to an affirmation: to doubt the legitimacy of "either/or" in favor of "both/and." (Rabbi Chaim Stern)

FROM CHAPTER IV

בֶּן זוֹמָא אוֹמֵר: אֵיזֶהוּ חָכָם? הַלּוֹמֵד מִכָּל־אָדָם. אֵיזֶהוּ גִבּוֹר?
הַכּוֹבֵשׁ אֶת־יִצְרוֹ. אֵיזֶהוּ עָשִׁיר? הַשָּׂמֵחַ בְּחֶלְקוֹ. אֵיזֶהוּ מְכֻבָּד?
הַמְכַבֵּד אֶת־הַבְּרִיּוֹת.

Ben Zoma says: Who is wise? One who learns from every person. Who is strong? One who shows self-control. Who is rich? One who is contented with his or her portion. Who is respected? One who respects others.

℘ And some say, strong is the one who turns an enemy into a friend. (Avot d'Rabbi Natan)

℘ The wise know themselves to be unknowing. The strong know themselves to be weak. The rich know themselves to be "poor" in days. The respectable fear they will be unmasked. (Rabbi Chaim Stern)

בֶּן עַזַּאי אוֹמֵר: הֱוֵי רָץ לְמִצְוָה קַלָּה כְּבַחֲמוּרָה; שֶׁמִּצְוָה
גוֹרֶרֶת מִצְוָה, וַעֲבֵרָה גוֹרֶרֶת עֲבֵרָה; שֶׁשְּׂכַר מִצְוָה מִצְוָה,
וּשְׂכַר עֲבֵרָה עֲבֵרָה.

Ben Azzai says: Run to do a minor Mitzvah as though it were a major. For one good deed leads to another, and one transgression leads to another; and the reward of one good deed is another, whereas the punishment of one transgression is another.

℘ The reward for doing a minor Mitzvah is the opportunity of doing an even greater one. (Machzor Vitry, 11th-12th century)

ℒ Some interpret this as follows: The reward for doing a Mitzvah [or a good deed, for that matter] is in having done it. (Nachmias)

הוּא הָיָה אוֹמֵר: אַל תְּהִי בָז לְכָל־אָדָם, וְאַל תְּהִי מַפְלִיג לְכָל־דָּבָר, שֶׁאֵין לְךָ אָדָם שֶׁאֵין לוֹ שָׁעָה, וְאֵין לְךָ דָּבָר שֶׁאֵין לוֹ מָקוֹם.

He [Ben Azzai] would say: Despise no one, and regard nothing as impossible, for you will find no one whose hour does not come, and not a thing that does not have its place.

ℒ It was the favorite saying of the sages of Yavneh: I am a creature of God and you are a creature of God. My work may be in the city, yours is perhaps in the field. As you rise early to your work, so I rise early to my work. As you do not claim that your work is superior to mine, so do I not claim that my work is superior to yours. And should one say, "I do more important work and the other does less important work," we have already learned: "More or less, it does not matter, so long as the heart is inclined toward Heaven." (Talmud Berachot 17a, quoting Berachot 5a)

רַבִּי יִשְׁמָעֵאל בְּנוֹ אוֹמֵר: הַלּוֹמֵד עַל מְנָת לְלַמֵּד, מַסְפִּיקִין בְּיָדוֹ לִלְמֹד וּלְלַמֵּד. וְהַלּוֹמֵד עַל מְנָת לַעֲשׂוֹת, מַסְפִּיקִין בְּיָדוֹ לִלְמֹד וּלְלַמֵּד, לִשְׁמֹר וְלַעֲשׂוֹת. רַבִּי צָדוֹק אוֹמֵר: אַל תַּעֲשֵׂם עֲטָרָה לְהִתְגַּדֶּל בָּהֶם, וְלֹא קַרְדֹּם לַחְפּוֹר בָּהֶם.

Rabbi Ishmael his son says: Learn in order to teach, and it is given you to learn and to teach. Learn in order to do, and it is given you to learn and teach, to keep and do. Rabbi Zadok says: Do not make them [learning and doing] a crown with which to glorify yourself, nor a spade to dig with.

ℒ The path to the Torah's truth is through error. (Talmud Gittin 43a)

רַבִּי יוֹחָנָן הַסַּנְדְּלָר אוֹמֵר: כָּל־כְּנֵסִיָּה שֶׁהִיא לְשֵׁם שָׁמַיִם
סוֹפָהּ לְהִתְקַיֵּם. וְשֶׁאֵינָהּ לְשֵׁם שָׁמַיִם אֵין סוֹפָהּ לְהִתְקַיֵּם.

Rabbi Yochanan ha-Sandlar said: Every assembly for the sake of
Heaven will in the end have enduring value. But one not for the
sake of Heaven will in the end not have enduring value.

רַבִּי שִׁמְעוֹן אוֹמֵר: שְׁלֹשָׁה כְתָרִים הֵם: כֶּתֶר תּוֹרָה, וְכֶתֶר
כְּהֻנָּה, וְכֶתֶר מַלְכוּת, וְכֶתֶר שֵׁם טוֹב עוֹלֶה עַל גַּבֵּיהֶן.

Rabbi Simeon said: There are three crowns: the crown of Torah,
the crown of priesthood, and the crown of royalty, yet the crown
of a good name is best of all.

‿ Each of us has three names: what our parents call us, what others call
us, and what we call ourselves. (Midrash Kohelet Rabbah 7)

רַבִּי יַעֲקֹב אוֹמֵר: הָעוֹלָם הַזֶּה דּוֹמֶה לַפְּרוֹזְדוֹר בִּפְנֵי הָעוֹלָם
הַבָּא. הַתְקֵן עַצְמְךָ בַּפְּרוֹזְדוֹר, כְּדֵי שֶׁתִּכָּנֵס לַטְּרַקְלִין.

Rabbi Jacob said: This world is like an anteroom to the world-to-
come. Prepare yourself in the anteroom, so that you may enter the
palace.

‿ Today is for doing; tomorrow is for the reward. (Talmud Eruvin 22a)

הוּא הָיָה אוֹמֵר: יָפָה שָׁעָה אַחַת בִּתְשׁוּבָה וּמַעֲשִׂים טוֹבִים
בָּעוֹלָם הַזֶּה מִכָּל־חַיֵּי הָעוֹלָם הַבָּא, וְיָפָה שָׁעָה אַחַת שֶׁל
קוֹרַת רוּחַ בָּעוֹלָם הַבָּא מִכָּל־חַיֵּי הָעוֹלָם הַזֶּה.

He would add: Better one hour of repentance and good deeds in
this world than all the life of the world-to-come, and better one
hour of bliss in the world-to-come than all the life of this world.

‿ One cannot explain a comparison of what cannot be compared.
(Midrash Shemuel)

רַבִּי שִׁמְעוֹן בֶּן אֶלְעָזָר אוֹמֵר: אַל תְּרַצֶּה אֶת־חֲבֵרְךָ בִּשְׁעַת כַּעֲסוֹ, וְאַל תְּנַחֲמֶנּוּ בְּשָׁעָה שֶׁמֵּתוֹ מֻטָּל לְפָנָיו, וְאַל תִּשְׁאַל לוֹ בִּשְׁעַת נִדְרוֹ, וְאַל תִּשְׁתַּדֵּל לִרְאוֹתוֹ בִּשְׁעַת קַלְקָלָתוֹ.

Rabbi Simeon ben Elazar says: Never try to pacify a neighbor who is in the grip of rage, nor try to console one who has only just been bereaved, nor question the wisdom of a vow newly made, nor rush to see your neighbor who has just been disgraced.

⅋ Even as we are commanded to speak up when our words will be listened to, so are we commanded to hold our peace when our words will not be listened to. (Talmud Yevamot 65b)

⅋ We do not condemn people for what they say when they are out of control. (Talmud Bava Batra 16b)

אֱלִישָׁע בֶּן אֲבוּיָה אוֹמֵר: הַלּוֹמֵד יֶלֶד: לְמַה הוּא דוֹמֶה? לִדְיוֹ כְּתוּבָה עַל נְיָר חָדָשׁ. וְהַלּוֹמֵד זָקֵן: לְמַה הוּא דוֹמֶה? לִדְיוֹ כְּתוּבָה עַל נְיָר מָחוּק.

Elisha ben Abuyah says: Learning as a child: what is it like? Ink inscribed on new paper. Learning in old age: what is that like? Ink inscribed on blotted paper.

⅋ Fortunate the generation in which the elder listens to the younger. (Talmud Rosh Hashanah 25b)

רַבִּי יוֹסֵי בַּר יְהוּדָה, אִישׁ כְּפַר הַבַּבְלִי, אוֹמֵר: הַלּוֹמֵד מִן הַקְּטַנִּים: לְמַה הוּא דוֹמֶה? לְאוֹכֵל עֲנָבִים קֵהוֹת וְשׁוֹתֶה יַיִן מִגִּתּוֹ. וְהַלּוֹמֵד מִן הַזְּקֵנִים: לְמַה הוּא דוֹמֶה? לְאוֹכֵל עֲנָבִים בְּשׁוּלוֹת וְשׁוֹתֶה יַיִן יָשָׁן. רַבִּי אוֹמֵר: אַל תִּסְתַּכֵּל בַּקַּנְקַן אֶלָּא בַּמֶּה שֶׁיֶּשׁ בּוֹ. יֵשׁ קַנְקַן חָדָשׁ מָלֵא יָשָׁן, וְיָשָׁן שֶׁאֲפִילוּ חָדָשׁ אֵין בּוֹ.

Rabbi Yose bar Judah of Kefar Habavli says: Who learns from the young is like one who eats unripe grapes and drinks wine straight from the vat. Who learns from elders is like one who eats ripe grapes and drinks vintage wine.

Rabbi [Judah ha-Nasi] says: Don't look at the flask but at what is in it. There are new flasks full of old wine, and old ones that don't even hold new wine.

℘ Learning when young has two advantages: it is easier to impress knowledge on the mind, and one has time left in which to teach others; learning when old has the correlative disadvantages: it is harder to absorb learning, and there is little time left for teaching others. (Midrash Shemuel)

℘ As elders would feel no shame to ask a younger person for water, so should they feel no shame to ask a younger person to teach them a chapter, verse, or even a letter of Torah. (Midrash Songs Rabbah 1:1)

רַבִּי אֶלְעָזָר הַקַּפָּר אוֹמֵר: הַקִּנְאָה וְהַתַּאֲוָה וְהַכָּבוֹד מוֹצִיאִין אֶת־הָאָדָם מִן הָעוֹלָם.

Rabbi Elazar ha-Kappar says: Envy, lust, and [the pursuit of] honor make one unfit for human society.

FROM CHAPTER V

שִׁבְעָה דְבָרִים בַּגֹּלֶם, וְשִׁבְעָה בֶחָכָם: חָכָם אֵינוֹ מְדַבֵּר בִּפְנֵי מִי שֶׁהוּא גָדוֹל בְּחָכְמָה וּבְמִנְיָן, וְאֵינוֹ נִכְנָס לְתוֹךְ דִּבְרֵי חֲבֵרוֹ, וְאֵינוֹ נִבְהָל לְהָשִׁיב, שׁוֹאֵל כָּעִנְיָן וּמֵשִׁיב כַּהֲלָכָה, וְאוֹמֵר עַל רִאשׁוֹן רִאשׁוֹן וְעַל אַחֲרוֹן אַחֲרוֹן, וְעַל מַה שֶּׁלֹּא שָׁמַע אוֹמֵר לֹא שָׁמַעְתִּי, וּמוֹדֶה עַל הָאֱמֶת. וְחִלּוּפֵיהֶן בַּגֹּלֶם.

A clod has seven traits, and so does a sage: The wise never speak before one whose wisdom and knowledge are greater; they do not interrupt their companions; they are not in a rush to reply; they ask to the point and their reply is pertinent; they speak of first things first and of last things last; when they don't know something they say, "I don't know", and [when shown to be wrong] they acknowledge their error. The reverse is true of clods.

& The fool thinks everyone is a fool. (Midrash Kohelet Rabbah 10)
& The one claimed wheat, and the other granted the claim—about barley! (Talmud Bava Kamma 35b)
& Teach your tongue to say, "I don't know," lest you be caught in error. (Talmud Berachot 4a)

חֶרֶב בָּא לָעוֹלָם עַל עִנּוּי הַדִּין וְעַל עִוּוּת הַדִּין.

The sword enters the world because of justice delayed and justice denied.

אַרְבַּע מִדּוֹת בָּאָדָם. הָאוֹמֵר: שֶׁלִּי שֶׁלִּי וְשֶׁלְּךָ שֶׁלָּךְ: זוֹ מִדָּה בֵּינוֹנִית. (וְיֵשׁ אוֹמְרִים: זוֹ מִדַּת סְדוֹם.) שֶׁלִּי שֶׁלְּךָ וְשֶׁלְּךָ שֶׁלִּי: עַם הָאָרֶץ. שֶׁלִּי שֶׁלְּךָ וְשֶׁלְּךָ שֶׁלָּךְ: חָסִיד. שֶׁלְּךָ שֶׁלִּי וְשֶׁלִּי שֶׁלִּי: רָשָׁע.

People come in four types. One says: What's mine is mine and what's yours is yours: average. (But some say: This is the way of Sodom.) What's mine is yours and what's yours is mine: stupid. What's mine is yours and what's yours is yours: saintly. What's mine is mine and what's yours is mine: wicked.

& Those who say that this is the way of Sodom are not in disagreement with the first view, but make an additional point, namely, that such an attitude is very close to the behavior of Sodom. Once you get into the habit of letting no one enjoy what is yours, you will eventually refuse to let people enjoy even that which is theirs. (Duran)

אַרְבַּע מִדּוֹת בַּדֵּעוֹת: נוֹחַ לִכְעוֹס וְנוֹחַ לִרְצוֹת—יָצָא שְׂכָרוֹ
בְּהֶפְסֵדוֹ. קָשֶׁה לִכְעוֹס וְקָשֶׁה לִרְצוֹת—יָצָא הֶפְסֵדוֹ בִּשְׂכָרוֹ.
קָשֶׁה לִכְעוֹס וְנוֹחַ לִרְצוֹת—חָסִיד. נוֹחַ לִכְעוֹס וְקָשֶׁה
לִרְצוֹת—רָשָׁע.

There are four temperaments: Quick to anger and quick to be appeased: its gain is canceled by its loss. Slow to anger and slow to be appeased: its loss is canceled by its gain. Slow to anger and quick to be appeased: saintly. Quick to anger and slow to be appeased: wicked.

♪ These "temperaments" are actually within our power to improve or make worse. Otherwise you could not call someone a saint for the one and wicked for the other. (Duran)

♪ The saintly person is "slow to anger"—that is, there is no requirement that one should *never* be angry: that is possible only for an angel. (Duran)

אַרְבַּע מִדּוֹת בַּתַּלְמִידִים: מַהֵר לִשְׁמוֹעַ וּמַהֵר לְאַבֵּד—
יָצָא שְׂכָרוֹ בְּהֶפְסֵדוֹ. קָשֶׁה לִשְׁמוֹעַ וְקָשֶׁה לְאַבֵּד—
יָצָא הֶפְסֵדוֹ בִּשְׂכָרוֹ. מַהֵר לִשְׁמוֹעַ וְקָשֶׁה לְאַבֵּד—חָכָם.
קָשֶׁה לִשְׁמוֹעַ וּמַהֵר לְאַבֵּד—זֶה חֵלֶק רַע.

Students come in four types: Quick to learn and quick to forget: their gain is canceled by their loss. Slow to learn and slow to forget: their loss is canceled by their gain. Quick to learn and slow to forget: wise. Slow to learn and quick to forget: a misfortune.

♪ If you give the Torah up for one day, it will give you up for two. (Jerusalem Talmud Berachot, end)

אַרְבַּע מִדּוֹת בַּנוֹתְנֵי צְדָקָה: הָרוֹצֶה שֶׁיִּתֵּן וְלֹא יִתְּנוּ אֲחֵרִים-
עֵינוֹ רָעָה בְּשֶׁל אֲחֵרִים. יִתְּנוּ אֲחֵרִים וְהוּא לֹא יִתֵּן-עֵינוֹ רָעָה
בְּשֶׁלוֹ. יִתֵּן וְיִתְּנוּ אֲחֵרִים-חָסִיד. לֹא יִתֵּן וְלֹא יִתְּנוּ אֲחֵרִים-רָשָׁע.

People who give charity come in four types: Who want to give but don't want others to give: they are misers for others. Who want others to give but not themselves: they are misers themselves. Who want to give and want others to give: saintly. Who won't give and don't want others to give: wicked.

ℒ Better one who gives a little of his own than one who steals and gives much. (Midrash Kohelet Rabbah 84)

אַרְבַּע מִדּוֹת בְּהוֹלְכֵי לְבֵית הַמִּדְרָשׁ: הוֹלֵךְ וְאֵינוֹ עוֹשֶׂה— שְׂכַר הֲלִיכָה בְּיָדוֹ. עוֹשֶׂה וְאֵינוֹ הוֹלֵךְ—שְׂכַר מַעֲשֶׂה בְּיָדוֹ. הוֹלֵךְ וְעוֹשֶׂה—חָסִיד. לֹא הוֹלֵךְ וְלֹא עוֹשֶׂה—רָשָׁע.

Four kinds of people attend the House of Study: Who attend but do not practice [what they have learned]: they have the reward of attending. Who practice but do not attend: they have the reward of doing. Who both attend and do: saintly. Who neither attend nor do: wicked.

ℒ To serve the Torah is greater than to learn it. (Talmud Berachot 7a)

כָּל־אַהֲבָה שֶׁהִיא תְלוּיָה בְדָבָר, בָּטֵל דָּבָר, בְּטֵלָה אַהֲבָה. וְשֶׁאֵינָה תְלוּיָה בְדָבָר, אֵינָה בְּטֵלָה לְעוֹלָם. אֵיזוֹ הִיא אַהֲבָה הַתְלוּיָה בְדָבָר? זֹאת אַהֲבַת אַמְנוֹן וְתָמָר. וְשֶׁאֵינָה תְלוּיָה בְדָבָר? זֹאת אַהֲבַת דָּוִד וִיהוֹנָתָן.

If love depends on an extraneous cause, it lasts only as long as that cause. If love does not depend on an extraneous cause, it never dies away.

What sort of love depends on an extraneous cause? The love of Amnon and Tamar [II Samuel 13]. What sort of love does not depend on an extraneous cause? The love of David and Jonathan [I Samuel 20].

🖙 This is what the Holy One said to Israel: "My children, what do I ask of you? Only this: that you love one another and honor one another." (Midrash Tanna D'Bei Eliyahu Rabbah 26)

כָּל־מַחֲלֹקֶת שֶׁהִיא לְשֵׁם שָׁמַיִם סוֹפָהּ לְהִתְקַיֵּם. וְשֶׁאֵינָהּ לְשֵׁם שָׁמַיִם אֵין סוֹפָהּ לְהִתְקַיֵּם. אֵיזוֹ הִיא מַחֲלֹקֶת שֶׁהִיא לְשֵׁם שָׁמַיִם? זוֹ מַחֲלֹקֶת הִלֵּל וְשַׁמַּאי. וְשֶׁאֵינָהּ לְשֵׁם שָׁמַיִם? זוֹ מַחֲלֹקֶת קֹרַח וְכָל־עֲדָתוֹ.

Every controversy that is for the sake of Heaven will bear fruit. And one that is not for the sake of Heaven will not bear fruit.

What is a controversy for the sake of Heaven? That of Hillel and Shammai. And one not for the sake of Heaven? That of Korach and his cabal [Numbers 16].

🖙 In their debates one of them would render a decision and the other would argue against it, out of a desire to discover the truth, not out of the wish to prevail. That is why, when he was right, the words of the one who disagreed, endured. (Meiri, Provence, 13th-14th century)

יְהוּדָה בֶן תֵּימָא אוֹמֵר: הֱוֵי עַז כַּנָּמֵר, וְקַל כַּנֶּשֶׁר, וְרָץ כַּצְּבִי, וְגִבּוֹר כָּאֲרִי לַעֲשׂוֹת רְצוֹן אָבִיךָ שֶׁבַּשָּׁמַיִם.

Judah ben Tema says: Be bold as a leopard, light as an eagle, swift as a gazelle, and strong as a lion to do the will of your God.

בֶּן בַּג בַּג אוֹמֵר: הֲפָךְ בָּהּ, וְהַפָךְ בָּהּ, דְּכֻלָּא בָהּ; וּבָהּ תֶּחֱזֵי, וְסִיב וּבְלֵה בַהּ, וּמִנַּהּ לָא תְזוּעַ, שֶׁאֵין לָךְ מִדָּה טוֹבָה הֵימֶנָּה.

Ben Bag Bag says: Turn it and turn it again, for everything is in it; reflect on it and grow old and gray in it and do not move away from it, for there is no better way than this.

ℒ Ben Bag Bag comes to warn us not to be content with a superficial reading of the Torah; on the contrary, let us go over it again and again. As the sages in the Talmud teach us (Chagigah 9b): "One who studies a text one hundred times cannot be compared with one who studies it one hundred and one times." (Meiri)

FROM CHAPTER VI

וְאוֹמֵר: וְהַלֻּחֹת מַעֲשֵׂה אֱלֹהִים הֵמָּה, וְהַמִּכְתָּב מִכְתַּב אֱלֹהִים
הוּא, חָרוּת עַל הַלֻּחֹת. אַל תִּקְרָא חָרוּת אֶלָּא חֵרוּת, שֶׁאֵין
לְךָ בֶּן חוֹרִין אֶלָּא מִי שֶׁעוֹסֵק בְּתַלְמוּד תּוֹרָה.

The Torah says (Exodus 32:16): And the tablets [given to Moses] were God's own work, and the writing was God's own writing engraved on the tablets. Do not read it as *charut* (engraved) but as *cheirut* (freedom), for no one is free except one engaged in the study of Torah.

❦

REFLECTIONS FOR TROUBLED HOURS

PSALM 23

❖ See "Selected
Psalms," pages
358-375, and
"A Daily
Psalm," pages
27-33.

מִזְמוֹר לְדָוִד

A SONG OF DAVID

יְהוָה רֹעִי, לֹא אֶחְסָר. בִּנְאוֹת
דֶּשֶׁא יַרְבִּיצֵנִי, עַל־מֵי מְנֻחוֹת
יְנַהֲלֵנִי. נַפְשִׁי יְשׁוֹבֵב; יַנְחֵנִי
בְמַעְגְּלֵי־צֶדֶק לְמַעַן שְׁמוֹ.
גַּם כִּי־אֵלֵךְ בְּגֵיא צַלְמָוֶת
לֹא־אִירָא רָע, כִּי־אַתָּה
עִמָּדִי: שִׁבְטְךָ וּמִשְׁעַנְתֶּךָ,
הֵמָּה יְנַחֲמֻנִי. תַּעֲרֹךְ לְפָנַי
שֻׁלְחָן נֶגֶד צֹרְרָי, דִּשַּׁנְתָּ
בַשֶּׁמֶן רֹאשִׁי, כּוֹסִי רְוָיָה.
אַךְ טוֹב וָחֶסֶד יִרְדְּפוּנִי
כָּל־יְמֵי חַיָּי, וְשַׁבְתִּי בְּבֵית־
יְהוָה לְאֹרֶךְ יָמִים.

Adonai, You are my shepherd, I shall not want. You make me lie down in green pastures, You lead me beside still waters. You restore my soul; You guide me in paths of righteousness for the sake of Your name.

Yes, even when I walk through the valley of the shadow of death, I shall fear no evil, for You are with me; with rod and staff You comfort me. You prepare a table before me in the presence of my enemies; You have anointed my head with oil; my cup overflows. Surely, goodness and mercy shall follow me all the days of my life, and I shall dwell in the house of my God forever.

ACCEPTANCE

I thank You, God, for the glory of late days and the excellent face of Your sun. I thank You for good news received. I thank You for the pleasures I have enjoyed and for those I have been able to confer. And now, when the clouds gather and the rain impends, permit me not to be cast down; let me

341

not lose the savor of past mercies and past pleasures; but, like the voice of a bird singing in the rain, let grateful memory survive in the hour of darkness. Amen.

SYMPATHY

I have always said that the way to deal with the pain of others is by sympathy, which in first-year Greek they taught me meant "suffering with," and that the way to deal with one's own pain is to put one foot after the other.

REFLECTIONS

Rabbi Samuel ben Nachmani said: At times the gates of prayer are open, at times the gates of prayer are barred. But the gates of repentance are never barred.

But it is reported that Rabbi Judah the Prince taught: In truth, the gates of prayer are never barred.

Rabbi Akiba taught: The gates of prayer are open, and the prayer of those who practice steadfast love is heard.

Rav Chisda taught: Though sometimes the gates of heaven seem shut to all prayers, they are open to the prayers of the wounded and the hurt.

CHOOSING OUR OWN SORROWS

Whenever the Chasidim would enter into competition, each claiming to have the most trouble and to have endured the greatest suffering (and therefore had earned the right to be the first to complain), the rebbe would tell them the story of the Tree of Sorrows.

"On Judgment Day," said he, "I, like everyone else, will be allowed to hang all my unhappiness on a branch of the great Tree of Sorrows. Then, when I have found a limb from which my sorrows can dangle, I will walk slowly around that tree. Do you know what I will do on that walk? I will search for a set of sufferings I might prefer to those I have hung on the tree. But search as I may, I will not find any. In the end, like everyone else, I will freely choose to reclaim my own personal set of sorrows rather than that of another. I will leave that tree wiser than when I got there."

HEALING OF THE SOUL

Help me, O God, help me; in my weakness, bring out the strength You have given me; in my fear, bring the faith that You have lodged within me; in my despair, renew my hope within me; and in my stumbling, show me that there is a rock on which I can stand firm. Above all, O God, remind me that even though I give myself over to my anger and pain, the sun will continue to shine.

FOR PEACE OF SOUL

In my great need for light I look to You, the source of life and light. Eternal God, help me to feel Your presence even when dark shadows fall upon me. When my own weakness and the storms of life hide You from my sight, help me to know that You have not deserted me. Uphold me with the comfort of Your love! Give me trust, O God; give me peace, and give me light. May my heart find its rest in You.

USING OUR PAINS TO HELP OTHERS

O God, help me to plant a flower in the scarred earth; show me a soul in pain whose suffering I can alleviate; grant me the grace to live through my own sorrow and not to give it to another. And what I cannot change, let me endure, until, unasked, it passes from my view.

HOPE

O God of hope, be with me when hope seems foolish; O God of light, be with me when day grows dark; O God of life, be with me when life seems to have lost its meaning.

ACCEPTING TIME AND CHANGE

We learn, slowly but undeniably, that nothing belongs to us, completely, finally. The job is ended, the children grow up and move away, even the money (when there is money) buys little that we want. For what we want cannot be bought. And it is then, if ever, that we learn to make our peace with destiny; to accept the fact that our dreams have been half-realized, or unrealized; that we did not do what we set out to do; that our goals have receded as we approached them. There may be a sadness in this prospect, but also a serenity. Illusions lose their power to disturb us; we value life by what it has given us, not by the promise of tomorrow. For only by accepting time can we, in a measure, learn to conquer it.

GOD REDEEMS US

Shall we live forever
and avoid the sight of a grave?
Alike the wise and the foolish end their days,
leaving their wealth to others.
They imagine their houses will last forever,
their homes for countless generations;
they give their names to streets and towns:
But human splendor does not last—
we are animals, we pass away.
But God, upon taking me,
will redeem my spirit from death's dark hand. (From Psalms)

COURAGE

In my darkness be a light to me,
in my loneliness help me to find
a soul akin to my own.
Give me strength
to live with courage.
And give me courage
to draw blessing from life:
even in the midst of suffering;
to hold fast against the storm,
and to smile at a loved one's glance.

VISION AND FAITH

When the darkness is too dark for me, give me light, O
source of light. Renew my vision, my hope, my dream, my
faith that the darkness does not last, the sense that despair
will not be the last word, and the courage to go on believing
in my vision.

ON SUFFERING

Each day must contain the service of God even if it is also a
day of suffering. Like much that is sent into our life,
suffering sometimes comes to us independently of our
volition; but we must shape it. Our task is to make that part
of our life into which suffering has entered a portion of
God's dominion. Thus to suffering, too, the command
applies: "You shall love Adonai your God with all your
heart, with all your mind, with all your being."

WHAT WE CAN PRAY FOR

Let us not pray that God make our lives free of problems. . . .
Nor ask God to make us and those we love immune to
disease. . . . Nor should we ask God to weave a magic spell
around us so that bad things will happen only to other

people, and never to us. . . . But people who pray for courage, for strength to bear the unbearable, for the grace to remember what they have left instead of what they have lost, very often find their prayers answered. They discover that they have more strength, more courage than they ever knew themselves to have. We cannot escape suffering, but we may find God in spite of it, and even within it.

ON TAKING GOOD HEALTH FOR GRANTED

After a long illness, I was permitted for the first time to step out-of-doors. And as I crossed the threshold sunlight greeted me. . . . So long as I live, I shall never forget that moment. . . . The sky overhead was very blue, very clear, and very, very high. . . . A faint wind blew from off the western plains, cool and yet somehow tinged with warmth—like a dry, chilled wine. And everywhere in the firmament above me, in the great vault between the earth and sky, on the pavements, the buildings—the golden glow of sunlight. It touched me, too, with friendship, with warmth, with blessing. And as I basked in its glory there ran through my mind those wonderful words of the prophet:

וְזָרְחָה לָכֶם יִרְאֵי שְׁמִי שֶׁמֶשׁ צְדָקָה וּמַרְפֵּא בִּכְנָפֶיהָ.

"For you who revere God's name the sun of righteousness shall rise with healing on its wings."

In that instant I looked about me to see whether anyone else showed on their face the joy, almost the beatitude, I felt. But no, there they walked—men and women and children, in the glory of the golden flood, and so far as I could detect, there was none to give it heed. And then I remembered how often I, too, had been indifferent to the sunlight, how often, preoccupied with petty and sometimes mean concerns, I had disregarded it. And I said to myself: How precious is the sunlight but alas, how careless of it we are.

LOOKING AT OURSELVES

OUR RANGE OF VISION

The astonishing thing about the human being is not so much his intellect and bodily structure, profoundly mysterious as they are. The astonishing and least comprehensible thing about him is his range of vision; his gaze into the infinite distance; his lonely passion for ideas and ideals . . . for which . . . he will stand until he dies; the profound conviction he entertains that if nothing is worth dying for nothing is worth living for.

CHANGING OUR MINDS

We sometimes find ourselves changing our minds without any resistance or heavy emotion, but told that we are wrong, we resent the imputation and harden our hearts. It is obviously not the ideas themselves that are dear to us, but our self-esteem, which is threatened.

TWO TRUTHS

One should always keep two truths in separate pockets and take them out as needed: In the first, *For my sake the world was created*. In the second, *I am but dust and ashes*. (Chasidic)

WHEN WE ARE WORTHY OF OURSELVES

Dust as we are, the immortal spirit grows
Like harmony in music; there is a dark
Inscrutable workmanship that reconciles
Discordant elements, makes them cling together
In one society. How strange that all
The terrors, pains, and early miseries,
Regrets, vexations, lassitudes interfused
Within my mind, should e'er have borne a part,
And that a needful part, in making up

The calm existence that is mine when I
Am worthy of myself! Praise to the end! . . .

WHAT DO WE TEACH OUR CHILDREN?

Each second we live is a new and unique moment of the
universe, a moment that never was before and never will be
again. And what do we teach our children in school? We
teach them that two and two make four, and that Paris is the
capital of France. When will we also teach them what they
are? We should say to each of them: Do you know what you
are? You are a marvel. You are unique. In all the world there
is no other child exactly like you. In the millions of years that
have passed there has never been another child like you.
And look at your body—what a wonder it is; your legs, your
arms, your cunning fingers, the way you move! You may
become a Shakespeare, a Michelangelo, a Beethoven. You
have the capacity for anything. Yes, you are a marvel. And
when you grow up, can you then harm another who is, like
you, a marvel? You must work—we must all work—to make
this world worthy of its children.

WHAT GIVES LIFE ITS WORTH?

It may be that death gives all there is of worth to life. If those
we press and strain within our arms could never die,
perhaps that love would wither from the earth. Maybe this
common fate treads from out the paths between our hearts
the weeds of selfishness and hate. And I had rather live and
love where death is king, than have eternal life where love is
not.

THE WORST QUALITY

Of all qualities, sadness is the worst. It is the attribute of the
incurable egotist, who is always thinking: "This should have

been mine; I have been wrongfully deprived of that." It is always I. (Chasidic)

I am afraid of things that cannot harm me, and I know it. I yearn for things that cannot help me, and I know it. What I fear is within me, and within me, too, is what I seek. (Chasidic)

WE MUST LOOK AT OURSELVES

I cannot find redemption until I see the flaws in my own soul, and try to correct them. Nor can a people be redeemed until it sees the flaws in its own soul, and tries to correct them. But whether it be an individual or a people, if we shut out the realization of our own flaws we are shutting out redemption. (Chasidic)

HOW TO LOOK AT YOURSELF

The Baal Shem Tov said: It is not good to be alone, for one cannot know one's own defects. Other people are mirrors, in which you can discover your own flaws by observing the acts you dislike in them. In fact, it is only because you share them yourself in some degree, that you can see another person's flaws. (Chasidic/Rabbi Chaim Stern)

WHAT YOU ARE

Tell me what you pay attention to and I will tell you what you are.

FALLING

O God, help me get up; I can fall down by myself. (Yiddish proverb)

We fall not because we are weak but because we think we are strong. (Yiddish proverb)

THE DOUBLE STANDARD

The vices we scoff at in others laugh at us within ourselves.

How easy to see another's fault, how hard to perceive one's own! We winnow our neighbor's faults like chaff and conceal our own, like a cheat with loaded dice.

FEAR

For hunger or for love they bite or tear,
Whilst wretched man is still in arms for fear;
For fear he arms, and is of arms afraid,
From fear to fear successively betrayed.

HUMILITY

I do not know what I may appear to the world, but to myself I seem to have been only a boy playing on the seashore, and diverting myself in now and then finding a smoother pebble or a prettier shell than ordinary, whilst the great ocean of truth lay all undiscovered before me.

THE ONE HUMAN BEING

Creation began with one human being: if you cause a single life to perish you cause a whole world to perish; and if you save a single life you save a whole world. . . . Therefore let every human being say: For my sake the world was created. (Mishnah Sanhedrin 4.5)

One righteous human being is equal to the whole world, as it is said (Proverbs 10.25): *The righteous is the foundation of the world.* (Midrash Tanchuma, Beshallach, 10)

IF ONLY

Could we but live at will upon this perfect height,
Could we but always keep the passion of this peace,
Could we but face unshamed the look of this pure light,

Could we but win earth's heart and give desire release,
Then were we all divine, and then were ours by right
These stars, these nightingales, these scents; then shame
would cease.

BOOMERANG

Whoever battles with monsters had better see to it that it
does not turn him into a monster. And if you gaze long into
an abyss, the abyss will gaze back into you.

THE COURAGE TO DECIDE

The greatest mistake you can make in life is to be continually
fearing you will make one.

There is always a multitude of reasons both in favour of doing a thing and against doing it. The art of debate lies in
presenting them; the art of life lies in neglecting ninety-nine
hundredths of them.

WHO WE ARE

What is the ultimate truth about ourselves? Various answers
suggest themselves. We are bits of stellar matter gone
wrong. We are physical machinery—puppets that strut and
laugh and die. But there is one inescapable answer. We are
that which asks the question. Whatever else there may be in
our nature, responsibility to truth is one of its attributes. . . .
In our own nature, or through the contact of our consciousness with a nature transcending ours, there are things that
claim the same kind of recognition—a sense of beauty, or
morality, and finally . . . an experience which we describe as
the presence of God.

LOOKING FOR GOD

REALIZATION

God does not want to be believed in, to be debated and defended by us, but simply to be realized through us.

KNOWLEDGE AND FAITH

It is not necessary to know something of God in order really to believe in God; many true believers know how to talk to God but not about God.

WITNESSING

Rabbi Simeon ben Yochai says: "You are my witnesses, says Adonai, and I am God." (Isaiah 43:10) When you *are* my witnesses, I am God; but when you are *not* my witnesses, I am, as it were, not God. (Midrash Sifre Deuteronomy 346)

TREMBLE AT THE LIGHT

The story is told of a Chasid who was ushered into the Tzaddik's presence for an audience. He was trembling with awe to be in the same room as the holy man. When the Tzaddik noticed this, he said: "Any piece of glass will reflect light. Tremble at the Light, not at the glass." (Chasidic)

TRUTH AND REPOSE

God offers to every mind the choice between truth and repose. Take which you please; you can never have both.

IN THE DEPTHS

Rabbi Uri of Strelisk taught: The psalmist says (Psalm 139): *If I ascend to the heavens, You are there; if I make my bed in the lowest depths, behold, You are there!* When I think myself great and think I can touch the sky, I discover that the higher I reach, God is higher still, and far beyond my grasp. But if I make my bed in the depths, if I bow my soul down to the depths, God is there with me. (Chasidic)

HIDE AND SEEK

Rabbi Baruch's grandson Yechiel was once playing hide-and-seek with another boy. He hid himself well and waited for his playmate to find him. When, after a long wait, he came out of his hiding-place, the other was nowhere to be seen. It seemed his friend had not looked for him at all!

That made him cry and, crying, he ran to his grandfather and complained of his friend. Then tears brimmed in Rabbi Baruch's eyes, and he said: God says the same thing: I hide, but no one comes looking for Me. (Chasidic)

SEEING HEAVEN

Earth's crammed with heaven,
And every common bush afire with God!
But only he who sees, takes off his shoes.

THE UNKNOWABLE

All religious reality begins with what Biblical religion calls the "fear of God." It comes when our existence between birth and death becomes incomprehensible . . ., when all security is shattered through the mystery. This is not the relative mystery of that which is inaccessible only to the present state of human knowledge and is hence in principle discoverable. It is the essential mystery, the inscrutableness of which belongs to its very nature; it is the unknowable.

ONLY METAPHOR WILL DO

We can speak only in metaphor of the eternal and infinite. If we wish to describe the indescribable, we can do so only by poetry. All endeavors to reach God by words resolve themselves into religious poetry. When we experience the hidden, the unfathomable, we can respond with the devoutness of silence . . . and with poetry and prayer we can sing of the ineffable.

WORSHIP

The best worship of God is silence and hope.

THE COURAGE TO DOUBT

In the saints [doubt] appears, according to holy legend, as a temptation that increases in power with the increase of saintliness. In those who rest on their unshakable faith, . . . fanaticism [is] the unmistakable symptom of doubt which has been repressed. Doubt is overcome not by repression but by courage. Courage does not deny that there is doubt. . . . Courage does not need the safety of unquestionable conviction. It includes the risk without which no creative life is possible.

CONFINING GOD

The men and women in the Bible are sinners like ourselves, but there is one sin they do not commit, our arch-sin: they do not dare confine God to a circumscribed space or division of life, "religion." They have not the insolence to draw boundaries around God's commandments and say: "Up to this point You are sovereign, but beyond these bounds begins the sovereignty of science or society or the state."

GOD IN THE WORLD

God is in the world, or nowhere, creating continually in us and around us. This creative principle is everywhere, in animate and so-called inanimate matter, in the ether, water, earth, human hearts. . . . In so far as . . . [we] partake of this creative process . . . [do] we partake of the divine, of God.

GIVING THANKS

The older we get, the greater becomes our inclination to give thanks, especially heavenwards. We feel more strongly . . . that life is a gift. . . .

But we also feel . . . an urge to thank our brothers and sisters, even if they have not done anything special for us. For what, then? For really meeting me when we met; for opening your eyes, and not mistaking me for someone else; for opening your ears, and listening carefully to what I had to say to you; indeed, for opening up to me what I really want to address—your securely locked heart.

SEEING GOD

Why should I wish to see God better than this day?
I see something of God each hour of the twenty-four, and each moment then;
In the faces of men and women I see God, and in my own face in the glass,
I find letters from God dropt in the street, and ev'ry one is sign'd by God's name,
And I leave them where they are, for I know that where-soe'er I go,
Others will punctually come forever and ever.

THE MYSTERY

Rabbi Chanina bar Isi said: There are times when the entire universe cannot contain the glory of God, yet there are times when God speaks to us even in the trembling of the hairs on our heads. (Midrash Genesis Rabbah 4:4)

Looking for God

FROM PSALM 139

אָנָה אֵלֵךְ מֵרוּחֶךָ? וְאָנָה מִפָּנֶיךָ אֶבְרָח?

אִם־אֶסַּק שָׁמַיִם, שָׁם אָתָּה! וְאַצִּיעָה שְׁאוֹל, הִנֶּךָּ!

❖ See
"Selected
Psalms,"
pages 358-375,
and "A Daily
Psalm," pages
27-33.

Whither can I go from your spirit?
Whither can I flee from your presence?
If I go up to the heavens, You are there!
If I make my home in the lowest depths, behold,
You are there!

אֶשָּׂא כַנְפֵי־שָׁחַר, אֶשְׁכְּנָה בְּאַחֲרִית יָם,

גַּם־שָׁם יָדְךָ תַנְחֵנִי, וְתֹאחֲזֵנִי יְמִינֶךָ.

If I fly up on the wings of the morning,
and dwell on the ocean's farthest shore,
even there your hand leads me,
your strong hand holds me.

וָאֹמַר: אַךְ־חֹשֶׁךְ יְשׁוּפֵנִי, וְלַיְלָה אוֹר בַּעֲדֵנִי,

גַּם־חֹשֶׁךְ לֹא־יַחְשִׁיךְ מִמֶּךָ, וְלַיְלָה כַּיּוֹם יָאִיר!

And if I say: Yes, the darkness will hide me,
the light will turn into night for me—
even darkness is not dark for You,
for whom night is bright as the day!

אוֹדְךָ, עַל כִּי נוֹרָאוֹת נִפְלֵיתִי; נִפְלָאִים מַעֲשֶׂיךָ,

וְנַפְשִׁי יֹדַעַת מְאֹד.

I who am a miracle of your making, praise You;
wonderful are your works; my heart knows it well.

חָקְרֵנִי, אֵל, וְדַע לְבָבִי; בְּחָנֵנִי, וְדַע שַׂרְעַפָּי.

וּרְאֵה אִם־דֶּרֶךְ־עֹצֶב בִּי, וּנְחֵנִי בְּדֶרֶךְ עוֹלָם.

356

Search me, O God, and know my heart;
test me, and consider my thoughts.
See if my ways lead to sorrow,
and lead me, instead, on a way that is everlasting.

FAITH

In Judaism, faith is the capacity of the soul to perceive the abiding in the transitory, the invisible in the visible.

Give me a God worthy of worship, worthy of the stars in all their radiance, of the splendor in which we walk, and of the mystery that surrounds us at every turning. O, and make me aware of this grandeur!

Faith is not an insurance but a constant effort, constant listening to the eternal voice. . . . To have faith means to justify God's faith in us. . . . Religion is not a feeling for something that is, but an answer to the One who is asking us to live in a certain way. It is in its very origin a consciousness of duty, of being committed to higher ends.

(

I wonder if
anything is impossible
to a God
who can make
evergreen trees with black trunks
cast blue shadows
on white snow.

&

SELECTED PSALMS

FROM PSALM 3—SAFE IN GOD'S HAND

יְהוָה, מָה־רַבּוּ צָרָי, רַבִּים קָמִים עָלָי!

רַבִּים אֹמְרִים לְנַפְשִׁי, אֵין יְשׁוּעָתָה לּוֹ בֵאלֹהִים! סֶלָה.

✣ See "A Daily Psalm," pages 27-33.

HOW MANY ARE MY FOES, ADONAI, how many rise up against me! How many say of me, O God, that You will not help me!

וְאַתָּה יְהוָה מָגֵן בַּעֲדִי, כְּבוֹדִי וּמֵרִים רֹאשִׁי!

קוֹלִי אֶל־יְהוָה אֶקְרָא, וַיַּעֲנֵנִי מֵהַר קָדְשׁוֹ. סֶלָה.

אֲנִי שָׁכַבְתִּי וָאִישָׁנָה, הֱקִיצוֹתִי, כִּי יְהוָה יִסְמְכֵנִי.

O, but You are the shield that covers me,
my glory who keeps my head high!
I cry out to You, Adonai,
and from Your holy mountain
Your answer comes.
I lie down and sleep,
and then I am awake, safe in Your hands.

קוּמָה, יְהוָה; הוֹשִׁיעֵנִי, אֱלֹהַי,

לַיהוָה הַיְשׁוּעָה, עַל־עַמְּךָ בִרְכָתֶךָ. סֶלָה.

Rise up, Adonai; help me, O my God,
for You are the one from whom help comes,
and Your blessing rests upon Your people.

FROM PSALM 4—WE CAN LIVE UNAFRAID

בְּקָרְאִי, עֲנֵנִי, אֱלֹהֵי צִדְקִי.

בַּצָּר הִרְחַבְתָּ לִּי; חָנֵּנִי וּשְׁמַע תְּפִלָּתִי.

בְּנֵי אִישׁ, עַד־מֶה כְבוֹדִי לִכְלִמָּה,

תֶּאֱהָבוּן רִיק תְּבַקְשׁוּ כָזָב? סֶלָה.

רִגְזוּ וְאַל־תֶּחֱטָאוּ;

אִמְרוּ בִלְבַבְכֶם עַל־מִשְׁכַּבְכֶם, וְדֹמּוּ. סֶלָה.

WHEN I CRY OUT, BE MY ANSWER, O God, my champion.
From every tight spot You have set me free;
show me grace again and hear my plea.

Great ones of the world,
how long will you try to dishonor me, put me to shame?
How long will you love illusions and run after lies?
Tremble, then, and sin no more;
look into your hearts as you lie abed, and hold your peace.

זִבְחוּ זִבְחֵי־צֶדֶק, וּבִטְחוּ אֶל־יהוה.

רַבִּים אֹמְרִים: מִי־יַרְאֵנוּ טוֹב, נְסָה־עָלֵינוּ אוֹר פָּנֶיךָ, יהוה!

נָתַתָּה שִׂמְחָה בְלִבִּי, מֵעֵת דְּגָנָם וְתִירוֹשָׁם רָבּוּ.

בְּשָׁלוֹם יַחְדָּו אֶשְׁכְּבָה, וְאִישָׁן;

כִּי־אַתָּה, יהוה, לְבָדָד לָבֶטַח תּוֹשִׁיבֵנִי.

Let your offering be justice, and trust in Adonai.
Many say, "O, that we could be shown some good,
but the light of Your countenance has fled from us, Adonai!"

Yet You have put joy in my heart,
more than others rejoice from a rich crop of grain and wine.
Now I will lie down in peace, and sleep;
for You alone, Adonai, make me live unafraid.

FROM PSALM 13—
WHEN WE ARE DOWN AND SEEMINGLY ABANDONED

עַד־אָנָה, יהוה, תִּשְׁכָּחֵנִי נֶצַח?

עַד־אָנָה תַּסְתִּיר אֶת־פָּנֶיךָ מִמֶּנִּי?

HOW LONG, ADONAI, must I go unremembered?
How long will You turn Your face from me?

עַד־אָנָה אָשִׁית עֵצוֹת בְּנַפְשִׁי, יָגוֹן בִּלְבָבִי יוֹמָם?

עַד־אָנָה יָרוּם אֹיְבִי עָלָי?

How long must my soul be torn,
my heart be filled with grief day after day: how long?
How long shall my enemy have the upper hand?

הַבִּיטָה עֲנֵנִי, יהוה אֱלֹהָי; הָאִירָה עֵינַי, פֶּן־אִישַׁן הַמָּוֶת,

פֶּן־יֹאמַר אֹיְבִי: יְכָלְתִּיו, צָרַי יָגִילוּ כִּי אֶמּוֹט.

Look at me and answer, Adonai my God; give light to these
eyes of mine, lest I sleep death's sleep, lest my enemy say: "I
have prevailed," and my foes rejoice to see me fall.

וַאֲנִי, בְּחַסְדְּךָ בָטַחְתִּי; יָגֵל לִבִּי בִּישׁוּעָתֶךָ.

אָשִׁירָה לַיהוָה, כִּי גָמַל עָלָי!

As for me, I will trust in Your unfailing love;
my heart will rejoice in Your deliverance.
I will sing to Adonai, who has shown me such goodness!

FROM PSALM 25—FINDING OUR WAY

אֵלֶיךָ, יהוה, נַפְשִׁי אֶשָּׂא.

אֱלֹהַי, בְּךָ בָטַחְתִּי; אַל־אֵבוֹשָׁה;

גַּם כָּל־קֹוֶיךָ לֹא יֵבֹשׁוּ.

TO YOU, ADONAI, my soul ascends. In You, O God, have I put my trust; I shall not be shamed. Indeed, none who wait for You shall be shamed.

דְּרָכֶיךָ יהוה, הוֹדִיעֵנִי; אֹרְחוֹתֶיךָ לַמְּדֵנִי.
הַדְרִיכֵנִי בַאֲמִתֶּךָ וְלַמְּדֵנִי, כִּי־אַתָּה אֱלֹהֵי יִשְׁעִי,
אוֹתְךָ קִוִּיתִי כָּל־הַיּוֹם.

Let me know Your ways, Adonai; teach me Your paths.
In Your faithfulness lead me and teach me,
as You are God my help,
the one for whom I wait all the day.

זְכֹר־רַחֲמֶיךָ, יהוה, וַחֲסָדֶיךָ, כִּי מֵעוֹלָם הֵמָּה.
חַטֹּאות נְעוּרַי וּפְשָׁעַי אַל־תִּזְכֹּר; כְּחַסְדְּךָ זְכָר־לִי־אַתָּה;
לְמַעַן טוּבְךָ יהוה.

Remember Your compassion and Your unfailing love,
Adonai, for they are from time's beginning.
Remember no more the sins of my youth;
no, remember me with Your unfailing love;
Adonai, make Your goodness manifest.

טוֹב־וְיָשָׁר יהוה, עַל־כֵּן יוֹרֶה חַטָּאִים בַּדָּרֶךְ,
יַדְרֵךְ עֲנָוִים בַּמִּשְׁפָּט, וִילַמֵּד עֲנָוִים דַּרְכּוֹ.
כָּל־אָרְחוֹת יהוה חֶסֶד וֶאֱמֶת.

How good God is, teaching sinners the right way,
leading the humble toward justice,
teaching the humble God's way.
All God's paths are kindness and truth.

מִי־זֶה הָאִישׁ יְרֵא יהוה יוֹרֶנּוּ בְּדֶרֶךְ יִבְחָר.
נַפְשׁוֹ בְּטוֹב תָּלִין, וְזַרְעוֹ יִירַשׁ אָרֶץ.

Those who fear God are taught the way to choose.
Their souls dwell in goodness,
their children shall inherit the earth.

FROM PSALM 27—WHAT TO ASK OF GOD

אַחַת שָׁאַלְתִּי מֵאֵת־יהוה, אוֹתָהּ אֲבַקֵּשׁ׃
שִׁבְתִּי בְּבֵית־יהוה כָּל־יְמֵי חַיַּי.
כִּי יִצְפְּנֵנִי בְּסֻכֹּה בְּיוֹם רָעָה,
יַסְתִּרֵנִי בְּסֵתֶר אָהֳלוֹ, בְּצוּר יְרוֹמְמֵנִי.

THIS ONLY DO I ASK, Adonai, only this:
to live in Your house all the days of my life:
Keep me safe in Your tent when evil days come,
shelter me, set me high upon a rock.

שְׁמַע־יהוה קוֹלִי אֶקְרָא, וְחָנֵּנִי וַעֲנֵנִי.
לְךָ אָמַר לִבִּי: בַּקְּשׁוּ פָנָי,
אֶת־פָּנֶיךָ, יהוה, אֲבַקֵּשׁ.
אַל־תַּסְתֵּר פָּנֶיךָ מִמֶּנִּי,
אַל־תִּטְּשֵׁנִי וְאַל־תַּעַזְבֵנִי, אֱלֹהֵי יִשְׁעִי.

Hear my voice when I call, Adonai,
be gracious and answer me.
My heart tells me to seek You,
and Your presence is what I seek.
God my help, do not hide Your face, do not forsake me!

הוֹרֵנִי, יהוה, דַּרְכֶּךָ,
וּנְחֵנִי בְּאֹרַח מִישׁוֹר,
לוּלֵא הֶאֱמַנְתִּי לִרְאוֹת בְּטוּב־יהוה בְּאֶרֶץ חַיִּים.

Selected Psalms

Teach me Your way, Adonai,
and lead me in a straight path,
still believing I shall see Your goodness
in the land of the living.

FROM PSALMS 42 AND 43—A PLEA FOR LIGHT AND TRUTH

כְּאַיָּל תַּעֲרֹג עַל־אֲפִיקֵי־מָיִם, כֵּן נַפְשִׁי תַעֲרֹג אֵלֶיךָ, אֱלֹהִים.

צָמְאָה נַפְשִׁי לֵאלֹהִים, לְאֵל חָי: מָתַי אָבוֹא וְאֵרָאֶה פְּנֵי אֱלֹהִים?

הָיְתָה־לִּי דִמְעָתִי לֶחֶם יוֹמָם וָלָיְלָה, בֶּאֱמֹר אֵלַי כָּל־הַיּוֹם:

אַיֵּה אֱלֹהֶיךָ?

AS A DEER LONGS for flowing streams,
so does my soul long for You, O God.
My soul thirsts for God, for the living God:
when shall I come to see God's face?
Day and night my tears have been my bread,
as all day long they say to me: Where is your God?

אֵלֶּה אֶזְכְּרָה וְאֶשְׁפְּכָה עָלַי נַפְשִׁי: כִּי אֶעֱבֹר בַּסָּךְ אֶדַּדֵּם

עַד־בֵּית אֱלֹהִים, בְּקוֹל־רִנָּה וְתוֹדָה הָמוֹן חוֹגֵג.

This I remember as I pour out my soul:
going with the festive crowd to the house of God,
to the sound of song and thanksgiving.

תְּהוֹם־אֶל־תְּהוֹם קוֹרֵא לְקוֹל צִנּוֹרֶיךָ; כָּל־מִשְׁבָּרֶיךָ וְגַלֶּיךָ

עָלַי עָבָרוּ. יוֹמָם יְצַוֶּה יהוה חַסְדּוֹ, וּבַלַּיְלָה שִׁירֹה עִמִּי,

תְּפִלָּה לְאֵל חַיָּי.

Deep calls to deep at the roar of the cataracts;
Your waves and breakers have passed over me.
By day Adonai ordains kindness, and at night
God's song is in me, a prayer to the God of my life.

363

שְׁלַח־אוֹרְךָ וַאֲמִתְּךָ, הֵמָּה יַנְחוּנִי, יְבִיאוּנִי אֶל־הַר־קָדְשְׁךָ,
וְאֶל־מִשְׁכְּנוֹתֶיךָ, וְאָבוֹאָה אֶל־מִזְבַּח אֱלֹהִים, אֶל־אֵל
שִׂמְחַת גִּילִי, וְאוֹדְךָ בְכִנּוֹר, אֱלֹהִים אֱלֹהָי!

Send out Your light and Your truth; let them lead me, let
them bring me to Your holy mountain, to Your dwelling-
place, that I may come to the altar of God, to God my highest
joy, and praise You with the harp, O God my God!

FROM PSALM 51—WHAT GOD WANTS FROM US

חָנֵּנִי אֱלֹהִים כְּחַסְדֶּךָ, כְּרֹב רַחֲמֶיךָ מְחֵה פְשָׁעָי.
כִּי־פְשָׁעַי אֲנִי אֵדָע; וְחַטָּאתִי נֶגְדִּי תָמִיד.

IN YOUR KINDNESS show me grace, O God;
wipe out my transgressions in the fullness of Your mercy.
For I acknowledge my transgressions, and my sin is ever
before me.

לְךָ לְבַדְּךָ חָטָאתִי, וְהָרַע בְּעֵינֶיךָ עָשִׂיתִי—לְמַעַן תִּצְדַּק בְּדָבְרֶךָ,
תִּזְכֶּה בְשָׁפְטֶךָ. הֵן־אֱמֶת חָפַצְתָּ בַטֻּחוֹת; וּבְסָתֻם חָכְמָה תוֹדִיעֵנִי.

You alone have I sinned against, doing wrong in Your sight—
so let Your word be seen as just, Your decrees as right.
For it is inner truth You want from us;
You show me the wisdom of the heart's secret places.

תַּשְׁמִיעֵנִי שָׂשׂוֹן וְשִׂמְחָה;
לֵב טָהוֹר בְּרָא־לִי, אֱלֹהִים, וְרוּחַ נָכוֹן חַדֵּשׁ בְּקִרְבִּי.

Let me hear tidings of joy and gladness;
Create in me a clean heart, O God,
and renew a willing spirit within me.

אַל־תַּשְׁלִיכֵנִי מִלְּפָנֶיךָ, וְרוּחַ קָדְשְׁךָ אַל־תִּקַּח מִמֶּנִּי.
הָשִׁיבָה לִּי שְׂשׂוֹן יִשְׁעֶךָ, וְרוּחַ נְדִיבָה תִסְמְכֵנִי.

Do not drive me away from Your presence,
and do not deprive me of Your holy spirit.
Return to me the joy of Your help,
and let a generous spirit uphold me.

אֲדֹנָי, שְׂפָתַי תִּפְתָּח, וּפִי יַגִּיד תְּהִלָּתֶךָ.
כִּי לֹא־תַחְפֹּץ זֶבַח וְאֶתֵּנָה; עוֹלָה לֹא תִרְצֶה:
זִבְחֵי אֱלֹהִים רוּחַ נִשְׁבָּרָה; לֵב־נִשְׁבָּר וְנִדְכֶּה אֱלֹהִים לֹא תִבְזֶה.

Adonai, open my lips,
and my mouth will declare Your praise.
For if You desire sacrifices I would give them;
but burnt-offerings do not please You:
The sacrifice God wants is a humbled spirit;
God does not reject a humble heart brought low.

FROM PSALM 63—A THIRST FOR GOD

אֱלֹהִים, אֵלִי אַתָּה; אֲשַׁחֲרֶךָּ.
צָמְאָה לְךָ נַפְשִׁי, כָּמַהּ לְךָ בְשָׂרִי,
בְּאֶרֶץ־צִיָּה וְעָיֵף בְּלִי־מָיִם.
כֵּן בַּקֹּדֶשׁ חֲזִיתִיךָ, לִרְאוֹת עֻזְּךָ וּכְבוֹדֶךָ.
כִּי־טוֹב חַסְדְּךָ מֵחַיִּים; שְׂפָתַי יְשַׁבְּחוּנְךָ.
כֵּן אֲבָרֶכְךָ בְחַיָּי,
כִּי־הָיִיתָ עֶזְרָתָה לִי, וּבְצֵל כְּנָפֶיךָ אֲרַנֵּן.

GOD, YOU ARE MY GOD; at first light I seek You.
My soul thirsts for You, my flesh longs for You,
as in a dry and weary land, where there is no water.
So in Your sanctuary I look for You,

to behold Your power and Your glory.
For Your love is better than life;
my lips extol You.
So I praise You with my life,
for You are my help,
and in the shadow of Your wings
I sing for joy.

FROM PSALM 103—GOD'S LOVE REDEEMS OUR BRIEF LIVES

בָּרְכִי, נַפְשִׁי, אֶת־יהוה, וְכָל־קְרָבַי אֶת־שֵׁם קָדְשׁוֹ.

בָּרְכִי, נַפְשִׁי, אֶת־יהוה, וְאַל־תִּשְׁכְּחִי כָּל־גְּמוּלָיו.

PRAISE ADONAI, O my soul,
and let all that is in me praise God's holy name.

Praise Adonai, O my soul,
and do not forget the blessings of God,

הַגּוֹאֵל מִשַּׁחַת חַיָּיְכִי, הַמְעַטְּרֵכִי חֶסֶד וְרַחֲמִים.

עֹשֵׂה צְדָקוֹת יהוה, וּמִשְׁפָּטִים לְכָל־עֲשׁוּקִים.

who redeems your life from emptiness,
surrounding you with love and compassion.

Adonai is just, demanding justice for the oppressed.

רַחוּם וְחַנּוּן יהוה, אֶרֶךְ אַפַּיִם וְרַב־חָסֶד.

כִּי־הוּא יָדַע יִצְרֵנוּ, זָכוּר כִּי־עָפָר אֲנָחְנוּ.

Adonai is merciful and gracious,
endlessly patient and full of love.

For God knows how we are made,
and remembers that we are dust.

אֱנוֹשׁ כֶּחָצִיר יָמָיו; כְּצִיץ הַשָּׂדֶה כֵּן יָצִיץ.

כִּי רוּחַ עָבְרָה־בּוֹ, וְאֵינֶנּוּ; וְלֹא־יַכִּירֶנּוּ עוֹד מְקוֹמוֹ.

וְחֶסֶד יהוה מֵעוֹלָם וְעַד־עוֹלָם עַל־יְרֵאָיו, וְצִדְקָתוֹ
לִבְנֵי בָנִים, לְשֹׁמְרֵי בְרִיתוֹ וּלְזֹכְרֵי פִקֻּדָיו לַעֲשׂוֹתָם.

Our days are like grass;
we blossom like the flower of the field.

The wind blows, and it is gone; its place knows it no more.

But Your love, Adonai, rests forever on all who revere You,
and Your goodness rests on their children's children, who
keep Your covenant:
to remember and observe Your precepts.

FROM PSALM 108—A HYMN OF PRAISE

נָכוֹן לִבִּי, אֱלֹהִים,
אָשִׁירָה וַאֲזַמְּרָה אַף־כְּבוֹדִי!
עוּרָה, הַנֵּבֶל וְכִנּוֹר; אָעִירָה שָּׁחַר.

MY HEART IS READY, O God,
I will make melody and sing with all my heart!
Awake, harp and lyre;
I will rouse the dawn!

אוֹדְךָ בָעַמִּים, יהוה, וַאֲזַמֶּרְךָ בַּל־אֻמִּים.
כִּי־גָדוֹל מֵעַל־שָׁמַיִם חַסְדֶּךָ, וְעַד־שְׁחָקִים אֲמִתֶּךָ.
רוּמָה עַל־שָׁמַיִם, אֱלֹהִים, וְעַל כָּל־הָאָרֶץ כְּבוֹדֶךָ!

I will praise You among the peoples, Adonai,
and sing Your song among the nations.
For Your love is higher than the heavens,
Your faithfulness reaches to the sky!
You are exalted above the heavens, O God,
and Your glory is over all the earth!

PSALM 121—CONFIDENCE IN GOD OUR SHIELD

אֶשָּׂא עֵינַי אֶל־הֶהָרִים: מֵאַיִן יָבֹא עֶזְרִי?

עֶזְרִי מֵעִם יהוה, עֹשֵׂה שָׁמַיִם וָאָרֶץ.

אַל־יִתֵּן לַמּוֹט רַגְלֶךָ, אַל־יָנוּם שֹׁמְרֶךָ.

הִנֵּה לֹא־יָנוּם וְלֹא יִישָׁן שׁוֹמֵר יִשְׂרָאֵל.

יהוה שֹׁמְרֶךָ, יהוה צִלְּךָ עַל־יַד יְמִינֶךָ.

יוֹמָם הַשֶּׁמֶשׁ לֹא־יַכֶּכָּה, וְיָרֵחַ בַּלָּיְלָה.

יהוה יִשְׁמָרְךָ מִכָּל־רָע, יִשְׁמֹר אֶת־נַפְשֶׁךָ.

יהוה יִשְׁמָר־צֵאתְךָ וּבוֹאֶךָ מֵעַתָּה וְעַד־עוֹלָם.

I LIFT UP MY EYES to the mountains:
Where will I find my help?
My help comes from Adonai,
maker of heaven and earth.
God will keep your foot from slipping;
your guardian does not slumber.
Behold, Israel's guardian neither slumbers nor sleeps.
Adonai is your guardian,
Adonai is your shade at your side.
The sun shall not strike you by day,
nor the moon by night.
Adonai will guard you from evil,
will watch over your life.
Adonai will guard you, going out and coming in,
now and forever.

FROM PSALM 130—DE PROFUNDIS

מִמַּעֲמַקִּים קְרָאתִיךָ, יהוה.

אֲדֹנָי, שִׁמְעָה בְקוֹלִי,

תִּהְיֶינָה אָזְנֶיךָ קַשֻּׁבוֹת לְקוֹל תַּחֲנוּנָי.

OUT OF THE DEPTHS I cry out to You, Adonai.
Hearken to my voice, Adonai,
let Your ears be attentive to the sound of my plea.

אִם־עֲוֹנוֹת תִּשְׁמָר־יָהּ, אֲדֹנָי, מִי יַעֲמֹד?
כִּי־עִמְּךָ הַסְּלִיחָה, לְמַעַן תִּוָּרֵא.

If You kept account of sins, Adonai,
who could stand before You?
But forgiveness is Yours, that You may be held in awe.

קִוִּיתִי יהוה, קִוְּתָה נַפְשִׁי, וְלִדְבָרוֹ הוֹחָלְתִּי.
נַפְשִׁי לַאדֹנָי מִשֹּׁמְרִים לַבֹּקֶר שֹׁמְרִים לַבֹּקֶר.

Adonai is my hope; my soul hopes, as I wait for God's word.
My soul longs for Adonai
more than sentinels do for the morning.

יַחֵל יִשְׂרָאֵל אֶל־יהוה, כִּי־עִם־יהוה הַחֶסֶד, וְהַרְבֵּה עִמּוֹ פְדוּת.
וְהוּא יִפְדֶּה אֶת־יִשְׂרָאֵל מִכֹּל עֲוֹנֹתָיו.

Let Israel wait for Adonai,
for with Adonai is loyal love and abundant deliverance,
and God will deliver Israel from all its sins.

FROM PSALM 131—TRUST

יהוה, לֹא־גָבַהּ לִבִּי; וְלֹא־רָמוּ עֵינַי.
וְלֹא־הִלַּכְתִּי בִּגְדֹלוֹת וּבְנִפְלָאוֹת מִמֶּנִּי.

MY HEART IS NOT PROUD, Adonai,
my eyes are not haughty.
On things beyond me,
too wonderful for me,
I brood no more.

אִם־לֹא שִׁוִּיתִי וְדוֹמַמְתִּי נַפְשִׁי.

כְּגָמֻל עֲלֵי אִמּוֹ, כַּגָּמֻל עָלַי נַפְשִׁי.

יַחֵל יִשְׂרָאֵל אֶל־יהוה מֵעַתָּה וְעַד־עוֹלָם.

But I have calmed and quieted my soul.
Like a child at its mother's breast,
my soul is like a comforted child.
Trust in God, O Israel, now and forever.

FROM PSALM 137—REFUSAL TO SURRENDER

עַל נַהֲרוֹת בָּבֶל, שָׁם יָשַׁבְנוּ, גַּם־בָּכִינוּ, בְּזָכְרֵנוּ אֶת־צִיּוֹן.

עַל־עֲרָבִים בְּתוֹכָהּ, תָּלִינוּ כִּנֹּרוֹתֵינוּ.

כִּי שָׁם שְׁאֵלוּנוּ שׁוֹבֵינוּ דִּבְרֵי־שִׁיר, וְתוֹלָלֵינוּ שִׂמְחָה:

שִׁירוּ לָנוּ מִשִּׁיר צִיּוֹן.

BY THE WATERS OF BABYLON we sat down and wept,
as we remembered Zion.
On the willows, there, we hung up our harps.
For there our captors and tormentors
demanded of us song and mirth, saying:
"Sing us some songs of Zion."

אֵיךְ נָשִׁיר אֶת־שִׁיר־יהוה עַל אַדְמַת נֵכָר?

אִם־אֶשְׁכָּחֵךְ יְרוּשָׁלָיִם, תִּשְׁכַּח יְמִינִי;

תִּדְבַּק־לְשׁוֹנִי לְחִכִּי אִם־לֹא אֶזְכְּרֵכִי,

אִם־לֹא אַעֲלֶה אֶת־יְרוּשָׁלַיִם עַל רֹאשׁ שִׂמְחָתִי.

How can we sing Adonai's song on alien soil?
If I forget you, Jerusalem, let my right hand wither;
let my tongue cleave to the roof of my mouth
if I do not remember you,
if I do not set Jerusalem above my highest joy!

PSALM 146—ON WHOM SHALL WE RELY?

הַלְלוּיָהּ! הַלְלִי, נַפְשִׁי, אֶת־יהוה! אֲהַלְלָה יהוה בְּחַיָּי;

אֲזַמְּרָה לֵאלֹהַי בְּעוֹדִי.

אַל־תִּבְטְחוּ בִנְדִיבִים, בְּבֶן־אָדָם שֶׁאֵין לוֹ תְשׁוּעָה.

תֵּצֵא רוּחוֹ, יָשֻׁב לְאַדְמָתוֹ; בַּיּוֹם הַהוּא אָבְדוּ עֶשְׁתֹּנֹתָיו.

HALLELUYAH! Praise Adonai, O my soul!
I will sing to Adonai as long as I live;
I will sing praises to my God as long as I breathe.
Do not rely on princes, on mortals powerless to save.
Their breath departs, and they are dust;
that very day their plans turn to dust.

אַשְׁרֵי שֶׁאֵל יַעֲקֹב בְּעֶזְרוֹ, שִׂבְרוֹ עַל־יהוה אֱלֹהָיו,

עֹשֶׂה שָׁמַיִם וָאָרֶץ, אֶת־הַיָּם וְאֶת־כָּל־אֲשֶׁר־בָּם,

הַשֹּׁמֵר אֱמֶת לְעוֹלָם, עֹשֶׂה מִשְׁפָּט לָעֲשׁוּקִים,

נֹתֵן לֶחֶם לָרְעֵבִים, יהוה מַתִּיר אֲסוּרִים.

Blessed are all whose help is the God of Jacob,
whose hope is Adonai their God,
maker of heaven and earth, the sea and all that is in them,
who keeps faith forever,
who does justice for the oppressed,
gives bread to the hungry, and sets captives free.

יהוה פֹּקֵחַ עִוְרִים, יהוה זֹקֵף כְּפוּפִים,

יהוה אֹהֵב צַדִּיקִים, יהוה שֹׁמֵר אֶת־גֵּרִים,

יָתוֹם וְאַלְמָנָה יְעוֹדֵד, וְדֶרֶךְ רְשָׁעִים יְעַוֵּת.

יִמְלֹךְ יהוה לְעוֹלָם, אֱלֹהַיִךְ, צִיּוֹן, לְדֹר וָדֹר. הַלְלוּיָהּ.

Adonai opens the eyes of the blind;
Adonai lifts up the downtrodden;

371

Selected Psalms

Adonai loves the righteous;
Adonai cares for the stranger,
supports the orphan and the widow,
but blocks the path of the wicked.
Adonai shall reign forever;
your God, O Zion, from generation to generation.
Halleluyah.

FROM PSALM 147—THANKING THE GOD OF HISTORY AND NATURE

הַלְלוּיָה!

כִּי־טוֹב זַמְּרָה אֱלֹהֵינוּ, כִּי־נָעִים נָאוָה תְהִלָּה.

HALLELUYAH!
How good to sing to our God,
how pleasant and fitting to praise.

בּוֹנֵה יְרוּשָׁלַיִם יהוה, נִדְחֵי יִשְׂרָאֵל יְכַנֵּס.
הָרֹפֵא לִשְׁבוּרֵי לֵב וּמְחַבֵּשׁ לְעַצְּבוֹתָם,

Adonai builds up Jerusalem,
and gathers Israel's scattered folk,
healing the brokenhearted
and binding up their wounds,

מוֹנֶה מִסְפָּר לַכּוֹכָבִים, לְכֻלָּם שֵׁמוֹת יִקְרָא.
גָּדוֹל אֲדוֹנֵינוּ וְרַב־כֹּחַ, לִתְבוּנָתוֹ אֵין מִסְפָּר.

numbering the stars,
calling them all by name.
Great is our God, immense in power,
unlimited in wisdom.

מְעוֹדֵד עֲנָוִים יהוה, מַשְׁפִּיל רְשָׁעִים עֲדֵי־אָרֶץ.
עֱנוּ לַיהוה בְּתוֹדָה; זַמְּרוּ לֵאלֹהֵינוּ בְכִנּוֹר.

Adonai heartens the humble
and throws the wicked to the ground.
Acclaim Adonai with thanksgiving;
sound praise to our God with the harp.

הַמְכַסֶּה שָׁמַיִם בְּעָבִים, הַמֵּכִין לָאָרֶץ מָטָר,
הַמַּצְמִיחַ הָרִים חָצִיר,

Who covers the sky with clouds,
showers the earth with rain,
makes grass to grow on the hills,

נוֹתֵן לִבְהֵמָה לַחְמָהּ, לִבְנֵי עֹרֵב אֲשֶׁר יִקְרָאוּ.
לֹא בִגְבוּרַת הַסּוּס יֶחְפָּץ, לֹא־בְשׁוֹקֵי הָאִישׁ יִרְצֶה.

giving animals their food,
ravens what they cry for.
God does not delight in the might of cavalry,
or take pleasure from the boasts of warriors.

רוֹצֶה יְהוה אֶת־יְרֵאָיו, אֶת־הַמְיַחֲלִים לְחַסְדּוֹ.
הַנֹּתֵן שֶׁלֶג כַּצָּמֶר, כְּפוֹר כָּאֵפֶר יְפַזֵּר.

No—Adonai is pleased by the reverent,
by those who trust in God's kindness.
God sends down the fleecelike snow,
scattering frost like ash.

מַשְׁלִיךְ קַרְחוֹ כְפִתִּים; לִפְנֵי קָרָתוֹ מִי יַעֲמֹד?
יִשְׁלַח דְּבָרוֹ וְיַמְסֵם; יַשֵּׁב רוּחוֹ, יִזְּלוּ־מָיִם.

Ice falls like bread crumbs;
who can withstand its cold?
Yet at God's command it melts;
the wind is stilled, and the water flows.

FROM PSALM 148—LET ALL CREATION GIVE PRAISE

הַלְלוּיָהּ !

הַלְלוּ אֶת־יהוה מִן־הַשָּׁמַיִם, הַלְלוּהוּ בַּמְּרוֹמִים.

הַלְלוּהוּ כָל־מַלְאָכָיו, הַלְלוּהוּ כָּל־צְבָאָיו.

HALLELUYAH!

Praise Adonai from the heavens,
praise God in the heights.
Give praise, all God's angels,
give praise, all God's hosts.

הַלְלוּהוּ שֶׁמֶשׁ וְיָרֵחַ, הַלְלוּהוּ כָּל־כּוֹכְבֵי אוֹר.

הַלְלוּהוּ שְׁמֵי הַשָּׁמָיִם, וְהַמַּיִם אֲשֶׁר מֵעַל הַשָּׁמָיִם.

Give praise, sun and moon;
give praise, O shining stars.
Give praise, O highest heavens,
and the waters above them.

יְהַלְלוּ אֶת־שֵׁם יהוה, כִּי הוּא צִוָּה וְנִבְרָאוּ,

וַיַּעֲמִידֵם לָעַד לְעוֹלָם, חָק־נָתַן וְלֹא יַעֲבוֹר.

Let them praise the name of Adonai,
at whose command they came to be,
establishing them to abide forever,
a decree that does not change.

הַלְלוּ אֶת־יהוה מִן־הָאָרֶץ: תַּנִּינִים וְכָל־תְּהֹמוֹת,

אֵשׁ וּבָרָד, שֶׁלֶג וְקִיטוֹר, רוּחַ סְעָרָה עֹשָׂה דְבָרוֹ,

הֶהָרִים וְכָל־גְּבָעוֹת, עֵץ פְּרִי וְכָל־אֲרָזִים,

הַחַיָּה וְכָל־בְּהֵמָה, רֶמֶשׂ וְצִפּוֹר כָּנָף,

Praise Adonai from the earth:
crocodiles and creatures of the deep,
fire and hail, snow and mist,
storm winds that obey the divine command,
mountains and hills, fruit trees and cedars,
wild animals and cattle, creatures that creep
and birds on the wing,

מַלְכֵי־אֶרֶץ וְכָל־לְאֻמִּים, שָׂרִים וְכָל־שֹׁפְטֵי אָרֶץ,
בַּחוּרִים וְגַם־בְּתוּלוֹת, זְקֵנִים עִם־נְעָרִים!

earth's rulers and all the nations,
princes and judges of the earth;
boys and girls alike,
old and young together!

יְהַלְלוּ אֶת־שֵׁם יהוה, כִּי־נִשְׂגָּב שְׁמוֹ לְבַדּוֹ.
הוֹדוֹ עַל־אֶרֶץ וְשָׁמָיִם, וַיָּרֶם קֶרֶן לְעַמּוֹ,
תְּהִלָּה לְכָל־חֲסִידָיו, לִבְנֵי יִשְׂרָאֵל, עַם־קְרֹבוֹ, הַלְלוּיָהּ.

Let them praise the name of Adonai,
whose name alone is exalted,
whose splendor covers heaven and earth.
Adonai, You are the strength of Your people,
making glorious Your faithful ones,
Israel, a people close to You. Halleluyah!

⚘

375

PRAYERS FOR HEALING

מוֹדֶה אֲנִי לְפָנֶיךָ, מֶלֶךְ חַי וְקַיָּם, שֶׁהֶחֱזַרְתָּ בִּי נִשְׁמָתִי
בְּחֶמְלָה. רַבָּה אֱמוּנָתֶךָ.

Mo-deh a-ni l'fa-neh-cha, meh-lech chai v'ka-yam,
sheh-heh-cheh-zar-ta bi nish-ma-ti b'chem-lah. Ra-bah eh-mu-na-teh-cha.

I give You thanks, O everliving God: each day, in compassion,
You restore and renew me. Great is Your faithfulness.

※

Mi sheh-bei-rach a-vo-tei-nu,
M'kor ha-b'ra-chah l'i-mo-tei-nu,
May the Source of strength
Who blessed the ones before us
Help us find the courage
To make our lives a blessing
And let us say: Amen.

Mi sheh-bei-rach l'i-mo-tei-u,
M'kor ha-b'ra-chah l'a-vo-tei-nu,
Bless those is need of healing
With *r'fu-ah sheh-lei-mah*
The renewal of body
The renewal of spirit
And let us say: Amen.

(Friedman and Setel)

376

MI SHEBEIRACH מי שברך

מִי שֶׁבֵּרַךְ אֲבוֹתֵינוּ אַבְרָהָם, יִצְחָק, וְיַעֲקֹב,
וְאִמּוֹתֵינוּ שָׂרָה, רִבְקָה, לֵאָה, וְרָחֵל, הוּא יְבָרֵךְ אוֹתָנוּ.
הַקָּדוֹשׁ בָּרוּךְ הוּא יְמַלֵּא רַחֲמִים עַל־ _____
וְעַל־כָּל הַחוֹלִים, וְיִשְׁלַח לָנוּ בִּמְהֵרָה רְפוּאַת הַנֶּפֶשׁ
וּרְפוּאַת הַגּוּף. וְנֹאמַר: אָמֵן.

May the one who blessed our ancestors Abraham, Isaac, and
Jacob, Sarah, Rebekah, Leah, and Rachel bless [_____ and]
all who are in need of healing. Holy One, in the fullness of
Your compassion bestow upon them renewed health and
strength. Guide their healers, O God; give them skill and
compassion, and the joy that comes from selfless service.
And let us say: *Amen.*

❧

We pray for all who are in need of healing.

Be with all Your children, O God: be with us all.

בָּרוּךְ אַתָּה יי, רוֹפֵא הַחוֹלִים.

Ba-ruch a-ta Adonai, ro-fei ha-cho-lim.

Praised be God, healer of the sick.

❧

We know that illness is not what defines us; for even when
we are beset by illness and its pains, we can find ways to be
useful: we can love and be loved.

*O God, even when I am weak and in pain help me to remember
the good I can do. And help me, on this and every day, to see
beyond my troubles, that I may be a blessing to others—and to
myself.*

❧

There are many who suffer pain from illness—either their own or of family members or good friends. Some we know, others we do not. We say this prayer with the hope that our love and concern may bring comfort and strength to all of them—all of us.

In sickness we turn to You, O God, and seek Your help. You create the healing powers that reside within every living creature. You are the source of the knowledge and skill of healers, and of the dedication that prompts them to give of their best. From You comes the comforting care of loved ones, and the tranquility of spirit needed by all in distress.

And so we pray: May all these forces combine to speed the recovery of our loved ones and instill within us sympathy for all who suffer, and a deep appreciation of life and its blessings.

❧

ברכי, נפשי, את־יהוה

ברכות

BLESSINGS

BLESSINGS

&

BEFORE SLEEP

Source of life and blessing, let me lie down in peace, and let me rise up to life renewed. Spread a shelter of peace over me and my loved ones.

בָּרוּךְ אַתָּה יי, הַפּוֹרֵשׂ סֻכַּת שָׁלוֹם עָלֵינוּ
וְעַל־כָּל־יוֹשְׁבֵי תֵבֵל.

Ba-ruch a-ta Adonai, ha-po-reis su-kat sha-lom a-lei-nu
v'al kol yo-sh'vei tei-veil.

Praised be God, whose shelter of peace covers all the living.

שְׁמַע יִשְׂרָאֵל: יהוה אֱלֹהֵינוּ, יהוה אֶחָד.

Shema Yisrael, Adonai Eh-lo-hei-nu, Adonai eh-chad.

Hear, O Israel: Adonai is our God, Adonai alone.

Holy One, may Your love bless me in my lying down, and keep me in my sleep. Let Your light be with me when I waken, and abide with me when I go out into the world.

UPON WAKING

מוֹדֶה אֲנִי לְפָנֶיךָ, מֶלֶךְ חַי וְקַיָּם, שֶׁהֶחֱזַרְתָּ בִּי
נִשְׁמָתִי בְּחֶמְלָה. רַבָּה אֱמוּנָתֶךָ.

Mo-deh a-ni l'fa-neh-cha, meh-lech chai v'ka-yam, sheh-heh-cheh-zar-ta bi
nish-ma-ti b'chem-lah. Ra-bah eh-mu-na-teh-cha.

I give You thanks, O everliving God. Each day, in compassion, You restore and renew me. Great is Your faithfulness.

שְׁמַע יִשְׂרָאֵל: יהוה אֱלֹהֵינוּ, יהוה אֶחָד.

Shema Yisrael: Adonai Eh-lo-hei-nu, Adonai eh-chad.

Hear, O Israel: Adonai is our God, Adonai alone.

בָּרוּךְ אַתָּה יי, אֱלֹהֵינוּ מֶלֶךְ הָעוֹלָם,
הַמֵּאִיר לָעוֹלָם כֻּלּוֹ בִּכְבוֹדוֹ.

Ba-ruch a-ta Adonai, Eh-lo-hei-nu meh-lech ha-o-lam,
ha-mei-ir la-o-lam ku-lo bi-ch'vo-do.

Praised be Adonai our God, who gives light to all the world.

Source of life and blessing, let me and all my loved ones awaken to a world filled with beauty; and may all that I do this day help to make this world more beautiful still.

בָּרוּךְ אַתָּה יי, אֱלֹהֵינוּ מֶלֶךְ הָעוֹלָם,
הַמַּעֲבִיר שֵׁנָה מֵעֵינַי וּתְנוּמָה מֵעַפְעַפָּי.

Ba-ruch a-ta Adonai, Eh-lo-hei-nu meh-lech ha-o-lam,
ha-ma-a-vir shei-na mei-ei-nai u-t'nu-mah mei-af-a-pai.

Praised be Adonai our God, who opens our eyes to greet the new day.

GIVING THANKS FOR FOOD

At home or on our way, may we be blessed with food that nourishes and sustains us, and may we be grateful for this, the most obvious of blessings, as it comes, in part, through the effort of others.

BEFORE EATING BREAD OR A FULL MEAL

בָּרוּךְ אַתָּה יי, אֱלֹהֵינוּ מֶלֶךְ הָעוֹלָם, הַמּוֹצִיא לֶחֶם מִן הָאָרֶץ.

Ba-ruch a-ta Adonai, Eh-lo-hei-nu meh-lech ha-o-lam,
ha-mo-tzi leh-chem min ha-a-retz.

We praise You, Adonai our God, sovereign of the universe, for the bread You bring forth from the earth.

FOR THE FRUIT OF THE VINE

בָּרוּךְ אַתָּה יי, אֱלֹהֵינוּ מֶלֶךְ הָעוֹלָם, בּוֹרֵא פְּרִי הַגָּפֶן.

Ba-ruch a-ta Adonai, Eh-lo-hei-nu meh-lech ha-o-lam, bo-rei p'ri ha-ga-fen.

We praise You, Adonai our God, sovereign of the universe, for the fruit You bring forth from the vine.

FOOD FOR THOUGHT

Ben Zoma said: "Blessed is the one who discerns secrets and blessed the one who created all these to serve me." For he would say: How hard Adam the First Man had to labor before he had a loaf to eat: he had to plow, sow, reap, bind sheaves, pound, winnow, clean, grind, sift, knead, bake—only then could he eat—and I wake up and find all this done for me! The same is true for the clothes I find waiting for me when I wake up. Every trade and craft is here at the door of my house! (Talmud Berachot 58a)

ברכת המזון   SHORT THANKSGIVING FOR FOOD

ON SHABBAT BEGIN HERE

PSALM 126

A SONG OF ASCENTS   שִׁיר הַמַּעֲלוֹת

בְּשׁוּב יהוה אֶת־שִׁיבַת צִיּוֹן, הָיִינוּ כְּחֹלְמִים. אָז יִמָּלֵא שְׂחוֹק

פִּינוּ, וּלְשׁוֹנֵנוּ רִנָּה. אָז יֹאמְרוּ בַגּוֹיִם: הִגְדִּיל יהוה לַעֲשׂוֹת

עִם־אֵלֶּה. הִגְדִּיל יהוה לַעֲשׂוֹת עִמָּנוּ, הָיִינוּ שְׂמֵחִים.

שׁוּבָה יהוה אֶת־שְׁבִיתֵנוּ, כַּאֲפִיקִים בַּנֶּגֶב. הַזֹּרְעִים בְּדִמְעָה

בְּרִנָּה יִקְצֹרוּ. הָלוֹךְ יֵלֵךְ וּבָכֹה, נֹשֵׂא מֶשֶׁךְ־הַזָּרַע, בֹּא־יָבוֹא

בְרִנָּה, נֹשֵׂא אֲלֻמֹּתָיו.

When Adonai restores the exiles of Zion, it will seem like a dream. Our mouths will fill with laughter and our tongues with song. Then they will say among the nations: "Adonai has done great things for them." Adonai has done great things for us, and we rejoice. Restore our fortunes, Adonai, as streams restore the desert. Then those who sowed in tears shall reap with shouts of joy. Those who went out weeping, bearing sacks of seed, shall come back with shouts of joy, bearing their sheaves.

ON WEEKDAYS BEGIN HERE

חֲבֵרַי, נְבָרֵךְ.

Cha-vei-rai n'va-reich.

Let us praise God.

יְהִי שֵׁם יי מְבֹרָךְ מֵעַתָּה וְעַד עוֹלָם.

Y'hi sheim Adonai m'vo-rach mei-a-ta v'ad o-lam!

Praised be the name of God, now and forever!

בִּרְשׁוּת הַחֲבֵרָה, נְבָרֵךְ אֱלֹהֵינוּ שֶׁאָכַלְנוּ מִשֶּׁלּוֹ.

Bi-r'shut ha-chev-rah, n'va-reich Eh-lo-hei-nu sheh-a-chal-nu mi-sheh-lo.

Praised be our God, of whose abundance we have eaten.

בָּרוּךְ אֱלֹהֵינוּ שֶׁאָכַלְנוּ מִשֶּׁלּוֹ, וּבְטוּבוֹ חָיִינוּ.

Ba-ruch Eh-lo-hei-nu sheh-a-chal-nu mi-sheh-lo, u-v'tu-vo cha-yi-nu.

Praised be our God, of whose abundance we have eaten,
and by whose goodness we live.

בָּרוּךְ הוּא וּבָרוּךְ שְׁמוֹ.

Ba-ruch hu u-va-ruch sh'mo.

Praised be the name of God!

בָּרוּךְ אַתָּה יְיָ, אֱלֹהֵינוּ מֶלֶךְ הָעוֹלָם, הַזָּן אֶת־הָעוֹלָם
כֻּלּוֹ בְּטוּבוֹ, בְּחֵן בְּחֶסֶד וּבְרַחֲמִים. הוּא נוֹתֵן לֶחֶם
לְכָל־בָּשָׂר, כִּי לְעוֹלָם חַסְדּוֹ. וּבְטוּבוֹ הַגָּדוֹל תָּמִיד לֹא
חָסַר לָנוּ, וְאַל יֶחְסַר לָנוּ מָזוֹן לְעוֹלָם וָעֶד, בַּעֲבוּר שְׁמוֹ
הַגָּדוֹל. כִּי הוּא אֵל זָן וּמְפַרְנֵס לַכֹּל, וּמֵטִיב לַכֹּל וּמֵכִין
מָזוֹן לְכָל־בְּרִיּוֹתָיו אֲשֶׁר בָּרָא. בָּרוּךְ אַתָּה יְיָ, הַזָּן אֶת־הַכֹּל.

Ba-ruch a-ta Adonai, Eh-lo-hei-nu meh-lech ha-o-lam, ha-zan et-ha-o-lam
ku-lo b'tu-vo, b'chein b'cheh-sed u-v'ra-cha-mim. Hu no-tein leh-chem
l'chol ba-sar, ki l'o-lam chas-do. U-v'tu-vo ha-ga-dol ta-mid lo
cha-sar la-nu, v'al yech-sar la-nu ma-zon l'o-lam va-ed, ba-a-vur sh'mo
ha-ga-dol. Ki hu eil zan u-m'far-neis la-kol, u-mei-tiv la-kol u-mei-chin
ma-zon l'chol b'ri-yo-tav a-sher ba-ra. Ba-ruch a-ta Adonai, ha-zan et ha-kol.

Adonai our God, sovereign of the universe, we praise You, whose goodness sustains the world with grace, love, and compassion. You are the source of bread for all who live—for Your love is everlasting. Because of Your great goodness we need never lack for food, for You provide food enough and sustenance for all Your creatures. We praise You, O God, source of food for all the living.

נוֹדֶה לְךָ, יְיָ אֱלֹהֵינוּ, עַל שֶׁהִנְחַלְתָּ לַאֲבוֹתֵינוּ
וּלְאִמּוֹתֵינוּ אֶרֶץ חֶמְדָּה טוֹבָה וּרְחָבָה, וְעַל אֲכִילַת מָזוֹן

שָׁאַתָּה זָן וּמְפַרְנֵס אוֹתָנוּ תָּמִיד, בְּכָל־יוֹם וּבְכָל־עֵת
וּבְכָל־שָׁעָה

No-deh l'cha, Adonai Eh-lo-hei-nu, al sheh-hin-chal-ta la-a-vo-tei-nu
u-l'i-mo-tei-nu e-retz chem-dah to-vah u-r'cha-vah, v'al a-chi-lat ma-zon
sheh-a-tah zan u-m'far-neis o-ta-nu ta-mid, b'chol yom u-v'chol eit
u-v'chol sha-ah.

Adonai our God, for this good earth that You have entrusted to our
mothers and fathers and to us; and for the food that sustains us day by
day, hour by hour, we give You thanks.

כַּכָּתוּב: וְאָכַלְתָּ וְשָׂבָעְתָּ, וּבֵרַכְתָּ אֶת־יהוה אֱלֹהֶיךָ
עַל־הָאָרֶץ הַטֹּבָה אֲשֶׁר נָתַן־לָךְ.

Ka-ka-tuv: V'a-chal-ta v'sa-va-ta, u-vei-rach-ta et Adonai Eh-lo-heh-cha
al ha-a-retz ha-to-vah a-sher na-tan lach.

As it is written: "When you have eaten and are satisfied give praise to
Adonai your God, who has given you this good earth."

וּבְנֵה יְרוּשָׁלַיִם עִיר הַקֹּדֶשׁ בִּמְהֵרָה בְיָמֵינוּ.
בָּרוּךְ אַתָּה יי, בּוֹנֶה בְרַחֲמָיו יְרוּשָׁלָיִם. אָמֵן.

U-v'nei Y'ru-sha-la-yim ir ha-kodesh bi-m'hei-ra b'ya-mei-nu.
Ba-ruch a-ta Adonai, bo-neh b'ra-cha-mav Y'ru-sha-la-yim. A-mein

Let Jerusalem, the holy city, be renewed in our time. We praise You, O
God, who in compassion rebuilds Jerusalem. Amen.

הָרַחֲמָן, הוּא יְבָרֵךְ אוֹתָנוּ וְאֶת־כָּל־אֲשֶׁר לָנוּ, כְּמוֹ
שֶׁנִּתְבָּרְכוּ אֲבוֹתֵינוּ אַבְרָהָם, יִצְחָק, וְיַעֲקֹב, וְאִמּוֹתֵינוּ
שָׂרָה, רִבְקָה, לֵאָה וְרָחֵל, בַּכֹּל מִכֹּל כֹּל, כֵּן יְבָרֵךְ
אוֹתָנוּ כֻּלָּנוּ יַחַד, בִּבְרָכָה שְׁלֵמָה, וְנֹאמַר: אָמֵן.

Ha-ra-cha-man, hu y'va-reich o-ta-nu v'et kol a-sher la-nu, k'mo
sheh-nit-ba-r'chu a-vo-tei-nu Av-ra-ham, Yitz-chak, v'Ya-a-kov, v'i-mo-tei-nu

*Sa-rah, Riv-kah, Lei-ah, v'Ra-cheil, ba-kol mi-kol kol, kein y'va-reich
o-ta-nu ku-la-nu ya-chad bi-v'ra'cha sh'lei-ma, v'no-mar: A-mein.*

Merciful One, bless us and all our dear ones. As You blessed our ancestors Abraham, Isaac, and Jacob; Sarah, Rebekah, Leah, and Rachel, so bless us, one and all; and let us say: Amen.

ON SHABBAT

הָרַחֲמָן, הוּא יַנְחִילֵנוּ יוֹם שֶׁכֻּלוֹ שַׁבָּת.

Ha-ra-cha-man, hu yan-chi-lei-nu yom she-ku-lo Shabbat.

Merciful One, help us to see the coming of a time that is all Shabbat.

ON YOM TOV

הָרַחֲמָן, הוּא יַנְחִילֵנוּ יוֹם שֶׁכֻּלוֹ טוֹב.

Ha-ra-cha-man, hu yan-chi-lei-nu yom she-ku-lo tov.

Merciful One, help us to see the coming of a time that is all good.

ON ROSH HASHANAH

הָרַחֲמָן, הוּא יְחַדֵּשׁ עָלֵינוּ אֶת־הַשָּׁנָה הַזֹּאת לְטוֹבָה וְלִבְרָכָה.

Ha-ra-cha-man, hu y'cha-deish a-lei-nu et ha-sha-nah ha-zot l'to-vah v'li-v'ra-cha.

Merciful One, bring us a year of renewed good and blessing.

ON ALL OCCASIONS

עֹשֶׂה שָׁלוֹם בִּמְרוֹמָיו,   *O-seh sha-lom bi-m'ro-mav,*

הוּא יַעֲשֶׂה שָׁלוֹם עָלֵינוּ   *hu ya-a-seh sha-lom a-lei-nu*

וְעַל־כָּל־יִשְׂרָאֵל, וְאָמְרוּ:   *v'al kol Yis-ra-eil, v'i-m'ru:*

אָמֵן.   *A-mein.*

May the source of peace on high let peace descend on us, on all Israel, and all the world, and let us say: Amen.

יְהוָה עֹז לְעַמּוֹ יִתֵּן; יְהוָה יְבָרֵךְ אֶת־עַמּוֹ בַשָּׁלוֹם.

Adonai oz l'amo yi-tein, A-do-nai y'va-reich et a-mo va-sha-lom.

Eternal God, You give strength to Your people; Eternal God, You bless Your people with peace.

A GOOD GUEST

Ben Zoma would say: A good guest says: "How much they exerted themselves for me! How much meat, how much wine, how many cakes—and all on my account!" Whereas an ungrateful guest says: "In what way did they trouble themselves? [I ate one loaf, one slice of meat, had one cup]—whatever they did, they did for themselves!" (Talmud Berachot 58a)

ברכת המזון   THANKSGIVING FOR FOOD

ON SHABBAT BEGIN HERE

PSALM 126

A SONG OF ASCENTS   שִׁיר הַמַּעֲלוֹת

בְּשׁוּב יהוה אֶת־שִׁיבַת צִיּוֹן, הָיִינוּ כְּחֹלְמִים. אָז יִמָּלֵא שְׂחוֹק

פִּינוּ, וּלְשׁוֹנֵנוּ רִנָּה. אָז יֹאמְרוּ בַגּוֹיִם: הִגְדִּיל יהוה לַעֲשׂוֹת

עִם־אֵלֶּה. הִגְדִּיל יהוה לַעֲשׂוֹת עִמָּנוּ, הָיִינוּ שְׂמֵחִים.

שׁוּבָה יהוה אֶת־שְׁבִיתֵנוּ, כַּאֲפִיקִים בַּנֶּגֶב. הַזֹּרְעִים בְּדִמְעָה

בְּרִנָּה יִקְצֹרוּ. הָלוֹךְ יֵלֵךְ וּבָכֹה, נֹשֵׂא מֶשֶׁךְ־הַזָּרַע, בֹּא־יָבוֹא

בְרִנָּה, נֹשֵׂא אֲלֻמֹּתָיו.

When Adonai restores Zion's exiles, it will seem like a dream. Our mouths will fill with laughter and our tongues with song. Then they will say among the nations: "Adonai has done great things for them." Adonai has done great things for us, and we rejoice. Restore our fortunes, Adonai, as streams restore the desert. Then those who sowed in tears shall reap with shouts of joy. Those who went out weeping, bearing sacks of seed, shall come back with shouts of joy, bearing their sheaves.

ON WEEKDAYS BEGIN HERE

חֲבֵרַי, נְבָרֵךְ.

Cha-vei-rai n'va-reich.

Let us praise God.

יְהִי שֵׁם יי מְבֹרָךְ מֵעַתָּה וְעַד עוֹלָם.

Y'hi sheim Adonai m'vo-rach mei-a-ta v'ad o-lam!

Praised be the name of God, now and forever!

בִּרְשׁוּת הַחֶבְרָה, נְבָרֵךְ אֱלֹהֵינוּ שֶׁאָכַלְנוּ מִשֶּׁלּוֹ.

Bi-r'shut ha-chev-rah, n'va-reich Eh-lo-hei-nu sheh-a-chal-nu mi-sheh-lo.

Praised be our God, of whose abundance we have eaten.

387

בָּרוּךְ אֱלֹהֵינוּ שֶׁאָכַלְנוּ מִשֶּׁלוֹ, וּבְטוּבוֹ חָיִינוּ.

Ba-ruch Eh-lo-hei-nu sheh-a-chal-nu mi-sheh-lo, u-v'tu-vo cha-yi-nu.

Praised be our God, of whose abundance we have eaten,
and by whose goodness we live.

בָּרוּךְ הוּא וּבָרוּךְ שְׁמוֹ.

Ba-ruch hu u-va-ruch sh'mo.

Praised be the name of God!

בָּרוּךְ אַתָּה יי, אֱלֹהֵינוּ מֶלֶךְ הָעוֹלָם, הַזָּן אֶת־הָעוֹלָם
כֻּלּוֹ בְּטוּבוֹ, בְּחֵן בְּחֶסֶד וּבְרַחֲמִים. הוּא נוֹתֵן לֶחֶם
לְכָל־בָּשָׂר, כִּי לְעוֹלָם חַסְדּוֹ. וּבְטוּבוֹ הַגָּדוֹל תָּמִיד לֹא
חָסַר לָנוּ, וְאַל יֶחְסַר לָנוּ מָזוֹן לְעוֹלָם וָעֶד, בַּעֲבוּר שְׁמוֹ
הַגָּדוֹל. כִּי הוּא אֵל זָן וּמְפַרְנֵס לַכֹּל, וּמֵטִיב לַכֹּל וּמֵכִין
מָזוֹן לְכָל־בְּרִיּוֹתָיו אֲשֶׁר בָּרָא. בָּרוּךְ אַתָּה יי, הַזָּן אֶת־הַכֹּל.

Ba-ruch a-ta Adonai, Eh-lo-hei-nu meh-lech ha-o-lam, ha-zan et-ha-o-lam
ku-lo b'tu-vo, b'chein b'cheh-sed u-v'ra-cha-mim. Hu no-tein leh-chem
l'chol ba-sar, ki l'o-lam chas-do. U-v'tu-vo ha-ga-dol ta-mid lo
cha-sar la-nu, v'al yech-sar la-nu ma-zon l'o-lam va-ed, ba-a-vur sh'mo
ha-ga-dol. Ki hu eil zan u-m'far-neis la-kol, u-mei-tiv la-kol u-mei-chin
ma-zon l'chol b'ri-yo-tav a-sher ba-ra. Ba-ruch a-ta Adonai, ha-zan et ha-kol.

Adonai our God, sovereign of the universe, we praise You, whose
goodness sustains the world with grace, love, and compassion. You are
the source of bread for all who live—for Your love is everlasting.
Because of Your great goodness we need never lack for food, for You
provide food enough and sustenance for all Your creatures. We praise
You, O God, source of food for all the living.

נוֹדֶה לְךָ, יְיָ אֱלֹהֵינוּ, עַל שֶׁהִנְחַלְתָּ לַאֲבוֹתֵינוּ וּלְאִמּוֹתֵינוּ
אֶרֶץ חֶמְדָּה טוֹבָה וּרְחָבָה; וְעַל שֶׁהוֹצֵאתָנוּ מֵאֶרֶץ מִצְרַיִם;
וּפְדִיתָנוּ מִבֵּית עֲבָדִים; וְעַל בְּרִיתְךָ שֶׁחָתַמְתָּ בְּלִבֵּנוּ; וְעַל
תּוֹרָתְךָ שֶׁלִּמַּדְתָּנוּ, וְעַל חֻקֶּיךָ שֶׁהוֹדַעְתָּנוּ, וְעַל חַיִּים חֵן
וָחֶסֶד שֶׁחוֹנַנְתָּנוּ, וְעַל אֲכִילַת מָזוֹן שָׁאַתָּה זָן וּמְפַרְנֵס אוֹתָנוּ
תָּמִיד, בְּכָל־יוֹם וּבְכָל־עֵת וּבְכָל־שָׁעָה.

Adonai our God, for this good earth that You have entrusted to our mothers and fathers, and to us; for our deliverance from the land of Egypt; for the covenant You have sealed into our hearts; for having taught us Torah by which to live; for the grace and kindness that give our life meaning; and for the food that sustains us day by day, hour by hour, we give You thanks.

ON CHANUKAH ADD

עַל הַנִּסִּים, וְעַל הַפֻּרְקָן, וְעַל הַגְּבוּרוֹת, וְעַל הַתְּשׁוּעוֹת, וְעַל
הַנֶּחָמוֹת שֶׁעָשִׂיתָ לַאֲבוֹתֵינוּ וּלְאִמּוֹתֵינוּ בַּיָּמִים הָהֵם וּבַזְּמַן הַזֶּה.
בִּימֵי מַתִּתְיָהוּ בֶּן־יוֹחָנָן כֹּהֵן גָּדוֹל, חַשְׁמוֹנָאִי וּבָנָיו, כְּשֶׁעָמְדָה
מַלְכוּת יָוָן הָרְשָׁעָה עַל עַמְּךָ יִשְׂרָאֵל, לְהַשְׁכִּיחָם תּוֹרָתֶךָ
וּלְהַעֲבִירָם מֵחֻקֵּי רְצוֹנֶךָ. וְאַתָּה בְּרַחֲמֶיךָ הָרַבִּים עָמַדְתָּ
לָהֶם בְּעֵת צָרָתָם, רַבְתָּ אֶת־רִיבָם, דַּנְתָּ אֶת־דִּינָם, מָסַרְתָּ
גִבּוֹרִים בְּיַד חַלָּשִׁים, וְרַבִּים בְּיַד מְעַטִּים, וּטְמֵאִים בְּיַד טְהוֹרִים,
וּרְשָׁעִים בְּיַד צַדִּיקִים, וְזֵדִים בְּיַד עוֹסְקֵי תוֹרָתֶךָ. וּלְךָ עָשִׂיתָ
שֵׁם גָּדוֹל וְקָדוֹשׁ בְּעוֹלָמֶךָ, וּלְעַמְּךָ יִשְׂרָאֵל עָשִׂיתָ יְשׁוּעָה גְדוֹלָה
וּפֻרְקָן כְּהַיּוֹם הַזֶּה, וְאַחַר כֵּן בָּאוּ בָנֶיךָ לִדְבִיר בֵּיתֶךָ, וּפִנּוּ
אֶת־הֵיכָלֶךָ, וְטִהֲרוּ אֶת־מִקְדָּשֶׁךָ, וְהִדְלִיקוּ נֵרוֹת בְּחַצְרוֹת קָדְשֶׁךָ,
וְקָבְעוּ שְׁמוֹנַת יְמֵי חֲנֻכָּה אֵלּוּ, לְהוֹדוֹת וּלְהַלֵּל לְשִׁמְךָ הַגָּדוֹל.

In days of old, at this season, You saved our people by wonders and mighty deeds. In the days of Mattathias the Hasmonean, the tyrannic Syrian-Greek Empire sought to destroy our people Israel by making them forget their Torah, and thus to abandon Your teaching.

But in great compassion You stood by them, so that the weak defeated the strong, the few prevailed over the many, and the righteous prevailed. Through this great deliverance Your name was exalted and sanctified in the world, as Your children returned to Your house to purify the sanctuary and to kindle its lights. And they dedicated these eight days to give thanks and praise to Your majestic glory.

ON PURIM ADD

עַל הַנִּסִּים, וְעַל הַפֻּרְקָן, וְעַל הַגְּבוּרוֹת, וְעַל הַתְּשׁוּעוֹת, וְעַל הַנֶּחָמוֹת שֶׁעָשִׂיתָ לַאֲבוֹתֵינוּ וּלְאִמּוֹתֵינוּ בַּיָּמִים הָהֵם וּבַזְּמַן הַזֶּה.

בִּימֵי מָרְדְּכַי וְאֶסְתֵּר בְּשׁוּשַׁן הַבִּירָה, כְּשֶׁעָמַד עֲלֵיהֶם הָמָן הָרָשָׁע, בִּקֵּשׁ לְהַשְׁמִיד לַהֲרֹג וּלְאַבֵּד אֶת־כָּל־הַיְּהוּדִים, מִנַּעַר וְעַד־זָקֵן, טַף וְנָשִׁים, בְּיוֹם אֶחָד, בִּשְׁלֹשָׁה עָשָׂר לְחֹדֶשׁ שְׁנֵים־עָשָׂר, הוּא־חֹדֶשׁ אֲדָר, וּשְׁלָלָם לָבוֹז. וְאַתָּה בְּרַחֲמֶיךָ הָרַבִּים הֵפַרְתָּ אֶת־עֲצָתוֹ וְקִלְקַלְתָּ אֶת־מַחֲשַׁבְתּוֹ.

In days of old, at this season, You saved our people by wonders and mighty deeds. In the time of Mordechai and Esther, the wicked Haman arose in Persia, plotting the destruction of all the Jews, young and old alike. He planned to destroy them in a single day, the thirteenth of Adar, and to plunder their possessions. But through Your great mercy his plan was thwarted, his scheme frustrated. We therefore thank and bless You, O great and gracious God!

ON ALL OCCASIONS

וְעַל הַכֹּל, יי אֱלֹהֵינוּ, אֲנַחְנוּ מוֹדִים לָךְ וּמְבָרְכִים אוֹתָךְ.
יִתְבָּרַךְ שִׁמְךָ בְּפִי כָּל־חַי תָּמִיד לְעוֹלָם וָעֶד,

כַּכָּתוּב: וְאָכַלְתָּ וְשָׂבָעְתָּ, וּבֵרַכְתָּ אֶת־יהוה
אֱלֹהֶיךָ עַל־הָאָרֶץ הַטֹּבָה אֲשֶׁר נָתַן־לָךְ.
בָּרוּךְ אַתָּה יְיָ, עַל־הָאָרֶץ וְעַל־הַמָּזוֹן.

Ka-ka-tuv: V'a-chal-ta v'sa-va-ta, u-vei-rach-ta et Adonai

Eh-lo-heh-cha al ha-a-retz ha-to-vah a-sher na-tan lach.

Ba-ruch a-ta Adonai, al ha-a-retz v'al ha-ma-zon.

For all this we thank You, Adonai our God. Let Your praise ever be on the lips of all who live, as it is written: "When you have eaten and are satisfied, give praise to Adonai your God who has given you this good earth." We praise You, O God, for the earth, and for sustenance. Amen.

רַחֵם, יְיָ אֱלֹהֵינוּ, עַל יִשְׂרָאֵל עַמֶּךָ, וְעַל יְרוּשָׁלַיִם עִירֶךָ,
וְעַל צִיּוֹן מִשְׁכַּן כְּבוֹדֶךָ. אֱלֹהֵינוּ אָבִינוּ, רְעֵנוּ זוּנֵנוּ,
פַּרְנְסֵנוּ וְכַלְכְּלֵנוּ וְהַרְוִיחֵנוּ, וְהַרְוַח לָנוּ, יְיָ אֱלֹהֵינוּ,
מְהֵרָה מִכָּל־צָרוֹתֵינוּ. וְנָא אַל תַּצְרִיכֵנוּ, יְיָ אֱלֹהֵינוּ,
לֹא לִידֵי מַתְּנַת בָּשָׂר וָדָם וְלֹא לִידֵי הַלְוָאָתָם, כִּי אִם
לְיָדְךָ הַמְּלֵאָה, הַפְּתוּחָה, הַגְּדוּשָׁה, וְהָרְחָבָה, שֶׁלֹּא נֵבוֹשׁ
וְלֹא נִכָּלֵם לְעוֹלָם וָעֶד.

Adonai our God, show compassion for Israel Your people, Jerusalem Your city, and Zion the ancient dwelling-place of Your glory. As a loving parent, O God, guide and sustain us in all our habitations, and be a help to us in all our troubles. Rather than having to rely on the generosity of others, may we be able to rely on the abundance that comes from Your open and generous hand. Thus shall we never be brought to shame.

ON SHABBAT

רְצֵה וְהַחֲלִיצֵנוּ, יְיָ אֱלֹהֵינוּ, בְּמִצְוֹתֶיךָ וּבְמִצְוַת יוֹם הַשְּׁבִיעִי
הַשַּׁבָּת הַגָּדוֹל וְהַקָּדוֹשׁ הַזֶּה, כִּי יוֹם זֶה גָּדוֹל וְקָדוֹשׁ הוּא
לְפָנֶיךָ, לִשְׁבָּת־בּוֹ וְלָנוּחַ בּוֹ בְּאַהֲבָה כְּמִצְוַת רְצוֹנֶךָ. וּבִרְצוֹנְךָ

הָנַח לָנוּ, יי אֱלֹהֵינוּ, שֶׁלֹּא תְהֵא צָרָה וְיָגוֹן וַאֲנָחָה בְּיוֹם
מְנוּחָתֵנוּ. וְהַרְאֵנוּ, יי אֱלֹהֵינוּ, בְּנֶחָמַת צִיּוֹן עִירֶךָ וּבְבִנְיַן יְרוּשָׁלַיִם
עִיר קָדְשֶׁךָ, כִּי אַתָּה הוּא בַּעַל הַיְשׁוּעוֹת וּבַעַל הַנֶּחָמוֹת.

Adonai our God, strengthen our resolve to live by Your Mitzvot, and
especially the Mitzvah of the seventh day, the great and holy Sabbath
that we may lovingly pause from our labors and rest. Adonai our God,
supreme source of deliverance and consolation, shelter us on this day
from sorrow, anguish, and pain, and show us a vision of Zion
comforted, of Jerusalem restored, and of a world that prospers in peace.

ON ROSH CHODESH AND YOM TOV

אֱלֹהֵינוּ וֵאלֹהֵי אֲבוֹתֵינוּ וְאִמּוֹתֵינוּ, יַעֲלֶה וְיָבֹא וְיִזָּכֵר
זִכְרוֹנֵנוּ וְזִכְרוֹן כָּל־עַמְּךָ בֵּית יִשְׂרָאֵל לְפָנֶיךָ לְטוֹבָה
לְחֵן לְחֶסֶד וּלְרַחֲמִים, לְחַיִּים וּלְשָׁלוֹם בְּיוֹם

❖ רֹאשׁ הַחֹדֶשׁ הַזֶּה.

❖ חַג הַמַּצּוֹת הַזֶּה.

❖ חַג הַשָּׁבוּעוֹת הַזֶּה.

❖ הַזִּכָּרוֹן הַזֶּה.

❖ חַג הַסֻּכּוֹת הַזֶּה.

❖ הַשְּׁמִינִי חַג הָעֲצֶרֶת הַזֶּה.

זָכְרֵנוּ, יי אֱלֹהֵינוּ, בּוֹ לְטוֹבָה. אָמֵן.

וּפָקְדֵנוּ בוֹ לִבְרָכָה. אָמֵן.

וְהוֹשִׁיעֵנוּ בוֹ לְחַיִּים. אָמֵן.

Our God, God of our fathers and our mothers, be mindful of Your
people Israel on this

❖ Day of Rosh Chodesh,
❖ Festival of Pesach,

❖ Festival of Shavuot,

❖ Day of Remembrance (Rosh Hashanah)

❖ Festival of Sukkot,

❖ Festival of Sh'mini Atzeret (Simchat Torah),

and renew in us love and compassion, goodness, life, and peace.
This day remember us for well-being. Amen.
Bless us with Your nearness. Amen.
Help us to renew our life. Amen.

וּבְנֵה יְרוּשָׁלַיִם עִיר הַקֹּדֶשׁ בִּמְהֵרָה בְיָמֵינוּ.

בָּרוּךְ אַתָּה יְיָ, בּוֹנֶה בְּרַחֲמָיו יְרוּשָׁלָיִם. אָמֵן.

U-v'nei Y'ru-sha-lay-im ir ha-kodesh bi-m'hei-ra b'ya-mei-nu.

Ba-ruch a-ta Adonai, bo-neh b'ra-cha-mav Y'ru-sha-lay-im. A-mein

Let Jerusalem, the holy city, be renewed in our time. We praise You, O
God, who in compassion rebuilds Jerusalem. Amen.

בָּרוּךְ אַתָּה יְיָ, אֱלֹהֵינוּ מֶלֶךְ הָעוֹלָם, הָאֵל אָבִינוּ, אִמֵּנוּ,

אַדִּירֵנוּ, בּוֹרְאֵנוּ, גּוֹאֲלֵנוּ, יוֹצְרֵנוּ, קְדוֹשֵׁנוּ, קְדוֹשׁ יַעֲקֹב,

רוֹעֵנוּ, רוֹעֵה יִשְׂרָאֵל, הַמֶּלֶךְ הַטּוֹב וְהַמֵּטִיב לַכֹּל,

שֶׁבְּכָל־יוֹם וָיוֹם הוּא הֵטִיב, הוּא מֵטִיב, הוּא יֵטִיב לָנוּ.

הוּא גְמָלָנוּ, הוּא גוֹמְלֵנוּ, הוּא יִגְמְלֵנוּ לָעַד, לְחֵן, לְחֶסֶד

וּלְרַחֲמִים וּלְרֶוַח, הַצָּלָה וְהַצְלָחָה, בְּרָכָה וִישׁוּעָה, נֶחָמָה,

פַּרְנָסָה וְכַלְכָּלָה, וְרַחֲמִים וְחַיִּים וְשָׁלוֹם, וְכָל־טוֹב,

וּמִכָּל־טוּב אַל־יְחַסְּרֵנוּ.

We praise You, Adonai our God, sovereign of the universe, divine parent
of Israel, our creator and redeemer, Holy One of Jacob, source of all that
is holy and good. You have shown us love and kindness always; day
after day You grant us grace and compassion, deliverance and freedom,
prosperity and blessing, life and peace, and all that is good.

הָרַחֲמָן, הוּא יִמְלוֹךְ עָלֵינוּ לְעוֹלָם וָעֶד.

Merciful One, be our God forever.

הָרַחֲמָן, הוּא יִתְבָּרַךְ בַּשָּׁמַיִם וּבָאָרֶץ.

Merciful One, heaven and earth alike are blessed by Your presence.

הָרַחֲמָן, הוּא יִשְׁתַּבַּח לְדוֹר דּוֹרִים, וְיִתְפָּאַר בָּנוּ לְנֵצַח נְצָחִים,
וְיִתְהַדַּר בָּנוּ לָעַד וּלְעוֹלְמֵי עוֹלָמִים.

Merciful One, let all the generations proclaim Your praise, and glory in You forever, to the end of time.

הָרַחֲמָן, הוּא יְפַרְנְסֵנוּ בְּכָבוֹד.

Merciful One, help us to sustain ourselves in honor.

הָרַחֲמָן, הוּא יִשְׁבּוֹר עֻלֵּנוּ מֵעַל צַוָּארֵנוּ.

Merciful One, help us break the yoke of oppression from off our necks.

הָרַחֲמָן, הוּא יִשְׁלַח בְּרָכָה מְרֻבָּה בַּבַּיִת הַזֶּה,
וְעַל שֻׁלְחָן זֶה שֶׁאָכַלְנוּ עָלָיו.

Merciful One, bring abundant blessing on this house and on this table at which we have eaten.

הָרַחֲמָן, הוּא יִשְׁלַח לָנוּ אֶת־אֵלִיָּהוּ הַנָּבִיא, זָכוּר לַטּוֹב,
וִיבַשֶּׂר־לָנוּ בְּשׂוֹרוֹת טוֹבוֹת, יְשׁוּעוֹת וְנֶחָמוֹת.

Merciful One, send us Elijah the Prophet—tidings of good to come, a glimpse of redemptive and consoling days.

הָרַחֲמָן, הוּא יְזַכֵּנוּ לִימוֹת הַגְּאוּלָה וּלְחַיֵּי הָעוֹלָם הַבָּא.

Merciful One, find us worthy of witnessing a time of redemption and of eternal life.

הָרַחֲמָן, הוּא יְבָרֵךְ אוֹתָנוּ וְאֶת־כָּל־אֲשֶׁר לָנוּ, כְּמוֹ
שֶׁנִּתְבָּרְכוּ אֲבוֹתֵינוּ אַבְרָהָם, יִצְחָק, וְיַעֲקֹב, וְאִמּוֹתֵינוּ

394

שָׂרָה, רִבְקָה, לֵאָה וְרָחֵל, בַּכֹּל מִכֹּל כֹּל, כֵּן יְבָרֵךְ
אוֹתָנוּ כֻּלָּנוּ יַחַד, בִּבְרָכָה שְׁלֵמָה, וְנֹאמַר: אָמֵן.

Ha-ra-cha-man, hu y'va-reich o-ta-nu v'et kol a-sher la-nu, k'mo
sheh-nit-ba-r'chu a-vo-tei-nu Av-ra-ham, Yitz-chak, v'Ya-a-kov, v'i-mo-tei-nu
Sa-rah, Riv-kah, Lei-ah, v'Ra-cheil, ba-kol mi-kol kol, kein y'va-reich
o-ta-nu ku-la-nu ya-chad bi-v'ra'cha sh'lei-ma, v'no-mar: A-mein.

Merciful One, bless us and all our dear ones; as You blessed our ancestors Abraham, Isaac, and Jacob; Sarah, Rebekah, Leah, and Rachel, so
bless us, one and all; and let us say: Amen.

בַּמָּרוֹם יְלַמְּדוּ עָלֵינוּ זְכוּת שֶׁתְּהֵא לְמִשְׁמֶרֶת שָׁלוֹם; וְנִשָּׂא
בְרָכָה מֵאֵת יְיָ וּצְדָקָה מֵאֱלֹהֵי יִשְׁעֵנוּ, וְנִמְצָא־חֵן וְשֵׂכֶל
טוֹב בְּעֵינֵי אֱלֹהִים וְאָדָם.

May we receive blessings from on high, kindness from God our help,
and may we all find divine and human grace and favor.

ON SHABBAT

הָרַחֲמָן, הוּא יַנְחִילֵנוּ יוֹם שֶׁכֻּלוֹ שַׁבָּת.

Ha-ra-cha-man, hu yan-chi-lei-nu yom sheh-ku-lo Shabbat.

Merciful One, help us to see the coming of a time that is all
Shabbat.

ON YOM TOV

הָרַחֲמָן, הוּא יַנְחִילֵנוּ יוֹם שֶׁכֻּלוֹ טוֹב.

Ha-ra-cha-man, hu yan-chi-lei-nu yom sheh-ku-lo tov.

Merciful One, help us to see the coming of a time that is all good.

ON ROSH HASHANAH

הָרַחֲמָן, הוּא יְחַדֵּשׁ עָלֵינוּ אֶת־הַשָּׁנָה הַזֹּאת לְטוֹבָה וְלִבְרָכָה.

Ha-ra-cha-man, hu y'cha-deish a-lei-nu et ha-sha-nah ha-zot l'to-vah v'li-v'ra-cha.

Merciful One, bring us a year of renewed good and blessing.

ON ALL DAYS

עֹשֶׂה שָׁלוֹם בִּמְרוֹמָיו, *O-seh sha-lom bi-m'ro-mav,*

הוּא יַעֲשֶׂה שָׁלוֹם עָלֵינוּ *hu ya-a-seh sha-lom a-lei-nu*

וְעַל־כָּל־יִשְׂרָאֵל, וְאִמְרוּ: *v'al kol Yis-ra-eil, v'i-m'ru:*

אָמֵן. *A-mein.*

May the source of peace on high let peace descend on us, on all Israel,
and all the world, and let us say: Amen.

הוֹדוּ לַיהוה כִּי־טוֹב, כִּי לְעוֹלָם חַסְדּוֹ.

פּוֹתֵחַ אֶת־יָדֶךָ וּמַשְׂבִּיעַ לְכָל־חַי רָצוֹן.

בָּרוּךְ הַגֶּבֶר אֲשֶׁר יִבְטַח בַּיהוה, וְהָיָה יהוה מִבְטַחוֹ.

Give thanks to Adonai, who is good, whose love is everlasting,
whose hand is open to feed all that lives.
Blessed are you who trust in God; God is your stronghold.

יהוה עֹז לְעַמּוֹ יִתֵּן; יהוה יְבָרֵךְ אֶת־עַמּוֹ בַשָּׁלוֹם.

Adonai oz l'a-mo yi-tein, Adonai y'va-reich et a-mo va-sha-lom.

Eternal God, You give strength to Your people;
Eternal God, You bless Your people with peace.

⚘

GIVING THANKS FOR FOOD
WHEN NOT EATING A FULL MEAL

FOR AN APPLE OR ANY OTHER FRUIT THAT GROWS ON TREES

בָּרוּךְ אַתָּה יי, אֱלֹהֵינוּ מֶלֶךְ הָעוֹלָם, בּוֹרֵא פְּרִי הָעֵץ.

Ba-ruch a-ta Adonai, Eh-lo-hei-nu meh-lech ha-o-lam, bo-rei p'ri ha-eitz.

We praise You, Adonai our God, sovereign of the universe, for the fruit of the tree.

FOR FRUITS THAT GROW IN THE SOIL AND FOR VEGETABLES

בָּרוּךְ אַתָּה יי, אֱלֹהֵינוּ מֶלֶךְ הָעוֹלָם, בּוֹרֵא פְּרִי הָאֲדָמָה.

Ba-ruch a-ta Adonai, Eh-lo-hei-nu meh-lech ha-o-lam, bo-rei p'ri ha-a-da-mah.

We praise You, Adonai our God, sovereign of the universe, for the fruit of the earth.

FOR WATER, JUICE, OR OTHER LIQUIDS

בָּרוּךְ אַתָּה יי, אֱלֹהֵינוּ מֶלֶךְ הָעוֹלָם, שֶׁהַכֹּל נִהְיֶה
בִּדְבָרוֹ.

Ba-ruch a-ta Adonai, Eh-lo-hei-nu meh-lech ha-o-lam, sheh-ha-kol ni-h'yeh bi-d'va-ro.

We praise You, Adonai our God, sovereign of the universe, for all that came to be by Your word.

TREES

He that plants trees loves others besides himself. (Proverb)

EARTH

Let me enjoy the earth no less
Because the all-enacting Might
That fashioned forth its loveliness
Had other aims than my delight.

See *On the
Doorposts of
Your House*
(Central
Conference of
American
Rabbis), for a
more extensive
selection of
blessings and
rituals for the
home and the
individual.

BLESSINGS FOR VARIOUS OCCASIONS

&

GIVING THANKS FOR A WORLD OF WONDERS

The Baal Shem Tov said: The first time something occurs in nature, people call it a miracle. When it recurs they call it "natural." And when it occurs again and again, they disregard it entirely. Make your service of God a fresh miracle every day. (Chasidic)

The world is charged with the grandeur of God./It will flame out, like shining from shook foil. . . .

IN A GARDEN

בָּרוּךְ אַתָּה יי, אֱלֹהֵינוּ מֶלֶךְ הָעוֹלָם, בּוֹרֵא עִשְׂבֵי בְשָׂמִים.

Ba-ruch a-ta Adonai, Eh-lo-hei-nu meh-lech ha-o-lam, bo-rei i-s'vei v'sa-mim.

Thank You, Adonai our God, sovereign of the universe, for fragrant flowers and herbs.

AT THE OCEAN

בָּרוּךְ אַתָּה יי, אֱלֹהֵינוּ מֶלֶךְ הָעוֹלָם, שֶׁעָשָׂה אֶת־הַיָּם הַגָּדוֹל.

Ba-ruch a-ta Adonai, Eh-lo-hei-nu meh-lech ha-o-lam, sheh-a-sah et yam ha-ga-dol.

Thank You, Adonai our God, sovereign of the universe, for the life-giving waters of the sea.

IN A WOODS OR FOREST

בָּרוּךְ אַתָּה יי, אֱלֹהֵינוּ מֶלֶךְ הָעוֹלָם, בּוֹרֵא עֲצֵי בְשָׂמִים.

Ba-ruch a-ta Adonai, Eh-lo-hei-nu meh-lech ha-o-lam, bo-rei a-tzei v'sa-mim.

Thank You, Adonai our God, sovereign of the universe, for the fragrance of trees.

FOR LIGHTNING OR OTHER NATURAL WONDERS

בָּרוּךְ אַתָּה יי, אֱלֹהֵינוּ מֶלֶךְ הָעוֹלָם, עֹשֶׂה מַעֲשֵׂה בְרֵאשִׁית.

Ba-ruch a-ta Adonai, Eh-lo-hei-nu meh-lech ha-o-lam, o-seh ma-a-sei v'rei-sheet.

Thank You, Adonai our God, sovereign of the universe, for creation and its wonders.

FOR THUNDERSTORMS

בָּרוּךְ אַתָּה יי, אֱלֹהֵינוּ מֶלֶךְ הָעוֹלָם, שֶׁכֹּחוֹ וּגְבוּרָתוֹ מָלֵא עוֹלָם.

Ba-ruch a-ta Adonai, Eh-lo-hei-nu meh-lech ha-o-lam, sheh-ko-cho u-g'vu-ra-to ma-lei o-lam.

Thank You, Adonai our God, sovereign of the universe, Your power and might pervade the world.

ON SEEING A RAINBOW

בָּרוּךְ אַתָּה יי, אֱלֹהֵינוּ מֶלֶךְ הָעוֹלָם, זוֹכֵר הַבְּרִית, וְנֶאֱמָן בִּבְרִיתוֹ, וְקַיָּם בְּמַאֲמָרוֹ.

Ba-ruch a-ta Adonai, Eh-lo-hei-nu meh-lech ha-o-lam, zo-cheir ha-b'rit, v'neh-eh-man bi'v'ri-to, v'ka-yam b'ma-a-ma-ro.

Thank You, Adonai our God, sovereign of the universe, You remember Your covenant with creation.

IN THE PRESENCE OF NATURAL BEAUTY, SUCH AS A MOUNTAIN RANGE OR A SUNSET

בָּרוּךְ אַתָּה יי, אֱלֹהֵינוּ מֶלֶךְ הָעוֹלָם, שֶׁכָּכָה לוֹ בְּעוֹלָמוֹ.

Ba-ruch a-ta Adonai, Eh-lo-hei-nu meh-lech ha-o-lam, sheh-ka-chah lo b'o-la-mo.

Thank You, Adonai our God, sovereign of the universe, for this world so filled with beauty.

Blessings for Various Occasions

ON FIRST SEEING TREES BLOSSOM IN SPRINGTIME

בָּרוּךְ אַתָּה יי, אֱלֹהֵינוּ מֶלֶךְ הָעוֹלָם, אֲשֶׁר בָּרָא בְּעוֹלָמוֹ
בְּרִיּוֹת טוֹבוֹת וְאִילָנוֹת טוֹבִים לֵהָנוֹת בָּהֶם בְּנֵי אָדָם.

*Ba-ruch a-ta Adonai, Eh-lo-hei-nu meh-lech ha-o-lam, a-sher ba-ra b'o-la-mo
b'ri-yot to-tot v'i-la-not to-vim lei-ha-not ba-hem b'nei a-dam.*

We praise You, Adonai our God, sovereign of the universe: You have
created goodly creatures and goodly trees that bring us delight.

REJOICING IN THE DIVERSITY OF THE HUMAN / NATURAL WORLD

בָּרוּךְ אַתָּה יי, אֱלֹהֵינוּ מֶלֶךְ הָעוֹלָם, מְשַׁנֶּה הַבְּרִיּוֹת.

Ba-ruch a-ta Adonai, Eh-lo-hei-nu meh-lech ha-o-lam, m'sha-neh ha-b'ri-yot.

Thank You, Adonai our God, source of life and blessing, for the wondrous diversity of creation.

BEFORE PERFORMING A MITZVAH

ON MAKING A CHARITABLE DONATION

בָּרוּךְ אַתָּה יי, אֱלֹהֵינוּ מֶלֶךְ הָעוֹלָם, אֲשֶׁר קִדְּשָׁנוּ
בְּמִצְוֹתָיו וְצִוָּנוּ עַל הַצְּדָקָה.

*Ba-ruch a-ta Adonai, Eh-lo-hei-nu meh-lech ha-o-lam, a-sher ki-d'sha-nu
b'mitz-vo-tav v'tzi-va-nu al ha-tz'da-kah.*

We praise You, Adonai our God, sovereign of the universe: You hallow
us with Your Mitzvot, and command us concerning the duty of charity.

BEFORE AN ACT OF SOCIAL SERVICE

בָּרוּךְ אַתָּה יי, אֱלֹהֵינוּ מֶלֶךְ הָעוֹלָם, אֲשֶׁר קִדְּשָׁנוּ
בְּמִצְוֹתָיו וְצִוָּנוּ עַל גְּמִילוּת חֲסָדִים.

*Ba-ruch a-ta Adonai, Eh-lo-hei-nu meh-lech ha-o-lam, a-sher ki-d'sha-nu
b'mitz-vo-tav v'tzi-va-nu al g'mi-lut cha-sa-dim.*

400

We praise You, Adonai our God, sovereign of the universe: You hallow us with Your Mitzvot, and command us to aid one another.

WHEN MEETING FOR THE BENEFIT OF THE COMMUNITY

בָּרוּךְ אַתָּה יי, אֱלֹהֵינוּ מֶלֶךְ הָעוֹלָם, אֲשֶׁר קִדְּשָׁנוּ
בְּמִצְוֹתָיו וְצִוָּנוּ לַעֲסוֹק בְּצָרְכֵי צִבּוּר.

*Ba-ruch a-ta Adonai, Eh-lo-hei-nu meh-lech ha-o-lam, a-sher ki-d'sha-nu
b'mitz-vo-tav v'tzi-va-nu la-a-sok b'tzor-chei tzi-bur.*

We praise You, Adonai our God, sovereign of the universe: You hallow us with Your Mitzvot, and command us to attend to the needs of the community.

GIVING THANKS FOR VARIOUS EVENTS

UPON EXPERIENCING A WONDER, AN EXCEPTIONAL JOY, OR A DELIVERANCE

בָּרוּךְ אַתָּה יי, אֱלֹהֵינוּ מֶלֶךְ הָעוֹלָם, שֶׁעָשָׂה לִי נֵס
בַּמָּקוֹם הַזֶּה.

*Ba-ruch a-ta Adonai, Eh-lo-hei-nu meh-lech ha-o-lam, sheh-a-sa li neis
ba-ma-kom ha-zeh.*

Thank You, Adonai our God, sovereign of the universe, for the wonder I have experienced in this place.

AFTER AN ENCOUNTER WITH THE SUBLIME OR MYSTERIOUS

בָּרוּךְ אַתָּה יי, אֱלֹהֵינוּ מֶלֶךְ הָעוֹלָם, חֲכַם הָרָזִים.

Ba-ruch a-ta Adonai, Eh-lo-hei-nu meh-lech ha-o-lam, cha-cham ha-ra-zim.

Praised be Adonai our God, sovereign of the universe, our answer to the mysteries that surround us.

REJOICING IN A NEW EXPERIENCE, OR ON A HAPPY OCCASION

בָּרוּךְ אַתָּה יי, אֱלֹהֵינוּ מֶלֶךְ הָעוֹלָם, שֶׁהֶחֱיָנוּ
וְקִיְּמָנוּ וְהִגִּיעָנוּ לַזְּמַן הַזֶּה.

*Ba-ruch a-ta Adonai, Eh-lo-hei-nu meh-lech ha-o-lam, sheh-heh-cheh-ya-nu
v'ki-y'ma-nu v'hi-gi-ya-nu la-z'man ha-zeh.*

We praise You, Adonai our God, sovereign of the universe, for keeping
us alive, for sustaining us, and for enabling us to reach this season.

ON HEARING GOOD NEWS

בָּרוּךְ אַתָּה יי, אֱלֹהֵינוּ מֶלֶךְ הָעוֹלָם, הַטּוֹב וְהַמֵּטִיב.

Ba-ruch a-ta Adonai, Eh-lo-hei-nu meh-lech ha-o-lam, ha-tov v'ha-mei-tiv.

Thank You, Adonai our God, source of life and blessing, origin of all
good, for helping me rejoice.

ON HEARING SAD NEWS

בָּרוּךְ אַתָּה יי, אֱלֹהֵינוּ מֶלֶךְ הָעוֹלָם, דַּיַּן הָאֱמֶת.

Ba-ruch a-ta Adonai, Eh-lo-hei-nu meh-lech ha-o-lam, da-yan ha-eh-met.

We praise You, Adonai our God, sovereign of the universe: Your
faithfulnes and justice are everlasting.

OR

בָּרוּךְ אַתָּה יי, נוֹטֵעַ בְּתוֹכֵנוּ חַיֵּי עוֹלָם.

Ba-ruch a-ta Adonai, no-tei-a b'to-chei-nu cha-yei o-lam.

Thank You, Adonai our God, source of life and blessing, for You have
implanted everlasting life within us.

ADDITIONAL BLESSINGS

ON GOING FOR A WALK OR A HIKE

בָּרוּךְ אַתָּה יי, אֱלֹהֵינוּ מֶלֶךְ הָעוֹלָם, הַמֵּכִין מִצְעֲדֵי־גָבֶר.

*Ba-ruch a-ta Adonai, Eh-lo-hei-nu meh-lech ha-o-lam, ha-mei-chin
mitz-a-dei ga-ver.*

We praise You, Adonai our God, sovereign of the universe, for making
firm our steps.

AT A MUSEUM OR GALLERY

בָּרוּךְ הַיּוֹצֵר בְּתוֹכֵנוּ חָכְמָה וְכִשְׁרוֹן לִיַצֵּר אֶת־הַיּוֹפִי.

Ba-ruch yo-tzeir b'to-chei-nu choch-mah v'kish-ron l'ya-tzeir et ha-yo-fi.

Praised be the one who has fashioned within us the wisdom and skill to
create beauty.

ON SEEING A SCHOLAR LEARNED IN TORAH

בָּרוּךְ אַתָּה יי, אֱלֹהֵינוּ מֶלֶךְ הָעוֹלָם, שֶׁחָלַק מֵחָכְמָתוֹ לִירֵאָיו.

*Ba-ruch a-ta Adonai, Eh-lo-hei-nu meh-lech ha-o-lam, sheh-cha-lak
mei-choch-ma-to li-rei-av.*

We praise You, Adonai our God, sovereign of the universe, for sharing
Your wisdom with those who revere You.

ON SEEING A SCHOLAR DISTINGUISHED IN SECULAR LEARNING

בָּרוּךְ אַתָּה יי, אֱלֹהֵינוּ מֶלֶךְ הָעוֹלָם, שֶׁנָּתַן מֵחָכְמָתוֹ לְבָשָׂר וָדָם.

*Ba-ruch a-ta Adonai, Eh-lo-hei-nu meh-lech ha-o-lam, sheh-na-tan
mei-choch-ma-to l'va-sar va-dam.*

We praise You, Adonai our God, sovereign of the universe, for giving of
Your wisdom to flesh and blood.

403

BEFORE A JOURNEY

יהוה יִשְׁמָר־צֵאתְךָ וּבוֹאֶךָ מֵעַתָּה וְעַד־עוֹלָם.

Adonai yish-mor tzei-t'cha u-vo-eh-cha mei-a-ta v'ad o-lam.

"Adonai shall guard your going forth and your coming in from this time forth and forever." (Psalm 121:7)

Source of life and blessing, Your presence pervades the world. Wherever I go, may I always feel You near me. "If I take up the wings of the morning, and dwell on the ocean's farthest shore, even there Your hand will lead me, Your strong hand will hold me." (Psalm 139:9-10)

Be a light to my path. May I safely reach my destination. And let me return in contentment to my home and my dear ones. Then will my travels be truly blessed. Amen.

בָּרוּךְ אַתָּה יי, שׁוֹמֵר הַנּוֹסְעִים.

Ba-ruch a-ta Adonai, sho-meir ha-no-s'im.

Praised be God, protector of wayfarers.

UPON RETURNING FROM A JOURNEY

Before going forth from home I spoke the words of the Psalmist:

יהוה יִשְׁמָר־צֵאתְךָ וּבוֹאֶךָ מֵעַתָּה וְעַד־עוֹלָם.

Adonai yish-mor tzei-t'cha u-vo-eh-cha mei-a-tah v'ad o-lam.

"Adonai shall guard your going forth and your coming in from this time forth and forever." (Psalm 121:7)

Now I have "come in," and I give thanks with these words of Scripture:

בָּרוּךְ אַתָּה בְּבֹאֶךָ וּבָרוּךְ אַתָּה בְּצֵאתֶךָ.

Ba-ruch a-ta b'vo-eh-cha u-va-ruch a-ta b'tzei-teh-cha.

"Blessed are you in your going out, blessed are you in your coming in." (Deuteronomy 28:6)

May I always know myself to be blessed, and may blessing surround all my loved ones on their life's journey.

UPON ARRIVING IN ISRAEL

In this, the ancient home of our people, we pray for the welfare of the Land of Israel and all who dwell here:

Rock and redeemer of Israel, grant blessing to this land. Let it ever be filled with life, and a beacon of liberty, justice, and peace for all its inhabitants.

FROM PSALM 122

✤ See "Selected Psalms," pages 358-375, and "A Daily Psalm," pages 27-33.

שָׂמַחְתִּי בְּאֹמְרִים לִי: בֵּית יהוה נֵלֵךְ!
עֹמְדוֹת הָיוּ רַגְלֵינוּ בִּשְׁעָרַיִךְ, יְרוּשָׁלָםִ!
יְרוּשָׁלַםִ הַבְּנוּיָה, כְּעִיר שֶׁחֻבְּרָה־לָהּ יַחְדָּו.

I rejoiced when they said to me:
"Let us go to the house of Adonai!"
Our feet have stood within your gates, O Jerusalem!
Jerusalem rebuilt, a city tied together and whole.

שַׁאֲלוּ שְׁלוֹם יְרוּשָׁלָםִ: יִשְׁלָיוּ אֹהֲבָיִךְ.
יְהִי־שָׁלוֹם בְּחֵילֵךְ, שַׁלְוָה בְּאַרְמְנוֹתָיִךְ.
לְמַעַן אַחַי וְרֵעָי אֲדַבְּרָה־נָּא שָׁלוֹם בָּךְ.
לְמַעַן בֵּית־יהוה אֱלֹהֵינוּ אֲבַקְשָׁה טוֹב לָךְ.

Pray for the peace of Jerusalem:
May those who love you prosper.
Let there be peace within its walls, prosperity in its homes.
For the sake of my kin, my friends, I pray you find peace.
For the sake of the house of Adonai our God,
I will seek your good.

שירו ליהוה שיר חדש

שירים וזמירות

SONGS

שירים SONGS

אדון עולם ADON OLAM

אֲדוֹן עוֹלָם אֲשֶׁר מָלַךְ, בְּטֶרֶם כָּל־יְצִיר נִבְרָא,
לְעֵת נַעֲשָׂה בְחֶפְצוֹ כֹּל, אֲזַי מֶלֶךְ שְׁמוֹ נִקְרָא.

A-don o-lam, a-sher ma-lach, b'teh-rem kol y'tzir niv-ra,
L'eit na-a-sa v'chef-tzo kol, a-zai meh-lech sh'mo nik-ra.

וְאַחֲרֵי כִּכְלוֹת הַכֹּל, לְבַדּוֹ יִמְלֹךְ נוֹרָא;
וְהוּא הָיָה וְהוּא הֹוֶה, וְהוּא יִהְיֶה בְּתִפְאָרָה.

V'a-cha-rei kich-lot ha-kol, l'va-do yim-loch no-ra;
V'hu ha-ya, v'hu ho-veh, v'hu yi-h'yeh b'tif-a-ra.

וְהוּא אֶחָד, וְאֵין שֵׁנִי, לְהַמְשִׁיל לוֹ, לְהַחְבִּירָה,
בְּלִי רֵאשִׁית, בְּלִי תַכְלִית, וְלוֹ הָעֹז וְהַמִּשְׂרָה.

V'hu eh-chad, v'ein shei-ni l'ham-shil lo, l'hach-bi-ra,
B'li rei-sheet, b'li tach-lit, v'lo ha-oz v'ha-mis-ra.

וְהוּא אֵלִי, וְחַי גֹּאֲלִי, וְצוּר חֶבְלִי בְּעֵת צָרָה,
וְהוּא נִסִּי וּמָנוֹס לִי, מְנָת כּוֹסִי בְּיוֹם אֶקְרָא.

V'hu Ei-li, v'chai go-a-li, v'tzur chev-li b'eit tza-ra,
V'hu ni-si u-ma-nos li, m'nat ko-si b'yom ek-ra.

בְּיָדוֹ אַפְקִיד רוּחִי, בְּעֵת אִישַׁן וְאָעִירָה,
וְעִם רוּחִי גְּוִיָּתִי, יְיָ לִי, וְלֹא אִירָא.

B'ya-do af-kid ru-chi, b'eit i-shan v'a-i-ra,
V'im ru-chi g'vi-ya-ti, Adonai li, v'lo i-ra.

God of the world who reigned before creating all things—You willed all
things to be, You were sovereign.

406

אין כאלהינו   EIN KEILOHEINU

אֵין כֵּאלהֵינוּ, אֵין כַּאדונֵינוּ,
אֵין כְּמַלְכֵּנוּ, אֵין כְּמוֹשִׁיעֵנוּ.

Ein kei-lo-hei-nu, ein ka-do-nei-nu,
ein k'mal-kei-nu, ein k'mo-shi-ei-nu.

מִי כֵאלהֵינוּ? מִי כַאדונֵינוּ?
מִי כְמַלְכֵּנוּ? מִי כְמוֹשִׁיעֵנוּ?

Mi chei-lo-hei-nu? Mi cha-do-nei-nu?
Mi ch'mal-kei-nu? Mi ch'mo-shi-ei-nu?

נוֹדֶה לֵאלהֵינוּ, נוֹדֶה לַאדונֵינוּ,
נוֹדֶה לְמַלְכֵּנוּ, נוֹדֶה לְמוֹשִׁיעֵנוּ.

No-deh lei-lo-hei-nu, no-deh la-do-nei-nu,
no-deh l'mal-kei-nu, no-deh l'mo-shi-ei-nu.

בָּרוּךְ אֱלהֵינוּ, בָּרוּךְ אֲדונֵינוּ,
בָּרוּךְ מַלְכֵּנוּ, בָּרוּךְ מוֹשִׁיעֵנוּ.

Ba-ruch Eh-lo-hei-nu, ba-ruch a-do-nei-nu,
ba-ruch mal-kei-nu, ba-ruch mo-shi-ei-nu.

אַתָּה הוּא אֱלהֵינוּ, אַתָּה הוּא אֲדונֵינוּ,
אַתָּה הוּא מַלְכֵּנוּ, אַתָּה הוּא מוֹשִׁיעֵנוּ.

A-ta hu Eh-lo-hei-nu, a-ta hu a-do-nei-nu,
a-ta hu mal-kei-nu, a-ta hu mo-shi-ei-nu.

There is none like our God, our supreme ruler, our redeemer.

YIGDAL יגדל

יִגְדַּל אֱלֹהִים חַי וְיִשְׁתַּבַּח, נִמְצָא וְאֵין עֵת אֶל־מְצִיאוּתוֹ.
אֶחָד וְאֵין יָחִיד כְּיִחוּדוֹ, נֶעְלָם וְגַם אֵין סוֹף לְאַחְדוּתוֹ.

Yig-dal Eh-lo-him chai v'yish-ta-bach, nim-tza v'ein eit el m'tzi-u-to.
Eh-chad, v'ein ya-chid, k'yi-chu-do, neh-lam v'gam ein sof l'ach-du-to.

אֵין לוֹ דְּמוּת הַגּוּף וְאֵינוֹ גוּף, לֹא נַעֲרוֹךְ אֵלָיו קְדֻשָּׁתוֹ.
קַדְמוֹן לְכָל־דָּבָר אֲשֶׁר נִבְרָא, רִאשׁוֹן וְאֵין רֵאשִׁית לְרֵאשִׁיתוֹ.

Ein lo d'mut ha-guf, v'ei-no guf, lo na-a-roch ei-lav k'du-sha-to.
Kad-mon l'chol da-var a-sher niv-ra, ri-shon v'ein rei-sheet l'rei-shi-to.

הִנּוֹ אֲדוֹן עוֹלָם, לְכָל־נוֹצָר. יוֹרֶה גְדֻלָּתוֹ וּמַלְכוּתוֹ.
שֶׁפַע נְבוּאָתוֹ נְתָנוֹ, אֶל־אַנְשֵׁי סְגֻלָּתוֹ וְתִפְאַרְתּוֹ.

Hi-no a-don o-lam, l'chol no-tzar. Yo-reh g'du-la-toh u-mal-chu-to.
Sheh-fa n'vu-a-to n'ta-no, el an-shei s'gu-la-to v'tif-ar-to.

לֹא קָם בְּיִשְׂרָאֵל כְּמֹשֶׁה עוֹד, נָבִיא וּמַבִּיט אֶת־תְּמוּנָתוֹ.
תּוֹרַת אֱמֶת נָתַן לְעַמּוֹ אֵל, עַל יַד נְבִיאוֹ נֶאֱמַן בֵּיתוֹ.

Lo kam b'yis-ra-eil k'Mo-sheh od, na-vi u-ma-bit et t'mu-na-to.
To-rat eh-met na-tan l'a-mo Eil, al yad n'vi-o neh-eh-man bei-to.

לֹא יַחֲלִיף הָאֵל, וְלֹא יָמִיר דָּתוֹ, לְעוֹלָמִים לְזוּלָתוֹ.
צוֹפֶה וְיוֹדֵעַ סְתָרֵינוּ, מַבִּיט לְסוֹף דָּבָר בְּקַדְמָתוֹ.

Lo ya-cha-lif ha-eil, v'lo ya-mir da-to, l'o-la-mim l'zu-la-to.
Tzo-feh v'yo-dei-a s'ta-rei-nu, ma-bit l'sof da-var b'kad-ma-to.

גּוֹמֵל לְאִישׁ חֶסֶד כְּמִפְעָלוֹ, נוֹתֵן לְרָשָׁע רַע כְּרִשְׁעָתוֹ.
יִשְׁלַח לְקֵץ יָמִין פְּדוּת עוֹלָם, כָּל־חַי וְיֵשׁ יַכִּיר יְשׁוּעָתוֹ.

Go-meil l'ish cheh-sed k'mif-a-lo, no-tein l'ra-sha ra k'rish-a-to.
Yish-lach l'keitz ya-min p'dut o-lam, kol chai v'yeish ya-kir y'shu-a-to.

חַיֵּי עוֹלָם נָטַע בְּתוֹכֵנוּ, בָּרוּךְ עֲדֵי עַד שֵׁם תְּהִלָּתוֹ.

Cha-yei o-lam na-ta b'to-chei-nu, ba-ruch a-dei ad sheim t'hi-la-to.

You, the sovereign, willed all things to be. In Your greatnes You sustain Your people and all creation.

יה רבון   YAH RIBON

יָהּ רִבּוֹן עָלַם וְעָלְמַיָּא, אַנְתְּ הוּא מַלְכָּא, מֶלֶךְ מַלְכַיָּא.

Yah ri-bon a-lam v'al-ma-ya (v'al-ma-ya), ant hu mal-ka, meh-lech mal-cha-ya (meh-lech mal-cha-ya).

עוֹבַד גְּבוּרְתֵּךְ, וְתִמְהַיָּא, שְׁפַר קֳדָמַי לְהַחֲוָיָה.

O-vad g'vur-teich, v'tim-ha-ya, sh'far ko-do-mai l'ha-cha-va-yah.

יָהּ רִבּוֹן ...

Yah ri-bon . . .

שְׁבָחִין אֲסַדֵּר, צַפְרָא וְרַמְשָׁא; לָךְ, אֱלָהָא קַדִּישָׁא דִּי בְרָא כָל־נַפְשָׁא.

עִירִין קַדִּישִׁין, וּבְנֵי אֱנָשָׁא, חֵיוַת בָּרָא, וְעוֹפֵי שְׁמַיָּא.

Sh'va-chin a-sa-deir, tzaf-ra v'ram-sha; lach, eh-la-ha ka-di-sha di v'ra chol naf-sha.
I-rin ka-di-shin, u-v'nei eh-na-sha, chei-vat ba-ra, v'o-fei sh'ma-ya.

יָהּ רִבּוֹן ...

Yah ri-bon . . .

רַבְרְבִין עוֹבְדָיךְ, וְתַקִּיפִין, מָכֵךְ רְמַיָּא וְזָקֵף כְּפִיפִין.

לוּ יְחֵא גְבַר שְׁנִין אַלְפִין, לָא יֵעֹל גְּבוּרְתֵּךְ בְּחֻשְׁבְּנַיָּא.

Rav-r'vin o-v'dach, v'ta-ki-fin, ma-cheich r'ma-ya v'za-keif k'fi-fin.
Lu y'chei g'var sh'nin a-l'fin, la yei-ol g'vur-teich b'chush-b'na-yah.

יָהּ רִבּוֹן ...

Yah ri-bon . . .

Sovereign God of this and all worlds, You are the supreme ruler of human rulers.

TCHIRI BIRI BIM טשירי בירי בים

אַז אִיך וועל זאָגען לְכָה דוֹדִי, זאָלסט דו זאָגען טשירי בירי
בִּים. אַז אִיך וועל זאָגען לִקְרַאת כַּלָה, זאָלסט דו זאָגען
טשירי בירי בֶּם.
לְכָה דוֹדִי, טשירי בירי בִּים, לִקְרַאת כַּלָה, טשירי בירי בֶּם,
לְכָה דוֹדִי, לִקְרַאת כַּלָה, טשירי בירי בירי בֶּם.
טשירי בִּים, טשירי בֶּם, טשירי בִּים בֶּם בִּים בֶּם בֶּם,
טשירי בֶּם, טשירי בִּים, טשירי בִּים בֶּם בִּים בֶּם בֶּם,
הי טשירי בירי בירי בִּים בֶּם, בֶּם. (4)
טשירי בִּים, טשירי בֶּם, טשירי בִּים בֶּם בִּים בֶּם בֶּם,
טשירי בֶּם, טשירי בִּים, טשירי בִּים בֶּם בִּים בֶּם בֶּם,
טשירי בירי בירי בֶּם.

Az ich vel za-gen, "L'cha Dodi," zolst do za-gen, tchi-ri bi-ri bim.
Az ich vel za-gen, "Lik-ras Ka-lah," zolst do za-gen, tchi-ri bi-ri bam.
"L'cha Dodi," tchi-ri bi-ri bim. "Lik-ras Ka-lah," tchi-ri bi-ri bam.
"L'cha Dodi," "Lik-ras Ka-lah," —tchi-ri bi-ri bi-ri bi-ri bam.
Tchi-ri bim —tchi-ri bi-ri bam, tchi-ri bim bam bim bam bim bam.
Tchi-ri bam —tchi-ri bim, tchi-ri bim bam bim bam bim bam.
Hei tchi-ri bi-ri bim bam bam, Hei tchi-ri bi-ri bim bam bam,
Hei tchi-ri bi-ri bim bam bam, Hei tchi-ri bi-ri bim bam bam,
Tchi-ri bi-ri bi-ri bi-ri bam.

When I say "L'cha Dodi," you say "tchi-ri bi-ri bim." When I say "Lik-ras Ka-lah, you say "tchi-ri bi-ri bam." Etc.

410

ישמחו השמים   YISM'CHU HASHAMAYIM

יִשְׂמְחוּ הַשָּׁמַיִם וְתָגֵל הָאָרֶץ; יִרְעַם הַיָּם וּמְלֹאוֹ.

Yis-m'chu ha-sha-ma-yim v'ta-geil ha-a-retz; yir-am ha-am u-m'lo-o.

Be glad, O heavens; rejoice, O earth; let the sea and its fullness roar.

לא ישא גוי   LO YISA GOI

לֹא יִשָּׂא גּוֹי אֶל־גּוֹי חֶרֶב, לֹא יִלְמְדוּ עוֹד מִלְחָמָה.

Lo yi-sa goi el goi cheh-rev, lo yil-m'do od mil-cha-mah.

Nation shall not lift up sword against nation, neither shall they study war any more.

דוד מלך   DAVID MEHLECH

דָּוִד מֶלֶךְ יִשְׂרָאֵל, חַי וְקַיָּם.

Da-vid meh-lech Yis-ra-eil, chai v'ka-yam.

David king of Israel, lives and endures.

אלה חמדה לבי   EILEH CHAMDAH LIBI

אֵלֶה חָמְדָה לִבִּי, חוּסָה נָא וְאַל נָא תִּתְעַלֵּם.

Ei-leh cham-dah li-bi, chu-sah na v'al na tit-a-leim.

This is my heart's desire: Have pity, do not hide Yourself.

יוֹם זֶה לְיִשְׂרָאֵל YOM ZEH L'YISRAEIL

יוֹם זֶה לְיִשְׂרָאֵל אוֹרָה	Yom zeh l'Yis-ra-eil o-ra
וְשִׂמְחָה, שַׁבַּת מְנוּחָה.	v'sim-cha, Shabbat m'nu-chah.
צִוִּיתָ פִּקוּדִים בְּמַעֲמַד	Tzi-vi-ta pi-ku-dim b'ma-a-mad
סִינַי,	Si-nai,
שַׁבָּת וּמוֹעֲדִים לִשְׁמוֹר	Shabbat u-mo-a-dim lish-mor
בְּכָל־שָׁנַי,	b'chol sha-nai,
לַעֲרוֹךְ לְפָנַי מַשְׂאֵת	La-a-r-och l'fa-nai mas-eit
וַאֲרוּחָה,	va-a-ru-cha,
שַׁבַּת מְנוּחָה.	Shabbat m'nu-cha.
יוֹם זֶה לְיִשְׂרָאֵל אוֹרָה	Yom zeh l'Yis-ra-eil o-ra
וְשִׂמְחָה, שַׁבַּת מְנוּחָה.	v'sim-cha, Shabbat m'nu-chah
קִדַּשְׁתָּ בֵּרַכְתָּ אוֹתוֹ	Ki-dash-ta bei-rach-ta o-to
מִכָּל־יָמִים,	mi-kol ya-mim,
בְּשֵׁשֶׁת כִּלִּיתָ מְלֶאכֶת	B'shei-shet ki-li-ta m'leh-chet
עוֹלָמִים,	o-la-mim,
בּוֹ מָצְאוּ עֲגוּמִים הַשְׁקֵט	Bo ma-tz'u a-gu-mim hash-keit
וּבִטְחָה,	u-vi-t'cha,
שַׁבַּת מְנוּחָה.	Shabbat m'nu-cha.
יוֹם זֶה לְיִשְׂרָאֵל אוֹרָה	Yom zeh l'Yis-ra-eil o-ra
וְשִׂמְחָה, שַׁבַּת מְנוּחָה.	v'sim-cha, Shabbat m'nu-chah.

This is our day of light and joy: a Sabbath of rest.

יום זה מכבד   YOM ZEH M'CHUBAD

יוֹם זֶה מְכֻבָּד מִכָּל־יָמִים,	Yom zeh m'chu-bad mi-kol ya-mim,
כִּי בוֹ שָׁבַת צוּר עוֹלָמִים.	ki vo sha-vat tzur o-la-mim.
שֵׁשֶׁת יָמִים תַּעֲשֶׂה מְלַאכְתֶּךָ,	Shei-shet ya-mim ta-a-seh m'lach-teh-cha,
וְיוֹם הַשְּׁבִיעִי לֵאלֹהֶיךָ;	v'yom ha-sh'vi-i lei-lo-heh-cha;
שַׁבָּת לֹא תַעֲשֶׂה בוֹ מְלָאכָה,	Shabbat lo ta-a-seh vo m'la-chah,
כִּי כֹל עָשָׂה שֵׁשֶׁת יָמִים,	ki chol a-sah shei-shet ya-mim.
יוֹם זֶה מְכֻבָּד מִכָּל־יָמִים,	Yom zeh m'chu-bad mi-kol ya-mim,
כִּי בוֹ שָׁבַת צוּר עוֹלָמִים.	ki vo sha-vat tzur o-la-mim.
הַשָּׁמַיִם מְסַפְּרִים כְּבוֹדוֹ,	Ha-sha-ma-yim m'sa-p'rim k'vo-do,
וְגַם הָאָרֶץ מָלְאָה חַסְדּוֹ;	v'gam ha-a-retz ma-l'ah chas-do;
רְאוּ כִּי כָל־אֵלֶּה עָשְׂתָה יָדוֹ,	r'u ki chol ei-leh a-s'tah ya-do,
כִּי הוּא הַצּוּר פָּעֳלוֹ תָמִים.	ki hu ha-tzur po-o-lo ta-mim.
יוֹם זֶה מְכֻבָּד מִכָּל־יָמִים,	Yom zeh m'chu-bad mi-kol ya-mim,
כִּי בוֹ שָׁבַת צוּר עוֹלָמִים.	ki vo sha-vat tzur o-la-mim.

This day is honored above the others, for on it rested the Rock of Ages.

ידיד נפש · YEDID NEFESH

יְדִיד נֶפֶשׁ, אָב הָרַחֲמָן, מְשׁוֹךְ עַבְדְּךָ אֶל רְצוֹנֶךָ.

יָרוּץ עַבְדְּךָ כְּמוֹ אַיָּל, יִשְׁתַּחֲוֶה אֶל מוּל הֲדָרֶךָ.

יֶעֱרַב לוֹ יְדִידוֹתֶיךָ מִנּוֹפֶת צוּף וְכָל־טָעַם.

הָדוּר נָאֶה, זִיו הָעוֹלָם, נַפְשִׁי חוֹלַת אַהֲבָתֶךָ.

וָתִיק, יֶהֱמוּ נָא רַחֲמֶיךָ, וְחוּסָה נָא עַל בֵּן אֲהוּבֶךָ.

כִּי זֶה כַּמָּה נִכְסוֹף נִכְסַפְתִּי לִרְאוֹת בְּתִפְאֶרֶת עֻזֶּךָ.

אָנָּא אֵלִי, חֶמְדַּת לִבִּי, חוּסָה נָא וְאַל תִּתְעַלָּם.

הִגָּלֶה נָא, וּפְרוֹס, חֲבִיבִי, עָלַי אֶת־סֻכַּת שְׁלוֹמָךְ.

תָּאִיר אֶרֶץ מִכְּבוֹדֶךָ, נָגִילָה וְנִשְׂמְחָה בָּךְ.

Y'did neh-fesh, av ha-ra-cha-man, m'shoch av-d'cha el r'tzo-neh-cha.

Ya-rutz av-d'cha k'mo a-yal, yish-ta-cha-veh el mul ha-da-reh-cha.

Yeh-eh-rav lo y'di-do-teh-cha mi-no-fet tzuf v'chol ta-am.

Ha-dur na-eh, ziv ha-o-lam, naf-shi cho-lat a-ha-va-teh-cha.

Va-tik, yeh-heh-mu na ra-cha-meh-cha, v'chu-sah na al bein a-hu-veh-cha.

Ki zeh ka-mah nich-sof nich-saf-ti li-r'ot b'tif-eh-ret u-zeh-cha.

A-na ei-li, chem-dat li-bi, chu-sa na v'al tit-a-lam.

Hi-ga-leh na, u-f'ros, cha-vi-vi, a-lai et su-kat sh'lo-mach.

Ta-ir eh-retz mi-ch'vo-deh-cha, na-gi-la v'nis-mach bach.

Soul's beloved, source of mercy, draw Your servant to Your will.
Let me leap like a deer to stand in awe before Your glory.
Your love is sweeter than the taste of honey.
Shining glory, light of the world, my heart is faint for love of You.
Show compassion, O Ancient One, pity for the child You love.
How long I have yearned to see Your glorious might.
O God, my heart's desire, have pity, and hide no more.
Show Yourself, beloved, and spread over me the shelter of Your peace.
Illumine the world with Your presence, and we will rejoice and be glad
in You.

אל אדון EIL ADON

אֵל אָדוֹן עַל כָּל־הַמַּעֲשִׂים, בָּרוּךְ וּמְבֹרָךְ בְּפִי כָּל־נְשָׁמָה.

גָּדְלוֹ וְטוּבוֹ מָלֵא עוֹלָם, דַּעַת וּתְבוּנָה סוֹבְבִים אוֹתוֹ.

זְכוּת וּמִישׁוֹר לִפְנֵי כִסְאוֹ! חֶסֶד וְרַחֲמִים לִפְנֵי כְבוֹדוֹ!

טוֹבִים מְאוֹרוֹת שֶׁבָּרָא אֱלֹהֵינוּ! יְצָרָם בְּדַעַת, בְּרָאָם בְּהַשְׂכֵּל.

כֹּחַ וּגְבוּרָה נָתַן בָּהֶם, לִהְיוֹת מוֹשְׁלִים בְּקֶרֶב תֵּבֵל.

מְלֵאִים זִיו וּמְפִיקִים נֹגַהּ, נָאֶה זִיוָם בְּכָל־הָעוֹלָם.

שְׂמֵחִים בְּצֵאתָם וְשָׂשִׂים בְּבוֹאָם, עוֹשִׂים בְּאֵימָה רְצוֹן קוֹנָם.

פְּאֵר וְכָבוֹד נוֹתְנִים לִשְׁמוֹ, צָהֳלָה וְרִנָּה לְזֵכֶר מַלְכָם.

קָרָא לַשֶּׁמֶשׁ וַיִּזְרַח־אוֹר, רָאָה וְהִתְקִין צוּרַת הַלְּבָנָה.

שֶׁבַח נוֹתְנִים־לוֹ כָּל־צְבָא מָרוֹם!

God is supreme over all creation, blessed and praised by every soul.

Your greatness and goodness fill the world; knowledge and insight are all around You.

In Your majestic presence are purity and justice; love and compassion are Your constant glory!

How good are the stars our God has made! You formed them with knowledge, and made them with wisdom.

You endowed them with power, and enjoined them to rule in the midst of the world.

Filled with splendor, radiant with brightness, their brilliance is lovely in all the world.

They rejoice in their rising and delight in their setting, obeying in awe the will of their maker.

Honor and glory they give to Your name, singing with joy to their royal God.

You call the sun, and it blazes with light; You look at the moon, and it circles the earth. All the hosts of heaven praise You!

הכל יודוך HAKOL YODUCHA

הַכֹּל יוֹדוּךָ וְהַכֹּל יְשַׁבְּחוּךָ וְהַכֹּל יֹאמְרוּ: אֵין קָדוֹשׁ כַּיְיָ.
הַכֹּל יְרוֹמְמוּךָ סֶּלָה, יוֹצֵר הַכֹּל.
הָאֵל הַפּוֹתֵחַ בְּכָל־יוֹם דַּלְתוֹת שַׁעֲרֵי מִזְרָח, וּבוֹקֵעַ חַלּוֹנֵי
רָקִיעַ, מוֹצִיא חַמָּה מִמְּקוֹמָהּ, וּלְבָנָה מִמְּכוֹן שִׁבְתָּהּ.
הַמֵּאִיר לָאָרֶץ וְלַדָּרִים עָלֶיהָ בְּרַחֲמִים, וּבְטוּבוֹ מְחַדֵּשׁ
בְּכָל־יוֹם תָּמִיד מַעֲשֵׂה בְרֵאשִׁית.
הַמֶּלֶךְ הַמְּרוֹמָם לְבַדּוֹ מֵאָז, הַמְשֻׁבָּח וְהַמְפֹאָר וְהַמִּתְנַשֵּׂא
מִימוֹת עוֹלָם.
אֱלֹהֵי עוֹלָם, בְּרַחֲמֶיךָ הָרַבִּים רַחֵם עָלֵינוּ: אֲדוֹן עֻזֵּנוּ, צוּר
מִשְׂגַּבֵּנוּ, מָגֵן יִשְׁעֵנוּ, מִשְׂגָּב בַּעֲדֵנוּ.

All shall thank You, and all shall praise You, and all shall say: "There is none holy as Adonai." All shall exalt You, creator of all things.

Day by day You unlock the gates of the east, and open the windows of heaven, bringing forth the sun from its place, and the moon from its dwelling.

In Your mercy You give light to the earth and all who dwell on it, and in Your goodness You renew the work of creation continually, day by day.

You alone, O sovereign, have been exalted since earliest times, praised and glorified from days of old.

O everlasting God, in Your abundant mercy have mercy on us! You are the source of our strength, the rock of our refuge, the shield of our salvation, and our mighty stronghold.

אלי, אלי   EILI, EILI

אֵלִי, אֵלִי,

שֶׁלֹּא יִגָּמֵר לְעוֹלָם:

הַחוֹל וְהַיָּם,

רִשְׁרוּשׁ שֶׁל הַמַּיִם,

בְּרַק הַשָּׁמַיִם,

תְּפִלַּת הָאָדָם.

הַחוֹל וְהַיָּם,

רִשְׁרוּשׁ שֶׁל הַמַּיִם,

בְּרַק הַשָּׁמַיִם,

תְּפִלַּת הָאָדָם.

Ei-li, Ei-li

sheh-lo yi-ga-mer l'o-lam:

ha-chol v'ha-yam,

rish-rush shel ha-ma-yim,

b'rak ha-sha-ma-yim,

t'fi-lat ha-a-dam.

Ha-chol v'ha-yam,

rish-rush shel ha-ma-yim,

b'rak ha-sha-ma-yim,

t'fi-lat ha-a-dam.

O God, my God,
I pray that these things never end:
the sand and the sea, the rush of the waters,
the crash of the heavens, the prayer of the heart;
the sand and the sea, the rush of the waters,
the crash of the heavens, the prayer of the heart.

והאר עינינו   V'HAER EINEINU

וְהָאֵר עֵינֵינוּ בְּתוֹרָתֶךָ, וְדַבֵּק לִבֵּנוּ בְּמִצְוֹתֶיךָ,

וְיַחֵד לְבָבֵנוּ לְאַהֲבָה וּלְיִרְאָה אֶת־שְׁמֶךָ.

V'ha-er ei-nei-nu b'to-ra-teh-cha, v'da-beik li-bei-bu b'mitz-vo-teh-cha,
v'ya-cheid l'va-vei-nu l'a-ha-va u-l'yir-ah et sh'meh-cha.

Open our eyes to Your teaching, make our hearts faithful to Your commandments, and make us wholehearted in the love and awe of Your name.

הַיָּמִים חוֹלְפִים DAYS PASS

הַיָּמִים חוֹלְפִים, שָׁנָה עוֹבֶרֶת,
הַיָּמִים חוֹלְפִים, שָׁנָה עוֹבֶרֶת,
אֲבָל הַמַּנְגִּינָה, אֲבָל הַמַּקְהֵלָה,
אֲבָל הַחֶבְרַיָּה, תָּמִיד נִשְׁאֶרֶת.

Ha-ya-mim cho-l'fim, sha-nah o-veh-ret,
Ha-ya-mim cho-l'fim, sha-nah o-veh-ret,
A-val ha-man-gi-nah, a-val ha-mak-hei-lah,
A-val ha-chev-ra-yah, ta-mid nish-eh-ret.

Days pass and years go by, ever and ever.
Days pass and years go by, ever and ever.
And yet the hope we bring,
And yet the love we sing,
Friends to whose hands we cling,
Go on forever.

שָׁלוֹם חֲבֵרִים SHALOM CHAVEIRIM

שָׁלוֹם חֲבֵרִים, *Sha-lom cha-vei-rim,*
שָׁלוֹם חֲבֵרִים *sha-lom cha-vei-rim,*
שָׁלוֹם, שָׁלוֹם. *sha-lom, sha-lom.*
לְהִתְרָאוֹת, לְהִתְרָאוֹת. *L'hit-ra-ot, l'hit-ra-ot.*
שָׁלוֹם, שָׁלוֹם. *Sha-lom, sha-lom.*

Our hope is for peace,
Our prayer is for peace,
Shalom, shalom.
Let all now be friends,
Let all now be free.
Shalom, shalom.

שחקי SACHAKI

שַׂחֲקִי, שַׂחֲקִי, עַל הַחֲלוֹמוֹת,	Sa-cha-ki, sa-cha-ki, al ha-cha-lo-mot,
זוּ אֲנִי הַחוֹלֵם שָׂח,	zu a-ni ha-cho-leim sach,
שַׂחֲקִי כִּי בָאָדָם אַאֲמִין,	sa-cha-ki ki va-a-dam a-a-min,
כִּי עוֹדֶנִּי מַאֲמִין בָּךְ.	ki o-deh-ni ma-a-min bach.
כִּי עוֹד נַפְשִׁי דְּרוֹר שׁוֹאֶפֶת,	Ki od naf-shi d'ror sho-eh-fet,
לֹא מְכַרְתִּיהָ לְעֵגֶל פָּז,	lo m'char-ti-ha l'ei-gel paz,
כִּי עוֹד אַאֲמִין גַּם בָּאָדָם,	ki od a-a-min gam ba-a-dam,
גַּם בְּרוּחוֹ רוּחַ עָז.	gam b'ru-cho ru-ach az.
אַאֲמִינָה גַּם בֶּעָתִיד,	A-a-mi-nah gam beh-a-tid,
אַף אִם יִרְחַק זֶה הַיּוֹם.	af im yir-chak zeh ha-yom.
אַךְ בֹּא יָבוֹא יִשְׂאוּ שָׁלוֹם	Ach bo ya-vo yis'u sha-lom
אָז, וּבְרָכָה לְאֹם מִלְאֹם.	Az, u-v'ra-chah l'om mi-l'om.

Smile, friend, smile away my dreams!
What I dream shall yet come true,
Smile that I believe in people,
As I still believe in you.
My spirit still for freedom yearns,
Unbartered for a calf of gold;
In men and women I believe,
And in their spirit, strong and bold.
And in the future I believe—
Though it be distant, come it will—
When nations shall each other bless,
And peace at last the earth shall fill.

שההיינו SHEHECHEYANU

בָּרוּךְ אַתָּה יי, אֱלֹהֵינוּ מֶלֶךְ הָעוֹלָם,
שֶׁהֶחֱיָנוּ וְקִיְּמָנוּ וְהִגִּיעָנוּ לַזְּמַן הַזֶּה.

Ba-ruch a-ta Adonai, Eh-lo-hei-nu meh-lech ha-o-lam,
sheh-heh-cheh-ya-nu v'ki-y'ma-nu v'hi-gi-a-nu la-z'man ha-zeh.

We praise You, Adonai our God, sovereign of the universe, for giving us life, for sustaining us, and for enabling us to reach this season.

הבה נגילה HAVAH NAGILAH

הָבָה נָגִילָה וְנִשְׂמְחָה. *Ha-vah na-gi-lah v'nis-m'chah.*

הָבָה נְרַנְּנָה וְנִשְׂמְחָה. *Ha-vah n'ra-n'nah v'nis-m'chah.*

עוּרוּ, אַחִים, בְּלֵב שָׂמֵחַ. *U-ru, a-chim, b'leiv sa-mei-ach.*

Come, let us rejoice and be happy. Come, let us sing and be happy. Wake up, brothers and sisters, with a joyful heart.

גשר צר מאד GESHER TZAR M'OD

כָּל־הָעוֹלָם כֻּלּוֹ גֶּשֶׁר צַר מְאֹד,
וְהָעִקָּר לֹא לְפַחֵד כְּלָל.

Kol ha-o-lam ku-lo geh-sher tzar m'od,
v'ha-i-kar lo l'fa-cheid k'lal.

This world is a very narrow bridge, and the main thing is not to be afraid at all.

MAYIM מים

וּשְׁאַבְתֶּם־מַיִם בְּשָׂשׂוֹן,	U-sh'av-tem ma-yim b'sa-son
מִמַּעַיְנֵי הַיְשׁוּעָה. (2)	mi-ma-a-y'nei ha-y'shu-a. (2)
מַיִם, מַיִם, מַיִם, מַיִם	Ma-yim, ma-yim, ma-yim, ma-yim
הֵי מַיִם בְּשָׂשׂוֹן. (2)	hei ma-yim b'sa-son. (2)
הֵי, הֵי, הֵי, הֵי,	Hei, hei, hei, hei,
מַיִם (6) בְּשָׂשׂוֹן. (2)	ma-yim (6) b'sa-son (2)

With joy you shall draw water from the fountains of salvation.

MIPI EIL מפי אל

אֵין אַדִּיר כַּיְיָ וְאֵין בָּרוּךְ כְּבֶן אַמְרָם.
אֵין גְּדוֹלָה כַּתּוֹרָה וְאֵין דַּרְשָׁנֶיהָ כְּיִשְׂרָאֵל.
מִפִּי אֵל וּמִפִּי אֵל יְבֹרַךְ כָּל יִשְׂרָאֵל.

*Ein **A**-dir ka-do-nai v'ein **B**aruch k'ven Am-ram.*
*Ein **G**'dolah ka-Torah, v'ein **D**ar-sha-neh-ha k'Yis-ra-eil.*
Mi-pi Eil u-mi-pi Eil y'vo-rach kol Yis-ra-eil.

אֵין הָדוּר כַּיְיָ וְאֵין וָתִיק כְּבֶן אַמְרָם.
אֵין זַכָּה כַּתּוֹרָה וְאֵין חֲכָמֶיהָ כְּיִשְׂרָאֵל.
מִפִּי אֵל וּמִפִּי אֵל יְבֹרַךְ כָּל יִשְׂרָאֵל.

*Ein **H**a-dur ka-do-nai v'ein **V**a-tik k'ven Am-ram.*
*Ein **Z**a-kah ka-Torah, v'ein **C**ha-cha-meh-ha k'Yis-ra-eil.*
Mi-pi Eil u-mi-pi Eil y'vo-rach kol Yis-ra-eil.

אֵין טָהוֹר כַּיְיָ וְאֵין יָחִיד כְּבֶן אַמְרָם.
אֵין כַּבִּירָה כַּתּוֹרָה וְאֵין לַמְדָנֶיהָ כְּיִשְׂרָאֵל.
מִפִּי אֵל וּמִפִּי אֵל יְבֹרַךְ כָּל יִשְׂרָאֵל.

Ein Ta-hor ka-do-nai v'ein Ya-chid k'ven Am-ram.
Ein Ka-bi-rah ka-Torah, v'ein Lam-da-neh-ha k'Yis-ra-eil.
Mi-pi Eil u-mi-pi Eil y'vo-rach kol Yis-ra-eil.

אֵין מֶלֶךְ כַּיְיָ וְאֵין נָבִיא כְּבֶן אַמְרָם.
אֵין סְגוּלָה כַּתּוֹרָה וְאֵין עוֹסְקֶיהָ כְּיִשְׂרָאֵל.
מִפִּי אֵל וּמִפִּי אֵל יְבֹרַךְ כָּל יִשְׂרָאֵל.

Ein Meh-lech ka-do-nai v'ein Na-vi k'ven Am-ram.
Ein S'gu-lah ka-Torah, v'ein O-s'keh-ha k'Yis-ra-eil.
Mi-pi Eil u-mi-pi Eil y'vo-rach kol Yis-ra-eil.

אֵין פּוֹדֶה כַּיְיָ וְאֵין צַדִּיק כְּבֶן אַמְרָם.
אֵין קְדוֹשָׁה כַּתּוֹרָה וְאֵין רוֹמְמֶיהָ כְּיִשְׂרָאֵל.
מִפִּי אֵל וּמִפִּי אֵל יְבֹרַךְ כָּל יִשְׂרָאֵל.

Ein Po-deh ka-do-nai v'ein Tza-dik k'ven Am-ram.
Ein K'do-shah ka-Torah, v'ein Ro-m'meh-ha k'Yis-ra-eil.
Mi-pi Eil u-mi-pi Eil y'vo-rach kol Yis-ra-eil.

אֵין קָדוֹשׁ כַּיְיָ וְאֵין רַבִּי כְּבֶן אַמְרָם.
אֵין שְׁמִירָה כַּתּוֹרָה וְאֵין תּוֹמְכֶיהָ כְּיִשְׂרָאֵל.
מִפִּי אֵל וּמִפִּי אֵל יְבֹרַךְ כָּל יִשְׂרָאֵל.

Ein Ka-dosh ka-do-nai v'ein Ra-bi k'ven Am-ram.
Ein Sh'mi-rah ka-Torah, v'ein To-m'cheh-ha k'Yis-ra-eil.
Mi-pi Eil u-mi-pi Eil y'vo-rach kol Yis-ra-eil.

None are exalted as Adonai, and none as blessed as Amram's son. There is nothing as great as the Torah, and none interprets it as Israel does. Out of God's mouth, God's alone, shall Israel be blessed. . . .

אויפֿן פּריפּעטשיק   OIFN PRIPETCHIK

אויפֿן פּריפּעטשיק ברענט אַ פֿייערל, און אין שטוב איז הייס.

און דער רבי לערנט קלײנע קינדערלך דעם אלף־בית. (2)

זאָגט־זשע קינדערלך, געדענקט־זשע טײַערע,

וואָס איר לערנט דאַ,

זאָגט־זשע נאָך אַמאָל און טאַקע נאָך אַמאָל: קמץ־אַלף: אָ! (2)

Oifn pri-pet-chik brent a fa-y'rl, un in shtub iz heis.

Un der rebbe leh-rnt klei-neh kin-der-lach dem a-leph beis.(2)

Zugt-zheh kin-der-lach, geh-denkt zheh ta-y'reh,

vos ir leh-rent do,

Zugt-zheh noch a-mol un ta-keh noch a-mol: ko-metz-a-leph: O! (2)

A fire burns in the stove, the house is hot, and the rebbe teaches little children the "aleph-beis." See, little ones, remember, dear ones, what you're learning here. Say it again, yes, and once again: "ko-metz-aleph" is "O!"

מעוז צור   MA-OZ TZUR

מָעוֹז צוּר יְשׁוּעָתִי,   *Ma-oz tzur y'shu-a-ti,*

לְךָ נָאֶה לְשַׁבֵּחַ,   *l'cha na-eh la'sha-bei-ach.*

תִּכּוֹן בֵּית תְּפִלָּתִי,   *Ti-kon beit t'fi-la-ti,*

וְשָׁם תּוֹדָה נְזַבֵּחַ.   *v'sham to-dah n'za-bei-ach.*

לְעֵת תָּכִין מַטְבֵּחַ   *L'eit ta-chin mat-bei-ach,*

מִצָּר הַמְנַבֵּחַ,   *mi-tzar ha-m'na-bei-ach,*

אָז אֶגְמוֹר, בְּשִׁיר מִזְמוֹר,   *az eg-mor, b'shir miz-mor,*

חֲנֻכַּת הַמִּזְבֵּחַ.   *cha-nu-kat ha-miz-bei-ach.*

Refuge, rock of my salvation, to You our praise is due.
Let Your house become a house of prayer

and thankgiving for all peoples.
When by Your will all bloodshed ends
and enemies cease to scream hate:
Then we shall celebrate with joyful song
the true dedication of Your altar.

Rock of ages, let our song
Praise Your wondrous saving power.
You, amid the raging foes,
Were our safe and sheltering tower.
Furious, they assailed us,
But Your arm availed us,
And Your word
Broke their sword
When our own strength failed us.

Kindling new the holy lamps,
Priests, approved in suffering,
Purified the nation's shrine,
Brought to You their offering.
And, Your courts surrounding,
Hear, in joy abounding,
Happy throngs
Singing songs
With a mighty sounding.

Children of the Maccabees,
Whether free or fettered,
Wake the echoes of the songs
Where you may be scattered.
Yours the message cheering
That the time is nearing
Which will see
All go free,
Tyrants disappearing.

עצו עצה- UTZU EITZAH

עֵצוּ עֵצָה וְתֻפָר; דַּבְּרוּ דָבָר וְלֹא יָקוּם; כִּי עִמָּנוּ אֵל.

U-tzu ei-tzah v'tu-far; da-b'ru da-var v'lo ya-kum; ki i-ma-nu Eil.

Conspire, and it will fail; plot, and it will not stand; for God is with us.

דודי לי DODI LI

דּוֹדִי לִי וַאֲנִי לוֹ, הָרֹעֶה בַּשׁוֹשַׁנִּים. (2)

מִי זֹאת עֹלָה מִן־הַמִּדְבָּר, מִי זֹאת עֹלָה?

מְקֻטֶּרֶת מוֹר וּלְבוֹנָה, מוֹר וּלְבוֹנָה.

דּוֹדִי לִי וַאֲנִי לוֹ, הָרֹעֶה בַּשׁוֹשַׁנִּים. (2)

לִבַּבְתִּנִי, אֲחֹתִי כַלָּה, לִבַּבְתִּנִי כַלָּה. (2)

דּוֹדִי לִי וַאֲנִי לוֹ, הָרֹעֶה בַּשׁוֹשַׁנִּים. (2)

עוּרִי צָפוֹן, וּבוֹאִי תֵימָן. (2)

דּוֹדִי לִי וַאֲנִי לוֹ, הָרֹעֶה בַּשׁוֹשַׁנִּים. (2)

Do-di li va-a-ni lo, ha-ro-eh ba-sho-sha-nim. (2)

Mi zot o-lah min ha-mid-bar, mi zot o-lah?

M'ku-teh-ret mor, (mor) u-l'vo-na, mor u-l'vo-na.

Do-di li va-a-ni lo, ha-ro-eh ba-sho-sha-nim. (2)

Li-bav-ti-ni, a-cho-ti ka-la, li-bav-ti-ni ka-la. (2)

Do-di li va-a-ni lo, ha-ro-eh ba-sho-sha-nim. (2)

U-ri tza-fon, u-vo-i tei-man. (2)

Do-di li va-a-ni lo, ha-ro-eh ba-sho-sha-nim. (2)

My beloved is mine, and l am his, who grazes among the lilies. Who is that coming out of the desert, who is it? She is anointed with myrrh, myrrh and frankincense. You have taken my heart, my sister, my bride; you have taken my heart. Rise up, O North Wind, and come, O South Wind. My beloved is mine, and l am his, who grazes among the lilies.

אל גנת אגוז   EL GINAT EGOZ

אֶל־גִּנַּת אֱגוֹז יָרַדְתִּי, לִרְאוֹת בְּאִבֵּי הַנָּחַל,

לִרְאוֹת הֲפָרְחָה הַגֶּפֶן, הֵנֵצוּ הָרִמֹּנִים.

לְכָה דוֹדִי, נֵצֵא הַשָּׂדֶה, נָלִינָה בַּכְּפָרִים,

נַשְׁכִּימָה לַכְּרָמִים,

נִרְאֶה אִם פָּרְחָה הַגֶּפֶן, פִּתַּח הַסְּמָדַר.

עוּרִי צָפוֹן, וּבוֹאִי תֵימָן,

הָפִיחִי גַנִּי, יִזְּלוּ בְשָׂמָיו,

יָבֹא דוֹדִי לְגַנּוֹ, וְיֹאכַל פְּרִי מְגָדָיו.

El gi-nat eh-goz ya-ra-d'ti, li-r'ot b'i-bei ha-na-chal,

li-r'ot ha-fa-r'cha ha-geh-fen, hei-nei-tzu ha-ri-mo-nim.

L'cha do-di, nei-tzei ha-sa-deh, na-li-na ba-k'fa-rim,

nash-ki-ma la-k'ra-mim,

nir-eh im par'cha ha-geh-fen, pi-tach ha-s'ma-dar.

U-ri tza-fon, u-vo-i tei-man,

ha-fi-chi ga-ni, yiz-lu v'sa-mav.

Ya-vo do-di l'ga-no, v'yo-chal p'ri m'ga-dav.

I went down to the grove to see the valley break into flower, to see if the vines had blossomed, if the pomegranates were in bloom. Come, my beloved, let us go into the field and lie down among the flowers. Let us go early to the vineyards; let us see if the vine has flowered, if its blossoms have opened. Awake, O North Wind, come, O South Wind! Blow upon my garden, that its perfume may spread. Let my beloved come to his garden and enjoy its luscious fruits!

ערב של שושנים   EREV SHEL SHOSHANIM

עֶרֶב שֶׁל שׁוֹשַׁנִים,	*Eh-rev shel sho-sha-nim,*
נֵצֵא נָא אֶל הַבּוּסְתָּן,	*Nei-tzei na el ha-bus-tan,*
מוֹר, בְּשָׂמִים וּלְבוֹנָה,	*Mor, b'sa-mim, u-l'vo-nah,*
לְרַגְלֵךְ מִפְתָּן.	*L' rag-leich mif-tan.*
לַיְלָה יוֹרֵד לְאַט,	*Lai-lah yo-reid l'at,*
וְרוּחַ שׁוֹשָׁן נוֹשְׁבָה,	*V'ru-ach sho-shan no-sh'vah,*
הָבָה אֶלְחַשׁ לָךְ שִׁיר בַּלָּאט,	*Ha-va el-chash lach shir ba-lat,*
זֶמֶר שֶׁל אַהֲבָה.	*Ze-mer shel a-ha-vah.*
שַׁחַר, הוֹמָה יוֹנָה,	*Sha-char, ho-mah yo-nah,*
רֹאשֵׁךְ מָלֵא טְלָלִים,	*Ro-sheich ma-lei t'la-lim,*
פִּיךְ אֶל הַבֹּקֶר שׁוֹשַׁנָּה,	*Pich el ha-bo-ker sho-sha-nah,*
אֶקְטְפֶנּוּ לִי.	*Ek-t'feh-nu li.*

On an evening of roses let us go out to the orchard, where myrrh, spices, and perfumes will be a carpet for your feet. Slowly descends the night, and the perfumed wind is a caress. I whisper a quiet song to you, a song of love. At dawn a dove coos, and your head is covered with dew. Your mouth is a rose in the morning: let me gather it to myself.

ירושלים של זהב   YERUSHALAYIM SHEL ZAHAV

אֲוִיר הָרִים צָלוּל כַּיַּיִן, וְרֵיחַ אֳרָנִים,
נִשָּׂא בְּרוּחַ הָעַרְבַּיִם, עִם קוֹל פַּעֲמוֹנִים.
וּבְתַרְדֵּמַת אִילָן וָאֶבֶן, שְׁבוּיָה בַּחֲלוֹמָהּ,
הָעִיר אֲשֶׁר בָּדָד יוֹשֶׁבֶת, וּבְלִבָּהּ חוֹמָה.

A-vir ha-rim tza-lul ka-ya-yin, v'rei-ach o-ra-nim,
ni-sa b'ru-ach ha-ar-ba-yim, im kol pa-a-mo-nim.

U-v'tar-dei-mat i-lan va-eh-ven, sh'vu-yah ba-cha-lo-mah,
ha-ir a-sher ba-dad yo-sheh-vet, u-v'li-bah cho-mah.

 יְרוּשָׁלַיִם שֶׁל זָהָב וְשֶׁל נְחֹשֶׁת וְשֶׁל אוֹר,
הֲלֹא לְכָל־שִׁירַיִךְ אֲנִי כִּנּוֹר.

Y'ru-sha-la-yim shel za-hav v'shel n'cho-shet v'shel or,
Ha-lo l'chol shi-ra-yich a-ni ki-nor.

חָזַרְנוּ אֶל בּוֹרוֹת הַמַּיִם, לַשּׁוּק וְלַכִּכָּר,
שׁוֹפָר קוֹרֵא בְּהַר הַבַּיִת, בָּעִיר הָעַתִּיקָה.
וּבַמְּעָרוֹת אֲשֶׁר בַּסֶּלַע, אַלְפֵי שְׁמָשׁוֹת זוֹרְחוֹת,
נָשׁוּב נֵרֵד אֶל יַם הַמֶּלַח, בְּדֶרֶךְ יְרִיחוֹ.
יְרוּשָׁלַיִם ...

Cha-zar-nu el bo-rot ha-ma-yim, la-shuk v'la-ki-kar,
sho-far ko-rei b'har ha-ba-yit, ba-ir ha-a-ti-kah.
U-va-m'a-rot a-sher ba-seh-la, al-fei sh'ma-shot zor-chot,
na-shuv nei-eid el yom ha-meh-lach, b'deh-rech y'ri-cho.
Y'ru-sha-la-yim . . .

אַךְ בְּבוֹאִי הַיּוֹם לָשִׁיר לָךְ, וְלָךְ לִקְשׁוֹר כְּתָרִים,
קָטֹנְתִּי מִצְּעִיר בָּנַיִךְ, וּמֵאַחֲרוֹן הַמְשׁוֹרְרִים.
כִּי שְׁמֵךְ צוֹרֵב אֶת־הַשְּׂפָתַיִם, כִּנְשִׁיקַת שָׂרָף,
אִם אֶשְׁכָּחֵךְ יְרוּשָׁלַיִם, אֲשֶׁר כֻּלָּהּ זָהָב.
יְרוּשָׁלַיִם ...

Ach b'vo-i ha-yom la-shir lach, v'lach lik-shor k'ta-rim,
ka-ton-ti mi-tz'ir ba-na-yich, u-mei-a-cha-ron ha-m'sho-r'rim.
Ki sh'meich tzo-reiv et ha-s'fa-ta-yim, ki-n'shi-kat sa-raf,
im esh-ka-chech Y'ru-sha-la-yim, a-sher ku-lah za-hav.
Y'ru-sha-la-yim . . .

Your ancient trees all stand in silence,
As though immersed in dream;
Your fragrant breeze now comes to meet me,
As light begins to gleam.
My yearning heart has long remembered
The sun that gilds your face;
Jerusalem, how I have loved you,
How we have been embraced!

יְרוּשָׁלַיִם ...

Y'ru-sha-la-yim . . .

The mountain air is clear as wine, and the scent of pine trees is carried on the evening breeze with the sound of bells. As tree and stone slumber, so the city that dwells alone, whose heart is a wall, is held captive by its dream.

Jerusalem of gold, of copper and of light,
am I not a harp for all your songs?

We have returned to the water cisterns, the market and the square. A shofar sounds on the Temple Mount in the Old City. In the caves among the rocks a thousand suns gleam. Let us go down again to the Dead Sea by way of Jericho.

But now that I come to sing to you and to weave garlands for you, I am less than the least of your children and the last of your poets. For your name burns the lips like a serpent's kiss, if I forget you, O Jerusalem, who are all gold.

&